¶	paragraph
no ¶	no paragraph
p	error in punctuation (pp. 482–498)
paral	faulty parallelism (pp. 461–462)
pas	unnecessary or ineffective passive construction (pp. 472–473)
prom	paragraph is faulty—try the promise pattern (pp. 101–106)
pron	error with pronoun (pp. 436–439)
pv	check point of view
ref	vague pronoun reference (pp. 433–435)
rep	unnecessary repetition
ro	run-on sentence (pp. 471, 527)
sb	check the sentence unit rule (pp. 85–86)
sp	spelling error
split	split construction (pp. 457–458)
ss	check sentence structure (pp. 453–473)
sub	faulty subordination (p. 464)
t	error in verb tense (p. 438)
th	clarify the thesis (pp. 39–47)
tr	effective transition needed (p. 87)
un	unity—check for unnecessary shifts in wording, tone, or attitude
vb	error with verb (pp. 508–509)
wdy	wordy
wr	write out—do not abbreviate or use numbers (pp. 499, 501–502)
ws	check your writer's stance (p. 476)
x	obvious error
^	insertion (p. 512)
?	I don't understand

STRATEGIES

A RHETORIC AND READER
WITH HANDBOOK

FIFTH EDITION

CHARLENE TIBBETTS
ARN TIBBETTS
UNIVERSITY OF ILLINOIS (URBANA-CHAMPAIGN)

 LONGMAN

An imprint of Addison Wesley Longman, Inc.

New York • Reading, Massachusetts • Menlo Park, California • Harlow, England
Don Mills, Ontario • Sydney • Mexico City • Madrid • Amsterdam

Executive Editor: Anne Elizabeth Smith
Project Coordination, Text and Cover Design: Interactive Composition Corporation
Cover Illustration: *Dunan #1,* ©1996 Neal Parks (http://www.ccnet.com/~nparks)
  commissioned for Jack Menendez
Art Studio: Interactive Composition Corporation
Electronic Production Manager: Eric Jorgensen
Manufacturing Manager: Hilda Koparanian
Electronic Page Makeup: Interactive Composition Corporation
Printer and Binder: RR Donnelley & Sons Company
Cover Printer: The Lehigh Press, Inc.

For permission to use copyrighted material, grateful acknowledgment is made to the
copyright holders on pp. 532–534, which are hereby made part of this copyright page.

Library of Congress Cataloging-in-Publication Data

Tibbetts, Charlene.
    Strategies : a rhetoric and reader with handbook /
Charlene Tibbetts, Arn Tibbetts. — 5th ed.
        p.   cm.
    Includes bibliographical references and index.
    ISBN 0–673–98035–9 (pbk.)
    1. English language—Rhetoric. 2. English
language—Grammar—Handbooks, manuals, etc.
3. College readers.   I. Tibbetts, A. M.
II. Title.
PE1408.T494 1997
808'.0427–dc20   95–47739
                                            CIP

0–673–98035–9

12345678910–DOC–99989796

Brief Contents

Contents

Preface

With this new edition of *Strategies* we provide a complete text for a college course in writing—Rhetoric, Readings, and Handbook. The Rhetoric covers the major problems and principles of composition, from prewriting to editing and revising. The Readings give a broad sampling of modern prose from which students can learn both writing and reading techniques. The Handbook offers brief answers to typical problems in grammar and usage.

The Theme of this Book: Choice

When we picked the term *strategies* for our first book in 1969, we did so to stress the idea that there are many ways to create a good piece of writing. At every stage, the writer faces options and makes decisions.

So the theme of this book is, simply: *Writers have choices*. At different times and for different purposes, they will make different choices. At the same time, instructors want a textbook that gives them flexibility in organizing the course to meet the needs of students and society. We hope that this new edition provides that flexibility.

The Student's Choices

For the student, the opportunity to choose arises first in the process of finding and limiting an idea. It continues as he or she selects a method for developing and organizing the idea. Choice is ever-present as the student decides which words are most clear and appropriate, as sentences are written and revised, and as the entire paper is revised and edited.

The Instructor's Choices

We have arranged the parts of the book around the elements of composition—stance, organization, paragraphs, sentence structure, and so on. The Rhetoric provides the theory, along with a wealth of exercises and practices. The Readings allow the instructor to apply theory—to show how writers in a real world solve their problems. Sometimes they bend the theory a good bit, sometimes they violate it entirely: a very good thing for students to know! Writing may have rules, but one has to know when and how to apply them.

In addition, the Readings provide ideas for discussion and topics for papers. For instance, if student Jane Smith does not agree with Linda Hasselstrom's idea that she should pack a pistol to defend herself (pages 398–403), then Jane can write an argument detailing her disagreement. Writing (we insist to students) is a free-for-all affair in the realm of ideas. Dive into the Readings, get your intellectual bearings, and surface with a viewpoint. All students have a stake in contemporary debates, and an essay of their own to nail on the classroom door.

What Distinguishes this Edition?

We have added a new chapter on rhetorical ethics. This chapter—"The Question of Ethics in Writing and Reading"—now introduces the book. We hope that this echo of classical rhetoric will be useful to students as they struggle with the difficult problem of making their writing believable as well as effective.

We have rewritten the Argument chapter completely, using new material and examples, along with a new section on fallacies. Chapter 6, "What Words Should You Avoid?" is also new. For foreign speakers, we have added a section on the articles (*a, an,* and *the*)—pages 449–452 in the Handbook.

Chapter 7, on basic sentence structure, has been partly rewritten to clarify some elements of what we call the *sentence base system.*

We have continued to use charts and tables in the text, and to revise them where necessary. For example, note the practical tables on documentation systems for the research paper (pages 142–151). These tables allow students to see, *in visual form,* the MLA system as it applies to all parts of documentation in a research paper.

The Reader, based on the Fourth Edition of our HarperCollins reader *Strategies: A Rhetoric and Reader* (1992), has nine new readings (Don Holt, "Leaving the Farm"; Oliver Sacks, "The Man Who Mistook His Wife for a Hat"; William Oscar Johnson, "Sports and Beer—There's Trouble Brewing"; Lars Eighner, "On Dumpster Diving"; Joshua Janoff, "A Gen-X Rip Van Winkle"; Kay S. Hymowitz, "'American Cool' is Killing Love"; Alex Kozinski, "Ten Reasons Skiing is Dead"; Robert Hughes, "Take This Revolution. . . "; and Linda Hasselstrom, "Why One Peaceful Woman Carries a Pistol"), along with new exercises and examples.

Here and there in the Rhetoric, we have replaced older professional and student examples of writing with new ones.

Like its predecessors, this edition of *Strategies* owes much to many people. In particular, we would like to thank the following reviewers: Cynthia Becerra, Humphreys College; Herb Smith, Southern College of Technology; Tahita Fulkerson, Tarrant County Junior College, NW; Anne C. Armstrong, Walters State Community College; Linda Rollins, Motlow State Community College; and Kirk Adams, Tarrant County Junior College, NW.

And hosannas to our editors!

Charlene and Arn Tibbetts

PART ONE

The Rhetoric

CHAPTER 1

The Question of Ethics in Writing and Reading

> *Ethics* is concerned with good and bad, with moral obligations or duties. In creating "ethical proof," writers demonstrate their good character by showing that they know their subject and by writing so as to convince the reader honestly and without trickery.

We were discussing an essay with students, an essay written by a well-known journalist.

"I don't believe the author," said one student. "I'll bet his statistics are not accurate."

"Well, what, exactly, don't you believe?" someone asked.

Before he could answer, another student broke in, "That statement at the top of page 301—I never heard of this kind of thing happening. I don't think it's likely. It doesn't seem real."

The first reader agreed: "I have trouble accepting that, too. The author doesn't give any *examples* of the type of food being bought by people on food stamps—I'm not sure if it's luxury food or just staples. But I also wonder about his earlier description of those retired people spending their social security checks entirely on food. Does that really happen? Is it true?"

The words these student-readers used were significant:

don't believe

not accurate

It doesn't seem real.

I have trouble accepting that, too.

Does that really happen?

Is it true?

These words and phrases imply an unfortunate conclusion, so far as the author of the essay is concerned. The readers weren't convinced by his work. They lacked *confidence* in him. Indeed, "Is it true?" may be the most profound question that can be asked of any writer's nonfiction work, because the answer to the question is fundamental to his or her success. In one way or another, your readers must believe you—and believe in you. If they don't, you lack something fundamental—ethical proof.

Here are four paragraphs for class discussion. As you read them, consider the writer's use of ethical proof, and then answer the questions that follow.

1   I build eight to ten homes a year. Mainly these are for middle-class families who are making their first step up to a house that they themselves designed. For many of them, buying these relatively modest houses is the achievement of a lifetime. I've been doing this work for 20 years—it is the most satisfying job I can think of. You're working with people's dreams.

2   But I really shouldn't be writing this article for the newspaper. I am putting myself at risk. For what I report here will alienate other builders, my suppliers, and probably affect my future in the community. Yet I must say something about the poor quality of home-building that I see every day.

3   Consider these true descriptions: There is a new house going up on Pickering Street that has badly built walls on the first floor. I counted a dozen crooked, deformed studs on one wall alone. Some of these studs are around window frames, which as a consequence aren't square. In another house going up in Southvale, the builder put in a basement but did not regrade the drainage pattern behind the house. Three acres of ground will drain right into that basement on the first heavy rain. In the old house south of the city library— the one that's being remodeled—the remodeler has improperly handled the cold-air returns. In the cold winter months, the owner is going to wonder why half his house is hot and the rest is unpleasantly cold. One final example from yet a different house: When vandals tore off the vapor-barrier sheeting on an inside wall, the builder did not replace it before the dry wallers came to work. Lack of a vapor barrier means eventual wall and paint damage, and expense to the owner.

4   Who will pay for this carelessness and (sometimes) downright incompetence? You, the homeowner.

—Webb McKinney, "You Don't Always Get What You Pay For"

▼ Questions For Discussion

Check McKinney's text and be specific in your answers.

1. McKinney wants us to believe that he knows his subject. How does he persuade us that he knows it?

2. McKinney complains about "the poor quality of home-building" that he sees. What does he tell us that makes us believe this judgment has some validity? Make a list. Give your reaction to the material on the list.

3. Why does McKinney give all the specific detail in paragraph (3)? How would you answer the criticism that some of this is boring and unnecessary?

4. Do you believe that at any point McKinney overstates his case, or overdramatizes?

5. Refer to the boxed note at the beginning of the chapter. For the sake of discussion, using these four paragraphs only, would you say that McKinney is an ethical writer? Defend your judgment.

▼ Ethical Proof: Good Character in Prose

Most readers are friendly enough at the start. Unless you do something to put them off, they will usually give you the benefit of the doubt. But you want more than that—you want them on your side, rooting for you and eager to believe.

In teaching oratory, the ancient rhetoricians used to emphasize what they called *ethical proof*, the word *ethical* being associated with *ethos* or "character." They taught that speakers (and writers too, of course) should try, so far as they could, to be persons of good character; such people are more easily believed. But the mere appearance of goodness, said the ancients, is hardly sufficient. Speakers should live their lives as good human beings. As one famous authority put it, the best orator is "a good man speaking."

In modern times, for our own practical purposes, the idea of *ethos* can be expressed in the writer's answers to three questions concerning ethical proof:

1. Do you *know* what you are talking about? (Have you had any experience with the subject?)

2. How do you *show* your reader that you know? (What's the evidence?)

3. Is your writing *honest*?

For the rest of this book, we will assume that to determine ethical proof, *writers* will ask these three questions of their own work and that *readers* will ask the same questions of the writers.

▼ Three Examples of How Writers Create Ethical Proof

1. Adam Liptak, *a second-year law student, writes to undergraduate students:*

> People go to law school for a lot of different reasons—and many of these are foolish. I should know. My rationale for entering the study of the law has little to do with

why I now consider it worthwhile. Knowing what I know now, and thinking back to what I thought then, I'm moved to help prospective law students make their decisions on a sound basis. In particular, I want to clarify the misconceptions which lie behind four very popular and bad reasons for attending law school. While, certainly, these may be valid for some people, to a large extent they represent a willful blindness to the central fact of law school: It is a trade school, and the trade itself can be esoteric, dull, and of questionable utility.

—Adam Liptak, "Bad Reasons to Study Law"

Liptak provides ethical proof in three ways: (1) He says he writes to help "prospective law students" make better decisions. (2) He has had experience being a law student and therefore should be a reliable witness. (3) He shares an important secret with the reader—law school is only a trade school, a disarming admission indeed, and one that makes us ready to believe him.

2. Perri Klass, *a new intern in pediatrics, writes for a general audience* (her argument, not explicitly stated here, concerns the problem of overtired young doctors in training):

1   Internship, that all-important, terrifying first year as a doctor, brings you up against many of the life-and-death issues of the day. You turn off respirators and allow people to die, or else you fight death with all the pharmacology and technology you have. You tell the truth to patients, or you lie to them. You treat the rich and the poor alike, or else you make distinctions. Life and death, pain and relief. And so on. But right now I want to talk about the biggest issue of all, the concern that dominates an intern's life, the subject with which we grapple constantly. I mean, of course, fatigue.

2   I mean, I'm so tired you wouldn't believe it. I mean, right now, while I'm writing this, I can barely see farther than how tired I am. I mean, I got to the hospital this morning at 7:15 (ridiculous already; I've never been able to think clearly before noon) and I stayed there until 7 p.m. And this was one of the good days. Oh, am I tired!

— Perri Klass, "ZZZZZZZZZZ"

We believe Klass for several reasons. We know that she is an intern, and we know that interns work hard. She emphasizes the point about fatigue at the end of her first paragraph. Yet it's the painful weariness that she describes in the next paragraph that really convinces us as readers the most. She even sounds as if she is about to fall asleep.

3. *Scientist* Dixy Lee Ray *tells a general audience why we shouldn't be afraid of our radioactive world:*

1   The simple fact is, we live in a radioactive world—always have, always will. Our bodies receive the impact of 15,000 radioactive particles every second; we don't feel them or suffer any ill effect from such bombardment. One of the difficult aspects of radiation phobia is that our ability to measure radiation has become so accurate and precise that it is now possible to detect unbelievably small amounts, e.g. one part per billion. How much or rather how little is that? How can we visualize one part per billion? One

way is by analogy—one part per billion is equivalent to one drop of Vermouth in five rail-road carloads of gin! (A very dry martini?) Or—look at it another way—there are now about five billion people living on this planet. Therefore, one family of five persons represents one part per billion of the entire human population.

2   And what about one part per trillion? That would be *one thousand times less.* When radioactivity from the Chernobyl accident in the USSR in April 1986 reached the west coast of the United States, the popular press warned residents about the dangers of possible fallout, speaking of the number of picocuries of radioactivity detected in the high clouds, without ever explaining that one picocurie is one part per trillion and to receive from that "Chernobyl cloud" as much radioactivity as a patient would get in a diagnostic test for thyroid problems, a person would have had to drink 63,000 gallons of the "radioactive" rainwater—a formidable task!

3   Remember, everything is radioactive—our homes, buildings, everything we use. So is the forest primeval, our lakes, our streams, the ocean, and even our gardens. Because we have no human sense to detect radioactivity (no smell, sound, or sight reveals it), it has been like magnetism, gravity, or molecules; undetectable until instruments were built that can measure it with incredible precision. Now we know that even the ground we walk on is radioactive.

— Dixy Lee Ray, "Who Speaks for Science?"

From the standpoint of ethical proof, Ray's article is different from the other two we read. She does not introduce herself anywhere in the text. We have no direct sense of her personality, of her experience or scientific authority. We do not know, for example—from the material we have here—that she was once Chair of the Atomic Energy Commission and professor of Zoology at the University of Washington, or that she was awarded the United Nations Peace Medal.

We know only that she is generous with evidence, piling up the facts line after line. She is also considerate of her readers, helping them to visualize *one part per billion* ("equivalent to one drop of Vermouth in five railroad carloads of gin"). And she appeals to what we know, to familiar things: "Remember, everything is radioactive—our homes, buildings, everything we use. So is the forest primeval, our lakes, our streams, the ocean, and even our gardens."

Ray's ethical proof depends mainly on two things—the factuality of her account and what we *intuit* from the passage. She seems friendly, sane, unbiased. Furthermore, we sense that she has a strong interest in us, her readers. She appeals to our common sense and our ability to accept a case on its merits. In other words, she compliments us, thereby encouraging us to accept her views.

All three writers we've discussed—Liptak, Klass, and Ray—try to make themselves believable to their readers. They give the impression of being solid, decent human beings, people of good character who can be trusted. They have moved us toward acceptance of their writing by showing us that they know what they are talking about and—in the cases of Liptak and Klass—by explaining how they know it. To varying extent, they use facts to support the point they are making.

▼ Postscript

We have deliberately kept our examples of ethical proof varied and short. Longer examples (we tried using them in an earlier draft) tended to be indigestible and disguised our point. You will discover, as you continue through the book, that ethical proof can be complicated and difficult to analyze. But it is important to think about the issue. And, in various places, this textbook gives you ample opportunity to do so.

For example, one difference between the active and the passive constructions in sentence structure (pages 472–473) is that the active assigns responsibility while the passive may not:

> Active: The *mechanic failed to change* the oil in your car.
>
> Passive: The *oil was not changed.*

If the owner of your gas station uses the passive, he blurs the sense of responsibility, thereby creating an ethical problem which may be important to you as owner of the car.

So far as this book is concerned, the place to study an ethical question is in its context. If it occurs in sentence structure, consider it there. If it occurs in organization, discuss it when it arises. A common breakdown in organization occurs when writers promise readers they will deal with something, but don't—for example, that they will discuss both X and Y, but fail to consider Y. Failure to honor the contract between writer and reader is a lapse in rhetorical ethics. Promises made should be kept.

Each chapter in the Rhetoric section will suggest its own problems in ethical proof.

The Readings, of course, are a gold mine of issues in rhetorical ethics. We trust that you and your instructor will mine this ore in whatever way you see fit when you study each reading.

▼ A Checklist for Considering Ethical Proof

NOTE: This Checklist is useful for both writers and readers.

Writing has an ethical or a moral dimension, apart from the artistic, aesthetic, or technical. Note that items in the checklist may be usefully discussed from various angles other than an ethical standpoint.

1. *Thesis or Main Point.* Does the writer let you know what his or her point is? Does he promise one thing but write another? Does he try to pull the wool over your eyes?

2. *Content.* Does the writer give enough evidence—facts, details, or examples— to convince you? Is this evidence relevant? Believable?

3. *Organization.* Can you follow the main points of the essay? Does the writer keep his or her promises in the main organization *and* in each paragraph? Is the writer so careless that you get lost in the organization?

4. *Sentences.* Do the sentences reflect the material and the facts? Are they clear? If a coach tells a reporter, "Our quarterbacking failed in terms of receivers," someone is failing the demands of ethical proof. Is it the coach's

fault? (He didn't coach the players properly.) The quarterback's fault? (He didn't perform as he was coached.) The receivers' fault? (They ran the wrong routes). And so on.

5. *Words.* As George Orwell pointed out in "Politics and the English Language" (and elsewhere), much modern use of words is hot air at best and pure lies at worst. Is the word choice of the writer *clear, accurate,* and *honest?*

6. *Total Effect.* As the writer, have you fulfilled the ethical contract with your readers? As the reader, are you convinced by the writer's ethical proof?

CHAPTER 2

Finding Subjects~

An Introduction

"Growl!" the student said. At least that is what she wrote (and underlined) at the top of the page. Here is the rest of what she wrote:

> I'm working on a new paper, one which is causing me a good deal of trouble. I hope it's worth the trouble. Topics and subjects for papers don't come easily to me, and when they do come, they aren't docile. I beat on them until they submit. Stop! they cry. I'll cooperate if you will just let me alone. For this new paper I have developed new techniques of harassment to get the subject tamed.
>
> Today I feel like a hunter. I go tiptoeing around, hoping the subject won't suspect I'm coming, making sure to stay downwind; then I slowly sneak up on it, watching out for all the pitfalls of the past, when I have scared it off—I'm very superstitious. When I finally get close I pounce. The subject remains very cool through this. It pretends to ignore me. I grapple and bite. The subject must enjoy being pursued a little; it has to like my grip, I suppose.
>
> Finally, I get it pinned down on paper, get it all written out in several pages (by now I am really sick of the thing). I hand it to someone, and they read it and say: "That's very good!" Then the subject hisses in my ear, "I told you so." I yell back, "What do you mean, 'Told you so?' I did all the work!"

This is a chapter about finding subjects—finding, trapping, caging them; and then keeping them under control once you've got them in mind. We subtitle this chapter "an introduction" because it is just that—the beginning of a program in writing which continues through the rest of the book. At almost any stage in writing, you can "find" an idea. Ten years after you write something, you can read it over and have an idea pop into your head about the subject. Indeed, as long as you are alive, your brain never stops its process of discovering ideas. What it needs is encouragement. In that last sentence is a major theme of this chapter—and also of the following three chapters.

Psychologically speaking, our "needs" as writers are somewhat different. A device for finding ideas for papers may be useful to you but not to your friend, sister, or roommate. A method of organizing may satisfy your roommate but drive you to distraction. Every human being has a creative engine, but not all engines run at the same rate or on the same fuel. Accordingly, the strategies for finding ideas for subjects given here are meant to be suggestions rather than hard-and-fast rules.

▼ Finding Subjects

■■■ *Brainstorming*

Originally, *brainstorming* was a term used to describe a "conference method" for solving problems. The method has been used for many years in business. You get a group of people around a table, and they try to solve a problem—for example, to find new uses for a resealable plastic bag. The people around the table simply start talking and reacting to each other (the example is from an early description of brainstorming):

>   *Joan:* "Use it for wet bathing suits."
> *Chairman:* "How about album covers for phonograph records."
>   *Joan:* "Toothbrushes . . . Soap."
>   *Sally:* "How about the fisherman."
> *Chairman:* "How about for bait. Live bait, you could put that in this."
>   *Jim:* "How about taking something down when you go skin diving."
>   *Joan:* "How about for vegetables or cheeses."
> *Chairman:* "How about using it to contain paint or coloring material."
>   *Bill:* "Put the fish in it after you catch it."
>   *Sam:* "Use it as a rain shoe."
>   *Albert:* "How about the invalids who have to take a certain type of prescribed pill so many times a day . . . a very small package in place of a box which is cumbersome."
> *Chairman:* "Maybe it could even have little packages inside the major package."
>   *Joan:* "Artists could use that for carrying pastels and oils."
> *Chairman:* "Or for their wet brushes."
>   *Mary:* "Women could carry their makeup."
>   *Joan:* "Yes."
>   *Paul:* "Packaging food for restaurants."
>   *Bill:* "Use it to take the bones home to feed the dog."

—Charles Whiting, *Creative Thinking*

Brainstorming is particularly valuable to the writer because it offers a technique for getting *suggestions* and *leads* for a subject. You can do it with roommates or friends, but most of us brainstorm alone, using sheets of scratch paper. Done alone, brainstorming becomes an association game on paper. You start with something—anything—and with a pencil and paper you talk to yourself (see page 13).

Here you see an example of *controlled brainstorming,* in which at first you let your thoughts freely associate, writing down whatever comes to mind. After a few phrases appear, you gently apply pressure and *shape* some of the material as it emerges. Don't use too much pressure at first. Only when the ideas tend to get specific should you come to a conclusion that may provide a subject. Then, as in the example, try to shape the conclusion into a sentence: *Prevent thefts in college lots by adding lights and regular police patrols.* This may not be your final subject (it may not even be close to the final one), but at least it is a beginning.

You will note that we suggest ending a brainstorming session—whether you are doing it alone or with other people—with a sentence that is written down. Writing the sentence is not meant to be a final act in your search for a subject. Rather it is merely a "closure" on the brainstorming session, one that enables you to pick up easily where you left off if you think more work is necessary.

In the pages that follow, we will give more suggestions for finding and shaping subjects. As you read them, keep in the back of your mind what we have said about *brainstorming*—a technique which is useful in combination with other subject-hunting devices.

■■■ Freewriting

Freewriting is a form of brainstorming, the difference being that in freewriting you tend to use "running prose"—sentences and parts of sentences that run from margin to margin of the page. Most brainstorming, as we use the term, consists of words and phrases in list form. Most freewriting looks like ordinary writing on the page, although it is somewhat choppier and often rather disconnected.

The advantage of freewriting is that it loosens you up psychologically and allows your brain and hand to coordinate and warm up together (many writers have cold engines). The point of it is to start and keep going: write from the left margin to the right margin and don't stop until you feel like a baseball pitcher after a good warm-up—loose and ready for action. Here's an example of freewriting:

Here I am, sitting under this tree, half dozing in the sun. Shouting and bellowing; it started almost without warning. One minute, silence on the quad. Long curves of flights of frisbees and oofs of pleasure when the frisbee is caught. Whirl and turn and throw again. "HAVE YOU THOUGHT ABOUT GOD TODAY?" No, and I didn't yesterday, nor the day before nor the day before—tomorrow and tomorrow creeps in . . . what's the rest of that and what's it from? "GOD IS WITH YOU, HE WANTS TO KNOW. . . ." I want to know why I can't sit here in the sun without somebody bellowing in my ear. 100 ft. away and he's the noisiest thing in 6 acres of quadrangle. What do preachers want to come here and bother us for anyway? Do they ever get converts? I don't need them—I'm

```
            Here comes Mickey up the stairs wearing his Walkman

            Walkman—radio

            radio what? Lost. No, stolen

            Cherie's car, they stole radio & stereo, broke into car

            (in college lot)

            parking lot

            why steal?

            why not keep from stealing?

            cars broken into often in college lots

            stop it!!!

            how to stop them from stealing (breaking into?)

            add lights

            regular patrols—use 'em
            _____

            Prevent thefts in college lots by adding lights and

            regular police patrols.
```

already a believer. They are raucous, noisy, tiresome, irrelevant, and a plain bore. UNDERLINE THAT!

The idea that the student told himself to underline suggested a subject for writing. He eventually wrote a paper that described how he felt about the event he freewrote into his notebook. He called his paper: *Godspelling the Quad: One Form of Noise Pollution.*

■■■ *Keep a Journal*

A *journal* is a set of scribbled notes and personal remarks that you put down when something intriguing happens, or when you hear about an idea that you want to remember. A journal is useful because it is full of information, and also of little observations that trigger the imagination. The entries can consist of a sentence, a phrase, a conversation, a quotation from a magazine article, or a line from a movie or story. It can be your reaction to an event. It is also a good warm-up device; write for awhile, and then find an idea.

A JOURNAL ENTRY:

Went to lunch with Lillian, who said that she found the concert last night "sickening." The movie two nights before she said was "sickening." The lunch was "sickening." Lillian is becoming, well, repetitive.

Worked on the report due in Psych until 5:00. Then played a little touch football for a while. Knee still hurts.

Lillian called and said she got a job at the bookstore and would I come over and talk about it with her. She seemed subdued, and didn't say that the thought of 20 hours of work a week would make her sick. As it turned out, she *was* subdued. I can't decide whether she is 12 years old or 22. She can run the range of 10 years in a few seconds. She's not as bad as Duane [his roommate] tho, who acts like he's 12 all the time.

Lillian proofread my psych paper and found six errors that I had missed. "Sickening," she said.

I went home and went to bed.

NEXT DAY: I found an idea! *Discuss the current slang on the campus.*

▚▚▚ Look around You

In a lecture, a professional writer told her audience: "If it's ideas you're after, get out of your chair *and go look*. Walk around; listen." After the great flood in Corning, N.Y., in 1972, R. N. Hoye wondered: What is a flooded house like after the water is gone? What do people face when they return to their homes? He went to look:

1   The first problem is just to get in. If the front door has swollen, is blocked by mud, or has something jammed against it, it may be necessary to break a window to gain entry. Inside, the first thing observed is a waterline four or six or ten feet high all around the walls. The floors themselves are warped into unbelievable waves of wood six to ten inches high, very easy to stumble over. Everything in every room is coated with mud between two and four inches deep, and the mud not only is still wet, but has an unforgettable odor. Rugs, sofas, pillows, tables, and chairs are all soaked, not just sodden or damp. Books have swollen and burst their bindings. Any ashtray or vase you pick up is full of brown, cold water. Everything drips.

2   Go into the kitchen. The doors on some cabinets are so swollen that it takes a few hard pulls to get them open. When you do open the cabinets, water runs out. The washing machine is filled with water; there is an ugly waterline on the refrigerator. Now go upstairs. In the bedrooms, the mattresses are soaked and covered with mud. The mattresses are so heavy that two people can barely drag one, and then only a few feet at a time. Everything folded in drawers and hanging in closets is soaked, too. Even the shoes on the floors of the closets have water in them.

3   Of course, if you have a basement, it's still full of water; you may be able to see the top of the furnace. There's nothing to do here until the pumpers start making their rounds. In your garage, bikes, sleds, lawnmowers, and tools already have begun to rust.

Nearly every sentence of Hoye's represents an observation—a going-to-look at something which could provide ideas for several papers: (a) A flood causes irreparable damage to a house, clothing, and equipment. (b) A flood leaves a mark on a family's possessions that can never be paid for. (c) Some flood-damaged goods can never be used again.

■■■ Surprise Yourself

One problem with looking for material is that you may find more of it than you know what to do with; life is full of surprises. But if surprising ideas won't come easily to you, go to them. Surprise yourself.

A student remarked in class one day: "It seems that every good idea I have about writing is just an ordinary one, seen from a new angle."

"Meaning what?"

"Well, if you take an ordinary idea and look at it from a different angle, it may come out unordinary—surprising. When I was in high school I read that statement of Admiral Oliver Hazard Perry's: 'We have met the enemy, and they are ours.' When my brother took the SAT test to get into college, he and thousands of others the same year had to write an essay for the SAT based on a statement from the comic strip *Pogo:* 'We have met the enemy, and he is us.' The change in the quote is surprising, and helps to suggest ideas."

Surprise yourself (and your reader) with a *description* one might not normally expect. The scholar Elaine Partnow writes: "Through all this sleuthing I have come to feel that the public regards women in past and current history very much like fine character actors—we recognize them but do not know their names; we need them but do not pay them homage; we make demands on them but do not document their contributions." Women as character actors: the surprise inherent in the description is itself a "found idea," one which helps find and shape other ideas.

■■■ Other Options for Finding Subjects

Another student writes home regularly. Before mailing her letters, she copies them on the copy machine in the library. Into the letters she puts everything she can think of, making her parents happy and also supplying ideas for papers and essays to come. A third student is an annotator of books and magazines. Never lend him a book unless you want it back full of underlinings and remarks in the margin like *This is not true!!* He also keeps a notebook of observations and quoted material from his reading. We would hesitate to use his notebook method by itself. Think of having to read all the way through a notebook to find a remark you were sure you remembered putting down— somewhere. But his notebook works for him.

And that, of course, is the point. If brainstorming, freewriting in books, or keeping a diary, notebook, or journal works for you, do it. Indeed, don't be afraid to try anything that may produce or trap an idea. *Skim* a magazine or book; *watch* a TV channel you seldom watch; *read* a newspaper as if you were from a foreign country; *chat* with a stranger at the laundromat or supermarket. Interview a professor who teaches a course you've never heard of: "How did the course come to be taught? What do your students learn in it?"

PRACTICE

Read the student paper below. Work backwards from the paper, and make guesses on the strategies the student used in choosing and shaping the subject. How might she have used *brainstorming, freewriting, a journal, "looking around,"* and *surprise?*

ONE DOZEN WAYS TO PICK UP A CAT

1　　My brother, when he was little, picked up a cat (a small cat, to be sure—no more than a kitten) by both its ears. The kitten hung in the air, looking rather surprised, but without fear or noticeable resentment. Perhaps it understood that the little boy holding its ears was without experience or understanding and was more to be pitied than scratched. If one of us adults had tried this, that kitten would probably have located a few of our finger bones with its claws.

2　　You can pick up a cat by any one of four legs, or by all four legs at once. Or by its head—or, as we all know, by that favorite handle, the tail. Marjorie, a tough old woman on the farm south of us, had a couple of cats on her property to keep down the mouse population. They were never allowed in her house. But they always tried to get in. Whenever Marjorie opened the screen door, it was a signal for at least one cat to make a dash for the warm kitchen inside.

3　　Usually the cat never got more than a few inches inside the kitchen. As it whipped through the half-open door, tail at full mast, Marjorie would lean gracefully down like a ballet dancer, close her hand on ten full inches of tail, and smoothly swing the cat through the air and out of doors, where it would land on the porch with a light thump and look around with a great pretense of disinterest and fall to licking one paw. If the cat got safely into the kitchen, which seldom happened, it was allowed to stay for a while, and perhaps even to dip its nose into a saucer of milk.

4　　On the farm, we had a cat named Furde which got into the basement furnace when Dad was working on the machinery. Furde—a fine, intelligent, if overly curious calico cat—climbed into the open furnace and then into the cold-air ducting system. Dad closed up the furnace and departed. Not being able to get out of the furnace, Furde climbed up the cold-air duct to the second floor until she found a cold-air entrance (with tiny holes in it) from the duct into a bedroom. There she uttered horrible noises which, amplified by the metal ducting system, frightened my two-year-old sister so badly she ran into the bathroom and refused to come out.

5　　We took off the cover to the duct and discovered Furde barely visible and wedged sidewise in the hole. Taking a pair of tongs from the fireplace, we gently pulled at what we could see of her, and finally picked her up out of her predicament.

6　　Including the use of fireplace tongs, one can think of about a dozen ways to pick up a cat, some of them more appropriate than others. The cat itself has natural handles on both ends. Oddly enough, a full-grown cat does not like to be picked up by the scruff of the neck, the way a mother cat picks up her young. In fact, most cats don't like to be picked up by any method, as the barely healed scratches on my arms remind me. As of last week, I have finally determined that the thirteenth and best way to pick up a cat is not at all.

■■■ *Hooking an Idea*

One cold winter day we were talking to a student who had too many ideas. His father was a high school principal, and he was planning to write about the joys and sorrows of being a school principal in a small town.

The student showed us a dozen pages of false starts. We read them and asked, "How many subjects have you got here?"

"That's the trouble," he said. "I've got so many ideas about being a principal and so much to say that I don't know where to begin. If I could just get started . . ." We pointed to the back of the classroom. Along the wall was a line of coat hooks, and his coat was hanging on one of them. "Look at your coat," we said. "When you came in, you didn't throw your coat at the wall and hope it would miraculously stay up there off the floor. You hung it high and dry on a hook. You are trying to throw your next piece of writing at a rhetorical wall, hoping it will stay there. But your writing keeps falling down in a heap. Try some hooks. For example:

> *Why* school principals *fail.*

The hooks are provided in the words *why* and *fail.* As you plan your paper, keep hanging your ideas on those two words."

We told the student about other possible word-hooks for this paper:

> The *successful* principal *listens.*
>
> How a *good* principal *prepares.*
>
> A principal who keeps his job is *lucky.*
>
> A principal and town *politics.*
>
> Should you be a principal? Yes, if you have *patience* and physical *stamina.*

For two reasons, we recommend the hook strongly to writers. First, it dramatizes clearly and simply one of the natural ways the human brain works, and so helps us find and clarify ideas. It is natural for us to characterize and capsulize our experiences in single words (and, sometimes, phrases):

— That course is *boring.*
— For some American citizens. President Reagan was a *teflon* president.
— But I'm not *ready* to get married!
— All he wanted in life was *to act on the stage.*
— The Civil War was a *bloody disaster,* the first *modern war.*
— To me, God is a woman, and everything about Her reminds me of the *female.*
— A *partial solution* to terrorism is *phone tapping* suspected terrorists.

Each italicized word or phrase represents an idea-hook on which you can hang a paper or theme. Note, by the way, that the hook can be more than one device of grammar. In the previous examples:

Boring, teflon, and *ready* are adjectives.

Female, and *life* are nouns.

To act is an infinitive.

Bloody disaster and *modern wars* are noun phrases.

Phone tapping is a gerund phrase.

A second reason why we recommend the hook is that it supplies control throughout the writing process. No matter where you are in the process—whether in finding ideas, outlining, or rewriting—the hook provides a check on what you are doing. If, for instance, you are writing on why principals *fail,* throughout the writing process keep checking the *fail* hook to see that your paper is still hanging on it. For example: You will *fail* as a principal if you are not a good listener, an adept politician, and an organized planner. A student writing about a successful principal might use a different hook(s): A principal's job is not an easy one, but if you have *patience* and *physical stamina,* you will be successful.

Here, at the stage of finding ideas, we suggest only that you consider hanging your paper on something—or on something*s*. (Some ideas need two, even three, hooks.) Also, in this early stage, it is not important whether your hooks are expressed in a title, a sentence fragment, or a full sentence. The main thing is to get those hooks on paper so you can think about them and get started writing.

PRACTICE

Discussion

1. Let us assume that you want something changed. This change may involve better service for your car, different scheduling of classes, more money from home, getting the highway in front of your house repaired, or improved funding for women's sports at your college, etc.

   Look back at the strategies for finding ideas that we have examined. Prepare a few specific answers to these questions for class discussion:

   a. What change do you want?

   b. How did you decide on the change?

2. Sue Hubbell writes about "manhandling" a chainsaw:

   1   When the man in my life moved out, he left his chain saw behind, but it was a heavy, vibrating, ill-tempered thing. I weigh 105 pounds, and although I could lift it, once I had it running, it shook my hands so much that it became dangerous to use. The first year, I hired a man to cut my wood, but I wasn't pleased with the job he did. The next year, I needed money badly and wrote articles for a women's

magazine, articles that embarrassed me when I saw them in print below my name. Shame finally won out over cupidity and I quit, but as a reward and celebration I took some of the money I'd earned and bought the finest, lightest chain saw I could find.

2   All chainsaws are formidable and dangerous. A neighbor who earns his living in timber was cutting wood overhead when a branch snapped the saw back toward him. He switched off the engine, but the chain's continuing momentum carried the blade forward. It stopped after it had cut through the bill of his cap. When I told him I had bought my own chainsaw, he advised me, "The time to worry about a chainsaw is when you stop being afraid of it."

3   So I'm careful with my saw. I spend a lot of time sizing up a tree before I fell it. Once it's down, I clear away the brush around the tree before I start cutting it into lengths so I won't trip and lose my balance with the chainsaw running. And I simply let the widow-makers go, those trees that after being cut snag in another tree as they fall, because they require fancy cuts that are beyond my skill. A dull chain and a poorly running saw are dangerous, so I've learned to keep mine in good shape, and I sharpen the chain each time I use it. My chainsaw is a tool that does what I want it to do, and woodcutting is a job in which I take pleasure.

—Sue Hubbell, "Careful with a Chainsaw"

Work backwards from these paragraphs. Make a scratch list of ideas that might have occurred to Hubbell as she prepared to write. What were her *surprises?* Her *hooks?*

3. Titles are often a good way to create (and express) a *hook* for writing. Suppose you are writing a paper about the number of still-useful appliances that homeowners throw away. You want to emphasize that something else can be done with them, so you title your paper, "Repair, Don't Buy." The hook is in that word *repair* and your point is going to be: Don't buy a new toaster or lawnmower—repair the old one.

   Another example. A friend of yours pays a professional résumé company to write and print his job application for summer work. You look at the application and say to him, "You could have done that yourself on your own computer." You write a paper using a similar argument, titling it: "Student Résumés—Self-Design Is the Best Design." Your hook is in the words *self-design* and *best design.*

   Make up five titles for papers. Try to build in the *hook* for each title. Prepare to defend two of your titles in class.

▼ Avoiding Writer's Block

Writers find that blocks often occur when the message *"hooks"* are not sharp, when they are unsure of their facts, or when they are unsure of what they want the reader to *believe* or *do.*

When this happens to you, there is really only one thing to do: go back and fill in on your areas of ignorance. Get the facts. Make sure you know what your reader should believe or do.

After you have done that, start again. Are you blocking now? If so, don't waste time getting angry with yourself. Put pencil to paper and just start to write the familiar words in your hook or main point:

project finance Evans finance
Evans Evans Evans project finance

And write your reader's name over and over:

Marsh Marsh Marsh Marsh

Do both of these at once, loosening your muscles and keeping your brain warm and focused on the subject of your message. Now start to write . . .

Mr. Marsh, I really wish you would change your mind about financing the Evans project. The Evans project is dear to my heart; it is also one that will help the company in our fall campaign click Mr. Marsh, would you please reconsider the financing of the Evans projects. . .

Right at that *click* everything fell into place. You were relaxed; your mind was engaged on the problem; you knew where the message was going; your muscles were warmed up. The block just disappeared. You exercised it out of existence.

Some people never suffer from writer's block. Good for them. But for those of us who do, we are like baseball pitchers who need extra warm-up time before beginning to throw hard. If we don't warm up carefully, there goes the old arm, tied in knots and extremely painful. The main cure is to warm up carefully and not to worry.

Our example, as you have seen, is of a writer who uses pencil and paper. The same method works for those who dictate. For those who type or use a computer, warm up by hitting keys at random and then typing clichés:

```
cnvmbj24343434 45trtfgf hjhjykopdhs ajcbghtuypio Now is the time
for Now is the time Now is Now Now Now Now Now for the all good
men to come to the aid of their country men and women.
```

```
To be or not to be that is the question Who cares whether that is the
question Hamlet was a dummy he should have run away from the
castle with Ophelia and had a bunch of little great danes. etoain
shrdlu.
```

Now you are warmed up and can start writing.

The key to removing all blocks is action. Get your muscles, hands, and mind moving. When they are warm they will continue moving easily and with less effort on your part.

PRACTICE

Writing

1. Write a paper based on Practice 1, under *Discussion* questions (page 18).

2. Take a blank sheet of paper and start writing. Don't stop to think—simply begin. If nothing else gets you moving, write "One, two, three, four, get up and bar the door . . ." Write anything that crosses your mind until you get to the bottom of the page.

    Pick up a second sheet. From the first sheet, make a few lists of words and phrases that strike your fancy, like: "I can hear the faucet dripping. I remember Lee left the cap off the toothpaste again. Sloppy roommate." Make a judgment: "He is sloppy but easy to live with." Generalize: "Sloppy roommates are tolerable if they are easy to live with."

    Spend a few minutes working back and forth between your first sheet of paper and your second. Listen for the meanings. On your second sheet, write a column heading: Hooks. How many hooks can you find from the first sheet? From the second? Can you find or create any surprises?

CHAPTER 3

The Writer's Stance

▼ An Example

Glen Bantz waved the engineer's report in the air, then dropped it on his desk. Bantz is the executive vice president of his company. We were interviewing him for an article on college graduates and what they should know about writing.

"If you want to know what to teach engineers about writing, I'll tell you," Bantz said. "It's the same thing I'd tell you to teach accountants, lawyers, technical editors, MBAs, anybody who works for this company—or any other outfit, for that matter."

Bantz picked up several folders from his desk.

"In each of these folders is a report from one of our field offices. In my in-basket, there's a bunch of letters and memos from these same offices. I'm going to tell my secretary to buy a great big rubber stamp. Without reading any of these letters and memos, I'm going to rubber-stamp each one on the first page and send it back to the author for rewriting. Here's what the stamp will look like."

We peered at the piece of paper he handed us. It had three questions on it:

> Who am *I??*
>
> Who are *YOU??*
>
> What is my *POINT??*

Ninety percent of the company's problems in communication, Bantz told us, come from writers not answering those questions before they write something. . . .

Who am I?—this question reminds the writer to identify the *role* he is assuming for that particular message. (As you will see later in this chapter, every writer can have many different roles.)

Who are YOU?—this question reminds the writer to identify the *reader* (or group of readers) he or she is writing to. One particular idea can have different "readerships," each of which may require a somewhat different strategy of writing.

What is my POINT?—this question reminds the writer to give the reason for the message. *Why is he writing it, and why should anybody be persuaded to read it?*

Before we left his office, Glen Bantz gave us several examples of messages rewritten with these questions in mind. One message—originally incomprehensible—was only a sentence in length; Bantz had cut it out of *Communication Briefings,* a magazine designed for all people who write, in or out of college. Here is the incomprehensible sentence:

> *The proposal for carrying out the self-study has been redesigned to facilitate more closely with ongoing strategic planning processes and to capitalize on pre-existing data.*

The revision suggested for this "putrid" sentence, as the magazine called it, is:

> *We have redesigned the self-study proposal to fit our strategic plan better and to get the most out of the data we have.*

"Look at the revision," Bantz said. "It shows why my rubber stamp should help to improve company writing. First, the writer puts himself—and his group—into the sentence with *we.* Second, he clearly has a reader in mind. Third, the point of the whole thing is much clearer."

"What would you say to the idea that the writer's difficulty is basically one of style?" we asked.

"Well," Bantz answered, "we've spent a thousand bucks a day on writing consultants to teach our people better style, and almost nothing happened. Their writing didn't show any significant change. Then we figured out that bad style was the *symptom,* not the disease."

"We needed to treat the disease," he went on. "So we made each employee in the home office answer my three questions before writing anything,—anything at all! Their reports and memos immediately became much clearer. And *shorter!* What this taught us was that the problem must be solved *before* writing—before the style has a chance to get bad."

The main idea of these introductory remarks has been made somewhat differently by Ernst Jacobi, an authority on writing:

1   There may be some writers in this world who never get stuck, writers whose fluency is so great that it carries them without a break from the beginning to a predetermined end. I am not one of them. I get stuck with depressing regularity, and I find that the best way to become unstuck is to start over as if I were writing a letter to a friend. This prescription also seems to work well for others who have tried it.

2   Writing in the form of a letter to a friend gives you several immediate advantages. It forces you to focus on one specific person, preferably one whom you respect and especially like; this immediately influences your communicative attitude. You will tend to be warm, direct, informal, and spontaneous. You will instinctively take care to stress why

you are writing and why you think that what you are writing will be of interest. And you will probably avoid being pompous, stiff, and self-important. You are, after all, writing to a friend. You are not trying to impress him. You know he knows you're not stupid, and you need not be afraid of his (or her) criticism. At least that's the kind of friend you should write the letter to—someone at your own level whose weaknesses and failings you know as well as he knows yours.

—Ernst Jacobi, *Writing and Work*

Although Glen Bantz and Ernst Jacobi come from very different places in the American scene, they agree on one thing about writing. *Before* writers write, they must decide on three things: the role to adopt, the point of the message, and the person(s) who will read it. Considered together as a unit, these three things are called *the writer's stance.* It is the subject of this chapter.

Incidentally, we do not mean to suggest that the problem of *writer's stance* is meant for "real-world" writing only. Indeed, the person who popularized the idea of stance was an English professor who based his original theory on the problems of a college English major who had trouble organizing material and writing clear sentences. The strategy of specifying a clear *stance* is for all writers at every level of school and profession.

▼ Applying the Principles of Stance

So far, we have been discussing *stance* in fairly general terms. Now let's be specific, and apply the principle to some writing problems you may have. Our examples will come from two student writers, Michael and Nancy. Michael's example is brief; Nancy's is longer, and we will follow it from conception to finished paper.

Michael drives a cab part-time. He has an interesting idea for a paper: that cab driving is an unglamorous job. Here is one of the paragraphs in his first draft:

> Traffic can destroy patience faster than threading heavy thread through a needle. City driving sneaks up on your nerves. It doesn't blast you; it just gnaws at your stomach. Cars are death traps. It takes so little to be behind a wheel—almost anyone can get a license. And there's not much money in it. Driving all day I saw them all, wild drivers, incompetent drivers, angry drivers. I made mistakes too and put lives in jeopardy; I came to respect the power of the automobile.

When he talked to us, Michael said that he did not feel comfortable with what he had written. Something, he wasn't sure what, had gone wrong; he was stuck and could not continue with any confidence.

The problem was that he had not yet found an appropriate stance for the essay. What was he trying to say about cab driving? His paragraph rambles, making three or four points without developing any one of them adequately. To improve his work, he needed to specify the three elements of stance:

Role: I am a student working part-time as a driver for a local cab company.
          I am nineteen years old.

Thesis: Driving a cab part-time is a poor way for a college student to make money.

Reader: The "general reader," who might be curious about what it's like to drive a cab.

About the general reader we will have more to say later. Michael began to rewrite his paper, getting this result for two paragraphs:

> On an average twelve-hour workday on Saturday or Sunday, I make twenty-five to thirty dollars after paying for half of the gas I use—a company requirement. I start at six o'clock in the morning, and finish at seven in the evening. But since the supper hour is the busiest time of the day, I often have to stay an hour late. The cabs eat gas like luxury cars. Twenty-five percent of my profits are lost in paying for gas. In the winter, between calls, I either turn off the engine or burn up all my profits. Cold, cold.
>
> I receive tips from perhaps one-fifth of the fares. If a person gives me a quarter he smiles benevolently as if he has finally proved to himself that he really has a philanthropic heart. "Well, how much do you get as a tip?" some will ask. Or: "What's the right amount to tip?" A common comment, after a toothy smile: "Well, you got me here safely, didn't you? I think you deserve a tip." An extra dime falls into my hand, and after my word of thanks, I hear a chuckle or two, and a pleasant, "You're welcome, you're quite welcome."

These paragraphs are not perfect, but they're better than Michael's first effort—more interesting, readable, and informative. We know who the writer is, why he wishes to communicate to us, what the point of his communication is.

As a part of a new assignment, Michael tried shifting his stance:

> Your cabs are in terrible condition; some are actually unsafe. The horn did not work on mine all last weekend. The brakes on No. 37 are so badly worn that they will not respond without pumping. Since most of us have to drive fast to get from one place to another to pick up a new fare, we are endangering our lives and other people's—just to do our jobs.

The writer's role here stays the same, but Michael has changed his thesis and his reader, who is now the owner of the cab company.

Let's consider another writer. Nancy was working on a paper for her composition class. But the paper—about her experiences backpacking in Europe last summer—refused to get written. She made several false starts, tried an outline that got nowhere, and filled parts of three pages with neat handwriting that turned into scrawls as she realized that the paper was not coming out right.

What to do? She remembered her instructor's suggestion: "If you get into trouble on a paper, don't keep fighting it—come see me right away!"

So, bundling up her material (false starts, scrawls, and the outline that went nowhere), off she went to her instructor's office. He looked at what she had written so far and said to her: "Surely we can do something with this. But before we go on, tell me—just how do you feel about your subject?"

"Traveling in Europe? A perfect subject for me," said Nancy. "I just spent over two months living it. I'm following your advice: 'Write about what you know.' I have a lot of concrete materials, so the paper ought to write itself. I don't usually have much trouble writing, but right now each word comes harder than the last one. I feel as if I should tear it all up and start over. But *how* do I get a better start? Talk about frustration!"

The basic solution to Nancy's problem, her instructor told her, may lie in improving her stance. She had forgotten that a successful paper is always written by somebody, to somebody, and for a purpose. Using her material as an example, let's examine the elements of stance—*role, thesis* (point), and *reader.*

■■■ The Role

You do not use a role to cover up your true self or to give a false impression to a reader. Nor do you use it to play out a fictional part, as you might if you were acting on stage or in film. Your role as writer is a legitimate part of you and your existence. Who are you and what do you do? How many roles do you adopt as a matter of course in your daily life?

Nancy is eighteen years old. She graduated from high school last spring. She lives in a dormitory and has a part-time job. She is taking a general science course, and hopes eventually to be a hospital technician. She saved her job money during her last year in high school in order to backpack through Europe in the summer with a friend. Here are some of her roles that she mentioned to her instructor:

— babysitter	— bicycle owner
— consumer	— stenographer/typist
— taxpayer	— cook
(five cents on every dollar)	— daughter
— sister	— amateur pottery maker
— U.S. citizen	— environmentalist
— college student	— member of Sierra Club

Her instructor told her that he could not find Nancy in the first drafts of her paper—that, in effect, he could not see one of her clear roles as a writer in them. "Before you start writing again," he told her, "pick a role and stick to it. What do you want to be?"

"An American traveling in Europe."

"Pretty vague," he said. "Politicians, movie stars, tourists, soldiers, business executives—they can all be 'Americans traveling in Europe.' Can you be more specific?"

"OK, I am a woman; I'm eighteen; I know a little French, but no other foreign languages. I took 2,500 hard-earned dollars out of my bank account—that was all there was in it—and flew off to another part of the world, not knowing any more what I was getting into than if I were flying to the moon. But I was going to see everything!"

"Good enough," he said. "There's a genuine role for you: a young American woman on the loose over there without much money who's going to see every castle and museum on the continent. Now—what is your thesis?"

■■■ The Thesis

Her instructor talked to Nancy about several possibilities for a *thesis*—the point of the paper, *its main idea stated in one specifically written sentence.* She could discuss the language problems she encountered, the difficulties of travel for someone without much money, the sights to see, and the problem of communicating with parents and friends thousands of miles away.

But Nancy kept coming back to one idea that she considered important. Too many young Americans, like herself, went off merrily to Europe without being properly pre-pared for what they would encounter. Her thesis suggested itself. Why not try to warn travelers about three or four problems they might encounter, and suggest how they could go about solving them? At this stage, then, her hooks for the paper were *traveling in Europe* and *problems.* (For a discussion of *hooks,* see Chapter 2, pages 17–18).

Her instructor agreed that this idea could lead to a sensible thesis. (The final version of her thesis is given below.)

▪▪▪ The Reader

Now Nancy needed to specify a reader.

"You already know," said her instructor, "that you seldom (if ever) write anything that is directed to every person who reads English. Most pieces of writing are directed to a special reader or group of readers. Your own composition textbook is directed to one group of readers; an article in *TV Guide* is directed to another; a set of directions on repairing a motorboat engine to yet another. While these groups of readers may overlap somewhat, they usually do have a certain distinctness. Write for a specific reader, Nancy; aim for a particular target."

Nancy commented that her thoughts about her role and thesis also seemed to suggest a certain group of readers—those young American backpackers with little money who intended to see Europe but wouldn't always know what to expect.

▪▪▪ A Completed Stance

Nancy's completed stance now looked like this:

My role: I am a young American who traveled through Europe this summer. I would like to show how other backpackers can do the same thing, but do it more easily than I did.

My thesis: In order to make traveling easier and more pleasant in Europe, buy three informative books, learn about youth hostels, and be prepared for the "male problem."

My reader: Young Americans who might want to travel as I did. My essay will be slanted somewhat to women, but men should definitely be inter-ested too.

Here is Nancy's completed paper.

WHAT YOU ALWAYS WANTED TO KNOW ABOUT BACKPACKING IN EUROPE (BUT DIDN'T KNOW ENOUGH TO ASK)

1   So you're going to hike around Europe! You have saved some money; you have your backpack all ready to go (complete with a box of bandages for the very sore feet you're going to get); and you have pored over your collection of travel folders, looking again at those glamorous canals and castles and mountains that will shortly be in front of your camera.

2   But have you talked to other young people who have recently been there? Do you know what to look for and what to expect? I thought I was well prepared in every way, but some problems came up I did not expect. I could have dealt with them much more easily if I had had the information I am giving you here. I'll omit a lot of little things in order to concentrate on three larger ones: certain useful books to buy, the nature of youth hostels, and the problem of men in southern Europe. (I assume that, like myself and most of the other young travelers I met, you are traveling light and on a small budget—I got home with twenty-five cents.)*

3   Before you begin your trip, there are two or three books I would recommend you buy and read. One is a budget guide, Arthur Frommer's *Europe on Fifty Dollars a Day.* This book tells you a great deal about all the major cities in Europe. It has descriptions of the fascinating places to go and often how to get there. It also includes names of inexpensive restaurants and hotels. The book is a reassuring thing to have when you arrive in a big city with no place to sleep. Also, by reading about what is in a city before you go, you can decide in advance if you want to visit it.

4   Another important book to get is a *Rail Schedule.* It includes train schedules for all of western Europe. If you have a Eurailpass, which is probably the cheapest and fastest way to travel in the western countries on the continent, this book will be a great help. Having a complete *Schedule* allows you to stop in little out-of-the-way places because you know when and where you can get connections *out* of them. It's usually not wise to jump on a train going to a tiny town if you have no idea when you can catch another train to leave. Also, having the *Rail Schedule* will inevitably save you long hours of waiting in train stations. Since many of the southern countries do not post schedules, it is extremely time-consuming to stand (sometimes for hours) in information lines trying to find out when you can leave.

5   A third book I recommend is the *Youth Hostel Guide.* This book tells you where the hostels are and how far they are located from the train stations. It gives hostel facilities, hours, and (sometimes) prices. I tried to get along without a hostel book some of the time by using the information offices at railway stations. The information clerk could usually tell me if there was a hostel and how to find it. But if you are planning to do any traveling in rural areas, like Normandy in France, as I did, you will definitely need a *Hostel Guide.* The townspeople in such areas often don't even know their hostel exists.

6   Staying in youth hostels can make your living expenses much lower, but sometimes the problems and restrictions of staying in a hostel may make other accommodations more desirable. Hostels are dormitory-type hotels that rent a cheap place to sleep. Their quality varies greatly. Some of them are very clean and have all the comforts of home. Others are incredibly dirty and primitive. Before you plan to make a habit of staying in hostels you should know that they have two large drawbacks.

7   First, hostels are usually located far away from the center of the city, sometimes too far to make staying in one economical. Be prepared either to walk a long way into town or to spend money on subways and buses. Second, the early curfews in most hostels makes staying in them a problem if you want to go out on the town. Most of them have a curfew as early as 10 P.M. Although there are a few hostels that will charge a small fine for being late, most of them simply lock the doors at 10:00 so no one can get in *or* out. If you are in a city like Munich or London where you want to stay out late, I would advise staying in a cheap hotel rather than in a hostel.

---

* In order to make your sentences flow smoothly in your introduction, you may have to paraphrase your thesis rather than state it word for word. Note that Nancy's original thesis (pages 26–27) is paraphrased in paragraph 2.

8   Hostels are closed during the day between 9:00 and 5:00. This causes some difficulty if you arrive in a new town early in the afternoon and go straight to the hostel. You will end up wasting a lot of time just waiting for it to open. And you will have plenty of waiting ahead of you in the check-in line. Because hostels are closed all day and because many of them require that you reregister every night, you could end up in some very long lines, especially during the summer months. The fact that the hostels are closed from 9:00 to 5:00 means that you may have to keep walking around all day. In the southern countries like Italy and Spain, where an entire town closes up during the afternoon, you can end up with nothing to do and no place to go.

9   If you women are planning to spend any time at all in Italy, Greece, or Spain, you should be forewarned about the male population. (This section should be read by you men too because you will undoubtedly be approached by an American girl looking for someone to protect her or just to sit with her until her harassers leave.) The first thing you have to realize when traveling in these countries is that a local woman does not ordinarily walk out on the street without a sister or an older woman with her. So when you go out on the street alone you are automatically taken to be a tourist—and available. Also, the men have some kind of early detection device for American girls. It doesn't matter what you look like or what you are wearing. In Italy particularly, you will be leered at, jeered at, whispered to, pinched, and generally driven crazy by the men. Don't think you can go unnoticed; the mere fact that you are an American on the street draws attention to you. Being with a man helps sometimes, but not always. My girl friend and I were with eight British and American boys in Rome, and it made absolutely no difference. You can be wearing a potato sack and the men will still bother you—I wouldn't recommend wearing a dress or shorts and halter tops anywhere. Wearing jeans instead will save you a lot of trouble. All of this may sound exaggerated to you, but it isn't. And it's better to expect the worst. If you are bothered less than you expected to be, it's better than entering a country like Italy unprepared for the hassles.

10   A final point. Don't be discouraged by any of the things I have warned you about. Just know what to expect, and prepare carefully for your trip. Europe is a wonderful place, and I had a wonderful time. I have no regrets, and I would go again. Have a great time— and hang on to your Eurailpass!

▼ Avoiding the *You* Stance

You have just read a paper in which the author, Nancy, addressed her reader directly as *you,* or implied *you* in making suggestions or commands—as in ["*You*] be prepared to walk. . . ." Nancy did this because her stance (see page 27) called for a reader to whom she was speaking directly. This situation is fairly common, as the following examples show.

Situation	**Sample Sentence** *from the paper*
1. You are telling readers how to understand a satirical cartoon	If *you* look in the bottom left corner, *you* will see the tiny comment by the cartoonist's "stand-in," a comic mouse.
2. You are explaining a process	Before setting the margins, check the manual on the printer. (*You* is understood in [You] check the manual. . . .)

If, for any reason, you wish to avoid using the informal *you,* change your stance so that *you,* explicit or implied, can be smoothly avoided. Employing the two examples above, we can change the stance of each so that the *sample sentences* contain no *you:*

1   In the bottom of the left-hand corner, the cartoonist put his tiny comment in the mouth of his "stand-in," a comic mouse.
2   Before setting the margins, the operator checks the printer.

In both these examples, after adjusting the stance, the writer employs the objective third-person viewpoint, thus allowing *you* to disappear painlessly.

It is unwise to say that good writing either uses *or* does not use *you* as a matter of good taste or propriety. *You* appears in writing more as a consequence of stance than anything else. And like anything else in writing, *you* can be overworked—even tiresomely so.

In her paper on traveling in Europe, Nancy employed *you* throughout. She could have used the same material but changed her stance to avoid *you,* as this version of paragraph 3 shows (compare the same paragraph, page 28):

Before students begin their trip, there are two or three books I would recommend they buy and read. One is a budget guide, Arthur Frommer's *Europe on Fifty Dollars a Day.* This book tells the student a great deal about all the major cities in Europe. It has descriptions of the fascinating places to go and often how to get there. It also includes names of inexpensive restaurants and hotels. The book is a reassuring thing to have when students arrive in a big city with no place to sleep. Also, by reading about what is in a city before they go, they can decide in advance if they want to visit it.

PRACTICE

Discussion

Before discussing the following questions, review the summary of Nancy's *writer's stance* (page 27).

a. In her first two paragraphs, how does Nancy show a concern for her reader? How does she *involve* her reader in her topic?

b. The thesis of the essay is stated, in paraphrased form, at the end of paragraph 2. Given the nature of Nancy's topic, is this a natural place for the thesis? Are there other places where the thesis might comfortably be placed? Why must the reader's reactions be closely considered when you decide on a location for your thesis?

c. Why will the reader appreciate the expression *"Another important book* to get . . ." at the beginning of paragraph 4?

d. Toward the end of paragraph 5, Nancy writes: "But if you are planning to do any traveling in rural areas, like Normandy in France, as I did, you will definitely need a *Hostel Guide.*" How, if at all, does this sentence reinforce

Nancy's adopted role in her writer's stance? Do you find other sentences in other paragraphs that remind the reader of her role?

e. What other readers could this paper be directed to? What changes would be necessary in Nancy's role for other readers?

f. What kinds of readers (other than those we have already mentioned) would not find this paper very useful? Explain.

g. In paragraphs 6 and 7, how does Nancy make sure that her reader can follow the organization of her ideas?

h. A well-made paragraph can often be considered as a small "essay." Discuss the effectiveness of paragraph 9 as a little essay. Does it have a stance any different from that of the whole essay?

i. How does Nancy's conclusion fit her stance? Is there any contradiction in her conclusion?

j. The purpose of writing, of course, is to communicate ideas, attitudes, facts, and values. When a reader finishes a piece of writing, he should know more than he did when he started. Using brief phrases, make a list of "new knowledge" you have gained from Nancy's writing. What does this list tell you about her ethical proof?

k. As a typical reader, write a note to Nancy making comments or suggestions about her writer's stance and her material. What, for instance, would you wish she had covered in her paper that she did not?

▼ The Writer's Stance and *You*

Are you wondering whether Nancy's writing problem is typical of most of the problems you will face? It *is* pretty typical. She had started out simply to write a paper on her European experiences, and she specified her stance using that idea as a broad base on which to build. For most assignments (whether you choose a topic or it is given to you by your instructor), you can follow a procedure roughly similar to Nancy's when you specify your own stance.

To help you with your various stances in preparing to write your papers, we suggest that you ask (and answer) certain questions about role, thesis, and reader:

Role: In this paper, who am I? What role can I most reasonably adopt? Will I feel comfortable in this role? What are my purposes in adopting it? Can I maintain it consistently throughout the paper?

Thesis: What main point do I want to explain or prove to my reader? Can I state this point specifically in a single sentence?

Reader: What reader, or group of readers, do I want to inform or convince? Have I identified the most appropriate reader?

Overview: How does my writer's stance look as a whole? Are its three parts logically related?

■■■ *Your Role and Your Reader*

Of course you are limited to some extent by the roles and readers that, in a practical way, are available to you. A readership of middle-aged bankers or Los Angeles cab-drivers would not have been practical for Nancy's essay on traveling in Europe. And if she were given the topic "Defend or Attack Offshore Drilling for Oil," her writer's role would probably be limited because, as she mentioned in her list of possible roles, she is an environmentalist and a member of the Sierra Club, an organization pledged to pre-serve the coastline against offshore drilling. As to what this specific limitation would amount to, she would have to decide for herself. Each of you will have your own limi-tations in roles—limitations governed by age, philosophy, political and religious beliefs (or lack of them), experience, knowledge of the subject, and so on. But on most topics, even within the framework of such limitations, there should be several writer's roles you can choose for your papers.

For most topics, there are also several possible audiences. On the offshore drilling topic just mentioned, your readership might be one of these:

— legislators considering an offshore drilling proposal
— drivers of cars who buy gasoline
— other college students of your "type"
— anyone interested in the topic
— anyone uninterested in the topic (a challenge to the writer)
— a writer who has written an argument for or against offshore drilling

Some of these audiences are more general than others. On many topics you may find that it is practical to address these *general readers,* a class of people who vary somewhat in age, occupation, and interests. But you should always specify and describe even your general audience because it will usually have certain characteristics that set it off from the "whole world" of readers. A letter written to your local newspaper on rezoning prime farmland for industrial use should not be directed to all readers of the newspaper because all of them are not equally interested in the subject or able to do anything about it.

To take another example, a critical essay on a novel should not be written for "every-body," but only for those interested in serious fiction generally and in your novel specif-ically—usually someone who has read the novel. If your group of readers have not read the novel, then that fact affects your thesis and your essay, which in this instance is likely to take the form of a review ("For the following reasons, this book is good—read it").

Too many students believe that their audience consists of one person, the instructor. In some cases, he or she may be your only reader. But in reality, he or she is quite often your *teacher-editor,* a trained professional who stands between you and your readers, pointing out where you have gone wrong in your essay, what you have done well, and how you can make your work more convincing.

■■■ *Guidelines for Identifying "The Reader"*

Most papers are written for readers, in the plural. To see how we can identify them, let's look in on a brainstorming session (for *brainstorming,* see pages 11–12). The stu-dents in the session are brainstorming the audience for a short paper discussing requirements for the film study major at the college. The paper will argue that the requirements should be *increased.*

Arthur:	Audience is all students here.
Scott:	Not all are interested.
Catherine:	Just majors.
Wilda:	No, majors and minors.
Francisca:	They are not the ones who make the requirements.
Wilda:	Decide on one group.
Scott:	Who has the most power to make changes?
Instructor:	Faculty committee on Majors and Minors.
Scott:	Tenured professors on the committee, then.
Catherine:	Are all professors on the committee tenured?
Wilda:	What's the membership like?
Instructor:	(reading) Two full profs., one in 18th century lit., one in film study; two assistant professors, one in film study, one in composition; one student—five people total. Student's name is Gary Nelson.
Wilda:	Anyone know the student?
Francisca:	I think that's the Nelson who writes movie reviews for the paper.
Shannon:	Three people, then, who care about film; two unknown. Shall we write for the three we are sure of, and guess about the others?
Don:	They wouldn't be on the committee unless they were reasonably sympathetic to film study.
Shannon:	Assumption: The committee wants the film study courses to succeed. Would not mind increasing hours for the major.
Scott:	But another assumption: At least two people on this committee might think doing that would decrease the majors in either rhetoric or "straight" literature. Watch out for *them.*
Catherine:	You mean they might be hostile to the proposal in the paper?
Francisca:	OK, assume two hostiles in the audience.

We'll break off our account of the brainstorming session here. The group has clearly moved toward a good sense of their audience for an argument that requirements should be increased for the major in film. In essence, their conclusion was that the audience should be taken as mixed in several ways—student and professorial; possibly hostile to the argument, and non-hostile; knowledgeable about film study and not knowledgeable. The paper should be written to "spread" to this audience. In other words, no part of the audience should be ignored in certain parts of the argument. If, for example, the writer assumes that all members of the audience know the history of the major in film and why certain requirements have been put in, he or she may miss the student member and possibly the two professors who do not teach in the film program.

We can set up flexible guidelines for considering readership or audience:

1. If possible, list the people in the audience—or, at least, the *types* of people. Know who and what they are.

2. Consider their knowledge; how much do they *know* about your subject and its various parts? (Are they very familiar with one part but not another?)

3. What are their prejudices—or prejudgments? What kind of automatic acceptance or rejection of your ideas are you likely to encounter? Familiar (and controversial) subjects like abortion, capital punishment, and "big" government touch many nerves in people. But sometimes subjects that are less familiar and controversial can bring strong reactions you never expected. That can be awkward!

4. What parts of your argument—or of your material—are they likely to accept? For whatever reason, what parts are they not likely to accept? Shape your paper accordingly.

5. As you write, keep in mind the typical faces of your readers. Imagine, as you write, that you are speaking to them and that they are reacting to your ideas as listeners would. Doing this gives you an immediate imaginative feedback on your ideas as you write them.

■■■ *Your Thesis*

Much of what we have said on the practical limitations of role and reader also applies to the thesis. The thesis, discussed at length in the next chapter, is dependent on role and reader. If you change either of these latter two, your thesis will probably change as well. A thesis is also dependent on what you know about your subject. Nancy said that so far as foreign languages are concerned, she knows only "a little French." Given this fact, it is doubtful that any thesis of hers could easily deal with the Italian language, classical French literature, or modern Greek grammar. But given the knowledge about Europe gained in her travels, she might construct a number of interesting theses, as follows (for the purposes of illustration, we will ignore here the problems of role and reader):

— The average Englishman seems friendlier to the backpacker than the average Frenchman.
— If you want to stay healthy in Europe, stick to simple foods and carry plenty of stomach medicine.
— For an American traveling in Europe, French is the most useful foreign language to know.
— Although France has the reputation of being anti-American, France seems more Americanized than England, Germany, Greece, Italy, or Spain.
— The American Youth Hostel Association needs tighter control from its top administration.
— The beauty of Greece is undeniable, but its beauty is unvarying and, after a while, rather boring.

PRACTICE

Discussion

1. Here is a brief essay, that tries to influence the thinking of the reader. Answer the questions following the essay.

1   A traveler enters Maine at the very spot where John Paul Jones's *Ranger* slid from the ways in 1777. A flawless thoroughfare of cement has replaced the winding, rutted trail of olden days. . . .

2   It was a road, not long since, of small white farms nestling in the shadow of brooding barns and sheltering elms; of old square homes built by shipbuilders and shipmasters; of lilac-scented Junes, and meadows rich in the odors of mallow and sweet-grass; of irregular stone walls; ancient taverns; solid, mellow little towns happy in the possession of architecture and tradition and family pride; of long stretches of pine woods, cool and fresh in the heat of summer; of birch-clad hill slopes, forests of oaks and sugar maples, swelling fields and flat salt marshes shimmering mistily in the warm summer sun; of life-giving breezes from the strip of deep blue sea at the far edge of all these things.

3   It was a beautiful road; a road for health and rest and peace of mind; a priceless possession, to be cherished and forever held in trust for the descendants of those who laid it out and made it possible. It was the essence of Maine; the gateway to the great and beautiful Maine wilderness to the north and east.

4   Today it is a road of big signs and little signs and medium-sized signs; of cardboard signs tacked to pine trees and wooden fences and dilapidated barns; of homemade signs tilting drunkenly in ragged fields and peering insolently from the yards and walls of furtive-looking houses; of towering signs thrusting garish, mottled faces before forests, fields, and streams, like fat, white-faced streetwalkers posing obscenely in a country lane; of little indecent litters of overnight camps, crawling at the edges of cliffs and in trampled meadows as though the countryside had erupted with some distressing disease: of windrows of luncheon boxes, beer bottles, paper bags, wrapping paper, discarded newspapers, and the miscellaneous filth of countless thoughtless tourists; of doggeries, crab-meateries, doughnutteries, clammeries; of booths that dispense home cooking on oilcloth and inch-thick china in an aura of kerosene stoves, smothered onions, and stale grease; of roadside stands resembling the results of a *mésalliance* between an overnight camp and an early American outhouse; of forests of telephone and electric light poles entangled in a plexus of wires.

5   It was a road rich in the effluvia of clams in batter, frying doughnuts, sizzling lard; in tawdriness, cheapness, and bad taste, but in little else.

—Kenneth Roberts, "Roads of Remembrance"

a. What is Roberts' thesis? Has he supported it adequately?

b. Why should Roberts care about a road in Maine? What is his role?

c. For whom is Roberts writing? Do you consider yourself a member of his audience? How are you affected by his essay?

    d. What does this essay tell you about Roberts' values and character *(ethical proof)*?

2. One of us received this letter, quoted in its entirety. How do you think the writer viewed the reader? The subject of the letter? The writer himself? Is the letter effective?

> Dear Professor Tibbetts:
>   This letter is to inform you of the death of Mr. _____, who is currently enrolled in your English 302, Sec. B. The student's registration will be officially canceled by the appropriate college office in the near future.
>   Sincerely,
>   _____, Associate Dean

3. Read this extract from a student's research paper. Describe and justify the student's use of *stance*.

> 1   Most authorities agree that *handedness* is the tendency to use a certain hand to perform most tasks. Modern authorities agree that handedness is related neurologically to the brain. One popular theory is that of "cerebral dominance," which means that one side of the brain dominates the other, this dominance being translated into the preference of one hand over the other.
>
> 2   The researcher encounters difficulty finding good authorities on the subject of handedness. First, the subject itself has no common name. One may have to look in his sources under *left-handedness, right-handedness, laterality,* and *handedness* before he can find information. Many good reference works (for example, the *Collier's Encyclopedia)* have no material on the subject. Those authorities which are available fall roughly into two groups: (1) the medical and (2) the psychological and educational. Since these two groups of authorities often do not agree with each other, one must decide whether to use certain information or to throw it out as being unscientific or unreasonable. In the latter category may be put the theory of Professor _____ in Educational Psychology 280. He told his class that handedness was the result of accident, depending upon which hand a child used in his crib or ate with. If the professor were correct, the laws of probability should require that about half of the population be right-handed and half be left-handed.

4. Here are two short pieces that describe the same process—the emergence of a butterfly from its pupa. But the descriptions use somewhat different *stances*. How are they different? Explain, using examples from the writers' works.

> Many of the parts of the future butterfly—the antennae, eye, proboscis, leg and wings—can be seen pressed close to the thoracic region, and the segments of the abdomen are visible also. The pupa does not feed, and remains still except for occasional twitchings of the abdomen. Inside the pupa changes are taking place, for most of the larval tissues are being broken down and re-organized to form the adult organs.
>
> —Robert Hull, *The Language Gap*

> But now, inside the pupa, their moment has come. The giant cells of the caterpillar's body die and the dormant cell-clusters suddenly begin to divide rapidly, nourishing

themselves on the soup of the disintegrated caterpillar body. The insect, in effect, is eating itself. Slowly it builds a new body of a completely different form. Its shadowy features can be seen on the outside of the brown pupa like the anatomy of a mummy, vague beneath the wrappings. Indeed, the name 'pupa' derives from a Latin word meaning 'doll', for at this stage the insect within seems to be wrapped in swaddling clothes.

—David Attenborough, *Life on Earth*

5. The four paragraphs following represent the introduction to a longer article by Nancy Hunt. From these paragraphs, you should be able to describe the author's use of stance in the rest of the article. What is Hunt's role? Who is her audience? Identify her thesis.

1   When I landed in Utica, N.Y., one recent weekend, I had been flying 7½ hours with just one fuel stop at Youngstown, Ohio, to break the journey and wash my hands. Tired, dirty, and hungry, I wanted only to tie down my Piper Tomahawk, find a motel room, and get a drink.

2   I spotted the only vacant parking spot on the ramp and was heading for it when a Cherokee taxied past, whipped around directly in front of me, and grabbed my space. I jammed on my brakes and sat there in stupefied indignation. I've seen some pushy people on the ramp at Midway Airport [in Chicago], but not *that* pushy.

3   Welcome to the surly East, home of bad manners!

4   Because I was born in New York City and reared in Connecticut, I consider myself an expert on Eastern manners. Chicagoans often laugh derisively when I say that Midwesterners are kinder and more courteous, but a trip back East confirms my view. . . .

Writing

1. As a writer, some of your first questions are: Who are my readers? How do I want to affect them? That is,

— What do I want them to believe?
— Do I want them to take action? Of what kind? Why?
— How and where should I tell them the point of my paper?
— How can I tell them who *I* am? (I'm not a ghost, after all, but a human being.)

   Write two versions of the same essay. For your major you are required to take a course for which you believe there is no practical use.

   a. Write an essay directed to the dean of your college, explaining why you and your fellow majors should not be required to take the course. Be cool and objective in your ethical proof.

   b. Write to other students in your major field. Try to get them to support you in your efforts to have the requirement abolished. In this version, your stance and approach to the subject will be more personal.

2. There is a bill before the state legislature that will impose a severe punishment for hitchhiking in your state. (We will assume that the laws now

covering hitchhiking are often not enforced and the punishments, if any, are mild.) Consider these roles, along with the suggested readers. You are:

a. A state trooper writing to your state representative.

b. A student living 50 miles from campus; you are writing to your campus newspaper.

c. A trucker writing to the opinion column of your union's monthly magazine.

d. A female student writing to your worried mother who lives in another state.

Write a paragraph for each of these situations, filling out your stance with a clear thesis. Let your paragraph be the *introduction* to your letter or article.

Given the general problem, what other stances are citizens in your state likely to take?

3. Here is an exotic writing assignment, one which you should not consider unless your instructor—in his or her unwisdom—insists.

You are a "Sand Dolphin," a species of intelligent beings (as yet unknown to people) that live mainly in the South Seas. One day you discover a well-preserved 1974 Volkswagen "Bug" lying in ten feet of water. Of course, you don't know it's a VW. One door is open and swinging slightly in the current. Nothing on the VW is obviously broken. (Where did it come from? You don't know, and neither do we. Perhaps it fell off a ship transporting it.)

The Sand Dolphins have a highly developed culture, complete with an elaborate communication system. It is your responsibility to report the objects you have found to the Ministry of USO's (Unidentified Sunken Objects).

The members of the ministry—like you—look, feel, and (most important) think like sea creatures. For instance, their idea of measurement is based upon the dimensions and physiology of a fish. They would never describe any object as being so many "feet" long.

Taking a Sand Dolphin's role, write a report to the ministry describing *in detail* the object you have found.

CHAPTER 4

Making A Point~Your Thesis

Every written communication must make a point. A letter to your newspaper, a note to the postman, an article on Democrats in the state legislature, a memo to your boss at work, a textbook on the American colonial period, one of your papers—each makes a point about something. The sharper the point, the more successful the communication. In written form, your paper's point is its thesis—*the main idea stated in one specific sentence.* The thesis that you use to guide your early planning does not always appear word for word in the essay itself. Sometimes, in order to fit a thesis into the flow of your writing, you may have to reword it slightly or take two or three sentences to state it. But for the purposes of planning, practice putting each thesis in a single sentence.

Why is a thesis useful? First, it helps you respond to the essay assignment and shape your ideas before you write. Second, the thesis helps you organize your material as you write; it keeps you from wandering away from your topic. Third, after you have completed your essay, you can use your thesis to judge whether you have done what you set out to do. Fourth, in conferences both you and your instructor will refer to your thesis when you discuss your essay's effectiveness—for example, its organization and the relevance of supporting material. And, of course, the thesis as expressed in your essay is a great help to your reader.

PRACTICE

Read the following brief essay by Isaac Asimov and prepare to discuss it in class. What is Asimov's *thesis?* How does he organize his essay around that thesis?

1   What is intelligence, anyway? When I was in the army I received a kind of aptitude test that all soldiers took and, against a normal of 100, scored 160. No one at the base had ever seen a figure like that, and for two hours they made a big fuss over me. (It didn't mean anything. The next day I was still a buck private with KP as my highest duty.)

2   All my life I've been registering scores like that, so that I have the complacent feeling that I'm highly intelligent, and I expect other people to think so, too. Actually, though, don't such scores simply mean that I am very good at answering the type of academic questions that are considered worthy of answers by the people who make up the intelligence tests—people with intellectual bents similar to mine?

3   For instance, I had an auto-repair man once, who on these intelligence tests, could not possibly have scored more than 80, by my estimate. I always took it for granted that I was far more intelligent than he was. Yet, when anything went wrong with my car I hastened to him with it, watched him anxiously as he explored its vitals, and listened to his pronouncements as though they were divine oracles—and he always fixed my car.

4   Well, then, suppose my auto-repair man devised questions for an intelligence test. Or suppose a carpenter did, or a farmer, or, indeed, almost anyone but an academician. By every one of those tests, I'd prove myself a moron. And I'd *be* a moron, too. In a world where I could not use my academic training and my verbal talents but had to do something intricate or hard, working with my hands, I would do poorly. My intelligence, then, is not absolute but is a function of the society I live in and of the fact that a small subsection of that society has managed to foist itself on the rest as an arbiter of such matters.

5   Consider my auto-repair man, again. He had a habit of telling me jokes whenever he saw me. One time he raised his head from under the automobile hood to say: "Doc, a deaf-and-dumb guy went into a hardware store to ask for some nails. He put two fingers together on the counter and made hammering motions with the other hand. The clerk brought him a hammer. He shook his head and pointed to the two fingers he was hammering. The clerk brought him nails. He picked out the sizes he wanted, and left. Well, doc, the next guy who came in was a blind man. He wanted scissors. How do you suppose he asked for them?"

6   Indulgently, I lifted my right hand and made scissoring motions with my first two fingers. Whereupon my auto-repair man laughed raucously and said, "Why, you dumb jerk, he used his *voice* and asked for them." Then he said, smugly, "I've been trying that on all my customers today." "Did you catch many?" I asked. "Quite a few," he said, "but I knew for sure I'd catch *you*." "Why is that?" I asked. "Because you're so goddamned educated, doc, I *knew* you couldn't be very smart."

7   And I have an uneasy feeling he had something there.

—Isaac Asimov, "Intelligence"

▼ The Assignment and the Thesis

You write because you need to, whether the "need" is imposed from within or without. Ordinarily, in your composition class, you write in response to an instructor's assignment. So let's now turn to the problem of the typical writing assignment and consider how it can lead to a thesis.

There are, roughly, three kinds of assignments. Here are examples, ranging from the general to the specific:

1. A brief general request for written work:

   "Write a paper for next Friday."

2. A request for a type of essay or for a particular essay topic:

   a. "Write an essay convincing someone to take up your hobby."

   b. "Write an essay explaining a cause or effect."

   c. "In your essay, discuss the characterization of Willy Loman in *Death of a Salesman.*"

3. A more specific request that tends to control your response as you write:

   a. "Write a paper that supports an idea that some people ordinarily do not agree with—for example, that organized athletic programs do not foster team spirit or group loyalty in the players; that strongly religious people can be evil; that going to college may be a serious mistake for certain young people."

   b. "If you were to call for a change in any university (or college) policy or practice, what would that change be? Write a letter to someone in authority outlining the policy or practice and stating your reasons for suggesting the change."

   c. "Some people believe that Willy Loman is not a tragic character. Define the term *tragic character,* and argue that Willy either is or is not tragic. (You may take the position that he is partially tragic.)"

While assignments **1** and **2** give you more freedom than **3** does, they may be harder to prepare. You have to specify most of the elements of the topic yourself, and you may spend as much time finding and limiting a topic as you spend actually writing the paper. But instructors continue to use assignments like **1** and **2** because with them you can choose your own material and create your own stance. You can write essays that you might not otherwise get a chance to write with the more limited assignments.

■■■ The Thesis Journal

Journal entries can help you to develop an appropriate thesis in response to an assignment. After Jack's instructor spent two class periods discussing these, he gave assignment **3a** above. Jack thinks about the assignment in his dorm room, wondering what he will write about, when he hears a sharp blast on a car horn. This blast is followed by a howl of locked brakes, a yell from somebody, and then the familiar crashing sound of metal meeting metal. By the time he gets his eyes focused on the street, the accident is over. The two cars are locked together there on the street, one of them at a right angle to the other.

Jack watches from his window as the police come, and then he gets a glimmer of an idea for a paper. He writes in his journal:

Auto accidents are something that I know about. For two years I've worked as an assistant to the ambulance drivers for the Pemberton Funeral Home on weekends and during the summer. As a part of the ambulance team, I've seen thirty or forty accidents, a few of them fatal. Let me jot down a thesis or two for this assignment:

> Auto accidents should be prevented.

(Objection: Of course they should be prevented; who would argue that they shouldn't be?)

> There are fewer auto accidents in Tennessee than in Illinois. (Wait: I don't really know very much about auto accidents in Tennessee.)

Maybe I'd better take my instructor's advice and make a list:

autos	casket?
accidents	relatives worried
injury	cost—expensive!
mothers	cost of blood—how much?
fathers	cost of surgery?
worry for them because they're hurt	doctors' fees
auto accidents expensive	nurses
new engine—cost?	• ambulance costs
burial	ambulance driving

Look at all those items that have to do with the financial cost of the accident! If somebody pays money for accidents, someone earns it—doctors, nurses, hospitals, morticians, garages, mechanics. Everybody always talks about the cost of accidents but never about the profit in them.

I've found my hook! There's good money in accidents.

This is something that I know about because I had made good money as part of the ambulance team.

Here is my thesis: <u>Contrary to what many people think there is a lot of money to be made from automobile accidents</u>.

Now I need to establish my authority: I know the costs and also the money to be made from ambulance calls, and I know from being around Pemberton Funeral Home how much caskets and funerals cost. Other fees—those charged by garages and hospitals—I'm not so sure about. I guess I'd better check on that tomorrow.

Entries for the following day:

I just called two local hospitals and two garages and obtained a page of typical charges for typical injuries and damages, from broken legs to smashed fenders. I believe that I can write with reasonable authority on the subject. Or can I? I'd better check out my thesis again:

"... a lot of money to be made from auto accidents."
Where? New York State? Am I implying that auto accidents "cost" the same everywhere? I don't have any authority for making a judgment.

Maybe I'd better limit my thesis. How about this? <u>Contrary to what many people think, there is a lot of money to be made from auto accidents in the Phillipsburg area</u>.

Jack's essay now has a focus. In addition, he feels comfortable with the subject because he has available material, most of it taken from memory.

Another example of thesis development may be useful here. The assignment is: "Write an essay convincing someone to take up your hobby." In checking the assignment, you find that the key words or hooks are already in it: *convincing, take up,* and *hobby.*

These help in clarifying your subject. You settle quickly on a writer's role (that of a young person who needs to earn money for school expenses) and on a reader (a similar type of person, particularly one who can work with his or her hands).

Now you start specifying a point:

1. *My hobby* . . . used to be sports, but a compound fracture ended that . . . spend more time "clocking" now than in any other leisure-time activity . . . .

2. *Hobby is repairing clocks.* . . odd hobby for a kid . . . took it up by accident . . . money in it . . . tell why money in clock repair . . . .

3. *Good money in repairing clocks* . . . but it's interesting too . . . almost everyone is fascinated by an old clock . . . that's all I work on . . . remember I have to *convince* someone to take up my hobby . . . .

4. **Thesis:** *If you want an interesting and profitable hobby, take up clock repair.*

Since the thesis is clear, narrowed, and specific, it would be a good one to use when organizing and writing the paper.

▆▆▆ The Thesis as Answer to a Question

Finding a workable thesis often seems to involve "thinking out loud," as Jack did, picking your way through ideas as they occur to you, selecting and discarding as you go along. Look for key words in an assignment and underline them. If other key words or hooks occur to you, put them down on scratch paper before they get away. As you think out loud, ask yourself the questions in the following list. (The word *something* stands for your subject or an important idea about it.)

— What was the effect of *something?* Its cause?
— Can I break *something* down or analyze its main parts in order to understand it better?
— Can I compare *something* to another thing?
— Can I define *something?*
— Is *something* typical for some people and not for others?
— Is *something* good or bad, or partly good and partly bad?
— Who knows about *something?* Who would I see or what would I read to find out?
— What class or category of ideas or objects is *something* in?
— What are the facts about *something?* What things aren't known?
— Can I tell a story about *something?*
— Does *something* do any job that is necessary for a group, large or small?
— How is *something* made or created? Destroyed?
— How can one do or perform *something?*
— Can I recommend *something* to other people? Not recommend?
— Should I suggest changes in *something?*

Note: We discuss the development of answers to many of these questions in the Reader.

Here are two examples of how a thesis can be an answer to a question:

Question: How can one do *something?*

Thesis: *Anyone can put up a standard house wall if he buys good-quality, straight studs, can use a level accurately, and makes all measurements carefully.*

Question: What is a *computer program for writers?*

Thesis: *A computer program is a piece of computer software that is designed to help someone design, write, and revise a document.*

▼ Improving Your Thesis

As you work on your thesis, consider these suggestions for making it useful and effective:

1. Base Your Thesis on What You Know (Ethical Proof).

You know a lot about a variety of subjects. So write about them: your family; your friends; your hometown; the politicians, doctors, mechanics, plumbers, carpenters, or lawyers you know; the crabgrass on your front lawn; your parents' divorce; your stereo; your friend's broken arm; your first vote; failing trigonometry; or your A in Spanish.

Do not try to write about racial problems in our cities unless you have first-hand information on the subject. Do not write about the United Nations, violence in Bosnia, communism in Cuba, Lincoln's first administration, the creation of the American Constitution, the writings of Norman Mailer, or the movies of Humphrey Bogart, *unless* (1) in the past you have done considerable research on one of these subjects and know the field well; or (2) you are willing to commit yourself to hours of research in the library or elsewhere to make yourself reasonably knowledgeable on the subject.

This advice is necessarily somewhat general, so check with your instructor when you have doubts about your knowledge of a subject. (Review the section on *ethical proof,* pages 5–9.)

2. Narrow Your Thesis.

Because most essays are relatively short, you can't adequately support a very broad thesis in 500 words or so. Narrow your thesis to fit your essay's length by testing your tentative theses, as Jack did (page 44). You will find certain questions helpful, especially questions beginning with *why, what,* and *who.*

Tentative thesis: People in my hometown are selfish.

Questions: Why do you call them selfish? What do they *do?* Who are the *people* you refer to? *All* of them?

Revised thesis: Some people in my hometown will not give to the United Fund because they do not wish to support some of the agencies that receive money from the Fund.

Tentative thesis: Computers are a popular form of mass communication.

Questions:	*All* computers? What *kind* of communication do you mean? *Who* uses the computer for communication?
Revised thesis:	Among some of my friends, notes through the Internet are so popular that they have replaced the telephone as the chief method of talking to one another.

3. Unify Your Thesis.

In your essay, discuss one thing or group of things. You might ask yourself questions like *How many terms do I have in this thesis? Are they separate topics to be dealt with in different papers? Are some of my terms subtopics of the larger topic?*

Tentative thesis:	A blind child is often treated badly by other children because he or she is different from them; consequently they are embarrassed, because they don't realize how talented a blind child can be.
Questions:	If blind children are *talented,* does that still make them *different?* Are other children embarrassed by the blind child's "differences?"
Revised thesis:	A blind child is sometimes treated badly by other children on the playground because they do not know how to deal with his or her "differences."
Tentative thesis:	Motorcycles are fun, providing fast, inexpensive, and dangerous transportation.
Questions:	Is riding a motorcycle *fun* because it is *dangerous?* Is it *dangerous* because it is *fast?* What is the relationship between *inexpensive* and *dangerous?*
Revised thesis:	Motorcycles provide inexpensive but dangerous transportation.

The last tentative thesis would require the writer to juggle four somewhat illogically associated points about motorcycles. The improved thesis reduces these to two easily associated points by saying, in effect: the machine may not cost much, but it can kill you.

4. Specify Your Thesis.

As you have probably guessed by now, the whole business of improving a thesis is a continuous process. When you make your thesis authoritative, and when you narrow and unify it, you are simply sharpening your essay's point. And the best single way to make that point even sharper is to avoid general words and to use specific ones instead.

You might ask questions like: Can I tie my point to a more specific word than the one I have used here? What evidence do I have? How can that evidence be translated into specific terms?

Tentative thesis:	Sororities are getting better.
Questions:	What do I mean by "better?" If they are better, what difference does that make?

Revised thesis:	Sororities at this college are getting more pledges, because they offer better housing, better food, and better facilities for study than the dorms.
Tentative thesis:	America should have more freedom of speech.
Questions:	What do I mean by *freedom of speech? Where* in America should this happen? What do I propose to *do* in order to get more freedom of speech?
Revised thesis:	The Library Board in Paxton should have a strict procedure to follow whenever a citizen objects to one of the books in the library's collection. (Notice the hook in the phrase *strict procedure.*)

PRACTICE

Discussion

1. For class discussion read the following essay. What is its thesis? Where is the thesis stated? Discuss its unity and specificity. In what way has the writer "narrowed" her coverage of the topic?

HUSSIES AND HOLES IN YOUR EARS

1   In the old neighborhood, piercing ears of young girls was an exotic ritual.

2   All the neighborhood noseys would gather around in a kitchen like eager interns as someone's shaky and half-blind grandmother would miraculously become a surgeon, eagle-eyed and steady of hand. The girl's earlobes were anesthetized with an ice cube, and the largest needle in the sewing box would be heated on the stove and dipped in alcohol for the procedure. The patient would wear a loop of thread, then a piece of straw from a broom before getting her first ladylike pair of earrings.

3   But some of us were never initiated. "Only gypsies and hussies have pierced ears," Mother maintained. A few girlfriends proved Mother right, becoming bona fide hussies by the sixth grade, even wearing lipstick and stockings and unloosening their braids. There were no gypsies on the block, but Mother knew best.

4   Away from Mother's overprotectiveness, I finally had my ears pierced in my mid–20s. Not by anyone's grandmother, but in a sanitized doctor's office with no spectators. I should have listened to Mother.

5   One hole was pierced on an angle and began to stretch, nearly splitting the earlobe in two. A fortune in pierced earrings sat idle as I went back to clip-ons. I began to notice other casualties of ear piercing who had split lobes and infections, even some who had gone through the grandmother method. I pondered a malpractice suit, but too much time had passed. I consulted a plastic surgeon, but it was too costly to have the lobe sutured and the ears repierced.

6   Other friends, of course, had the fashionable two and three holes in their ears with no complications. My childhood desire never waned.

7   I'd look for free ear-piercing offers in department stores, even stood in line at one, but chickened out. Finally last month I relented on a lunch hour impulse and had both

ears repierced above the original holes. No grandmothers, no doctor, just your basic sales clerk.

8   I wore the training studs for the requisite 24 days, religiously and liberally applied the antiseptic twice a day, twirled the posts to keep the scar tissue from mending around the holes and polished my pierced earrings.

9   For not listening to Mother, not once but twice, I now have an infection. But I have no regrets. Fortunately, I still have the same two ears. I have four pierced earring holes, three of which are serviceable. And above all—look, Ma, I never became a hussy.

—Leanita McClain

2. Discuss and evaluate each of the following tentative theses. How can they be improved?

  a. Traffic destroys superhighways.

  b. Biking and hitchhiking through Maine are safe.

  c. The Berlin Wall was necessary to the Soviet Union.

  d. Adopting the metric system is a mistake.

  e. Working and eating in a pizza parlor is boring, hard work, and gives me indigestion, plus the boss is a jerk.

  f. The earth is getting hotter.

  g. Intercollegiate sports cost the university too much money.

  h. Nuclear power plants should be shut down.

  i. Welfare takes too much of the tax dollar.

Writing

1. You can learn much about writing useful theses by imitating those used in successful student essays. Here are six such theses with certain key words and phrases in italics. Imitate them using your own ideas and material. For example, an imitation of **a** might be: "Unlike my sister, who went out for the swimming team because she thought swimming was a challenging sport, I tried out only because I badly needed the exercise." Are any particular writers' stances suggested by the theses?

  a. *Unlike* my uncle, *who* was a compulsive *alcoholic,* my father *drank* too much simply because he *liked* the *comradeship* of other drinkers.

  b. *Racial problems* in Penant High School *existed* for two years *before busing started.*

  c. For good *apples* in September, *spray* the *trees* with dormant oil just before the *buds* open in the spring.

  d. We *lost* eight basketball *games* that year because we didn't *practice* our basic *plays* enough.

    e. To get a natural color on fresh hardwood, use *first* a light *stain* and *then* a quick-drying standard *varnish.*

    f. Since the independents did not *campaign* in all campus areas, *they failed* to reach many students and *lost* the *election.*

2. Here are some typical assignments you may encounter early in the term. For each assignment, (a) underline the important words or phrases; (b) write a narrowed, unified, and specific thesis.

    a. Tell your reader about the most important event in your life. Do not merely relate the event; describe it and explain in detail why you believe it is "important." (Do you need to define *important?* What might your hook be here?)

    b. In the past two or three years, several things have probably happened in your hometown, or area where you have been living, that you do not approve of. Write an essay explaining one of these events—a decision by an authority, a change in local government, and so on. State specifically why you do not approve. *Hint:* Don't spend so much time in description that you are unable to be specific concerning your disapproval.

    c. Write an essay about a clash of personalities that you have experienced or closely observed. What effect on friends or relations did this clash have? Explain by giving details and examples.

    d. Write a paper about a person—you or someone you know—who has been successful or unsuccessful doing something. Describe the person's success, or lack of it, and explain in detail why he was (or was not) successful.

3. Write a paper, using one of the theses you developed for **2** above.

4. For *two* of the following topics, develop a thesis that will form the basis of a 500-word essay. Be sure that your thesis is based on what you know and is narrowed, unified, and specific.

    a. seat belts in cars

    b. fishing

    c. intramural sports programs

    d. house plants

    e. movies

    f. hobbies

    g. video games

    h. reading

Choose one of the theses and write an essay.

CHAPTER 5

Shaping and Outlining Ideas

In this chapter, we will discuss a number of devices for organizing and planning a piece of writing. And that is what they are—plans. None of them is a fixed structure that you must follow blindly. Generally speaking, successful writers, whether amateur or professional, use whatever organizational devices they need—and use them flexibly. They may go through all the steps of a *shape, support diagram,* or *outline* (all of which will be discussed in this chapter). But writers may also work forward and backward through the process, refining, changing, switching main ideas or moving them about, inserting and deleting details. A writer may often consider, or actually follow, all the steps in the essay-writing process. But no successful writer allows the process to overrule his or her good judgment concerning any part of the final essay and its plan for organization.

For instance, if you can't make your plan fit your thesis exactly, it may be wise not to force a perfect fit. Theses and plans are *tools* for shaping materials, and sometimes materials refuse to be perfectly shaped. If you think it is necessary, try changing the thesis to fit the plan or changing both to fit each other. But don't change them so much that you distort the truths in your subject.

Sometimes you may have trouble following your planned organization as you write the essay. This may mean that the plan is poorly made—try inspecting it for logic and order. But this may also mean that a "logic of writing" is legitimately taking over. A piece of writing often seems to develop an order and a coherence all its own determined partly by the subject, by your supporting materials, and by the way you choose to organize it. If you like the way your paper is going, and its new direction appears to be appealing and honest, consider changing the plan to fit fresh developments. Plans are helpful and good, but they are not written on tablets of stone.

Let's see how John Jackson Chase, a successful writer of TV plays, used a plan in the form of a drawing. When he planned a new play (he planned as many as two or three at a time), he worked in a large room at the end of which was a big blackboard. On the blackboard was this drawing in white chalk:

As Chase worked on his play, he scribbled on this white-chalk drawing; the scribblings were in red chalk. What did the drawing mean? (It looks a little like a mountain peak with one steep side.) What were the scribblings in red about? If you questioned Chase, he would gladly tell you.

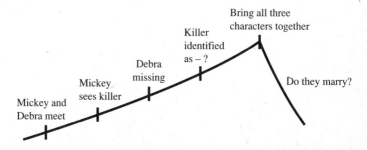

"I start every play with a *shape*," he said. "There on the blackboard in white chalk is my permanent shape for a story. Then I introduce (in red chalk) my characters at the left, give them some conflict to solve as the line moves upward to the right, and finally get to the peak of the shape with the climax of the story, where everything is brought together. The little drop-off after the climax is something almost every story has: a relaxing of tension—like somebody saying, "They lived happily ever after."

"Sometimes," Chase continued, "I start with the high point, the climax, and write that. Then I move backward to fill in parts of the story."

But why the blackboard with the shape on it?

"Oh, it reminds me to fill out the structure of the story. It gives me a feeling of where I'm going and where I've been. Besides, I'm a visual person. I like to see the skeleton of a play, the big bony pieces of it."

▼ Give Your Paper a Shape of Its Own

Chase's idea about the shape of a piece of writing is not new, although perhaps his application of it is. Most of us—at one time or another—have visualized a paper as starting at the top of a page and continuing downward, the result being the rough geometry of a composition (see Figure 1).

The total *shape* here is that of the classic argument, the thesis stated first, with the proofs or reasons coming after. The reasons are given in the order of importance, from least to most.

Indeed, the shape of a paper is a symbolic outline of your material. Using only the main ideas in your paper, you doodle a shape on a piece of scratch paper until you are satisfied that these main ideas are in the proper order and are given the proper emphasis, which is represented visually. For instance, in the argument we have been discussing you would *not* want a shape like that in Figure 2.

▼ Shaping a Sample Paper

In Chapter 2, we saw several students brainstorming an audience for a paper arguing that the requirements for the film major be increased. When one student (named Arthur) planned this paper, he first started with a list of ideas that he would include:

— Need more courses in film major
— Students don't know much about modern techniques of acting

Figure 1

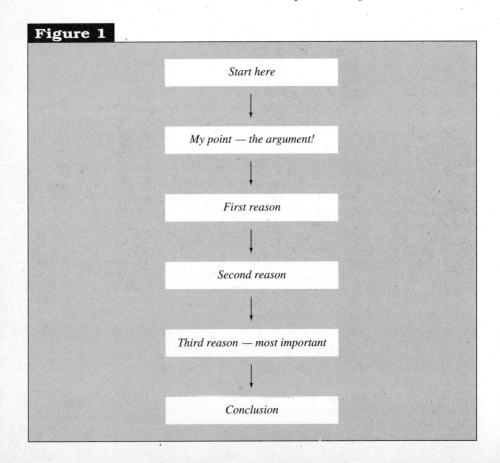

Start here

My point — the argument!

First reason

Second reason

Third reason — most important

Conclusion

— Students don't know much about modern films
— Students don't know much about modern directing
— Many things are right with the major

To deal with these logically, Arthur considered several shapes that the paper might take, using sheets of paper to draw on. He finally settled on the basic shape in Figure 3—question and answer. Why? Arthur said he thought that starting with a question would intrigue his readers and make them want to read on.

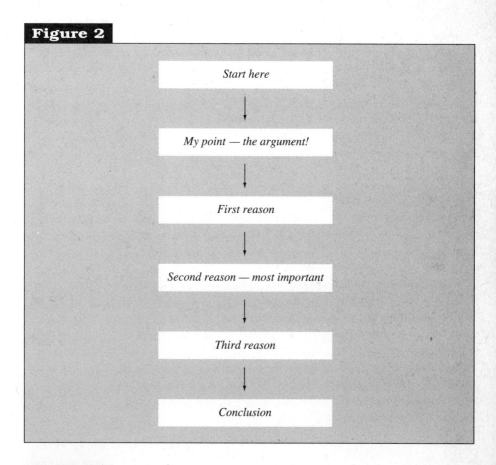

Figure 2

Start here

My point — the argument!

First reason

Second reason — most important

Third reason

Conclusion

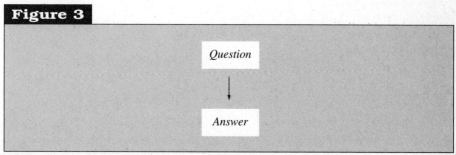

Figure 3

Question

Answer

To fill in the shape of his paper, Arthur made the drawing in Figure 4. In this drawing, he tried to illustrate to himself the parts of the argument, especially in the section where he notes that the film major is already being well managed. Arthur does not want to attack the major; he only wants to make it better. He wants to stress the three basic subpoints equally.

▪▪▪ Advantages and Disadvantages of the Paper "Shape"

The *shape* is a quick way of getting an overall pattern of your paper quickly in mind—and in your eye. It is essentially a big doodle on a large piece of scratch paper, taking only a few minutes to draw. In fact, on many subjects you can draw half a dozen shapes in a short time, each one supplying a different pattern or structure to your paper.

Figure 4

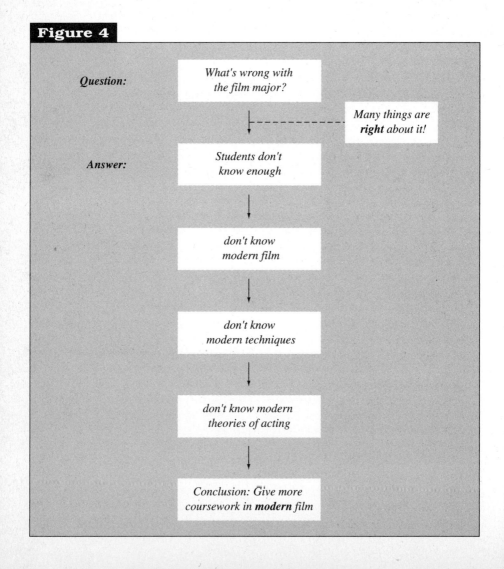

Question: What's wrong with the film major?

Many things are right about it!

Answer: Students don't know enough

don't know modern film

don't know modern techniques

don't know modern theories of acting

Conclusion: Give more coursework in **modern** film

A disadvantage is that the shape gives only the big pieces of the pattern, and if you don't have the smaller ones already in mind you have to search for them.

▼ Support Diagrams

The *support diagram* is another version of the planning *shape* (see pages 51–55). Both are "visuals." But there are two basic differences between these types of planning devices. First, the *shape* is linear; it represents the one-dimensional progress of your paper as it "develops" *down* the page. The support diagram works in two dimensions: up and down, and left and right. Second, the support diagram shows logical relations more clearly than the shape does.

Support diagrams typically connect pieces of evidence to your statement or generalization. That is, they show how examples, details, and facts *support* or explain a main point or idea in the paper. For example, see Figure 5, which illustrates how a basic support diagram can be drawn.

In Figure 6, we put material into the diagram.

As you add more evidence and specific facts to your main point, the more detailed your support diagram becomes. Now consider the diagram in Figure 7.

The support diagram *connects* and *explains* relationships. All of the arrows you use should tie ideas together logically.

Here is the paragraph we can write from the support diagram on "periods of sadness."

Short periods of sadness, discouragement and even suicidal thinking are a part of normal living, particularly after losses and physical illness. These depressed moods usually last a few days, perhaps a few weeks at the most. They are not severe enough to interrupt the business of everyday life. Most of us learn to live with them.

—Anne H. Rosenfeld

Figure 5

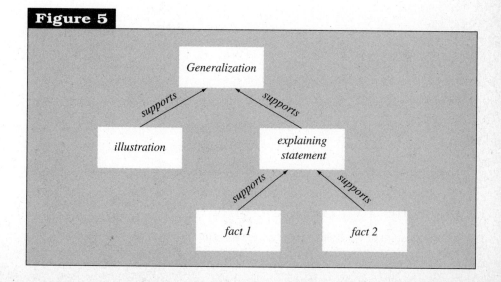

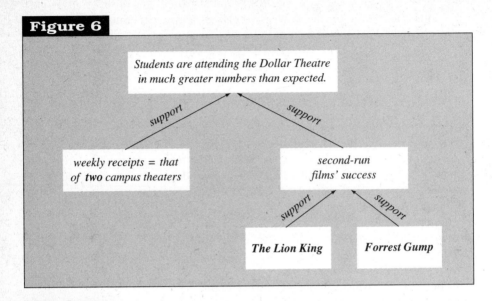

Figure 6

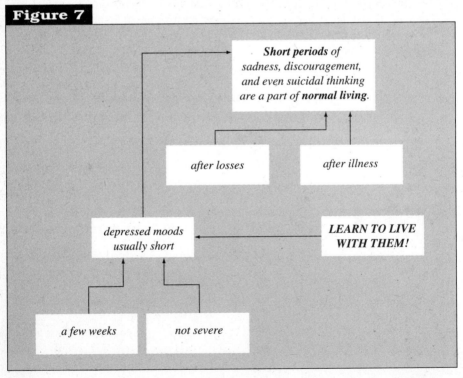

Figure 7

▼ The Formal Outline

The question of whether to make a formal outline or not depends upon the needs and the requirements of the course you are taking. Even professional writers disagree about outlining.

Stephen Jay Gould is Professor of Geology at Harvard University. In 1980 his columns in *Natural History* won the National Magazine Award for Essays and Criticism. In 1981 his book, *The Panda's Thumb,* won the American Book Award for science. Here is what Gould says about outlines (for his columns in *Natural History* he produces a paragraph-by-paragraph outline):

> I really do believe outlines exist in heaven. I'm a Platonist when it comes to articles. I really believe there is a correct organization for each article. Once you find it, everything fits in.

Jacques Barzun has had a brilliant career as Professor of History, Provost of Columbia University, and writer extraordinare. He has published more than two dozen books, several of them on writing and English usage. His opinion of outlines:

> Well, for my taste, outlines are useless, fettering, imbecile. Sometimes, when you get into a state of anarchy, or find yourself writing in circles, it may help to jot down a sketchy outline of the topics (or in a story, of the phases) so far covered. You outline, in short, something that already exists in written form, and this may help to show where you started backstitching.

—On Writing, Editing, and Publishing

To suggest that writers are either outliners or anti-outliners is an oversimplification. One reason is that *outline* is an ambiguous term. It can mean a few jottings on scrap paper, or a detailed piece of formal architecture covering several pages and with every roman numeral, arabic number, and upper- and lowercase letter reverently placed in its assigned niche. The important thing to remember is that an individual has many options for showing the plan of a paper.

Some writers and teachers have found that a formal outline clearly shows how pieces of evidence (A, B, and C) support the generalizations or main points (I, II, III) of a paper. Even if a writer has used another kind of planning, it is easy to convert such a plan into a *formal outline.* Note how the *support diagram* in Figure 7 can be converted into a formal outline, mainly because the writer has a clear notion of how her evidence supports her main idea.

Thesis: Recognizing that short periods of sadness are natural, psychologists are more concerned about long periods of depression.

I. Short periods of sadness, discouragement, and even suicidal thinking are a part of normal living.
   A. They often occur after losses.
   B. They may occur after physical illness.
   C. These depressed moods usually last a few days.
      1. They may last a few weeks at most.
      2. They are not severe enough to interrupt the business of everyday life.
   D. Most of us learn to live with these short periods of depression.
II. . . . (rest of outline omitted)

■■■ *The Relationship Between "Shapes" and Outline*

If a writer chooses one of the *shapes* for organizing a paper, it is possible to translate that shape into an outline. Here is how a girl named Cathy came up with some ideas about junk mail, and how she translated those ideas into a shape and later into two kinds of formal outlines.

LIST OF IDEAS ABOUT JUNK MAIL

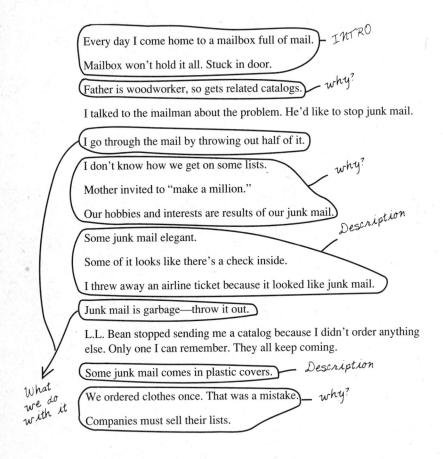

Every day I come home to a mailbox full of mail. — *INTRO*

Mailbox won't hold it all. Stuck in door.

Father is woodworker, so gets related catalogs. — *why?*

I talked to the mailman about the problem. He'd like to stop junk mail.

I go through the mail by throwing out half of it.

I don't know how we get on some lists. — *why?*

Mother invited to "make a million."

Our hobbies and interests are results of our junk mail. — *Description*

Some junk mail elegant.

Some of it looks like there's a check inside.

I threw away an airline ticket because it looked like junk mail.

Junk mail is garbage—throw it out.

L.L. Bean stopped sending me a catalog because I didn't order anything else. Only one I can remember. They all keep coming.

Some junk mail comes in plastic covers. — *Description*

We ordered clothes once. That was a mistake. — *why?*

Companies must sell their lists.

What we do with it

After grouping her main ideas, Cathy could see that she had a shape for her paper (see the figure on the next page).

▼ Topic Outline

Next, Cathy developed a thesis and a topic outline—an outline that lists topic ideas in the form of phrases or single words in the headings.

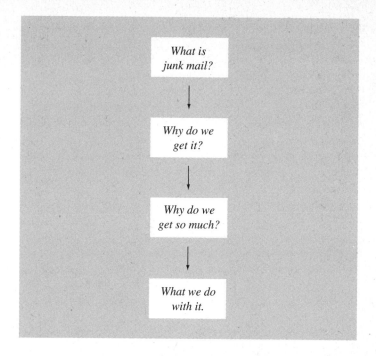

Thesis: Because our family has a variety of hobbies and interests, we get a lot of junk mail that we treat like junk.

   I. Definition of *junk mail*
     A. Bulk rate postage
     B. Advertising
  II. Hobbies and interests of the family
     A. Woodworking
     B. Investing
     C. Gardening and camping
 III. Lists sold by companies
     A. Farm, fleet, work clothes catalogs
     B. Financial brochures
     C. Camping, clothing, and gardening catalogs
 IV. Junk mail as *junk*
     A. Clutter
     B. Garbage

    Cathy decides that the topic outline isn't adequate for her needs because she wants better control of her paragraphing. She makes a sentence outline where she can see every idea in its complete form. She has found that a formal outline is useful when she wants to organize a paragraph deductively, going from the general (topic sentence) to the specific examples and details, as she eventually does in her paper on junk mail.

Thesis: Because our family has a variety of hobbies and interests, we get a lot of junk mail that we treat like junk.

I. Junk mail is a particular kind of mail. *(paragraph)*
   A. Junk mail goes for "bulk rate."
   B. Junk mail consists of advertising or soliciting brochures.
II. The hobbies and interests of our family reflect the kind of junk mail we receive. *(paragraph)*
   A. My father is a woodworker, so he gets everything connected with carpentry.
   B. My mother is an investor in stocks and bonds, so she gets investment brochures.
   C. I once had a garden, so I get garden catalogs.
   D. I ordered something from L.L. Bean, so now I get sporting goods catalogs from all over.
III. The companies we order from have sold their lists of customers. *(paragraph)*
   A. My father gets farm and fleet catalogs as well as work clothes catalogs.
   B. My mother gets invitations to "make a million."
   C. I get every conceivable kind of catalog related to clothing, camping, and gardening.
IV. We treat the catalogs like junk. *(paragraph)*
   A. We seldom look at them.
   B. We throw them in the garbage.

Conclusion: As a result of all our junk mail, we have reduced the number of things that we order by mail and have started buying from local stores.

■■■ The Form of Outlines

Since Cathy has been well trained in the conventions of formal outlining, she knows that it is customary to employ numerals and letters in this order, according to the rank of ideas or to the *levels of subordination.*

I. First level (main heading)
   A. Second level
      1. Third level
      2. Third level
         a. Fourth level
         b. Fourth level
   B. Second level
II. First level (main heading)

Headings on the same level of subordination should be roughly parallel—that is, equal in importance and grammatical form. The following example violates this principle in four ways:

I. Definition
   A. Bulk rate

B. Junk mail is a good way for advertisers to sell their merchandise.

II. The hobbies and interests of our family reflect the kind of junk mail we receive.

A. Father woodworker

A and B are improperly subordinated to Part I. A and B are not parallel in importance or grammar. Part II is put in sentence form, which violates the form established in Part I. (The rule is this: When for the first time you use a particular form for a heading—a full sentence, a phrase, or a single word, for example—*use the same form in subsequent entries for that level of heading.*) Furthermore, you should avoid single headings like II-A above. When you break a heading into subordinate headings, you must get at least two of these lower-level headings. Often when a single heading hangs out in space, you will find that it really belongs with the previous major heading.

▼ Four Typical Questions about Outlines

1. *What type of outline should I use?*

The answer to this depends on many factors—the length of your paper and the complexity of your material, to name only two. When preparing to write a long paper which presents a lot of material and complex issues, you might like to make a complete sentence outline that maps out every detail of your argument and its evidence. If you are going to do a short, relatively uncomplicated paper, perhaps a brief topic outline would be sufficient.

Not the least important factor in your choice of outline is your own preference. What type of outline do you feel most comfortable with? For most assignments, which type seems to work best for you?

2. *How specific should an outline be?*

Specific enough to do the job. It should suggest what your paper is going to do—what its thesis is and what its main supporting points are. It should also supply some examples of evidence or detail that you will use in developing your ideas. But the outline is, as we said earlier, just a skeleton; and it can suggest only the bare bones of your completed paper.

If you have any doubts about a particular outline, show it to your instructor.

3. *What can I do if I start an outline, get a point or two down, and then can't continue?*

When this happens, you may be trying to build a house before acquiring concrete, bricks, lumber, and shingles. Before you can build a paper, you need materials for it. Here is where the *shapes* or *support diagrams* can be useful. These forms may help to show you where you need more material.

Some writers find the card system useful: Get some 3×5 or 4×6 file cards, or small pieces of stiff paper cut to size. Next, write down your thesis on a sheet of paper and place it where you can see it. Start writing your ideas down on your cards, one idea to a card. Note that—*one idea to a card*; preferably, one complete sentence to a card. The point is to separate your ideas so that you can later classify and organize them.

4. *I know I shouldn't do it, but I always make an outline after I write the paper. How can I train myself to make one before writing?*

Writers often check their organization *after* they have written a paper. It is usually a good practice, however, to plan before you write. Consider your outline as a figurative road map—refer to it before you start on your trip so that you won't end up at the seashore when you wanted to go to the mountains.

How a Thesis Suggests an Outline

The phrasing of the thesis often suggests a pattern in the outline. A typical thesis:

I	II
Since St. James Catholic Church has recently been remodeled, it is a more pleasant place

III
to worship, and thus may draw members from other churches in the area.

In creating your stance, you direct your ideas to someone who is not directly familiar with the Catholic churches in your area. After considering the phrasing of the thesis, you can construct an outline like this:

 I. Description of the remodeling.
 II. Description of the effect of the remodeling.
III. Why this may bring new members to the church.

▼ The Hook and the Outline

As you recall, we recommended the hook as a useful device in finding ideas (see pages 17–18). Like the thesis and the outline, hooks are often valuable throughout the writing process. They provide control, a simple reminder of where you want to go and how effectively you are getting there. Here's an example of their value as related to the outline.

A student wrote a paper that, in its first draft, did not satisfy her. Something was wrong with the fit between the material and her organization. She thought of throwing the paper away, but then decided to make one last attempt to salvage the large amount of work she had put into it. So she wrote her title, hooks, and paragraph topic sentences on an outline page:

Title: Power to Both Parents

Hooks: *power, both parents*

Topic sentences: 1. Introduction (thesis): Neither the husband nor the wife should be the dominant figure in the family.

2. Both the husband and wife should share major financial decisions.

3. Both parents are responsible for the discipline of the children, and they should share this responsibility equally.

4. Both should share in the maintenance of the house.

5. The children also have a responsibility to the family unit.

Conclusion: 6. Cooperation is important between parents if a family is to be successfully maintained.

After inspecting this outline page, the student saw her own problem immediately. Paragraph 5 was hooked to an idea outside her topic, so she cut it.

▼ How to Check an Outline

If you choose to write from an outline, the following suggestions may be helpful to you.

1. See that all the *parts* of the outline are there—thesis, main headings, and subordinate headings.

2. Use the proper outline *form* (see pages 58–61). Make particularly sure that your headings are reasonably parallel. There are minor exceptions to this rule. Sometimes you can't quite get your headings parallel; the idiom of the language won't allow it. But you should get as close to complete parallelism as you can.

3. Make your outline reasonably *specific,* particularly in your thesis and the main headings (I, II, III, etc.).

4. Check the outline for *logic.* Do all the parts fit together? Does every supporting point firmly fit your thesis? If necessary, try the subject-predicate test. To make the test, write the major parts of your outline in full-sentence form, using subject-predicate patterns:

   I. MY CAR MECHANIC *was very thorough.*
       A. HE *checked the distributor twice.*
       B. HE *cleaned the carburetor, even though it did not appear to need cleaning.*
   II. But THE MANAGER *did not appreciate the mechanic's work.*
       A. THE MANAGER *said that the mechanic spent too much time on routine jobs.*
       B. HE *refused to give the mechanic overtime to complete important repairs.*

If your outline is logical, and all its parts fit together, you can draw connecting arrows (as shown above) from SUBJECT to SUBJECT and from *predicate* to *predicate*. You may also develop a *support diagram* of your ideas to check them for logic (see pages 55–56).

5. Check the outline for the proper *order*—that is, for a sensible sequence or organization of ideas. Check each level separately—first I, II, III, etc.; and then A, B, C, etc.; and so on. Except for the general rule that important ideas are often placed last, there is no special rule about order. The arrangement of your points should make sense and should not be incongruous. The order of points below, for example, would not be very sensible:

     I. The manager did not appreciate the mechanic's work.
    II. The mechanic was very thorough.

This order would force you to describe the manager's attitude toward the mechanic's work before you had described that work. It's hard to write a paper backwards.

PRACTICE

Writing

1. We borrowed the outline below from an essay and scrambled its main and subordinate points. We also took the thesis and put it into the list of points. Copy each item from the list below onto a separate card. You may rewrite for the sake of clarity or consistency. Identify the thesis. Arrange the cards into a logical order. Draw a *shape* that fits the material. Make a sentence or topic outline, as directed by your instructor.

A mover's workday can vary from 10 to 18 hours.

A mover has to work in temperatures that vary greatly.

Some days it is 95 degrees with 95% humidity.

Going in and out of air conditioning is hard on the body.

Moving furniture demands speed because movers must keep a schedule.

A mover is expected to lift at least 100 pounds alone.

When customers live in second- or third-floor apartments, moving furniture is difficult.

Sometimes a crew moves 2 or 3 households in a day.

Apartment buildings often have narrow stairs and landings.

Sometimes heavy furniture and appliances must be lifted over the head to get upstairs or downstairs.

Some furniture has sharp edges which cut into the hands.

Moving furniture, particularly on stairways, demands agility and strength.

A mover must hold onto the furniture to prevent accidents.

The boss-driver, not the furniture mover, sets the pace.

The mover has to please the driver, customer, and management.

Moving furniture in the summer requires stamina to work long hours in hot weather.

2. Outline the following student-written paper. Pick out the thesis, and write out the main and subordinate points in outline form. What kind of an outline—topic, sentence, or mixed—would be most satisfactory for a paper of this length? What kind of a *shape* would you develop at the planning stage of this paper?

1   I am writing this in reference to some letters that I have sent to you which were never answered. These letters concerned the possibility of my working full-time at your restaurant during my month-long vacation from college. The fact that you didn't answer any of my many inquiries regarding employment shows much inconsideration in your attitude toward me.

2   When I left my job at your restaurant at the end of August, you promised me a job any time that I would be home from school—Labor Day, Thanksgiving vacation, weekends, etc. I was also told that the Christmas season is one of the busiest times of the year at the restaurant. Many people travel by car during this period, and the restaurant is located near the intersection of several main interstate roads. More workers are needed if the restaurant is to be smoothly and efficiently run. Why didn't you keep your promise to me?

3   During the time that I worked for you, I worked hard—I did everything that I was told to do, and I did it quickly and efficiently. Besides keeping fifty tables in the cafeteria dining room cleaned off and ready for the customers, I was expected to unload dirty dishes from a cart and stack them on the dishwasher's counter. I was also told to vacuum the dining room carpet every day, clean and dust the booths and furniture, and fill condiment containers on every table. I was expected to do all of this alone, even when busloads of people would stop at the restaurant. I managed to always get all of my work done on time, and you complimented me frequently on the good job I had done.

4   When you had some other job for me to do, I always did it willingly. Several times I did dishes when other workers had too many other things to do or if they didn't come to work. Also, during the Fourth of July holiday period, I worked on the foodline serving customers. Several times, also, I gave up my day off to go in and work for other bus girls who got sick. I was never paid any extra wages for the extra jobs I did.

5   I am sure that you were satisfied with my work. I realize that I didn't have any experience working in a restaurant when you hired me, but you did give me a raise after I had only worked three days. As I said before, you complimented me often on the job I had done. The customers must have been satisfied with the appearance of the dining room, because many people left tips for me, which is not a common practice in a cafeteria-style restaurant.

6   I feel that I treated you fairly as my boss. I was never late to work, and I never stopped working early. I took my breaks only when you told me that I could, and I never took any "extra" breaks when a manager wasn't around (like many of the other workers did). Busing tables isn't a very interesting job, but I never

complained. I worked every day that I was scheduled to, and never asked for any extra days off.

7   I hope that you realize, after reading this, how inconsiderate you were by not answering my inquiries. I treated you with fairness and respect, but in this case, you didn't treat me in the same way. If I had been lazy and done a sloppy job while I worked for you, I probably would have expected my letters to be ignored. Because I waited weeks for a reply from you, I was unable to find any other type of work over vacation. I hope that in the future you will be more considerate and fair to the college students who work for you.

CHAPTER 6

What Words Should
You Avoid?

Most successful writers agree that there are some words which don't fit well in a piece of writing. For instance, they will object to the italicized words below:

1. People who do very good work should be *awarded* for it.

2. Although we are all very *conscientious with* the garbage disposal in our apartment, our garbage problem is still *yucky*.

3. Before attending a marriage class, you need an *extended pre-preparation base*.

When you ask successful writers why they object to these usages, you will usually get answers like these:

In the first example, *awarded* is the wrong word; it should be *rewarded*. In number 2, *conscientious* seems a bit formal for the subject of garbage. (Also, the idiom is conscientious *about,* not *with*.) *Yucky* is definitely too informal and slangy. In number 3, *extended pre-preparation base* is silly jargon. In addition, part of the phrase is redundant.

PRACTICE

This section is to be done before continuing—at your instructor's discretion.
You are the galaxy's expert on little furry beasts. Your boss gives you the following sentences and asks that you rearrange and "translate" them into a short, clear

paragraph. Your translation is to be designed for an individual (from another planet) who has pointy ears, no discernible sense of humor—and has never seen or heard of a mouse before.

> Mice have five appendages, and four of them are on the corners.
>
> Per unit-mouse, there exist five things sticking out.
>
> Mice have four leg-foot assemblies and one unleg-foot assembly per frame.
>
> Each mouse comes equipped with a series of appendages numbering four or five depending on the epistemological characterization of same.
>
> Each mouse has a foot at the end opposite the body; the anterior appendage is minus said foot.
>
> Allotment of appendages of mice will be (said the All-Knowing Spirit): four foot-leg assemblies, one tail assembly. Deviation from this policy is not permitted as it would constitute misapportionment of scarce appendage assets.
>
> Each foot of mouse in question is attached to a small item joined integrally with the overall mouse structure main system; the anterior appendage is nonfunctional and ornamental in nature.[1]

Avoid Formal Expressions If They Are Pretentious or Abstract

Using excessively formal language in ordinary situations is like wearing a top hat and tuxedo at a baseball game. Try to be natural:

Too Formal	*More Natural*
atmospheric residue	smog
cellular overabundance	fat
a sartorial anarchist	a streaker
facilitate	make something easier
functioning members of society	working people
utilize	use
implement	do or make
currently	now
presently	in a minute
intensive labor	hard work
stated	said
inoperative	it doesn't work
medical complex	hospital
social misfit	thief, crook, robber, thug, murderer, criminal, etc.

Use Slang Sparingly

Slang is language used on the bottom fringes of society, where verbal color counts for everything and speech is all. Slang is a nickname for a name, like *Jackie* instead of

---

[1]Adapted from T. C. Wyld, "Pentagonese Be Gone."

Jacqueline. Slang is intimate and draws a circle around itself: *fun city, Sun City, fat city.* To get this stuff, you must be in the know.

Good writers object to slang when it is tired or trite; when readers might not understand it; or when it is foolishly out of date—in short, when it is the lazy writer's answer to the problem. These, in most instances, would be objectionable slang (some examples are deliberately dated):

freak out	hot shot
she *goes* [for she *says*]	bluebelly [what does it mean?]
OK	goldbrick [ditto]
far out	the cat's pajamas
glitz	real cool
ticked off	fancy pants
foodaholic	ace an exam
downer	funky
the boonies	stylin'
neatnick	

▼ Keep Your Wording Idiomatic

When we say that someone's English is *idiomatic,* we mean that it is natural, particularly in the writer's use of the many *linguistic formulas* that are embedded in the language like pebbles in a sandbank. And like a pebble, the typical idiom is as hard, firm, unchangeable as a rock can be. To *catch a cold* cannot be changed to *receive a cold* or *take on a cold.* You cannot substitute *dash and hide* or *run and disappear* for *run and hide.* Nor can you turn the idiom around: *hide and run.*

As a little linguistic formula, an idiom is a special expression that is (above all) peculiar. Ordinarily, you can't analyze it by logic or by appealing to its grammatical constituents. The idiom merely *is,* and you have to accept it as a given in the language. In *strike a bargain,* nothing is "struck"; in *be your age,* "you" are not equivalent to the number 20 or 34.

You seldom have any choice except to use idioms as they already are. Any significant change in most common idioms will disturb your reader.

Not Idiomatic	**Idiomatic**
capable to do something	*capable of doing* something
not for *money or love*	not for *love or money*
knuckle *to*	knuckle *under*
a doubting *Frederick*	a doubting *Thomas*
read the *small lines*	read the *small print*
dining room comedy	*drawing room* comedy
There was no necessity *of* him to . . .	There was no necessity *for* him to . . .
object *with*	object *to*

▼ Avoid Jargon and Gobbledygook

The phrase *jargon and gobbledygook* has become an idiomatic pair like *ham and eggs* or *run and hide.* To say that something is jargon implies that it is also gobbledygook, and vice versa.

No one knows who invented the word *gobbledygook,* although it is associated with Maury Maverick, a Texas congressman. Maverick was enraged by the incomprehensible polysyllabic language of government memos and reports. He wrote to his department in Washington DC:

> Be short and say what you're talking about. Stop "pointing up" programs. No more "finalizing," "effectuating," or "dynamics." Anyone using the words "activation" or "implementation" will be shot.

What are the characteristics of jargon and gobbledygook? They are:

1. Long words with many syllables

2. Abstract, formal words

3. Noisy words. Say these slowly: *ef fect u a ting, im ple men ta tion, ag glu ti na tive, lo go syn thet ic skills.* Such ugly noises these words make!

4. A psychological tendency in writers toward *cir cum loc u tory verb u la tive crap u la tion* (big words uttered by idiots)

5. A second psychological tendency in writers to make simple things unbearably complicated

The distinction between real English and gobbledygook can be seen in this exchange between an editor and Isaac Asimov, the famous science fiction writer (Asimov was also a scientist):

Editor (speaking gobbledygook):   Do you think the current environmental situation necessitates a halt or substantial curtailment of technical progress?

Asimov (speaking normally):   If it does, we will be in the same sort of trouble that we would be in if we simply allowed technology to proceed without concern for pollution.

▼ Avoid Clichés If They Are a Substitute for Clear Thinking

A cliché is a trite, overworked expression:

right as rain

Such-and-such *is a must.*

That *goes without saying.*

this day and age

bright and early

the last straw

Clichés have a bad name, and many people condemn them without qualification. As you read that sentence did you stop to identify *have a bad name* as a cliché? Over several years, we tested that sentence on about a hundred people, using a different context. Only four or five commented that the phrase could be considered a cliché, and only two of them blanketly condemned it as such.

If clichés communicate meaning quickly and neatly, writers may find them to be satisfactory. They use them for the same reason they use small coins when buying things at a store. Small coins may be a nuisance, but they are still part of our medium of exchange. We can't get along without them. We can't get along without the small coinage of clichés either, as we go about our daily business [*cliché*] of communicating with one another.

We object to clichés when they are the lazy writer's way out or when they are a substitute for clear or vivid wording. In these instances they can irritate the reader:

Irritates: He made the *supreme sacrifice* for his country.

Better: He died for his country.

Irritates: Uncle Tom was *a sight for sore eyes.*

Better: I was happy to see Uncle Tom.

Irritates: Their action *rubbed me the wrong way.*

Better: I thought their action was dishonest.

As these examples illustrate, the objectionable cliché is usually vague or ambiguous, and it's almost always lazy. To improve the usage, make the statement more specific:

Vague: Jameson was a *pillar of the church.*

Specific: Jameson gave more of his free time to church work than any other member did.

Vague: *Much water has flowed under the bridge* since she graduated from high school.

Specific: She graduated from high school in 1927.

▼ Avoid Vogue Words

A *vogue word* comes into fashion overnight. People take it up with great enthusiasm for a period of time, and then (as often as not) drop it. Vogue words come in and out of style like wide neckties and bell bottoms. Such words often are empty abstractions that seem to have more meaning than they really do. They sound important:

charisma   relevant

credit crunch   synergy

dynamic	peer group
escalation	parameter

We have deliberately mixed new—and not so new—vogue words in this list. Twenty years ago, *relevant* was so voguish that no careful writer would have used it without shame. Nowadays, one could argue that it no longer belongs on the list at all. *Parameter* comes from a somewhat later period than *relevant;* but it is still a vogue word, and writers use it fairly often.

Readers—particularly, educated readers—often react to vogue words with surprising negativism. Of the vogue word *structured,* the *Harper Dictionary of Contemporary Usage* says: "It is a borrowing from the Jargon of sociologists, a group that has probably done more calculated harm to the English language than any other scholarly or quasi-scholarly group. *Structure* is very popular with people who use words like *crunch, thrust,* and *seminal.* Such people are best avoided."

▼ Use Euphemisms Only Where Necessary

A *euphemism* is a "soft" word that replaces a harsh or unpleasant one.

Harsh **or** *Unpleasant*	*Euphemism*
bastard	illegitimate
die	pass away
toilet	bathroom
syphilis	social disease
old person	senior citizen
pain	discomfort
lie	fib
drunk	under the weather
stupid	underachiever

Your motives in using a euphemism will vary. It is not necessarily a bad thing to use a euphemism in place of an obscenity, an unkind expression, or a strongly irreverent expression. Would you call your kindly old aunt *drunk* when she gets *tipsy* on wine?

PRACTICE

---

1. In the sentences below, the writer has used some words poorly. Rewrite each sentence in clear, standard English. Use your imagination, where you can, to fill out a sentence. For some words, your dictionary may be of help.

   a. I'll jet back to the dorm and hang out.

   b. The personnel who arose in the balloon freaked out when they saw the tornado.

c. In reference to your epistle, I am stalling on an answer for the time being.

d. Your achievement in the realm of chemical endeavors makes the old lady and me very happy.

e. It is a privilege and a compliment for me to address this great group today.

f. I have indubitably mellowed out.

g. We were nearing the mountain top when our vehicle went topsy turvy.

h. If the coach doesn't win, the populace shouldn't heap him with vilification.

i. That class was a regular old *auto–da–fé*.

j. The vagaries of my present condition indicate a kid's in the oven.

2. Supply the proper *idiomatic* word(s) in the empty spaces below.

a. Now that he has left home, he is free _____ his father's influence.

b. Can you compare the snow of February _____ the snow of November?

c. Why do you always agree _____ me?

d. Her attitude differed _____ his.

e. She _____ herself into the part of Juliet with great energy.

f. It is impossible to _____ coat the pill of grammar.

g. He was out in the middle of the lake, _____ ing water and yelling for _____ .

h. You'd better make _____ while the sun _____ .

i. Jeannie is not angry at me any _____ —she has no hard _____ .

j. Well, the shoe is on the other _____ now, isn't it?

k. Yes, and two can play at that _____ .

l. Earlier, they had been quarreling loudly and making the _____ fly.

m. Lady Figg said: "It's bedtime, so I am going up to my room and turn _____ . Would you ask the upstairs maid to turn _____ my bed? I am so tired; all this rock and roll has been a great turn- _____ . Being rejected by Lord Dorg has worn me _____ too; it was such an unexpected turn- _____ . The next time Lord Dorg turns _____ at my door, I am going to turn him _____ . I never wanted to marry old Dorg anyway; Dorg Enterprises has never _____ ed a fair profit. And he is so ugly, he _____ my stomach. In re _____ for what he has done to me, I am going to _____ all his friends against him. But I am not worried about the future; something is _____ to _____ up."

3. Translate the following examples of *gobbledygook* and *jargon* into
   English—clear, simple English. Of course, you will have to guess at what
   some of the authors are trying to say. Be bold and imaginative!

   a. If Miss Muffet had developed a second-strike capability instead of
      squandering her resources on curds and whey, no spider on earth would
      have dared launch a first strike capable of carrying him right to the heart
      of her tuffet.

   —Russell Baker

   b. "In recent years [said Tommy John, major league pitcher], my ball has had
      good movement, but not much sinkage."

   c. Sign on a computer in a college library: *We are in an interrupt
      environment, and have to minimize student consulting.*

   d. While current models of communication adequately represent information
      flow within organization, a new interactive model based on human mental
      processes and structures needs to be developed which will effectively
      represent a business communication event in an organizational context.

   —professor of business writing

   e. To effectuate equality, we need affirmative action, comparable worth, and
      co-determination.

   f. Television, the true medium of the inflated and the phony, is the nutrient
      of choice for this linguistic superhype. . . .

   —Alvin Kernan, commenting ironically on gobbledygook

   g. Sign in public park: RESTRICTED FIRE USE

   h. Sinistrality in most of the human population is a developmental anomaly
      of preferred laterality.

   i. A massive restructuring of the dean's office is contraindicated.

4. In a class exercise, trying to make firm distinctions between *euphemisms, vogue
   words,* and *clichés* can lead to unnecessary disagreement and confusion. A
   euphemism can be voguish, a cliché can be euphemistic, etc. In the sentences
   below, identify any expression that is working "lazily" and rewrite the sentence.
   Then make whatever tentative comment you can as to identification, bearing in
   mind that some unfortunate usages can fall into one, two, or even three
   categories.

   a. "I now pronounce you interfaced."

   —minister, concluding the marriage
   ceremony in a "modern marriage"

b. We need to finalize our discussion in relation to Professor Michaels' research project.

c. Firefighters who refuse to train according to proper professional parameters should be thrown out of the department on their ear.

d. He continues to rationalize in terms of spiritualism—a Force freak, always trying get in tune with a *Star Wars* concept of religion.

e. She authored a news story about the Constitution Committee that did not render its members accountable for their mendacious published remarks on the U.S. Attorney General.

f. "I need to focus in and prioritize my objectives so I'll feel good about myself—let's share feelings another time, shall we? Ciao!"

> —Nathan Goodvibes, guidance counselor at
> Bypass High [from the comic strip *Kudzu*]

g. When all the social notables and their yuppie friends came to perambulate around the ski slopes, we ran for cover.

h. He was as drunk as a skunk, lit up like a Christmas cake.

i. In grammar school, it is a known fact that if you are confronted with irrelevant instructions you are up a creek.

j. A place of ill repute is not a residential domicile.

CHAPTER 7

Effective Sentence Structure

The study of sentences can be quite complicated. For example:

> The sentence under discussion begins with a subordinating signal (*when*), followed by a subordinating adverbial clause, after which there is a main clause with a phrasal subject and an adjective clause (both of which are the subject of the main-clause verb). The subordinating signal in the adjective clause is omitted and understood (*etc.!*).

We would begin to describe the same sentence this way:

> The sentence has a unit *that does not stand alone,* followed by a unit *that does stand alone.*

The sentence under discussion in both descriptions? It is:

Does not stand alone   Does stand alone

When I get up, the first thing I do is put on my shoes. (two units)

Once you understand the principle of *sentence units* and *"standing alone,"* you are ready for this chapter.

1. A *stand-alone unit* is a complete thought by itself:

   She speaks Spanish.

2. A *non-stand alone unit* (it can be a single word, phrase, or clause) is an incomplete thought:

   When she speaks Spanish,

3. Sentence *units* are defined by *punctuation:*

If I see you before Saturday,

I saw you last Saturday.

Important: Punctuation *separates* and *defines* sentence units; that is, it shows where the *units start and stop.* We treat punctuation as something you do as you write—not as something you add after you have written.

Below are some examples of sentence units (note their punctuation).

SA = unit stands alone.

Not SA = unit does not stand alone.

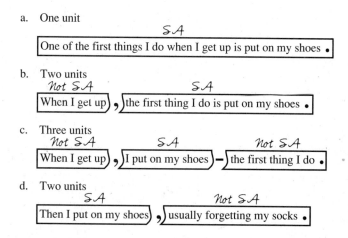

a.   One unit

SA

| One of the first things I do when I get up is put on my shoes . |

b.   Two units

Not SA   *SA*

| When I get up) ,) the first thing I do is put on my shoes . |

c.   Three units

Not SA   *SA*   *Not SA*

| When I get up) ,) I put on my shoes) —) the first thing I do . |

d.   Two units

SA   *Not SA*

| Then I put on my shoes) ,) usually forgetting my socks . |

▼ The Sentence Base

The stand-alone unit of a sentence is called a *sentence base.* Some examples are:

— Roger was my best friend.
— Saturday will be my wedding day.
— What has been done should never happen again.

The examples below are not *bases* because they cannot stand alone:

— Although Roger was my best friend. . .
— Saturday being my wedding day. . .
— What has been done. . .

From a structural standpoint, the sentence base has *no punctuation inside it.* Note that there is no punctuation inside the three sentence bases above. *Exception:* Bases may use certain *non-structural* commas, as in:

Coordinate adjectives: the *exhausted, dust-covered* soldier
Parallel elements: flowers, candy, and *paper hats*

For examples of *structural punctuation,* see the table on page 79.

Here is a piece of professional writing that shows how sentence bases work. The bases are in heavy type:

> *The octopus has a remarkable trace of adaptability. Dumas determined that,* by patiently playing with them until he met some response. Usually, *octopi were most submissive when very tired. Dumas would release an exhausted octopus and let it jet away with its legs trailing. The octopus has two distinct means of locomotion. It can crawl efficiently on hard surfaces.* (Guy Gilpatric *once saw an octopus let loose in a library. It raced up and down the stacks,* hurling books on the floor, possibly a belated revenge on authors.) *Its method of swimming consists of inflating the head,* or valve, *with water and jetting the fluid to achieve moderate speed. Dumas could easily overtake the animal. The octopus discharged several ink bombs and then resorted to its last defense,* a sudden plunge to immobility on the bottom, where it instantly assumed the local color and pattern. Keeping a sharp eye out for this camouflage stunt, *Didi confronted the creature again.* At the exhaustion of its psychological warfare effects, *the octopus sprang hopelessly from the bottom, fanned its legs and dribbled back to the floor.*

> —Jacques Cousteau, with Frédéric Dumas, *The Silent World*

PRACTICE

Each sentence below is a sentence base standing by itself, but part of the base is missing. Supply (make up) the missing material. Be sure that your base requires no punctuation inside it.

a. Sir Gewgaw was the worthiest knight _____ .

b. The invention of the automobile_____ the greatest _____ of the century.

c. What the Rockies lack _____ .

d. _____ want to visit New Orleans, Nashville, and San Antonio.

e. _____ my new umbrella in the cafe yesterday.

f. _____ why Shakespeare wrote *Henry VIII.*

g. Calvin Coolidge _____ very little.

h. I _____ from _____ with lowest honors this spring.

i. Why Bill Clinton ran for president against George Bush _____ _____ .

j. _____ into the elevator and hid their faces.

Punctuation in the Sentence Unit System

The purpose of punctuation in the system is very simple—to show where the *sentence bases* and the *free units* start and stop in the sentence.

We diagram the *base* with a heavy line: ━━━━━━━

We diagram the *free unit* with a light line: ───────

An opener, followed by a base, followed by a closer, looks like this:

opener		base		closer	
──────────── ,		━━━━━━━━━ _		─────────── .	

Sentence bases have no punctuation *inside* them. Major exceptions: *series* (dogs, cats, and rats); *coordinate adjectives* (smart, alert students).

Free units are punctuated in various ways, as shown below.

       Openers . . . . .use a comma:

        ──────────── , ──────────────────── .

       Interrupters . . . . . . .use commas, dashes, or parentheses:

   (1) ━━━━━━━ , ──────── , ━━━━━━ .

   (2) ━━━━━━━ — ──────── — ━━━━━━ .

   (3) ━━━━━━━ (────────) ━━━━━━ .

       Closers . . . . .use parentheses, or one dash or one comma:

   (1) ━━━━━━━━━ (────────────────) .

   (2) ━━━━━━━━━ — ──────────────── .

   (3) ━━━━━━━━━ , ──────────────── .

Typical sentence patterns, with their punctuation:

- opener, base: ──────────── , ━━━━━━━━━ .
- two bases: ━━━━━━━━━ ; ━━━━━━━━━ .
      (A semicolon after a base implies another base coming.)
- two bases with conjunction:
      ━━━━━━━━━━━━━ , and ━━━━━━━━━ .
- two bases with conjunctive adverb: ━━━━━━━━ ; therefore, ━━━━━━━ .
- a base, followed by an opener for a second base: ━━━━ ; ──── , ━━━━ .
- a base, followed by a closer, followed by a second base: ━━━━━ , ──── ; ━━━━ .

k. Running for treasurer of the club _____ .

l. In the morning is the best time _____ .

m. To lie [fib] _____ .

n. "On Top of Old Smoky" _____ .

o. Parting _____ .

▼ The Free Units of the Sentence

The *free unit* in a sentence differs from the *base unit* in one fundamental way (*this is very important*):

> The free unit *cannot* stand alone.

The *base unit,* by definition, *can* stand alone. Note these contrasts between *base* and *free* units:

Base unit: I am feeling cheerful.

Free unit: Whenever I am feeling cheerful. . .

Base unit: He still smokes too much.

Free unit: . . . although he still smokes too much.

Base unit: The wind had been blowing hard.

Free unit: . . . which had been blowing hard. . .

Now let's take each of the *free units* shown above and put them into a full sentence (where they would normally appear):

— *Whenever I am feeling cheerful,* it rains.
— He has stopped drinking, *although he still smokes too much.*
— The wind, *which had been blowing hard,* suddenly died down.

This distinction between *free* and *base* units is simple and consistent. If the unit you are writing can stand alone, you are writing a *base.* If it cannot stand alone, it is *free.*

There are three other important characteristics of the *free unit:*

1. The beginning and end of the free unit are shown by *punctuation.*

   . *Whenever I am feeling cheerful,* (The period ends the previous sentence.)

   , *although he still smokes too much.*

   , *which had been blowing hard,*

2. The free unit is often *movable* in the sentence.

   We will continue to drill for oil—*even though the equipment is very expensive.*

   Even though the equipment is very expensive, *we will continue to drill for oil.*

   However, *it is your decision.* [A free unit can be only one word. See number **3.**]

   It is your decision, *however.*

3. A free unit can be of various lengths—it can be *one word*, a *phrase*, or a full *subordinate clause*.

> *Consequently,* Ms. Hoskins decided to go to Europe by ship. *(single word)*
>
> She made her decision quickly, *thus clearing the way for other activities. (phrase)*
>
> *When nuclear power is made completely safe,* we should reconsider using it. *(clause)*

▪▪▪ The Free Unit as Opener

Note the punctuation in the examples.

The *opening* free unit comes *before* the sentence base and is punctuated with a comma. Examples:

> *To show their condemnation of the Vietnam war,* some young Americans emigrated to Canada.
>
> *Incidentally,* the fireplace needs more wood before evening.
>
> *After the parade was over,* the antique cars were driven away.
>
> *No matter how frightened Tammy was,* she always walked home alone from work at 2 a.m.
>
> *Before eating peanut butter,* take out your false teeth.

▪▪▪ The Free Unit as Interrupter

Note the punctuation in the examples.

The *interrupting* free unit is placed *inside* the sentence base, where it is punctuated with commas, dashes, or parentheses.

NOTE: Always remember that in this pattern the sentence base is "interrupted" by the free unit, and that the same base exists on both sides of this unit. It's as if you broke a stick into two pieces and inserted a fresh piece of wood between the pieces:

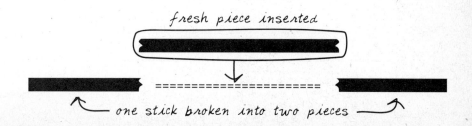

Example:

Interrupter inserted

I shocked Bob, *who was a careful driver,* when I told him I'd wrecked his car.

— one base —

Here are examples of interrupters (note the variety of possible punctuation):

The prisoner, *who was starving,* threatened to kill himself.

My aspirin bottle—*already opened when I bought it*—was taken by the police for evidence.

The child *(now hiding behind his mother)* peeked fearfully out at the two tall men.

The anti-abortion movement, *however,* continued in full force.

The college needs a new standards committee, *one with students on it,* to frame a reasonable set of rules for campus behavior.

■■■ The Free Unit as Closer

Note the punctuation in the examples:

The *closing* free unit is placed *after* the sentence base and (like the interrupter) can be punctuated with a comma, dash, or parentheses. Examples:

A student needs success—*not constant failure.*

I anticipate the best of all possible worlds, *one in which TV shows Monday Night Football every night of the week.*

Check the spelling of all words *(using a dictionary if necessary).*

Patrick stumbled toward me, *his feet getting more tangled up every second.*

Some authorities believe that a certain amount of sexual censorship is inevitable—*that human beings have a rage for moral order which must be satisfied.*

Then Thompson intervened in the argument, *his voice shaking with emotion.*

NOTE: At this point, we suggest that you carefully review the table on page 79, "Punctuation in the Sentence Unit System."

PRACTICE

---

1. *First:* Identify all *free units* as *openers, interrupters,* or *closers.*

   Second: Explain each punctuation mark. In **a,** you would say:

Opener: *As he rose to his feet,* [comma separates opener from the base]

Base: *he held high the ancient bible*—[dash separates the base from the closer]

Closer: *a tattered leather-bound book.*

Third: With the help of the table on page 79, diagram each unit as a base [——————] or as a free unit [——————]. Be sure to insert punctuation marks between the heavy and light lines that represent units.

a. As he rose to his feet, he held high the ancient bible—a tattered leather-bound book.

b. All this time, people in the crowd were silent, not even shuffling their feet.

c. That idea is, of course, a good explanation of the device (one which almost anyone could understand).

d. Running almost sideways down the line, the quarterback tried to hand off to his halfback.

e. The halfback got the ball for a second, juggling it furiously and then dropping it.

f. The linebacker, who had been charging into the play, suddenly found the ball bouncing right into his hands.

g. He ran desperately for the goal, his great heavy legs churning furiously.

h. Loping almost lazily after this new ball carrier, the cornerback reached out with one hand and grabbed at the linebacker's jersey.

i. The jersey ripped away. The cornerback seemed to drift for a moment in the air.

j. Then everything happened at once.

k. The cornerback, now tumbling on the ground, was out of the play.

l. The huge linebacker, still on his feet, continued to lumber goalward.

m. From out of nowhere came the quarterback, galloping uncertainly on his ruined knees.

n. According to the head coach's orders, this gimpy-legged ancient (38 years old to the day) was never supposed to amble out of the pocket.

o. But there he was, grabbing at the bouncing shoulder pads of a 240-pound linebacker—who had crossed the goal line one second earlier.

2. In this exercise, you will make up units (or parts of units).

a. Like her sisters, Margaret _____ .

b. Obviously, it was not a good idea (considering _____ _____) to take a train home for Christmas.

c. Because _____ , the chipmunk raced frantically around to the other side of the tree.

d. The old farmhouse had only one stove, which _____ .

e. And the stove—which _____—had always burned coal.

f. Generosity is my best trait, one that _____ .

g. Before we can make a decision between the two new cars, _____

_____ .

h. This group of alumni (_____) have never given any money to the college.

i. Believing that I had stood her up, _____ .

j. I was ashamed that I had forgotten the date, although _____

_____ .

▼ Punctuating Base and Free Units

For reference, continue to review the table on page 79.

The marks of punctuation in typical sentences act as small signals for your readers, warning them that a certain kind of construction is about to appear in the sentence. For example, if your readers see a comma after this free unit,

At the end of the second hour,

they can guess that a new sentence unit is coming. What will it be? Possibly a sentence base:

At the end of the second hour, stop writing the exam.

Or they can guess that a second opening unit is coming:

At the end of the second hour, before you go on to the multiple choice section, stop writing the exam.

By contrast, if readers see a base followed by a comma, they may expect a closing unit to follow:

Stop writing the exam at the end of two hours, *even if you are not finished.*

Readers would *not* expect a base to follow the comma, because that mispunctuation would create a *comma splice* (see page 468), which is considered a bad error.

Error of the comma splice: ━━━━━ **,** ━━━━━ **.**

As the table on page 79 shows, commas can be used between all base and free units, *but not between two bases* (unless they are joined by a *coordinating conjunction*—see page 468.

In fact, trained writers use the comma energetically when they need it, but otherwise tend to ration commas rather stingily. If they already have two commas in a sentence, they may turn to dashes or parentheses to clarify the relationship of units to each other.

Consider the variety of punctuation in these sentences:

— "These men, you understand, now say (at least in private to younger working women in their office) that they are bored with women who 'don't do anything.'"

—Ellen Goodman

— "If I were a man, I would be a hellion, I would; the kind of man a woman like myself would fall in love with—and probably live to regret it."

—Marya Mannes

— "After breakfast we would go up to the store and the things were in the same place—the minnows in a bottle, the plugs and spinners disarranged and pawed over by the youngsters from the boys' camp, the Fig Newtons and the Beeman's gum."

—E. B. White

▼ The Rhetoric of Sentence Units

Obviously, as a writer you have to make decisions about where to put the units of a sentence. Should you use an opener at a certain point in a paragraph? Two bases joined by a conjunction? Many such questions take care of themselves. For instance, if you want to add one idea to another, and if the two ideas are balanced in importance, you may well put them in two bases:

> The store asked her to work overtime, and she said that she would.

But when such opportunities don't present themselves, you will have to choose among units. In the sections that follow, we suggest some strategies in the *rhetoric* of sentence units. (For further information, see the table on page 86, "The Sentence Unit Rule.")

■■■ Using Openers

For reference, see "The Sentence Unit Rule," page 86.

Base units sometimes become lengthy or awkward. As long as you keep them short and specific, you are probably safe. But let them start to get long and snaky and your reader is in trouble:

> The second week of college that I had experienced in September was one of the worst things that had ever happened to me and one that my brother Zack had repeatedly warned me about before I left home.

This sentence snake needs cutting up. An opener may help:

In my second week of college, I had an experience that was one of the worst of my life. [This is followed by another sentence.]

As in the last example, the opening "position" is often an excellent place to put material that is cluttering your sentence:

Cluttered: His energy in doing his job on most Saturday nights when the rest of us don't have to work was one of the most disgusting things about him.

Revised: On Saturday nights, when most of us didn't have to work, he performed his job with disgusting energy.

Cluttered: The assistant to the professor who taught the lecture was sometimes in charge of the lab and drove us all crazy with his constant demands to "keep this place clean!"

Revised: When the lecturer's assistant was in charge of the lab, he drove us crazy. . . [Note also that we compressed some of the original material in this opener.]

The Sentence Unit Rule

Given its nature, the rule must be stated in several parts. But it is based on a simple premise—that you will find it easier to write clear, readable sentences if you think of the sentence as a series of *punctuated units*. Each unit represents a little idea (or piece of an idea) of its own. And each unit has its boundaries; you know how long it is because punctuation indicates where each unit begins and ends. There are only two types of units, *base* and *free*.

Sentence pointers (see pages 88–90) help your reader to predict where your sentence is going. A *pointer* is defined as a word (or, less often, a phrase) that begins an *opener* or *base unit* and suggests the kind of statement to come. See the list of sentence pointers on page 89.

The **sentence unit rule** is not a grammatical law, but a set of techniques. Use them, when you can, to improve the clarity of your sentence. Here is the four-part rule:

1. Break up your sentences into clearly defined *units*.

2. Use *punctuation* to show where the units *begin* and *end*.

3. Use *sentence pointers* to predict ideas.

4. *Vary* your units. Don't use the same pattern over and over.

As an example of the four-part rule, here are two sentences. They are made of a short base, followed (in a new sentence) by an opener and its base, followed by a closer:

We should learn from this tragedy. Whenever you have the urge to keep a gun at home for protection, remember the father who mistakenly shot his own ten-year-old daughter, believing that she was a burglar.

In both of these examples, you look for a nugget of information that can be moved out of the sentence, rewritten if necessary, and put into an opening position.

Openers provide a great variety of partial statements that can be completed in the bases that follow:

> *Although she was ambitious, . . .*
>
> *During the last war, . . .*
>
> *After the period was over, . . .*
>
> *Because they had no money, . . .*
>
> *When we had just about given up, . . .*
>
> *Derided by nearly the whole town, . . .*
>
> *Springing to the defense of her client, . . .*

Openers are also valuable as *transitions:*

> *In addition to these properties, . . .*
>
> *After that second attempt to reach the pole, . . .*
>
> *Before you finish this experiment, . . .*
>
> *In accepting such a solution to the problem, . . .*

> *In the first place, . . .*
>
> *In spite of my objections, . . .*
>
> *No matter how we cheered them on, . . .*
>
> *After taking into account every variable, . . .*

■■■ Using Interrupters

Use "The Sentence Unit Rule" on page 86 for reference.
Interrupters help to *explain, identify,* or *add detail.*

> The garden flowers, *blooming late that year,* were all killed by my spray of 2-4-D.
>
> General Sherman, *driven by pride and ferocity,* led his army relentlessly through Georgia.
>
> There sat Teddy, *stubborn and balky to the end,* snarling out orders to his trembling family.

Interrupters are often *who* or *which* clauses:

> Jezebel, *who was one of the most awkward horses you ever saw,* actually won her first race.
>
> The garden flowers, *which bloomed late that year,* were all killed by my spray of 2-4-D.

General Sherman, *who was driven by pride and ferocity,* led his army relentlessly through Georgia.

Our new car, *which we had bought only last week,* was now a total wreck.

■■■ Using Closers

See the table on page 86 for reference.

Like *interrupters,* closers explain, identify, or add detail:

> Bates stopped going to his barber, *who always refused to give him a simple, uncompli-cated haircut.*
> Emily loved airplanes—*any airplane, any size, any kind.* (three closers)

> So far as I am concerned, PBS radio has become tiresome: *full of classical music and boring intellectuals talking only to each other.*
> This is the age of electronics, *of microchips and tiny "dedicated" computers.*
> Then the motion picture was invented, *which was at first a toy that grew into a cultural monster.*

You will observe from these examples that closers tend to "look backward" at the idea you have just written, in order to add something about that idea:

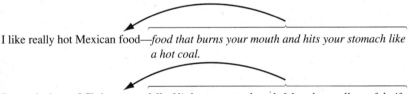

I like really hot Mexican food—*food that burns your mouth and hits your stomach like a hot coal.*

It was the best of Christmases, *full of little presents, thoughtful and actually useful gifts.*

Where you use two closers, they may both say something about an idea in the base. Or, as in the last example above, the first closer may refer to the base while the second closer refers to the first closer.

Is there a limit to the number of closers you can write? Theoretically, no. But practically speaking, your readers may get lost if you use more than two or three. One or two will usually suffice. A writer like William Faulkner will sometimes use dozens—some of his long, seemingly complicated sentences are no more than a sentence base followed by a profusion of narrative closers.

▼ Sentence "Pointers"

The great dramatist George Bernard Shaw once said of the word *but* that it "is the most important conjunction in the English language." Shaw didn't say why, but we can guess. It has great "pointing" power—it points vividly and suggestively to the kind of idea coming up in a sentence:

She: I intend to vote for President X.

He: But...

Anybody listening is reasonably sure that *but* is going to lead to a contradiction.

Sentence pointers are words that lead a reader toward an idea that is about to appear in the sentence. Like a flashing yellow light at a highway intersection, they are highly suggestive of something important to come. They are most effective *when they start a sentence, when they begin an opener* or *sentence base.* In fact, we will define a *sentence pointer* as "a word (or, less often, a brief phrase) that begins an opener or base, and suggests the kind of statement to come." Examples of such pointers are:

Yet, we had not anticipated...

Also, this magnificent liar told us...

Unlike Monroe, Farquhar had no reason to...

After his depression, my father never regained...

Sentence pointers give direction to a sentence in various ways. They can indicate time, place, reason, cause, effect, and so on. Some of the strongest pointers indicate cause or effect:

Because the Russians must understand our motives,...

Consequently, the law has nothing to tell us about...

As a result, I looked into my thesaurus and found...

Any list of sentence pointers would be incomplete because a large number of adverbs, conjunctions, conjunctive adverbs (and even some prepositions) can act as pointers. Here is a list of some of the most common:

but	first, second, third	still
and	then	yet
so	however	as a result
consequently	next	thus
also	before	like, unlike
for example	in fact, indeed	finally
therefore	whenever	although

■■■ Classes of Pointers

There are four general classes of pointers:

1. Pointers of *time:*

While spraying the plant, he discovered mites on its leaves.

Before lighting the pilot light, be sure that the heat exchanger is clean.

2. Pointers of *logical relation:*

Thus inflation continues to be a major problem in the Western democracies.

Because the ice was more than two inches thick on the telephone poles, repair crews were unable to work in Sapulpa.

3. Pointers of *similarity* and *contrast:*

Like the other teachers, she went on strike.

But the school board refused to grant pay raises.

Yet the Supreme Court seems determined to stay out of obscenity questions as long as possible.

4. Pointers that *count* or *differentiate:*

First, let us define the term correctly.

Then, at this point, it is possible to see the precipitate in the tube.

Finally, all passengers should observe the no-smoking rule.

PRACTICE

1. In the following exercises, we show successful writers using the *Sentence Unit Rule.* For each sentence given below, (a) identify each *base* and *free unit* (opener, interrupter, closer); (b) circle the punctuation used between units; (c) identify the *sentence pointers;* (d) comment on the *effectiveness* of the placement and content of the units. (Part **d** may be done as an oral class exercise.)

First Group

a. In Moulmein, in lower Burma, I was hated by large numbers of people—the only time in my life that I have been important enough for this to happen to me.

—George Orwell

b. But anyone who tries to tell me that youngsters who work for their "allowance" at crummy hamburger joints are low-class had better stay away from me, particularly on the day when I get my pitiful paycheck, and most particularly when I have to ask my kids for a few bucks to help pay for groceries for the rest of the week.

—Sammie Pagitt

c. Presumably, 50 percent of the sentences that writers—teachers, students, and scholars—produce may contain *parallelism,* "faulty" or otherwise.

—Mary Hiatt

d. Striding along, matching Charlie's pace as best I could, I soon saw someone approaching from the other direction.

—Susan Allen Toth

e. But the truth is—and I hope this admission will not disappoint too many of my friends—that I had already shaken my university president's hand and accepted my bachelor's degree from him by the time they started demanding he resign.

—Joseph Goodman

f. Of course equality is needed. Yet, in the long run, we are facing a permanent war between the haves and the have-nots, a war that may destroy many of us and leave our children emotionally destitute.

—Angela Muniz

g. Although Ridgeway proved his point time and again, the response of the American public was (in almost every instance) to turn its back on his evidence. They just didn't want to listen to him.

—Isaac Parklin

h. Locke erects the transit on a tripod. He turns the brass wheels until the bubble, encased in glass beneath the eyepiece, floats to the center of the chamber. Then, bending over, putting one eye to the lens of the transit and squinting the other, he transforms his view of this patch of open ground into a narrow, well-lighted tunnel divided by cross hairs.

—Tracy Kidder

i. To oppose one class perpetually to another—young against old, manual labor against brain-worker, woman against man—is to split the foundations of the state; and if the cleavage runs too deep, there remains no remedy but force and dictatorship.

—Dorothy L. Sayers

j. All cultures, we know, place boundaries around the passions; they construct powerful defenses against murder and incest, to say nothing of derivative transgressions.

—Peter Gay

Second Group

a. I have no dress [for my wedding] except the one I wear every day. If you are going to give me one, please let it be practical and dark so that I can put it on afterwards to go to the laboratory.

—Marie Curie

b. Finally, I have left nothing undone that might have made you happy—
nothing, ever, from the very beginning. And now my end is your beginning.

—Evan Taylor, before his suicide

c. Our society treats sex as a sport, with its record-breakers, its judges, its rules
and its spectators.

—Susan Lydon

d. Gossip is the opiate of the oppressed.

—Erica Jong

e. What a crowd of snobs and slobs! The leftist students of the sixties did not
like learning; they had a positive and lasting prejudice against thinking; and
they considered the common decencies of society a plot against the young.

—Stuart Kramer

f. Women are natural guerrillas. Scheming, we nestle into the enemy's bed,
avoiding open warfare, watching the options, playing the odds.

—Sally Kempton

g. If you are lucky enough to have lived in Paris as a young man, then
wherever you go for the rest of your life, it stays with you, for Paris is a
moveable feast.

—Ernest Hemingway

h. When I get sick of what men do, I have only to walk a few steps in another
direction to see what spiders do.

—E. B. White

i. Don't compromise yourself. You are all you've got.

—Janis Joplin

j. The right to trial by jury shall be preserved.

—Seventh Amendment [1791] to the Constitution of the United States

Third Group

1. a. In science, the credit goes to the man who convinces the world, not to the
man to whom the idea first occurs.

—William Osler

b. Before I leave the dorm for vacation, I lock my stereo in the closet (a useless gesture, considering that the lock is breakable).

c. Obviously, a stationary population—one in which the birth rate matches the death rate—is out of the question for many years to come.

—David E. Lilienthal

d. Dean McIntyre (he's the one who has been calling you long-distance) has also written a letter of congratulation about your award.

e. Drug addiction is *not* increasing; in all probability, it has declined since the turn of the century.

—William McCord

f. She disagrees with you, but she respects your opinion.

g. She disagrees with you; she respects your opinion, however.

h. In the summer before the French Revolution, all of France was, it seems, gripped by a deep malaise, an underlying panic to which contemporaries gave the name of *la grande Peur*—the great Fear.

—Adlai Stevenson

i. He struggled in a wild frenzy of fury and terror, almost mad terror.

—D. H. Lawrence

j. The storm took the helicopter ten miles from the airport.

k. Ten miles from the airport, the storm overtook the helicopter.

l. For instance, violence—accidents, suicides, and homicides—accounts for fully three out of four deaths among males age 15 to 24, making the American death rate for this age group 62 percent higher than the Swedish rate.

m. I was raised to farm work, which I continued till I was twenty-two.

—Abraham Lincoln

2. For class discussion and writing practice, consider again the sentences in Practice on pages 90–93. Pick out six of the sentences and write imitations of them. Use your own ideas, and modify or switch the units around if you wish. For instance, for **e** (third group), you could write:

Highway accidents are not increasing; in all probability, they have declined since 1984.
Since 1984, highway accidents probably have not increased.

Highway accidents—judging from the evidence—have not increased since 1984.

Highway accidents seem to have decreased recently (since 1984, to be exact).

▼ Variations on the Typical Sentence

Here are some interesting sentences:

Among those whom I like or admire, I can find no common denominator, but among those whom I love, I can: all of them make me laugh.

—W. H. Auden

These are the times that try men's souls: The summer soldier and the sunshine patriot will in this crisis, shrink from the service of his country; but he that stands it Now, deserves the love and thanks of man and woman. Tyranny, like hell, is not easily conquered; yet we have this consolation with us, that the harder the conflict, the more glorious the triumph. . . .

—Thomas Paine

The afternoons were long; sunsets were sad glories: allegorical wars between dark heroes and the lords of light.

—Jack Vance

I had not known my father very well. We had got on badly, partly because we shared, in our different fashions, the vice of stubborn pride. When he was dead I realized that I had hardly ever spoken to him. When he had been dead a long time I began to wish I had. It seems to be typical of life in America, where opportunities, real and fancied, are thicker than anywhere else on the globe, that the second generation has no time to talk to the first.

—James Baldwin, *Notes of a Native Son*

Sentences like these provide variety and drama. The techniques for writing them are relatively simple, and you might like to try them out yourself. Write a few sentences every day in which you imitate the sentence patterns and techniques discussed in the rest of this chapter. Create your own variations. Take off and fly a little. But don't worry about crashes—nobody ever got hurt from falling off a sentence.

■■■ *Try Different Beginnings*

By changing the way your sentences begin, you can add variety to your writing almost automatically. Here is a sentence that follows the subject-verb-object pattern:

She has a new sports car.

By using various kinds of beginnings, you can work variations on this:

With object as subject:	Her new sports car is easy to drive.
With change of subject:	Her prized possession is a sports car.
With -*ing* subject:	Driving a sports car is a sign of status in a university community.
With infinitive subject:	To drive a sports car is a sign of affluence.
With subordinate clause:	After her grandfather's estate was settled, she bought a sports car.
With -*ing* phrase:	Having received her inheritance, she bought a sports car.
With prepositional phrase:	After the model change, she bought a sports car.
With *it/there*:	There is nothing more fun than a sports car.
With *that/what*:	That she spent her money on a new sports car is obvious. What she wanted more than anything else was a new sports car.
With a question:	A new sports car? She just bought one.

■■■ *Employ Inversion*

Most sentences are written using this normal word order: "They did not say a word." In creating an *inversion,* or *inverted order,* you shift a sentence element into an *earlier* position in the arrangement of words: *"Not a word* did they say." An occasional inversion makes your writing more interesting and dramatic:

Normal order:	He slid down the slope, scraping skin from his elbows.
Inversion:	*Down the slope he slid,* scraping skin from his elbows.
Normal order:	The vampire stalked through the castle, his eyes glowing.
Inversion:	*Through the castle stalked the vampire,* his eyes glowing. [a double inversion]

Precisely because inverted sentences are dramatic, they should be used sparingly.

■■■ *Try a Periodic Sentence*

For richness and suspense, use an occasional *periodic sentence,* which keeps your main thought suspended until the end as a position of emphasis. The periodic sentence has two virtues: (1) you can pile many ideas into its versatile and flexible structure; and (2) it holds the reader's interest like a detective story. How, the reader wonders while reading through a periodic sentence, will it all turn out? Here are some examples (italics added):

At that great moment in history, ranking with the moment in the long ago when man first put fire to work for him and started on his march to civilization, *the vast energy locked within the hearts of the atoms of matter was released for the first time in a burst of flame such as had never before been seen on this planet.*

—W. L. Laurence

Cleanliness is a great virtue; but when it is carried to such an extent that you cannot find your books and papers which you left carefully arranged on your table—when it gets to be a monomania with man or woman—*it becomes a bore.*

—C. B. Fairbanks

There is a homely adage which runs, "Speak softly and carry a big stick; you will go far." If the American nation will speak softly and yet build and keep at a pitch of the highest training a thoroughly efficient navy, *the Monroe Doctrine will go far.*

—Theodore Roosevelt

■■■ Use Qualifying and Balancing Devices

In your writing you will sometimes need to qualify your statements. That is, you will need to limit the range of an assertion or include an exception to an idea expressed in the base. Suppose you write: "I like Wagner's music, even though some of it is excessively dramatic." Here you qualify the idea in the sentence base ("I like Wagner's music") with an idea in a closer that is introduced by the phrase *even though*.

In balancing ideas, you can use certain *signs of correlation* to indicate that the ideas are equal in importance and emphasis. Here are some typical signs:

Either-or:	Sandy wants *either* strawberry *or* vanilla ice cream.
Neither-nor:	We wanted to go swimming, but *neither* Judy *nor* Alice was able to go.
Both-and:	We went to Hawk Beach because the water there was *both* safe *and* warm.
Not only-but also:	Howells should be admired *not only* for his vivid storytelling *but also* for his knowledge of human beings.

Sometimes you will need to express *opposing* ideas that are equal in importance. So you should use a special kind of balancing structure known as *antithesis:* "Linda likes swimming but not baseball." Antithesis is an art beloved of satirists, preachers, and politicians: "Woolworth was not brave; he was a coward. He was not fair; he played favorites. He was not moral, but righteous; not honest, but slyly dutiful; not skillful, but lucky; not . . ." Poor Woolworth. It is easy to get carried away by this sort of thing.

■■■ Let Meaning Determine Your Structure

Surely, the most important suggestion of all is: *Let meaning determine the structure of your sentences.* If your meaning demands a certain type of sentence or a certain construction, use that sentence or construction. A sentence expresses an idea. If your idea is one of cause and effect, for example, your sentence construction in some way must show cause and effect: "Since all children should be able to read, we must build schools to teach them." The *since* tied to the opener, which is in turn tied to the sentence base, helps give the reader a sentence that moves clearly from opener to period and that also neatly marries structure and sense. Of course there are other ways to state this idea: "We must build schools because all children should be able to read." Here, *because* signals the cause-and-effect relation. Many cause-and-effect sentences have either a *since* or *because* in them.

As you allow the meaning to determine the structure of your sentences, you will combine several of the structures discussed in this chapter. For example, Tom dislikes baseball. Perhaps he dislikes football and tennis too. And he loathes swimming. To express these ideas accurately, you write something like: "Tom dislikes football, tennis, and baseball—but swimming he actually loathes." To express a rather simple set of ideas you have created a complex and interlocked set of constructions:

Sentence base:	Tom dislikes football, tennis, and baseball
Parallel elements:	football, tennis, and baseball
Signal:	but
Inversion:	swimming he actually loathes.

All these guidelines end with a bit of practical and general advice: Use different sentence structures and lengths. Occasionally sneak up on your readers with a sentence they do not expect. Don't plod along writing one *subject-verb-object* sentence after another. Make your sentences show a little sparkle and life—but remember that too much sparkle, like too much champagne, will only make your readers dizzy. Here is a sparkling bit of prose that illustrates many of the variations we've been talking about:

> It is curious to be awake and watch a sleeper. Seldom, when he awakes, can he remember anything of his sleep. It is a dead part of his life. But watching him, we know he was alive, and part of his life was thought. His body moved. His eyelids fluttered, as his eyes saw moving visions in the darkness. His limbs sketched tiny motions, because his sleeping fancy was guiding him through a crowd, or making him imagine a race, a fight, a hunt, a dance. . . .. he sweated. He felt the passage of time and was making himself ready for the morning with its light and noise. And all that time he was thinking—vaguely and emotionally if he was intellectually untrained, in symbols, animals, and divinities if he was a primitive man, often in memories, sometimes in anticipation of the future, and far oftener than he himself would believe, forming intricate and firm decisions on difficult problems carried over from his waking life.
>
> —Gilbert Highet, *Man's Unconquerable Mind*

PRACTICE

1. Identify the sentence structures in the following sentences. Look for inversions, periodic sentences, and qualifying and balancing devices.

   a. All animals are equal, but some animals are more equal than others.

   —George Orwell

   b. Though I speak with the tongues of men and of angels, and have not charity, I am become as sounding brass, or a tinkling cymbal.

   —1 Cor. 13:1

c. In some sort of crude sense which no vulgarity, no humor, no overstatement can quite extinguish, the physicists have known sin; and this is a knowledge which they cannot lose.

—J. R. Oppenheimer

d. All in green went my love riding/on a great horse of gold/into the silver dawn.

—E. E. Cummings

e. We must conquer war, or war will conquer us.

—Ely Culbertson

f. In the free billowing fender [of the automobile], in the blinding chromium grilles, in the fluid control, in the ever-widening front seat, we see the flowering of the America that we know.

—E. B. White

g. Through all his life one idea runs— "Avoid the intelligent men and embrace the mediocre."

h. A man may be old, he may be ugly, he may be burdened with grave responsibilities to the nation, and that nation be at a crisis of its history; but none of these considerations, nor all of them together, will deter him from sitting for his portrait.

—Max Beerbohm

2. Discuss these two passages. How are they similar and different in their use of the sentence variations discussed on pages 94–97?

1   Here is what we know about the state of poverty: its boundaries do not appear on any map; it has no flag or official song, but once you are there it is difficult to get your zip code changed; as a character-building experience it is overrated by the rich and overpopulated by the poor; and it's a place where nobody goes for the weekend.

2   Earl Campbell had never given much thought to being poor, had never really realized how deprived his family had been, until—in the space of a single year— he won the Heisman Trophy, signed a contract worth $ 1.4 million to play for the Houston Oilers and became the hottest thing to hit the NFL since *Monday Night Football*. When the full weight of his family's privation hit him, Campbell decided to take some of his NFL greenbacks and build a spacious new house for his mother and then turn the rundown plank shack where he had grown up into a museum where other underprivileged kids could come see firsthand that the NFL was, indeed, the land of opportunity.

3   And so, as Campbell's fortunes soared on football fields across America last season, his mama's new house went up. And lest the contrast between his past and his present would be too subtle to grasp, Campbell had the new house built about 25 feet from the old one, with only a large gray septic tank between them.

—Bruce Newman, "The Roots of Greatness"

1   Dogs fare ill in proverbs. They are greedy, fierce, filthy, and servile. They defile cisterns, return to their vomit, drive the patient ox from the manger, bark at their own fleas, eat each other, bay the moon, suffer under a bad name, get themselves hanged and beaten, and whine, snarl, cringe, fawn, and slaver in a myriad dangerous and disgusting ways. Dogs are mentioned many times in the Bible, but only with abhorrence. That they licked Lazarus' sores was intended not as an indication of their pity but of his degradation. They fare even worse in Shakespeare than in the Scriptures; their combined servility, ferocity, and filthiness seems to have fascinated the poet with revulsion.

2   Until fairly recently the dog was a scavenger. His food consisted exclusively of garbage and his residence was the kennel or channel, the loathsome trickle down the center of the street into which refuse was thrown. Great houses, having much garbage, had many dogs, and there was a regular functionary the dog whipper, to keep them in subjection. Blows and kicks were the rule and for the slightest offense dogs were hanged. Sometimes just for the fun of it.

3   In such an atmosphere and under such a regime *a dog's life* was, no doubt, a wretched one to lead. *To go to the dogs* was to descend low indeed, and *to die like a dog* to make a miserable end. The sayings might be trite, even then, but at least they had meaning.

—Bergen and Cornelia Evans,
A Dictionary of Contemporary American Usage

3. Using the ideas supplied in the sentences below, create new sentences that employ the variations suggested in this chapter. Omit any sentences or sentence parts that seem irrelevant in your new sentences. But try to use as much of the detail as possible.

   a. I read *Dracula.* It frightened me. I did not understand some of it. After reading it, I dreamed of blood and castles. I did not understand much of the story.

   b. Darwin College needs a new rugby field. The players are unhappy. The trustees will not approve the funds for it. The players are thinking of trying to raise money by charging people to watch the games for the rest of the season. The field is very bumpy and rough. It has a shallow irrigation ditch running through it.

   c. The desert is full of killers. The desert seems empty. The desert is hot, but the heat does not kill all life. Many forms of life live off other forms. Many inhabitants of the desert look like bugs from another planet.

d. His mother screamed when she first saw it. Spiders did not frighten him. He got a big black spider as a pet. He kept it in a coffee can. He was curious, not fearful. The spider was more afraid of him than he of it.

e. Censorship is wrong. Censorship at times is necessary. Society has certain rights. Individuals should be able to read or view what they please without censorship. Books that show pictures of people being tortured are an evil.

f. The child was bored. The professor was angry at being interrupted. The mother stayed in class with her child. The child ran out of paper and crayons. The student brought her five-year-old child to class.

g. She wanted to experiment with the new. She did not care for tales of failure in the past. She liked chemistry most of all. Tales of dusty kings bored her. She enjoyed working with figures and test tubes and chemical unknowns.

Organizing Clear Paragraphs and Essays

▼ The Promise Pattern

There are many ways to organize a piece of writing. The most frequently used—and for many purposes, probably the best—employs what we call the *promise pattern*. You "promise" your readers at the beginning of your paper that you will tell them certain things, and as you write you fulfill your promise. The promise pattern is most easily seen in a typical paragraph. (This kind of paragraph is often called *deductive* because it begins with a general statement supported by particular details and examples.)

Near the beginning of the following paragraph about surviving in the desert, the author makes a promise (note italics) to his reader:

> These few examples make one thing clear: for anyone who has to survive in the desert, the heat of the day, both cause-and-effect of the lack of water, is the chief danger. *Temperatures reach an amazing height.* In Baghdad the thermometer in the hot summer months often climbs to 150°F., occasionally even to 180° and over (in the sun). In the Sahara near Azizia (Libya) temperatures of 134° in the shade have been recorded, and in July 1913 that was also the temperature in the Great Salt Lake Desert (also in the shade). But if the thermometer is put in the sand there at noon during the summer, the mercury goes up to 176°. On the side of Highway 91, which goes through the Mohave Desert, it has sometimes been 140° in the shade at noon; in the evenings the thermometer sinks to a "low" of 90°. In Libya, Montgomery's and Rommel's soldiers sometimes fried eggs on the armor plate of their tanks.
>
> —Cord-Christian Troebst, *The Art of Survival*

In the rest of the paragraph after the italicized sentence, Troebst keeps his promise—to discuss and illustrate amazingly high desert temperatures.

Much of what we say here concerning the organization of paragraphs applies generally to complete papers. For example:

A paper's promise = the paper's *thesis*

A paragraph promise = the paragraph's *topic idea*

The *topic idea* of a paragraph is its main, controlling statement, which is often expressed in a *topic sentence*. The topic idea of Troebst's paragraph is expressed in the italicized topic sentence, *Temperatures reach an amazing height.* Some paragraphs need two or three sentences to express their topic ideas (or promises), while a few paragraphs have no topic ideas at all. A paragraph that contains no topic ideas may fulfill the promise made in a preceding paragraph, or it may provide a transition between paragraphs.

Consider the *promise pattern* in the two paragraphs below. In an earlier section (not given here) the writer promised his reader that he would relate how immigrant Jews lived in a big American city. In the first paragraph, he keeps that promise; in the second he makes and keeps another:

<table>
<tr><td>*Previous topic idea developed (promise kept)*</td><td>1</td><td>The Jews in Lawndale cut down the trees for firewood and tramped out the grass in the parking strips. They removed the doorknobs and the light fixtures from the flats they rented and sold them for junk. They allowed the drains in their sinks to become clogged with debris, and when you went into their kitchens, you would see the sink full of water to the brim with fishtails and other remains of food products floating in it. I know because my aunt owned her house in Lawndale for some time after she had moved out of it and gone to Oak Park, and when I was in my teens I used to go in and collect the rent for her.</td></tr>
<tr><td>*Transition from previous paragraph New topic idea (promise)*

Promise kept</td><td>2</td><td>Obviously this was a situation ideally calculated to inspire racial and religious prejudice. But the dreadful mistake which many persons made was that they supposed that these people were behaving as they did because they were Jews. *The truth of the matter is of course that they were behaving thus because they were peasants. They had not yet learned how to live in an American city.* They, or their fathers, had come from Polish and Russian villages (most of the older members of the community had not even learned to speak English), and when they first came to America they had been herded into slums where it would have been impossible for anybody to live in any other way than they were living. They were now in the first stage of their escape from the slums, but they did not yet know any better than to take the slums with them. All this was straight sociological conditioning, and it had nothing whatever to do with their being Jews. I am sure that most of us would have been astonished if we had been told that their children and grand-children would have made their adjustment with complete success and that, long before the date at which I am writing, some of these would have made important contributions to American welfare and become distinguished</td></tr>
</table>

citizens in music, science, philanthropy, and many other areas of our corporate life.

—Edward Wagenknecht,
As Far As Yesterday: Memories and Reflections

It is important to understand that when you make a promise to your readers you set up an expectation. Suppose you make this statement near the beginning of an essay: *The problem of recreation at Windsor College is not as great as the administration believes.* Immediately your readers expect you to show them in some detail why the problem is not as great as some might think. If you wander off into another subject (like academic achievement, for instance), or do not give details concerning your thesis/promise, you will fail to satisfy the expectations of the readers. They will then say you haven't done your job of communication—and they will be right.

Idealized, the promise pattern for a typical paper appears below.

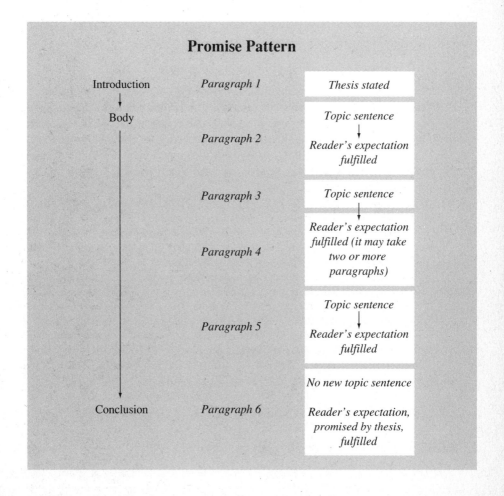

Promise Pattern

Introduction	*Paragraph 1*	*Thesis stated*
Body	*Paragraph 2*	*Topic sentence* ↓ *Reader's expectation fulfilled*
	Paragraph 3	*Topic sentence*
	Paragraph 4	*Reader's expectation fulfilled (it may take two or more paragraphs)*
	Paragraph 5	*Topic sentence* ↓ *Reader's expectation fulfilled*
Conclusion	*Paragraph 6*	*No new topic sentence* *Reader's expectation, promised by thesis, fulfilled*

PRACTICE

Discussion

1. The following sentences from student papers were written to act as statements of promise. For class discussion, answer these questions: (a) What do these statements promise the reader? (b) Can each promise be reasonably fulfilled by the writer in a paragraph? In a paper of 500–1000 words? (c) If you answered *yes* to either part of (b), explain briefly how *you* might go about fulfilling the reader's expectation for each statement.

   a. _____ is becoming one of the most popular art forms in America today.

   b. The history of war proves that human beings can never get along.

   c. The _____ car is less popular now because its snob appeal is gone and it costs too much to repair and operate.

   d. Contrary to what many students think, our chemistry lab has more expensive equipment than the beginning student needs.

   e. There are no good Chinese/French/Italian restaurants in my hometown.

2. June Kronholz, a professional writer, wrote an essay from which we have taken (1) the first two sentences, and (2) selected sentences from paragraph beginnings. Write two or three paragraphs guessing how Kronholz used the promise pattern in the completed essay as published. Her article appeared on the front page of *The Wall Street Journal,* a newspaper with a highly educated readership. The article was well received and widely praised. Why do you think this was the case?

   1   This is a story about power, sex, predation and violence in Africa.
   2   It's about crocodiles.
   3   First, the power. A crocodile can grow to a length of 20 feet, weigh half a ton and tackle a 900-pound buffalo that wanders past at lunchtime. . . .
   4   Now for the sex. A crocodile reaches [sexual] maturity when he is 2.5 feet long, which can take anywhere from 10 to 20 years, depending on how well he has been eating. . . .
   5   Here's where the predation comes in. An adult crocodile has only one predator: a man with a rifle (a Soviet-designed AK–47 is preferred in these parts). . . .
   6   Now, finally, the violence. Given the choice between a man and a buffalo, a crocodile almost always will opt for a fish. But occasionally a man will happen along the river bank. . . .

▼ Writing Successful Paragraphs

■■■ *Support Your Paper's Promise*

A paragraph is a collection of sentences that helps you support your thesis. Itself a small "essay," a paragraph should be clearly written and specific; and it should not wander or make irrelevant remarks. Each paragraph should be related in some way to the thesis or the paper's "promise." Since a paragraph is usually part of a larger piece of writing (essay, research paper, report, etc.), use your *shape, plan,* or *outline* to help you construct paragraphs that support the thesis.

KEEP YOUR TOPIC SENTENCE IN MIND.   After you have decided on your paragraph topic sentence, jot down all the facts and details that you have previously collected by brainstorming, freewriting, or thinking about your subject. Arrange these ideas in a logical form and sequence, with your details and *specific* examples fulfilling the paragraph promise.

Consider this ex-smoker's support of his topic sentence:

Topic sentence *(promise)*	*My body was sicker than I thought it would be.* The joints in my arms and shoulders and the muscles in my chest and my calves hurt so badly the first night I hid in the dark and cried. That pain lasted
Joints, muscles, and calves hurt	only one day, but for at least a week I was always aching somewhere. My mouth, nose, throat, stomach, and each tooth were deprived of
General aching	smoke and nicotine, and their reactions lasted much longer. I kept arching my mouth wide open as if adjusting cheap store-bought teeth.
Results of deprivation in mouth, throat, nose	My throat was sore as if I had smoked too much, perhaps from inhaling too hard on an absent cigarette. I blew my nose needlessly. It is staggering how many parts of me—phalange, organ, membrane, and hair—wanted a smoke, each in its own sore way. For two full weeks I
Nausea	was nauseated. Peanuts and Irish whiskey are as good a way as I found to calm this sick desire of the body for tobacco. The cure, however, is expensive.

—Budd Whitebook, "Confessions of an Ex-Smoker"*

GET TO THE POINT.   Don't waste time or words in stating your topic sentence. Consider this good example of getting to the point—the writer is explaining the ancient Romans' technique for conquering their world:

The technique of expansion was simple. *Divide et impera* [divide and conquer]; enter into solemn treaty with a neighbouring country, foment internal disorder, intervene in support of the weaker side on the pretense that Roman honour was involved, replace the legitimate ruler with a puppet, giving him the status of a subject ally; later, goad him into rebellion, seize and sack the country, burn down the temples, and carry off the captive gods to adorn a triumph. Conquered territories were placed under the control of a provincial governor-general, an ex-commander-in-chief who garrisoned it, levied taxes, set up courts of summary justice, and linked the new frontiers with the old by so-called Roman roads—usually built by Greek engineers and native forced labour. Established social and religious practices were permitted so long as they did not threaten Roman administration or offend against the broad-minded Roman standards of good taste. The new province presently became a spring-board for further aggression.

—Robert Graves, "It Was a Stable World"

Graves makes his promise in the first nine words, in which he mentions the "simple" technique the Romans had for "dividing" and "conquering" in order to expand their empire. Suppose Graves had started his paragraph this way:

> The technique of expansion was interesting. It was based upon a theory about human nature that the Romans practically invented. This theory had to do with how people reacted to certain political and military devices which . . .

Do you see what is wrong? Since the beginning sentences are so vague, the paragraph never gets going. The writer can't fulfill a promise because he hasn't made one. Here's another example of a poor paragraph beginning:

> The first step involves part of the golf club head. The club head has removable parts, some of which are metal. You must consider these parts when deciding how to repair the club.

Specify the beginning of this paragraph and get to the point quicker:

> Your first step in repairing the club head is to remove the metal plate held on by Phillips screws.

This solid, specific paragraph beginning gives your reader a clear promise which you can fulfill easily without wasting words. (Observe, by the way, that establishing a writer's stance—as we did in the last example—can help you write clearer paragraph beginnings.)

AVOID FRAGMENTARY PARAGRAPHS.   A fragmentary paragraph does not develop its topic or fulfill its promise. A series of fragmentary paragraphs jumps from idea to idea in a jerky and unconvincing fashion.

1   My freshman rhetoric class is similar in some ways to my senior English class in high school, but it is also very different.
2   In my English class we usually had daily homework assignments that were discussed during the class period. If we were studying grammar, the assignments were to correct grammatical errors in the text. If we were studying literature, we were supposed to read the material and understand its ideas.
3   In rhetoric class, we do basically the same things, except that in the readings we are assigned, we look much deeper into the purpose of the author.
4   In my English class. . .

Fragmentary paragraphs are often the result of a weak stance. In this case, the writer has no clear idea of his role or audience, and so needs to revise his stance.

KEEP YOUR THOUGHTS RELATED.   Don't allow any paragraph to be a collection of unrelated statements that looks like freewriting or brainstorming. Notice that the following paragraph contains at least six paragraph promises, none of them properly supported.

Paul Schrader's remake of the *Cat People* (1942) has come to the screen as a chilling horror film. The story revolves around a young woman named Irene who believes that making love will cause her to change into a leopard. Irene switches back and forth between cat and human. The actors—Nastassia Kinsky, Malcolm McDowell, and Annette O'Toole—are caught up in this dilemma with anthropological overtones. Nastassia Kinsky, a Russian, is well-known for the Avedon photograph of her with a snake. She is considered one of the most beautiful women in film today. Malcolm McDowell, playing her incestuous brother, is British and married to Mary Steenbergen, who played Marjorie Kinnan Rawlings in *Crosscreek*. In fact, McDowell played the famous editor Maxwell Perkins in the same film.

AVOID IRRELEVANCIES IN YOUR PARAGRAPHS.   As with the fragmentary paragraph, the problem of irrelevancies in a paragraph is often the result of a vague *stance*. Notice how the italicized sentence does not fit the development of this paragraph, probably because it does not seem to be written for any particular reader:

We need a better working atmosphere at Restik Tool Company. The workers must feel that they are a working team instead of just individuals. If the men felt they were part of a team, they would not misuse the special machine tools, which now need to be resharpened twice as often as they used to be. Management's attitude toward the union could be improved too. The team effort is also being damaged by introduction of new products before their bugs have been worked out. Just when the men are getting used to one routine, a new one is installed, and their carefully created team effort is seriously damaged.

■■■ Try Different Organizational Patterns

Experiment with variations on the promise pattern. Read this student's paper in which she uses *time* and *space* as a means of organizing her paragraphs.

A TRIAL

Introduction (promise) 1 About two years ago, my brother was charged with armed robbery, and I attended all the sessions of the trial. Three days stand out in my memory as being the most difficult of my life—the first day, the day the jury brought in the verdict, and the day my brother was sentenced.

Space and Time 2 The first day I became acquainted with the unfamiliar surroundings of the courtroom. When our family entered, it was full of spectators sitting in rows at the back of the court. We sat on two benches near the front. My brother and his lawyer sat on the left side of the room, facing the judge. The prosecuting attorney sat at the right front. The jury sat in a box along the wall on my right. As I sat there, I could feel all the eyes in the courtroom moving back and forth along the row where we were sitting. Whenever I glanced up I saw people smiling at us, but I knew what they thought. If someone laughed, I felt ashamed, and when someone whispered, I was offended.

Time 3 On that first day, a young man told the jury that he recognized my brother. He pointed to him and said, "That's the man. That's him!" The girls who worked at the place he supposedly robbed were the next witnesses, and they said they were unsure of his identity. That first day I had to get used to the humiliation of the prosecuting attorney and the witnesses talking about my brother and the robbery.

Time   4   The day the jury returned and announced the verdict of guilty, I felt a lump in my throat. I did not want to cry in front of all those people. Instead, I cried inside. I could see a tear on my father's face, and that made my agony worse. My mother was shaking her head and tears trickled down her cheeks.

5   A few days later, my brother was sentenced to a term in the state penitentiary. This time I could not hold back the tears. It seemed that the pool of tears I had cried inside were now rushing up at once. They kept flowing. I tried to wipe them away with my hands, but I couldn't. Crying uncontrollably, I rushed past the people sitting behind us to the restroom to clean my face, but all I could find were rough paper towels that wouldn't absorb the tears. I stayed in the restroom, crying, until they took my brother, handcuffed, downstairs to the jail.

Use the *suspense paragraph*—a class of paragraph that writers organize differently from the promise pattern. We call them *suspense paragraphs* because the writer does not put the topic idea near the beginning, but places it later, near the middle or even the end. This technique allows the writer to concentrate on details and keep the reader in suspense. The point is held back in order to make the paragraph more dramatic, interesting, or emphatic. This kind of paragraph is often called *inductive,* because it develops from the particular to the general. (It is the reverse of the promise paragraph.) Here is an example:

Details and observations   My generation of actors were trained to entice our prey. We kept an eye open, a claw sharpened, even when we professed to slumber. However deep the tragedy or shallow the farce, we never forgot to face front. Nowadays, the relation between player and public tends to be more sophisticated. Together they share a mutual experience of pain and sorrow. Sometimes the actor seems able to dispense with his audience—to no longer need them. He may choose or chance to perfect his performance on a wet afternoon in Shrewsbury, with hardly anyone watching, and thereafter the repetition for him may stale. For me this never happens. I never perfect a performance, though obviously I am sometimes better or worse, but I have learned that without a perfect audience, my struggle to the summit is impossible. I am aware as the curtain rises of the texture of the house. Some nights they will appear eager and willing; on others, listless and reluctant to follow the play. Once or twice during the evening they will change course, become willing and cooperative or grow sullen and bored. *Topic idea (point)*   Suddenly the laughter is stilled, the coughing commences. Is it our fault or theirs? I have long ceased to wonder. *An audience is like the sea, ever changing, never to be taken for granted.*

—Robert Morley

Here is another suspense paragraph, written by Alistair Cooke, who had been asked to write about the American oil industry, a subject he knew nothing about. He panicked until he found an old man in Texas who knew "more about oil than anybody."

Details and examples

I went to see the old man, and right away he said, "What do you know about oil?" Absolutely nothing, I said. "Fine," was his comment. I sat with him for one day, and went over the fields for another; and in forty-eight hours he took me step by step over the history and practice of the industry. It was like sitting at the feet of Aristotle and having your mind rinsed out at frequent intervals with such drafts of common sense as "A play has a beginning, a middle, and an end." I went off on many more expeditions after that, and remember with pleasure the tricks of a couple of Irishmen growing spray orchids in an Oregon hothouse, or tramping out at night into the mountains of Arizona with an infrared lamp to spot strategic minerals embedded in

Topic idea (point)

the rocks like petrified tropical fish. *From all these safaris and interviews I came to the tentative, but for me amazing, conclusion that the first-rate businessman in this country is more precise, more imaginative, watchful, and intelligent about his trade than 90 percent of the writers and academics who despise him.*

—Alistair Cooke, *Talk About America*

PRACTICE

Discussion

Prepare some notes for a class discussion of the following paragraphs. Center your analysis of the paragraphs on the *promise pattern*. How well do the paragraphs get to the point and fulfill their promises? Do the authors need a different stance? What suggestions for improvement, if any, would you make? Optional: Rewrite the first paragraph, which is from the middle of a student's paper on body surfing.

The physical sensations of body surfing are pleasurable. The cold water is invigorating. The churning water is exhilarating. The activity makes me feel more alive and receptive to the sensations I receive. The activity also relieves tension. Besides feeling the power around me working for me, I like to smell and taste the salt water. It reminds me of the difference between the world on land and the ocean world and its vastness. With my experiences in skin diving I can see the beginnings of its vast depths. Standing on the beach I can see its vastness as it disappears over the horizon. It all combines to overwhelm me. I respect the ocean for its vastness and beauty and am somewhat awed by its majesty. Body surfing is a way of escaping the everyday world and entering a more perfect, ideal one.

1   In this confusion, with cigar butts lying about, his large assortment of pipes scattered on whatever would support them, matchboxes everywhere—he was a large consumer of matchboxes, for he struck an incredible number of matches in order to keep a cigar or a pipe alight—and with the air filled with the decaying smell of tobacco, he passed his working hours in supreme contentment. He enjoyed writing, even though it was always difficult for him, and he enjoyed wrestling with ideas. He could not afford a large and extensive library, and at no time did he possess more than a thousand books. But in a hundred notebooks he preserved the important passages from the books he had read in the British Museum, and the library therefore represented only a

part of his available literary resources. He was an inveterate notetaker, and the habit grew even more pronounced as he grew older.

2   What Marx did not know was that this mode of life was slowly killing him. It was not only that he smoked too much, but he spent eight or nine hours a day breathing tobacco smoke in a room where, except on calm summer days, the windows were permanently closed. He was taking less and less exercise, and less and less sensible food, for now that he was reasonably affluent he was indulging himself more and more with highly seasoned foods. The only physical exercise came from the Sunday walks on Hampstead Heath, but these were neither so frequent nor so prolonged as in the days when he was younger. Sometimes he would go for a short stroll on Hampstead Heath in the evening.

—Robert Payne, Marx

Writing

1. Assume that you must get rid of every appliance in your home in order to save electricity. Using *time* organization, write a paragraph in which you describe your decision about which appliances must go first—down to the very last one.

2. Write a paragraph, organized by *space,* on:

   a. The stage as it appeared to you the first time you were in a play.

   b. The college registration procedure the first time you registered.

   c. Your first visit to your dormitory room or apartment.

   d. Your mouth after your dentist applied braces.

   e. Your car after it was wrecked.

   f. Your _____ before/during/after _____ .

3. Write a *suspense* (inductively organized) paragraph on one of the following topics:

   a. A description of a problem, with your solution at the end.

   b. A series of details reporting an event in college life, with a generalizing explanation at the end.

   c. A series of statements or descriptions building up to a prediction.

4. Do a complete rewrite of an old paper, concentrating on paragraph organization.

▼ How to Arrange Your Ideas: Lead Your Reader by the Hand

It is likely that you know more about your subject than your readers do. Much of your material may be unfamiliar to them. A capable writer is often much like a professional guide in a jungle who leads a group of travelers toward an objective by avoiding wild animals, pitfalls, and quicksand traps. It is easier to lose a reader on the page than a traveler in a jungle. Here are a few suggestions that can help you become a more experienced guide through such dangers.

■■■ Start with a Simple or Familiar Idea

If your subject warrants such treatment, you can plan the paper to *lead* the readers from a simple (or familiar) idea to a more complex (or unfamiliar) one. Be sure that they understand each idea before the next is introduced. In the following two examples, each writer uses this strategy.

Familiar detail: beach ball
1   To help us get a better picture of this solar system let us imagine a model of it reduced some five billion times. In this model, the sun is a beach ball about twelve inches across. Now, how far away would you imagine the planets to be from the sun on this scale? . . .

Familiar details: dust specks and pinhead
2   Mercury, the closest planet to the sun and as small as a speck of dust in this scale, would be forty-two feet away. Venus, the second speck, about twice as big as Mercury, would be seventy-eight feet away. Earth, about the size of a pinhead next to the twelve-inch beach-ball sun, would be one hundred eight feet away; Mars, fifty-four yards; Jupiter, one hundred eighty yards; Saturn, three hundred forty yards; Neptune, one thousand eighty yards; and more than a mile away, tiny Pluto would move along its slow orbital path around the sun.

Application of familiar detail to scale of solar system
3   Beyond this model of the solar system, the nearest star, on this same beach-ball scale, would be four thousand miles away. And farther still, the nearest galaxy would be almost four million miles out.

—John Rublowsky, *Life and Death of the Sun*

First paragraph of article
1   Most studies of atmospheric diffusion carried out heretofore have relatively little relevance to air pollution. The theoretical studies have been concerned (with some exceptions) with ideal situations which are sufficiently simple to be solved, at least approximately, and the experimental investigations have been carried out in situations which approximate the idealizations as nearly as possible in order to test the theory.

Use of familiar detail: cream in coffee
2   Perhaps I should interrupt myself long enough to explain to nonspecialists just what is meant by *atmospheric diffusion.* In the old days when people took cream in their coffee it was simple to illustrate from their daily experience. If poured into the coffee very slowly and not stirred, the cream would remain a long time where it was poured, and only slowly mix with the dark brown brew. Stirring with a spoon creates an irregular motion we call *mechanical turbulence,* which speeds up the horizontal and vertical spread of the cream and its rapid mingling with the coffee to form a uniform mixture. This spread and mixing is the process known as *diffusion.*

Application of knowns, by analogy, to "atmospheric diffusion"
3   If the cream were poured first and then the coffee, the tendency of the light cream to rise to the top and the heavy coffee to sink would create convection, which would further tend to mix the two, even in the absence of mechanical stirring. In this case we speak of the

stratification as *unstable,* whereas when the heavier fluid is at the bottom we say it is stable. The degree of stability and the amount of mechanical turbulence are the factors which determine the rate of diffusion in the atmosphere.

—Morris Neiburger, "Where Is Science Taking Us?"

In the first example, Rublowsky gives his readers a relevant familiar detail (the beach ball) and works from it in order to lead us to a partial understanding of the vast distances in the solar system.

Since the second example is the beginning of Neiburger's article on *atmospheric diffusion,* he explains the term here in his introduction. To do so, he needs to define related terms—*mechanical turbulence, diffusion,* and *stability.* Instead of throwing these words at the reader without explanation, he uses an analogy: the familiar act of putting cream in one's coffee. After the reader has understood how diffusion and turbulence work in familiar liquids, he can better understand how they work in the atmosphere.

■■■ Use a Graded Order of Ideas

In a piece of writing you may deal with ideas or actions that vary in interest, importance, usefulness, practicality, or value. For example, there are five ways to leave our college town when vacation starts and one could "grade" them according to:

— How expensive they are
— How fast they are
— How dangerous they are
— How practical they are
— How interesting they are
— How reliable they are

Here is an example of a student's graded order using the organizing principle of *reliability:*

For you new students who have not yet fought the battle of the student exodus, let me suggest the best way to get out of town before Christmas. Hitchhiking is illegal and dangerous—not very reliable. Planes are fast, but they don't go to enough hometowns, and airports get snowed in this time of year. Somewhat more reliable is the train, but the locals recently have had a nasty habit of running six or seven hours late. A car is better than the train, if you have one or know someone who does—and he happens to be going your way. The most reliable transportation for the average student is the bus. Buses aren't crowded and they are inexpensive. Also they are surprisingly fast, since if you plan ahead you can get an express bus that does not stop at small towns.

It is customary when employing any graded order to go from the least to the most— for example, from the *least reliable* to the *most reliable,* as in the paragraph above. You should follow this pattern partly because you want to get the less important ideas out of the way quickly so that you can get on with the more important ones. Also, you build up interest if you leave your best point until last. If you give readers your best idea first they may quit reading in the middle of your paper.

Here is another example of graded order:

Lowest class of the poor
The *idea* of poverty is simple enough—it means that one does not have very much money. Beyond this simplicity, poverty in our real American world is surprisingly complex. It is the worst poverty we continually talk about in Congress and the media, the grinding poverty of the ghetto where at the bottom of the life-chain of the poor we find our standard example: the single illiterate parent with hungry children who don't attend school. They all live (on welfare) in a wretched household where there is no food, and drug use leaches away money, life, and hope.

Middle class of the poor
But let's look at two other examples of the poor in the same ghetto, indeed in the same apartment building. On the fourth floor of the building lives a two-parent family with three children. Nobody is on drugs, and the children go to school. The mother works as a maid, and the husband is often sick; the children barely get enough to eat. What they do eat is bad for teeth and growing bones. But here in this second example there is some decent life, and perhaps even a little hope.

Highest class of the poor
Now consider another step up in the life chain of the poor. In this same building lives Mrs. X, a widow, aged 70. She is fairly healthy, eats pretty well, has a working television that she watches all day long. She lives on social security and a small pension. True, she is afraid to go out, and has been mugged two times in the past four years. (She has learned never to carry money or valuables in a purse.) But she is not as bad off—as "poor"—as my first two examples.

All three of these examples have one thing in common: they have almost the same amount of money coming in every month. But as examples of the wretchedness of poverty, they are significantly different, representing three classes of the ghetto poor: low-, middle- and upper-class. The seventy-year-old widow actually has more creature comforts than millionaire Queen Victoria of the nineteenth century. And, paradoxically, since she lives in perfect anonymity, the widow is usually safer than was Queen Victoria, who lived permanently in the public eye. The queen was shot at several times and once smashed on the head with a heavy cane.

—Lewis Hornick

PRACTICE

Writing

Write a paper in which you use a *graded order* to explain an unfamiliar process, device, or activity. Where you can, help your reader by moving from simple or familiar ideas to more difficult ones.

■■■ Use Signposts

USE SINGLE-WORD OR PHRASE TRANSITIONS.   Transitions point forward and backward. They are the reader's signposts; without them he or she might easily get lost. The simplest and most obvious transitions are those that count in order: "This is my *first* idea. . . . Now for the *second* idea. . . . *Third,* I think. . . ." Less obvious are those transitions that do not so much lead readers by the hand as smooth their way: *"It is certain that the reactor could not have been shut down so easily if . . . . Nevertheless,* the men in the black suits were blowing up the bridge. . . . *Moreover,* the two physicists could not agree on what to do."

Here are some typical transitional words and phrases:

— To explain or introduce ideas: *for instance, for example, such as, specifically, in particular, to illustrate, thus*
— To count or separate ideas: *first, second, third* (but not *firstly, secondly, thirdly*), *moreover, in addition, another, furthermore, also, again, finally*
— To compare ideas: *likewise, similarly, in the same way*
— To contrast or qualify ideas: *however, on the other hand, on the contrary, but*
— To show cause or effect: *as a result, consequently, therefore, thus*

Such a listing could continue indefinitely, for under special circumstances hundreds of words and phrases that are not ordinarily thought of as being transitional (like pronouns and certain key words) can be used to link words, ideas, or sentences. As an example, here is a brief passage taken from the middle of a magazine article (linking expressions are in italics):

1   Today it is no secret that our official, prison-threat theory of crime control is an utter failure. Criminologists have known *this* for years. When pocket-picking was punishable by hanging, in England, the crowds that gathered about the gallows to enjoy the spectacle of an execution were particularly likely to have their pockets picked by skillful operators who, to say the least, were not deterred by the exhibition of "justice." We have long known that the perpetrators of most offenses are never detected; *of those detected,* only a fraction are found guilty and still fewer serve a "sentence." *Furthermore,* we are quite certain now that of those who do receive the official punishment of the law, many become firmly committed *thereby* to a continuing life of crime and a continuing feud with law enforcement officers. Finding themselves ostracized from society and blacklisted by industry *they* stick with the crowd they have been introduced to in jail and try to play the game of life according to *this set of rules. In this way* society skillfully converts individuals of borderline self-control into loyal members of the underground fraternity. . . .

2   What might deter the reader from conduct which his neighbors would not like does not necessarily deter the grown-up child of vastly different background. The *latter's* experiences may have conditioned him to believe that the chances of winning by undetected cheating are vastly greater than the probabilities of fair treatment and opportunity. He *knows* about the official threats and this social disapproval of *such acts.* He knows about the hazards and the risks. *But despite all this "knowledge,"* he becomes involved in waves of discouragement or cupidity or excitement or resentment leading to episodes of social offensiveness.

3   *These episodes* may prove vastly expensive both to him and to society. *But* sometimes they will have an aura of success. Our periodicals have only recently described the wealth and prominence for a time of a man described as a murderer. Konrad Lorenz, the great psychiatrist and animal psychologist, has beautifully described in geese what he calls a "triumph reaction." *It* is a sticking out of the chest and flapping of the wings after an encounter with a challenge. All of us have seen *this primitive*

biological triumph reaction—in some roosters, *for example,* in some businessmen and athletes and others—and in some criminals.

—Karl Menninger, "Verdict Guilty—Now What?"

USE TRANSITIONAL PARAGRAPHS.   The transitional paragraph, which usually acts as a bridge between two other paragraphs, is often found in a fairly long piece of writing. As the short italicized paragraph below illustrates, it can prepare the reader for a plunge into a new topic.

> There was, however, a darker and more sinister side to the Irish character. They are, said a land agent on the eve of the famine, "a very desperate people, with all this degree of courtesy, hospitality, and cleverness amongst them."
> *To understand the Irish of the nineteenth century and their blend of courage and evasiveness, tenacity and inertia, loyalty and double-dealing, it is necessary to go back to the Penal Laws.*
> The Penal Laws, dating from 1695, and not repealed in their entirety until Catholic emancipation in 1829, aimed at the destruction of Catholicism in Ireland by a series of ferocious enactments.

—Cecil Woodham Smith, *The Great Hunger: Ireland, 1845–1849*

In the longer transition, you may sum up what you have been saying before introducing a new subject, and so give your readers a chance to catch up before you go on to a new topic.

> So far, we have spoken only about that portion of the stellar population that falls within the main sequence. All these stars, as we have seen, are very much the same. They differ mainly in their stages of evolution, which in turn is a result of their mass and the speed at which they use up their original fuel supply. But what happens to a star after it has used up its allotment of hydrogen? Can we find examples of such stars that have reached old age in their life cycle? Or can we find examples of stars that are still in their babyhood as far as the stellar cycle is concerned?

—John Rublowsky, *Life and Death of the Sun*

■■■ Organize by Repeating Key Words

Repetition, we are told, is an evil in writing; and it seems that we are told this practically from the time we begin to write. Yet the skillful writer instinctively recognizes that carefully repeating certain key words and phrases can help tie ideas together. The mathematician Norbert Wiener begins his discussion of Brownian motion in this way: "To understand the Brownian motion, let us imagine a *push-ball* in a field in which a *crowd* is milling around. Various people in the *crowd* will run into the *push-ball* and will move it about. Some will *push* in one direction and some in another."

To use repetition effectively, you repeat certain words or phrases in order to keep the reader's mind firmly on the subject. Sometimes you change the grammatical form slightly in order to prevent the repetition from becoming a bore. Note the following example:

1   Its signal characteristic, as the reader and all other critics of businesese will recognize, is its uniformity. Almost invariably, businesese is marked by the heavy use of the passive construction. Nobody ever *does* anything. Things happen—and the author of the action is only barely implied. Thus, one does not refer to something; reference is made to; similarly, while prices may rise, nobody raises them. To be sure, in businesese there is not quite the same anonymity as is found in federal prose, for "I" and "we" do appear often. Except when the news to be relayed is good, however, there is no mistaking that the "I" and "we" are merely a convenient fiction and that the real author isn't a person at all but that great mystic force known as the corporation.

2   Except for a few special expressions, its vocabulary is everywhere quite the same. Midwesterners are likely to dispute the latter point, but a reading of approximately 500,000 words of business prose indicates no striking differences—in the Midwest or anywhere else. Moreover, in sounding out a hundred executives on the subject, *Fortune* found that their views coincided remarkably, particularly so on the matter of pet peeves (principally: "please be advised," "in reference to yours of . . . ," "we wish to draw attention," "to acknowledge your letter"). The phrases of businesese are everywhere so uniform, in fact, that stenographers have a full set of shorthand symbols for them.

3   Because of this uniformity, defenders of businesese can argue that it doesn't make for misunderstanding. After all, everybody knows the symbols, and furthermore, wouldn't a lot of people be offended by the terseness of more concise wording? There is something to this theory. Since businesese generally is twice as wordy as plain English, however, this theory is rather expensive to uphold. By the use of regular English the cost of the average letter—commonly estimated at 75 cents to $1—can be cut by about 20 cents. For a firm transmitting a million letters a year, this could mean an annual savings of $200,000. Probably it would be even greater; for, by the calculations of correspondence specialist Richard Morris, roughly 15 percent of the letters currently being written wouldn't be necessary at all if the preceding correspondence had been in regular English in the first place.

> —William H. Whyte, "The Language of Business," *Fortune magazine*

Whyte employs *businesese* as a catchy technical term, and so he doesn't need to vary the word. Every time he refers to the "sameness" of business prose, however, he varies the word or phrase: *uniformity, quite the same, uniform, this uniformity.* Each use of this "word-idea" is just close enough to the last to keep the reader on the track of the essay's main point. Whyte's article is more than thirty years old, but it is still the standard discussion of *businesese,* a fact which says something about the effectiveness of repeating key words.

PRACTICE

Discussion

For discussion prepare some notes on the organization of the following passage. Describe the writer's stance. How well does the writer keep his *promise* to the reader and fulfill the reader's expectations? Consider both the paragraph promises (topic ideas) and the essay promise (thesis). Where is the thesis stated? Where are the topic ideas in each paragraph?

Does the writer use any special techniques for arranging his ideas? Discuss his use of transitions, and of organizational devices such as repetition of key words.

1   Three seconds after you leap from the Golden Gate Bridge, perhaps the most popular location for suicide in the western world, you hit the water 226 feet below at about 75 miles an hour. The trip is nearly always one-way: It's cold down there, fierce crosscurrents pull a body under in seconds, and the water is 300 feet deep. Only 10 out of the more than 500 people who have jumped since the bridge opened in 1937 are around to tell the story.

2   Each year more and more people are doing it, or trying to, and the experts agree that an antisuicide barrier is needed at once. It is not about to happen: A special committee studying the question in San Francisco has just voted against the idea, unanimously, after spending $27,000 on the design and testing of a model. "Much as I hate to say it," sighed Edwin Fraser, bridge district president, "we have to forget it until it's more financially feasible." A barrier would cost between $1 and $2 million and it seems the city has other priorities.

3   The committee chairman said mail was running strongly against the barrier anyhow. It was not just the expense: The view would be ruined, and besides, folks would only find another place to do it. San Francisco is full of skyscrapers.

4   "It's nonsense to say that blocking the bridge will merely send suicides elsewhere," says Dr. Richard Seiden, a psychologist at the University of California at Berkeley. "It is the bridge itself that's fatally attractive." The great russet span of the Golden Gate Bridge, with its sweeping, soaring lines poised over the sparkling blue water, is a glamorous place, and nearly all the suicides choose to jump from the landward side, facing the amphitheaterlike ring of cities around the bay.

5   Six survivors of the leap agreed with Dr. Seiden when asked: If they couldn't have used the bridge as backdrop for their attempt, they wouldn't have tried at all. Each of them was in favor of the barrier; none has tried to repeat his act elsewhere. . . .

6   For thousands, San Francisco is the end of the rainbow, the lovely dream-city where all the rootless, dissatisfied, lonely people come from elsewhere expecting that all their troubles will be cured. It does not work out that way and for some it is the final disappointment. If you cannot make it in this fun city, where can you make it?

7   At least eight agencies and hospitals here are working to help the suicidal, with "hot lines" and crisis centers. But beyond that, doctors agree, there is a great need for more study, research, clinical investigation and social openness about suicide, and, of course, for that Golden Gate barrier. Says Dr. Seiden, "We really don't have to make it so easy."

—Charles Foley, "The Leap from Golden Gate Bridge"

▼ Introductions and Conclusions

An effective introduction ordinarily does two things: (1) it catches the readers' interest and makes them want to read on; (2) it tells them what the essay is about, perhaps by stating the thesis or suggesting the main points.

An effective conclusion rounds off the paper. As you will see in the following examples, a conclusion often "matches" its introduction by referring to or restating the writer's early material. If the rest of the paper has been planned carefully, conclusions often seem to write themselves. Here are two examples of effective introductions and conclusions. Note that the second example delays the main point and puts it in the conclusion.

Introduction

Very few people would sit at the TV for hours to watch a cargo of potatoes take off from planet earth in a spaceship. Yet a single potato orbiting the sun could hold infinitely greater significance for the future of humanity than would the landing of a man on the moon. For a man on the moon can tell us nothing new about injecting happiness into life on earth. *But a potato in solar orbit might lead to the secret*

Thesis   *of how all growth—hence life itself—is regulated.*

Conclusion

References to material   The last of the comments above concern Professor Brown's exper-
in the article   iments principally. They convey some sense of the values inherent in
          orbiting a potato around the sun. NASA has not yet set a date for this
Allusion to thesis   expedition, but a "Spudnik" has been designed and if the conven-
          tional scientific opposition to innovation can be overcome, the chosen
          potato may take off next year.

                                        —John Lear, "The Orbiting Potato"

Introduction

Questions interest   Why should any words be called obscene? Don't they all describe
the reader   natural human functions? Am I trying to tell them, my students de-
          mand, that the "strong, earthy, gut-honest"—or, if they are fans of
          Norman Mailer, the "rich, liberating, existential"—language they use to
          describe sexual activity isn't preferable to "phony-sounding, middle-
          class words like 'intercourse' and 'copulate'?" "Cop-you-late!" they
          say with fancy inflections and gagging grimaces. "Now, what is *that*
          supposed to mean?"

Conclusion

          And yet how eloquently angered, how piously shocked many of
          these same people become if denigrating language is used about any
          minority group other than women; if the obscenities are racial or eth-
          nic, that is, rather than sexual. Words like "coon," "kike," "spic,"
          "wop," after all, deform identity, deny individuality and humanness
          in almost exactly the same way that sexual vulgarisms and obsceni-
          ties do. No one that I know, least of all my students, would fail to
          question the values of a society whose literature and entertainment
          rested heavily on racial or ethnic pejoratives. Are the values of a soci-
Thesis stated as   ety whose literature and entertainment rest as heavily as ours on sex-
question   ual pejoratives any less questionable?

                                        —Barbara Lawrence

There are as many ways to write introductions and conclusions as ways to write papers. A short, blunt beginning may make an effective promise: "The amateur productions in the University Playhouse are poorly directed this year." One-sentence conclusions are occasionally worth trying, although you should be wary of using conclusions that are too brief, for they may leave the reader with a feeling of having been let down.

Here are some ideas for writing introductions. You might start with:

— An apt quotation
— A literary allusion
— A story or an incident relating to your subject
— A statement that shows how interesting your subject is
— A question that limits your subject; the answer to the question is your paper
— A statement of a problem that readers should know about
— A simple statement of thesis that limits your subject
— A definition of an important word or phrase relating to your subject
— The historical background of your subject (be brief)
— A statement that popular ideas about your subject are wrong and that you intend to refute them in a specific way
— A statement that your subject needs new examination; your paper is the examination
— Pertinent facts about your subject
— Combinations of some of these methods

For a conclusion, you might end your paper with:

— An allusion to the hook of your introduction
— A reference to the question, definition, statement of thesis, historical background, etc., that you started the paper with
— A restatement of your thesis
— A brief answer to the question you raised in the introducion
— A brief statement of the solution to the problem you raised in your introduction
— A new question that relates to your paper, a question that gives the reader something to think about (but be careful not to introduce an undeveloped idea)
— A summary of the main points in your paper (this is often useful if materials are complex, but beware—a summary can be dull and redundant)
— A punchy, single sentence—don't punch too hard
— A new story or incident that relates to your subject

Avoid these errors in writing introductions:

— Writing a vague or ambiguous introduction, leaving the thesis of the paper unclear
— Failing to define terms that the reader is not familiar with; terms should be defined if you are using them in a special sense
— Writing an introduction that is too long; for most short papers, it is a mistake to write more than a one-paragraph (or, at most, a two-paragraph) introduction

And these errors in writing conclusions:

— Failing to fill out a conclusion, leaving the reader hanging
— Adding irrelevant or unnecessary details
— Adding an undeveloped idea; a conclusion is not the place to develop or
  introduce ideas

PRACTICE

Discussion

For class discussion, review the suggestions for writing introductions and conclusions. Then read the pairings below and evaluate how well they fulfill the requirements for introductions and conclusions.

1. *Introduction*

During my life I've had seven dogs, two snakes, one frog, three turtles, ten fish, four gerbils, four wild baby rabbits, and two guinea pigs. Having so many pets has turned our house into a virtual zoo with all of the smells and messes of one. Life is often wild and confusing, but living with all of these animals can also be really fun. One nice aspect of living with pets is that we share a "trade-off" relationship. I feed them, wash them, train them, clean up after them and try to keep them happy. But what have my pets done for me? Owning pets has made me more responsible, relaxed, and outgoing.

Conclusion

Although owning a number of pets can be a very hectic and confusing experience, I would never live without one. Both the responsibilities and pleasures of pet ownership have enriched my life. They have made me a responsible, relaxed and sociable person. I would not care to speculate about how different my life would be without pets.

2. *Introduction*

Many geologic features of the Midwest define the terrain of that area and indicate to scientists that glaciers once covered this portion of the continent. The effect of glacial activity is evident throughout the Midwest—in moraines, eskers, kettles, and erratics. If a traveller knows about these features and can identify them, driving through the flat agricultural area known as the "bread basket of the world" can be more meaningful and less dull.

Conclusion

The flat but rich and productive topsoil of the Midwest region known as Illinois is not the only result of the former presence of the glaciers. Such features as moraines, eskers, kettles, and erratics are all remnants of a bygone age which help to define the Midwest, at least geologically.

3. *Introduction*

Last summer my friend Debbie cut her foot on broken glass while playing in a lake. Because the water was murky, she failed to see the glass and accidentally pushed it into her foot when she stepped in the area. This incident illustrates how senseless littering really is. Littering is not only harmful to people (and animals), it causes needless destruction of the environment, destruction which is very hard to undo.

Conclusion

A clean environment is less likely to harm someone than a polluted one. A landscape is much more breathtaking if there aren't any beer bottles to mar it. More important, it is much harder to clean up our environment than it is to contaminate it. And just how hard is it to find a garbage can, anyway?

4. Introduction

Waiting is a kind of suspended animation. Time solidifies: a dead weight. The mind reddens a little with anger and then blanks off into a sort of abstraction and fitfully wanders, but presently it comes up red and writhing again, straining to get loose. Waiting casts one's life into a little dungeon of time. It is a way of being controlled, of being rendered immobile and helpless. One can read a book or sing (odd looks from the others) or chat with strangers if the wait is long enough to begin forming bond of shared experience, as at a snowed-in airport. But people tend to do their waiting stolidly.

Conclusion

Waiting can seem an interval of nonbeing, the black space between events and the outcomes of desires. It makes time maddeningly elastic: it has a way of seeming to compact eternity into a few hours. Yet its brackets ultimately expand to the largest dimensions. One waits for California to drop into the sea or for "next year in Jerusalem" or for the Messiah or for the Apocalypse. All life is a waiting, and perhaps in that sense one should not be too eager for the wait to end. The region that lies on the other side of waiting is eternity.

—Lance Morrow

Writing

1. Choose one of your papers written for this class or another one. Rewrite the introduction and conclusion.

2. After studying the major strategies in organizing paragraphs and papers, you should now be able to use all the skills you have learned in the chapter. Write a paper on a "technical" subject for a reader who knows little or nothing concerning the matter. *Technical* here refers to any subject that may have some mystery or complexity for the average person—for example, putting (in golf), county primary elections, balancing tires on a car, using shorthand in secretarial work, etc.

   In your paper concentrate on using the promise pattern, writing clear paragraphs, arranging your ideas clearly, and writing a good introduction and conclusion. Use transitions where necessary.

CHAPTER 9

*The Research Paper**

▼ Follow Four Research Steps

In writing the research paper, you will go outside your own experience and use mainly the ideas of others, usually authorities on the subject you have chosen. In most cases, the research paper is based on library sources (books, periodicals, and newspapers), but you may also consult authoritative living people. The research paper should not be a new or unusual rhetorical problem. Find and limit your subject, as you have always done. Evaluate and organize your materials and evidence and create a stance, as you have learned to do. For most students, the only difficulty is how to mesh these activities with library research. How do you get into the maze of a library and safely get out, several days later, armed with dozens of neatly written note cards which can be turned into a documented paper?

Following a series of four steps in your library research will help:

Step 1:   Choose your subject, ask a question, and write a narrative.

Step 2:   Use Library and Information Sources.

Step 3:   Make a working bibliography.

Step 4:   Read, take notes, and evaluate the evidence.

---

* Kathryn Howard, Graduate Student, School of Library and Information Science, University of Illinois (U–C), acted as consultant for this chapter.

▼ Step 1: Choose Your Subject, Ask a Question, and Write a Narrative

■■■ Choose Your Subject

If your instructor has not assigned subjects for the research paper, you should choose a subject that interests you and that you will enjoy working with. Consider the following suggestions:

1. Begin with your own hobby, special interest, or academic major. Look through some of the dictionaries and encyclopedias in your major for subjects that appeal to you.

   Do not choose highly technical subjects, particularly those that require technical terminology, or you may have to spend so much time explaining the terms that you will not be able to develop your ideas clearly. For instance, Ben Stokes, the student who wrote the model research paper " 'Rational Magic'—Hypnosis and the Control of Pain" (pages 152–163), made that mistake in his first draft. In reporting the research on pain, he used so many technical terms that to define each one would have kept him from proving his *point*—how hypnosis helps patients control the acute pain associated with certain medical procedures.

NOTE: We will be using Ben's work throughout this chapter to show examples of research technique.

2. Look through current magazines and newspapers. What kinds of subjects are being discussed? Do any of them interest you? Keep a file of photocopied or clipped newspaper and magazine articles on two or three topics that you think might be of use later. Ben Stokes—whose research paper we are using as an example—is a psychology major who wants to go to graduate school immediately after he earns his B.A. Ben is always searching for a subject in his field that might lead him toward a graduate specialty. One specialty that has fascinated him is hypnotherapy—hypnosis used by therapists. He had read an interview with Professor Ernest Hilgard, a well-known hypnotherapist. The interview, published in *Psychology Today,* caught his attention because Professor Hilgard called the use of pain hypnosis an example of "rational magic." This magazine article helped Ben to choose his subject.

   Be wary of subjects so current that there may be little or nothing in the library about them. Even though hypnotherapy for controlling pain can be considered a fairly recent subject (Hilgard called it a "promising use of hypnosis"), Ben had no problem finding books and magazines on the subject.

3. Choose a subject that you will enjoy working with over a period of time. If your subject bores you, you may have trouble convincing your reader that

you believe in your thesis. Ben had the opposite problem. Because he became so interested in the research studies of pain control, he incorporated their results in an early draft of his paper and spent too much time reporting their findings. As a result, in that early draft he neglected his reader and his promise to deal with *how* hypnosis helps to reduce pain.

Be prepared to change your mind about a subject during the process of researching it. The facts may be different from what you imagined them to be. At first, Ben thought that the medical establishment was prejudiced against the use of hypnosis with medical procedures. However, he learned that much of the prejudice has been eliminated because of research conducted in the late twentieth century.

4. Choose a subject about which you can prove a point. A research paper that merely explains or surveys the situation isn't very meaningful. You are in the business of convincing your reader, so you should take a stand on your subject, proving that your position is valid and reasonable. Ben's first draft was a survey of pain research done on children with leukemia, but he had no *point*. In his revision, he focused on a point (*how* hypnotherapy helps to control pain), and he used the research studies to prove that point.

■■■ Ask a Series of Questions That You Hope to Answer

Identify questions about your subject that you know you will have to answer before you can develop a thesis. These questions will help you get a focus for your research. Ben asked the following set of questions:

a. What are the connections between hypnosis and therapy?

b. Who is qualified to use hypnosis as therapy?

c. Who are the best subjects for hypnotherapy?

d. What is the history of hypnosis in the relief of pain?

e. What are the techniques used?

f. Under what conditions do therapists find hypnosis for pain most successful?

g. Why do some doctors and patients call hypnotherapy "rational magic"? (This question was important because Ben wanted to use the term "rational magic" as a hook. See pages 17–19 for a discussion of *hook*.)

h. What does the hypnotherapist actually do to help relieve a patient's acute pain?

i. What part does the patient play in hypnosis?

After you have answered all of your questions, you can narrow to one single question. Ben's final question: *How does the "rational magic" of hypnosis (as used by a therapist) help to control pain?*

▪▪▪ Write a Narrative Describing Your Research

Write a narrative explaining to yourself—and to anyone else who might be in a position to help you —what you want to know. In your narrative, describe your *role* and your *audience* (see *stance,* pages 22–24). You may not be ready to develop your *thesis,* but you should state your question. In your narrative, use specific terms to describe the research you are about to do.

Ben wrote the following, underlining certain *key words* or *subject headings* (relating to his subject) that could be helpful in his research.

Role	I'm a freshman in college, majoring in psychology.
	I have always been interested in <u>hypnotism</u>, particularly its
Subject Headings	use in <u>psychotherapy</u>. I know that many people consider <u>hypnosis</u>
	something that performers do on stage, so they don't realize that it
Subject Headings	has <u>therapeutic uses</u>. I want to research the topic to find out how it is
	used for relief of <u>pain</u> in patients. I would also like to know just how
	hypnosis works in the hands of therapists. As a result of my research.
Subject Heading	I might decide to become a <u>hypnotherapist</u>.
Question posed	My question is: *How does hypnotherapy help patients control pain?*
	My audience is the young men and women in my psychology
Audience	classes who will read my paper. I am sure that my psychology professor will also be interested in it because one of his concerns is how psychology relates to other fields.

Writing a narrative has provided several *key words* or *subject headings* that may be useful to Ben when he uses catalogs, indexes, and encyclopedias. But before he begins his search, he should check guides such as *Sears List of Subject Headings* or *The Library of Congress Subject Headings* to see if his own headings or key words match the ones used by libraries. If his headings or key words do not match, he should skim these references, looking for different headings that fit his topic.

▼ Step 2: Use Library and Information Sources

Keeping in mind your *subject headings* or *key words,* run a brief check on (1) catalogs, (2) indexes, and (3) general encyclopedias.

▪▪▪ Search Catalogs

The On-line Catalog

When researching any subject, the best place to start is the *on-line catalog* (the print card catalog may not be kept up to date). New books will probably be cataloged directly into the computer and will never be added to the print card catalog. (If you want historical information or information from older books, the print card catalog may be the best place to look.)

The on-line catalog contains information on every book that is added to the library's database. For each book, you have at least three ways to find it—the same as in the print card catalog: by *author, title,* and *subject.*

Ben learned that *Hypnotism* is a subject heading in the on-line catalog. His library uses the Library of Congress Subject Headings, and its classification system uses these headings: *Hypnotism* with a subheading, *Therapeutics.* Once the on-line catalog identified some books on the subject, Ben followed the program's commands, which gave him the call number, the location of the book, and whether it was checked out. The program even gave him the option of reserving a book that was currently checked out by another student.

Here is a title entry from the on-line catalog on Ben's subject:

```
                    BIBLIOGRAPHIC DISPLAY
         Hypnotherapy : a handbook / edited by Michael Heap and
Wendy Dryden. Milton Keynes :England: ; Philadelphia : Open
University Pr c1991.
              207 p. ; 24 cm. (Psychotherapy handbooks series)
              Includes bibliographical references and index.
              ISBN 0335098878 (pbk.)
              ISBN 0335098886
                1. Hypnotism--Therapeutic use  I. Heap, Michael.  II.
Dryden, Wendy.  III. Series.
              ocm23-017881
Wish to see circulation information? (Press <Y> if "YES",
<ENTER> otherwise


Subject Search: Hypnotism--Therapeutic use   Press Exit
```

Ben will press <Y> in answer to the question, "Wish to see circulation information?" At that point, the program will give him the call number and the location of the book in his library system.

The Print Card Catalog

The print card catalog is an alphabetized collection of index cards that carry information on books in your library. Like the on-line catalog, it will have three categories of books classified by *author, title,* and *subject.*

Here is the kind of *subject* card that Ben found in the card catalog under *Hypnotism—Therapeutic Use.*

```
                    HYPNOTISM—THERAPEUTIC USE

   RC281   Hilgard, Josephine Rohrs
   C4H55     Hypnotherapy of pain in children with cancer / by
             Josephine R. Hilgard, Samuel LeBaron; foreword
             by Fred H. Frankel.—Los Altos, Calif.: Kaufman,
             c1984.
                x. 250 p.: ill.; 24cm.
                Includes index.
                Bibliography: p. 229-241.
                ISBN 0865760748

        1. Pain—Treatment. 2. Hypnosis—Therapeutic use.
     3. Tumors in children—Palliative treatment. 4. Sick
     children—Psychology. I. Title II. LeBaron, Samuel, 1943-
```

Note the numbered subject headings listed at the bottom of the card; similar to those at the bottom of the on-line display.

Check Out the Books

You may already know from the on-line and card catalogs which books are available in your library (and their location). If not, now is the time to see if the important books on your subject are actually in the stacks.

PRACTICE

---

1. Look up the following books in the on-line card catalog. Record the call number and other relevant information so that a student in your class could easily find the book in your library. If your library doesn't have the books, check the on-line catalog or with interlibrary loan to see if they are available in another library in your area.

   a. Sterne, Richard S. *Delinquent Conduct in Broken Homes.*

   b. Keith, Lawrence H., ed. *Acid Rain.*

   c. Kirkpatrick, Jeane J. *Political Woman.*

   d. Mandel, Ruth B. *In the Running: The New Woman Candidate.*

2. What *subject headings* (or *key words*) were used to classify the books in the list above?

3. In the print card catalog, find three subject cards for your research topic. Describe the procedure you followed in finding *subject headings* to fit your topic.

4. Using the on-line catalog, look up sources that discuss the five topics listed below. Write a short description of your search in which you evaluate whether adequate information is available on these possible research topics.

   a. Dr. Pritikin's diet

   b. Dangerous chemicals in skin makeup

   c. Gun control

   d. Antiballistic missiles

   e. The Iran Hostage Crisis of 1979–1981

■■■ Search Indexes

Indexes on CD-ROM

Some of the periodical and newspaper indexes are on CD-ROM, a small disc that may be permanently loaded into one of the computers in the reference room of your library. These CD-ROM indexes allow you to find more than one year's references on the computer. Using a CD-ROM index is much faster than using a print index. You can also get a printed copy of the information available on your subject. Unfortunately, most CD-ROM indexes cover only the most recent years, and most do not go back any further than 1980–82. So you will have to use the paper indexes if you have a subject that was popular before 1980. Ben chose to look at the CD-ROM version of *The Readers' Guide to Periodical Literature* because he wanted the most current information.

The CD-ROM version of most indexes allow you to do a *key word* or *subject heading* search. The computer program will match every word in the title, author, or abstract to the key word you use for your search. These indexes usually allow you to combine terms such as "hypnotism *and* therapeutic use." Or "hypnotherapy *and* pain." The illustration below uses the slash: "Hypnotism/Therapeutic use."

Here is a typical printout entry from the CD-ROM *Readers' Guide:*

```
    5 RDG
Not held by Morris Library.

     AUTHOR:  Callahan, Jean
      TITLE:  Hypnosis can bring pain relief
     SOURCE:  New Choices for Retirement Living
              (ISSN 1061-2157) v33 p44-7 July/August '93
   CONTAINS:  illustration(s)


SUBJECTS COVERED:
Hypnotism/Therapeutic use
```

Print Indexes

Most of the major newspapers in the United States publish their own print indexes. Print periodical indexes for specific academic disciplines are also available. For instance, there is an *Education Index* that covers educational issues and a *Social Sciences Index* that covers information on history, sociology, and economics. You will probably find the print *Readers' Guide to Periodical Literature* the most useful because it lists recent articles published in 198 popular magazines.

Most print periodical indexes employ roughly the same format. To use them efficiently, you need to be aware of the information presented in the front of each issue: (1) suggestions for using the index; (2) abbreviations of the periodicals indexed; (3) a list of the periodicals indexed; and (4) the key to other abbreviations.

To look up your subject, use a specific subject heading. If you can't find it, move to a broader one. Print periodical indexes use cross references in the same way that the catalogs do.

After you have identified the items in the CD-ROM or print indexes containing information on your subject, check the on-line and card catalogs to see if your library has the magazines in bound form.

Most CD-ROM indexes allow the library to add information to the computer disk. This information may tell you the location and call number of a particular periodical. It may also tell you whether (or how long) the library has subscribed to the periodical.

PRACTICE

---

1. Look up one of your subject headings in the CD-ROM *Readers' Guide.* Write a short paragraph on your search procedure. What did you find? Did you have to go to a broader heading or term?

2. Do the same for the print *Readers' Guide.*

3. Using your library's resources, answer the following questions.

   a. What is the most recent issue of *New Republic* in your library?

   b. Are the back issues of *Vital Speeches* bound? If so, where are they shelved? If they are not bound, what happens to old issues?

   c. Identify four professional journals in your major or minor field. Check to see if your library carries them.

■■■ Search General Encyclopedias

Search Encyclopedias on CD-ROM

CD-ROM encyclopedias are usually taken from the text of print encyclopedias. Sometimes pictures and short video clips are added. Each CD-ROM allows you to print either portions of the article, the complete article, or pictures.

One commonly used CD-ROM encyclopedia is *Encarta,* made by Microsoft and based on the *Funk and Wagnalls Encyclopedia.*

When Ben searched *Encarta,* using his subject heading *Hypnosis,* he found a brief article and a bibliography. But the most important things he found were "see also" references that referred him to other articles.

Other CD-ROM general encyclopedias that might be in your library are *Grolier's Encyclopedia* and *Compton's Multi-Media Encyclopedia.* All of these CD-ROM encyclopedias will provide background information and give you leads for the next step in the research process.

■■■ Print Encyclopedias

The most efficient way to use a multivolume print encyclopedia is to turn first to the index, which is contained in a separate volume. There you may find the main entry for your subject. In addition to the main entries, you may find a *See also* reference, which indicates there are other related subjects in the index that you should check. You may also find a *See* reference, which tells you that a particular subject is listed under a slightly different heading.

Note particularly the bibliographies that follow most articles of any importance.

■■■ *Search Other Electronic Databases*

After checking the cataloges, indexes, and encyclopedias, you may discover that little has been written on your subject or that much of what has been written is not available in your library. Before you give up on your chosen subject, consider using an *electronic data base*. An electronic database can be either on-line (like DIALOG) or a CD-ROM (like ERIC). DIALOG is actually a collection of indexes, directories, and full-text databases. ERIC is a CD-ROM index to a collection of books and articles on microfiche, covering topics on education. With the help of a librarian and payment of a small fee, you can find quantities of stored information on specific subjects in databases like these. If your librarian believes that searching an electronic database would be useful, show him or her your list of subject terms and your narrative (page 125).

Let's assume that your research strategy has turned out to be successful, and that you intend to research your first choice as a subject. Now you are ready for Step 3, *Make a working bibliography.*

▼ Step 3: Make a Working Bibliography

At this point, many students start using shortcuts, some of which may actually work. But unless students have done a lot of research and writing, shortcuts can lead only to errors and frustration. The best researchers are usually both careful and lazy—careful in taking all the steps, but lazy in not wanting to repeat any of them unnecessarily. For instance, if you don't make your working bibliography cards right the first time, you may not be able to find some of your sources in the library. Or you may have to go back to look up a source before typing your list of *Works Cited*. The best rule is to do everything right—once.

Study the Modern Language Association (MLA) form for list of *Works Cited—End of Paper* (pages 142–150). Notice that the following bibliographic card gives all the material necessary for this list.

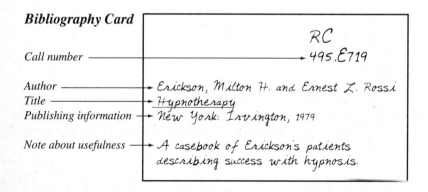

Therefore, if you have done the step properly, all you need to do is alphabetize your bibliography cards and type them for your final draft.

Go slowly through any encyclopedias, other reference works, periodicals, and books that looked promising when you were searching for a workable subject. Take brief notes on the bibliography cards, indicating what you feel to be the particular *usefulness* of each source. If a source doesn't look useful, abandon it.

In other words, even at this early stage, it is wise to anticipate Step 4 and start evaluating your sources and evidence. Begin with the most informative and most interesting sources. Skim through them and look for aspects of your subject that are repeatedly emphasized. This repetition often gives a clue to important developments in your subject. Don't get lost in a blind alley—a small part of a subject which one source treats voluminously but which the others ignore.

▼ Step 4: Read, Take Notes, and Evaluate the Evidence

You may believe that the four elements in Step 4 are distinct operations that must be tackled separately. Actually, you can do them at nearly the same time if you are careful. By now, you should have some idea of what is the best source material available on your subject. If you aren't sure, the following guidelines should help you to evaluate your sources.

1. *Check the date.*   If your topic needs up-to-date information, a book or article written before the last decade or even in the last five years may be too old. On the other hand, a source that is older than a decade may be useful, particularly if you need a historical perspective on your topic. Needless to say, statistics and other quantitative data must be recent.

2. *Check the viewpoint.*   Does the author take a particular position on the topic that would bias his or her objectivity?

3. *Skim the table of contents, introduction, and index.*   See if the content of the book deals with the sort of question you need to answer.

4. *Check the author's ethical proof.*   See pages 3–9.

■■■ Taking Notes

As you take notes, you should consider both their form and how they may be used in your paper.

Take notes on four-by-six cards, not on sheets of regular notebook paper—they are too large to handle. Do not use three-by-five cards because you might mix them with your bibliography cards. *Put only one idea*—a paraphrase, summary, or quotation—on each card.

Typical Note Card (4 x 6 inches)

      ⓐ *How hypnosis helps patient*   ⓒ*Quote, p.293*
          bear pain
      ⓑ *Pain not eradicated, just distant*

      ⓓ *"As is sometimes the case during a hypnotic
          trance, pain sensations may not be entirely
          eradicated; they may simply become more
          distant, less relevant, and therefore less
          upsetting and painful."*

      ⓔ *Kuttner, "Favorite Stories"*

      ⓐ *broad title* covering material on card
      ⓑ *subtitle* covering material on card
      ⓒ gives *page number* and the fact that the words are *quoted*
      ⓓ the *material* taken from the source
      ⓔ the *source* (bibliography card will give the full reference)

Look at the typical note card above. The two-part title in the upper-left corner is useful because it tells you what is on the card without having to read it. When you come to arrange the note cards before outlining your paper, such careful labeling will pay off. In the upper-right corner is a reminder that this material is quoted (a good way to avoid accidental plagiarism) and that it was taken from page 293. At the bottom, the card provides the author's name and the title of the book or article.

Always give the complete citation on at least one note card. That way, if you lose your bibliography cards, you will have the reference without having to backtrack.

As you take notes, keep one fact in mind: Students often use too much of others' work. Some research papers turn out to be no more than a loose sewing together of other writers' thoughts. A good general rule can be stated in two parts:

1. Use the materials and opinions of others mainly *as support* for your ideas, not in place of them.

2. When using sources, paraphrase as much as possible. A *paraphrase* restates a passage, using words *different* from those in the original. A *quotation* uses the *original* words of the passage. Quote only when the writer says something better or more vividly than you can, or when for the sake of evidence you

choose to present the author's own words. Keep paraphrases and quotations short.

■■■ *Accurate Paraphrasing*

To illustrate paraphrasing, we will use this sample selection from Fletcher Pratt's *A Short History of the Civil War:*

> In 1862 Abraham Lincoln was only the spokesman of an angry people, and no one realized more clearly than he that he did not have *carte blanche* from the nation—a fact which has been obscured by the halo that has since surrounded his name. To the majority he was at that time still the low, cunning clown, the President by hazard, and Chase, Stanton or Seward (according to whether one lived in the West, the Atlantic states or New England) the frequently thwarted brain of the administration. It must be remembered that the arrangement was then the normal one in American politics: the last seven Presidents had all been Merovingians ruled by some Mayor of the Palace. Lincoln's shambling gait, awkward movements and low jokes made him appear as the most inept of all the presidential ventriloquist's dummies. Beside him Zachary Taylor looked like a drawing-room fop and Franklin Pierce like a courtier. When he leaned over and patted the leg of a Congressman who was urging some unfeasible scheme and threw him off balance with the remark "My, my, what big calves you do have." the discomfited legislator could see nothing in it but a piece of *gaucherie*. Even the skill with which the President charmed Kentucky, Maryland and Missouri out of the rebels' lap made no impression. His part in the intrigues was largely secret and both Southerners and Northerners regarded the series of events as fortuitous. The surprising thing in the North was not that the border states remained in the Union but that so many of the others left it.

Here are two paraphrases of the passage:

Paraphrase 1

> Abraham Lincoln did not have *carte blanche* from the nation. Even so, he was a very effective president who charmed many southern states out of the rebels' lap. He was the first president in many years to act on his own without being another powerful politician's mouthpiece; he was never just a political ventriloquist's dummy.

Paraphrase 2

> According to Fletcher Pratt's *A Short History of the Civil War,* Abraham Lincoln's political skill during the early years of the war was a study in contrasts. While appearing to be a buffoon who made irrelevant remarks at the wrong times, a politician who became president only by accident, he was actually involved in partly successful attempts to save the border states. Since the power given him by the country was incomplete (in Pratt's phrase, "he did not have *carte blanche* from the nation"), he had no choice but to move slyly and by indirection.

You can see that Paraphrase 1 is not a paraphrase at all but rather a careless mixture of summary and unmarked quotation. A paraphrase like that is considered a form of *plagiarism* (see below). Paraphrase 2 fairly states Pratt's ideas and honestly places in quotation marks words that the writer has taken directly from Pratt.

■■■ *Plagiarism*

Plagiarism is using the words or ideas of another writer without giving proper credit. The plagiarist usually intends to pass off his paper as being an original creation when it is not. Borrowing other people's ideas and their wording without giving due credit will create problems for you as a student because teachers can take severe action against the writer of a plagiarized paper.

Plagiarism can take several forms:

1. *Word-for-word copying without using quotation marks or crediting your source.*

2. *Using another student's work but turning it in under your own name.*

3. *Using a catchy or clever phrase or comment without giving credit.*

4. *Taking materials from a variety of sources and tying them together to make the paper look original.*

Most colleges and universities define "plagiarism" in their student codes. If you want further information, check the rules on written work in your own institution. Your instructor undoubtedly will give you more complete advice on this problem, which proves vexing to students and teachers alike.

■■■ *Proper Techniques for Quoting*

Short Quotations

Always quote accurately. Short prose quotations (those of fewer than four lines) should be worked into your own material smoothly and coherently. Note how the writer of the following sentences has varied the way *Fletcher Pratt* has been identified as the source.

> As *Fletcher Pratt states,* "the skill with which the President [had] charmed Kentucky, Maryland and Missouri out of the rebels' lap made no impression" (15).

> In light of our admiration of Lincoln, *Fletcher Pratt's comment* concerning the President's "shambling gait, awkward movements and low jokes" (15) may seem oddly inappropriate.

(The numbers in parentheses are page numbers, an appropriate use of MLA parenthetical documentation form described on pages 142–151.)

In the first quotation, the brackets indicate *editorial insertion*—words or phrases put into the quotation for the sake of grammar or explanation.

You must copy a quotation *exactly as it is printed.* You may show your reader that a grammatical error or a misspelling in the text is not yours by inserting [sic] immediately after the error.

Long Quotations

Prose quotations of more than four lines are usually put in *block form* and indented ten spaces from the left-hand margin. And quotation marks are *not* used to set off the entire quotation. Here is an example of how a block quotation is set up in relationship to the regular text of a paper.

It is very easy to forget that during much of his administration. Lincoln was an unpopular president. For one thing, as Fletcher Pratt points out, he did not look or act much like a president:

> Lincoln's shambling gait, awkward movements and low jokes made him appear as the most inept of all the presidential ventriloquist's dummies. Beside him Zachary Taylor looked like a drawing-room fop and Franklin Pierce like a courtier. When he leaned over and patted the leg of a Congressman who was urging some unfeasible scheme and threw him off balance with the remark, "My, my, what big calves you do have," the discomfited legislator could see nothing in it but a piece of *gaucherie* (15).

Ellipsis Marks

An *ellipsis* is an omitted portion of a quotation. *Ellipsis marks* (three or four spaced periods) indicate the place in the quoted material from which the words were removed. Ellipsis marks usually appear in the middle or at the end of the quotation. Here are two examples:

> Pratt's comment on the political history of the time was: "It must be remembered that . . . the last seven Presidents had all been Merovingians ruled by some Mayor of the Palace" (15).

> As Fletcher Pratt states, "To the majority he was at that time still the low, cunning clown, the President by hazard. . . ." (15).

The three periods in the first example indicate that a phrase has been removed from the middle of Pratt's sentence. The four periods in the second example indicate that material from the end of the quoted sentence has been omitted.

Four ellipsis marks are also used when a *full sentence or more* is removed from a quotation. The four periods in the following example represent the omission of a full sentence:

> "Lincoln's shambling gait, awkward movements and low jokes made him appear as the most inept of all the presidential ventriloquist's dummies. . . . Even the skill with which the President charmed Kentucky, Maryland and Missouri out of the rebels' lap made no impression" (15).

Ordinarily, you do not use ellipsis marks at the *beginning* of a quotation; that is, you do not write:

> Pratt's opinion is that Lincoln was " . . . at that time still the low, cunning clown . . . ."

Instead you fit the beginning of the quotation smoothly into your own sentence without the ellipsis marks:

> Pratt's opinion is that Lincoln was "at that time still the low, cunning clown . . . ." (15).

PRACTICE

Read Claudia Dowling's "The Relative Explosion", pages 250–252. Then, on five separate note cards, write down:

a. a quotation from a passage that is worked into your own sentence;

b. a longer quotation to be used as a block quote in a paper;

c. a one-sentence paraphrase of an entire passage;

d. a quotation using an ellipsis inside one sentence;

e. a quotation using an ellipsis that "bridges" two or three sentences. You may use the same passage from Dowling for all five cards.

▼ Follow Four Writing Steps

After doing your research carefully and before beginning the step of classifying your evidence, you should have three kinds of information: (1) bibliography cards that give accurate and brief descriptions of all your sources; (2) note cards, keyed to the bibliography cards, that contain paraphrases and quotations of important material; (3) bits of information that you have retained from reading. (In a general way, this last kind of information is of subtle but considerable help in writing your paper.)

Now set aside your bibliography cards and follow these four steps:

Step 1:   Classify your evidence: develop a preliminary plan and thesis.

Step 2:   Study documentation, make a list of *Works Cited*, and write a rough draft.

Step 3:   Revise the rough draft.

Step 4:   Write the final draft, and proofread.

▼ Step 1: Classify Your Evidence: Develop a Preliminary Plan and Thesis

When you finish your research, you will have piles of note cards—a mass of material that you must get control of somehow. If you have taken our suggestion and used *titles* and *subtitles* for your note cards (pages 131–132), you will have a ready-made device for controlling (and understanding) the results of your research. The first step is to classify and group your cards.

Group your note cards by title and subtitle. Observe that the resulting groups suggest possible outline headings, which in turn can give you ideas for a preliminary plan, organization, and thesis. You may, of course, change any or all of these several times before settling on those that you like.

We have already introduced Ben Stokes, who wrote the sample research paper on hypnotism and pain (see pages 152–163). We now pick up Ben's story as he develops his *preliminary plan.*

After Ben made his first plan from a grouping of note cards, he discovered that he had to make adjustments to the plan twice before he was satisfied with his final outline. For instance, since he knew that he had to narrow his topic, he wouldn't be able to use all of the material in all his groupings. So he checked his note-card headings against his research question (page 124). As a result of this checking, he decided to cut everything concerned with the dangers of hypnosis because most of the dangers occur when un-qualified people use it for entertainment.

Next Ben diagrammed a rough plan—using support diagrams—from which he would test his preliminary thesis (see support diagrams, pages 55–56).

Ben now made a preliminary thesis based on his first groupings: *Hypnosis used by therapists on hypnotizable patients is a kind of "rational magic" that reduces the pain and anxiety associated with surgery, bone marrow removal in cancer patients, severe burns, migraine headaches, and phantom limb pain.*

Although too long, this preliminary thesis helped Ben to continue shaping his work.

In the process of doing research on his topic, Ben learned that hypnotherapists divide pain into two categories—*chronic* and *acute*. As a result of this new knowledge, he de-cided to narrow his topic even further to a discussion of the effect of hypnosis on *acute* pain only. Ben's new thesis: *As used by medical therapists, hypnosis can be described as a form of "rational magic" that can reduce the acute pain and anxiety associated with certain medical procedures.* This is the thesis of the model research paper, pages 152–163. (*Important:* As you will see in Ben's final draft, his thesis does not appear word for word in the paper. Such paraphrasing is often necessary to make the writing flow smoothly.)

From this second thesis, Ben developed his final outline. (See page 153 for his out-line.) Ben included an outline with his final paper because his instructor asked him to do so. Ask your instructor what his or her requirements are. See Chapter 5 for more infor-mation about writing an outline.

▼ Step 2: Study Documentation, Make a List of *Works Cited*, and Write a Rough Draft

You are now ready to write your rough draft, using your outline to guide you and keep you on track. But before you start to write, study the MLA documentation forms. We have presented the documentation forms in charts so that you can see how the par-enthetical form relies on the list of *Works Cited*.

1. Alphabetize your bibliography cards, the works you cite (or refer to) in your paper.

2. Make a list (alphabetized) from your cards, leaving plenty of white space between items. This will help you to add new items in case you find a reference you had previously missed, but one that you want to quote or paraphrase.

3. Whenever you draw on material from a note card—direct quotation, paraphrase, or summary—put a number in your rough draft where you have

used the material. Put that same number on the note card. This system will keep you from losing track of where your references were used in your text. If your rough draft uses 20 separate references, you should have 20 cards numbered consecutively in the same way that you use them in your paper. If you use a content or bibliography note (see page 150) use an identifying letter, such as 2a.

After you have listed your sources in your preliminary *Works Cited* (MLA), start to write from your plan or outline. Keep checking your thesis to see that you are staying on track. Some writers find that keeping paragraphs on separate sheets of paper will allow them to edit parts of the paper before putting them all together. Writing a little piece now and then may be a less onerous task than facing the entire paper all at once, particularly if your blocks of time are limited to an hour or two. After all the pieces are put together, you can edit and revise.

▼ Step 3: Revise the Rough Draft

After you have written your rough draft from your outline or plan, use the following checklist to see if your material is as logically organized, clear, and accurate as you can make it.

■■■ *Checklist for the Rough Draft*

Outline

1. Is your thesis placed at the top of the outline page so that it can be checked against the outline?

2. Do each of your first-level points (I, II, III, etc.) support the thesis?

3. Do your second-level points (A, B, C, etc.) support your first-level ones?

4. Are the items in the outline parallel in content and in form? Did you use complete sentences for all first- and second-level points? (The sentence outline is preferred for research papers, but your instructor may want you to use another form.)

Introduction

1. Is your thesis clearly stated?

2. Have you shown why the topic is important enough to interest your reader?

3. Have you defined any terms that the reader should clearly understand?

Body

1. Have you checked your reasoning in the paper?

   a. Are your generalizations supported by well-chosen evidence?

   b. Are your causal relationships logical?

   c. Have you checked your facts? Your sources?

2. Are your paragraphs unified and logical?

3. Have you used your sources properly?

   a. Do your sources support your ideas and points?

   b. Are your quotations integrated with your own ideas?

4. Have you reviewed the material on paraphrasing and quoting (pages 133–135)?

5. Have you used correct quotation, note, parenthetical, and *Works Cited* or *Reference* forms?

   a. If you used footnotes or end notes, did you give a complete note reference for the first time you used a source in the paper?

   b. Did you check the *Works Cited* (or list of *References*) against your parenthetical citations to see that you included all sources?

Conclusion

1. Do you have a concluding paragraph which restates the thesis and rounds off the paper?

2. Have you introduced any new or significant ideas in the conclusion (usually a poor idea)?

Proofreading

1. Have you read the paper aloud at least once, listening and watching for anything that doesn't sound and look right?

2. Did you avoid shifts in tense and person?

3. Are your parallel ideas stated in parallel form?

4. Have you overused the passive voice?

5. Are your signals and transitions clear so that your reader can follow your organization?

6. Have you used words precisely and accurately?

7. Have you avoided errors in spelling, grammar, and punctuation?

8. Have you proofread for typographical errors?

See pages 475–479 on revision to guide you further. Most of the same rules apply to the research paper that you have used for revising other forms of writing.

▼ Step 4: Write and Proofread the Final Draft

The final draft of your paper should be typed, double-spaced, on 8½ by 11-inch sheets. Write on one side of the paper, leaving top, bottom, and left margins of an inch. Except for the title page, number all pages consecutively in the upper-right corner, beginning with page one, one-half inch from the top. Type your last name just before the page number, but without any punctuation marks or *p.* for *page.*

■■■ Research Paper without a Title Page

On the first page, keeping a margin of one inch from the top, type your name, instructor's name, course number, and date on separate lines, double-spaced, and flush with the left margin. Center the title, and double-space between the title and the text. Place your name and page number in the upper-right corner one-half inch from the top.

■■■ Research Paper with a Title Page

The same kind of information is provided on a title page, but arranged differently (see title page of model research paper, page 152).

Page 1 Without Title Page of Research Paper

```
                                                        Stokes 1


    Ben Stokes

    Professor Daugherty

    English 101, Section A

    June 8, 1995

            "Rational Magic"—Hypnosis and the Control of Pain

        The use of hypnosis to control pain—called hypnotherapy—
```

Before handing in the paper, proofread it one last time.

Be sure to copy your research paper and keep it in a safe place in case you wish to refer to it at a later date.

▼ Modern Language Association (MLA) Forms

■■■ *The List of* Works Cited *(Bibliography)*

The *Works Cited (bibliography)* provides your reader with an alphabetized list of sources you used in the paper—those you cited in parentheses. Your instructor may also want you to list all the sources you have read or consulted. If that is the case, you may add another section entitled *"Works Consulted."*

Arrange the entries in your *Works Cited* in alphabetical order by the surname of the author. When no author is given, use the first word of the title; when the title begins with an article (*a, an,* or *the*) or with a preposition, use the second word. If you have two sources written by the same author, it is not necessary to repeat the author's name in the second entry. (See entry under *Two or more books by the same author* in the table, page 142.)

■■■ *Parenthetical Documentation*

Documentation gives the reader the source of the fact, paraphrase, or quotation you use in your paper. It says to the reader: "Here is where I found this information in case you are interested in pursuing the subject further." Parenthetical documentation provides the reference in the text so that your readers can tell immediately where you found your material. If readers want the complete citation, they can look at your alphabetized *Works Cited* to find the complete reference. All parenthetical references must be clear enough so that an exact match in the *Works Cited* section can be found. If you keep your readers in mind, you can give them information in the text itself or in parentheses so they know exactly who or what you are quoting or paraphrasing.

In the first column of the *Works Cited* chart (pages 142–150), we give examples of typical bibliographic items. In the second column (pages 143–150), we show how you might cite the item in the text of your paper, using the parenthetical form of documentation.

To show you how the chart works, let's use as an example the first item, *Mack, Maynard. Alexander Pope: A Life.* Assume that in researching the works of Alexander Pope, you use an important biography, written by Maynard Mack. In your paper, you write a section on Pope's translation of the *Iliad,* citing Mack in the text. All that you need, when using the parenthetical form of documentation, is to give a page reference (in parentheses at the end of the sentence) referring to Mack. If you don't name Mack in your own sentence, you give his name, along with the page number *without a comma,* in the parenthetical reference: (Mack 348).

How to Use MLA Styles of Documentation

Works Cited—End of Paper
(same as bibliography and bibliography cards)

BOOKS

One author
Mack, Maynard. *Alexander Pope: A Life.* New York: Norton, 1985.

Two or three authors
Douvan, Elizabeth, and Joseph Adelson. *The Adolescent Experience.* New York: Wiley, 1966.
[Note that the second author's first name comes before his last name. Indent second line five spaces.]

More than three authors
Quirk, Randolph, et al. *A Comprehensive Grammar of the English Language.* London: Longman, 1985.

Two or more books by the same author
Leacock, Stephen. *The Garden of Folly.* New York: Dodd, 1924.
—. *How to Write.* New York: Dodd, 1944.
[Instead of naming Leacock again, type three unspaced hyphens.]

Anonymous author or no author
My Secret Life. New York: Grove, 1966.

A literary work in an anthology with editor, translator, or compiler
Swift, Jonathan. "A Modest Proposal." *Major English Writers of the Eighteenth Century.* Ed. Harold E. Pagliaro. New York: Free, 1969. 464–71.

Article in non-literary anthology with editor, translator, or compiler
Kantor, Kenneth J. "Classroom Contexts and the Development of Writing Intuitions: An Ethnographic Case Study." *New Directions in Composition Research.* Eds. Richard Beach and Lillian S. Bridwell. New York: Guilford, 1984. 72–94.

Cross reference to anthology or collection
[If Kantor is one of two or three articles or literary selections from an anthology, list the anthology itself, then cross-reference]:
The anthology cited:
Beach, Richard, and Lillian S. Bridwell, eds. *New Directions in Composition Research.* New York: Guilford, 1984.
The work from the anthology cited:
Kantor, Kenneth J. "Classroom Contexts and the Development of Writing Intuitions: An Ethnographic Case Study." Beach and Bridwell, 72–94.

How to Use MLA Styles of Documentation

Parenthetical Documentation (Inside Paper)

BOOKS

One author
Maynard Mack reminds us that Pope's translation of the *Iliad* is not our *Iliad* because
Pope knew nothing of the nineteenth- and twentieth-century discoveries in
archaeology and anthropology (348).
[If Mack isn't cited in the text, give his name in the parentheses: (Mack 348).]

Two or three authors
The death of a father creates serious financial problems for both adolescent boys and
girls, causing them to take increased responsibility for household duties and financial
assistance (Douvan and Adelson 269–70).

More than three authors
Even though English does not have the word *longly,* the adverb *shortly* has many uses
(Quirk et al. 405).

Two or more books by the same author
Leacock claims that writers often pack too much information in their subordinate clauses,
particularly in clauses introduced by relative pronouns (*How to Write* 73).)
[Shorten the title if possible. In this case, shortening the title to *How* would look
ridiculous, so use the entire title.]

Anonymous author or no author
The author says, "We had a very large playground; beyond it were fields, orchards, and
walks of large extent. . . ." (*My Secret Life* 90).

A literary work in an anthology with editor, translator, or compiler
Swift in "A Modest Proposal" confuses some readers because his persona uses the word
humble so many times that the reader actually believes that he is serious (466).

Article in non-literary anthology with editor, translator, or compiler
Kenneth Kantor identifies five characteristics of ethnography: "contextuality,
participant observation, multiple perspectives, hypothesis-generating, and meaning-
making" (72).

Cross reference to anthology or collection
Kenneth Kantor identifies five characteristics of ethnography: "contextuality,
participant observation, multiple perspectives, hypothesis-generating, and meaning-
making" (Beach 72).

How to Use MLA Styles of Documentation

Works Cited—End of Paper
(same as bibliography and bibliography cards)

BOOKS

An Introduction, Preface, Foreword, or Afterword
McFee, William. Introduction. *A Conrad Argosy.* By Joseph Conrad. New York:
  Doubleday, 1942.

A multivolume work
The Society for Pure English. 7 vols. New York: Garland, 1979.

Edition or revision
Gibaldi, Joseph, and Walter S. Achtert. *MLA Handbook for Writers of Research Papers.*
  4th ed. New York: MLA, 1995.

Corporate author
National Education Association. *NEA Handbook*, 1985–86. Washington: NEA, 1985.

REFERENCE WORKS

Signed article
Springer, Stewart. "Shark." *Americana.* 1983 ed.

Unsigned article
"Washington, George." *Encyclopaedia Britannica: Macropaedia.* 1984.

GOVERNMENT PUBLICATIONS

United States. Arms Control and Disarmament Agency. *World Military Expenditures and
  Arms Transfers 1968–1977.* Publication 100. Washington: U.S. Arms Control and
  Disarmament Agency, 1979.

How to Use MLA Styles of Documentation

Parenthetical Documentation (Inside Paper)

BOOKS

An Introduction, Preface, Foreword, or Afterword
Joseph Conrad resented being called "a sea writer" because he wrote about other
   things—life in the jungle, spies, and Latin America (McFee x).

A multivolume work
[Give volume number, a colon, a space, and the page reference.] The simplicity of
   English grammar makes it superior to other languages (*Society* 7: 108).

Edition or revision
The Modern Language Association recommends that all notes be endnotes, rather than
   footnotes (Gibaldi 243).

Corporate author
[Since corporate authors are often several words long, it is preferable to identify them in
   the text rather than in a long parenthetical entry.]
The National Education Association in 1984 passed an amendment taking a position
   on video games in public schools, recommending that communities "support the
   enactment of zoning, time, and age restrictions" against video arcades (216).

REFERENCE WORKS

Signed article
Sometimes sharks in large groups will attack each other in a "frenzied and
   indiscriminate" manner (Springer).
[Omit page number because not needed in an encyclopedia.]

Unsigned article
Even though George Washington was not an expert in military tactics, his personality
   and character gained the loyalty of his army and his people, so he was able to win the
   war ("George Washington").

GOVERNMENT PUBLICATIONS
The U.S. Arms Control and Disarmament Agency reports that because of higher pay
   for military personnel it costs more to support an army in a developed country
   than in an undeveloped one (6).
[Since government agencies usually have such long titles, treat like a corporate
   author and include the authorship in the text.]

How to Use MLA Styles of Documentation

Works Cited—End of Paper
(same as bibliography and bibliography cards)

PERIODICALS: JOURNALS, MAGAZINES, AND NEWSPAPERS

Journal with continuous pagination
Martin, Anne. "Teachers and Teaching." *Harvard Educational Review* 58 (1989): 488–50.
[Learned journals that may publish only three or four times a year, page each year's
   issues continuously. For example, the fall issue will end with page number 110, then
   the winter issue will begin with page 111. That is why the volume number (58 in the
   example above) is important in documenting such journals.

Journal that pages each issue separately using issue numbers
Levine, Edward. "The Inflated Image: Satire and Meaning in Pop Art." *Satire Newsletter*
   6.1 (1968): 43–50.

Weekly or monthly magazine
"The Hewing Ax." *Wood Magazine* Oct. 1986: 24.
[If the magazine is published weekly, put the day just before the month: *16 Oct. 1986.* If
   the article is signed, the author comes before the title of the article, and is
   alphabetized by the author's name.]

Newspaper
Signed Article, editorial, review
Emmerman, Lynn. "Middle-aged Bosses Becoming Obsolete." *Chicago Tribune* 10 Aug.
   1986, final ed., sec. 3:1.

Unsigned article, editorial, review
"Trade Deficit Bad, But Not Worse." Editorial. *Chicago Tribune* 8 Nov. 1986, final ed.,
   sec. 1:10.
[Unsigned articles, editorials, reviews alphabetize by title.]

DISSERTATIONS AND THESES

Unpublished
Park, Young Mok. "Writing Performance and its Relationship to Writing Task." Diss. U
   of IL, 1986.

Published
Selby, Stuart Allen. *The Study of Film as an Art Form in Secondary Schools.* Diss.
   Columbia U, 1963. New York: Arno. 1978.

Abstract from Dissertation Abstracts International
Wynne, James Howard. "Determining the Internal Consistency of English Compositions
   Using Selected Criteria." Diss. Louisiana State U, 1977. *DAI* 38 (1977): 3347A.

How to Use MLA Styles of Documentation

Parenthetical Documentation (Inside Paper)

PERIODICALS: JOURNALS, MAGAZINES, AND NEWSPAPERS

Journal with continuous pagination
Martin deplores the use of the term *children at risk* because it is "a prediction of danger and implicitly a call for immediate strong action to avert disaster" (490).

Journal that pages each issue separately using issue numbers
Edward Levine claims that Pop art is a combination of representational painting and abstract expressionism (44).

Weekly or monthly magazine
There are three ways to tell the date of an ax:(1) axes from the 17th century don't have a *poll*, (2) an eye in the ax head dates it in the 18th century, and (3) a wrought-iron head dates it before 1800 ("Hewing Ax" 24).

Newspaper
Signed article, editorial, review
Lynn Emmerman reports that younger men and women of the baby boom generation are making it difficult for older executives to find jobs after they have been laid off (6).

Unsigned article, editorial, review
In the month of September, exports and imports are down, a good sign for the economy (Chicago Tribune 10).

DISSERTATIONS AND THESES

Unpublished
Using protocol analysis to draw a correlation between performance and planning is often inconclusive (Park 23).

Published
[Same as above.]

Abstract from Dissertation Abstracts International
[Same as above.]

How to Use MLA Styles of Documentation

Works Cited—End of Paper
(same as bibliography and bibliography cards)

PAMPHLETS, BULLETINS, AND CONFERENCES

Signed
Mitchell, Richard. *Underground Grammarian.* Glasboro. NJ: Underground Grammarian.
   November. 1986.

Unsigned
Communication Briefings. Blackwood, NJ: Encoders, April 1984.

CD-ROMS AND ON-LINE DATABASES

CD-ROM databases
"Michael Jordan." *Encarta.* 1994. CD-ROM. Microsoft: 1991–93.

On-line data bases
Fee-Fulkerson, Katherine C. "Cognitions on Performance of High and Low Math Anxious
   College Men and Women." *DAI* 43 (1983): 3729. University of North Carolina at Chapel
   Hill, 1982. *Dissertation Abstracts On-line.* On-line. DIALOG. 2 May 1995.

PERFORMANCES, LECTURES, AND SPEECHES

Individual performance
Blossom, Beverly. *Beverly Blossom Solo.* Studio Theater, Krannert Center for the
   Performing Arts, Urbana, IL. 8 Nov. 1986.

Group performance
The Midday Witch. By Anton Dvořak. Cond. Sir Charles Mackerras. With Michele
   Campanella and Men of the Chicago Symphony Chorus. Chicago Symphony
   Orchestra. Orchestra Hall, Chicago, IL. 20 Nov. 1986.

Speech with title
Knoll, Harold. "The Arrow or the Ring?" Winona Exchange Club. Winona. MN., Nov.
   1977.

Speech without title
Knoll, Harold. Speech. Winona Exchange Club. Winona, MN., Nov. 1977.

INTERVIEWS

Recorded or published
Harrod, John. "English and Public Policy." Natl. Public Radio WILL. Urbana, IL.
   5 March 1978.

Personal
June Mank. Personal interview. 15 August 1995.

How to Use MLA Styles of Documentation

Parenthetical Documentation (Inside Paper)

PAMPHLETS, BULLETINS, AND CONFERENCES

Signed
[Treat as signed book or article.]

Unsigned
[Treat as unsigned book or article.]

CD-ROMS AND ON-LINE DATABASES

CD-ROM databases
Encarta gives Michael Jordan credit for being the second player in history to score 3,000 points in one season—1986–87 ("Michael Jordan").

On-line database
As early as 1982, studies addressed math anxiety among college men and women (Fee-Fulkerson).

PERFORMANCES, LECTURES, AND SPEECHES

Individual performance
Beverly Blossom's dance, "Dad's Ties," uses 200 men's ties for its effect (Performance).

Group performance
In its rendition of Dvořak's *The Midday Witch* the Chicago Symphony Orchestra used a variety of unusual effects, such as the sound of the men's chorus (Performance).

Speech with title
Knoll describes two ways of communicating in business—the simplest and most direct, but perhaps not the most effective, is like shooting an arrow (Speech).

Speech without title
[same as above.]

INTERVIEWS

Recorded or published
The use of jargon and gobbledygook is damaging the bargaining power of the English-speaking world, according to Harrod (Interview).

Personal
June Mank states that any political party needs strong precinct representatives in order to reach the citizens at the neighborhood level (Interview).

How to Use MLA Styles of Documentation

Works Cited—End of Paper
(same as bibliography and bibliography cards)

FILM, TELEVISION, AND RECORDINGS

"Wonders Are Many." *The Soul of Science.* Betamax Televideo. Madison: Hawkhill Video, 1983.

MUSICAL COMPOSITIONS AND WORKS OF ART

Wyeth, Andrew, *Groundhog Day.* Philadelphia Museum of Art.

■■■ *Exceptions in Parenthetical Documentation*

Indirect source cited

If you cannot cite the primary source of a quote, use *qtd. in*:

One executive reports how he felt when he lost his job as a financial manager: "I got at least 70 percent of my identity from my job" (qtd. in Emmerman 6).

General reference to entire work

Put author's name in the text.

Citing more than one work

Use semicolons between each item cited:

(Mack 348; Leacock 73)

■■■ *Content (or Explanatory) Notes*

Sometimes you will have reason to give your reader information that is too bulky or inappropriate for the text itself. Or perhaps you will need to cite several sources that would interfere with the readability of your paper if you listed all of them parenthetically. In these two cases, use notes. Number them consecutively and place them at the bottom of each page (where the citation occurs) or, better yet, at the end of the paper before the *Works Cited.* (See content notes #1 and #2 in the model research paper.)

■■■ *Bibliographic Notes*

Use bibliographic notes to evaluate a source or to list several citations.

Text:

Urie Bronfenbrenner has a constant theme that the present trend toward individualism—everyone doing his own thing—has created alienated children and adolescents.[2]

Bibliographic note:

[2]See *Current* 39–47, *Phi Delta Kappan* 431–436, and *Psychology Today* 39–47.

How to Use MLA Styles of Documentation

Parenthetical Documentation (Inside Paper)

FILM, TELEVISION, AND RECORDINGS

Even though the large bulk of the human population in ancient times produced many of the advances in science, they were kept in a subservient position ("Wonders" Televideo).

MUSICAL COMPOSITIONS AND WORKS OF ART

Wyeth's *Groundhog Day* is an accurate representation of the late-winter sun in Maine (Philadelphia Museum).

■■■ *Endnote and Footnote Forms*

Some instructors prefer that you use the endnote (or footnote) form rather than the parenthetical form. Endnotes appear at the end of the paper. Footnotes appear at the bottom of each page. Both notes are *numbered* consecutively, using the MLA form. Your notes are also keyed to the matching item in the list of *Works Cited*.

▼ Sample Research Paper

The sample research paper and outline written on the subject of hypnotherapy will show you the culmination of one student's efforts. The paper contains many of the techniques and forms discussed in this chapter so that you can see how they work together in an actual situation. Here are a few things you should note about the format of the paper:

1. The body is double-spaced, with block quotations indented 10 spaces and also double-spaced.

2. The outline, notes, and *Works Cited* are double-spaced both within and between each entry.

3. The boxed numbers in the margin beside each paragraph have been added so that you can refer to specific paragraphs when discussing the paper. (You should *not* use such numbers in your own paper.)

The Practice (pages 164–165) not only should give you a better understanding of the principles and conventions illustrated in the paper; it should also help you apply them to your own efforts.

NOTE: If your paper does not begin with an outline or abstract, it does not require a title page. See instructions (page 140).

"Rational Magic" — Hypnosis and the Control of Pain

by

Ben Stokes

English 101, Section A

Professor Daugherty

8 June 1996

OUTLINE

Thesis: As used by medical therapists, hypnosis may be described as a form of "rational magic" that can reduce the acute pain and anxiety associated with certain medical procedures.

I. Introduction

   A. The history of *hypnotherapy* is long and complex.

   B. Hypnotherapy can be considered a form of "rational magic."

II. We do not really know how hypnosis itself works—or why.

   A. Some authorities believe that hypnosis creates a sleeplike condition.

   B. Other authorities prefer to define hypnosis operationally, by how the subject feels or acts.

   C. Hypnosis may work analogously to meditation and biofeedback.

   D. Professor E. Hilgard believes that there are seven characteristics of the hypnotic state.

III. Patients use hypnotism as a form of "rational magic" to help themselves control pain.

   A. Patients learn to employ an individualized trance.

   B. *Pain* is classified into two categories.

   C. Patients respond to the memory of pain, and to its duration.

IV. Children who are in pain provide an excellent instance of the use of "rational magic."

   A. A typical painful procedure for children is bone-marrow removal.

   B. The therapist encourages the child to fantasize during a hypnotic trance.

      1. The therapist picks the child's own favorite story.

      2. The therapist uses the child's favorite doll.

V. How does the "rational magic" of hypnosis control pain?

   A. The pain is not really eliminated; it becomes a part of the background of the situation.

   B. Fantasizing creates a "competition" with the pain.

   C. The patient controls the *theater of pain*.

VI. Conclusion

Stokes 2

[1]   The use of hypnosis to control pain—called *hypnotherapy*—has a long
history. In 1829, before anesthesia was developed, a doctor in Paris
performed a mastectomy on a woman he had hypnotized. A little later,
in England and the United States, hypnotism was used to relieve the
pain of amputations, tumor operations, and dental surgery (Gravitz
(A)   202–203). Even though there was no chemical anesthesia available, and
some doctors used hypnosis successfully to deaden the pain of surgery,
the medical establishment was basically against the procedure. Doctors
who used hypnosis were often attacked and, in some instances, forced to
resign their professorships and hospital posts. Some doctors even
believed that it was necessary for a patient to suffer pain. Professor
Melvin Gravitz reports one doctor's belief that pain is "a wise provision
of nature, and patients ought to suffer pain while the surgeon is
operating; they are all the better for it, and recover better" (203).

[2]   In the United States, doctors in small villages and out-of-the-way places
were most likely to use hypnosis as an anesthetic because they weren't
closely scrutinized by the medical establishment. Gravitz explains that
they were freer to experiment with hypnosis at a time "when surgery
was a distinct risk and frequently a death sentence" (207). He
compliments these early doctors who practiced hypnosis for being
"courageous, innovative, and competent professionals who used hypnosis
(B)   because it worked effectively and without negative side effects" (207).

[3]   The practice of hypnosis as anesthesia for controlling pain in surgery
died out a few years after ether and chloroform were developed in the
1830s and 40s. It wasn't until the mid-twentieth century that the
medical profession accepted hypnosis as a science. Today, specialists
from medicine, dentistry, and psychology form professional groups such
as The American Society of Clinical Hypnosis (J. Hilgard 223). They
conduct scientific research on the therapeutic uses of hypnosis, the
results of which are published in their journals. Much of this research

deals with the use of hypnosis to alleviate pain in medical procedures other than surgery. A good example is bone-marrow removal in children afflicted with leukemia. This procedure, using a large needle driven through the skin and bone, is repeated often, creating a great deal of acute pain and anxiety for the children. According to Professor Ernest R. Hilgard, one of the pioneers in hypnosis research, hypnosis for pain in this kind of medical procedure works as "rational magic"—hypnotizing the patient can work wonders, but nobody knows quite why (Study 27).

At the heart of the mystery is hypnosis itself. No one knows just what it *is*. According to *The Oxford Companion to the Mind*, hypnosis is a sleeplike condition psychically induced, usually by another person, through "sustained mental concentration" (331). To be successful, a "very real mutual cooperation between the hypnotist and his subject must occur" (332). As a result of this *cooperation*, the subject responds, with certain limitations, to the suggestions of the hypnotist. The root of the word *hypnosis* is the Greek word *hypnos*, meaning *sleep*. So the term *sleeplike* is important to our understanding of hypnosis.

However, it is a mistake to take the sleep analogy too seriously because electroencephalograms (or EEG's), which measure the electric potential in the brain, show that people under hypnosis are in a waking state (E. Hilgard, Hypnotic 150).[1] It is this waking state, described as "sleeplike," that makes hypnosis used by doctors and therapists seem to may patients like "rational magic." They are awake enough to help themselves deal with pain but asleep enough to lessen its effects.

Hypnotherapists—doctors, dentists, and psychologists who combine hypnotism with therapy—usually do not even try to define *hypnosis*. Instead, in discussing their work, they describe how a subject *feels* or *acts* while in a hypnotic trance. Their descriptions vary considerably. For instance, Frank Marlowe, a Philadelphia plastic surgeon and otolaryngologist who uses hypnosis as anesthesia, calls it "a very focused, intense form of concentration" on the part of the patient (qtd.

Ⓔ in Silberner 188). But other hypnotherapists call it "an induced state of relaxation" (Gelman 74). Dr. Jacob Conn calls hypnosis the patient's "role playing" (358), and other authorities call it a "believed-in fantasy" ("Hypnosis").

⑦ In order to explain how hypnosis works, hypnotherapists note that it is partly similar to Zen meditation and biofeedback. In comparing hypnosis to meditation, Professor Ernest Hilgard explains that Zen meditation is a private process in which the meditator relies completely on the self, freeing the mind of extraneous thoughts. But during hypnosis, the subject requires instruction from the hypnotist, and the

Ⓕ resulting trance is to some extent created by an agent outside the self (Study 26). In comparing hypnosis to biofeedback (sometimes called *self-hypnosis*), Josephine Hilgard says that biofeedback depends upon patients being aware of their physiological processes in order to control them. With the help of the feedback of these processes, represented in heart rate or blood pressure, they learn to control their pain.[2] Yet the opposite is true of hypnosis: the patient tries to ignore the physiological processes in order to deny the existence of pain (226–227).

⑧ Professor Ernest Hilgard identifies seven characteristics of the hypnotic state. All of these are related to the subject's (a patient's) behavior:

(1) The subject loses all desire and initiative to act on his or her own, even though he has the ability to do so.

(2) The subject selects what will get his attention.

(3) The subject is able to recall the past and produce fantasy.

(4) The subject is unable to test reality, and consequently distorts it.

(5) The subject is highly suggestible.

(6) The subject will enthusiastically play a role.

(7) The subject will forget what occurred during hypnosis

Ⓖ (Hypnotic 6–10).

[9]
(H) The hypnotherapist is trained to use the resources of patients to help themselves control pain through hypnosis (J. Hilgard 40–41). Dr. Milton H. Erickson, one of the pioneers in the therapeutic uses of hypnosis, explains how hypnotherapists encourage patients to use this "rational magic." First, they prepare the patients for the therapy by interviewing and observing them. The purpose of the preparation stage is to encourage the patients to trust the therapist so that pain control is possible. In the next stage, therapists use what they have learned to develop an individualized trance so that the patients can help themselves "solve" their pain problems. And last, by observing physical clues provided by the patient during the trance, the therapist verifies that a trance has occurred and that a "therapeutic change" has taken place (1–14).

[10] According to Dr. Erickson, a therapist helps patients "learn to use their mental skills and potentials to achieve their own therapeutic goals" (14). David Rigler, Chief Psychologist at Children's Hospital of Los Angeles, provides a simplified version of how he uses the Erickson method of hypnotherapy in a pediatric hospital: "(1) Get the patient's attention; (2) communicate to the patient's satisfaction that change is possible; and (3) enlist the patient's commitment to the service of positive change" (306).

[11] Hypnotherapists classify pain into two categories, both associated with time—*chronic* and *acute*. Chronic pain lasts over a long period of
(I) time, and it recurs.[3] Acute pain, whether recurring or not, is usually short-lived. While experiencing acute pain, the patient is unable to withstand either its severity or duration (J. Hilgard 214). It is acute pain that the patient experiences during medical procedures such as bone-marrow removal, spinal taps, and injections into a muscle. Since *time* is so important, Dr. Erickson explains the relationship:

> Pain is a complex, a construct, composed of past
> remembered pain, of present pain experience, and of

Stokes 6

anticipated pain in the future. Thus, immediate pain is
augmented by past pain and enhanced by the future
Ⓙ   possibilities of pain. . . . Nothing so much intensifies pain as the
fear that it will be present on the morrow. It is likewise
increased by the realization that the same or similar pain was
experienced in the past, and this and the immediate pain
render the future even more threatening. (95–96)

Ⓚ   Because anxiety about future pain is so much a part of certain medical
procedures, it isn't any wonder that children and adults are eager to
accept the help of hypnotic "rational magic."

⑫   Two research studies (one conducted at Children's Hospital at
Stanford and one at British Columbia Children's Hospital) show how
effective hypnotherapy can be in the reduction of anxiety and pain in
children. (The study of pain therapy in children is particularly
important because children react so violently—and straightforwardly—to
pain and its alleviation.) The first study, begun in 1975 by Josephine
Hilgard and Samuel Lebaron at Stanford, will hereafter be referred to as
Ⓛ   the *J. Hilgard study*. The other study, conducted in the early 80s by
Leona Kuttner at British Columbia Children's Hospital, will be referred
to as the *Kuttner study*.

⑬   The children in both studies were leukemia patients who had to
undergo intensive drug chemotherapy and radiotherapy to slow down
the effects of the disease. The only way a physician can determine
whether the therapy is affecting the leukemic cells is by frequently
removing a sample of the bone marrow. It is a very painful procedure:

Ⓜ   In a bone marrow aspiration [removal], a large needle is
pushed into the hipbone (iliac crest) in order to withdraw a
sample of marrow for diagnostic purposes. There are three
sources of discomfort reported by most patients: first, a
sharp, stinging pain as the needle penetrates the skin; then

pain and heavy pressure as the needle penetrates the periosteum, or covering of the bone; and finally an intense, excruciating pain as the sample of bone marrow is sucked into the needle. This "suction pain" may be brief and localized, but it is reported by some patients to remain in their entire upper leg for 30 seconds or more. Although local anesthesia can alter the degree of pain felt when the large bone marrow needle penetrates sensitive outer tissues and possibly the periosteum, no local anesthesia can relieve the sharp pain that accompanies the actual aspiration. (J. Hilgard 16)

Children who must have this procedure repeated over fairly short periods of time have a great deal of anxiety which is often manifested in sleeplessness, nausea, and vomiting (J. Hilgard 85).

[14]   Both the J. Hilgard and Kuttner studies based their hypnotic technique on the ability of children to fantasize, a characteristic of easily hypnotizable subjects. Kuttner used the child's favorite story to induce and maintain the hypnotic trance. Before the bone-marrow removal, she asked each child to recount his or her favorite story. Then she accompanied the child to the surgery room where she put him in a trance, using the story he favored. During the surgical procedure, the trance was maintained by adding to the story as the procedure caused pain (291). For example, while one child was in a trance, Kuttner added points about courage to the story of "Cinderella" during the worst part of the surgical procedure:

> Cinderella wanted to do fun-things [sic], but her three sisters said that she had to do horrid things like wash and clean up the kitchen. Well, one day while she was sweeping the floor, Cinderella said, "Oh I wish I were brave and not scared at all of my sisters." Well, as soon as she said, "I wish," a Magic Fairy suddenly appeared in the room and said, "Cinderella, you are a wonderfully brave girl. You have handled some tough things so

Stokes 8

I am going to reward you for your courage. You can have your
wish come true." What do you think Cinderella wished for? . . .
That's it, to go to the King's Ball. Cinderella took a deep breath
in and sighed it out. She felt marvelous because she knew she'd
soon be having fun and all the hardship would be over. (293)

15   The J. Hilgard study also used fantasy to induce and maintain a trance.
Annette, a six-year-old, was hypnotized by focusing on a cartoon-fantasy
"funny face" drawn on her thumbnail. After she was fully "under," her
trance was maintained by the fantasy that her favorite doll was having a
birthday party, complete with birthday cake and candles. When Annette
underwent bone-marrow removal, she blew on the therapist's fingers
(which had become birthday candles) during the most painful parts of the
procedure (58–59). Her fear and pain were considerably alleviated.

O 16   How does the "rational magic" of hypnosis help patients to control
their pain? Hypnotherapists explain the phenomenon in several ways.
Dr. Kuttner says that the pain suffered during a hypnotic trance is not
eliminated. Rather it retires into the background, becoming simply
"more distant, less relevant, and therefore less upsetting and painful"
(293). Or putting it in different words, she says that the favorite story
(or fantasy) creates *competition* with the painful procedure (298). Dr.
Erickson explains that hypnosis is effective when the pain is a result of
a "single event" (as in certain medical procedures) because knowing
that the pain won't recur helps to diminish it (96). Professor Ernest
Hilgard uses a theater metaphor to explain the effect of hypnosis on
pain: "Some hidden part of the mind registers things that are going on,
while another part is occupied with something else and is unaware of
what's going on . . . part of you is on this stage and part of you is out in
the wings watching" (qtd. in Gelman 75).

17   In modern medical science, the control of pain in the "theater" of
hypnosis remains an oddity. Hypnotherapy is partly a science, and is

therefore *rational.* It is partly an ancient mystery, and is therefore *magical.* Medically speaking, does the procedure work? The answer is *yes*—for many people and for certain kinds of pain. Yet we do not know how much of the credit for alleviating pain belongs to hypnosis and how much to suggestion (or self-suggestion, as the case may be). And what is truly changed, the pain itself or the patient's perception of it? Final answers elude both doctors and patients.

Notes

[1]Hilgard also reports that sometimes a hypnotist will tell the subject that he or she will experience a dream, but the dream the subject experiences will be different from a sleep dream in two ways. The dream and time of the dream (and sometimes the subject of the dream) in the hypnotic state is set by the hypnotist. Furthermore, the subject expects to report the subject of his dream after being taken out of the hypnotic state. Both of these requirements are absent in a sleep dream (Hypnotic 151).

[2]Jacknow's research studies the effect of self-hypnosis (or biofeedback) on chemotherapy-related nausea in children and young adults. The results show that self-hypnosis is an effective treatment for "reducing the anticipatory nausea associated with chemotherapy in pediatric oncology patients" (261).

Findlay reports that researchers have come to believe that self-hypnosis may have an effect on the limbic system, a center in the brain controlling involuntary bodily functions such as digestion. Under hypnosis, the limbic system may respond to patients' efforts to change their reactions to nausea or pain (71).

[3]Hypnotherapists have been successful in helping patients deal with the chronic pain of ulcerative colitis, migraines, angina, phantom limb pain, herpes, and damaged facial nerves (Long 28).

Stokes 10

Works Cited

Conn, Jacob H. "The Myth of Coercion Under Hypnosis." *Zeig* 357–367.

Erickson, Milton, and Ernest L. Rossi. *Hypnotherapy, An Exploratory Casebook*. New York: Irvington, 1979.

Findlay, Stephen, Doug Podolsky, and Joanne Silberner. "Wonder Cures from the Fringe." *U.S. News & World Report* 23 Sept.1991: 69–74.

Gelman, David. "Illusions That Heal." *Newsweek* 17 Nov. 1986: 74–76.

Gravitz, Melvin A. "Early Uses of Hypnosis as Surgical Anesthesia." *American Journal of Clinical Hypnosis* 30 (1988): 201–208.

Hilgard, Ernest R. *Hypnotic Susceptibility*. New York: Harcourt, 1965.

———. "A Study in Hypnosis." *Psychology Today* Jan. 1986: 23–29.

Hilgard, Josephine, and Samuel Lebaron. *Hypnotherapy of Pain in Children with Cancer*. Los Altos, CA: Kaufmann, 1984.

"Hypnosis." *The New Grolier's Multimedia Encyclopedia*. CD-ROM. Danbury, CT: Grolier Electronic Publishing, Inc. 1994.

Jacknow, Dale S. et al. "Hypnosis in the Prevention of Chemotherapy-Related Nausea and Vomiting in Children: A Prospective Study." *Developmental and Behavioral Pediatrics* 15. 4 (1994): 258–264.

Kuttner, Leona. "Favorite Stories: A Hypnotic Pain-Reduction Technique for Children in Acute Pain." *American Journal of Clinical Hypnosis* 30 (1988): 289–295.

Long, Patricia. "Medical Mesmerism." *Psychology Today* Jan. 1986: 28–29.

Rigler, David. "Ericksonian Techniques in a Pediatric Hospital." *Zeig* 301–309.

Silberner, Joanne. "Hypnotism Under the Knife." *Science News* 22 (1986): 186–87.

Zangwill, O. L "Hypnotism, History of." *The Oxford Companion to the Mind*. Oxford: Oxford UP, 1987.

Zeig, Jeffrey K., ed. *Ericksonian Approaches to Hypnosis and Psychotherapy*. New York: Brunner, 1982.

Explanations for Sample Research Paper

(A)   Gravitz' name has not been used in the text, so the parenthetical notation must give his name. Note: No comma comes after *Gravitz*, and the period is after the parenthesis.

(B)   The antecedent for the pronoun *He* in paragraph 2 is <u>Gravitz</u>. Therefore, his name is not in the parenthetical notation.

(C)   Ben introduces the *hook* or controlling term "rational magic" here. Note that he gives Professor Ernest Hilgard credit for the term; consequently, the term is always in quotation marks in the paper.

Important: Note that the last sentence of this third paragraph is the restated thesis found on the outline (p. 153). For a discussion of the "restated thesis," see page 28 (footnote).

(D)   Transition from the *Introduction* (*history*) to the definitions of *hypnosis*.

(E)   Since Silberner quotes Marlowe, the documentation includes *qtd. in* for *quoted in*.

(F)   Ben uses two references by Ernest Hilgard, so he uses a shortened title *Study* ("A Study in Hypnosis") in the parenthetical documentation.

(G)   Since Ben paraphrased the seven characteristics of the hypnotic state, he does not use a block quote here. See items *J* and *M* below.

(H)   The discussion of the process of hypnosis as "rational magic" begins in paragraph 9.

(I)   This informational content note (3) describes the kinds of conditions that hypnotherapists say cause "chronic" pain.

(J)   Ben blocked the quotation in paragraph 11 because it is longer than 4 lines. Notice that no quotation marks are necessary around block quotations, and that the parenthetical reference is set off from the block at the end by two spaces. The period comes at the end of the quote, not after the parenthetical reference. Block quotations are always indented 10 spaces from the left-hand margin, and are double-spaced in the same style as the balance of the paper.

Ⓚ   Ben ties the long quotation from Dr. Erickson to his point about anxiety, and repeats his hook "rational magic."

Ⓛ   Hereafter the two studies which exemplify how hypnosis is used to control acute pain will be referred to by author's name rather than the hospital where they were conducted. This helps the reader because the *Works Cited* is alphabetized by author's name.

Ⓜ   Another block quote. Ben uses brackets around *removal* as an editorial insertion (page 134) to define the meaning of *aspiration*.

Ⓝ   Ben uses information about hypnotizability here. You will recall that he decided it was a topic that would break the flow of his paper if he had devoted an entire section to it.

Ⓞ   Ben uses a transition in the form of a question, and he repeats his hook, "rational magic." This helps the reader to make a connection with Annette's actions and rational magic.

PRACTICE

1. Check Ben's outline (page 153) against the body of his paper by putting outline symbols (I, A, B, C; II, A, etc.) in the margin of the paper where the various topics and subtopics are discussed. How well does the student follow his outline?

2. Why does Ben put so much information identifying himself and the course before the title of the paper?

3. Explain the purpose of the first three paragraphs. Are all three necessary?

4. What is the writer's stance? Who in particular is Ben writing to?

5. In paragraph 2, Ben quotes twice from page 207 of the Gravitz article. Why does he find it necessary to use (207) after "sentence" and also after "effects"?

6. Why did Ben use the material about dreams in an endnote rather than using it in the text itself?

7. Here is the card for the Hilgard quotation in paragraph 16. How did the writer integrate the material in his paper?

Card for Hilgard Quotation in Paragraph 16

```
How hypnosis works                          Quote p. 76

Theater metaphor

    Hilgard says, "Some hidden part of the mind registers

things that are going on, while another part is occupied

with something else and is unaware of what's going on."

It is as if, says Hilgard, "part of you is on this stage

and part of you is out in the wings watching."


Newsweek, Nov. 17, 1986, p. 75
```

8. In paragraphs 9 and 10, Ben gives two views of the process that the therapist and patient go through to deal with the pain. First is a long one-paragraph description from Dr. Erickson's perception. Then Ben gives a shorter version as perceived by Dr. David Rigler. Evaluate the usefulness of Dr. Rigler's quote after Dr. Erickson's.

9. How are brackets around *remo*val the long quote in paragraph 13 different from the parentheses used in the same quote?

10. Why does Ben use [sic] after "fun-things" in the long block quote in paragraph number 14?

11. Why does Ben use three periods after "Cinderella wished for?" in the same block quote in paragraph 14?

12. What are the rhetorical patterns used in paragraphs 4 and 7?

13. How did Ben use the quotation as a transition device between paragraph 16 and the conclusion in paragraph 17?

PART TWO

The Reader

CHAPTER 10

Mixed Strategies

▼ Introduction—Strategies of Development

As we have indicated in previous chapters, writing situations are not all alike. Each of them tends to present its own problems. For this reason you need to investigate every situation carefully and create a special *stance* that will work best for it.

But while stances and writing situations may often vary greatly, your choices of methods for developing papers are somewhat more limited. These methods include a variety of techniques and rhetorical devices that we call *strategies.*

The *strategies* are actually thinking techniques that you have employed in a variety of ways in and out of school since you were very young. For example, when you had a choice between two flavors of ice cream, you made a *comparison-contrast.* If you made a list of homework assignments, you *classified.* In changing your bicycle tire, you were engaged in a *process.* In history classes you studied the *causes and effects* of the Civil War. In science you *defined* the elements, and in English you identified *analogies* in literature. Whenever you were asked to give an example to prove your point, you used *illustration.* You use *narration* and *description* every day when you talk about your personal experiences. So you can see that the strategies are not elements related only to composition. They are natural ways of dealing with information so that we can think and communicate more effectively.

To see how the strategies can be used to organize a paper, we will follow Greg, a pre-med student, as he thinks about a very real problem: The college Board of Trustees has voted to increase tuition at his school by 30 percent in the next academic year. Then the trustees plan to increase tuition the following year by 10 percent. Since he is one of five college-age children in a family, he cannot depend on his parents for much financial help. The federal government is cutting its funding for Guaranteed Student Loans (GSLs), so he isn't sure if he will be able to borrow enough to pay his tuition. He is a pre-med major; consequently he cannot transfer to a "cheaper" college because pre-med programs aren't offered in other state schools close by. He works summers as a lifeguard and he works 20 hours a week in the college cafeteria during the school year. That income, combined with his GSL, barely covers expenses.

Greg considers the effect that a 40 percent hike in tuition will have on him. He gets increasingly angry about the prospect of having to go in debt, and this anger is reflected in his comments jotted down quickly on scratch paper:

> Not fair. The debt is going to be impossible to pay back.
>
> Mom doesn't work.
>
> Parents proud of me wanting to be a doctor.
>
> Dad is a self-made man who works hard in his own business. Never took anything from anyone.
>
> Never any money left over, after paying debts and mortgage.
>
> Pre-med expensive.
>
> University charges more tuition for pre-med courses.
>
> Chose a public university because cheaper.
>
> Job at cafeteria barely covers room and board—no tuition or books.
>
> If I leave school to get some money for school, can I pick up my studies again?
>
> John and Susie barely managing to stay in school, even with loans.
>
> Takes a lot of persistence to apply for work.
>
> The total cost for college is increasing twice as fast as the inflation index. Does this make sense?
>
> The government is decreasing funds for loans. Harder to get in future.
>
> What could I do if I left school?

Certain observations that Greg has jotted down can be translated into *the strategies of development* mentioned earlier. Applied to Greg's situation as a pre-med student, the strategies could be used as follows:

1. *Description*—A description of the financial situation of Greg's family: number of children, amount of mortgage, and other debts.

2. *Narration*—A true story narrating his finding and keeping jobs in order to supplement his student loan.

3. *Process*—An accounting of the steps in applying for a student loan.

4. *Cause-effect*—An analysis of the effect of his having to leave school since he may not be able to qualify for a student loan to pay the increased tuition.

5. *Classification*—A breakdown of the kinds of loans available, most of which he is not eligible for.

6. *Illustration*—An account of three friends who will have a difficult time staying in school with increased tuition and reduced student loans.

7. *Definition*—An extended definition of *student loans.*

8. *Comparison-contrast*—An explanation of the kind of program Greg is enrolled in, compared with the program he could get in other colleges.

9. *Analogy*—An extended comparison in which he shows that the rate of tuition increases over a period of years in the college is higher than the rate of inflation. Nationally, college tuitions are increasing at double the rate of inflation, and experts believe that this will be the pattern for years to come.

10. *Argumentation*—An argument proving that tuition hikes are unnecessary.

After thinking about the subject of increased tuition, and after studying his jottings, Greg decides that the best argument he can make is to write to the Board of Trustees and his state legislator, objecting to the tuition increase. He knows that all the points in his jottings won't be relevant because he can't deal with all the possible topics on the subject. Nevertheless, he chooses those points that he believes would be most convincing and those that would perhaps be applicable to other students in his predicament. For instance, using *cause and effect* as a strategy to show that he—and others—might have to leave school (as a result of an increase in tuition) should convince his readers that the increase will cause unnecessary hardship.

After choosing this strategy, Greg outlines his stance.

Role:	College sophomore (pre-med) who has relied on part-time jobs and student loans to pay college expenses.
Audience:	The Board of Trustees and a state legislator.
Thesis:	The proposal to increase tuition over 40 percent by the school year 1998 should be reconsidered because restrictions on federally subsidized Guaranteed Student Loans (GSL's), and the inability of most students to get high-paying jobs, will result in many students having to drop out of school.

As the thesis implies, Greg's thesis is one of *cause* and *effect,* and the developmental strategy of his paper will reflect that fact.

Whether your choice of strategy is appropriate often depends on the nature of your subject. Some subjects seem to encourage a writer to employ certain methods of development; for example:

1. *Subject:* A relative

 Thesis: *My grandmother is not a stereotypical grandmother; she is young, independent, and athletic.*

 Strategy: **Description**

2. *Subject:* Vacations

 Thesis: *A trip to Russia last summer taught me that the Russian educated class is often discriminated against.*

 Strategy: ***Narration***

3.   *Subject:*   Running for student office

      Thesis: *There are three important steps in running for student office: applying, campaigning, and developing a constituency.*

      Strategy: **Process**

4.   *Subject:*   Nervous headaches

      Thesis: *My headaches are caused by the pressures of having to meet strict course deadlines.*

      Strategy: **Cause and effect**

5.   *Subject:*   Nonflowering house plants

      Thesis: *Of the foliage house plants, succulents and cacti are the easiest to grow in a dry climate.*

      Strategy: **Classification**

6.   *Subject:*   Camping

      Thesis: *Campers who travel in recreational vehicles are typically congenial people who bring their television sets, motor bikes, and the like to camp in commercial or park campsites.*

      Strategy: **Illustration**

7.   *Subject:*   "Pass/fail" courses

      Thesis: *"Pass/fail" courses are an educational opportunity to study a subject without having to face the pressure of a conventional grading system.*

      Strategy: **Definition** *(of the term* "pass/fail" *course)*

8.   *Subject:*   Two science-fiction movies.

      Thesis: The Empire Strikes Back *is a movie with a thin plot, unconvincing characters, and bizarre situations;* Close Encounters of the Third Kind *is a film with a strong plot, realistic characters, and situations based on actual happenings.*

      Strategy: **Comparison-contrast**

9.   *Subject:*   Hand guns

      Thesis: *Like automobiles, hand guns are dangerous but controllable.*

      Strategy: **Analogy**

10.   *Subject:*   Liability law suits

      Thesis: *Physicians who provide emergency medical treatment to accident victims should be exempt from liability law suits.*

      Strategy: **Argumentation**

▼ Mixed Strategies

Proper use of the ten strategies can help you express your ideas precisely and efficiently, and after you have learned to employ them you will find that writing most essays and papers is much easier. But you may—and you should—use the strategies in combination. In dealing with the subject of running for student office, for example, it is likely that you could use narration and process. In managing the subject of hand guns, you might need to employ the strategies of definition analogy, and comparison-contrast. While you will probably use one of the strategies as the main unifying principle behind your paper, you will often employ some of the others in creating your supporting material.

To give you an example of mixing the strategies, we will describe one student's method for handling a topic.

Jane is frustrated with the lack of transportation between her home-town and her college town, Collegeview—no train or plane, only buses. She believes that, since the bus transportation in and out of Collegeview is undependable, the college should charter buses for weekends and holiday traffic so that students can go home more efficiently and cheaply than they presently do. In supporting her thesis she could use combinations of certain strategies.

As we pointed out earlier, the strategies involve thinking skills, so in the prewriting stage Jane thinks through her topic, considering how the strategies can be used. The most obvious connection she sees between her topic and the strategies is that she has had personal experience with the buses and her experience has not been happy. She decides that narrating her experience would be a good way to get the attention of the reader. As she works through her facts and ideas, thinking about the strategies, she develops a scratch outline. Here is her outline showing how she will use combinations of strategies to write her *argument,* her basic strategy.

Introduction

Thesis: *The University should charter buses so that students can leave and return to Collegeview efficiently and cheaply.*

Strategy: Narration—Jane will recount her experiences of being forced to stay alone in her dorm because no transportation was available when she wanted to go home. Intertwined with her *narration* she will use *description* to illuminate her feelings.

Strategy: Definition—The reader must understand what Jane means by *charter.* She will support her definition with *illustration* by giving examples of the variety of ways the school may charter buses.

Body

I. The college needs better transportation out of Collegeview on weekends and holidays.

A. Not enough buses come into Collegeview for the number of students who want to leave on weekends and holidays.

Strategy: Description—Jane will describe the bus station on a Friday afternoon when all the students are clamoring to get seats on too few buses. She will support her *description* with *illustration.*

B. Alternate forms of transportation are too expensive—or dangerous (hitchhiking, for example).

Strategy: Comparison and contrast—She will show how bus transportation is cheaper than owning a car or hiring a taxi, the only feasible alternatives to buses.

Strategy: Cause and effect—Because Jane wanted to get home in a hurry, she tried to hitchhike—a harrowing experience. *Narration* of her experience mixed with *cause and effect.*

C. Fighting for bus tickets and waiting to get a seat on the bus is a waste of student time and resources.

Strategy: Process—Jane will identify the steps of getting a ticket and a seat on the bus. She will supplement process with *cause and effect,* showing how wasted time limits educational productivity. Wasted time also creates frustration and anger.

II.   Chartered buses are practical and will benefit the school.

A. Bus companies are willing to make a contract with the school.

Strategy: Classification—Jane has made inquiries and has classified the rates and companies who are willing to make a contract to provide bus service.

B. Students will be happier, and enrollment may increase if transportation is easier.

Strategy: Cause and effect—The college has had trouble keeping students after the freshman year, so Jane shows that this new system may help solve the problem.

Conclusion

Strategy: Analogy—An *analogy* is useful for concluding remarks. Perhaps Jane could draw an analogy between being stuck on the weekends and being a prisoner.

Before studying each of the strategies in more detail, we will look at three selections—two student-written models and one professional one. These writers have combined some of the strategies in their essays. At this point you may think that you do not know enough to identify all of the strategies. If so, do not hesitate to review the list of strategies on pages 170–171. You may look ahead to later chapters if you feel you need additional information.

But remember, the purpose of this analysis is not to test you, but to help you see how writers—both student and professional—use the strategies to support a *point* or *thesis.*

▼ Student Essay 1

The student-written paper below uses seven of the 10 strategies to prove her thesis: *The bumper sticker is basically an argument.* The writer has taken a position about bumper stickers that is debatable, so she herself has written an argument. It is important to define terms early in an argument, a point the writer seems to understand, because her *definition* of *bumper sticker* comes close on the heels of the thesis. Since there is a wide variety of bumper stickers, the writer classifies them in order to give some kind of logic to her paper. (Listing all the bumper stickers without any kind of order would create an indigestible mass). Another important reason for classifying is to support a particular point in the paper: *Bumper stickers aren't always serious. Illustration* is intertwined with *classification* because the reader needs to understand exactly what the writer means by the categories of *serious* and *unserious*.

The other strategies—*narration, process, comparison,* and *cause and effect*—the writer uses with some degree of success to help her build an argument in support of her thesis.

STICKING TO BUMPERS

1 Four children in the back of a car can drive vacationing parents crazy. At least our parents told us this often enough. "Shut up, and quit fighting! Look at the scenery!" (The scenery was hot dog stands and Taco Bells.)

2 Suddenly, right in the middle of Flagstaff, Arizona, my father said: "God bless America—and please hurry." A minute later he said: "Become a doctor—and support a lawyer." And then: "You touch-a my car, I break-a you face."

Introduction
Narration

3 He was, of course, reading bumper stickers in busy traffic. My mother is smart; she knew that if you can keep four hot, unhappy young people—ranging in age from nine to eighteen—from killing each other for only a short time, you are ahead of the game. The other kids were appointed look-outs, and I was made secretary for the Great Sticker Hunt. I was also appointed Drawer of Conclusion—father is a lawyer.

4 For the next few days, we saw enough bumper stickers to fill a small notebook, and I outlined my conclusions. First, the bumper sticker appears everywhere. It is glued on old rusty VWs and new Cadillacs—more on the former than the latter, however. Drivers of very expensive cars—foreign or domestic—do not, we think, buy bumper stickers.

Thesis and
Definition

5 *The bumper sticker is basically an argument.* It may or may not be serious; but it has to be short. It tends to be epigrammatic. It can state a "fact"—SOFT JUDGES MAKE HARDENED CRIMINALS—or a call for action—FIGHT ORGANIZED CRIME: ABOLISH THE IRS. The subject of the argument is seldom much older than last month's newspaper.

Elaboration of thesis
Classification—
first large category:
unserious
Illustration—
two subcategories of unserious

6 Bumper stickers seem to fall into seven broad groups. Four groups are relatively unserious, or even represent overt attempts at humor. The first of these is personal. Examples:

I'M A TENNIS BUM.
I TRAVEL THE FIFTH ST. BRIDGE. PRAY FOR ME.
In a second group are the determinedly wacky:
GET STONED—DRINK WET CEMENT
SURF NAKED
CLEAN AIR SMELLS FUNNY
FIGHT SMOG—RIDE A HORSE

DON'T STARE; I'M DANGEROUSLY ATTRACTIVE.

Illustration—
third subcategory
of unserious

7   In a third group of the relatively unserious stickers are derivations of other messages: HAVE YOU HUGGED YOUR KID TODAY? becomes HAVE YOU HUGGED YOUR HARLEY TODAY? and KEEP ON TRUCKIN' becomes KEEP ON TOLKIEN. Such derivations—or "echoes"—are important to the determined collector. On a dull day of vacationing you can trace eight or ten themes that undergo relatively unsubtle variations. On different bumpers you can be asked whether "today" you have hugged your wife, husband, grandparents, kids, motorcycle, and the defensive line of the Pittsburgh Steelers.

Illustration—
fourth
subcategory of
unserious

8   A fourth group of the unserious stickers makes little sense—at least to me. Examples:
FLOWERS DO IT!
JOHANN'S BACH (printed in gothic script)
CUSTER HAD IT COMING.
I FOUND IT!
WOULDN'T YOU RATHER BE RIDING A MULE ON MOLOKAI?
I BRAKE FOR UNICORNS AND HOBBITS
SUPPORT ONOMATOPOEIA

Classification—
second large
category: serious
Illustration—
first subcategory
of serious

9   The next three groups are relatively more serious. In the first of these, the driver of the car makes a clear pitch for his or her profession:
FIREMAN STILL MAKE HOUSECALLS
LOVE A NURSE
IF YOU CAN READ THIS THANK A TEACHER
ENGINEERS DO IT WITH PRECISION
IF YOU DON'T LIKE HOW WE TAKE CARE OF YOUR GARBAGE,
     WE'LL RETURN IT. (seen on the bumper of a garbage truck)

Illustration—
second
subcategory of
serious

10   In the second group of serious stickers, we find arguments that are related to marriage, sex, and the family:
ANOTHER FAMILY FOR ERA
CELEBRATE FAMILY VALUES. THIS IS FAMILY YEAR!
WE BELIEVE IN MARRIAGE
A WOMAN WITHOUT A MAN IS LIKE A FISH WITHOUT A BICYCLE
SOULS OF GREAT LIFE ARE WAITING TO BE BORN: HAVE ONE!
ABORTION NOW!!

Illustration—
third subcategory
of serious

11   The last group of serious stickers argues a political point, sometimes with an unpleasant edge of meanness or satire:
TAKE A WOLF TO LUNCH. FEED HIM AN ENVIRONMENTALIST.
SPLIT WOOD, NOT ATOMS
NUCLEAR POWER PLANTS ARE BUILT BETTER THAN JANE
     FONDA
A BUSHEL OF GRAIN FOR A BARREL OF OIL
CLEAN UP AMERICA—SHOOT A REDNECK

Process

12   In furthering our attempts to understand the bumper sticker syndrome, we tried writing a few, and in doing so learned a little about how to produce them. What you try for is a short statement that is both pointed and relevant to a recent event which most people are aware of. So first pick such an event. Next, associate it with another thing, idea, or person that is well known. Then, try to use a play on

End point

words or a pun. The readers should have "instant recognition" when they read the message, and perhaps be persuaded by the argument, serious or not. You can see the elements of the process working in this sticker: KEEP AIR CLEAN AND SEX DIRTY. (I won't reproduce any of the stickers we made up—they are too awful.)

Cause-effect

13 Why do thousands of American drivers go to the trouble to buy bumper stickers? They seem like such trivial messages to display to the world. One answer may be that they reflect the triviality of modern "media journalism." News stories on television, for example, are typically short and abbreviated, as are bumper stickers. Only one point is highlighted in both types of messages, so that the viewer gets a dramatic, but distorted idea of the complexities involved. When the President spoke in Chicago, the evening TV news account of his long speech showed him speaking only two sentences, both taken out of context. One of them was not even the full sentence as he spoke it.

Comparison
(*with other short communications*)

14 We live in an age of bumper-sticker journalism. The Letters columns in magazines and newspapers often use letters of one sentence. These deliver no more than an opinion without evidence or reasons given. Like the chopped-up TV interview and the one-sentence letter in a national magazine the bumper sticker gives us a message lacking background, context, or development. These are messages without authority or anybody standing behind them; and they are as forgettable as today's comic page. They are meant to last only a few seconds in one's consciousness and then disappear.

15 Given the way we live today, the bumper sticker probably satisfies an American need to make to a point quickly, painlessly, and—most of all—anonymously. The car involved may be identified clearly as a Ford, Chevrolet, Plymouth, etc. But when was the last time you saw a signed bumper sticker?

PRACTICE

Discussion

1. A definition should clarify, limit, and specify. Taking these requirements into account, how satisfactory and complete is the writer's definition of *bumper stickers?*

2. It was necessary for the writer to *divide* bumper stickers into two groups and then sub-classify. Do you agree with the writer's classifications, considering the thesis she wished to prove? How would another classification be more or less useful in proving her thesis?

3. How is the narrative in the introduction important to the writer's *role*? Is the narrative important for an understanding of the writer's *thesis*? What revision would you suggest for the introduction in relation to the thesis and the paper?

4. Except for the intertwining of illustration with classification, the other strategies used in this paper are discrete paragraph units (paragraphs 12–14). How is the

thesis supported by these three strategies? For example, is it important to know *how* to write a bumper sticker if you are being persuaded that they are short arguments?

5. If you were to make suggestions to this writer about revising her paper, what would you recommend? Can you think of other strategies she might have used to support her thesis?

▼ Student Essay 2

This student writer of this next essay has used a variety of strategies to support his point that how one sings the national anthem has nothing to do with patriotism. The writer has found at least five of the strategies useful. Read the essay and evaluate the effectiveness of the strategies in supporting the thesis. You may find more than one strategy employed in one paragraph, which was not always the case in "Bumper Stickers."

POP SINGERS AND THE NATIONAL ANTHEM

A

1   When I was a little kid, my Dad would take me to baseball and football games in the sports stadiums around the country—Busch in St. Louis, Tiger's in Detroit, and Soldier's Field in Chicago. I remember distinctly my first reaction to the singing of "The Star Spangled Banner." When the woman's voice came over the public address system, the men around us put down their beers and took off their hats. The children stopped jumping up and down and stood quietly. The players, all standing in a row, hats off, bright and shining in their colorful uniforms, filled me with awe. As my father put his hand over his heart. I asked. "What the heck is going on?" He shushed me and told me to stand still. It was obvious to

Thesis implied

me from the very beginning that the singing of the national anthem at a sporting event was a serious affair and had something to do with patriotism and respect.

B

2   Up until the time I got to high school, the singers who opened the game at sporting events were usually concert musicians like Beverly Sills and Robert Merrill. The national anthem is a difficult song to sing because its range is over an octave and a fifth, spanning the range of twenty notes on the scale. It takes a concert musician to sing it right—a singer who performs opera or presents recitals in places like Carnegie Hall or the Lincoln Center for the Performing Arts. Such singers go through a long, intensive training in order to sing the range of two or more octaves—or twenty-five notes. They do not usually depend upon sound systems when they perform because they are trained to sing for long periods of time, using their own volume to fill an auditorium. As a result, they can reach all the notes—top and bottom—of "The Star Spangled Banner," and with a microphone their voices can fill a stadium seating thousands of people.

3   After I got in college. I noticed a big change in the musicians who sang at athletic events. The trained concert singer was replaced in many instances with popular recording stars. Apparently, the man-

C { agers of athletic events wanted to boost their television ratings, thinking that popular names and faces would draw better than trained
opera singers.

4   José Feliciano was one of the first of the pop singers to sing the
national anthem at an athletic event. His rendition of the song was
controversial because it was different from the accurate and precise
performances of concert singers. Called undignified and unpatriotic
by some, José used a swinging style, pausing in unusual places, and
cutting out the high and low notes. Ray Charles, the blind jazz singer

D { and pianist, was also criticized because his rendition was different
from those who had customarily sung the song. But perhaps the most
controversial rendition was by the soul singer Marvin Gaye, who
sang at a famous NBA All-Star game. He used a gospel-rock synco-
pation and vocal inflection. His interpretation was called "creative"
and "soulful" by those who approved and "unpatriotic" and "disre-
spectful" by those who disapproved.

5   But does patriotism, respect, or devotion to country have anything
to do with the way a singer interprets the national anthem? Pop musicians like Marvin Gaye change the notes and give the song a different
beat because they are not trained singers. They have a limited range,
so they can't hit the top or low notes of the song as it was written.
They depend upon sound systems in the recording studios to provide

E { volume and range. In an athletic stadium, they do not have that kind
of back-up to make them sound better than they are. So they aren't
necessarily "soulful" in their rendition—they just can't sing it. Since
they have a limited musical talent, the only way they can sing the
song is to change it according to their "style." Their interpretations
have nothing to do with patriotism, loyalty, or respect.

6   So people who criticize a pop singer for interpreting the national an-

Thesis   them in an original way shouldn't assume that he loves his country less
than the trained singer or give him too much credit for being creative.
*He isn't less patriotic or devoted to his country because he can't sing
the song. He is doing all that he knows how to do*—making the national
anthem a pop song or gospel hymn so that he can reach the notes.

PRACTICE

Discussion

1. The writer of "Pop Singers and the National Anthem" uses the three *hooks*
   (*national anthem, patriotism,* and *respect* or *devoted*) in three different
   places in the paper: *implied thesis* (paragraph 1), rhetorical question
   (paragraph 5), and *thesis* (paragraph 6). How are these *hooks* related to the
   strategies employed in specific paragraphs and in the paper as a whole?

2. The writer introduces Beverly Sills, Robert Merrill, and the difficulty of
   signing the national anthem before the strategy in bracket B. Why does the
   reader need that information?

3. You will notice that many student-written papers begin the same way this one does. Why do students find this strategy useful in introductions? Discuss the writer's *stance,* and his *role* in particular. How is the writer's role established in the introduction?

4. Discuss the amount of detail and illustration in bracket C (paragraph 3). How well does the paragraph use the strategy? What advice for revision would you offer the writer about this paragraph?

5. Where in the paper is most of the proof for the thesis? What strategies have been used to present the proof? Is it adequate? If you wrote this paper, what causation would you attribute to the different renditions of the national anthem?

6. Reread the writer's conclusion. How does he prove to the reader that she is honest and unbiased?

▼ Professional Essay

"My Fat Problem and Theirs" (written by a professional writer) is a *cause and effect* essay which uses a variety of other strategies to answer the writer's question: *"Why had I equated being thin with happiness?"* The strategy of *process* is also important in this selection because the writer wants the reader to understand *how* her fat problem affected her parents' treatment of her and also her own behavior.

MY FAT PROBLEM AND THEIRS

Subject **1**   I think I'm the appropriate age to write about growing up as an *introduced:* overweight child. While I have enough perspective to look at the fat *Growing up* child who endured my first 18 years, I haven't lost the ability to re-*overweight* experience the painful emotions she felt. At any moment I could be stripped of the new confidence that two years of college have brought and could plunge backward into the sea of insecurities that almost drowned my younger self.

Contrast: **2**   The difference between us, me then and me now, is that I used *Differences* to think: "if I were thin I'd be perfect." And being perfect of course *between* meant getting male approval. I used to fantasize about being thin *fantasy and* on a seasonal basis. Every April I'd dream of a thin me by the first *reality* day of camp. I'd create elaborate and detailed scenarios of a sum-mer full of romance—I knew what color Lacoste shirt I'd be wear-ing when the boy of my dreams would confess his deeply felt love for me. But when the fateful June day arrived and the still fat me boarded the bus for camp, I moved my dreams one season ahead. I began to imagine the thin me on the first day of school. September came; nothing had changed. So I dreamed of Thanksgiving. Then of Christmas. Then spring vacation. By then I was back at camp again.

Transition: **3**   It was only after nine summers at camp and nine first days at *Thesis Implied* school that I became bored with this obsessive daydreaming and rec-

Thin is not necessarily happy

ognized its drain on me. That's when I set out to try and understand why I had equated being thin with being happy.

Contrast: *Differences between ideal weight in 1940 and now*

4   Had I been born years ago, when America worshiped a different beauty ideal, I might have been not only happy as is, but a sex object. In 1940, according to the company, the nude woman pictured on the label of the White Rock soda bottle was five feet four and weighed 140 pounds (my proportions exactly). Today's White Rock "girl" is five feet eight and weighs 118 pounds. Imagine! Forty years ago I could have appeared naked on a soft-drink bottle, while today I cannot leave my house in anything less than long wide-legged pants and a roomy, long-sleeved shirt.

Refutation of **cause-effect:** *Teasing is not a cause of unhappiness*

5   Many people blame the unhappiness of overweight people on the teasing of other children. Of course I encountered my share of jests from my classmates—such as altering my last name to "Pork-Noy." But attributing all my misery to kids' bullying just didn't explain it. Most children find ways to chide their playmates whether they are called "braceface," "foureyes," "metalmouth," or "pizzaface." The difference is that no one tells pizzaface or foureyes to do *something* to get rid of those pimples or glasses. And bracefaces can eat anything they want for dinner—and know someday their braces will be gone.

Effect *of fatness on other children's parents*

6   Others who were overweight as children have told me that it was their parents' reaction that made them feel the worst. Some parents refused to acknowledge the existence of excess weight: one woman remembers her mother yelling at a saleswoman for suggesting that she buy the "chubby" styles for her daughter. Other parents overreacted: panicked that the weight gain would increase geometrically for the rest of the child's life—and had to be stopped NOW! Looking back on my family's response, I simply wonder why everyone made such a *fuss* over my weight.

Effect *of fatness on her parents:* *(1) character flaw* *(2) diet workshop*

7   I had my share of talents, I took lessons, I was busy with a lot of activities, and yet the importance of my weight overshadowed those virtues. My fat was treated as a behavioral trait, *a character flaw.* So, along with art classes, piano lessons, Little League, and Hebrew school, came diet workshops. I started going in the fifth grade. More precisely, my mom, dad, and I went together—a team effort.

Process *of diet workshop*

8   Every Tuesday night I was taken behind a royal-blue curtain where one of the formerly fat group leaders subjected me to a battery of questions and my weekly weigh-in. I had to tell the woman if I'd cheated (and I always had). "Yes, I had an extra piece of fruit on Tuesday." I admitted, which really meant that I'd had Oreos and milk, or I ate the hamburger I was allowed on Friday and Saturday as well. (On Fridays I was allowed four ounces of broiled hamburger meat on half a bun. That was supposed to be a *treat*). This confession would explain my one-and-a-quarter-pound gain. Outside the blue curtain I was met by my parents "How'dja do?" they'd chime brightly and in unison. I had three choices: gained, lost, or stayed the same. All I ever answered was lost or stayed the same, even if I'd gained.

Process continued

9   After the weigh-in came the lecture. One I distinctly remember is the lecture on ridding oneself of the unsightly flab that forms beneath the chin when one loses weight. We were instructed to look up at the ceiling and pretend to kiss it while slowly oscillating our heads—now left, now right. There I was, 11 years old, doing exercises to renew the elasticity of the skin on my neck.

Effect of diet workshop: cheating and feeling cheated

10   Since I started that diet in the fifth grade I have been a habitual cheat. "You're really only cheating yourself," my mother would say. Maybe so, but it always felt as if I was the one being cheated. Every day my lunch box contained a sandwich on thin bread and a piece of fruit. Who wouldn't feel deprived when Cindy Goldman unpacked her bulging brown bag full of peanut butter and jelly sandwiches, Fritos, Yodels, miniature Hershey bars, and Hawaiian Punch? And on visitor's day at camp, when other kids got obscenely delightful arm-loads of Doritos, Oreos, and Twinkies, I got a grocery bag of plums, peaches, and sugarless bubble gum.

Cause-effect: Effect of mother's reprimand causes cheating

11   I perceived my mother's choice of foods for me as a reprimand. I fought back by eating whenever no one was looking. Train rides were a great opportunity to eat *M & Ms* among strangers. I also loved the afternoons when I would get home earlier than my mom and eat whatever was in the fridge—cheese and crackers, cold cereal, left-over Chinese food. Nor was I above sneaking down to the kitchen while my parents were asleep and stuffing Oreos into the pockets of my pajamas. Or holding a handful of Mallomars behind my back while poking my head in to say an innocent good-night.

Effect of cheating: secret food

12   I had perfected my indispensable trick of soundlessly opening and closing the refrigerator doors. What you do is first slide your fingers inside the rubber gasket around the door edge so that you break the suction seal and it doesn't make that telltale smack. Then pull the door open very, very slowly so that the horseradish and mustard jars on the inside of the door don't rattle. Then grab your Mallomars and close the door in the same fashion. This cheating habit has been hard to break. I still have ice cream for breakfast when I wake up earlier than everyone else. Food can be a secret pleasure.

Effect of weight on father: rage (cause) for effect of rage on her: never be thin

13   As much as I resented my mother's constant hinting, at least she tried to tiptoe around my feelings. My father, on the other hand, approached my weight problem with the sensitivity and tact of a sledge-hammer. Once he told me I looked like a horse. I could see the rage rising in him. It was weird, actually. Of all the times I'd been scolded—for being stubborn or selfish or fresh—I'd never seen that rage before. After that I vowed never to give him the satisfaction of my being thin.

Effect of overweight on father: blow to his ego

14   How could a few extra pounds have provoked such uncharacteristic behavior from an otherwise generous and gentle man? Why did *my* being overweight mean so much to *him*? *He* had never been over-weight. Is it really so important? Yes, he was telling me by the intensity of his reaction. No, I would now argue back: I think my being overweight was a blow to his ego, a blight on his otherwise aesthetically correct family.

Refutation of
cause and effect:
*thinness does not
solve all your
problems*

15   The myth that "thin is in" and that "in" is happy is used as an incentive to keep you in these diet programs. But after all that hype, thinness is anti-climatic. Your problems don't disappear with the pounds. And a better brain and love life do not suddenly appear with the new silhouette. I know this because I did go through my thin phases. But I never felt any different. I didn't feel "in."

Effect *of thinness
on others*

16   I look at myself among my friends. We're women of all shapes and sizes. Are the thinner ones happier than I? My friend Sara recently traded in 30 pounds for a five-feet-one, 105-pound frame. I asked her if she liked her new body. She said it was nice, but she'd had more bouts of depression in the year she'd been petite than ever before. Sara says thinness isn't all it's cracked up to be, and by believing her, I shed a burden much heavier than 30 pounds. I felt relieved, but also angry—at my parents, the media, and society for having misled me, and at myself for having been duped.

Narrative Thesis
stated

17   A few nights after my talk with Sara I shared this realization with my parents. Their voices quavered in congratulations and approval. Their words said, "We're glad you're happy," but the quaver betrayed their fear that I'll give up trying to control my weight and blow up like a balloon. I told them that thin doesn't mean happy and I'm happy as I am right now. I'm not certain that they believed me, but soon they will have to accept my attempt to accept my body.

Narrative Thesis
continued
Conclusion

18   I bombarded my parents will all my old resentments, angers, and fears. I reminded them of the summer before I went to college when they put me on an expensive diet. "You can go to college as a new person," my mother beamed. It didn't occur to either of us at the time that this "supportive" statement concealed a very damaging opinion. Why did I need to go as a new person? What was wrong with the *old* me? I told them that from now on my weight problem is my own and the sooner they stop worrying about it, the sooner I'd stop resenting them. My mom said that she was shocked that she had transmitted so many negative unspoken messages. I said I was shocked that she was shocked: a sensitive child feels whatever you're feeling without hearing a single word. My dad said he was sorry. So did my mom. I said it was okay. And it is okay. Things happen, so it's okay now. Okay.

—Sharon Portnoy

PRACTICE

Discussion

Reread Portnoy's essay and answers the following:

1. At what point in the essay does the author introduce the theme of insecurity/unhappiness? Cite the examples by paragraph number where she supports that theme.

2. What strategy does Portnoy use in paragraph 5 to refute the idea that teasing causes unhappiness in fat children?

3. Discuss the use of the implied thesis in paragraph 3. In what way would the paper have been different if she had stated her thesis in this paragraph, rather than in paragraph 17? What is the effect of her saying that she had "set out to try and understand why I had equated being thin with being happy"? Evaluate how effectively she learned what she set out to do.

4. What strategy does the writer use to describe her method of opening a refrigerator door? How well could you imitate her method?

5. Why does Portnoy use questions in paragraphs 14, 16 and 18? Are the questions in all three paragraphs used for the same reason?

6. In her conclusion, Portnoy describes her parents' reactions to the resentment she felt toward them in the in the past. Discuss the honesty and fairness (ethical proof) she displays in her responses to the problem.

Description

▼ Description

When you describe a thing, you explain its qualities, nature, or appearance. The word *describe* comes from the Latin *describere* ("to copy" or "to sketch"), which implies that the thing described has a material existence. Customarily, the words *describe* and *description* have been used to refer to material things, although of course one may describe abstractions such as states of mind or moral attributes.

You will find description useful in either single paragraphs or full papers. It is often necessary when you want to talk about a person or place; but description can be used to support your point in any kind of writing.

■■■ Sensory Images

Good descriptions often appeal to one or more of the five senses. The writer tries to make the reader see, hear, feel, smell, or taste the experience being described. These word pictures or sensory images help the reader experience vicariously what the writer has felt. They also help to create the mood that the writer wishes to achieve.

Descriptions usually support a larger purpose. Not only must you be an astute and careful observer, but you also need to relate your observations to a point or a descriptive purpose. Notice how Anaïs Nin, through her description of sights and smells in Fez, Morocco, makes the point about the importance of women's eyes.

Sight   Colors seep into your consciousness as never before: a sky-blue jellaba with a black face veil, a pearl-grey jellaba with a yellow veil, a black jellaba with a red veil, a shocking-pink jellaba with a purple veil. The clothes conceal the wearers' figures so that they remain elusive, with all the intensity and expression concentrated in the eyes.

Point:
Importance of eyes
The eyes speak for the body, the self, for the age, conveying innumerable messages from their deep and rich existence.

Smell
After color and the graceful sway of robes, the flares, the stance, the swing of loose clothes, come the odors. One stand is devoted to sandalwood from Indonesia and the Philippines. It lies in huge round baskets and is sold by weight, for it is a precious luxury wood for burning as incense. The walls of the cubicle are lined with small bottles containing the essence of flowers—jasmine, rose, honeysuckle, and the rose water that is used to perfume guests. In the same baskets lie the henna leaves that the women distill and use on their hands and

Importance
of eyes
feet. For the affluent, the henna comes in liquid form. And there is, too, the famous *kohl*, the dust from antimony that gives the women such a soft, iridescent, smoky radiance around their eyes.

Behind every good description there is a point being made: the sunset is *beautiful,* the earthquake was *frightening,* the birth of a baby is *miraculous,* the political ideas of Theodore Roosevelt were *pragmatic.* Consider the point in the passage below, which describes a bicycle-truck accident.

The sounds of traffic, three lanes south, three lanes north. I was in the left lane on my mountain bike, the Stumpjumper, my husband on his Stumpie in the right lane crossing with the green light. The red flag he always used on his bike danced in the late afternoon sunlight.

He did not wait for the light to change, but turned left and moved forward across the intersection against the light. Had he misread the signal?

I watched, my throat closing, as the traffic whizzed toward him. He made it across two lanes. Then a large pickup blocked my view and he disappeared, only his red flag showing above the pickup roof.

From the pickup came the sound of brakes; a loud horn went off behind me (what was he honking back there for?); and my husband's body rose over the roof of the pickup. It paused in the air, legs and arms relaxed in the gesture of someone sleeping. The truck slewed sidewise. My husband came slowly down in the air and disappeared behind the pickup again.

I braked and stepped off my bike before it stopped, a movement which should have been impossible. Something dribbled down my chin, and I wiped at it. My mouth was bleeding where I had bitten my tongue. I ran forward and around the pickup. My husband was spread carefully out on the pavement, as if he were a doll arranged by a three-year-old girl humming to herself. I fell on my knees on the concrete and cradled his head so he could not move it in case his back was broken.

I could feel nothing. In me, I mean. I touched the rough break in his bicycle helmet, but the jagged plastic made no impression on my fingertips.

Someone knelt by me and said, "You're bleeding."

I looked down. My mouth was dripping blood on my husband's face.

Later, in the ambulance, my husband started to talk quietly to himself. A small dead pain started to grow in my stomach.

What I remember from the accident was more than my husband's misreading of the traffic signal or the horror of the accident that followed. It was also—for a terrible quarter of an hour—the complete cessation of all feeling in my body.

—Marnie Guth

The point behind the description is that Marnie Guth was so affected by seeing her husband get hit by a truck that her body's physical sensations shut down. For a time, her "self" refused to function except automatically (she kept his head from moving, for example).

■■■ Point of View

Guth wrote her description some time after the accident, a fact which partly controls her point of view. *Point of view* is the angle—psychological or physical (or both)—from which a writer views a subject. To re-create the scene, Guth blends the physical and psychological points of view. You (the reader) see the events as she saw them. The husband is struck by the pickup, but this contact cannot be seen from her physical view-point, and therefore cannot be shown. Guth and the reader see only the body rising in slow motion and then falling and disappearing.

All the physical details are rigorously limited to what Marnie Guth could see (1) from her bicycle, and (2) from her perspective as she ran around the pickup.

The climax of the passage comes as pain enters her body in the ambulance. Although she does not say so, Guth had gone into shock. All her descriptive details fulfill a double purpose: to show the horror of the accident itself, and her psychological reaction to it at the time.

PRACTICE

Discussion

Discuss the point of view, use of details, and sensory images in the following description of a boy's father:

1   My father's world was monstrous. He knew places like Corsicana, Waxahachie, Nacogdoches, Wichita Falls, Monahans. His world was more than half the size of Texas. He would come home and tell us about it and expand our boundaries. He knew what the road looked like between Sonora and Eldorado, between Borger and Pampa. He loved roads and the way they looked. We would be driving to Grandma Hale's farm and come to a place that wasn't characteristic of our immediate world and he would say, "This looks like the road between Cuero and Yoakum."

2   He brought home the very best kind of gifts. A puppy in a shoe box. A chicken with a bad leg. A 25-pound sack of peanut brittle. Once he brought two milk goats. He had traded the old Ford for a smoking Chevy with the door wired shut on the driver's side. I can see him turning in off the road, grinning behind the cracked windshield, those two goats riding on the back seat with their heads poked out the windows.

3   Another time he brought an entire stalk of bananas. I wrote a theme about it for school. He brought home the first loaf of sliced bread our neighborhood ever saw. Bread, cooked in a bakery 150 miles away and sliced on a machine, and every slice just perfect. People came from two streets over, to see and taste. It was sure fine having a hero for a father.

4   The sweetest times of my growing up came when he'd take me with him on the road, beyond my world, to the edges of his own. We'd go smoking along at 35 miles an hour.

He'd push the brim of his hat up in front, and he'd brace the wheel between his thin old knees and steer that way. He'd take out his harmonica and play "Red River Valley" and "Coming Around the Mountain," and "Springtime in the Rockies." I am so grateful now for those days, inside my father's world.

—Leon Hale, "My Father's World"

■■■ *Writing*

1. Observe someone (on a bus, train, elevator, or in a classroom) engaged in some activity, unaware of being watched. Make eye contact and keep it for as long as possible. Write a short description of the person's reaction. For example, here is a description of a child:

   One day, as my bus swerved around a corner, and I was clinging tightly to the edge of my seat to keep from sliding onto the floor, I noticed across from me a young black girl, no more than ten years old. She was singing. Her white hat, perched on her braided hair, bobbed up and down, and her scuffed brown boots tapped on the floor, keeping time to her song. She had a soft, high voice, but she didn't stay in tune. My eyes met hers, and I smiled. Her mouth snapped shut and she quit singing. Her brown eyes turned icy cold, then she slowly and deliberately turned her head to look out the window, her mouth clamped tightly shut for the rest of the ride home.

2. Visit one of the following places. Spend some time there observing the people and taking notes. Try to record the way the place smells and feels; brainstorm for a possible hook. Then, using your notes, write a description. Before you begin to write, decide on the particular point you intend to make.

   a. A college cafeteria at lunchtime

   b. A clothing store that caters to the well-to-do

   c. A warehouse clothing outlet or an army surplus store

   d. A boutique

   e. A beauty salon

▼ Suggestions for Writing Description

1. Limit the focus of your description in order to make a single point.

2. Keep a consistent *point of view.*

3. Use sensory images when relevant and suitable.

4. *Show* with vivid language and specific details.

▼ Writing and Revising Description (An Example)

When Jan set out to describe her grandmother, she had a point that she wanted to make: *Even though my grandmother was stiff, formal, and countrified, I respect her for giving me a sense of pride in my heritage.* However, in her first jottings taken from notes in her journal, Jan has only the bare bones of a paper.

GRANDMA

1   I remember Grandma all right—but not really as a preferred member of the family. She was Polish and a very rigid person, always preferring the harsh idea or the harsh saying to the warm grandmotherly one.

2   Actually, I didn't know her very well, although I can remember that she always seemed the same: rather stiff, formal, countrified. It seems odd that she was both countrified and formal, but that is the way she appeared to me. She only understood me if I talked loud to her, which meant that I always talked slowly, pronouncing each word carefully in a formal way.

3   The only time I can remember when she seemed human and warm was the time when she came down to her basement with a jug full of alcoholic beverage. We had been hauling firewood and stacking it in the basement, and she said that since we had been working as hard as men we could drink like men. The four of us (my cousins and my sister, and I) drank down the foul stuff and really enjoyed it, just because Grandma had finally noticed us.

4   When Grandma died, I did not feel anything. I stood by her grave and tried to cry. But the tears would not come. I have never understood why. I respected her but could not grieve for her.

As Jan rereads her journal, she is struck by her use of particular terms to describe her Grandma: *rigid, countrified, formal,* and *stiff.* She also notes that she has given no examples to support those descriptive terms. She searches her memory to find specifics in the form of anecdotes, sensory details, and examples. She remembers:

> How Grandma made chicken soup
>
> How she looked in her wedding picture
>
> How she accepted gifts
>
> How her house smelled
>
> How she gave us liquor
>
> How her funeral left us feeling, etc.

With these and other details, Jan fleshes out her paper. After several drafts, the paper supports her main point.

GRANDMA (REVISED)

1   Some people remember deathdays as naturally as others remember birthdays. Without hesitation my father can recall the exact month, day, and year she died—but I can't. It was June, I think, about six or seven years ago and I was at work with my dad. I didn't

cry because I didn't really know her. I had to tell my father that she died. "She" was his mother, but he didn't cry either.

2   I referred to her as "Grandma," not using more affectionate names like "Gram," "Granny," or "Grams." Grandma was a rigid, aloof elf of a woman who was foreign by birth and by nature. She spoke Polish to my dad. She called my mom Re VeRand for undeterminable reasons. She preferred the outhouse to the upstairs bathroom. And when she made chicken soup she left both chicken feet adrift in the pot—claws and all. She rarely baked bread; she never baked cookies. Her house wasn't full of the sweet, warm smells that accompany such activities. It smelled of coal dust and time. Much to my dismay our biannual family vacations inevitably led to backwoods Pennsylvania and that idiosyncratic immigrant.

3   I didn't really know her as a person, much less as a grandmother. In my entire sixteen years of life she had never taken me on a picnic, or told me a bedtime story, or even tucked me into bed. She never initiated conversation and, on the rare occasions I addressed her, I had to shout. To this day I don't know if she was deaf, or if I just thought she understood shouted English better than spoken English.

4   Looking back, I can remember her wedding picture on top of the china cabinet in her dining room. She wasn't smiling—her arms were akimbo and her fists were clenched. A look of grim determination overpowered any bridely radiance she might have possessed. Surprisingly, she never changed. I have always envisioned grandmothers as being silver-haired ladies with gentle voices, adoring eyes, and eager smiles. My grandmother didn't possess any of those qualities—in her pictures or in person.

5   It isn't hard to recall the many incidents that helped me formulate and later strengthen my opinion of Grandma. When I was seven my family spent Christmas with her. I was just learning to crochet, and my first project was a present for her. I remember spending months working on that ugly aquamarine potholder—crocheting, unraveling, starting over, until I was satisfied that it was perfect. I was bursting with pride when I finally finished it. I somehow thought she would appreciate all the work that went into that gift and love me for it, as a grandma should. I don't remember being hugged or thanked. I don't even remember seeing it around the kitchen, ever. I never gave her another gift, and my father never dragged our family back to Pennsylvania for Christmas again.

6   Several years later, when I was fourteen, my two cousins, my sister, and I spent an entire afternoon hauling firewood and stacking it in Grandma's basement. We had wanted to go shopping in Johnstown, but Grandma hadn't, so no one went anywhere. Grudgingly we stayed home to work instead. That evening Grandma appeared with a dusty old jar filled with a powerful-looking concoction. She declared that if we could work like men we could drink like men too. I think that was a peace offering, because Grandma catered to her sons and grandsons while virtually ignoring her daughters and grand-daughters.

7   Now, at twenty-three, I can remember standing under the canopy at her funeral and honestly trying to cry, to feel some sort of loss. I am one of the few grandchildren that bear the family name and I thought that should have made us closer. I didn't feel anything. Time, experience, and knowledge have made me realize that she had reasons for being different and aloof. She had a hard life: thirteen children, an alcoholic husband, the depression, and war—she had proven that she was a survivor, and that she wasn't obligated to live up to my standards or anyone else's. She may not have fit my definition of what a grandmother should be, but I had no right to place demands on her. She didn't owe me anything. No matter, when I think of her now I'm proud of my heritage. I gladly carry her name. Most importantly, I'm grateful for the priceless gifts she left me . . . a stubborn Polish pride in the family name and the will to be a survivor too.

PRACTICE

Discussion

Read the final version of "Grandma", and answer these discussion questions:

a. Why does the writer spend so much time describing the negative or bad qualities of her grandmother?

b. Discuss the effectiveness of using the past to discuss the present.

c. Discuss the writer's use of sensory images.

d. What is the writer's point of view?

e. The writer tells us that she now understands why her grandma was not typical. Discuss her realization in light of her ethical proof.

Mark Twain

THE CAT

Samuel Langhorne Clemens (1835–1910) took his pen name, Mark Twain, from the term for "safe water" used on Mississippi riverboats. Born in Hannibal, Missouri, along the Mississippi River, Twain traveled around the country and, later, the world as a journalist and lecturer. Among his many famous novels and stories are Tom Sawyer *(1876) and the classic American novel* Huckleberry Finn *(1885). Twain is considered the master American humorist, and he used his humor for the purpose of social criticism that good-naturedly prodded Americans from their parochialism, pettiness, and greed. Humor, a keen eye for detail, and a touch of irony are apparent in his description of a cat, taken from* The Mysterious Stranger *(1906). While* The Mysterious Stranger *as a whole reflects the gloomy bitterness of Twain's later years, his perspective on the cat shows that he had not entirely lost his famous sense of humor, at least not where an honest, straightforward cat with incredible aplomb was concerned.*

1   The cat sat down. Still looking at us in that disconcerting way, she tilted her head first to one side and then the other, inquiringly and cogitatively, the way a cat does when she has struck the unexpected and can't quite make out what she had better do about it. Next she washed one side of her face, making such an awkward and unscientific job of it that almost anybody would have seen that she was either out of practice or didn't know how. She stopped with the one side, and looked bored, and as if she had only been doing it to put in the time, and wished she could think of something else to do to put in some more time. She sat a while, blinking drowsily, then she hit an idea, and looked as if she wondered she hadn't thought of it earlier. She got up and went visiting around among the furniture and belongings, sniffing at each and every article, and elaborately examining it. If it was a chair, she examined it all around, then

jumped up in it and sniffed all over its seat and its back; if it was any other thing she could examine all around, she examined it all around; if it was a chest and there was room for her between it and the wall, she crowded herself in behind there and gave it a thorough overhauling; if it was a tall thing, like a washstand, she would stand on her hind toes and stretch up as high as she could, and reach across and paw at the toilet things and try to rake them to where she could smell them; if it was the cupboard, she stood on her toes and reached up and pawed the knob; if it was the table she would squat, and measure the distance, and make a leap, and land in the wrong place, owing to newness to the business; and, part of her going too far and sliding over the edge, she would scramble, and claw at things desperately, and save herself and make good; then she would smell everything on the table, and archly and daintily paw everything around that was movable, and finally paw something off, and skip cheerfully down and paw it some more, throwing herself into the prettiest attitudes, rising on her hind feet and curving her front paws and flirting her head this way and that and glancing down cunningly at the object, then pouncing on it and spatting it half the length of the room, and chasing it up and spatting it again, and again, and racing after it and fetching it another smack—and so on and so on; and suddenly she would tire of it and try to find some way to get to the top of the cupboard or the wardrobe, and if she couldn't she would look troubled and disappointed; and toward the last, when you could see she was getting her bearings well lodged in her head and was satisfied with the place and the arrangements, she relaxed her intensities, and got to purring a little to herself, and praisefully waving her tail between inspections—and at last she was done—done, and everything satisfactory and to her taste.

2   Being fond of cats, and acquainted with their ways, if I had been a stranger and a person had told me that this cat had spent half an hour in that room before, but hadn't happened to think to examine it until now, I should have been able to say with conviction, "Keep an eye on her, that's no orthodox cat, she's an imitation, there's a flaw in her make-up, you'll find she's born out of wedlock or some other arrested-development accident has happened, she's no true Christian cat, if I know the signs."

3   She couldn't think of anything further to do, now, so she thought she would wash the other side of her face, but she couldn't remember which one it was, so she gave it up, and sat down and went to nodding and blinking.

PRACTICE

Discussion

1. Has the cat in the description ever been in the room before? How can you tell?

2. What senses does the cat use to get her bearings? What senses does the narrator use to observe her observations?

3. What is the purpose of the second to last paragraph? Would you have considered cutting it from a final draft?

4. What frame does Twain place around his picture, that is, what scene both opens and closes his piece?

5. List the verbs that Twain uses to describe the cat's actions. What does the length and variety of the list tell you about Twain's effort? How does he use adverbs? participles?

6. Study the sentence that begins, "If it was a chair . . . " Is it outrageous or effective? Explain.

7. How does the word "if" appear and function in the piece?

8. Mark Twain was once a riverboat pilot, and the vocabulary of the trade stuck with him for useful assignments to later writings. Where can you find "river talk" in his description of the cat? Why is it especially appropriate to her?

Vocabulary

disconcerting	overhauling	spatting
cogitatively	archly	orthodox
elaborately	cunningly	arrested-development

Writing

1. Observe a cat or other animal in action for about fifteen minutes and describe in careful detail its movements. Like Twain, try to figure out what it may be thinking.

2. Describe the same scene that Twain describes but from the point of view of the cat.

3. Find a room where something is happening. Close your eyes and listen carefully for the sounds of that activity. By describing the progression of sounds, try to create a picture of the room for your reader.

Carole Treasure

THE MIDNIGHT SHIFT DOES MURDER SLEEP

In a letter dated October 17, 1990, Carole Treasure wrote us: "I was born 48 years ago today, in Cumberland, Maryland. I have been variously, public health sanitarian, insurance salesperson, and power plant operator. On the side, I run a farm, raise horses and cattle, read a lot, and write a little. I have one son, who has turned out to be my most successful project so far. I write a column for the local Mensa publication, and am trying to figure out how to become gainfully employed as a writer. So far, I'm still working at the coal-fired power station,

Fort Martin, on the Monongahela River, near Morgantown, West Virginia. Still working swing shift." And the swing shift, as Ms. Treasure tells us in her essay, causes some problems for human beings.

1   Imagine you are an owl: a nice, middle-class barn owl. You raise 3.2 owlets, commute to the meadow, and have mousie-o's for breakfast.

2   One day, one of the farmer's kids, mistaking you for a football, grabs you off your perch, heads out to the yard, and makes a long forward pass.

3   You are stunned. Your beak is wide in soundless terror, and you are too shocked even to spread your wings. You plummet into the waiting hands of the receiver, who is immediately tackled by every sibling in sight, and you are on the bottom.

4   Welcome to the world of overnight shift. That's about what it feels like.

5   On the midnight shift, you are forever picking your metabolism up by the scruff of its neck, giving it a good shake and letting it down on a new track. It shudders groggily, and staggers off. Who on earth would want to do that, one wonders? Hardly anyone. But those who must include hospital care-givers, police, firefighters, utilities operators, anyone whose services are round-the-clock.

6   One out of four workers is enmeshed in this schedule, and its effects are all-pervasive.

7   Would you like to attend academic courses? Count on missing at least one out of three meetings. It will probably affect your grade. Join an organization? Don't expect to participate much. You'll either be at work or sleeping to get ready to go to work. The odds of getting child care that meets your schedule approximate those of walking to the moon. You may very likely have to trade shifts or take vacation to see your kid off to a prom, or play important games, or participate in other functions.

8   Would you like to sit on a school board, run for local office, run a small business on the side? Remotely possible, if you're very motivated and have good help. Don't buy season tickets to anything unless you have someone who wants to attend a free game or symphony. Get an answering machine. Even if you hate them, you will learn a grudging affection for it, not unlike the smiling regard of a medieval castle dweller for his moat.

9   Would you like to guess what we talk about on the midnight shift? We discuss sleep, with the intensity the starving reserve for food. We talk of sleep, its length and qualities, the way gourmets discuss wine. There is Shakespearean sleep, knitting up its raveled sleeve of care; Montaignesque sleep, sleeping wake and waking sleep; but mostly it is Frostian sleep, deferred to miles and promises.

10   There are good days for sleeping and bad days. A good day is cold and rainy, slate-gray and dull. A bad day is sparkling and clear, a first warm day of spring, a multicolored day in fall, enticing and seductive to activity. Misery is lying there, desperate to sleep, exhausted and blank, summoning an elusive wraith. Mantras, prayers, multiplication tables, envisioning lower curtains, encroaching numbness, sinking . . . 10 past, half-past, quarter'til . . . writhing like a lovesick cat, seeking a more comfortable position, the position that with luck will grant sleep. Always there is the haunting knowledge that, if the day was bad, the night will be worse.

11   And it is. A blink erases a corner of white flirting peripherally in my sight. Is this a ghost, a phantom? No, just a sheet, a 200-count percale, sleek and silky, beckoning me to enter. My mind sighs with desire and begins to conjure up a pillow to cradle my head.

My spine protests the vertical, each vertebra urging recline. I think of you out there, mindlessly snug under your electric blanket, coolly inert behind your air conditioner.

12   You take us so for granted, you blessed with a nine-to-five, Monday-to-Friday job. Of course, if you are rushed to the hospital at four in the morning, staff will care for you. If you hear a prowler, the police will come. Have the urge for a late-night snack? Somewhere there's an all-nighter.

13   We get paid a few cents more on the hour for the midnight shift. We pay, in turn, with higher rates of divorce, strokes and heart attacks, shortened life spans. Our spouses pay, our children pay.

14   Perhaps companies could declare a shorter work-week the norm for overnight workers or concede some more vacation. Society as a whole, benefits from our discomfort. Remember Three Mile Island? Happened on the midnight shift. And Chernobyl? Also on the midnight shift.

15   It's called burning out the midnight owl—after a while, you don't give a hoot about anything.

PRACTICE

Discussion

1. Treasure's title does two things for the reader. What are they?

2. The author's use of *point of view* is very important. Explain.

3. Explain the *technique* and *content* of the introduction and conclusion (paragraphs 1–4, 15). Do you find any weakness in the introduction and conclusion?

4. How do you suppose Treasure would justify the "wildness" of some of her metaphors? Do the metaphors have anything in common?

5. Many good descriptions strive for a single overriding effect. Discuss Treasure's description in light of this statement.

6. Where is the argument of action in the author's description? Why didn't the author build it up more?

7. How does the author use repetition to build her description?

8. Treasure describes the events and activities that she misses because she works the overnight shift. Discuss the effect of these descriptions on her ethical proof.

Vocabulary

mousie-o	enmeshed	wraith
sibling	medieval	mantra
metabolism	Montaignesque	

Writing

1. Write a description of one of your activities (past or present). Use Treasure's technique of exaggeration and hallucinatory metaphor.

2. Pick a comic strip that uses some or all of Treasure's technique of description in telling a story. Explain how the creator of the strip creates his or her effects.

3. Consider this thesis: "Life's too short to dance with ugly men/women." Write a description of why this is true—or not true.

The New Yorker
MY FATHER

Every week The New Yorker *magazine opens with "The Talk of the Town," a collection of short essays on a variety of topics and in a variety of modes and moods. These essays are written by current* New Yorker *staff writers and occasionally by staff writers* emeriti, *all of whom possess the qualities of writing upheld by the magazine's editors for more than fifty years: clarity, accuracy, discipline, and style. No individual credit is given these writers, although veteran* New Yorker *readers can easily identify essays penned by Anthony Hiss, Roger Angell, or others of their favorites. The essay printed here from the first issue in 1983 was written, according to a brief editorial note, by "a young woman." That it is loaded with specific details is soon obvious, but note also the implied but important generalities which dictate these details.*

1   The carpenter is at my house replacing the frames and glass panes of some windows. She (it is a woman, a round, fair woman who looks more like a cook than like a carpenter, but she is a good carpenter, as I soon see) has around her strips of wood, panes of glass, a glass cutter, a large portable electric saw, nails, hammers, and something called a caulk gun. She measures, she saws, she cuts, she sighs: it is a much more complicated job than she at first thought, the house being a very old and crooked house. The work is taking place in a bedroom, and I sit on the edge of a bed all the time, watching her. There are many things for me to do around the house; I should also go out and run some errands. But I cannot leave the carpenter's presence. Perhaps I will be able to assist in some way; perhaps she will say something to me.

2   My father was a carpenter, and a cabinetmaker, too. In the world (and it was a small world: a hundred and eight square miles, a population of sixty thousand, no deep-water harbor, so large ships had to anchor way offshore), my father was the second-best carpen-

ter and cabinetmaker. The best carpenter was Mr. Walters, to whom my father had been apprenticed as a boy and for whom he had worked when he was a young man. Mr. Walters had been dead for a long time, even before I was born, but he was still the best carpenter and cabinet maker. My father was so devoted to this man that he did everything just the way Mr. Walters would have done it. If, for instance, in 1955 you asked my father to build you a house and make you some simple chair to sit on in it, he would build you a house and make you a chair exactly like the house and the chair Mr. Walters would have built in 1915.

3   My father left our house for work every weekday morning at seven o'clock, by the striking of the Anglican church bell. If it was his first day on a new job, one of his apprentices would come by a little before seven o'clock to pick up my father's toolbox. If it was one of the older apprentices, he could walk along with my father, and they might talk. If it was one of the younger boys, he would have to walk a few steps behind. At around four o'clock in the afternoon, my father returned home. If he saw me then, he would say, "Well, we got everything in place today." And I would say, in reply, "Oh, sir, that's very good." After that, he would disappear into his shop, where he made furniture.

4   In my father's shop, everything was some shade of brown. First, there was the color of his skin; and he wore khaki trousers and khaki shirts, brown shoes, and a brown felt hat. He smoked cigarettes (Lucky Strikes) one after another, and he smoked so much that the thumb and the index and middle fingers of his right hand were stained brown. His hands were stained another shade of brown from handling stained wood, wood oils, and glues. Everything was brown, that is, except the red, flat carpenter's pencil (such an unusual, distinctive shape for a pencil, I thought, and I was sadly disappointed when I discovered that it was not a good writing pencil) that he carried perched always behind his right ear. Sometimes when I went to watch him work, he would tell me little things about himself when he was a young man. He would talk about himself as if he were someone he used to know very well, someone he thought really an admirable person, someone he would like very much. Mostly, they were stories about himself as a cricketer. He never told me that he was good at playing cricket; I already knew that.

5   My father made very beautiful furniture. Everybody said so—especially my mother, who would then point out that unfortunately none of this furniture was in our own house. I think almost every time she saw my father make something she would say to him that it would be nice to have one like that, and he would then promise to make another one, for her specially. But he never did. Finally, one day, he told her that the reason he was reluctant to make us up lots of furniture was that the furniture in Mrs. Walters' house (the widow of the man to whom he had been apprenticed) was really his: that he had made it up for himself when he was a very young man; that he had lent it to Mrs. Walters after her husband died and she had moved into a smaller house, the house she still lived in; that he would ask for it back one day; and that he would ask her for it soon. He never, of course, asked for the furniture—I don't think he could bring himself to. My mother could not believe that we were never to have that beautiful furniture; that at Christmastime, when our friends stopped by to have a glass of rum, if too many of them came by at once some of them would always have to sit on the floor. My father would visit Mrs. Walters quite often, and every once in a while my mother would go along with him. Afterward, she would always be furious that she had had to leave what she began calling "my furniture" behind, and she would have a big row with herself, for

my father never quarrelled with anyone—not even his wife. Once, my father took me with him on one of the visits. I got a good look at the furniture, and I began to understand my mother's point of view. There was a dining table with six matching cane-bottomed chairs (my father did all his own caning); there was a little round table the edge of which was scalloped; there was a table with fancy decorative carvings on its sides and, above it, a mirror in a frame with decorative carvings that matched the ones on the table; and there was a sofa, a cabinet with delicate woodworking on the glass front, and two Morris chairs. (At the time, I did not know—nor, for that matter, do I think anyone else knew—that there was someone named Morris who had made chairs of which these two were replicas.) We had nothing like any of this in our house.

6   Once, my father got sick, and the doctor said that it was his heart, and gave him some medicine and told him to stay home and rest. My mother, looking up heart diseases in one of her numerous medical books, said that the sickness was from all the cigarettes he smoked. At the same time, I took sick with a case of hookworm, and my mother, looking up hookworm in one of her numerous medical books, said that it was because I had walked around barefoot behind her back, and it was true that I did that. (I was disappointed when it was discovered that I had hookworm, and not beriberi. I would have liked to say to my friends when they asked why I wasn't in school, "Oh I have beriberi.") Since my father couldn't go to work and I couldn't go to school, we spent all day together. In the mornings, I would go and lie with him in my parents' bed. We would lie on our backs, our hands clasped behind our necks (me imitating him), and our feet up on the windowsill in the sun. We would lie there without saying a word to each other, the only sound being *pttt, pttt* from my father as he forced small pieces of tobacco from his mouth. He continued to smoke, though not as much as before. At midmorning, my mother would come in to look at us. As soon as she came into the room, she would always ask us to take our feet off the windowsill, and we would do it right away, but as soon as she left we would put them back. When she came, she would bring with her little things to eat. Sometimes it was barley water and a special porridge, made from seaweed; sometimes it was a beaten egg-yolks-and-milk drink, sweetened with powdered sugar; sometimes it was a custard of some kind. Whatever it was, she would say that it would help to build us up. Before she left, she would kiss us on our foreheads and say that we were her two invalids, the big one and the little one. In the afternoons, after our lunch, my father and I would go off to look for a wild elderberry bush and pick elderberries. He was sure that a draught prepared from the elderberries would make his heart get better faster than the medicine the doctor had prescribed. In fact, I think he took the medicine the doctor gave him only because he thought my mother might perhaps die herself if he didn't. After we had picked the elderberries, we would go and sit in the Botanical Gardens under a rubber tree. Then he would tell me stories about his own father. He had not known his father very well at all, since his father was always going off somewhere—usually somewhere in South America—to work, but he never said anything that showed he found his father at fault. Once, he said, his father had taken a boat to Panama to build the Panama Canal. The boat got caught in a storm and sank. His father was in the sea for eleven days, just barely hanging on to a raft. He was rescued by a passing ship, which took him on to Panama, where he built the Panama Canal. For a long time, I thought that my father's father had built the Panama Canal single-handed except perhaps with the help of one or two people, the way my father himself built things single-handed except with the help of one or two people.

PRACTICE

Discussion

1. What is the point of the opening paragraph? Why is it significant that the carpenter is female? What is significant in the narrator's staying to help or listen?

2. The narrator obviously admires her father. How would you characterize her feelings for her mother? How would you characterize her parents' feelings for each other? In what way do these feelings contribute to our confidence in the writer?

3. Describe the community in which the narrator grew up. What values are apparent among the people of the community?

4. Draw up a list of the father's characteristics. Opposite that list make two columns, one for direct statements and another for indirect statements, then note in the appropriate columns the direct statements or indirect details that communicate the characteristics. What does your completed chart tell you about the author's descriptive method?

5. How does the author appeal to different senses? Which senses are neglected? What details can you suggest for appealing to those senses?

6. If you were the editor of this essay, would you suggest cutting the opening paragraph and/or the final part about the grandfather? Defend your editorial suggestion.

7. Is the author wise in using so many parenthetical remarks? Try your hand at cutting the more unrelated ones and rewriting without parentheses the more necessary ones. Are you pleased with the result? Explain.

8. One usually thinks of description as relying on straightforward facts, but this descriptive essay uses many symbols effectively. What larger ideas are represented by the carpenter's pencil, Mrs. Walter's furniture, the elderberries, and the Panama Canal? What other symbols can you find in the essay? What ideas do they represent? How do they contribute to the author's ethical proof?

Vocabulary

caulk	cricket	Morris chairs
Anglican	row	beriberi
khaki	caning	botanical

Writing

1. Write an essay describing your father or mother. Try to show that parent's connection to you and, if possible, to his (or her) father or mother.

2. Describe someone you know at rest; then describe that person in action; finally, describe that person interacting with someone else. Now try combining all three descriptions into a single essay.

3. Choose a concept that you value (for example, *honesty*) and a person who represents that concept to you. Write an essay about the concept without once referring to it. Rely entirely on the description of the person to communicate what you value.

CHAPTER *12*

Narration

▼ Narration

A *narrative* is an account of an incident, or series of closely related incidents, that makes or illustrates a specific point. Since a narrative is a story, a writer can use narration when it is important for the reader to know "what happened." When writing a narrative, you need to ask yourself two questions: (1) Is the narrative relevant to my purpose? (2) Assuming that it is relevant, how can I tell it effectively? The first question you have to answer for yourself, as circumstances arise. To the second question we can suggest some partial answers.

In order to be effective, a narrative must get smoothly and quickly to its point and make that point dramatically. A narrative that dawdles along, introducing unnecessary people and irrelevant detail, is usually a failure. The reader will skip over it to get to something else. In writing vivid and convincing narratives, you should know how to compress certain details and expand others in order to give shape and emphasis to the incident you are relating. Here is how one writer uses narrative to emphasize the general ideas he is conveying:

Compressed description and historical account

From birth, the Fijians are in and out of the jungle. They understand the tangled greenery that covers the South Pacific Islands the way a New Yorker understands Times Square. Their senses are sharper than the white man's and their strength and endurance are greater. There is very little left for them to learn about the jungle. Certainly the

Story

news, a year or so ago, that they were to be "trained for jungle fighting" by the Allies must have struck them as comical, though none of them ever said so. In fact, I was recently told by a New Zealand captain stationed at the Fiji camp on Bougainville that the men there had been unfailingly deferential and kind to their white tutors. They are a

people with an extraordinary sense of humor, but they have an almost
pathological aversion to hurting the feelings of a friend. However, at
the end of their training, which took place in the Fijis, they allowed
their sense of humor a fairly free hand. The company of white soldiers who had trained them arranged to fight a mock battle with them
in the bush. After dark, each side was to try to penetrate as far as possible into the other's lines. The main idea was to see how well the
new Fiji scouts had learned their lessons. It turned out that they had

Climax   learned them pretty well. During the night some of the white scouts
worked thirty or forty feet into the Fiji lines, and figured they had the
battle won, since they hadn't caught any Fijians behind *their* lines.
When they came to check up at daylight, it developed that most of the
Fijians had apparently spent the night in the white headquarters. They
had chalked huge crosses on the tents and the furniture and had left
one of the most distinct crosses on the seat of the commanding officer's trousers, which he had thrown over a chair around 4:00 a.m.

—Robert Lewis Taylor, "The Nicest Fellows You Ever Met"*

The climax of the story nicely points up the ideas presented in the first part of the
passage: that Fijians are at home in the jungle and that they have a sense of humor.

Sometimes, for reasons of space or economy of effect, you may wish to compress
many details. Edward Iwata compresses years of life into just a few paragraphs, but the
narrative he calls "Barbed-Wire Memories" is hard to forget.

1   My parents rarely spoke about it, and I rarely asked them to.
2   Manzanar has emerged in recent years as a symbol of racial oppression for many
Asian Americans, but it remained a painful subject in my family home. For my parents,
the very word "Manzanar" calls up shameful memories of a four-year period of their
lives when their citizenship and patriotism, their simple belief in the unalienable
goodness of America, meant nothing amid the flood of wartime racism. I never asked
them about it in any detail because a fearful part of me had refused to believe that my
parents had been imprisoned by their own country. Their only crime was their color of
skin and slant of eye.
3   It was as if too long a glimpse into their tragic past would shatter the rules of our
relationship, a relationship peculiar to Japanese people that relies heavily on unspoken
but deeply understood values, emotions, and expectations. My knowledge of their stay in
Manzanar was scant, a hazy mix of childhood tales and harmless anecdotes they told with
a smile whenever their curious kids asked about "that camp in the desert."
4   Until recently, I did not know that my mother and father had met and fallen in love
while behind barbed wire at Manzanar. I did not know that my grandmother cried daily
the first two weeks in camp, hoping somehow that the tears would wash away the
injustice of it all. I did not know that my mother's youngest brother, who later died in
the Korean War, dreamed of fighting for the United States while he grew up as a little
boy in Manzanar.
5   I learned all of this in what seems the most absurd, impersonal manner: while
interviewing my parents for a newspaper story. In my role as reporter, I was able for

the first time to ask them about their concentration camp experience. In their roles as interview subjects, they spoke about Manzanar for the first time in an unashamed manner to their son.

6   Japanese Americans learn the stark facts early: On February 19, 1942, President Roosevelt issued Executive Order 9066, sanctioning the evacuation of our people. One hundred ten thousand, most of them citizens, were evacuated to ten camps throughout the United States, where they would remain for four years. Most of the evacuees were given two to seven days to sell a lifetime of belongings, although some ministers and language instructors were arrested immediately with not even that much notice.

7   The sudden evacuation order shocked the Issei, the industrious first generation in this country, and the Nisei, their children. One Pismo Beach man shot himself in the head to spare his family from his shame. He was found clasping an honorary citizenship certificate from Monterey County, which thanked him for his "loyal and splendid service to the country in the Great World War."

8   In my own family, my uncle, a minister, was not given the customary notice to evacuate. He was visited at his San Fernando home by two FBI agents at nine o'clock one evening. Within the hour, he was carted off, without his wife, for an undisclosed location.

9   Ironically, the evacuations came despite the fact that the only pre-war government study found a high degree of loyalty among Japanese Americans and concluded, "There is no Japanese 'problem' on the (West) Coast."

—Edward Iwata, "Barbed-Wire Memories"

■■■ *Dialogue in Narration*

Dialogue, the written representation of conversation, is often useful when you wish to relate an incident or describe something—a state of mind, an attitude, a belief, etc. In most nonfiction works, writers use dialogue sparingly, compressing or reporting it indirectly when they can. In employing dialogue, you may find these suggestions useful:

1. Where it is possible, avoid unnecessary repetition of the speakers' names or unnecessary description of the way they speak. It is old-fashioned and tiresome to write:

   "I see you in the corner," whispered Baker softly.
   "How did you find me?" inquired Charles curiously.
   "I smelled the pipe you've been smoking," purred Baker evilly.
   "Oh!" exclaimed Charles alarmedly.

2. Present dialogue simply:

   I'll not forget my first—and last—meeting with that old Texan. He came striding down the line I had just surveyed on his property, pulling up my line stakes and tossing them over his shoulder as he came. When he got up to my surveying truck, he wasn't even out of breath:

   "Get off my land."
   "O.K., I will—in just a minute. If you'll just—"
   "Get off *now.*"
   "Yes sir, right now, just like you say."
   And I did leave, as fast as possible.

3. Above all, remember to compress and shorten your dialogue whenever you can. Harry Crews reports a "conversation" he had as a farm boy in Georgia with his dog Sam:

1   The moment I sat down in the shade, I was already wondering how long it would be before they quit to go to the house for dinner because I was already beginning to wish I'd taken two biscuits instead of one and maybe another piece of meat, or else that I hadn't shared with Sam.

2   Bored, I looked down at Sam and said: "Sam, if you don't quit eatin' my biscuit and meat, I'm gone have to cut you like a shoat hog."

3   A black cloud of gnats swarmed around his heavy muzzle, but I clearly heard him say that he didn't think I was man enough to do it. Sam and I talked a lot together, had long involved conversations, mostly about which one of us had done the other one wrong and, if not about that, about which one of us was the better man. It would be a good long time before I started thinking of Sam as a dog instead of a person. But I always came out on top when we talked because Sam could only say what I said he said, think what I thought he thought.

4   "If you was any kind of man atall, you wouldn't snap at them gnats and eat them flies the way you do," I said.

5   "It ain't a thing in the world the matter with eating gnats and flies," he said.

6   "It's how come people treat you like a dog," I said.

PRACTICE

Discussion

Discuss the effectiveness of the narrative and dialogue in the following passage. How does Roberts achieve the sound of real people talking? Identify his introductions to dialogue. What is Roberts' thesis? What is his point of view?

1   I rounded a bend (on my recumbent bicycle), and suddenly, through an opening in the trees, saw a great splash of spilt truck on the landscape. Two semis had recently collided, and one was strewn in dramatic disarray down the hill, its cargo a giant splat on the countryside.

2   As I paused to gaze at the scene, I heard a rustling in the leaves behind me. Turning to look, I saw five of the biggest, meanest-looking characters I have ever seen heading toward me from the nearby Potomac. I nodded in friendly but uneasy greeting.

3   "What's this?" asked a mountainous black man.

4   "It's a recumbent bicycle," I replied, "with solar panels to power the electronic equipment. I'm traveling cross-country."

5   "Where you coming from, buddy?" asked a burly redhead.

6   "Columbus, Ohio. I'm doing a 14,000-mile loop around the United States that should take about a year," I said, mouthing my standard response.

7   "Yeah? You crazy, or what?"

8   "Sorta." I grinned. "What are you guys doing here?"

9   A white guy with long black hair in a ponytail answered, "We're convicts, man, from the Maryland Correctional Facility over in Hagerstown."

10   "Hey, is that right?" I chuckled nervously. "Well whaddya know. You escaping?"

11   "Naw, man," spoke the giant black. "You kiddin' me? We workin', man. We out here to clean up that truck." He gestured over his shoulder.

12   "Ah, I see," I answered with some relief.

13   After a bit more banter, I prepared to leave. "Well, I better hit the road," I said, "I'm shootin' for Shepherdstown. . . ."

14   "Whoa!" interrupted the redhead. "We gotta fix you up, man!" He turned on his heel and motioned for me to follow. The others set off in the same direction—toward the truck—laughing.

15   I apprehensively followed them through the woods, arriving at a couple of yellow state trucks and a few armed guards. Other inmates milled about. We took a turn into another part of the woods and came upon a large bundle under a tarp set back in the bushes. "Our stash, man," explained the huge black guy.

16   He pulled back the trap, exposing their private stock of the truck's cargo. Beneath the cover . . . what else but a giant mound of Sara Lee pastry!

17   He grabbed a box and shoved it into my hands. "Have some walnut cake, my man."

18   Another spoke up. "Oh, man, you don't want no walnut cake. Cheese danish, man. Cheese danish. *That's* where it's at!" Another box was placed on the first.

19   The redhead handed over another. "You want some of these apple things, buddy?"

20   Before long I was standing there in the beautiful Maryland woods amid a jovial crowd of murderers and bank robbers, laughing helplessly as my armload of Sara Lee pastries grew to an absurd height. "I'm on a bicycle," I finally managed to blurt out. "I can't carry all this!"

21   "C'mon," suggested the giant. We returned to the bike, still sitting in the middle of the towpath with a crowd of decidedly rough characters standing around it. Nothing appeared to be missing.

22   I started struggling with a box of apple danish, at least securing it under a bungee cord. The giant grabbed the walnut cake. "Gimme that." He stuffed it between the fairing and the electronics package on the front of the machine. "Don't worry, it'll stay." I managed to hang a bit more here and there, then diplomatically declined the rest.

23   We said our goodbyes and I set off again down the quiet trail, festooned with pastry, laughing for miles. You just never know in an enterprise like this. You just never know.

—Steve Roberts, *An Encounter in the Woods*

▼ Suggestions for Writing Narration

1. Choose an event that has a point. At one time or another each of us has had a friend or acquaintance who goes on and on about personal experiences. But the stories never get anywhere. Our reaction to them is, "So what? Why are you telling me all this?" In order for you to avoid this kind of reaction from your reader, narrow your thesis so that your essay has meaning for you *and* your reader.

2. Make your experience come to life. Use dialogue, if you wish, to show an interaction or conflict between people, but don't overuse it so that your essay reads like a film script. Describe the scene or situation with detail, using sensory impressions of touch, smell, sight, hearing, and taste. Try to build some

suspense if possible. Use vivid words to show emotional and physical response. (See pages 185–187 for more advice on vivid writing.)

▼ Planning and Writing a Narrative

Jon starts to write:

> My teacher told me that when I have a conflict, I should try "writing it out." I don't have any conflict with anyone now, but I remember one that has bugged me for many years. Maybe if I think it through and try to write an essay about the experience, I will look at it from a different perspective. Now that I am more mature, writing about it can help me understand just what happened.
>
> I had a conflict with a guy named Joe Haller when I was fifteen. We were on the same baseball team.
>
> I can remember how I hated him, always bugging me and making me feel inferior. He used to holler at me and humiliate me in front of the other players. Why couldn't I get back at him in some way, I kept thinking. I still feel rage when I think about him. Even though I guess I got back at him a little when I caught that high pop-up, I wonder why I don't feel better about that event than I do. Perhaps I'm letting my rage get into the way of understanding the effect of that event. Maybe I should act cooler about the whole thing and look at what actually happened:
>
> 1. Joe was a perfectionist.
>   He would chew out other players.
>   He would humiliate me in front of people.
>
> 2. He got support from the coach, his father.
>
> 3. I was obsessed with hoping that he would make a mistake.
>
> 4. I used to dream about his making a mistake.
>
> 5. Then one day he did make a mistake:
>   What did I do? Did his mistake help me to resolve my rage at him for humiliating me? Did I behave well or did I behave as badly as he had always done toward me?

Jon searches his memory for other details about his experiences with Joe Haller, asking questions: What did the field look like? What did the ball do? What did the crowd do? What was Haller's mistake? After he remembers some of these details, he sees that he has a basis for an essay, and a resolution of his anger because he remembers that he behaved rather well. He didn't gloat or humiliate Joe Haller in front of the team. He just ran toward the dugout, head held high. Below is his final essay.

1   When I was fifteen I played on the same baseball team with Joe Haller, who ten years later was the batting champion of the American Association. The year after that he played three games with the parent club before he ruined his knee and had to retire. At fifteen, he was already a brilliant, locally famous shortstop. He was a perfectionist, and would chew out any player who made an error. Since I played second base, my mistakes were right under his nose, and I got the benefit of his advice more than any other player on our team.

2   Occasionally an opposing player would steal second base, sliding neatly under my tag—a mistake that made Joe furious. He would shout, "That's not how you do it!" As the baserunner left the bag to retrieve his cap, Joe would straddle second base. He would sweep his glove across the shallow groove the runner had just made in the dirt, crying "Get your glove *down!* Don't let him slide *under* you!" The umpire watched respectfully. The stands were silent. Joe's father, our coach, nodded in agreement from the dugout. Then Joe would throw the ball to our pitcher, and the runner would take his place on second base, and the game would resume.

3   Joe never made a mistake that summer until one night-game late in August. We were winning; we were in the field; the bases were empty; there were two outs. The batter hit a very high pop-up behind the pitcher's mound, and Joe called for it, loudly. But for some reason he didn't move from his position deep at shortstop. The ball went so high that it almost disappeared into the blackness of the sky. I glanced at Joe, who still stood still, peering up, searching for the ball. Again, he called out, "I got it!" but he didn't move, and he was at least a dozen yards away from where the ball would land. "He's lost it," I thought, and I started running as fast as I could toward that spot behind the mound, peering up through the haze of lights. I caught sight of the ball as it descended, like a bullet. I went on running; I had a bead on it. But suddenly I lost my nerve; I was afraid of crashing into another player—and I glanced down. In that instant I saw the rows of white shirts in the stands and beyond them the black impenetrable summer sky; and I saw how brilliantly green was the infield grass: the stadium lights gave it a sort of electric glow. When I looked up again the ball was *there,* an inch above my outstretched, open glove.

4   Joe trotted toward me, smiling sheepishly. I nodded to him, and turned my back, and, buoyed along by the bleacher-rattling crowd, I went across the gleaming grass to the dugout.

PRACTICE

Discussion

Read Jon's essay, and answer the following questions:

1. How does the writer set up the situation? For instance, how are Joe Haller and the writer contrasted?

2. How does paragraph 2 develop the contrast?

3. In what way does paragraph 3 contradict the first two paragraphs?

4. Do you think that the conflict is satisfactorily resolved?

5. Discuss the effectiveness of the conclusion. What would you recommend to the writer?

6. Dialogue is used sparingly in this selection. Is it sufficient or insufficient for the author's point? What *is* the point?

Writing

Think about and list the details of an event that made an impression on you or one that you remember vividly. In particular, try to "relive" any conversations that occurred so that you can write the dialogue with the sound of real people talking.

Write a narrative about the event, keeping a consistent point of view. For example, if you were to narrate your experience of being locked in a fruit cellar as a child, the point of view would be affected by being directly involved. However, if you were narrating an event from the viewpoint of a bystander, it would be more objective.

Suggestions:

— My first visit to a hospital (either as a patient or visitor)
— Walking into a house after a burglary
— The fire that nearly destroyed our house (or neighbor's, or friend's)
— My hardest assignment—giving bad news
— Selling an old car

Ron Hoff

TO LIVE IS TO RAGE AGAINST THE DARK

Ron Hoff has sharpened his presentation skills as a creative director and executive vice president in the fiercely competitive advertising and marketing business. For the past decade, he has coached corporate executives at the highest level and conducted presentation seminars and workshops for the American Marketing Association and dozens of communications companies throughout the United States and Canada. His bylined articles have appeared in the New York Times, the Wall Street Journal, the Chicago Tribune, Advertising Age, and other publications. He is a frequent keynote and banquet keynote and banquet speaker, addressing business groups and college audiences nationally. Hoff's essay, as you will see, shows another side of a successful businessman.

1   It's funny how bad news makes you want to get up and get out. I'd taken all of the bad news I could take in one day—two projects canceled, another put on hold, I could hardly wait to get out of the office.

2   Outside, it was raining and the sky was a sheet of gray. I headed for the corner, feeling the rain against my face. I had decided, as I shut my office door, to get myself a Dr Pepper—an act of self-indulgence with few, if any, redeeming virtues.

3   As I approached the corner, I wasn't prepared for the shock of her. We got there at almost the same time, only she was moving faster than I—her cane flicking out in front of her, sweeping from side to side like radar, tapping the sidewalk with a hard, clicking sound. She was hatless in the rain, black hair that looked chopped rather than cut, and a coat as gray and sodden as the day. She seemed to be in her 30s.

4   The cane cast a wide arc in front of her, as if it were "claiming the territory" ahead. It had a red band around the end. The rest of it was white, at least what I could see, and was discolored—bruised by countless collisions. When she reached the curbing, she stopped—holding the cane in front of her.

5   Then, she screamed.

6   It didn't sound like a word or a phrase. It was just a noise, cutting sharply through the wet afternoon. No, it was more than that. It was a command. Sharp, shrill, a bit scary.

7   I started to turn the corner, moving from her. But she wasn't more than three feet away, and the rapping of the cane was so insistent.

8   I turned back and slipped my hand gently under her elbow. "Here," I said, "this way . . ."

9   Instantly, her arm clutched mine. I could feel the strength in it. I was no longer controlling the situation—she was. We stepped out to cross the street. A few steps and she veered to the right—heading out of the crosswalk.

10   I tried to move her back, within the crosswalk, steering against the strength of her arm. Another few feet, and she pulled her arm away from me, angry now, and cursed. It was a familiar four-letter word, but coming from her—it seemed eerie.

11   "I thought you wanted to stay on Clark, to cross the street," my words sounded feeble, even to me. She jerked herself loose from me, cane flicking in its full arc again, and continued in the direction that she obviously wanted to go.

12   I stood in the middle of the street, rejected, watching. She headed for the double doors of a small coffee and doughnut shop on the corner—on the other side of the street. But she was moving too fast. She banged into the first set of doors and disappeared behind the second set.

13   Then, it dawned on me. She knew where she was. She simply wanted somebody to start her across the street when no cars were coming.

14   I saw her take a booth near the window. Suddenly, her cane rapped against the base of the table where she was sitting. I couldn't hear it, but I saw the people inside react. The young man behind the counter heard it, and reacted. He filled a cup of coffee, placed a chocolate-covered doughnut on a plate, and hurried over to her.

15   I was looking through the window at her, and she was looking out—eyes closed, scar tissue surrounding them. Her face was gray, almost purplish. She was older than I had thought. As she was looking out, unseeing, and I was looking in, seeing her really for the first time, she looked content.

16   What were the lines of Dylan Thomas? Oh yes. "Do not go gentle into that good night . . . Rage, rage against the dying of the light." They seemed right for her.

17   She looked away. I turned and headed back up Clark, toward the deli. I was walking faster now, intent on my mission and, for some reason, I did not feel the rain.

PRACTICE

Discussion

1. In what way(s) does the narrator change? Would it hurt the story if he didn't change? How does his change influence our estimation of him as a "person of good character." (ethical proof)

2. Should the woman's obscenity (paragraph 10) be recorded exactly as spoken? And was it necessary that the narrator explain his reaction as he did?

3. As the reader, you know nothing about the woman beyond what she does in a few moments in the street. Is this information sufficient?

4. What sensory images do you carry away from the narrative?

5. If you were filming the incident, where would you put your camera? Explain.

6. Does any part of the story require more compression?

7. Explain the job of paragraph 4.

8. Make a list of the things, actions, and ideas that could have been put in the narrative, but are left out.

Vocabulary

Make a list of words in the story that could not be removed without damaging the total effect. In a sentence or two, explain each of your choices.

Writing

1. Try outlining this story from a different point of view. (How many different points of view are possible, given the situation? Are any of them "impossible"?)

2. This is a "surprise story"; most of what happens surprises—and teaches—the narrator. Write a surprise story of your own based on occurrences in your life.

Don Holt

LEAVING THE FAMILY FARM

Don Holt is Director of Research for the University of Illinois College of Agriculture. He grew up on a farm about 65 miles southwest of Chicago. After obtaining degrees in agriculture from the University of Illinois, he returned to operate his home farm until 1963, when he went to Purdue to work on a Ph.D. in Agronomy. After receiving his degree in 1967, he stayed on as a member of the faculty. He left Purdue in 1982 when he became Associate Dean of the College of Agriculture and Director of the Illinois Agricultural Experiment Station. Dr. Holt and his wife, Marilyn, a musician, have four children. Their oldest daughter married a farmer and is the only one of the family directly involved with a family farm.

1   Farmers are entrepreneurs who, like all entrepreneurs, must sometimes make the difficult decision to give up their businesses and move on. If this decision is treated in a businesslike manner, entrepreneurs can walk away from their creations with dignity and without the stigma of failure.

2   This is one man's story. Every year in this country many farm families face the trauma of having to quit farming. Almost all of these people worked very hard, risked

everything they had, and tried to do everything right. But the unpredictable and mostly uncontrollable vagaries of economics, world politics and weather converged to smash their dreams, disrupt their lives and change the course of their family histories forever. For one reason or another, many of them were vulnerable.

3   They were either strung out too far financially, not quite efficient enough or not able to tighten their belts enough to head off disaster. In many cases, absolutely nothing they could have done would have prevented this personal tragedy.

4   It is to these people that I dedicate my story, not to comfort them, because this story isn't comforting. I want to tell them to hold up their heads and be proud to have played this risky and dangerous game. They haven't lost everything.

5   It was just before dawn on a frosty morning in early November of 1962. I wheeled the tractor, corn husker and wagon through the gate of our lower eighty and started up along the headland to the last 12 rows of corn I had to pick that year. I could have finished those three rounds easily the night before, but I wanted to save them for this moment, for this special time when I would be there alone, just me and the machines and the crop and the land.

6   Even now, years later, I can't sit here and write about the sights and sounds of that morning without a lump in my throat and the tears welling in my eyes. It was a milestone in my life, a transition. This would be the last time I would ever harvest my own crop from my own land with my own machine.

7   In a few weeks, we would have our sale and my seven-year career as a farmer and my 31 years on the farm would end. My great-great-grandfather and everyone between him and me had farmed this land. My sons would never farm it. While I made the decision myself, I felt dragged to it, not by any one circumstance but by a combination of many factors and events.

8   I was born and raised on that farm in northeastern Illinois, in the southeast corner of Kendall County, near Minooka. My grandfather and his two brothers and my father farmed 480 acres, three quarter-section farms. They owned the farms individually but did their field work together, with my dad doing most of it in later years.

9   My dad was the engine mechanic and tractor driver of the group. He had learned engines in flight school in St. Louis. He always lamented the fact that the Depression prevented him from becoming a commercial pilot.

10   I remember well as a child, riding with him on the big diesel truck tractor, perched up on the fuel tank. I marveled at his ability to steer so accurately that the end blade on a 20-foot tandem disk rig exactly cut out the ridge of the previous pass, hour after hour, day after day, and he hardly ever seemed to look back.

11   He loomed big in my eyes in those days, and still does. My grandfather had a blacksmith shop on the farm. He was a real artist with metal and wood and a great inventor and builder of gadgets and gizmos that were useful around the farm. As a child, I spent many happy hours with him, working and watching him work in his shop.

12   He was a burly, powerful man, one of the strongest, toughest men I've ever known. But the things about Grandpa that stick most in my memory are his calmness, his steadiness, his gentleness, his artistry, and his unflinching, rock-like integrity. If somehow it could be that my grandchildren would come to think of me the way I think of him, I would regard my life as a complete success.

13   But that probably won't happen. Even if I had his qualities, my grandchildren will never know me as well as I knew him. They will never spend the days working with me in the shop and in the fields. They will never really see the fruits of my labor. Even my own children know little about what I do. Only our daughter, who was 9 when we left the farm and who married a farmer, inherited my love of agriculture.

14   I thought about this many times while Marilyn and I were wrestling with the decision to quit farming. We knew that by taking our children away from the farm at an early age, we were depriving them of the joy of growing up on a farm, of exploring the fields, the ditches and the fence rows. They would never again pet a new calf or play with a baby pig, one that belonged to them.

15   They would not know what it was like to share their youth with the young of other species, from time to time embracing them in warmth and affection. They would not know the discipline of chores nor the responsibility of having a group of fellow creatures totally dependent on them for water, food and shelter.

16   They would be deprived of the great cultural advantage of growing up on a farm, of developing a farmer's perspective on the relationship between man and other animals, plants and the powerful forces of nature.

17   Farmers and others fear that the unique American family farm, with its history of great economic, moral and spiritual contributions to our culture, is being destroyed by forces beyond their control. Americans in general, and farmers in particular, are compassionate people who do not like to see their neighbors beset by bad luck. Their inherent sense of fair play rebels at the thought of good, dedicated, hard-working farm families going down to financial destruction and personal tragedy because of the vagaries of weather and world politics.

18   Further, the American family farm is close to the hearts of Americans. Many see it as the last bastion of our American heritage, of family, faith, rugged individuality and self-reliance. But the forces that shaped and molded the American family farm into what it is are harsh forces.

19   If life were easy for farm families, there would be little incentive to stand together as families, to use each family member's talents and energies fully, and for neighbors to help each other through tough times. If there had never been opportunities to build — and to lose — farming empires, farming would never have attracted the daring, dedicated, rugged individuals who, aided by some good luck and enormous amounts of hard work, put together the big, productive farms that characterize American agriculture today. Since the agricultural revolution started in this country in the 1800s, millions of people have quit farming.

20   The hard facts of farm life are that the more successful and efficient a nation's agriculture is, the more people will quit farming. Before about 1950, most farmers had the dream that they might be able to send their children to school so they could get a better job, so they could escape the back-breaking labor and drudgery of farming, maybe even become a doctor, a lawyer or a professor.

21   The small, relatively self-sufficient farm of the past, with its garden and a few cows and chickens, now viewed by many as the idyllic family farm, looks better from here than it did from there. It is no wonder people hate to quit farming now. A modern, efficient, productive farm is a good place to live and work. It provides a good living at least

part of the time. It brings out the best of each person's technical skills, managerial abilities and sense of family solidarity.

22   Above all, the American family farm is one of the few remaining situations where people are free to make their own decisions about their lives, about their business operations, to control their own daily work activities, and to set their own schedules.

23   The price of this freedom is that there is little security on the farm, except what you can make for yourself. In a period like the 1980s, farms and farmers are ravaged by low prices, and there is no workmen's compensation, seniority system or welfare that will prevent it or minimize its consequences.

24   The PIK program probably delayed the inevitable for some farmers, but the public will not tolerate expensive subsidy programs very long.

25   This is history repeating itself. American agriculture has always been a boom and bust proposition. The very technological advances that make it possible for two of every 100 people to produce the food for the other 98 dictate that not more than two of 98 are going to support themselves well by farming.

26   As supplies and demand fluctuate in our agricultural system, there are low periods that move some people out of farming. The same periodically extreme economic pressures that force some people out, keep the rest sharp and efficient, foster competition and innovation, expand markets, and force the necessary adjustments in prices, costs and production.

27   The American family farm doesn't get its special character by being small. It is no longer characterized by being totally self-sufficient, by utilizing only family labor, by having a few cows or chickens or a little garden patch. It may have these things, but those are not its essential characteristics. The American family farm is unique because the people who operate it are unique.

28   Traditionally, they have been willing to play the game, win or lose, to risk their worldly goods and even their lives, to expend their energies and to put themselves in a position where nothing stands between them and failure but their own wits, muscle, faith and determination. Often even these are not enough to prevent a personal disaster.

29   The reality is that not everybody that wants to farm can farm, and the public is not obligated to support me on the farm just because I like it. Farming should be left to those who can survive in this tough business.

30   For 20 years we have been among the ranks of the non-farmers. I've been a part of American agriculture, however, and that's good. While I rarely use any of the specific skills I picked up on the farm, I regard the farm experience as extremely valuable. My tendency to try new ideas too early turned out to be an asset in research. Farmers generally do very well in other jobs because they know the value of timeliness and the necessity of persistence and hard work.

31   They know how important it is to be ready, and they know how to bend without breaking. I've enjoyed my work, my family has thrived, and there are many great challenges ahead. I'm not one to look back on decisions or cry over spilt milk.

32   But sometimes I see or hear something that reminds me, and the memories come flooding back, the good and the bad. The smell of the furrow slice, the bite of a January wind, the muted roar of a big tractor engine and the feeling of power as you throttle up;

the depression of a down market and all that work for nothing; the exuberance of cattle frisking in the bedding straw; the heat and dust of the haymow; the raw power of big animals; a mounted cultivator stuck in a mudhole, having to be removed piece by piece; a 20-mile, unobstructed view; a 20-mile, unobstructed windsweep; fishing in the creek; deterring a salesman by insisting that he talk to you in the open on a blustery winter day; a fresh jug of water and a few minutes in the shade; the crib driveway in summer and in winter; callouses; getting the check after the sale of a bunch of high-choice steers; straight back furrows and neat dead furrows; sitting on the porch; and many, many others.

33   And the one memory that will stay with me forever, that last pass through the cornfield. I made a figure eight with the picker and wagon, lined up on those last two rows of my farming experience and headed east, into the red half-circle of the rising sun.

34   I stood on the tractor platform, the seat flipped up, and drank in the sights and sounds of that moment, the glint of the sun off the corn stubble, the crisp passage of frosty stalks through gathering chains and snapping rolls, the river of golden, clean-husked ears streaming up the elevator, the muffled roar of the tractor, the smooth function of that long train of machinery moving slowly, but, somehow, inevitably through the field, devouring the last few stalks of my final harvest as a farmer. Only the other farmers who read this will know what that was like.

PRACTICE

Discussion

1. Identify the thesis. In paragraph 2, Holt tells the reader that this is his *story*. Discuss the appropriateness of his using the term *story*.

2. In Holt's introduction (paragraph 1–3), he gives three reasons why people have had to leave the farm. Later he elaborates on these same reasons. Which of the three reasons gets the most attention in his discussion? Why?

3. Discuss the author's point of view and its effectiveness.

4. Where does the writer use description? How do these descriptions show the consequences on his children of leaving the farm?

5. The author provides many reasons why people do not want to see the family farm disappear. Make a list of those reasons. Discuss his credibility and ethical proof in the analysis of these reasons.

6. Where does the author use sensory images in describing his memories of the farm? Choose those that are most effective. The least effective? Do you need to have lived on a farm to identify with his images?

7. Discuss whether you empathize with the writer's regret and sadness at leaving the family farm. Would you call his essay *romantic* or *realistic*?

8. How well does the writer prove his point or thesis?

Vocabulary

entrepreneurs	innovation
furrow	vagaries

Writing

1. Write an essay about something that you look back on with nostalgia. Show that times and circumstances have changed; things will never again be as you remembered them.

    Possible subjects: your high school class reunion; going back to visit your first job; visiting an old friend.

2. Thomas Wolfe wrote a book entitled, *You Can't Go Home Again.* Write a narrative essay with that title, using sensory images, and explaining how you felt when you went back to a place where you once lived.

3. Write a paper in which you describe events and situations that you have experienced that your children will never experience. Possible subjects: living in a home with two parents; playing games in an empty lot; walking to school.

Harry Crews

A CHILDHOOD

Born June 7, 1935, in Alma, Georgia, Harry Crews grew up on a farm, joined the Marines at the age of 18, and eventually, after earning bachelor's and master's degrees from the University of Florida, became a teacher and a writer. The rural South and the process of becoming a man in tune with the earth are central subjects of Crews' essays and novels, the best known of which are Karate Is A Thing of the Spirit *(1971) and* The Hawk Is Dying *(1973). Similar themes run through* A Childhood: The Biography of a Place *(1978), from which is excerpted the following story of fearful and loving intensity. The sharp twist of a pop-the-whip line of children leads to horror and pain and to a story that also contains a number of ironic twists.*

1   It was a bright cold day in February 1941, so cold the ground was still frozen at ten o'clock in the morning. The air was full of the steaming smell of excrement and the oily, flatulent odor of intestines and the heavy sweetness of blood—in every way a perfect day to slaughter animals. I watched the hogs called to the feeding trough just as they were every morning except this morning it was to receive the ax instead of slop.

2   A little slop *was* poured into their long communal trough, enough to make them stand still while Uncle Alton or his boy Theron went quietly among them with the ax, using the flat end like a sledgehammer (shells were expensive enough to make a gun out of the question). He would approach the hog from the rear while it slopped at the

trough, and then he would straddle it, one leg on each side, patiently waiting for the hog to raise its snout from the slop to take a breath, showing as it did the wide bristled bone between its ears to the ax.

3   It never took but one blow, delivered expertly and with consummate skill, and the hog was dead. He then moved with his hammer to the next hog and straddled it. None of the hogs ever seemed to mind that their companions were dropping dead all around them but continued in a single-minded passion to eat. They didn't even mind when another of my cousins (this could be a boy of only eight or nine because it took neither strength nor skill) came right behind the hammer and drew a long razorboned butcher knife across the throat of the fallen hog. Blood spurted with the still-beating heart, and a live hog would sometimes turn to one that was lying beside it at the trough and stick its snout into the spurting blood and drink a bit just seconds before it had its own head crushed.

4   It was a time of great joy and celebration for the children. We played games and ran (I gimping along pretty well by then) and screamed and brought wood to the boiler and thought of that night, when we would have fresh fried pork and stew made from lungs and liver and heart in an enormous pot that covered half the stove.

5   The air was charged with the smell of fat being rendered in tubs in the backyard and the sharp squeals of the pigs at the troughs, squeals from pure piggishness at the slop, never from pain. Animals were killed but seldom hurt. Farmers took tremendous precautions about pain at slaughter. It is, whether or not they ever admit it when they talk, a ritual. As brutal as they sometimes are with farm animals and with themselves, no farmer would ever eat an animal he had willingly made suffer.

6   The heel strings were cut on each of the hog's hind legs, and a stick, called a gambreling stick, or a gallus, was inserted into the cut behind the tendon and the hog dragged to the huge cast-iron boiler, which sat in a depression dug into the ground so the hog could be slipped in and pulled out easily. The fire snapped and roared in the depression under the boiler. The fire had to be tended carefully because the water could never quite come to a boil. If the hog was dipped in boiling water, the hair would set and become impossible to take off. The ideal temperature was water you could rapidly draw your finger through three times in succession without being blistered.

7   Unlike cows, which are skinned, a hog is scraped. After the hog is pulled from the water, a blunt knife is drawn over the animal, and if the water has not been too hot, the hair slips off smooth as butter, leaving a white, naked, utterly beautiful pig.

8   To the great glee of the watching children, when the hog is slipped into the water, it defecates. The children squeal and clap their hands and make their delightfully obscene children's jokes as they watch it all.

9   On that morning, mama was around in the back by the smokehouse where some hogs, already scalded and scraped, were hanging in the air from their heel strings being disemboweled. Along with the other ladies she was washing out the guts, turning them inside out, cleaning them good so they could later be stuffed with ground and seasoned sausage meat.

10   Out in front of the house where the boiler was, I was playing pop-the-whip as best I could with my brother and several of my cousins. Pop-the-whip is a game in which everyone holds hands and runs fast and then the leader of the line turns sharply. Because he is turning through a tighter arc than the other children, the line acts as a whip with each child farther down the line having to travel through a greater space and

consequently having to go faster in order to keep up. The last child in the line literally gets *popped* loose and sent flying from his playmates.

11   I was popped loose and sent flying into the steaming boiler of water beside a scalded, floating hog.

12   I remember everything about it as clearly as I remember anything that ever happened to me, except the screaming. Curiously, I cannot remember the screaming. They say I screamed all the way to town, but I cannot remember it.

13   What I remember is John C. Pace, a black man whose daddy was also named John C. Pace, reached right into the scalding water and pulled me out and set me on my feet and stood back to look at me. I did not fall but stood looking at John and seeing in his face that I was dead.

14   The children's faces, including my brother's, showed I was dead, too. And I knew it must be so because I knew where I had fallen and I felt no pain—not in that moment— and I knew with the bone-chilling certainty most people are spared this, yes, death does come and mine had just touched me.

15   John C. Pace ran screaming and the other children ran screaming and left me standing there by the boiler, my hair and skin and clothes steaming in the bright cold February air.

16   In memory I stand there alone along with the knowledge of death upon me, watching steam rising from my hands and clothes while everybody runs and, after everybody has gone, standing there for minutes while nobody comes.

17   That is only memory. It may have been but seconds before my mama and Uncle Alton came to me. Mama tells me she heard me scream and started running toward the boiler, knowing already what had happened. She has also told me that she could not bring herself to try to do anything with that smoking ghostlike thing standing by the boiler. But she did. They all did. They did what they could.

18   But in that interminable time between John pulling me out and my mother arriving in front of me, I remember first the pain. It didn't begin as bad pain, but rather like maybe sandspurs under my clothes.

19   I reached over and touched my right hand with my left, and the whole thing came off like a wet glove. I mean, the skin on the top of the wrist and the back of my hand, along with the fingernails, all just turned loose and slid on down to the ground. I could see my fingernails lying in the little puddle my flesh made on the ground in front of me.

20   Then hands were on me, taking off my clothes, and the pain turned into something words cannot touch, or at least my words cannot touch. There is no way for me to talk about it because when my shirt was taken off, my back came of off with it. When my overalls were pulled down, my cooked and glowing skin came down.

21   I still had not fallen, and I stood there participating in my own butchering. When they got the clothes off me they did the worst thing they could have done; they wrapped me in a sheet. They did it out of panic and terror and ignorance and love.

22   That day there happened to be a car at the farm. I can't remember who it belonged to, but I was taken into the backseat into my mama's lap—God love the lady, out of her head, pressing her boiled son to her breast—and we started for Alma, a distance of about sixteen miles. The only thing that I can remember about the trip was that I started telling mama that I did not want to die. I started saying it and never stopped.

23   The car we piled into was incredibly slow. An old car and very, very slow, and every once in a while Uncle Alton, who was like a daddy to me, would jump out of the car and

run alongside it and helplessly scream for it to go faster and then he would jump on the running board until he couldn't stand it any longer and then he would jump off again.

24   But like bad beginnings everywhere, they sometimes end well. When I got to Dr. Sharp's office in Alma and he finally managed to get me out of the sticking sheet, he found that I was scalded over two-thirds of my body but that my head had not gone under the water (he said that would have killed me), and for some strange reason I have never understood, the burns were not deep. He said I would probably even outgrow the scars, which I have. Until I was about fifteen years old, the scars were puckered and discolored on my back and right arm and legs. But now their outlines are barely visible.

25   The only hospital at the time was thirty miles away, and Dr. Sharp said I'd do just as well at home if they built a frame over the bed to keep the covers off me and also keep a light burning over me twenty-four hours a day. (He knew as well as we did that I couldn't go to a hospital anyway, since the only thing Dr. Sharp ever got for taking care of me was satisfaction for a job well done, if he got that. Over the years, I was his most demanding and persistent charity, which he never mentioned to me or mama. Perhaps that is why in an age when it is fashionable to distrust and hate doctors, I love them.)

PRACTICE

Discussion

1. Crews has remembered clearly many vivid, specific details from his childhood experience. But what alterations or omissions of memory, his own or others', does Crews cite in his narrative? What false conclusion is reached by John C. Pace, the other children, and Crews himself? At what points do words fail Crews as he writes of the experience? Why does he mention these failures of memory, perception, and expression in an otherwise accurate, realistic, and vivid story?

2. At what points does Crews imply or specifically draw a comparison between himself and a hog? What effect does the comparison have on the story?

3. Crews details a horrifying experience but also cites several examples of love. What are they? How do these examples contribute to our confidence in him as a good person (ethical proof)?

4. What is the point of Crews' story? (Reflect a moment; it may be more complex than you first think. Hint: His thesis is a two-part, contrasting, balanced concept. Look to paragraphs 14, 21, 24, and 25 for help.) Where does he specifically state the dichotomy of his theme? How does Crews' organization reflect his two-part balance?

5. At what point in the story does Crews make an abrupt turn from factual description to more impressionistic observations? How does he emphasize this turn with writing techniques?

6. Although Crews does not use direct dialogue in his narrative, where does he resort to indirect dialogue (for example, "He said that . . . ")? How does that

indirect dialogue briefly develop the character of the indirect speakers, in addition to advancing the factual report of the experience? In what way does he create a vivid characterization of two other figures?

7. Make a list of all the phrases or images with a surprising, ironic ironic twist that Crews employs in his narrative. Why are there so many in this particular story?

8. What is the narrator's point of view in relation to his own story here? What methods and phrases especially reinforce this point of view? How does this point of view affect the theme?

Vocabulary

flatulent	rendered	disemboweled
communal	defecates	interminable
consummate		

Writing

1. Narrate a childhood experience that led to an insight.

2. Have you ever felt such great pain or joy that it could not be expressed? Try to convey that deep emotion to a reader by narrating the story that surrounds it.

3. Crews' final line, "I love them," sums up his gratefulness to doctors as a class. Write a paper in which you describe an event in your life which made you love a class of people. Suggestions: firefighters, teachers, lawyers, law-enforcement officers.

CHAPTER 13

Process

▼ Process

If you want to tell your reader how something happens, you can use *process,* a writing strategy that describes a series of steps leading to a particular end point. Process is useful because it can be as short as a paragraph or as long as a full paper. It can also be used with other strategies.

One of the two basic kinds of process development is the *artificial* process, which traces the development of a situation or set of circumstances created by human beings. When you give directions or tell someone how to do something, you explain an artificial process. The manufacture of gasoline is such a process:

Steps in process	1	Heat the raw petroleum.
	2	Cool the resulting vapor into liquid.
	3	Use further refining processes.
End point	4	Blend liquids and treat chemically to get grades of commercial gasoline.

The second kind of process is *natural,* one which occurs in the real world around us. A natural process, for instance, may be the result of an instinctive reaction to some basic drive. Birds instinctively migrate every year. In this natural process they begin by losing some of their feathers and growing new ones, taking many trial flights, and eating a great deal to store up fat. The steps and end point in this process are:

Steps in process	1	Molting
	2	Trial flights
End point	3	Building a reserve of fat to get ready for migration

Natural processes are also often dependent upon timing. For instance, birds migrate south in the fall of the year and north in the spring of the year.

PRACTICE

Discussion

Here are examples of both types of process. Read each and answer the questions at the end.

1   The marriage flight is one of the most important days in the life of an ant colony. Its date varies according to the species but, in the case of the *rufa,* it falls between May and September. On one day—and on only one day in a single season—the reproducers must leave the nest, and workers chase out any reluctant ones.

2   They fly out on an August morning and, in the air, they mingle with the sexed ants from neighboring nests. A pursuit begins until each female offers herself to a male on a neighboring tree. Then, in turn, the males mate with her and, in so doing, they accomplish the only act for which they were created. The next day, they all will be dead and many of the females as well. Of the surviving females, some may return to their original nests. Others will be adopted by nests in need of a queen or big enough to require more than one.

3   Finally, others will go out alone and found a new nest. The female digs herself in about five inches below the surface of the earth and carves out a cell for herself with no exit. There she lays her eggs. Some of them will become larvae, but not all—most of them serve for food for their mother and for the larvae which she chooses to raise. If winter falls, the larvae must wait until the following spring before they become ants. On the other hand, if workers are born before the cold weather sets in, they immediately begin to dig galleries, the beginning of a future nest. They start foraging for food, and the normal life of an ant-nest has been founded.

—"Ants," *Realities* magazine

EXTINGUISHING AN OVEN FIRE

1   The blazing oven is another appliance problem, although it doesn't usually indicate anything is wrong with the appliance. But it calls for a mighty quick remedy. It usually shows up first as smoke trailing out of the oven vent. If, as is usually the case, the broiler is in action, the whole kitchen may be full of smoke. If you open the oven door, all the blazes in hell seem to sail out at you. In this event, try to hang on to your nonchalance and just shut the oven door again. The chances are the big, beautiful sirloin inside isn't ruined, the house won't burn down, and the entire mess isn't as bad as it looks.

2   First, turn off the broiler. Then yank the top off your biggest salt container. Next open the oven again and slide the broiler rack and the steak out a little with a carving fork or some other long utensil that won't burn and doesn't make you reach in so close you get spattered with fiery fat. (Fiery fat can set your clothing afire.) Then *pile* on the salt by the fistful—at the points the flames are coming from. This salt business is a sort of old wives'

tale, but it works if you have plenty of the stuff. It doesn't act chemically by creating some fancy fire-smothering gas. It simply stifles the fire by covering it up and shutting off its air supply—like a load of sand. But it's better than sand from the culinary standpoint because you can wash it off, and if a few grains remain they won't chip your teeth. Whatever you do, *don't* throw water on the fire. This blasts into steam, floats and spatters blazing grease all over the place, and can give you some very nasty burns and possibly set the kitchen on fire.

3   Actually things cool off surprisingly fast with the broiler turned off and salt piled on the conflagration. Everything usually is under complete control in a minute or two. But even with the fire out, you're likely to have a case of jitters. Just remember it's not anywhere near as horrible as it looks.

4   In the rare event that you can't put the fire out (most unlikely), shove the whole works back in the oven and shut the door—also the oven vent if possible. This, at least, keeps your private inferno locked up where it can do the least harm until the fire trucks arrive.

—George Daniels

1. Identify the *steps* and *end point* of each process.

2. Which process is *natural,* which is *artificial?* In what ways are the processes fundamentally different?

3. In a process paper, there are usually certain transitional "signals" (*first, later, after this, before,* and *so on*) which help the reader discriminate among the various parts of the process. List the signals in the examples. Do most of the signals fall into any particular class or type?

4. Describe the writer's stance in each passage. The two kinds of processes ordinarily have different stances. Explain why this should be so.

▼ Suggestions for Writing Process Papers

When you use process strategies of development, you are essentially describing how something is done, how it works, or how it "happens."

■■■ *Artificial Process*

In the artificial process, you often give directions to a specific person or group (people who want to learn how to put out an oven fire, for example), and your writer's stance is clear and precise. You will probably use a time or chronological order because some steps should be done before others. For instance, when showing the process of how detergents work, it is logical to discuss adding the detergent to the water *before* you discuss what happens when water and detergent are combined. You must, therefore, give careful thought to the sequence of steps or stages when describing a process.

Keep in mind that your reader may know little about your subject and may need definitions of terms and clear signals showing how the steps or stages are separated. You may wish to speak directly to the reader and address him or her as *you.* Certain suggestions may help you to use artificial process:

1. Decide if you are giving directions or making an explanation. Then choose the writer's stance that is most appropriate.

2. Determine the end point or purpose of the process.

3. Determine the relevant, main steps of the process that lead to the end point or purpose. *State the steps clearly,* and *use transitions.*

4. If possible, keep to a clear chronological sequence of events in the process, but avoid irrelevancies.

■■■ Natural Process

The natural process is somewhat more difficult to write because you have to look carefully at the sequence of steps in order to find them and the end point. Natural processes often involve scientific subjects, so you must be well informed in order to describe the process. However, neither you nor your reader is necessarily *in* that process. You are both standing off from it—watching it and trying to understand how it works. Instead of addressing the reader, try using the *who (or what) does what* formula:

[Who] *The male* [does what?] *mates and dies.*

PRACTICE

Discussion

1. Read the following artificial-process paper that uses process to inform.

    a. How does the student use the *who does what* formula to describe how she adapted to partial deafness?

    b. Note the order of steps. How long do you think this process took?

    c. If you were writing a paper like this, how would you change the sequence of steps? How useful are the abstract terms *physical, mental,* and *social?*

    d. Discuss the student's use of definition.

    e. Describe her stance.

Introduction	1	When I was eight, I had a radical mastoidectomy—a surgical procedure consisting of chiselling out the infected bone (behind the ear) called the *mastoid.* This is a serious operation, often leaving the patient with little hearing in the affected ear. Thanks to miracle drugs, mastoid operations are infrequently done today. However, since I lived in a remote area of North Dakota where the health care was not
Definition by		
classification and		
operation		

easily accessible, I developed a mastoid infection before my family realized how seriously ill I was.

Effect 2   Young people are adaptable, so I didn't realize that being deaf in one ear was anything to worry about. My friends and family didn't treat me any differently. Even though the operation had been very painful and disagreeable, I was so glad to be back in school, doing the things I liked to do, that I really didn't pay much attention to the stages I went through in adapting to partial deafness. As I look back over the years, I can see that I developed a conscious process of adapting to deafness. I made physical, mental, and social adjustments.

Introduces the strategy: process
Thesis

First step: physical 3   The first step in adapting to deafness was physical. I had to position my body so that I could hear my friends and family. Since my right ear was my "bad" ear, I learned to tip my head to the right so that the sound entered my left or "good" ear. Over the years it has become such a habit that all my photographs show me with my head tipped to the right. Another way I found that I could position my body was to get on the right-hand side of people. Even today, when I sit on a couch or ride in the back seat of a car, I always sit on a person's right. When we walk down the street, I always get on the "outside" or right-hand side. This sometimes causes me some problems with men who think they should be on the "outside." I never talk when I drive a car because I can't hear well enough to carry on a conversation, without losing track of my concentration.

Four examples

Second step: mental 4   I realized early that consciously positioning my body to the situation was not enough, so I progressed to the second step—being alert. I knew that I had to concentrate and listen very carefully to those around me. Other people were not going to go out of their way to help me hear. Besides, I wasn't willing to go around explaining that I heard with only one ear. Who cares! Therefore, I learned that by concentrating I could increase my hearing ability dramatically. By watching faces and lips, I taught myself lip-reading. Today, I can tell what is going on in television shows when the sound is off by reading the actor's lips. I also became alert to body language—unusual gestures, facial expressions and movements—that helped tell me what people were thinking.

Two examples

Third and final step: social 5   My final step was to adjust my social life to partial deafness. I couldn't have much fun at large parties because the commotion created too much "surface noise" for me to carry on conversations. However, when I was forced into large groups, I tried to figure out the general conversation and make suitable noises like "Oh?" "Is that so?" "Well!" and "I agree." I'm afraid there were times when I agreed when I shouldn't have. Occasionally, I received some peculiar looks when my pat answers didn't quite fit the discussion.

One example

Conclusion 6   I am lucky that I became partially deaf when I was very young. I have since met older people who became deaf late in life. Instead of working on the process of hearing, they have become lazy and resentful. They make *other* people do the work. No one wants to shout while conversing. It is better to answer with an occasional "I agree," even when it doesn't fit, than to be a demanding, irritable deaf person.

End point implied: adaptation successful

2. Here is part of a magazine article written by a doctor describing a process. Is this a natural or an artificial process? Identify the steps and the end point.

1   At 11 p.m. on Dec. 22, 1963 fire broke out aboard the Greek luxury liner *Lakonia* as it cruised the Atlantic near Madeira, and passengers and crew were forced into the water. The air temperature was over 60°, the sea almost 65° and rescue ships were in the area within a few hours. Nevertheless, 125 people died, 113 of these fatalities being attributed to hypothermia, the lowering of the body's inner heat, perhaps no more than 6° from the normal 98.6°. . . .

2   The moment your body begins to lose heat faster than it produces it, hypothermia threatens. As heat loss continues, the temperature of the body's inner core falls below normal. Hands and arms (the extremities most needed in order to survive) are affected first. When body temperature drops to 95°, dexterity is reduced to the point where you cannot open a jackknife or light a match.

3   According to recent research by the Mountain Rescue Association, the body reacts in a series of predictable ways when inner-core temperature falls. At 2.5° below normal, shivering begins, an automatic body process to create heat. But it takes energy to shiver—comparable to what is expended sawing wood—and the heat loss continues. The more the core temperature drops, the less efficient the brain becomes. Although you may have a pack on your back with a sleeping bag and food in it, you may not have the sense to use them.

4   If the core temperature drops to 94°, you will stop shivering but every now and then will experience uncontrollable shaking. Your system, automatically getting rid of carbon dioxide and lactic acid, also releases blood sugar and a little adrenaline, giving you a surge of energy, which causes the violent shaking. This last desperate effort by the body to produce heat utilizes a tremendous amount of energy.

5   "Now," you think, "I must be getting warmer because I am not shivering anymore." By this time you are pretty irrational. If someone were to ask you your name and telephone number, you probably wouldn't know them, for the brain has become numb.

6   If nothing is done, death usually occurs within 1 1/2 hours after the shivering starts. In fact, a shivering person can go from fatigue to exhaustion to cooling beyond the recovery point so quickly he may perish before rescuers can build a shelter or get a fire started.

—J. Clayton Steward, "Growing Cold by Degrees"

▼ Planning and Writing a Process (An Example)

Jack has a collection of old comic books that are becoming valuable with age. He belongs to a collector's association, which has invited him to write an article describing his process of storing comics in order to protect them from moisture, acids, and sunlight. He writes a paragraph on how he will plan his article:

My comic books don't fall into just one class. I have three different kinds: run-of-the-mill, more valuable, and *very* expensive. They all require particular treatments that overlap. What is the best way to describe the storage process without confusing my audience? Perhaps I should give the basic method of storing the least valuable comics, and then build on that method in a discussion of storing the more expensive ones. My steps in the process might look like this:

	Run-of-the-Mill	**More Valuable**	**Very Expensive**
Step 1:	omit	use Mylar bags	same
Step 2:	use acid-free box	same	use acid free notebook
Step 3:	use acid free millboard	omit	omit
Step 4:	store in dry place	same	same

This kind of pattern made writing his process easier than if he hadn't identified the relationship shown above.

KEEPING COMICS

1   Comic book collectors who are serious (like me) are known as "hard-core" collectors. There are, so one hobby magazine recently stated, tens of thousands of ordinary collectors, but only a few thousand hard-core ones. And for us, the problem is not just collecting—but keeping. Comic books were printed on very cheap paper using terrible techniques of production. Put a valuable comic book in the sun, and it may be ruined in a matter of hours. Store it improperly in a damp place, and it may be ruined in a matter of months or a few years. The answer is to store them properly and thus save your collection.

2   Like most collectors, you probably have a large number of run-of-the-mill comics. Place these on edge (never flat) in acid-free millboard boxes. When putting them in the box, take special care of the corners. Nothing protects the edges from bending, so put them in carefully. After packing every group of 10 or 15 comics, insert a piece of acid-free millboard. These supports will keep the comics from sagging. Bags are not necessary for these comics. Stack the boxes in a dark, cool place with relatively low humidity.

3   For your more valuable comics, an extra precaution is necessary. Place the valuable ones in three mil Mylar snugs before putting them in an acid-free box. These snugs are inert polyester bags that will last hundreds of years without decomposing. Normal polyethylene bags last only five years. When putting comics in the bags, again be careful of the edges and corners, since the corners bend easily. Mylar is quite stiff and holds the comic in a vise-like grip. This is beneficial if the comic is flat and straight in the bag, but detrimental if the corners are allowed to remain folded. Use a popsicle stick or some other blunt, flat instrument to push the corners down after the comic is in the bag. Also, watch the back cover and see that it is in straight also.

4   Store these bagged comics in small or large acid-free cartons. The small cartons are a little more expensive, but provide slightly easier access to the comics.

5   If you have *very* expensive comics costing $100 and up, give them the best treatment. Use a snug especially made for a three-ring binder. This snug, which clamps the comic like the regular snugs, is four mils rather than three mils thick. It also has an edge with punched holes for the binder. The binder, which should be well constructed and sturdy, makes it easy to display your valuable collection. The binders should also be stored in a dark, cool place.

6   Actually, any of the storage schemes for the expensive comics can be used for less expensive varieties. The best methods cost a lot of money though, up to $1.20 per stored

comic. The scheme for run-of-the-mill comics costs only twenty cents per comic. The best rule is: Spend in proportion to what your comics are worth to you.

PRACTICE

Discussion

Read Jack's paper on storing comic books.

1. Outline the stance. How does the writer's *point of view* influence his *role?*

2. Where in each paragraph are the basic steps described? Discuss the applications of the steps to the three divisions (or *classes*) of comic books.

3. Discuss the importance of the materials necessary in the *process.* How is the choice of materials relevant to the *purpose* of the process?

Writing

1. Think about a medical problem you or one of your family has had. Consider *one* of the following:

   a. What was the process your body went through when you had your medical problem?

   b. What kind of process did you develop to adjust to your problem?

   You may want to interview some experts or do research in order to deal with **a** above. (You will develop a process yourself when you deal with one of these topics—search your memory, freewrite everything you can remember, group your material, identify a hook, plan your stance, and write.)

2. Choose one of the following topics. If possible, practice the process, keeping notes on what you do and in what order. Identify a suitable audience, outline your stance, and write a paper.

   a. How to write exams

   b. How to make a house burglar-proof

   c. How to pierce your ear in more than one place

   d. How to talk to an answering machine

   e. How to pack a bag for backpacking

3. Choose one of the following topics and write a process paper. If you have had no experience with any of these processes, identify one of your own.

   a. How to use psychology in dealing with _____

   b. How you defeated computer anxiety

   c. How a shopping mall changes a community

   d. How a coach taught me to _____

Peter Elbow

FREEWRITING EXERCISES

Peter Elbow knows his way around a classroom. Educated at Williams College, Oxford, Harvard, and Brandeis universities, he has taught at the Massachusetts Institute of Technology and Franconia College. Currently he teaches at Evergreen State College in Olympia, Washington. He has directed writing programs in both academic and community settings, and his ideas have had a strong influence on teachers of writing and writing programs throughout the United States. Despite all his academic connections, the title of his 1973 writing text, from which the following piece is taken, is Writing Without Teachers. *Teachers, Elbow writes in the preface, are more useful if they are not necessary. That philosophy of self-reliance is apparent in the very first words of the book, reproduced below.*

1   The most effective way I know to improve your writing is to do freewriting exercises regularly. At least three times a week. They are sometimes called "automatic writing," "babbling," or "jabbering" exercises. The idea is simply to write for ten minutes (later on, perhaps fifteen or twenty). Don't stop for anything. Go quickly without rushing. Never stop to look back, to cross something out, to wonder how to spell something, to wonder what word or thought to use, or to think about what you are doing. If you can't think of a word or a spelling, just use a squiggle or else write, "I can't think of it." Just put down something. The easiest thing is just to put down whatever is in your mind. If you get stuck it's fine to write "I can't think what to say, I can't think what to say" as many times as you want; or repeat the last word you wrote over and over again; or anything else. The only requirement is that you *never* stop.

2   What happens to a freewriting exercise is important. It must be a piece of writing which, even if someone reads it, doesn't send any ripples back to you. It is like writing something and putting it in a bottle in the sea. The teacherless class helps your writing by providing maximum feedback. Freewritings help you by providing no feedback at all. When I assign one, I invite the writer to let me read it. But also tell him to keep it if he prefers. I read it quickly and make no comments at all and I do not speak with him about it. The main thing is that a freewriting must never be evaluated in any way; in fact there must be no discussion or comment at all.

3   Here is an example of a fairly coherent exercise (sometimes they are very incoherent, which is fine):

I think I'll write what's on my mind, but the only thing on my mind right now is what to write for ten minutes. I've never done this before and I'm not prepared in any way— the sky is cloudy today, how's that? now I'm afraid I won't be able to think of what to write when I get to the end of the sentence—well, here I am at the end of the sentence— here I am again, again, again, again, at least I'm still writing—Now I ask is there some reason to be happy that I'm still writing—ah yes! Here comes the question again— What am I getting out of this? What point is there in it? It's almost obscene to always ask but I seem to question everything that way and I was gonna say something else pertaining to that but I got so busy writing down the first part that I forgot what I was lead-

ing into. This is kind of fun oh don't stop writing—cars and trucks speeding by somewhere out the window, pens clittering across people's papers. The sky is cloudy—is it
symbolic that I should be mentioning it? Huh? I dunno. Maybe I should try colors, blue,
red, dirty words—wait a minute—no can't do that, orange, yellow, arm tired, green
pink violet magenta lavender red brown black green—now that I can't think of any
more colors—just about done—relief? maybe.

PRACTICE

Discussion

1. In what ways is freewriting completely different from the way you usually
   write a paper or a letter? In what ways is it the same?

2. Why is it so important not to get any feedback on freewriting? What is the
   point of having Elbow (or your instructor) read a freewriting assignment if
   there is to be "no discussion or comment at all"?

3. What is the most interesting point for you in the example of a freewriting
   exercise that Elbow gives? Why do you find that spot interesting? (Since
   the author of the piece is not here to hear your feedback, it is all right to
   comment.)

4. Does Elbow sound like a writing instructor? If not, how does his voice
   sound? What parts of this essay especially contribute to establishing his
   voice? Is that voice appropriate to the particular essay he is writing? Is that
   voice an honest one (ethical proof)?

5. Would Elbow's essay be improved by moving his example to the beginning?
   Why or why not? How would such a move affect the rest of the essay?

6. Elbow uses a couple of incomplete sentences in his part of the essay, exclusive
   of the example. (And he calls himself a writing instructor!) Where are they?
   Rewrite them as complete sentences. What did the essay gain from your
   revisions? What did it lose?

7. Besides fragments, Elbow uses several very short sentences in the essay. In
   which paragraphs do most of them occur? They are mixed in with some very
   long sentences in that same paragraph. Examine the construction of those
   long sentences. Does the mixture of short and long sentences vary the rhythm
   of the paragraph? Is the rhythm of the first paragraph the same as the of the
   second? Why or why not?

8. What tricks are used by the author of the freewriting exercise to keep the
   exercise moving? What tone do these ploys lend to the exercise?

Vocabulary

freewriting	feedback	pertaining
babbling	coherent	clittering
jabbering	obscene	magenta
squiggle		

Writing

1. Freewriting and proofreading are at opposite ends of the writing process. Write a guide to proofreading, explaining clearly to student writers how to go about proofreading a paper.

2. Freewriting is to writing as, perhaps, stretching is to running or sketching is to painting. Choose a type of exercise preparatory to something else with which you are familiar and tell someone interested in it about how to go about warming up. You may also want to tell your reader why he or she *should* warm up.

3. Freewrite for 10 minutes. Then examine what you should have written and note any interesting spots where you might have shifted gears or become stuck, for example. Write a brief analysis of your freewriting exercise: how you got started, the steps your mind and hand took together, and how you stopped.

Patrick McManus

THE PURIST

Patrick McManus writes a regular column for Field and Stream *magazine. "The Purist" is one of the essays in McManus' book* A Fine and Pleasant Misery *(1978). While readers concerned with writing styles and strategies will note how McManus explains several processes and how he uses understatement, they should read through the essay once just for fun.*

1   Twelve-year-olds are different from you and me, particularly when it comes to fishing, and most of all when it comes to fishing on Opening Day of Trout Season.

2   The twelve-year-old is probably the purest form of sports fisherman known to man. I don't know why. Perhaps it is because his passion for fishing is at that age undiluted by the multitude of other passions that accumulate over a greater number of years. Say thirteen.

3   Now I am reasonably sure that I can catch a limit of trout faster on Opening Day than the average twelve-year-old, but any angler knows that speed and quantity are not true measures of quality when it comes to fishing. It's a matter of style, and here the twelve-year-old beats me hands down. You just can't touch a twelve-year-old when it comes to style.

4   Preparation is the big part of his secret. If Opening Day of Trout Season is June 5, the twelve-year-old starts his preparation about the middle of March. He knows he should have started earlier, but at that age he likes to put things off. With such a late start, he will be hard pressed to be ready in time.

5   The first thing he does is to get his tackle out and look at it. He removes from one of his shoe boxes a large snarly ball of lines, hooks, leaders, spinners, flies, plugs, weeds, tree branches, and a petrified frog. He shakes the whole mass a couple of times and nothing comes loose. Pleased that everything is still in good order he stuffs it all back into his shoe box. The next time he will look at it will be on Opening Day Eve, fifteen minutes before he is supposed to go to bed. The tackle snarl will then provide the proper degree of wild, sweaty panic that is so much a part of the twelve-year-old's style.

6   The next order of business is to check his bait supplies. The best time to do this is in the middle of a blizzard, when it's too cold to be outside without a coat on or to have all the windows in the house open. The large jar of salmon eggs he has stored next to the hot-water pipes that run through his closet seems to look all right, but just to be sure he takes the lid off. He drops the lid on the floor and it rolls under something too large to move. Something must be done immediately, he knows, because uneasy murmurs are rising in distant parts of the house, and besides he won't be able to hold his breath forever. The best course of action seems to be to run the jar through every room in the building, leaving in his wake mass hysteria and the sound of windows being thrown open. Later, standing coatless with the rest of the family in the front yard while a chill north wind freshens up the house, he offers the opinion that he may need a new bottle of salmon eggs for Opening Day.

7   Occasionally the young angler will do some work on his hooks. There is, however, some diversity of opinion among twelve-year-olds whether it is better to crack off the crust of last year's worms from the hooks or to leave it on as a little added attraction for the fish. The wise father usually withholds any advice on the subject but does suggest that if his offspring decides to sharpen his hooks on the elder's whetstone, the worm crusts be removed *beforehand*. Nothing gums up a whetstone worse than oiled worm dust.

8   The twelve-year-old takes extra-special pains in the preparation of his fly rod. He gets it out, looks at it, sights down it, rubs it with a cloth, sights down it again, rubs it some more, and finally puts it away with an air of utter frustration. There is, after all, not much that you can do to a glass rod.

9   The reel is something else again. A thousand different things can be done to a reel, all of which can be grouped under the general term "taking it apart." The main reason a kid takes his reel apart is to take it apart. But most adults can't understand this kind of reasoning, so the kid has to come up with some other excuse. He says that he is taking his reel apart to clean it. No one can deny that the reel needs cleaning. It has enough sand and gravel in it to ballast a balloon. During most of the season it sounds like a miniature rock crusher and can fray the nerves of an adult fisherman at a hundred yards. For Opening Day, however, the reel must be clean.

10   There are three basic steps used by the twelve-year-old in cleaning a reel. First it is reduced to the largest possible number of parts. These are all carefully placed on a cookie sheet in the sequence of removal. The cookie sheet is then dropped on the

floor. The rest of the time between March and Opening Day of Trout Season is spent looking for these parts. The last one is found fifteen minutes before bedtime on Opening Day Eve.

11   Some twelve-year-olds like to test their leaders before risking them on actual fish. Nothing is more frustrating to a kid than having a leader snap just as he is heaving a nice fat trout back over his head. Consequently, he is concerned that any weakness in a leader be detected beforehand. There are many methods of doing this, but one of the best is to tie one end of the leader to a rafter in the garage and the other end to a concrete block. The concrete block is then dropped from the top of a stepladder. The chief drawback of this method is the cost involved in replacing cracked rafters.

12   Eventually the big night comes—Opening Day Eve.

13   The day is spent digging worms. Early in the season there is a surplus of worms and the young angler can be choosy. The process of worm selection is similar to that used in Spain for the selection of fighting bulls. Each worm is chosen for his size, courage, and fighting ability. One reason kids frequently have poor luck on Opening Day is that their worms can lick the average fish in a fair fight.

14   Approximately four hundred worms are considered an adequate number. These are placed in a container and covered with moist dirt. The container is then sealed and placed carefully back in the closet by the hot-water pipes, where it is next found during a blizzard the following March.

15   The twelve-year-old angler really peaks out, however, during that fifteen minutes before bedtime. He discovers that his tackle has become horribly snarled in his tackle box. No one knows how, unless perhaps the house has been invaded by poltergeists. The reel is thrown together with an expertise born of hysteria and panic. Four cogs, six screws, and a worm gear are left over, but the thing works. And it no longer makes that funny little clicking sound!

16   Finally, all is in readiness and the boy is congratulating himself on having had the good sense to start his preparation three months earlier. As it was, he went right down to the last minutes. Only one major task remains: the setting of the alarm clock.

17   Naturally, he wants to be standing ready beside his favorite fishing hole at the crack of dawn. The only trouble is he doesn't know exactly when dawn cracks. He surmises about four o'clock. If it takes him an hour to hike down to the fishing hole, that means he should set the alarm for about three. On the other hand, it may take longer in the dark, so he settles on 2:30. He doesn't have to allow any time for getting dressed since he will sleep with his clothes on.

18   Once in bed he begins to worry. What if the alarm fails to go off? He decides to test it. The alarm makes a fine, loud clanging sound. After all the shouting dies down and his folks are back in bed, he winds up the alarm again. As a precautionary measure, he decides to set the alarm for two, thus giving himself a half-hour safety margin. He then stares at the ceiling for an hour, visions of five-pound trout dancing in his head. He shakes with anticipation. He worries. What if the alarm fails to awaken him? What if he shuts it off and goes back to sleep? The horror of it is too much to stand.

19   Midnight. He gets up, puts on his boots, grabs his rod and lunch and brand-new bottle of salmon eggs, and heads out the door.

20   It's Opening Day of Trout Season, and there's not a minute to spare.

PRACTICE

Discussion

1. On what grounds is the twelve-year-old judged the purest form of fisherman? What is the prominent feature of his inimitable style?

2. How is the whole family involved in the mystique of the pure fisherman? What emotions are felt by other family members as the pure fisherman indulges his passion?

3. What are the three basic steps used by a twelve-year-old in cleaning a reel? How are these steps each symbolic of different aspects of the ultimate fisherman's style?

4. Is the process explained by McManus an artificial or a natural process? What phrases in the essay support your answer?

5. The main process discussed in the essay contains steps that involve mini-processes. Identify every process explained in the essay.

6. Where does McManus use a delayed statement to create a humorous effect? Where does he use understatement humorously? Where does he juxtapose two completely contradictory phrases or ideas to make us laugh?

7. Spot all the ways time and dates are mentioned in the essay. Why is a concern with time appropriate to a process explanation? What does McManus do with time in this essay that one does not usually expect in a process explanation?

8. Does McManus employ dialogue anywhere in the essay? How is the voice of the twelve-year-old occasionally introduced?

Vocabulary

diversity	ballast	cogs
whetstone	leaders	worm gear
fly rod	poltergeists	surmises
reel		

Writing

1. What did you really enjoy doing as a child? Explain how you did it in such a way that the explanation also conveys your enjoyment to the reader.

2. Observe a five-year-old (or a seventy-five-year-old) performing an activity that is important to him or her. Explain how the activity is performed. You may wish to be humorous, like McManus, but another perspective—admiring or sad, for example—may be more appropriate for your subject.

3. McManus distinguishes between style and output in fishing. Define style and, using illustration, support or refute the contention that style is a more important aspect of any activity than output.

Roger Welsch

SHELTERS ON THE PLAINS

Roger L. Welsch has been interested in folk architecture ever since graduate school. A professor of folklore at the University of Nebraska, Welsch would like to spend more of his time getting psychologically inside the buildings of the past—"thinking about them, feeling them, building them, tearing them down, driving nails, and cussing." As you will see in his essay, Welsch finds some unusual attitudes in the people who built the first "houses" on the American plains, people who may have been dominated by fear—but not fear of hostile Indians or marauding gunslingers.

The hinges are of leather
And the windows have no glass;
The board roof lets the howling
    blizzards in;
I can hear the hungry coyote
As he slinks up through the grass
'Round the little old sod
    shanty on my claim.

—Chorus of a Pioneer Plains Folksong

1   Even today the Great Plains crush travelers between the endless sky and a landscape that undulates like swells of the sea. But now, there are at least occasional trees and farmsteads, roads and telephone lines that delineate and articulate spaces within a land otherwise devoid of landmarks. Most of today's plains dwellers know the landscape and regard the climate and space as slight discomforts at worst, in contrast to the migrant homesteaders of the nineteenth century who had never imagined such a place in their worst dreams.

2   Then there were even fewer trees than now and the grasslands were not so neatly and re-assuringly divided into sizes the mind could digest. The term "prairie schooner" was only barely a metaphor. Ole E. Rölvaag, the Norwegian-born author, portrayed the life of the immigrants and described the vastness of the plains in his 1927 novel, *Giants in the Earth,*

> Bright clear sky over a plain so wide that the rim of the heavens cut down on it around the entire horizon. . . . Bright clear sky, today, tomorrow, and for all time to come. . . .
> And sun! And still more sun! It set the heavens afire every morning; it grew with the day to quivering golden light—then softened into all the shades of red and purple as evening fell. . . . Pure color everywhere. A gust of wind, sweeping across the plain, threw into life waves of yellow and blue and green. Now and then a dead black wave would race over the scene. . . a cloud! . . .

It was late afternoon. A small caravan was pushing its way through the tall grass. The track it left behind was like the wake of a boat—except that instead of widening out astern it closed in again.

3   The agony of frontier life on the plains is immortalized on tombstones, in the lyrics of folksongs, and in journals and daybooks. But archives often do not contain information on how people responded to specific conditions. I therefore turned to a source usually ignored by those who study folk architecture—the writers of the plains. I reasoned that these poets and novelists had based their hopes of success on a sensitive perception and faithful rendering of the pioneer experience. Such subjective and creative data necessitated careful evaluation; but then so must any field-gathered information.

4   I reread the works of such writers as Rölvaag, Willa Cather, Mari Sandoz, and Bess Streeter Aldrich, as well as the essays of architectural historian Amos Rapoport, architectural philospher Gaston Bachelard, and demographer John Demos, looking for clues to an understanding of the nature and degree of the impact of plains geography on the mind of the migrant. The message was clear: the plains were a mysterious land of frightening, unbounded space.

5   The intensity of plains geography was made all the sharper by the lens through which it was first seen by the pioneers: the eyes of hopeful immigrants—from Norway, Germany, Czechoslovakia—or of settlers from other parts of the United States, such as Wisconsin, Illinois, and Connecticut, where landscapes were more manageable. These people were accustomed to a perspective foreshortened by trees, rocks, lakes, and streams—rural scenes relieved by stone or timber fences a few hundred feet apart, by farmsteads numbering two or three to an eyeful.

6   The German farmers were accustomed to walking in the morning to fields they could shout across and then returning in the evening to a house among other houses, where there was company and communion. On the plains they farmed areas ten times bigger than they had in the Old Country. There were no fences, trees, or rocks, few neighbors within an hour's ride, and the nearest town was days away.

7   The distances were only one of the brutalities the Great Plains region dished up for its challengers. The temperature range exceeded, by twenty degrees at the top of the thermometer and forty at the bottom, any they had ever experienced in their homelands. The daily range could equal the annual range in Holland. In Czechoslovakia, there had been no prairie fires racing through the tinder-dry grass faster than a man on horseback. There had been no rattlesnakes and swarms of grasshoppers in Belgium; no cacti, buffalo, or vengeful Indians in Sweden. On the plains, the wind tore the covers from wagons and thunder shook the dishes from shelves. Hailstones, of a size that could kill horses, fell with terrifying abruptness. Trickles that would not have been worthy of a name in Germany were called rivers here, and like the Platte, they flowed—as some said—upside down, "with the sand on the top and the water underneath."

8   Thus the geography of America's northern plains region—Kansas, Nebraska, the Dakotas—offered climatic, social, and emotional violence that demanded the sturdiest of shelters. Yet, paradoxically, the plains withheld all the materials the settlers had traditionally used for building. There was little stone, even for chimneys; little wood, even for cooking. The most logical first thought would be hasty retreat.

9   Rölvaag's powerful writing grew from his own experience in the wilderness: one of his characters faces a future on the plains and cries, "How will human beings be able to

endure this place? Why, there isn't even a thing that one can hide behind!" Retreat is a universal motif in plains literature and folklore. A character in Willa Cather's novel *O Pioneers!* agonizes, "The country was never meant to live in; the thing to do was to get back to Iowa, to Illinois, to any place that had been proved habitable."

10   Consider just one aspect of what the pioneers experienced as they moved westward—the change in forestation. During the nineteenth century, Indiana was almost totally forested in hardwoods—mostly oak and walnut. Forty percent of Illinois was forested; Iowa only 18 percent, hinting, perhaps, at what lay ahead. Nebraska, Kansas, and the Dakotas were 3 percent forested, mainly in a line along the Missouri River at the eastern edge of the Great Plains.

11   And yet the promise of owning land, a farm many times the size of farms in the Old Country (where the possibility of ever possessing even a small one was unlikely) steeled the settlers' resolve to stay and blurred the impact of the catalog of trials they encountered. Besides, most of them had spent everything they had, in both money and pride, to get here, and they could scarcely turn back.

12   These people had to build houses. They quickly used up the trees crowding the river and creek banks in building their traditional log houses. The next alternative, one that made homesteading on the plains a possibility, was the earth, the sod, or "Nebraska marble." And for thirty years the standard on the plains was the sod house. (How sod came to be used as a building material is uncertain. The settlers may have borrowed the idea from the Mormons, who began building with sod in the mid-1850s. The Mormons, in turn, probably got the idea from the earth lodges of the Omaha and Pawnee Indians.)

13   Today we make every effort to design houses that bring the out-of-doors indoors and take the indoors out-of-doors. Patios serve as dining rooms; huge windows provide the illusion that we are outside when we are inside. We open the house walls and break down barriers. But for nineteenth-century plains dwellers, perceptions were different. After a day of being squeezed between sky and earth, of being exposed to the withering sun or a razor-sharp wind, there was little desire on the part of the pioneers to bring the environment into their houses.

14   The house was meant to be a fortress, a bastion for shutting out the outside. The thick walls, the few small windows and close rooms were not seen as disadvantages—as they might be now—but rather as an integral part of the sod house's advantages. Far from being discomfited by the cramped quarters, plains settlers sought the closeness of family members in the evening hours, after a day spent out of sight and hearing of each other or, for that matter, of any other human being. The close contact and association with the family took on a very special, desirable quality.

15   Writers' words resound with echoes of this premise. To be sure, the settlers saw the plains as a source of wealth, but the riches could be won only by facing nature. The plains, with their promise of treasure and freedom, demanded an ardent suitor, one willing to face tasks and trials much like those required of fairy-tale heroes in their quest for a princess bride. The land was an adversary, an enemy, to be conquered and tamed. Sod was first and foremost an expedient response to plains geography. It not only answered the absence of conventional building materials but also countered the problems of heat, cold, wind, and defense. The two- to three-foot-thick walls kept the sod house warm in winter and cool in the summer. Neither wind nor bullets could pass through them. Grass

fires, a constant threat, would sweep by the soddies, singeing the door and window frames but leaving the interiors cool. Inside the cavelike buildings, the roar of the wind and thunder was only a faint murmur.

16   The settlers usually built their sod houses on a slight rise or hillside, never in a low-land or valley bottom where a spring flood might destroy them. They first leveled out a floor area with spades, then wetted and tamped it solid with a fence post or wagon tongue. This was the only foundation the house would have.

17   Moist bottomlands produced the best sod. Here the grass was toughest and the soil was more likely to hold together during the processes of cutting, moving, and house construction. Preferred grasses were buffalo grass (*Buchloë dactyloides*), cordgrass (*Spartina pectinata*) and big bluestem (*Andropogon gerardii*). Only enough sod for a day's work—about a quarter acre—was cut at one time so that no sod would lie in the open overnight and dry out. A standard 12-by 14-foot soddie required about one acre of sod. Wherever possible, oxen were used to cut sod because they gave a smoother pull on the plow than horses, which tended to lurch under the heavy task.

18   The tool used for cutting sod was not the conventional farming plow, the purpose of which was to tumble and break up the soil. Rather, a grasshopper plow, which had a horizontal blade, was used to shave away a ribbon of sod, three to four inches thick and eighteen inches wide, which passed smoothly over a rod moldboard and rolled over up-side down behind the plow. Workers used sharp spades to cut this ribbon into "bricks" about two feet long. The bricks were then loaded onto a wagon or sledge and hauled to the house site.

19   The bricks formed the walls and were laid up grass-side down (for reasons I have never been able to discover) without any sort of mortar. To increase their stability and discour-age tunneling by mice or snakes, the bricks were staggered. When the walls reached a height of two to three feet, simple board frames for the door and windows were set in place and propped with sticks. The rest of the walls then went up around them. Later, dowels were driven through the frames and into the walls to hold the windows in place.

20   The slightly pitched roofs were made of from three to five heavy cedar beams, running from gable to gable on each side of the building. Over these beams the builders laid willow or cottonwood rods from peak to eave. Chokecherry or plum brush, then a layer of long grass—usually bluestem or prairie cordgrass—and finally, a layer of sod bricks followed. Here the sod was laid grass-side up so it would continue to grow and hold the roof together.

21   This early, expedient form of dwelling, often as much cave as house, had severe shortcomings, however. As the lyrics of "Starving to Death on a Government Claim," a folksong of the period, depict it,

My house it is built out of
national soil,
The walls are erected according
to Hoyle;
The roof has no pitch, it is level
and plain,
But I never get wet—unless
it happens to rain.

22   Even after a rain had ended, water from the thick sod roof would continue to drip inside a house for several days.

23   Before many years this *ad hoc* house type began to undergo the polishing processes of tradition. A technology of sod construction quickly developed; within twenty years it had transformed the miserable sod hovel into the sometimes elegant sod home. The walls of these more elaborate dwellings were shaved with a spade, giving them clean, sharp lines. Window frames were slanted to permit more light to come through. Commercial or homemade plaster and stucco covered the house inside and out to increase its durability and reduce a major problem of sod houses—fleas. These insects infested the porous walls and plagued the occupants.

24   Windows, the most expensive component of the house (and one required by many homesteading laws), often cracked or broke with the uneven settling of the heavy walls. Builders ingeniously solved the problem by leaving a four- to-six inch gap above the window during construction. This space was stuffed with paper or grass; as the walls settled, the gap simply closed.

25   Leaking roofs—the perpetual bane of sod houses—were made watertight either by adding a layer of plaster on the thatch under the roof sod or by using commercial cedar shingles brought in by railroad. Most houses still retained a sod covering over the shingles for insulation and to add enough weight to hold the roof on during high winds.

26   At the end of the nineteenth century, the suitability of the sod house for plains conditions became most apparent. The Nebraska State Historical Society's photographic collection of sod houses reveals ample amounts of milled lumber lying near the dwellings. Those who had settled on the plains during the early part of this century told me that while frame construction was fine for animals, sod was best for people. Wood burns, rots, warps, swells, and shrinks; insects and mice chew through it; and the cold penetrates it. The large number of still standing, and frequently still occupied, sod houses that are fifty to eighty years old offers further substantiation of the durability of sod.

27   Why then did plains dwellers almost universally abandon sod for frame construction during the late nineteenth century? The primary cause was class consciousness. Those who had achieved financial security could advertise their success through the frame house.

28   As another reason, the initial impact of plains geography had begun to wear off. As a familiar plains' line goes, "Living in Nebraska is a lot like being hanged; the initial shock is a bit abrupt but once you hang there for a while you sort of get used to it." In the demise of sod houses, the forbidding mystery of the plains had dissipated to the extent that inhabitants no longer felt the need for the physical and psychological security that these dwellings offered.

29   Sod houses still dot the plains. Some are still lived in, but most are just derelicts—abandoned, their roofs overgrown, their door and window frames sagging. These ghosts, however, are more than merely abandoned houses. They are reminders of the grip the plains had on their early settlers. Behind their dark sod, these houses offered protection from a lonely and inhospitable land. They also offer another reminder—their abandonment and replacement by wood frames are symbolic of a reversal in attitude. Now, it appears that plains dwellers have a grip on the land instead of the other way around. Thus the sod house was as much a product on the impact of the plains on the human mind as it was a product of the geography of the plains.

30   A farmer friend of mine commented a short time ago, "We seem to forget that we may have made this land what it is, but first it made us what we are."

31   It also made the plains' houses of our parents and grandparents.

PRACTICE

Discussion

1. Is the process the author describes *natural* or *artificial?*

2. Is the author giving directions or making an explanation?

3. List and explain the major *sentence pointers* (pages 88–90).

4. How many paragraphs does the author take to get to the description of the process? Why is the introduction so long?

5. State the thesis of Welsch's essay. Is the thesis directly related to the process he describes?

6. How does the author's discussion of the psychological effects of living on the plains contribute to his ethical proof?

7. Give the *steps* of the process and its *end point.*

8. Explain the structure of paragraph 7.

Vocabulary

delineate	discomfited	substantiation
devoid	resound	derelicts
demographer	expedient	

Writing

1. Consider the last sentence to paragraph 29. Write a paper on a similar theme as applied to something else in your own culture. For example: *The family van is as much a product of American lifestyle as it is a method of getting from one place to another.*

2. Welsch used *process* because he wanted to show how a certain group of people adapted to negative forces on them. Write a process paper in which you show how a group or individual you are aware of undergoes a process for a similar reason. Sample topic: *the process my brother created to adapt to the demands placed by our ambitious parents on his meager athletic skills.*

3. If you were under house arrest for a year (no visitors allowed), what major process would you create to combat your loneliness and boredom? You can use everything in your house but phone, radio, and TV, which have been removed.

CHAPTER 14

Cause and Effect (Causation)

Cause and effect (or simply causation) refers to a specific relationship between events in time. If you fail to look both ways before crossing a street and get hit by a car, the *cause* is failing to look and the *effect* is getting hit. If a doctor tells you that you have a broken leg from the accident, the broken leg is the effect of getting hit by the car, which is the cause. An event (in this case, the accident) can be *both* a cause and an effect of other events.

As a strategy of development, *causation* answers the question "Why did it happen?" You will find causation useful not only by itself but also combined with other strategies. It is often used with *process* because *how* something happened (process) is often related to *why* something happened (causation).

For many subjects—particularly those related to social and political matters—causes and effects are ambiguous or indistinct, leaving you unsure about the truth of the situation. Therefore, you must be very careful when you discuss causes and effects. For many subjects you also have the reactions of your reader to worry about because your analysis of a cause-and-effect relationship might be controversial, and your reader may not agree with you. For example, in discussions about causes and effects in certain social issues—such as crime or government spending—some readers may object to your analysis. Therefore, stance is very important in this strategy.

■■■ Recognizing the Signs of Causation

In order to identify and determine whether or not a cause-and-effect relationship is logical, you should look for certain signs. Two of the most common are:

THE SIGN OF ASSOCIATION.   Suppose you find two events, A and B, in association. Their being together could imply that A causes B, or vice versa. However, B must ordinarily occur whenever A does—otherwise you probably don't have a genuine cause-and-effect relationship. For instance, hair should bleach when a strong solution of peroxide is applied to it; the cook should burn his hand every time he touches a very hot skillet handle.

THE SIGN OF TIME-SEQUENCE.   If B comes after A in time, this fact may imply a causal relationship. If a student stays up all night studying, the fatigue he suffers the next day is an effect signaled by time. But determining time-sequence is so tricky that a special name has been given to the fallacy of misinterpreting it. The fallacy is called *post hoc* (short for *post hoc, ergo propter hoc*—"after this, therefore because of this"). You create the *post hoc* fallacy if you say that A causes B merely because B comes after A. In other words, if the 8:30 train comes after the 8:15 train, you cannot say that the earlier train "causes" the later one.

In brief, the signs of causation are no more than signs—they are not proofs. To avoid making fallacies in thinking about causation, you must take each sign and investigate it carefully. Never assume that a causal relationship exists until you find proof.

One cause ———————————————————————→ One effect

A strong head wind will cause the biker   to gear down.

One cause ———————————————————————→ Two
or more
effects

A slight rise in the road causes   increased pressure
on the pedal
so   the biker gears down.

Two
or more ———————————————————————→ One effect
causes

Failing to gear down   can create
while going uphill   serious knee problems.
or against a strong headwind

Two ———————————————————————→ Two
or more   or more
causes   effects

Short toe clips and   serious knee problems
a seat too high can cause   and pain in the legs.

The diagram on page 241 shows four types of cause-and-effect sequences that you should be aware of. (The examples support the thesis: *Proper gearing and equipment may help a biker avoid leg and knee problems.*)

In most situations, more than one cause or effect is involved. Drug addiction, for example, may have several causes, and these causes may have more than a single effect.

Following is an annotated cause-and-effect paper written by a student. Notice the writer's use of transitions, examples, and summary statements, making the cause-and-effect relationship clear.

Definition of term by negation	1	Student-watchers have long identified a common type on campus—the "Joiner." I don't mean the woman who belongs to the band and the Pi Phis, and maybe in her junior year joins an accounting
Question posed; answered by succeeding pars.		honorary. Nor do I mean the engineer who belongs to a mere three organizations. Nothing so limiting works for the true Joiner, who may belong to six or eight organizations, and who may pop up in student government as well. What makes Joiners join?
First cause, supported by three examples	2	First, Joiners like the limelight. Most of the groups they belong to are visible. On the dorm council they write petitions, or collect the petitions of others. In the marching band they perform before thousands of people. In fraternities, they are the treasurers who hound people for money and make long reports in meetings on the state of fraternal economy.
Transition, introducing second cause with one example Summary statement, explaining effect of cause	3	As these remarks imply, Joiners like to run things. My sister is a Joiner, and one can be sure that any group she belongs to, she is president or leader of it. If the group has no important office to fill, she will run it by indirection, volunteering to do this or that job, writing any necessary letters or memos, being the first one at the meeting and the last to leave. No job is too small for her to take on cheerfully. By the end of the semester, any group she joins discovers that she has become its chief bottle-washer and major spokesman. She has fulfilled her desire to control events and people.
Last cause with transition, finally *Example Surprise ending*	4	Finally, Joiners join because they must have something to do with themselves. They are usually hyperactive. Have you ever seen a Joiner sitting alone, perhaps in the Union, just reading a book? Sam, on the men's side of my dorm, is a Joiner; and for all the time I have known him, he has never been alone. People in the dorm say that Sam even goes to the bathroom with somebody. He belongs to eight organizations, and will someday be president of the country—if he can just decide which political party to join.

Occasionally, it is necessary and rhetorically useful to organize a cause-and-effect essay or paragraph by introducing the effect first, then giving an explanation of the causes. Note how the writer in the following excerpt explains why the poor have more garbage than the rich.

Effect	1	. . . low-income neighborhoods in Tucson discard 86 percent more garbage per week per household than do high-income areas, and 40 percent more waste than medium-income districts. There is a trick to that statistic. There are more people per household in low-income areas. But, even dividing on a per person basis, the poor pro-

duce more garbage than the middle class and only slightly less than the rich.

Question: why? 2   Why? It's not so hard to figure out. The rich buy antiques, the poor buy and throw away cheap or used furniture. The rich give their old clothes to the "Goodwill," the poor buy them there, wear them out and throw them away. And it is the poor and the working people who discard most of the packaging waste. They are the ones who drink soft drinks and beer and eat low-cost canned vegetables and canned

Causes   stews, fish sticks, pot pies, and T.V. dinners. And, if they eat out at all, it is at McDonalds or Burger King or Kentucky Fried Chicken, with the packaging which that entails. It is the rich who have their food flown in fresh daily from Florida or Spain. It is the rich who eat in the fancy French restaurants with all those superb dishes prepared from scratch, sans packaging and sans disposable dinner ware.

—Judd Alexander, "Truth and Consequences"

▼ Suggestions for Writing Cause-and-Effect Papers

When describing causation, remember this advice:

1. *Investigate your subject thoroughly, either from your own firsthand knowledge or from research.* Identifying the causes and effects in a subject that you know firsthand can be easy to do. Your dissatisfaction with your roommate, for instance, may be based on the fact that he won't do his share in keeping the apartment clean. The *cause* is his laziness or carelessness. The *effect* is your anger and frustration. But identifying the causes of pollution in Los Angeles is much more difficult because pollution is a complex problem, and without doing research, you will not know enough to write about the subject.

2. *Qualify your generalizations carefully when you draw cause-and-effect relationships.* Do not hesitate to use qualifiers such as "it seems to me," "it may be," or "the evidence points to." In most cause-and-effect relationships, you deal in probabilities rather than certainties, particularly when you get out of the realm of scientific subjects.

3. *Be sure that your time-sequence is accurate and inclusive.* This is especially true when you are explaining scientific causes and effects. You should present the chronology of the steps as they actually occur, and you should include every important link in the chain of events in order to ensure the accuracy of your paper. Here is an effective explanation of why Mexican jumping beans jump:

1   A simple explanation reveals the secret of the fascinating twisting, turning and jumping of the beans. Inside each bean is a tiny yellow caterpillar, the larvae of a

small moth. How does it get there? The moth lays an egg in the flower of the spurge shrub. In time the eggs hatch and the larvae are said to work their way deep into the blossom, where they are eventually encased in the seeds.

2   The caterpillar devours a large part of the inside of the seed, so that it occupies about one-fifth of the interior of its little home. To move the bean, the caterpillar grasps the silken wall of the bean with its legs and vigorously snaps its body, striking its head against the other end of the bean and sending it this way or that. The bean may actually travel several inches at a time, or leap in the air. Some people call them bronco beans because of the way they jump.

3   A jumping bean may keep up its antics for as long as six months. Then the caterpillar finally emerges from its house and becomes a moth.

—"Why Mexican Jumping Beans Jump," *Awake!*

4. *Separate "sufficient" from "contributory" causes.* An event may contribute to a cause, but it will not be sufficient in itself to create an effect. Failing to add baking powder or soda to biscuit dough is *sufficient* cause for the dough's failure to rise. A *contributory* cause to the flat biscuits might be a distracting phone call you had just when you were about to add the leavening agent. However, it isn't the phone call that caused the biscuits to be flat, but rather your forgetting to add the soda or baking powder. So you separate the phone call (*contributory* cause) from the lack of leavening agent (*sufficient* cause).

5. *Do not ignore immediate effects in a chain of multiple effects.* Note this description of the multiple effects of the cholera organism:

For centuries, men had known that cholera was a fatal disease, and that it caused severe diarrhea, sometimes producing as many as thirty quarts of fluid a day. Men knew this, but they somehow assumed that the lethal effects of the disease were unrelated to the diarrhea; they searched for something else: an antidote, a drug, a way to kill the organism. It was not until modern times that cholera was recognized as a disease that killed through dehydration primarily; if you could replace a victim's water losses rapidly, he would survive the infection without other drugs or treatment.

—Michael Crichton. *The Andromeda Strain*

A diagram of this chain of cause and effect might look like this:

Cholera organism (first cause)
↘
    diarrhea (first immediate effect)
    ↘
        dehydration (second immediate effect)
        ↘
            death (ultimate effect)

In this case, the failure to investigate the implications of an important immediate effect led to disastrous consequences.

6. *Much of what we loosely call "cause and effect" is actually "correlation."* In the process of identifying causation, researchers study samples to see if they can establish a pattern from which a generalization can be drawn about why something occurred. For example, from many medical experiments, researchers have discovered that there is a *correlation* between high cholesterol level and heart disease. They do not conclude that high cholesterol level *causes* heart disease but that a significant *correlation* exists between the two. You may use correlation in an analysis of cause and effect, but do not identify as causes what may only be correlations.

▼ Planning and Revising Cause and Effect (An Example)

Jana writes:

Irritationnnn. Illritatatat . . . irrittt IRRITIATION what did I do, s hit the sf shift key?

This is the most . . . . ok back to electric typewriter.

The keyboard is unfamiliar. The screen hurts my eyes. The printer goes clack, brzzt, clack. If you punch the wrong button, the whole thing disappears. The screen talks back to me: ARE YOU SURE YOU WANT TO LOG OUT, JANA?

I say: Yes, you monster, LOG ME OUT OF THIS THING!!!

It says dutifully, JANA LOGGED OUT MONDAY OCTOBER 20, 1995, 2:35 PM.

Phooey.

Now Jana has it out of her system. Her mother, a freelance writer, has a new computer with a word processor and letter-quality printer added on. Jana can log into the computer whenever her mother isn't using it. But as you can see from her brainstorming, her early experience on the new and unfamiliar equipment was not a pleasant one.

After two days and hours of practice with the computer and word processor, Jana decides to write a cause-effect paper based in part on her brainstorming material.

What I want to show [she writes in her plan of attack on the paper] is that when you first use the computer and word processor, all the causes lead to one effect: confusion and anger—most of which are UNNECESSARY. That is my hook: *unnecessary.*

Writer: me.

Point: I just said it.

Reader: Anybody just starting out on a word processor.

Here's my order of main ideas:

Makes no sense, partic. keyboard

Machine confusing— *commands?*

Printer noise

――――――――――――――――――――――

*But now they don't seem to bother
me as much. (?)*

And here I go!

Jana's draft

1. All right monster, I have logged in. And I have named you . . .
ZARKON. (Wasn't Zarkon a villain on STAR TREK?) Well
irregardless, ZARKON, you are now (and forever will be) a
villain.

2. The first thing about you, ZARKON, is that you're crazy. Look
at your keyboard. The asterisk is above the 8 where the
apostrophe ought to be; so I keep writing *Mother*s Manuscript*,
*Jack*s foot*, etc. On the left side of the keyboard are 10 buttons
numbered F1 through F10. On the right side are buttons called
Num Lock and *Scroll Lock*, *End*, *Ins*, and so on. My favorite button
is named *PrtSc*. Didn't she win the Derby last year?

3. When I put my fingers on the keys, I inevitably place them
wrong because there are extra keys where no keys should be.
Also the key shift for capitals is one key too far to the left, so I
keep hitting the wrong key when I want to make a capital. The
result is I can't type decently and spend too much time
correcting.

4. On top of that, ZARKON, you are too hard to use when I try to
take the WordPerfect lessons. I log in, punch the buttons your
manual tells me to, and then you say WRONG COMMAND. How
could it be the wrong command when you told me to do it? Now I
just sit there with the cursor flashing at me. My lesson is gone from
the screen—how do I get it back? I punch the ESC [escape] button
and nothing happens. Listen, ZARKON, If I say *escape*, I mean
escape. Let me out! I called the dealer. He said type in DIR for
directory. Ok, now I am back to the lesson. But how did I get there?

5. Now ZARKON, a few words about your printer. It goes *clack, brzzt, clack*; and now and then *whirrpp*. Your daisy wheel is a real flower, too. It goes in two directions, almost at once. The noise this printer makes is awful, and in Mom's little office it scrapes on my ear like a fingernail noise on a blackboard. Then, ZARKON, you jammed your paper. When I got up to unjam your paper, I tripped over the plug and pulled it out of the wall and ERASED ALL MY WORK.

6. ZARKON, you are an idiot and a bore and noisy . . . two days ago. Now, for some reason you seem docile and even pleasant. Even dare I say it, even a little easy to use? Is it possible you have spiked my diet cola with a little outer-space dumb drug?

7. I am not yet ready to believe that the two ZARKONS are one and the same, that just because I get a little used to you, you are suddenly a pussy cat.

8. ZARKON—are you trying to tell me that all the pain and irritation were unnecessary?

9. *Brrzt, clack.*

PRACTICE

Discussion

1. Remember that Jana's paper on the computer (and word processor) consists at this point of (a) a short piece of brainstorming, (b) a scratch outline of topics to cover, and (c) a first draft.

   Go back over these three materials and make direct suggestions to Jana for her next draft, which we will assume will be her final one. Consider every part of her writing problem: hook, point of her paper, organization of draft, paragraphing, sentences, words, choice of detail, grammar. Do you recommend that she make many changes in her draft?

   Describe the cause-effect patterns implicit in the paper.

2. Discuss the accuracy and validity of the cause-and-effect relationships in these statements:

   a. The state's experiment in the abolition of capital punishment is going badly. During the first six months of the trial period, murders are up an estimated 20 percent and there has been a rash of sex crimes against children. Last week two child rapists got life imprisonment—which practically means, in this state, parole after twenty years.

   b. *Statistic:* If you change jobs very often, your chance of having a heart attack is two or three times greater than if you stay at one job for a long time.

c. Why do people who in private talk so pungently often write so pompously? There are many reasons: tradition, the demands of time, carelessness, the conservative influence of the secretary. Above all is the simple matter of status. Theorem: the less established the status of a person, the more his dependence on jargon. Examine the man who has just graduated from pecking out his own letters to declaiming them to a secretary and you are likely to have a man hopelessly intoxicated with the rhythm of businessese. Conversely, if you come across a blunt yes or no in a letter, you don't need to glance further to grasp that the author feels pretty firm in his chair.

—William H. Whyte, "The Language of Business," *Fortune* magazine

d. The dog [as a pet] has advantages in the way of uselessness as well as in special gifts of temperament. He is often spoken of, in an eminent sense, as the friend of man, and his intelligence and fidelity are praised. The meaning of this is that the dog is man's servant and that he has the gift of an unquestioning subservience and a slave's quickness in guessing his master's mood. Coupled with these traits, which fit him well for relation of status—and which must for the present purpose be set down as serviceable traits—the dog has some characteristics which are of a more equivocal aesthetic value. He is the filthiest of the domestic animals in his person and the nastiest in his habits. For this he makes up in a servile, fawning attitude towards his master, and a readiness to inflict damage and discomfort on all else. The dog, then, commends himself to our favour by affording play to our propensity for mastery, and as he is also an item of expense, and commonly serves no industrial purpose, he holds a well-assured place in men's regard as a thing of good repute. The dog is at the same time associated in our imagination with the chase—a meritorious employment and an expression of the honorable predatory impulse.

—Thorstein Veblen, *The Theory of the Leisure Class*

Writing

1. Choose one of the following hypothetical situations that could be appropriate for you. (If you don't have a car, situation **a** wouldn't fit your life.) If none of the situations suit you, develop one of your own, using the format: "If I . . . then . . . "

   Make a list of all the possible effects of taking such an action. Classify or group the effects, develop a generalization for each class or group, and use the generalizations as paragraph topic leads (or topic sentences) in a discussion of causation.

a. If I decide to sell my car, then . . .

b. If I get married this month, then . . .

c. If I decide to quit school and go to work full-time, then . . .

d. If my parents are unable to help pay my tuition next fall, then . . .

e. If I can move into an apartment, then . . .

f. If I change majors, then . . .

2. Pick a subject concerning your hometown. Write a paper discussing the possible cause-and-effect relationships in the subject. Possible broad subjects are: crime, education, religion, prosperity, government, sports, race relations, culture, economics. (Be sure to narrow your topic.)

3. Develop a cause-and-effect essay on one of the following familiar topics:

a. The effect of children on a family, or the effect of not having children.

b. The effect of the change of seasons on your behavior.

c. The effect of paperback books on reading.

d. The effect of compulsory attendance laws on education.

e. The effect of the Beatles on popular music.

f. The effect of moving a child from one community to another.

   The following topics are more specialized and may take some research:

g. The effect of salt on automobiles.

h. The effect of extreme cold or extreme heat on a machine or an animal.

i. The effect of loss of electricity, due to a storm, on a household.

j. The effect of public opinion polls on the news.

k. The effect of allergies on the body.

   You may find a combination of process and cause-effect useful for some of the above. For example, the *process* of salting the streets in the winter has an *effect* on automobiles.

4. Discuss the effects that would occur if one of the following were suddenly taken away from you and you had to live for a year without it:

a. a telephone

b. a television set

c. a refrigerator

d. a computer

e. a bicycle, car, or motorcycle

Claudia Dowling

THE RELATIVE EXPLOSION

The following article by journalist Claudia Dowling appeared in Psychology Today. *Dowling speaks from experience when she writes about the relative explosion of the nuclear family. She is both a mother and a stepmother. In "The Relative Explosion," Dowling takes for her subject a very complex sociological phenomenon and its attendant issues and uses the associations of cause and effect as the means to unravel a few of the complexities.*

1   There is a new family in America, riddled with ex-spouses and half siblings, stepchildren and former in-laws, lovers and their children, not to mention an unprecedented collection of other relationships. In family law, according to the *New York Times,* "concepts unheard of a decade ago—joint custody of children . . . visiting rights for grandparents, and so-called habitation contracts between those not married but living together—have become commonplace in the courts." Today, a four-member "nuclear family" can boast as many surnames; to sort out the ties that bind might faze a genealogist for whom *Debrett's Peerage* is light reading. Not surprisingly, these complicated connections of blood and lust have left many men, women, and children floundering, for no clear social rules exist to guide them through the forms of modern serial monogamy.

2   The tangled web of new relationships is arguably the legacy of the 60s. Almost anyone who lived through that era without suffering a chemically induced memory burnout can embark on a recitation of who lived with whom and then subsequently with whomever else, an account that would be as dull as the begats. In this chain of connections, moreover, all the people usually knew one another, often in the biblical sense. "One thing you can say about our friends," comments a survivor, "we didn't sleep with strangers."

3   That, in a sense, was the problem—or if not the problem, the ingredient that was to change everything. The so-called sexual revolution led these bedfellows to act out their loves and passions one after the other in something of a round-robin manner. Risqué types had been doing that in Hollywood for years, but actors and actresses usually married the people whom they went to bed with. The 60s kids did not. At first. But they grew up. They waited a little longer than their parents, but eventually they did marry. Then some of them got unmarried and did it again. Every relationship—legal and otherwise—was played out against the backdrop of who had lived with whom before. And as the various unions have been blessed with progeny, things have become really complex.

4   Perhaps as an extension of that charming but outmoded exhortation to "love everybody," the members of the 60s generation do not sever past ties with ease. Indeed, they take pleasure and sometimes pride in maintaining all their ties, à la Bo and John and Ursula and Linda. Divorced partners no longer cut each other dead as a matter of course, particularly when there are children in the picture. Child-rearing has become an activity for both parents, especially when the parents are no longer married. Fathers are demanding, and taking, an active role, a rarity in the past. Equal parenting is made easier by the

fact that divorces are by and large less acrimonious and certainly less beset by social stigma than even a decade ago. After all, these marriages were just legal chapters in the continuing serial. Besides, these days everybody's doing it: One out of two couples eventually hits the matrimonial skids. Children have become virtually communal property.

5   The effects of this shared responsibility are only beginning to be felt by the new generation, but the unprecedented technical difficulties for their fathers and mothers—and their grandparents—are already enormous. For one thing, each child is the beneficiary of at least two complete sets of holidays, in some instances divided by hours of solitary plane flights. A mitigating factor for the young travelers is that the holidays are all accompanied by presents. For another thing, each child, in all likelihood, now has two sets of parents, each with an arithmetically expanding flock of satellite relatives—uncles, aunts, and cousins, some of whom have also been married more than once—in addition to two sets of grandparents and at least one set of stepgrandparents. This is the Relative Explosion.

6   In the interests of simplicity, some divorced parents have found it advisable to combine forces. This is possible only for those of enlightened sensibilities, and even then it can lead to situations that are the stuff of television comedies. One modern man reports: "In the past three years, I have spent two Thanksgivings, one Christmas, one New Year's Eve, three spring breaks and two weeks at the shore with my present wife, my son from my first marriage, and my ex-wife. Plus her present mate and his child and various combinations of my parents and my present wife's parents. It made our heads spin at first. We all thought that we were being incredibly mature. But now we just think it's normal . . . "

7   Obviously, the skills appropriate to life in the Relative Explosion have yet to be defined. The most critical need is for large portions of forbearance and tolerance—what some circles call "keeping cool" and others call "being laidback." Certain groups may find that large quantities of alcohol or other depressants are stopgap aids for New Family gatherings. But such artificial de-stimulation was an Old Family gathering standby too, so it can hardly be considered ground-breaking.

8   Coming to a comfortable *modus operandi* requires, first of all, an ordering of priorities. Top priorities should be one's current partner and one's children by birth, marriage, or whatever. If some of the children are the result of a previous relationship, the demands may conflict. A parent will have to deal with his or her ex, which may annoy, anger, or frighten the current partner.

9   One way to defuse the threat of an ex is to include his or her present mate in any necessary gathering. Such coupling is particularly desirable if the occasion requires an overnight stay; it removes much of the awkwardness of bedtime for everyone. And if one is the guest ex, one feels much less like a marauder in enemy territory. An additional benefit is that the *status quo* is graphically illustrated for children who, however, accepting of their new circumstances, may still harbor a latent desire to see their parents get back together. Seeing each parent with his or her separate partner helps a child accept the original break.

10   In regard to children and exes, most parents and many of those *in loco parentis* are willing to put their own emotional games aside in a child's interest. If a child feels better knowing that his or her estranged parents are on speaking terms—and most do—mature adults will bow gracefully to their needs. Children need not, indeed should not, suffer the torment of divided loyalties. On the other hand, if it seems to make children uncomfortable to see their parents together, there is obviously no need to pursue conviviality for its own sake.

11   Stepparents will find that it is best in most cases to refrain from forcing a spouse's child to "think of me as your own father." The child already has parents and, if our own experiences are anything to go by, doesn't need any more. Loaded appellations like "Dad" or "Mama Sue" will not help children cope. First names are best, indicating intimacy but not family ties. This also goes for well-meaning step-uncles, -aunts, -grandparents, and so on. How many relatives can one youngster deal with?

12   All this suggests that the New Family is perhaps the most difficult of all for children. They may have half siblings who spend much more time with one parent than they themselves can. A child of a first marriage may view the child of a second as an interloper, stealing the attention of the father or mother. A child of the second marriage may be threatened by the older half sibling who comes like an invader for the summer and seems to have some prior claim on the parent. Fortunately, left to themselves, children are eminently capable of sorting out their own differences and will quickly arrive at a working relationship. The worst possible thing a parent can do is to disparage the absent parent of one child in the presence of another. "I can see where you got your temper, and it wasn't from me—little Johnny doesn't talk that way." Such remarks are unfair to both children and cast the parent in the role of a hanging judge. And who can trust a hanging judge?

13   It is particularly important to use self-control when embarked on New Family voyages. The one shoal to steer absolutely clear of is allusion to the past. "Before your mother and I were divorced . . ." or "You always used to . . ." are unwise beginnings to any sentence. With those former ties of love and lust omnipresent in the air, all reminiscences are emotionally volatile. Even if they don't offend the children or the ex, they will assuredly offend the current partner.

14   After all, we made our beds. And if we suffer a restless night or two coping with the perplexing intricacies, we have ourselves to blame, and we can find the way to resolve them. These struggles to integrate the past with the present are the growing pains of a new design for society. What the result of the struggle may be in emotional, social, linguistic, legal, and political terms, no one knows. But in striving to make their lives and relationships workable in an entirely new context, many of today's young adults are pioneers. Their performance will be measured by coming generations.

PRACTICE

Discussion

1. What is the cause or causes of the Relative Explosion according to Dowling? What are the effects? Can you think of other causes and effects that Dowling has not mentioned?

2. What advice does Dowling give for coping with the effects of the Relative Explosion? How does her advice contribute to her ethical proof?

3. Where do Dowling's sympathies and concerns in this article seem most to lie—with men, women, current spouses, ex-spouses, or children? How can you tell?

4. Dowling uses a number of foreign terms or references. Compile a list of all that you can find. What does this choice of words tell you about Dowling's expected audience?

5. This article appeared in *Psychology Today,* a popular magazine. Why could it never have appeared in its current form in a scholarly journal for professional psychologists? Cite specific examples that support your answer. What paragraph or paragraphs could have been published unchanged in such a journal? Is that paragraph or paragraphs inappropriate for *Psychology Today?*

6. Which type or types of cause-and-effect sequence does Dowling use to construct her essay? (Refer to your answer to the earlier question on causes and effects.)

7. Where does Dowling use dialogue in the essay? Is it used successfully? Explain your answer.

8. How carefully docs Dowling qualify her generalizations about cause and effect? Find as many examples as you can of qualification. How do her qualifications add to your confidence in her handling of evidence?

Vocabulary

faze	risqué	mitigating
monogamy	progeny	*modus operandi*
begats	acrimonious	*status quo*
round-robin	stigma	*in loco parents*

Writing

1. Are you a member of an exploded nuclear family or do you know someone well who is? Drawing on your experience or knowledge, write an essay delving further into the effects of the Relative Explosion. For example, Dowling deals mostly with effects on young children. What are the effects on teenagers and college students whose parents are divorced and, perhaps, remarried?

2. How do television and the movies depict the contemporary family? Are the media's family portraits causes or effects of the social changes Dowling describes? Write an essay presenting your ideas on these questions.

3. What other effects, besides the Relative Explosion, have resulted from the sexual revolution of the 60s? Write an essay exploring one or several related effects that you think are significant.

Oliver Sacks

THE MAN WHO MISTOOK HIS WIFE FOR A HAT

Neurologist Oliver Sacks, born in London in 1933, was educated at Queen's College, Oxford, where he received his medical degrees. After moving to the United States, he attended UCLA. Since 1965 he has practiced as a clinical neurologist at a variety of university hospitals in the United States. He is a fellow of the American Academy of Neurology.

His books employ the case study approach, using personal narrative to describe his patients. The following excerpt from The Man Who Mistook His Wife for a Hat *(1985) is his best-known book. His other major publications are* Awakenings *(1987, a study of the victims of sleeping sickness);* Migraine: Understanding a Common Disorder *(1970);* Seeing Voices: A Journey into the World of the Deaf *(1989); and his most recent,* An Anthropologist on Mars *(1995). Sacks' sympathy with his patients is reflected in his belief that patients who have serious neurological problems adapt in unusual and creative ways. The following chapter shows how one talented musician adapts to his neurological disorder.*

1   Dr P. was a musician of distinction, well-known for many years as a singer, and then, at the local School of Music, as a teacher. It was here, in relation to his students, that certain strange problems were first observed. Sometimes a student would present himself, and Dr P. would not recognise him; or, specifically, would not recognise his face. The moment the student spoke, he would be recognised by his voice. Such incidents multiplied, causing embarrassment, perplexity, fear—and, sometimes, comedy. For not only did Dr P. increasingly fail to see faces, but he saw faces when there were no faces to see: genially, Magoo-like, when in the street, he might pat the heads of water-hydrants and parking-meters, taking these to be the heads of children; he would amiably address carved knobs on the furniture, and be astounded when they did not reply. At first these odd mistakes were laughed off as jokes, not least by Dr P. himself. Had he not always had a quirky sense of humour, and been given to Zen-like paradoxes and jests? His musical powers were as dazzling as ever; he did not feel ill—he had never felt better; and the mistakes were so ludicrous—and so ingenious—that they could hardly be serious or betoken anything serious. The notion of there being 'something the matter' did not emerge until some three years later, when diabetes developed. Well aware that diabetes could affect his eyes, Dr P. consulted an ophthalmologist, who took a careful history, and examined his eyes closely. 'There's nothing the matter with your eyes,' the doctor concluded. 'But there is trouble with the visual parts of your brain. You don't need my help, you must see a neurologist.' And so, as a result of this referral, Dr P. came to me.

2   It was obvious within a few seconds of meeting him that there was no trace of dementia in the ordinary sense. He was a man of great cultivation and charm, who talked well and fluently, with imagination and humour. I couldn't think why he had been referred to our clinic.

3   And yet there *was* something a bit odd. He faced me as he spoke, was oriented towards me, and yet there was something the matter—it was difficult to formulate. He

faced me with his *ears,* I came to think, but not with his eyes. These, instead of looking, gazing, at me, 'taking me in', in the normal way, made sudden strange fixations—on my nose, on my right ear, down to my chin, up to my right eye—as if noting (even studying) these individual features, but not seeing my whole face, its changing expressions, 'me', as a whole. I am not sure that I fully realised this at the time—there was just a teasing strangeness, some failure in the normal interplay of gaze and expression. He saw me, he *scanned* me, and yet . . .

4   'What seems to be the matter?' I asked him at length.

5   'Nothing that I know of,' he replied with a smile, 'but people seem to think there's something wrong with my eyes.'

6   'But *you* don't recognise any visual problems?'

7   'No, not directly, but I occasionally make mistakes.'

8   I left the room briefly, to talk to his wife. When I came back Dr P. was sitting placidly by the window, attentive, listening rather than looking out. 'Traffic,' he said, 'street sounds, distant trains—they make a sort of symphony, do they not? You know Honegger's *Pacific 234?'*

9   What a lovely man, I thought to myself. How can there be anything seriously the matter? Would he permit me to examine him?

10   'Yes, of course, Dr Sacks.'

11   I stilled my disquiet, his perhaps too, in the soothing routine of a neurological exam— muscle strength, co-ordination, reflexes, tone . . . It was while examining his reflexes—a trifle abnormal on the left side—that the first bizarre experience occurred. I had taken off his left shoe and scratched the sole of his foot with a key—a frivolous-seeming but essential test of a reflex—and then, excusing myself to screw my ophthalmoscope together, left him to put on the shoe himself. To my surprise, a minute later, he had not done this.

12   'Can I help?' I asked.

13   'Help what? Help whom?'

14   'Help you put on your shoe.'

15   'Ach,' he said, 'I had forgotten the shoe', adding, *sotto voce,* 'The shoe? The shoe?' He seemed baffled.

16   'Your shoe,' I repeated. 'Perhaps you'd put it on.'

17   He continued to look downwards, though not at the shoe, with an intense but misplaced concentration. Finally his gaze settled on his foot: 'That is my shoe, yes?'

18   Did I mis-hear? Did he mis-see?

19   'My eyes,' he explained, and put a hand to his foot. '*This* is my shoe, no?'

20   'No, it is not. That is your foot. *There* is your shoe.'

21   'Ah! I thought that was my foot.'

22   Was he joking? Was he mad? Was he blind? If this was one of his 'strange mistakes', it was the strangest mistake I had ever come across.

23   I helped him on with his shoe (his foot), to avoid further complication. Dr P. himself seemed untroubled, indifferent, maybe amused. I resumed my examination. His visual acuity was good: he had no difficulty seeing a pin on the floor, though sometimes he missed it if it was placed to his left.

24   He saw all right, but what did he see? I opened out a copy of the *National Geographic Magazine,* and asked him to describe some pictures in it.

25   His responses here were very curious. His eyes would dart from one thing to another, picking up tiny features, individual features, as they had done with my face. A striking

brightness, a colour, a shape would arrest his attention and elicit comment—but in no case did he get the scene-as-a-whole. He failed to see the whole, seeing only details, which he spotted like blips on a radar screen. He never entered into relation with the picture as a whole—never faced, so to speak, *its* physiognomy. He had no sense whatever of a landscape or scene.

26   I showed him the cover, an unbroken expanse of Sahara dunes.

27   'What do you see here?' I asked.

28   'I see a river,' he said. 'And a little guest-house with its terrace on the water. People are dining out on the terrace. I see coloured parasols here and there.' He was looking, if it was 'looking', right off the cover, into mid-air and confabulating non-existent features, as if the absence of features in the actual picture had driven him to imagine the river and the terrace and the coloured parasols.

29   I must have looked aghast, but he seemed to think he had done rather well. There was a hint of a smile on his face. He also appeared to have decided that the examination was over, and started to look round for his hat. He reached out his hand, and took hold of his wife's head, tried to lift it off, to put it on. He had apparently mistaken his wife for a hat! His wife looked as if she was used to such things.

30   I could make no sense of what had occurred, in terms of conventional neurology (or neuropsychology). In some ways he seemed perfectly preserved, and in others absolutely, incomprehensibly devastated. How could he, on the one hand, mistake his wife for a hat and, on the other, function, as apparently he still did, as a teacher at the Music School?

31   I had to think, to see him again—and to see him in his own familiar habitat, at home.

32   A few days later I called on Dr P. and his wife at home, with the score of the *Dichterliebe* in my briefcase (I knew he liked Schumann), and a variety of odd objects for the testing of perception. Mrs P. showed me into a lofty apartment, which recalled fin-de-siècle Berlin. A magnificent old Bösendorfer stood in state in the centre of the room, and all round it were music-stands, instruments, scores . . . There were books, there were paintings, but the music was central. Dr P. came in and, distracted, advanced with outstretched hand to the grandfather clock, but, hearing my voice, corrected himself, and shook hands with me. We exchanged greetings, and chatted a little of current concerts and performances. Diffidently, I asked him if he would sing.

33   'The *Dichterliebe*!' he exclaimed. 'But I can no longer read music. You will play them, yes?'

34   I said I would try. On that wonderful old piano even my playing sounded right, and Dr P. was an aged, but infinitely mellow Fischer-Dieskau, combining a perfect ear and voice with the most incisive musical intelligence. It was clear that the Music School was not keeping him on out of charity.

35   Dr P.'s temporal lobes were obviously intact: he had a wonderful musical cortex. What, I wondered, was going on in his parietal and occipital lobes, especially in those areas where visual processing occurred? I carry the Platonic solids in my neurological kit, and decided to start with these.

36   'What is this?' I asked, drawing out the first one.

37   'A cube, of course.'

38   'Now this?' I asked, brandishing another.

39   He asked if he might examine it, which he did swiftly and systematically: 'A dodecahedron, of course. And don't bother with the others—I'll get the eikosihedron too.'

40   Abstract shapes clearly presented no problems. What about faces? I took out a pack of cards. All of these he identified instantly, including the jacks, queens, kings, and the joker. But these, after all, are stylized designs, and it was impossible to tell whether he saw faces or merely patterns. I decided I would show him a volume of cartoons which I had in my briefcase. Here, again, for the most part, he did well. Churchill's cigar, Schnozzle's nose: as soon as he had picked out a key feature he could identify the face. But cartoons, again, are formal and schematic. It remained to be seen how he would do with real faces, realistically represented.

41   I turned on the television, keeping the sound off, and found an early Bette Davis film. A love scene was in progress. Dr P. failed to identify the actress—but this could have been because she had never entered his world. What was more striking was that he failed to identify the expressions on her face or her partner's, though in the course of a single torrid scene these passed from sultry yearning through passion, surprise, disgust and fury to a melting reconciliation. Dr P. could make nothing of any of this. He was very unclear as to what was going on, or who was who or even what sex they were. His comments on the scene were positively Martian.

42   It was just possible that some of his difficulties were associated with the unreality of a celluloid, Hollywood world; and it occurred to me that he might be more successful in identifying faces from his own life. On the walls of the apartment there were photographs of his family, his colleagues, his pupils, himself. I gathered a pile of these together and, with some misgivings, presented them to him. What had been funny, or farcical, in relation to the movie, was tragic in relation to real life. By and large, he recognized nobody: neither his family, nor his colleagues, nor his pupils, nor himself. He recognized a portrait of Einstein, because the picked up the characteristic hair and moustache; and the same thing happened with one or two other people. 'Ach, Paul!' he said, when shown a portrait of his brother. 'That square jaw, those big teeth, I would know Paul anywhere!' But was it Paul he recognized, or one or two of his features, on the basis of which he could make a reasonable guess as to the subject's identity? In the absence of obvious 'markers', he was utterly lost. But it was not merely the cognition, the *gnosis*, at fault; there was something radically wrong with the whole way he proceeded. For he approached these faces—even of those near and dear—as if they were abstract puzzles or tests. He did not relate to them, he did not behold. No face was familiar to him, seen as a 'thou', being just identified as a set of features, an 'it'. Thus there was formal, but no trace of personal, gnosis. And with this went his indifference, or blindness, to expression. A face, to us, is a person looking out—we see, as it were, the person through his *persona,* his face. But for Dr P. there was no *persona* in this sense—no outward *persona,* and no person within.

43   I had stopped at a florist on my way to his apartment and bought myself an extravagant red rose for my buttonhole. Now I removed this and handed it to him. He took it like a botanist or morphologist given a specimen, not like a person given a flower.

44   'About six inches in length,' he commented. 'A convoluted red form with a linear green attachment.'

45   'Yes,' I said encouragingly, 'and what do you think it *is,* Dr P.?'

46   'Not easy to say.' He seemed perplexed. 'It lacks the simple symmetry of the Platonic solids, although it may have a higher symmetry of its own . . . I think this could be an inflorescence or flower.'

47   'Could be?' I queried.

48   'Could be,' he confirmed.

49   'Smell it,' I suggested, and he again looked somewhat puzzled, as if I had asked him to smell a higher symmetry. But he complied courteously, and took it to his nose. Now, suddenly, he came to life.

50   'Beautiful!' he exclaimed. 'An early rose. What a heavenly smell!' He started to hum 'Die Rose, die Lillie. . . ' Reality, it seemed, might be conveyed by smell, not by sight.

51   I tried one final test. It was still a cold day, in early spring, and I had thrown my coat and gloves on the sofa.

52   'What is this?' I asked, holding up a glove.

53   'May I examine it?' he asked, and, taking it from me, he proceeded to examine it as he had examined the geometrical shapes.

54   'A continuous surface,' he announced at last, 'infolded on itself. It appears to have'—he hesitated—'five outpouchings, if this is the word.'

55   'Yes,' I said cautiously. 'You have given me a description. Now tell me what it is.'

56   'A container of some sort?'

57   'Yes,' I said, 'and what would it contain?'

58   'It would contain its contents!' said Dr P., with a laugh. 'There are many possibilities. It could be a change-purse, for example, for coins of five sizes. It could . . . '

59   I interrupted the barmy flow. 'Does it not look familiar? Do you think it might contain, might fit, a part of your body?'

60   No light of recognition dawned on his face.*

61   No child would have the power to see and speak of 'a continuous surface . . . infolded on itself', but any child, any infant, would immediately know a glove as a glove, see it as familiar, as going with a hand. Dr P. didn't. He saw nothing as familiar. Visually, he was lost in a world of lifeless abstractions. Indeed he did not have a real visual world, as he did not have a real visual self. He could speak about things, but did not see them face-to-face. Hughlings Jackson, discussing patients with aphasia and left-hemisphere lesions, says they have lost 'abstract' and 'propositional' thought—and compares them with dogs (or, rather, he compares dogs to patients with aphasia). Dr P., on the other hand, functioned precisely as a machine functions. It wasn't merely that he displayed the same indifference to the visual word as a computer but—even more strikingly—he construed the world as a computer construes it, by means of key features and schematic relationships. The scheme might be identified—in an 'identiti-kit' way—without the reality being grasped at all.

62   The testing I had done so far told me nothing about Dr P.'s inner world. Was it possible that his visual memory and imagination were still intact? I asked him to imagine entering one of our local squares from the north side, to walk through it, in imagination or in memory, and tell me the buildings he might pass as he walked. He listed the buildings on his right side, but none of those on his left. I then asked him to imagine entering the square from the south. Again he mentioned only those buildings that were on the right side, although these were the very buildings he had omitted before. Those he had 'seen' internally before were not mentioned now presumably, they were no longer 'seen'. It was evident that his difficulties with leftness, his visual field deficits, were as much internal as external, bisecting his visual memory and imagination.

---

* Later, by accident, he got it on, and exclaimed 'My God, it's a glove!' This was reminiscent of Kurt Goldstein's patient 'Lanuti', who could only recognise objects by trying to use them in action.

63   What, at a higher level, of his internal visualization? Thinking of the almost hallucinatory intensity with which Tolstoy visualizes and animates his characters, I questioned
Dr P. about *Anna Karenina*. He could remember incidents without difficulty, had an
undiminished grasp of the plot, but completely omitted visual characteristics, visual
narrative or scenes. He remembered the words of the characters, but not their faces; and
though, when asked, he could quote, with his remarkable and almost verbatim memory,
the original visual descriptions, these were, it became apparent, quite empty for him,
and lacked sensorial, imaginal, or emotional reality. Thus there was an internal agnosia
as well.*

64   But this was only the case, it became clear, with certain sorts of visualization. The visualization of faces and scenes, of visual narrative and drama—this was profoundly impaired, almost absent. But the visualization of *schemata* was preserved, perhaps enhanced. Thus when I engaged him in a game of mental chess, he had no difficulty
visualizing the chessboard or the moves—indeed, no difficulty in beating me soundly.

65   Luria said of Zazetsky that he had entirely lost his capacity to play games but that his
'vivid imagination' was unimpaired. Zazetsky and Dr P. lived in worlds which were
mirror images of each other. But the saddest difference between them was that
Zazetsky, as Luria said, 'fought to regain his lost faculties with the indomitable tenacity
of the damned', whereas Dr P. was not fighting, did not know what was lost, did not indeed know that anything was lost. But who was more tragic, or who was more
damned—the man who knew it, or the man who did not?

66   When the examination was over, Mrs P. called us to the table, where there was coffee and a delicious spread of little cakes. Hungrily, hummingly, Dr P. started on the
cakes. Swiftly, fluently, unthinkingly, melodiously, he pulled the plates towards him,
and took this and that, in a great gurgling stream, an edible song of food, until, suddenly, there came an interruption: a loud, peremptory rat-tat-tat at the door. Startled,
taken aback, arrested, by the interruption, Dr P. stopped eating, and sat frozen, motionless, at the table, with an indifferent, blind, bewilderment on his face. He saw, but no
longer saw, the table; no longer perceived it as a table laden with cakes. His wife poured
him some coffee: the smell titillated his nose, and brought him back to reality. The
melody of eating resumed.

67   How does he do anything, I wondered to myself? What happens when he's dressing,
goes to the lavatory, has a bath? I followed his wife into the kitchen and asked her how,
for instance, he managed to dress himself. 'It's just like the eating,' she explained. 'I put
his usual clothes out, in all the usual places, and he dresses without difficulty, singing to
himself. He does everything singing to himself. But if he is interrupted and loses the
thread, he comes to a complete stop, doesn't know his clothes—or his own body. He
sings all the time—eating songs, dressing songs, bathing songs, everything. He can't do
anything unless he makes it a song.'

---

* I have often wondered about Helen Keller's visual descriptions, whether these, for all their eloquence, are
somehow empty as well? Or whether, by the transference of images from the tactile to the visual, or, yet more
extraordinarily, from the verbal and the metaphorical to the sensorial and the visual, she *did* achieve a power
of visual imagery, even though her visual cortex had never been stimulated, directly, by the eyes? But in
Dr P.'s case it is precisely the cortex that was damaged, the organic prerequisite of all pictorial imagery.
Interestingly and typically he no longer dreamed pictorially—the 'message' of the dream being conveyed in
non-visual terms.

68   While we were talking my attention was caught by the pictures on the walls.

69   'Yes,' Mrs P. said, 'he was a gifted painter as well as a singer. The School exhibited his pictures every year.'

70   I strolled past them curiously—they were in chronological order. All his earlier work was naturalistic and realistic, with vivid mood and atmosphere, but finely detailed and concrete. Then, years later, they became less vivid, less concrete, less realistic and naturalistic; but far more abstract, even geometrical and cubist. Finally, in the last paintings, the canvasses became nonsense, or nonsense to me—mere chaotic lines and blotches of paint. I commented on this to Mrs P.

71   'Ach, you doctors, you're such philistines!' she exclaimed, 'Can you not see *artistic development*—how he renounced the realism of his earlier years, and advanced into abstract, non-representational art?'

72   'No, that's not it,' I said to myself (but forbore to say it to poor Mrs P.). He had indeed moved from realism to non-representation to the abstract, but this was not the artist, but the pathology, advancing—advancing towards a profound visual agnosia, in which all powers of representation and imagery, all sense of the concrete, all sense of reality, were being destroyed. This wall of paintings was a tragic pathological exhibit, which belonged to neurology, not art.

73   And yet, I wondered, was she not partly right? For there is often a struggle, and sometimes, even more interestingly, a collusion between the powers of pathology and creation. Perhaps, in his cubist period, there might have been both artistic and pathological development, colluding to engender an original form; for as he lost the concrete, so he might have gained in the abstract, developing a greater sensitivity to all the structural elements of line, boundary, contour—an almost Picasso-like power to see, and equally depict, those abstract organizations embedded in, and normally lost in, the concrete . . . Though in the final pictures, I feared, there was only chaos and agnosia.

74   We returned to the great music room, with the Bösendorfer in the centre, and Dr P. humming the last torte.

75   'Well, Dr Sacks,' he said to me. 'You find me an interesting case, I perceive. Can you tell me what you find wrong, make recommendations?'

76   'I can't tell you what I find wrong,' I replied, 'but I'll say what I find right. You are a wonderful musician, and music is your life. What I would prescribe, in a case such as yours, is a life which consists entirely of music. Music has been the centre, now make it the whole, of your life.'

77   This was four years ago—I never saw him again, but I often wondered how he apprehended the world, given his strange loss of image, visuality, and the perfect preservation of a great musicality. I think that music, for him, had taken the place of image. He had no body-image, he had body-music: this is why he could move and act as fluently as he did, but came to a total confused stop if the 'inner music' stopped. And equally with the outside, the world . . .

78   In *The World as Representation and Will* Schopenhauer speaks of music as 'pure will'. How fascinated he would have been by Dr P., a man who had wholly lost the world as representation, but wholly preserved it as music or will.

79   And this, mercifully, held to the end—for despite the gradual advance of his disease (a massive tumor or degenerative process in the visual parts of his brain) Dr P. lived and taught music to the last days of his life.

PRACTICE

Discussion

1. What is the significance of the title? What are some other mistakes that Dr. P. made, particularly concerning inanimate objects? Is there a certain logic to his making those mistakes?

2. Discuss the descriptive effect of the mistakes made by Dr. P. How do these mistakes affect the tone of the essay?

3. What is the effect of Sacks' use of specific details on the reader? Describe his audience.

4. Discuss the effect of Sacks' use of dialogue when writing on a medical problem.

5. List the *effects* of Dr. P.'s disorder. Does Sacks balance the *causes* with the *effects*? Why or why not?

6. What is the relationship of paragraph 42 to paragraph 41? Discuss the effectiveness of this technique in cause-effect.

7. Consider what happens to Dr. P.'s art as "he progresses toward neurological destruction." How effective is this example as a climax to Dr. Sacks' diagnosis and the essay itself?

8. In the final scene with Dr. P. (paragraphs 75–76), did Dr. Sacks know what was wrong with his patient? What did he tell Dr. P.? What does this tell you about Dr. Sacks' relationships with his patients?

Vocabulary

Magoo-like	collusion	philistines
indomitable	barmy	dementia

Writing

1. Look up the words *paradox, tragic,* and *damned.* The author offers a paradox in paragraph 64, where he describes Zazetsky's attitude toward his mental deterioration compared with Dr. P.'s failure to recognize that he also has a serious mental deterioration. Who is more tragic—the man who knows he has lost his faculties (like Zazetsky) and fights to regain them, or the man who does not know he has lost them (like Dr. P.)? (This question also makes a good discussion question.)

2. Write an essay in which you isolate a cause or causes of a disease that you or one of your family members has suffered. Was the diagnosis clear-cut (as far as you know), or did the doctor have a problem identifying the cause of the disease?

3. Write an essay in which you identify the effects of a sickness you once experienced. If you knew the cause of the disease, did this make the effects more bearable? If you didn't know the cause, how did you cope with that fact? If you prefer, you may combine this assignment with Writing Assignment 2 above.

William Oscar Johnson

SPORTS AND BEER—THERE'S TROUBLE BREWING

1   There is a school of thought, that argues vehemently that sport is not a proper area for brewer sponsorship. To many physicians, psychologists and social critics our incessant blending of intoxicating drink with athletic excellence is hypocritical, irresponsible and hazardous to the nation's health. Dr. Jay Caldwell, director of the Alaska Sports Medicine Clinic, wrote a scathing column last August in the *Anchorage Daily News.* After he decried the fact that the Alaska Midnight Sun Triathlon Championship had been summarily rechristened the Bud Light Triathlon, he fired away: "For blatant, and apparently acceptable, commercial exploitation of our youth by drug merchants, this even takes first prize . . . Lest we forget, alcohol is the No. I drug of abuse in the United States . . . there are about 13 million alcoholics in this country and over 3 million of them are in the 14–17 age group . . . . I worry about the cozy connection between alcohol and sport. Beer merchants have very effectively linked the two. They have made it seem perfectly natural for an intoxicating drug to be consumed following a pleasant sporting activity. Through sponsorship of events such as a triathlon, beer comes to share the luster of healthy athleticism."

2   Dr. William J. Beausay, president of the Academy for Sports Psychology International in Columbus, Ohio, says, "It's really paradoxic that alcohol and all that it stands for should be associated with excellent athletic performance. You cannot have one and the other at the same time. If you're going to perform as a top-grade athlete, you have to cut out alcohol."

3   In Austria, laws prohibit all public references at sporting events to "alcoholic beverages, tobacco, pharmaceutical products, political parties and religious communities"—in that order. Ironically, in a country that brews some of the most beautiful beer in the world, the very idea of a brewery involved with sports is considered appalling. "We could never think of it," huffs Dr. Klaus Leistner, director of the Austrian ski federation. "Sports and alcohol should never be placed together."

4   Cynical, ironic, immoral, hypocritical as it may be, the juxtaposition of beer and sports in the U.S. is often simply a matter of cold business pragmatism. As Bob Whitsitt, president of the Seattle SuperSonics, puts it: "We would be seriously hurt without beer companies as sponsors. It is a sensitive issue because you need the money, but you don't want to be seen as promoting the idea that people come to our games, get drunk and drive home. We'd be foolish to say we don't want a beer sponsor on moral

grounds, but at the same time that doesn't mean we encourage 21-year-olds to down a case. We do make sure that our players are out in the community talking about the dangers of alcohol and drugs. That helps."

5   Four academicians under the auspices of the AAA Foundation for Traffic Safety recently compiled a study about beer commercials entitled *Myths, Men & Beer.* They analyzed the content of 40 such commercials broadcast on network television during February and March 1987. Their major concern was the effect of these messages on children, because as the report says, "between the ages of two and eighteen, the period in which social learning is most intense, American children see something like 100,000 television commercials for beer."

6   The study points out that through exposure to sales pitches for beer, children are given "a particular view of what it means to be a man," as well as particular "attitudes toward beer drinking and driving." According to the report, in the world according to beer commercials, men's work is mostly physical—"felling trees, loading hay, welding beams, rounding up horses." As for play, the "men of beer commercials fill their leisure time in two ways: in active pursuits usually conducted in outdoor settings (e.g., boat racing, fishing, camping, sports) and in 'hanging out,' usually in bars." The authors point out that some risk or challenge is nearly always involved in beer commercials, even if it is only the risk and challenge of "good-natured arguments" in the barroom. And always, in beer-commercial country, the final prize to any man who succeeds in overcoming a risk or mastering a challenge or completing his day's work is—what else?—a beer.

7   The researchers discovered that the men who inhabit beer commercials tend to be a limited and simplistic breed: "We found no sensitive men . . . nor any thoughtful men, scholarly men, political men, gay men or even complex men." Of the women who appear in beer commercials, they are "largely reduced to the role of admiring onlookers. Men appear to value their group of friends over their female partners, and the women accept this . . . they become the audience for whom men perform." The study summarizes the stereotyped men and women who populate beer commercials as being "almost laughably anachronistic . . . a peculiar set of figures to offer the young of the 1980s as models of adult females and males."

8   On a darker note the authors ask, "Does the link in beer commercials between masculinity and beer drinking also promote an association between beer drinking and driving? On the basis of the analyses reported here, we conclude that the answer to that question is 'Yes.'" The study refers to the many beer commercial scenes that associate beer with fast-moving cars, with the excitement of speed, with tests of manhood and with tests of self-control; it says that "by omitting any references to drinkers' conditions and modes of transportation when leaving the setting where beer is consumed, beer commercials imply that drinking has no consequences or, at least, no consequences that are cause for concern." The final recommendation by the authors is tough and uncompromising: "That the policy permitting the televising of commercials for beer be revised to prohibit such commercials."

9   Bubba Smith, the Ex-NFL defensive end, played a beer-commercial myth for a while in the celebrated Miller Lite series. In 1977, about a year after he left football because of a ruined knee, Smith was cast as a glowering, lovable, beer-can-ripping

giant. Smith told Scott Ostler of the *Los Angeles Times* that he had been depressed, lonely and in need of work when the Miller people approached him: "Making those commercials was a joy to me. I told myself I couldn't be doing nothing wrong. It seemed so innocent. . . . Making those commercials, we were a team. It was like football, without the pain."

10   Then, in the fall of 1985, Smith went back to his alma mater, Michigan State, and performed as grand marshal of the homecoming parade. "I was riding in the backseat of this car," he said, "and these people were yelling. But they weren't saying 'Go, State, go!' One side of the street was yelling 'Tastes great!' and the other side was yelling 'Less filling!' It just totally freaked me out. When I got to the stadium, the older folks are yelling 'Kill, Bubba, kill!' but the kids are yelling 'Tastes great! Less filling!' And everyone in the stands is drunk."

11   Smith decided he had to quit the Miller Lite team. "I didn't like the effect I was having on a lot of little people. People in school. When kids start to listen to what you say, you want to tell 'em something that's the truth. . . . Doing those commercials, it's like me telling everyone in school, Hey, it's cool to have a Lite beer. . . . As the years wear on, you got to stop compromising your principles."

12   Not everyone feels the same about these commercials, of course. After 10 years as a villainous but essentially faceless offensive lineman in the NFL, Conrad Dobler retired from football and was billed on a 1987 Miller Lite TV commercial as "Famous Troublemaker." His life changed instantly. "In all of my years in the NFL," he writes in his upcoming book, *They Call Me Dirty,* "a visit to my hometown of Twentynine Palms, Calif., barely generated enthusiasm among my own family, let alone strangers. But when I visited three months after 'Famous Troublemaker' came out, everyone who saw me wanted an autograph. Men bought me beers. Women offered me sexual favors. . . . It's especially gratifying to be walking down the street or sitting in a restaurant and have people yell 'Tastes great!' so I can yell back 'Less filling!'"

13   As things have progressed, beer and sports have come to be something like Siamese twins—inseparable but clearly facing a complicated existence together. After a 1988 riot between the fans and the Cincinnati Reds, Giamatti, president of the National League, told *The New York Times,* "Alcohol is a large part of this; I believe excessive drinking is at the heart of the deteriorating situation. But to think that if one declared prohibition there would no longer be any problems of fan violence is naive. If you turn the ballpark into a maximum-security situation, then you have changed the nature of the event. Not because the event depends on alcohol, but because it depends on the perception that the event is a pleasure."

14   True enough. But it doesn't require storm troopers and police dogs to keep our sporting environments (or our *perceptions* of our sporting environments) pleasant. Nor does it require an absolute ban on alcohol. The vast majority of people at sporting events drink one or two beers—or no beer at all. And of those who drink more, the great majority are not troublemakers or obscenity-shriekers or fistfighters. What has happened is that a small minority of louts and loonies have been allowed a kind of license in stadiums that they aren't given anywhere else. A drunken man shouting obscenities at the top of his voice over and over again for two consecutive hours in the middle of a crowd that includes women, children and even sober, civilized men is not

tolerated in any other public environment in America. Such a foulmouthed misfit would not last long at a sports event either if only ushers and guards were *required* by whatever authorities prevail to enforce the same standards of public behavior that govern the rest of society.

15   Why doesn't it happen? Well, in some places it does. Milwaukee, a city with a beer belly if there ever was one, is oddly enough not renowned for drunk and disorderly behavior at its stadium events—drunk, perhaps, but seldom disorderly. Bill Hanrahan, manager of County Stadium, says, "People from Milwaukee know that if they're out of order, they'll be caught and ejected promptly. We have drinking patrols and we might keep a better eye out for it than they do in some cities. People here are apt to complain sooner when there are disruptive fans. People know we're going to get right on any bad behavior, and they act better here than at some other stadiums." Seattle, with one of the most tranquil (some would say tranquilized) sporting populations, actually did have one venue in town where young drunken fans frequently ran riot. That was in the 4,100-seat Seattle Arena whenever the Seattle Breakers junior hockey team took the ice. It became so bad that attendance fell off, until in the 1983–84 season the Breakers' crowds averaged fewer than 1,800 a game. New owners took over four seasons ago, changed the team name to the Thunderbirds and completely revamped the drinking regulations—upgrading security, opening beer-free sections, limiting the beers bought by each customer and reducing cup sizes. The result? "We went 35 games in a row without any incidents in the seats," says Bob Kaser, the Thunderbirds' director of marketing, "and our attendance is now averaging 2,900 a game."

16   So why does action against obstreperous beer drinkers so often seem to be the exception instead of the rule? Is it the greed of beer wholesalers, team owners and ballpark concessionaires eager to sell every last dreg they can? Yes, it is. Is it also the fear of team owners, league officials and various commissioners that any moves against beer drinkers—however reasonable and logical—may displease the brewing corporations that spend untold millions of dollars on advertising, sponsorships and TV commitments? Yes, it is that too.

17   Despite heavy foot-dragging by some team owners and stadium operators, there has been a raft of new and encouraging ballpark policies instituted around the country, such as opening beer-free sections, offering low-alcohol beer, cutting off beer sales well before games are over, limiting sales per customer and—one of the most effective techniques of all—banning vending in the seats.

18   This last approach has been put into effect by nine major league baseball clubs over the past couple of years. It has proved to be a major revenue loser for concessionaires, but it has also been surprisingly effective in making those nine ballparks nicer places to visit. Why such a powerful effect? Vendors often work on commission and thus become supreme hustlers, pushing beer at both the sloshed and the sober as if their livelihoods depended on it—which, at $200 to $300 on a good night for a good vendor, they certainly do.

19   Boston's Fenway Park, which over the years has probably produced more hooligans on parade than any place but Yankee Stadium, has cut out vending in the seats and installed a beer-free zone. How is it working? Rico Picardi, for 45 years the concession manager for the Harry M. Stevens Company there, told the Boston *Herald*: "Yes, we're losing revenues—our beer sales are down 14 percent—but I can't say we mind. What

we want most is to be sure the people come back to the ballpark. Hey, they come more often, they spend more money. And anyway, soda sales are up."

20   Even the best efforts, of course, don't provide instant and perfect results. Last season the San Francisco Giants banned beer vending in the stands. But on a recent Tuesday night, July 26, in a doubleheader at Candlestick Park against the Dodgers, the fans, sparked by two Giants losses and a controversial balk call and fueled, undoubtedly, by many hours of drinking, created another ugly scene. The problem of fan violence is complex and has to do with more than beer. Still, recent efforts to slow the flow are encouraging. According to Pat Gallagher, vice-president of business operations for the Giants, the drop in profit from the ban on vending beer in the stands—which cost the club roughly $600,000 last season—has been well worth the increase in good times had by all. "We knew it would have a negative financial impact on our beer sales," he says, "but we also noted that 90 percent of the feedback from the fans was positive. They said thanks for making them feel safer and better about bringing families to the ballpark. And we also found that beer sales did go down, but the sale of other concessions like nonalcoholic beverages and food went up. Overall, our alcohol-related security problems went down. Overall, we're very pleased."

21   Aha! Overall, is it possible that we have stumbled upon the inspiration for a brave new beer chant for the future? Let's try it:

22   *Less profit!* More fun! *Less trouble!* More fun!

23   Yes, I think we've got it. All together now:

Less profit! More fun! *Less trouble!* More fun! *Less trouble!* More fans! *Less trouble!* More profit! *More fun!* More profit! *More fun . . .*

PRACTICE

Discussion

1. What is Johnson's thesis and where is it stated?

2. Identify the terms that were used by the authorities and the author to describe the brewer sponsorship of athletic events. How do these terms set the tone of the article?

3. How does the topic sentence of paragraph 4 operate as a summary of the first three paragraphs, and a transition to the next paragraphs?

4. What is the rhetorical effect of beginning paragraphs 8, 15, and 16 with questions?

5. Note the number and credibility of authorities that Johnson quotes in paragraphs 1–12. How does Johnson's use of the authorities cited affect your feelings about the issue of brewer sponsorship of athletic events? How is the title related to what the authorities say about this issue?

6. What are the effects of children's exposure to sales pitches for beer? How many major effects are cited? Do you believe that children are at risk because of beer commercials? Defend your position.

7. In paragraph 14, the author describes "A drunken man shouting obscenities at the top of his voice over and over again for two consecutive hours in the middle of a crowd . . ." Is the man's drinking a *sufficient* cause for the behavior described (see page 244)?

8. Paragraph 15 describes two cause-effect relationships. Diagram these two cause-effects (see page 241).

Vocabulary

anachronism	incessant	obstreperous
pragmatism	hypocritical	renowned

Writing

1. Look up *anachronism*. Write a cause-effect paper in which you agree or disagree with the following: If the beer industry's advertisements promote views of men and women that are out of date and not realistic, why are they profitable?

2. In paragraph 8, the authors of *Myths, Men & Beer* claim that there is a cause-effect relationship between beer advertising and auto accidents, but they don't provide a specific cause-effect. Based on the material provided and what you know about drunk driving, develop your own cause-effect relationships and create a graph similar to the one on page 241. Then write a paper in which you either criticize or agree with the cause-effect relationships implied in paragraph 8.

3. Write a paper about the effect a particular category of television commercials may have on some aspect of our society.

   Possible topics include: erotic underwear advertising on —— , cereal advertising on —— , toy advertising on ——, cosmetics advertising on —— , cigarette advertising on —— .

Classification

▼ Classification

Classifying or grouping things is a natural way to think. Young children playing with rocks separate large ones from small ones, rough ones from smooth ones. As they grow older, they become more sophisticated in their classifying, and they begin to group their playmates into those they like to play with and those they don't. When they enter school, they separate their school clothes from their play clothes. Then, as they learn to use abstractions in their thinking, they identify subjects in school that they are interested or successful in. In every one of these classifications, the grouping is made according to a *ruling principle*: rocks classified according to *size* or *smoothness;* friends classified according to *amiability;* clothes classified according to *use;* school subjects classified according to *success* or, perhaps, *interest.*

Although classifying is a process "natural" to human beings, it is useful to remember that classes as such do not exist in nature itself. We create classes and systems of classification to help us understand our world.

■■■ The Ruling Principle in Classification

Classifying is the act of grouping things, people, activities, ideas, and so on, according to their similarities and differences. By the time you are of college age you are so accustomed to classifying and to being classified that you are scarcely aware of the process. Yet classification affects nearly every part of your life. To mention only a few of the possibilities, you may be classified in religion as a believer, nonbeliever, or agnostic; a Christian or non-Christian; a Protestant, Jew, or Catholic; a Methodist, Baptist, or Episcopalian; etc. In politics, you are Republican, Democrat, or Independent. In school, you are a freshman, sophomore, junior, senior (or unclassified). In a university, you may be placed in the College of Arts and Sciences, Engineering, Education, etc. If you are in Arts and Sciences, you may be classified as an English major, math major, or psychology major, etc. (In classifying, the *et cetera* is important because the classifier must be sure that all the members of the class are included. However, listing all the possible options may be boring and unnecessary.)

A *classification,* to define the term more accurately, is a significant and informative grouping of things, people, activities, ideas, etc. The key words here are *significant* and *informative.* We classify in order to use information, and the most informative classifications are those based upon significant groupings. If, in order to understand them, we separate the students in a particular composition class into two groups, men and women, we have made a classification, but it does not seem significant nor does it satisfy our curiosity about the students.

To make such a classification useful, we must apply a significant *ruling principle,* which is a unifying idea or point of view used in the act of classifying. The division of a composition class into men and women is based upon a ruling principle of *gender,* which is not a particularly significant grouping here, and thus will not prove to be very informative. Other ruling principles of varying significance might be athletic ability, religion, major field, interest in composition, etc.

In the following passage, observe that there are two ruling principles, cloud *formation* and *altitude:*

1   Clouds are classified according to how they are formed. There are two basic types: (1) Clouds formed by rising air currents. These are piled up and puffy. They are called "cumulus" which means piled up or accumulated. (2) Clouds formed when a layer of air is cooled below the saturation point without vertical movement. These are in sheets or foglike layers. They are called "stratus," meaning sheetlike or layered.

2   Clouds are further classified by altitude into four families: high clouds, middle clouds, low clouds, and towering clouds. The bases of the latter may be as low as the typical low clouds, but the tops may be at or above 75,000 feet.

—Paul E. Lehr, R. Will Burnett, and Herbert S. Zim, *Weather*

As with the other strategies of development, classification is created by the writer *for a specific reason.* In the classification of clouds, the writer's aim was to explain cloud formations to a reader who is not a scientist and who knows very little about clouds.

The diagram on the following page may help you visualize how this strategy works.

▼ Suggestions for Writing a Classification Paper

Here are some suggestions that you should find useful for writing the classification paper.

1. The first step in classifying is to list your evidence. The evidence you collect is from your experience or reading. Your evidence may be the answer to a

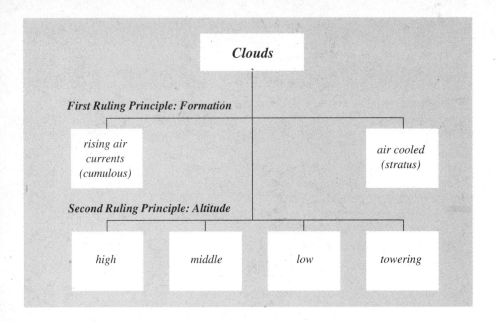

question such as "What kinds of . . . ?" or "What are the facts about . . . ?" After you have collected the evidence in order to answer the question, you have a list. Once you have your list, you should be able to see relationships, keep the evidence that is pertinent, and ignore the rest. Then you can identify your ruling principle and develop categories.

2. Next, remember to avoid artificial overlapping or illogical classifications. Simply chopping your subject into parts will not necessarily give you a valid classification. If you divide your composition class into (a) men and (b) good students, you have made a classification that is artificial and probably useless.

3. Be consistent with your ruling principle. You may change your principle if, after having investigated your subject thoroughly from one angle, you wish to investigate it from another. Note that the classification of clouds used two ruling principles. If you were studying political systems, for example, you might use several different ruling principles: (a) time-sequence or history, (b) causes and effects, (c) types of systems, (d) philosophies of systems, (e) success of systems, to name just a few.

4. Make sure your classification has a point. Don't try to write a classification paper without a specific stance.

5. Avoid most either-or classifications. For instance:

Voters are either left-wing or right-wing.

Financiers are either successful or unsuccessful.

Rhetoric students are either good writers or poor writers.

S-10
8:15

Richard.

Please call

Alice McCormick

544-9326

Re: Alumni dinner

REGISTRATION APPOINTMENT

INSTRUCTOR _____

NAME _____

SOCIAL SECURITY NO. _____

TELEPHONE NO. _____

DATE _____

TIME _____

MAJOR _____

REMARKS:

4Hp:11 (optional)

webster.commnet.edu/giannuri/

By its very structure, each of these either-or classifications probably distorts the truth because it omits certain members of the total group—those who would fall somewhere between the extremes of "left" or "right," "successful" or "unsuccessful," and "good" or "poor." Among a group of rhetoric students, for example, there are likely to be writers who are "excellent," "good," "fair," "poor," and (perhaps) "terrible."

▼ Writing and Revising a Classification Paper (An Example)

To understand more clearly how the process of classification works in the contexts of thinking and writing, let's follow a student named Tom who wants to understand the *behavior* of the fifteen eight-year-old boys that he supervised at summer camp. His purpose in using classification is to get some ideas for dealing with these boys when he returns to his counseling job next summer. He has made some scratch notes, and from those notes he writes the rough draft of a paragraph.

KIDS AT A SUMMER CAMP

Most campers fall into at least one emotional category that reveals a lot about the way they think about life. Every counselor should expect at least one of the following. *The Homesick Kid* is normally the one in his bunk while everyone else is playing soccer outside. Odds are he's writing home (at least three times a day). This kid has probably never been away from home much before, and normally he wishes that he is anywhere but camp. But at the end of camp, he'll cry even harder because he doesn't want to leave. *The Whiner* complains about everything. At meals, the food is always too gloppy, runny, bland, or spicy. At night, the bed is too hard or too soft, and the games are always too hard or too boring. Some kids are *Non-Existent,* and as their counselor you never meet them until their parents come to pick them up. They tend to be lethargic, hard to find, and exceptionally quiet— meaning that they sometimes end up being a counselor's favorite. *The Jock* is the all-around athlete, able to beat anyone in camp (including his counselors) in tetherball, football, soccer, etc. They're great to have around, though, if you need something heavy (a trunk, bed, or person) lifted. *The Super-Jock* is another story. He thinks he can do anything well, but his prime attribute is normally making excuses (sun too bright, glove too big or small, field too rough, not the way we play at home). Along these same lines is *the Veteran*—the kid who has done it all "many times," and is an expert at absolutely everything. Unfortunately for him, the camp never seems to do anything "his way," and he normally learns some big lessons in humility by the time the summer is over.

After Tom reviews what he has written, he discovers that he has failed to follow the steps for developing a clear classification system: He has no *ruling principle* and no *categories.* Instead, he has treated each boy as a separate class; consequently his grouping overlaps: *a homesick boy* can be a *whiner; a veteran camp-goer* can be a *jock.* Tom reconsiders his ruling principle. What each boy "thinks about life" is pretty vague, so he decides that a more important ruling principle would be to consider how various classes of boys contribute to the success of the camp, thereby helping the counselor run a better program. Tom believes that the classification system should be useful for the counselors,

so he changes his system to include three categories: *leader, follower,* and *obstructionist.*
His definitions help him to place the boys in these categories:

> A *leader* is a boy who takes initiative and has certain qualities that make other boys
> respect and follow him.
> A *follower* is a boy who does what the leader expects, but seldom acts on his own
> initiative.
> An *obstructionist* is a boy who exerts no positive leadership, but instead hinders the
> day-by-day progress of the camp with unacceptable behavior.

Keeping these three categories in mind, Tom can now see that whether or not a boy
is homesick is irrelevant. It is the way his homesickness keeps him from being a *leader*
or causes him to be a *follower* or *obstructionist* that is important. It isn't whether or not
a boy is selfish or generous that is the important thing, but how these traits affect his behavior and his leadership qualities.

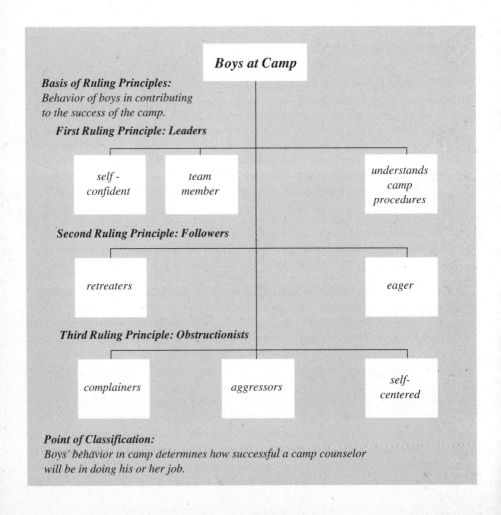

Boys at Camp

Basis of Ruling Principles:
*Behavior of boys in contributing
to the success of the camp.*

First Ruling Principle: Leaders

self-confident   team member   understands camp procedures

Second Ruling Principle: Followers

retreaters   eager

Third Ruling Principle: Obstructionists

complainers   aggressors   self-centered

Point of Classification:
*Boys' behavior in camp determines how successful a camp counselor
will be in doing his or her job.*

Tom tests his classification system by drawing a diagram similar to the one on clouds, page 270.

Tom develops a stance:

Role:	A college freshman who supervised a group of eight-year-old boys at YMCA summer camp the summer after graduating from high school.
Audience:	Other counselors of the YMCA camp or any other boys camp.
Thesis:	If you want to succeed as a camp counselor, you should recognize that eight-year-old campers fall into three categories, based on how each boy contributes to the success of the camp—leaders, followers, and obstructionists.

Here is Tom's completed paper.

CAN EIGHT-YEAR-OLD BOYS BEHAVE RESPONSIBLY?

1   When I took a job as counselor at the YMCA camp, I had hoped to work with older boys because I had experience with a twelve-year-old brother and his friends. Consequently, I was disappointed to be assigned to a group of eight-year-olds, an age I considered too childlike to interest me. I knew, however, that it was my job to understand the boys who come to the camp with varying backgrounds and personalities. It was apparent that I would be expected to teach, counsel, and clean up after these boys, so I had to learn something about them fast. Eight weeks—the length of the camp—isn't very long.

2   During the summer I learned that there are three kinds of eight-year-old boys— *leaders, followers,* and *obstructionists.* I knew that my life would be easier if I could get the best from each class of boy because I could make use of their abilities to lead or follow. The *leaders* I define as those boys who take initiative, and have certain qualities that make other boys respect and follow them. The *followers* are boys who do what the leader expects but who show no initiative. A *follower* seldom acts on his own initiative to help make camp successful. The *obstructionist* is a boy who exerts no positive leadership but instead hinders the day-by-day progress of the camp with unacceptable behavior.

3   The *leader* class may consist of only one or two boys. If a camp counselor can find any boy who others will look up to and one who will also support the counselor, he is lucky. A *leader* is usually self-confident, but not overbearing. He may be a good athlete, so he understands what team-work means. Other boys look up to athletes because they can beat other teams in tetherball, football, or soccer, making the camp team look good. The boys in the leader class have usually been to summer camp before, so they know the procedures and are not likely to be homesick. It is a good idea to identify any leaders in your group early because they can make your life as a camp counselor infinitely easier. They can cooperate with you by rounding up the followers at the end of a day, and they can get *followers* to cooperate with you.

4   The next largest class is *followers,* subclassified into *retreating* and *eager* boys. The *retreating boy* is usually homesick. He may stay in his bunk writing home every day. Sometimes he won't eat, so he is lethargic. A *retreater* will usually comply with directions because he is frightened. *Retreaters* are often generous. If a retreater gets a package of cookies from his parents, he shares it with the whole cabin. This kind of sharing helps to form a cohesive group.

5   *Eager* boys make good followers, particularly if they believe that they are lucky to be at any camp at all. Most boys camps try to admit each summer a few children from orphanages or foster homes. Their fees are usually paid by the YMCA or a service club like the Kiwanis or Rotary. Since these boys have no family and are used to institutional life, they think the camp food is great, the beds comfortable, and the counselor a good guy.

6   The largest class—and the biggest problem for a camp counselor—is the *obstructionist.* Perhaps eight-year-olds become *obstructionists* when they are away from home because they have to adapt to a new environment. Consequently, they are complainers. They whine about the food being too runny, bland, or spicy. Their beds are too hard or too soft. The games are boring. Some boys who fancy themselves good athletes complain when they don't succeed: the sun is too bright, the baseball glove is too small, the field is too rough, and the camp team doesn't play by the rules that they know. Some of the obstructionists are selfish because they are used to having people wait on them. They can't get used to doing the everyday chores of washing dishes, making beds, and sweeping floors. A selfish boy may draw a line around his bunk, padlock his food packages from home, and even steal food from other boys.

7   A counselor must put a great deal of effort into getting the obstructionists to accept responsibility for the group. One way of dealing with these boys is to be abrupt and order them about. However, this will probably make them even less cooperative than they were before. I have found a better way: Make them feel important. They are usually very insecure and frightened of a new experience, so they show their insecurity by aggressive and selfish behavior. I try to treat obstructionists as I treat my little brother when he displays similar behavior. I pay attention to him and make him think I'm interested in what he does. If I treat *obstructionists* as I treat my brother, by the end of eight weeks they usually become more cooperative—not completely cooperative—but *more* so!

8   Other counselors may find my classification incomplete, and they may not agree with my solutions. But these are the kinds of boys that I found in the YMCA camp. Knowing what I learned last summer will help me next year when I face another group of boys whose parents happily shipped their kids off to summer camp for my friends and me to civilize.

PRACTICE

Discussion

1. Study Tom's final draft. How well do the details and examples support each of his categories? Discuss the point of the paper. Is it clear enough that another counselor could follow Tom's advice? What suggestions do you have for improvements in the paper? Improvements in the classification system?

2. For class discussion, make a significant classification of the following items. You may need to subdivide to complete your classification. *Hint:* One of the category *names* may be in some of the lists. Give the ruling principle of your classification. Use the heading *Etc.* if an item doesn't fit your classifying system.

   a. *Time,* table, book, chair, magazine, divan, *Sports Illustrated,* newspaper, bookcase, *Fortune.*

   b. Truck, station wagon, automobile, luxury car, "semi," convertible, pickup, sports car, compact, economy car.

    c. Left-winger, Southern Democrat, socialist, communist, right-winger, Democrat, Republican, independent, middle-of-the-roader.

    d. Poet, novelist, journalist, editorial writer, TV commentator, textbook author, social philosopher, newspaper columnist, writer for *The National Enquirer,* writer on college paper, literary critic.

    e. Thugs, robbers, rascals, killers, arsonists, scoundrels, shoplifters, murderers, burglars, assassins, car thieves, rapists, traitors, villains.

    f. Various kinds of *rights:* moral, natural, political, original, acquired, absolute, relative, property, liberty, equality.

    g. Presidents, governors, prime ministers, mayors, kings, princes, queens, despots, princesses, commissars, dictators, rulers, wardens, magistrates.

3. For purposes of research, a major university has classified "human subjects" in the following categories. Discuss the accuracy of the classification. What is the ruling principle? Are all classes represented? Do any of the classes overlap?

Type of Subject:

a._____ Adult, non-student

_____ University student

_____ Minor

_____ Other (explain)

b._____ Normal volunteer

_____ In-patient

_____ Out-patient

_____ Mentally retarded

_____ Mentally disabled

_____ Individual with limited civil freedom

_____ Pregnant women, fetuses, and the dead

4. Discuss the following ideas for classification papers. Identify any flaws in the ruling principle.

    a. In her first classification exercise, a seventh-grader wrote, "I classify my friends by their loyalty, manners, or indifference toward me."

    b. Harp strings are classified according to the materials they are made of— cat gut, springs, or nylon—because the different materials influence the tone of the sound.

    c. When I put my stamp collection in order, I separate the stamps first by country, then by series and date.

d. From a U.S. government questionnaire: Check your nationality—
(a) white, (b) black, (c) Asian, (d) Hispanic, (e) Cuban.

e. People: There are two main categories, significant people and outsiders.
Significant people include family, friends, and business associates;
outsiders may be anyone from the cashiers at the local supermarket to
pedestrians on the street. People can be considered significant even when
they have a negative impact. Prison guards, for example, would be
extremely important to a prisoner.

—Shannon Brownlee

f. Casey Stengel, famous manager of the New York Yankees: "All right you
guys, line up alphabetically according to size."

g. Looters belong to three categories. There are everyday thieves—men and
women of no conscience—who would steal wherever and whenever no
authority existed to restrain them.

In the second group are those who feel deprived and frustrated and
seize the opportunity to express their grievances at being unemployed,
hungry, angry at society, their bosses or spouses, and who feel they have
little chance for revenge. These individuals are easily galvanized into
action by watching others behave wantonly.

The third category interests psychiatrists the most because any of us
could potentially become looters. In the wake of a disaster, impulses
usually contained—greed, naked aggression, lust for power, etc.—often
flow unchecked. The carnival atmosphere reigns, while the impulses to
help and to heal may be given short shrift.

—*Wall Street Journal*

Writing

1. Write a paper in which you classify your reactions to things around you. Be
sure to identify the significance of your classification. Examples:

a. Things you worry about.

b. Things you keep secret from your family.

c. Things you celebrate.

d. Things you laugh about.

e. Things you feel guilty about.

2. Choose a topic that can be classified, and write an essay. Be sure to keep in
mind the following: (1) choose the ruling principles(s) by which you plan to
classify; (2) identify your purpose in classifying (your reader should not read
your classification and say, "So what?"); (3) choose a writer's stance that

suits the ruling principle and the purpose of the classification; (4) write the paper.

3. Here are some possible topics (modify when necessary):

a. There are distinct kinds of people who patronize laundromats/sporting-goods stores/pizzerias/delicatessens; *therefore* . . .

b. I have encountered many types of people/ideas since coming to college. *My conclusions are* . . .

c. The subjects in my major field can be divided into several categories; *consequently* . . .

d. The parents of successful children fall into several categories, but *the most important category is* . . .

e. The summer and part-time jobs available to college students have certain characteristics, *so when you look for a job* . . .

Lars Eighner

ON DUMPSTER DIVING

Lars Eighner, born in Texas in 1948, attended the University of Texas, Austin (1966–1969). After dropping out, he became a drug counselor, and later, an attendant at Austin State Hospital, where he worked with the profoundly disabled. He discovered in 1988 that he would rather spend his time writing than working in a field where he had no training. He became homeless when he couldn't survive on the income from his publications in magazines such as The Threepenny Review, Advocate Men, The Guide, *and* Inches. *The excerpt below comes from* Travels with Lizbeth, *a best-selling collection of essays describing his life traveling the country, searching for editorial work. Eighner and his watchdog Lizbeth have been self-sufficient since the book's publication.*

1   I began Dumpster diving about a year before I became homeless.

2   I prefer the word *scavenging* and use the word *scrounging* when I mean to be obscure. I have heard people, evidently meaning to be polite, use the word *foraging,* but I prefer to reserve that word for gathering nuts and berries and such, which I do also according to the season and the opportunity. *Dumpster diving* seems to me to be a little too cute and, in my case, inaccurate because I lack the athletic ability to lower myself into the Dumpsters as the true divers do, much to their increased profit.

3   I like the frankness of the word *scavenging,* which I can hardly think of without picturing a big black snail on an aquarium wall. I live from the refuse of others. I am a scavenger. I think it a sound and honorable niche, although if I could I would naturally prefer to live the comfortable consumer life, perhaps—and only perhaps—as a slightly less wasteful consumer, owing to what I have learned as a scavenger.

4   I avoid trying to draw conclusions about the people who dump in the Dumpsters I frequent. I think it would be unethical to do so, although I know many people will find the idea of scavenger ethics too funny for words.

5   Dumpsters contain bank statements, correspondence, and other documents, just as anyone might expect. But there are also less obvious sources of information. Pill bottles, for example. The labels bear the name of the patient, the name of the doctor, and the name of the drug. AIDS drugs and anti-psychotic medicines, to name but two groups, are specific and are seldom prescribed for any other disorders. The plastic compacts for birth-control pills usually have complete label information.

6   Despite all of this sensitive information, I have had only one apartment resident object to my going through the Dumpster. In that case it turned out the resident was a university athlete who was taking bets and who was afraid I would turn up his wager slips.

7   Occasionally a find tells a story. I once found a small paper bag containing some unused condoms, several partial tubes of flavored sexual lubricants, a partially used compact of birth-control pills, and the torn pieces of a picture of a young man. Clearly she was through with him and planning to give up sex altogether.

8   Dumpster things are often sad—abandoned teddy bears, shredded wedding books, despaired-of sales kits. I find many pets lying in state in Dumpsters. Although I hope to get off the streets so that Lizbeth can have a long and comfortable old age, I know this hope is not very realistic. So I suppose when her time comes she too will go into a Dumpster. I will have no better place for her. And after all, it is fitting, since for most of her life her livelihood has come from the Dumpster. When she finds something I think is safe that has been spilled from a Dumpster, I let her have it. She already knows the route around the best ones. I like to think that if she survives me she will have a chance of evading the dog catcher and of finding her sustenance on the route.

9   Silly vanities also come to rest in the Dumpsters. I am a rather accomplished needleworker. I get a lot of material from the Dumpsters. Evidently sorority girls, hoping to impress someone, perhaps themselves, with their mastery of a womanly art, buy a lot of embroider-by-number kits, work a few stitches horribly, and eventually discard the whole mess. I pull out their stitches, turn the canvas over, and work an original design. Do not think I refrain from chuckling as I make gifts from these kits.

10   I find diaries and journals. I have often thought of compiling a book of literary found objects. And perhaps I will one day. But what I find is hopelessly commonplace and bad without being, even unconsciously, camp. College students also discard their papers. I am horrified to discover the kind of paper that now merits an A in an undergraduate course. I am grateful, however, for the number of good books and magazines the students throw out.

11   In the area I know best I have never discovered vermin in the Dumpsters, but there are two kinds of kitty surprise. One is alley cats whom I meet as they leap, claws first, out of Dumpsters. This is especially thrilling when I have Lizbeth in tow. The other kind of kitty surprise is a plastic garbage bag filled with some ponderous, amorphous mass. This always proves to be used cat litter.

12   City bees harvest doughnut glaze and this makes the Dumpster at the doughnut shop more interesting. My faith in the instinctive wisdom of animals is always shaken whenever I see Lizbeth attempt to catch a bee in her mouth, which she does whenever bees are present. Evidently some birds find Dumpsters profitable, for birdie surprise is al-

most as common as kitty surprise of the first kind. In hunting season all kinds of small game turn up in Dumpsters, some of it, sadly, not entirely dead. Curiously, summer and winter, maggots are uncommon.

13   The worse of the living and near-living hazards of the Dumpsters are the fire ants. The food they claim is not much of a loss, but they are vicious and aggressive. It is very easy to brush against some surface of the Dumpster and pick up half a dozen or more fire ants, usually in some sensitive area such as the underarm. One advantage of bringing Lizbeth along as I make Dumpster rounds is that, for obvious reasons, she is very alert to ground-based fire ants. When Lizbeth recognizes a fire-ant infestation around our feet, she does the Dance of the Zillion Fire Ants. I have learned not to ignore this warning from Lizbeth, whether I perceive the tiny ants or not, but to remove ourselves at Lizbeth's first pas de bourée. All the more so because the ants are the worst in the summer months when I wear flip-flops if I have them. (Perhaps someone will misunderstand this. Lizbeth does the Dance of the Zillion Fire Ants when she recognizes more fire ants than she cares to eat, not when she is being bitten. Since I have learned to react promptly, she does not get bitten at all. It is the isolated patrol of fire ants that falls in Lizbeth's range that deserves pity. She finds them quite tasty.)

PRACTICE

Discussion

1. What image do you get from the title? Why does Eighner provide so many definitions in paragraphs 1–3? Do the definitions contradict the title? Discuss the effectiveness of a more accurate title to replace "Dumpster Diving."

2. Eighner uses an implied comparison when he tells the reader that scavenging is a "sound and honorable niche." Does this comparison help to create the tone of the essay?

3. Identify Eighner's classification categories. Does he need sub-categories? Give him advice about making his classification system more logical. If he were to follow your advice, how would the tone of the essay change?

4. Identify Eighner's *ruling principle* (see page 268). Is he consistent?

5. How important is logic in Eighner's classification system?

6. Who is Lizbeth? How important are her antics and reactions to the essay?

Vocabulary

scrounge   forage
scavenger

Writing

1. Write a classification about the things that your pet, roommate, or family members do that you find amusing.

2. Choose one of the following subjects (or one of your own), and develop a logical classification. Then write a paper, based on your system. *On Cheerleading*; *On Hunting*; *On Dancing*; *On Swimming* (or any other sport); *On Part-time Working*; *On Studying*; *On collecting.* . . .

James T. Baker

HOW DO WE FIND THE STUDENT IN A WORLD OF ACADEMIC GYMNASTS AND WORKER ANTS?

Professor of history and director of the honors program at Western Kentucky University, James T. Baker is a graduate of Baylor University. He earned his Ph.D. at Florida State University. Baker has published biographies of Thomas Merton, Ayn Rand, Eric Hoffer, Jimmy Carter, and Brooks Hays. His latest book is about Studs Terkel. The recipient of two Fulbright Senior Lectureships, Baker has taught or studied in Florence, Italy; Seoul, Korea; Taipei, Taiwan; and Oxford, England. Here he describes students particularly and generally. Perhaps you can find yourself somewhere in his description.

1   Anatole France once wrote that "the whole art of teaching is only the art of awakening the natural curiosity of young minds." I fully agree, except I have to wonder if, by using the word "only," he thought that the art of awakening such natural curiosity was an easy job. For me, it never has been—sometimes exciting, always challenging, but definitely not easy.

2   Robert M. Hutchins used to say that a good education prepares students to go on educating themselves throughout their lives. A fine definition, to be sure, but it has at times made me doubt that my own students, who seem only too eager to graduate so they can lay down their books forever, are receiving a good education.

3   But then maybe these are merely the pessimistic musings of someone suffering from battle fatigue. I have almost qualified for my second sabbatical leave, and I am scratching a severe case of the seven-year itch. About the only power my malaise has not impaired is my eye for spotting certain "types" of student. In fact, as the rest of me declines, my eye seems to grow more acute.

4   Has anyone else noticed that the very same students people college classrooms year after year? Has anyone else found the same bodies, faces, personalities returning semester after semester? Forgive me for violating my students' individual "personhoods," but reality makes it so tempting to see them as types. Doubtless you will recognize at least some of them. They have twins, or perhaps clones, on your campus, too.

5   There is the eternal Good Time Charlie (or Charlene), who makes every party on and off the campus, who by November of his freshman year has worked his face into a case of terminal acne, who misses every set of examinations because of "mono," who finally burns himself out physically and mentally by the age of 19 and drops out to go home and recuperate, and who returns at 20 after a long talk with Dad to major in accounting.

6   There is the Young General Patton, the one who comes to college on an R.O.T.C. scholarship and for a year twirls his rifle at basketball games while loudly sniffing out

pinko professors, who at midpoint takes a sudden but predictable, radical swing from far right to far left, who grows a beard and moves in with a girl who refuses to shave her legs, who then makes the just as predictable, radical swing back to the right and ends up preaching fundamentalist sermons on the steps of the student union while the Good Time Charlies and Charlenes jeer.

7   There is the Egghead, the campus intellectual who shakes up his fellow students—and even a professor or two—with references to esoteric formulas and obscure Bulgarian poets, who is recognized by friend and foe alike as a promising young academic, someday to be a professional scholar, who disappears every summer for six weeks ostensibly to search for primeval human remains in Colorado caves, and who at 37 is shot dead by Arab terrorists while on a mission for the C.I.A.

8   There is the Performer—the music or theater major, the rock or folk singer—who spends all of his or her time working up an act, who gives barely a nod to mundane subjects like history, sociology, or physics, who dreams only of the day he or she will be on stage full time, praised by critics, cheered by audiences, who ends up either pregnant or responsible for a pregnancy and at 30 is either an insurance salesman or a housewife with a very lush garden.

9   There is the Jock, of course—the very-afternoon intramural champ, smelling of liniment and Brut, with bulging calves and a blue-eyed twinkle, the subject of untold numbers of female fantasies, the walking personification of he-man-ism—who upon graduation is granted managerial rank by a California bank because of his golden tan and low golf score, who is seen five years later buying the drinks at a San Francisco gay bar.

10   There is the Academic Gymnast—the guy or gal who sees college as an obstacle course, as so many stumbling blocks in the way of a great career or a perfect marriage—who strains every moment to finish and be done with "this place" forever, who toward the end of the junior year begins to slow down, to grow quieter and less eager to leave, who attends summer school, but never quite finishes those last six hours, who never leaves "this place," and who at 40 is still working at the campus laundry, still here, still a student.

11   There is the Medal Hound, the student who comes to college not to learn or expand any intellectual horizons but simply to win honors—medals, cups, plates, ribbons, scrolls—who is here because this is the best place to win the most the fastest, who plasticizes and mounts on his wall every certificate of excellence he wins, who at 39 will be a colonel in the U.S. Army and at 55 Secretary of something or other in a conservative Administration in Washington.

12   There is the Worker Ant, the student (loosely rendered) who takes 21 hours a semester and works 49 hours a week at the local car wash, who sleeps only on Sundays and during classes, who will somehow graduate on time and be the owner of his own vending-machine company at 30 and be dead of a heart attack at 40, and who will be remembered for the words chiseled on his tombstone:

> All This Was Accomplished Without Ever Having So Much As
> Darkened The Door Of A Library.

13   There is the Lost Soul, the sad kid who is in college only because teachers, parents, and society at large said so, who hasn't a career in mind or a dream to follow, who hasn't a clue, who heads home every Friday afternoon to spend the weekend cruising the local Dairee-Freeze, who at 50 will have done all his teachers, parents, and society said to do, still without a career in mind or a dream to follow or a clue.

14   There is also the Saved Soul—the young woman who has received, through the ministry of one Gospel freak or another, a Holy Calling to save the world, or at least some special part of it—who majors in Russian studies so that she can be caught smuggling Bibles into the Soviet Union and be sent to Siberia where she can preach to souls imprisoned by the Agents of Satan in the Gulag Archipelago.

15   Then, finally, there is the Happy Child, who comes to college to find a husband or wife—and finds one—and there is the Determined Child, who comes to get a degree—and gets one.

16   Enough said.

17   All of which, I suppose, should make me throw up my hands in despair and say that education, like youth and love, is wasted on the young. Not quite.

18   For there does come along, on occasion, that one of a hundred or so who is maybe at first a bit lost, certainly puzzled; who may well start out a Good Timer, an Egghead, a Performer, a Jock, a Medal Hound, a Gymnast, a Worker Ant; who may indeed have trouble settling on a major, who will be distressed by what sometimes passes for education, who might even be a temporary dropout; but who has a vital capacity for growth and is able to fall in love with learning, who acquires a taste for intellectual pleasure, who becomes in the finest sense of the word a Student.

19   This is the one who keeps the most jaded of us going back to class after class, and he or she must be oh-so-carefully cultivated. He or she must be artfully awakened, given the tools needed to continue learning for a lifetime, and let grow at whatever pace and in whatever direction nature dictates.

20   For I try always to remember that this student is me, my continuing self, my immortality. This person is my only hope that my own search for Truth will continue after me, on and on, forever.

PRACTICE

Discussion

1. Describe Baker's *role* as a writer.

2. Who is his *reader*? Give evidence from the essay that the reader will have confidence in Baker's ethical proof.

3. What is the ruling principle of Baker's classification? Are his classifications *significant* and *informative?*

4. What is Baker's purpose in making the classification?

5. Baker uses the *representative example* (see illustration, page 292). Where does he use it, and why? Discuss his attitude toward these representative examples. Does his attitude add or detract from his character?

6. Several descriptions of individual students begin one way and end another— for example, the egghead who ends up being killed while working for the CIA. Explain the technique.

7. Discuss the sentence construction of the paragraph *leads* (the first sentence in each paragraph) in the body of the essay. Explain particularly that of paragraph 18.

8. Respond to the final paragraph of the essay. How does this final paragraph contribute to Baker's ethical proof?

Vocabulary

sabbatical	primeval	plasticizes
pinko	mundane	Gulag Archipelago
esoteric	lush	

Writing

1. Reread paragraph 4. In the first line, substitute another clause for *the very same students people college classrooms.* Examples: *The very same professors people . . . : same janitors . . . : same secretaries people department offices; same columnists people the student paper;* etc.

2. Write a paper explaining why you agree or disagree (or partly agree) with Baker's *point* in writing the essay.

3. Write a classification paper explaining the motives of your high-school friends who decided to go to college.

James H. Austin

CHANCE

As a neurologist involved in biomedical research. James H. Austin has had many opportunities to observe the four varieties of chance he explores in the following essay. Austin was born in Cleveland, Ohio, on January 4, 1925. A graduate of Brown University, he received his medical degree from Harvard Medical School in 1948. Doctor and teacher, the combination has made him especially well suited to explain abstruse scientific issues to laymen, which he has done in his book on the psychology of creativity, Chase, Chance, and Creativity: The Lucky Art of Novelty. *The essay here is adapted from his article in* Executive Health Reports *that anticipated Austin's book. While one appreciates the scientific clarity of his classification of chance, one is also informed by Austin's definitions, his examples, and his enthusiasm.*

1   I am reminded of George Bernard Shaw's comment: "Never lose a chance: it doesn't come every day."

2   Of course, you get lucky sometimes. Everyone does! But is there something you can learn about the structure of chance that might improve your percentage?

3   As a physician-investigator, I began to wonder about these questions some years ago. What started me were some astonishing "happy accidents" . . . chance events that were completely unpredictable. Now, being a neurologist, raised in the conventional work ethic, I still believe that success in research comes from being hard-working, persistent, curious, imaginative, intuitive, and enthusiastic. . . . But when this is said and done, it still turns out that many of our lucky breaks will still be decided by our extracurricular activities—by those pivotal events that come only when we have reached out in a spirit of adventure and jousted at chance. Like the lowly turtle, man, too, lurches forward only if he first sticks his neck out and chances the consequences.

4   What is chance? Dictionaries define chance as something fortuitous that happens unpredictably without discernible human intention. *La cheance,* in old French, is derived from the Old Latin, *cadere,* to fall, implying that it is in the nature of things to fall, settle out, or happen by themselves.

5   Chance is unintentional, it is capricious, but we needn't conclude that chance is immune from human intervention. Indeed, chance enters in four different ways when we react creatively with one another and with our environment. You and I are each affected by the principles involved, and it is time we examine them more carefully.

6   The four kinds of chance each have a different kind of motor exploratory activity and a different kind of sensory receptivity. The varieties of chance also involve distinctive personality traits and differ in the way you, as a person, interact with them.

7   Chance I is the pure blind luck that comes with no effort on your part. If, for example, you are sitting playing bridge at a table of four, it's "in the cards" for you to receive a hand of thirteen spades, but statisticians tell us it will occur on an average only once in 635 billion deals. You will ultimately draw this lucky hand, but it may involve a rather longer wait than most have time for.

8   Chance II evokes the kind of luck Charles Kettering, the automotive engineer, had in mind when he said: "Keep on going and the chances are you will stumble on something, perhaps when you are least expecting it. I have never heard of anyone stumbling on something sitting down."

9   Consistent motion is what distinguishes Chance II; its premise is that *un*-luck runs out if you persist. An element of the chase is also implicit in Chance II, but action is still your primary goal, not results. The action is ill-defined, restless, driving, and it depends on your basic need to release energy, not on your conscious intellect. Of course, if you move around in more likely areas, Chance II may enter in to influence your results more fruitfully. For example, if orchids were your only goal, you wouldn't want to go tramping looking for them in the harsh desert.

10   So Chance II springs from your energetic, generalized motor activities, and, with the above qualification, the freer they are the better. A certain basal level of action "stirs up the pot," brings in random ideas that will collide and stick together in fresh combinations in your brain, lets chance operate. When someone, *anyone,* does swing into motion and keeps on going, he will increase the number of collisions between events. If you link a few events together, you can then exploit some of them, but many others, of course, you cannot. Kettering was right. Press on. Something will turn up. We may term this kinetic principle the Kettering Principle.

11   In our two previous examples, a unique role of the individual person was either lacking or minimal. Now, as we move on to Chance III, we see blind luck tiptoeing in softly

and dressed in camouflage. Chance presents the clue, the opportunity exists, but it would be missed except by that *one person* uniquely equipped to recognize it, visualize it conceptually, and fully grasp its significance. Chance III involves a special receptivity and discernment unique to the recipient. Louis Pasteur characterized it for all time when he said: "Chance favors only the prepared mind."

12   Pasteur himself had it in full measure. But the classic example of his principle occurred in 1928, when Alexander Fleming's mind instantly fused at least five elements into a conceptually unified nexus. He was in the laboratory at the bench one day, when his mental sequences went something like this: (1) I see that a mold has fallen by accident into my culture dish; (2) the staphylococcal colonies residing near it failed to grow; (3) therefore, the mold must have secreted something that killed the bacteria; (4) this reminds me of a similar experience I had once before; (5) if I could separate this new "something" from the mold, it could be used to kill staphylococci that cause human infections.

13   Actually, Fleming's mind was exceptionally well prepared for the penicillin mold. Nine years earlier, while he was suffering from a cold, his own nasal drippings had found their way onto a culture dish, for reasons not made entirely clear. He noted that bacteria around this mucus were killed, and astutely followed up the lead. His observations then led him to discover a bactericidal enzyme lysozyme, present in nasal mucus and tears. Lysozyme proved too weak to be of medical use, but imagine how receptive Fleming's mind was to the penicillin mold when nine years later it happened on the scene!

14   One word evokes the quality of the operations involved in the first three kinds of chance. It is *serendipity*. The term describes the facility for encountering unexpected good luck, as the result of: accident (Chance I), general exploratory behavior (Chance II), or sagacity (Chance III). Serendipity was coined by the English-man-of-letters, Horace Walpole, in 1754. He used it with reference to the legendary tales of the Three Princes of Serendip (Ceylon), who quite unexpectedly encountered many instances of good fortune on their travels. In today's parlance, we have usually watered down serendipity to mean the good luck that comes solely by accident. We think of it as a result, not an ability. We have tended to lose sight of the element of sagacity, by which term Walpole wished to emphasize that some distinctive personal receptivity is involved. The archaic meaning of sagacity is acuteness of smell, if we need further testimony of the word's entirely *sensory* connotation.

15   But now something is lacking—the motor counterpart to sagacity. The English Prime Minister Benjamin Disraeli summed up the principle underlying Chance IV when he noted that "we make our fortunes and we call them fate." Disraeli, the practical politician, appreciated that by our actions we each forge our own destiny, at least to some degree. One might restate the principle as follows: *Chance favors the individualized action. This is the fourth element in good luck . . . an active, but unintentional, subtle personal prompting of it.*

16   Chance IV is the kind of luck that develops during a probing action which has a distinctive personal flavor. It comes to you because of who you are and how you behave. It is one-man-made, and is as personal as your signature. Being highly personal, it is not easily understood by someone else the first time around. The outside observer may have to go underground to see Chance IV, for here we probe into subterranean recesses that autobiographers know about, biographers rarely. Neurologists may be a little more

comfortable with the concept because so much of the nervous system we work with exists as anatomically separate sensory and motor divisions. So, some natural separation does exist and underlies the distinction: Chance III concerned with personal *sensory receptivity;* its counterpart, Chance IV involved with personal *motor behavior.*

17   Unlike Chance II, Chance IV connotes no generalized activity, as bees might have in the anonymity of a hive. Instead, like a highly personal hobby, it comprehends a kind of discrete behavioral performance. Anyone might complete the lucky connections of Chance II as a happy by-product of a kind of circular stirring of the pot. But the links of Chance IV can be drawn together and fused only by *one* quixotic rider cantering in on his own home-made hobby horse to intercept the problem at an odd angle. Chance IV does resist straight logic and takes on something of the eccentric flavor of Cervantes' Spanish fiction.

18   Indeed, something about the quality of Chance IV is as elusive as a mirage. Like a mirage, it is difficult to get a firm grip on, for it tends to recede as we pursue it and advance as we step back. But we still accept a mirage when we see it, because we vaguely understand the basis for the phenomenon: a strongly heated layer of air, less dense than usual, lies next to the earth, and it bends the light rays as they pass through.

19   What psychological determinants enter into the varieties of chance? Chance I is completely impersonal. You can't influence it. Personality traits only start to enter in the other forms of chance. To evoke Chance II, you will need a persistent curiosity about many things coupled with an energetic willingness to experiment and explore. To arrive at the discernment involved in Chance III, you must have a sufficient background of firm knowledge plus special abilities in observing, remembering, recalling, and quickly forming significant new associations. Chance IV may favor you if you have distinctive, if not eccentric hobbies, personal life styles, and motor behaviors. The farther apart your personal activities are from the other area you are pursuing, the more strikingly novel will be the creative product when the two meet.

20   Many examples of luck exist in medical research, but if we return to the life of Alexander Fleming, we can see all four varieties of chance illustrated in one man.

21   Good examples of Chance I (pure blind luck) do not leap out from the medical literature because researchers feel guilty about mentioning luck when it replaces their more rational thought processes. However, Fleming tells us with refreshing candor how it was to be visited by Chance I. He said: "There are thousands of different molds, and there are thousands of different bacteria, and that chance put that mold in the right spot at the right time was like winning the Irish Sweepstakes."

22   Many investigators, like Fleming, are as energetic as bees, so their fast mental and physical pace stirs up a certain amount of Chance II for this reason alone. Examples of Chance II are surely all around us, but it is difficult to prove with scientific certainty that they exist, because studies of twins would be required. No medical researcher seems to have a twin who is indolent, but equal in all other abilities, to serve as a basis for comparison.

23   We have already considered Fleming's receptivity under Chance III, and we can also rely on him to serve as an example of the subtle workings of the personality in Chance IV. In Fleming's background was a boyhood shaped by the frugal economy of a Scottish hill farm in Ayrshire. Later, we find that much of his decision to train and work at old St. Mary's Hospital in London was not based on the excellence of its scientific facilities. Laboratories there were primitive by today's standards, damp and readily contaminated

by organisms swirling in out of the London fog. Instead, Fleming's decision hinged on the fact that he liked to play water polo, and St. Mary's had a good swimming pool. Without the *hobby*—swimming—that drew him to St. Mary's, Fleming would never have gone on to discover penicillin! Among the several elements that entered into the penicillin story, this is one crucial personal item usually lost sight of.

24 Still later, when he is 47, let us observe this same thrifty Scot in his laboratory at St. Mary's. His bench stands beneath a window open to the outside air, covered by a clutter of old culture dishes, for Fleming won't throw any dish out until he is certain that everything possible has been learned from it. He then picks up one culture dish of staphylococci that, with ingrained thrift, he has hoarded for many days. The delay has been critical. Had he thrown the dish out earlier, on schedule like the rest of us, the penicillin mold might not have had the opportunity to grow. But there the mold is now, growing in the over-age culture dish, and he alone also has the prepared mind, the sagacity, to realize its implications.

25 We now have seen Sir Alexander Fleming's modest comment about his Irish Sweepstakes luck under Chance I, and can infer that Chance II entered his life by virtue of his many industrious years in the laboratory. We later observed how receptive he was (Chance III) and finally how both his swimming hobby and his thrifty habits coalesced in Chance IV. In Fleming's life, then, we see a fusion of all four forms of chance, and from there follows a simple conclusion: *The most novel, if not the greatest, discoveries occur when several varieties of chance coincide.* Let us name this unifying observation the Fleming Effect. His life exemplifies it, and it merits special emphasis.

26 Why do we still remember men like Fleming? We cherish them not as Nobel Prize winning scientists alone. There is more to it than that. The fact is that, as men, their total contribution transcends their scientific discoveries. Perhaps we remember them, too, because their lives show us how malleable our own futures are. In their work we perceive how many loopholes fate has left us—how much of destiny is still in our hands. In them we see that nothing is predetermined. Chance can be on our side, if we but stir it up with our energies, stay receptive to its every random opportunity, and continually provoke it by individuality in our hobbies, attitudes, and our approach to life.

PRACTICE

Discussion

1. What are the four kinds of *chance* Austin describes?

2. What ruling principle does Austin use to classify chance? Where does he tell you? Does he use the ruling principle consistently?

3. What is the "Fleming Effect"? Why is it important in a discussion of chance? Is this more an essay about Fleming than a classification of chance? How does Austin's regard for Fleming support Austin's believability?

4. What purpose do paragraphs 20 through 26 fulfill? What would be the effect of ending the essay after paragraph 19?

5. Why did Austin present the four kinds of *chance* in the order he used? Could they be arranged in a different sequence? Why or why not?

6. Outline Austin's pattern of organization, taking into account the relationship between his classes and his examples.

7. James Austin is a doctor and no doubt has a large technical vocabulary. What "language" does he use for writing this essay? How does his use of language show that he has consideration for his reader?

8. What distinctions and relationships does Austin draw among the words *luck, chance,* and *serendipity?*

Vocabulary

fortuitous	nexus	candor
discernible	sagacity	indolent
capricious	parlance	implications
intervention	discrete	coalesced
camouflage	quixotic	malleable
conceptually		

Writing

1. Write an essay in which you describe how you have experienced at least three kinds of chance as classified here.

2. Using Austin's essay as a model, write a paper in which you classify an abstraction. Show how one person you know exemplifies each of your classes. Suggested topics: morality, intelligence, frugality, temperance, affection.

3. According to Austin, Disraeli suggested that "we each forge our own destiny, at least to some degree." Write a paper classifying the events in your life in which you "shaped your own destiny."

CHAPTER 16

Illustration

▼ Illustration

Illustration, as one dictionary says, is the "act of clarifying or explaining." It also refers to the material used to clarify or explain: the details, facts, or examples a writer employs to communicate specifics. Any time you support a generalization with evidence in the form of specific examples and details, you are using *illustration.* You can have a generalization at the paragraph-topic level, or a generalization that acts as your thesis for a paper. In either case, you must support those general- izations. But it isn't *where* you should use specifics that is important; rather it is that your evidence should be specific and convincing. As readers, we are often bored and put off by general or abstract statements. We enjoy examples and details because these give us a chance to picture situations for ourselves and to understand quickly what the writer is talking about.

■■■ Using Specific Examples and Details

Here are a few statements—written by a student—that give a reader little to under- stand and nothing to picture:

> I learned very quickly last summer that there was one thing you had to understand im- mediately when you worked around a waterhole drilling rig: safety was the watchword. Rigs are dangerous. I had to be careful and watch my step. One of the other roustabouts forgot this, and he got badly hurt.

The student gives us a general statement: "Rigs are dangerous." However, he doesn't specify *how* they are dangerous. Why was "safety" the "watchword"? How and why did another roustabout get hurt? Here in a second draft is the passage rewritten for specificity: Notice how the writer states a generalization first, then moves to more specific examples, finally ending with a statement about *one* roustabout.

Generalization	During the drilling operation, a *rig* is dangerous at *three times:* when the *head driller* is *breaking out, putting pipe on*, or *drilling hard.* Take *breaking out (removing pipe),* for instance. The driller *signals* when he wants his *helper* to put his *wrench* on the *pipe.* When he is ready, he will *clutch-out* and throw the *rotary table* into *reverse.*
Specific details	After the table begins to turn, if the helper does not take his *hands* off the *wrench* he will get his *fingers cut off* because the wrench *slams*
Application to one person—Billy Lawe	against the *drilling mast* with the force of 200 *horsepower* behind it. One *roustabout, Billy Lawe,* got careless one day and lost *three fingers* on his *left hand.*

Let's look at another example of dull, uninformative writing that lacks specific material:

The Model T Ford was versatile. It could do lots of things on the farm. It provided necessary power for emergencies and other things farmers needed to do.

By contrast, Reynald M. Wik uses illustrative *specific* detail to describe the versatility of the Model T:

Generalization	1	On the farm the Model T proved extremely versatile. In the fall when sparks from railroad locomotives often set prairie fires, farmers would use a car to pull a walking plow to make a fire guard to control the flames. Model Ts were used as early as 1913 to fight forest fires. In butchering hogs, the power from a car could be utilized to hoist the
Specific details		pig out of the hot water in the scalding barrel. In the fields, Model Ts pulled hay rakes, mowers, grain binders, harrows, and hay loaders. Pickup trucks stretched woven wire, hauled water to livestock, and distributed supplies where needed. Ford trucks hauled grain to elevators, brought cattle and hogs to market, and returned from town with coal, flour, lumber, and feed.
Specific details	2	To secure belt power, farmers attached pulleys to the crankshaft, or bolted them to a rear wheel to utilize the 20 horsepower motor for grinding grain, sawing wood, filling silos, churning butter, shearing sheep, pumping water, elevating grain, shelling corn, turning grind-
One fellow		stones, and washing clothes. One ingenious fellow used the spinning rear wheel to knock the shells off walnuts. One farmer said his Model T
One farmer		would do everything except rock the baby to sleep or make love to the hired girl.

Sometimes, however, specific examples and details alone do not stimulate the reader's interest. The material must also be presented vividly and vigorously so that the reader can identify with the person writing the essay. Consider Richard Wright's account of his early life. Notice how Wright uses a single example to support his paragraph lead: *My first lesson in how to live as a Negro came when I was quite small.*

1   My first lesson in how to live as a Negro came when I was quite small. We were living in Arkansas. Our house stood behind the railroad tracks. Its skimpy yard was paved

ILLUSTRATION   **291**

with black cinders. Nothing green ever grew in that yard. The only touch of green we could see was far away, beyond the tracks, over where the white folks lived. But cinders were good enough for me and I never missed the green growing things. And anyhow cinders were fine weapons. You could always have a nice hot war with huge black cinders. All you had to do was crouch behind the brick pillars of a house with your hands full of gritty ammunition. And the first woolly black head you saw pop out from behind another row of pillars was your target. You tried your very best to knock it off. It was great fun.

2   I never fully realized the appalling disadvantages of a cinder environment till one day the gang to which I belonged found itself engaged in a war with the white boys who lived beyond the tracks. As usual we laid down our cinder barrage, thinking that this would wipe the white boys out. But they replied with a steady bombardment of broken bottles. We doubled our cinder barrage, but they hid behind trees, hedges, and the sloping embankments of their lawns. Having no such fortifications, we retreated to the brick pillars of our homes. During the retreat a broken milk bottle caught me behind the ear, opening a deep gash which bled profusely. The sight of blood pouring over my face completely demoralized our ranks. My fellow combatants left me standing paralyzed in the center of the yard and scurried for their homes. A kind neighbor saw me and rushed me to a doctor, who took three stitches in my neck.

3   I sat brooding on my front steps, nursing my wound and waiting for my mother to come from work. I felt that a grave injustice had been done me. It was all right to throw cinders. The greatest harm a cinder could do was leave a bruise. But broken bottles were dangerous; they left you cut, bleeding, and helpless.

4   When night fell, my mother came from the white folks' kitchen. I raced down the street to meet her. I could just feel in my bones that she would understand. I knew she would tell me exactly what to do next time. I grabbed her hand and babbled out the whole story. She examined my wound, then slapped me.

5   "How come yuh didn't hide?" she asked me. "How come yuh awways fightin'?"

6   I was outraged and bawled. Between sobs I told her that I didn't have any trees or hedges to hide behind. There wasn't a thing I could have used as a trench. And you couldn't throw very far when you were hiding behind the brick pillars of a house. She grabbed a barrel stave, dragged me home, stripped me naked, and beat me till I had a fever of one hundred and two. She would smack my rump with the stave, and while the skin was still smarting, impart to me gems of Jim Crow wisdom. I was never to throw cinders any more. I was never to fight any more wars. I was never, never, under any conditions, to fight *white* folks again. And they were absolutely right in clouting me with the broken milk bottle. Didn't I know she was working hard every day in the hot kitchens of the white folks to make money to take care of me? When was I ever going to learn to be a good boy? She couldn't be bothered with my fights. She finished by telling me that I ought to be thankful to God as long as I lived that they didn't kill me.

7   All that night I was delirious and could not sleep. Each time I closed my eyes I saw monstrous white faces suspended from the ceiling, leering at me.

8   From that time on, the charm of my cinder yard was gone. The green trees, the trimmed hedges, the cropped lawns grew very meaningful, became a symbol. Even today when I think of white folks, the hard, sharp outlines of white houses surrounded by trees, lawns, and hedges are present somewhere in the background of my mind. Through the years they grew into an overreaching symbol of fear.

—Richard Wright, *Black Boy*

The word picture Wright draws of his life as a child is so distinct and strikingly alive that readers get the impression that they are there at the scene hearing the mother's tirade and feeling the boy's pain and frustration.

No writer can create reality. He can only create the illusion of reality by choosing details, examples, and words that are strikingly alive—*vivid*. As the novelist Joseph Conrad wrote: "My task which I am trying to achieve is, by the power of the written word, to make you hear, to make you feel—it is, before all, to make you *see*."

A basic strategy in writing vividly is: Don't just *tell* your readers—*show* them, too. General statements can explain a great deal, but they are often flat and colorless in comparison to the examples and details that *show* the reader what you have in mind.

■■■ The Representative Example

Magazines and newspapers are full of essays with titles like "The Typical College Student of the '80s," "The Workaholic in You," and "The Senior Citizen Today." In these essays, the writer gives a representative picture of a class. The writer understands that no person has all the traits described, but that it is often useful and informative to give the reader a composite picture of a particular group. We like to read such essays to see if we fit the picture. The writer of a representative example must be a keen observer of human behavior; otherwise, the picture will be unrepresentative and faulty. Following is an excerpt from an essay by Studs Terkel on the obstinate "hunger" for pride in one's work. Terkel gives three representative examples:

1   Conditions may be horrendous, tensions high, and humiliations frequent, yet Paul Dietch finds his small triumphs. He drives his own truck, interstate, as a steel hauler. "Every load is a challenge. I have problems in the morning with heartburn. I can't eat. Once I off-load, the pressure is gone. Then I can eat anything. I accomplished something."

2   Yolanda Leif graphically describes the trials of a waitress in a quality restaurant. They are compounded by her refusal to be demeaned. Yet pride in her skills helps her through the night. "When I put the plate down, you don't hear a sound. When I pick up a glass, I want it to be just right. When someone says, 'How come you're just a waitress?' I say, 'Don't you think you deserve being served by me?'"

3   Peggy Terry has her own sense of pride and beauty. Her jobs have varied with geography, climate, and the ever-felt pinch of circumstance. "What I hated worst was being a waitress, the way you're treated. One guy said, 'You don't have to smile, I'm gonna give you a tip anyway. I said, 'Keep it, I wasn't smiling for a tip.' Tipping should be done away with. It's like throwing a dog a bone. It makes you feel small."

▼ Suggestions for Using Illustration

As you plan an essay using illustration, keep the following suggestions in mind:

1. Make sure that you use specific details and examples in your illustrations.

2. Use appropriate examples. If you are trying to show that student shoplifting exists on your campus, do not use examples of nonstudents who shoplift. Do

not describe shoplifting that occurs off-campus in the downtown stores—unless that is part of your thesis.

3. Use appropriate and varied *sentence pointers* (pp. 88–90) for your examples, but don't "overpoint." You do not have to use "for example" or "another example of this is . . ." every time you introduce a new illustration. If you think your reader doesn't realize that another illustration is coming up, use a variety of pointers:

For instance. . .

Hence. . .

Thus. . .

Another case. . .

Additional evidence. . .

4. Develop some kind of order in your use of illustration.

▼ Writing and Revising Illustration (An Example)

One day, when Kathryn was out jogging, she took a rest in an old cemetery close to her college. It was a lovely fall day, so she decided to walk around and read the inscriptions on some of the gravestones and monuments. When she returned to her dormitory, she wrote about her impressions:

1   Mount Hope Cemetery was a very enjoyable place. I expected the graveyard to be less than pleasing, but I was surprised. Instead of seeing a piece of earth with dead bodies underneath and gravestones lined up like seats in a movie theatre, I found a place that made me think more of life than of death. Each gravestone, or at least each family plot, had its own personality. This gave me a feeling for the people who had died. They didn't seem like generic corpses, but rather people who had lived and done certain, unique things in their lives. This is what I caught myself thinking about as I walked through the cemetery.

2   There was a lot of life in the cemetery to take notice of. Though the trees screened the cemetery from the outside, out of the corner of my ear I could still hear traffic. Life existed inside the cemetery as well. I saw squirrels, chipmunks, birds, and insects galore. People were there jogging, and even doing their rhetoric assignments for their college course. I wouldn't say that the graveyard was absolutely bustling or anything, but it was more energetic than I expected. The foliage, too, was healthy and alive looking. The grass was green and thick, and the trees were plentiful.

3   The placement of the bushes, gravel roads, and land slopes gently separated the cemetery into small semi-private areas. Each family had its own place which was private, yet part of the rest of the graveyard community. Each family's place had its own feeling, its own personality. One spot I remember very well. In a hollow were several graves covered by a large, old maple. The grass grew in long, thin clumps the way it does under large, old trees, and dirt predominated. All the stones in this area were dark charcoal grey, and somewhat old. It made me think of an old, sad family who perhaps had no more children who would ever visit their graves.

4   The Paro family of tree stumps was one of my favorite groups. The family name was written on a huge stone shaped like a tree trunk with an anchor leaning up against it. Surrounding this was a forest of stubby little tree-stump stones for individual members of the Paro family. The anchor interested me. What seafaring family would live in Illinois?

5   The Campbell family had a stone shaped like the Eiffel Tower which almost shone. It looked more like a monument than a gravestone. I wondered if this family had anything to do with Campbell Hospital; they seemed to be flaunting their money. Even if they couldn't take it with them, they could still show it off.

6   Other areas were more touching. A family buried a 29-year-old daughter under a Greek temple ruin. The Waters family buried a child, their "darling," under a small stone shaped like a scroll, covered with lichen and discolored. An ornate stone, carved to look like a tree with day lilies, trillium, lily of the valley, and ivy winding around it, covered another grave. It was green with moss, and discolored with time. I found this to be the saddest stone of all. It was small, like a child's grave, and whispered sad things about death when young. This stone was sad and depressing, and didn't have much to do with life at all, but it had the right to be sad, if someone who died young was buried beneath it. At first I reacted the same way when I saw other stones with "mother" or "father" on them, but then I realized that although I personally would not like to be remembered only as the mother of someone, at least epitaphs like this made each grave different from the others. The epitaphs showed that people had done something that others, at least, considered unique and worthwhile in their lives.

7   Mount Hope was a cemetery that allowed the people buried there to retain something of their personalities. While death may make everyone equal, in Mount Hope death did not make everyone the same. Pieces of people's lives showed, even if they were very small, making each person different from the rest. I think this made the cemetery less sad. I felt better knowing that people can make a lasting impression on others. It seems to me that one of the saddest things about death is that people and what they did are so easily forgotten.

After reading her draft, Kathryn sees that not all of her paragraphs support her main point—that each gravestone or family plot in the Mount Hope cemetery gives the impression that a person who was unique is buried there.

For example, paragraph 2 is a pleasant description of a cemetery, but it doesn't do much to support her main point. Some of paragraph 3 needs to be better focused. Paragraphs 4–6 are really the only paragraphs that support her point, but they don't support it well.

As a result of her analysis, Kathryn goes back to revise the paper, tying her illustrations to her main point in a more organized, convincing fashion.

1   I expected a visit to a cemetery to be less than pleasing, but I was surprised. Paradoxically, I discovered that the cemetery made me think more about the people when they lived—in other words, think more about life than death. Each gravestone or family plot had its own "personality," giving me a feeling for the people buried there, that they had been unique in some way.

2   Mount Hope cemetery is an attractive, well-kept place. Trees, bushes, and small slopes separate the cemetery into semi-private areas. Each family has its own private place, and each family plot has its own personality. In an older part of the cemetery, a little hollow is covered by a large, old maple tree. The grass grows in long, thin clumps, typical of shady areas. All of the family stones in this area are in old, dark charcoal-grey

marble. The plot is not well-kept—weeds grow among the stones, and it is evident that no one has visited for many years. The area has been neglected and makes me think of a sad family made up of two old people with no children to visit their graves.

3   At another spot in the older area of the cemetery, I saw this simple phrase on a gravestone: "She lived for others." I could imagine a woman who was plump and rosy-cheeked, with many children to care for. Her death must have caused grief for those who had known and loved her.

4   Family names are important in some areas of the cemetery. Sometimes a grouping of gravestones with the family name makes a distinctive display. An example of this is the Paro family plot whose name is written on a huge stone shaped like a tree trunk. However, a peculiar addition to the tree trunk makes the monument most unusual— leaning against the trunk is an anchor. Surrounding the trunk is a forest of stubby little stone tree stumps designating the graves of individual members of the Paro family. I wondered if the anchor was a metaphorical symbol for stability and security of the main trunk of the family.

5   The Campbell family had a monument shaped like the Eiffel Tower that stood much higher than any other family gravestone in the cemetery. Compared with the other stones it seemed to be an ostentatious flaunting of wealth. One got the impression that the family believed if they couldn't take it with them, they could at least show it off.

6   One family buried a 29-year-old daughter under a monument that looked like the ruin of a Greek temple. Another family buried their child, called their "darling," under a small scroll-shaped tombstone. A small child was buried under the stone carving of a little tree with day lilies, trillium, lily of the valley, and ivy winding around it.

7   At first I was sad when I saw stones with "mother" or "father" carved on them. I thought that I wouldn't want to be remembered only as "the mother." However, I realized that designations like these made each grave different from the others, showing that these people had been considered special and worthwhile by their families or loved ones.

8   Mount Hope cemetery allows the people buried there to retain something of their uniqueness. While death may make everyone equal, in this cemetery death does not make everyone the same. I felt better knowing that people can make a lasting impression on others. It seems to me that one of the saddest things about death is that it is too easy to forget the specialness of the individual. A gravestone or burial plot may be the last place where people can be made special for those of us left behind.

PRACTICE

Discussion

1. Study the rewritten paper about the cemetery.

   a. Discuss the writer's use of *signals* and *examples.*

   b. Discuss the appropriateness of the examples.

   c. In what way(s) could Kathryn's essay be about other cemeteries? How is this cemetery different from others? How does the choice of examples indicate the difference or similarity?

   d. How does Kathryn use description as a means of exemplification or illustration?

Writing

1. Revise a paper of yours by adding vivid illustration: facts, details, and examples. Insofar as you can, avoid *telling* your readers; *show* them with specific detail—but avoid mere storytelling.

2. Write a paragraph giving a composite picture of the typical yearbook, autograph book, or picture album.

3. Write an essay in which you give at least four specific illustrations to support one of the following topics:

   a. In spite of efforts to abolish cheating, it still occurs on our campus.

   b. Photography is an expensive hobby.

   c. Collecting _____ satisfies my need for accumulating things.

   d. Old descriptions of my family do not reflect our present situation.

4. Write an essay in which you give a representative picture of a typical place or event. Suggestions:

   Amusement parks

   Recreation on campus

   Decorations in my dorm/rooming house/apartment complex

   The use of cosmetics in the 1980s

5. Using the composite picture of people who take pride in their work (page 292) as a model, write an essay. Possible topics include:

   The typical freshman

   Studyholics

   Partyboys/partygirls

   The typical part-time worker

   The sports nut

   The hobbyist

   The Internet addict

John Leo

A POX ON ALL OUR HOUSES

John Leo is a highly respected senior writer for U.S. News & World Report, *writing essays and cover stories on a wide range of social issues. Leo earned a B.A. with honors from the University of Toronto in 1957. He has been an associate editor for* Commonweal, *a reporter for the* New York Times, *and— before joining* U.S. News—*a senior writer for* Time *magazine for fourteen years.*

In more than thirty years of reporting the news, Leo has seen just about every stigma mankind has to offer—yet he has a kind word for (some) stigmas. Why?

1   Ed Koch, the former mayor of New York City, came out in favor of stigma the other day. He said we should probably try to revive the stigma against unwed mothers (he might have suggested a new one against absent unwed fathers, as well). This bold pro-stigma stance is a rare one. Since the Spanish Inquisition, at least, stigmatizing has had a terrible press. A Nexis computer search of recent newspapers turned up hundreds of awful stigmas, from the one against AIDS patients to the somewhat less revolting one against major-league pitchers who go only five innings. The computer uncovered stigmas against overly ignorant college jocks, careless home decoration and people with whiny voices. But there was only one stigma so positive that we can all get behind it: The stigma against chemical warfare.

2   In truth, stigmatization is the normal stuff of politics, from John Tower's troubles to former President Reagan's attempts to stigmatize and then destigmatize the "Evil Empire." Stigma contests, which clarify and define social values, go on all the time in every community, at every level.

3   An example of a recently concluded stigma contest is smoking. The battle is over and the antismokers have won. The burning and inhaling of dead plant matter will continue, but it is now a defiant, rear-guard activity, best undertaken in a spirit of sheepishness or shame. Now officially stigmatized, smokers are exposed to a level of harassment that would have been considered shocking three or four years ago. Ashtrays are vanishing. Lighting up anywhere is likely to draw a withering glance. Studies will continue to find that smoking a cigar, even in an open field on a breezy day, endangers the lives of innocent children for miles around. More and more pressure and regulations will be brought to bear on tobacco addicts. That is the way stigma works. And in this case, it will save many thousands of lives.

4   Another duel that is currently going well for the stigmatizers revolves around animal rights. The fur industry is very vulnerable because it is not in a position to mount a serious counterargument. Furs are not necessities, just status symbols, and such symbols change with blinding speed in America. Yesterday's glamorous mink wearer is tomorrow's accomplice in the mass murder of tiny furry creatures. Even though the issue has not yet burst full-blown upon the nation's consciousness, chances are that the animal-rights folks will win this contest fairly quickly, maybe in two or three years. Designers such as Bill Blass have already stopped making things with fur. Wealthy women are sneaking out the back of fur salons. How long can such furtive departures be associated with high status?

5   The main reason that the animal-rights people will win big is that the cause plays well on television. Researchers who experiment on animals have a serious case to make, but it is an abstract one: Your child's life may be saved by this dead monkey. Their arguments won't be able to stand up to all that horrendous film of bound animals, convulsed and screaming. Small-game hunting will very likely survive the animal-rights victory, and a drastically reduced amount of animal experimentation will take place under severe restriction, but prepare for a moving *Zeitgeist.* The '90s will not be a good time to invest in mounted animal heads, start a circus or even plan a municipal zoo. Stigma will forbid it.

6   Mothers Against Drunk Driving has taken a light stigma and converted it into a very heavy one. Alcohol may or may not be losing its glamour, but drunkenness has been stigmatized rather quickly, going from something humorous or cute just a decade ago to a strange loss of control. It is hard to watch the old Thin Man movies in quite the same way. William Powell's dawn-to-dusk martini drinking, played for laughs, now just seems pathetic.

7   Gay activists have turned a severe stigma into a much milder one. This long-running contest has now stabilized. On the whole, the straight majority has no stomach for isolating or penalizing gays, but it is not willing to grant that homosexual behavior has the same value and meaning as normal heterosexual sex. A gay male wrote to the *Village Voice* that he wants people to smile when they see him holding hands with his lover on the street. Smiles like this are unlikely to be extracted from most straights for the foreseeable future. The logic of this position, which offers tolerance but not approval, is a faint stigma. Gay-rights laws are now controversial only because many straights consider them exercises in stigma removal.

8   Efforts to stigmatize drug taking have always run afoul of the '60s generation and its tendency to identify drugs with liberation and, now, nostalgia. At the moment, the issue is not greatly relevant. The drug destroying us is crack, and it is consumed by people not known to respond well to middle-class stigma contests. For what it's worth, however, the snorting of cocaine may be about to join freebasing and heroin use as stigmatized pursuits. When the party-going novelist Jay McInerney says he no longer knows anybody who uses coke, this can be taken as a bulletin from the coke frontier.

9   Abortion is the most dramatic stigma contest now being fought. But there are also dozens of low-level skirmishes going on, such as attempts to restigmatize debt and to invent a brand-new stigma to cover the more rapacious expressions of greed. The first order of business, though, is to destigmatize stigma. In a sensible world, Ed Koch and opponents of poison gas should not be out there all alone defending this perfectly natural and healthy process. Any behavior that weakens and disorders social life is ripe for reform. And the first step is often sticking it with stigma.

PRACTICE

Discussion

1. The term *stigma* in the essay is all-important. What does it mean? A fact that you won't find explained in detail in some dictionaries is that originally the word referred to a brand in the flesh of a criminal, slave, or prisoner. It could be cut into the flesh or burned in with an iron.

2. Explain the structure of paragraphs 2 and 3.

3. At the end of paragraph 1, Leo says that "only one stigma [is] so positive that we can all get behind it: The stigma against chemical warfare." Can you think of any other stigmas in America that are equally positive?

4. What and where is the thesis of the essay? Defend or attack its location.

5. Do the illustrations in the essay support the thesis? Explain. Do the illustrations contribute to or detract from Leo's ethical proof?

6. Explain the job of the paragraph *leads* in paragraphs 3–4 and 6–8. (The lead is the first sentence of a paragraph.)

7. In his introduction, Leo seems to imply that this essay will be about unwed mothers and fathers—but it isn't. Did Leo mislead his readers?

8. Leo does not use a *representative example* (page 292) in his essay. Why?

Vocabulary

sheepishness	stomach (paragraph 7)	skirmish
furtive	nostalgia	rapacious
Zeitgeist	freebasing	

Writing

1. Pick (a) a topic (an idea, activity, or type of person) that you would like to see stigmatized; or (b) an idea, etc., that you would like to see destigmatized. Write a paper supporting your point of view. Use illustration as much as you can.

2. What stigma in America is presently undergoing change? Explain your answer, using illustrations.

3. Despite the many angry calls by Americans for a stigma against violence and sex in movies and TV, no real national stigma has formed against their use. Explain why this is generally true.

Joshua Janoff

A GEN-X RIP VAN WINKLE

Joshua B. Janoff was born in Summit, N.J. on September 8, 1972. At 17, he joined the U.S. Navy as a military journalist. He was decorated for service in Operation Desert Storm and received an honorable discharge as a non-commissioned officer at the age of 21. Since his discharge, he has been a full-time student at Emerson College, Boston, Massachusetts, majoring in print journalism. He is an avid runner, free-lance writer, and columnist who has written for numerous military and civilian publications.

1   Ever read the story of Rip Van Winkle? These days I'd recommend it to anyone. The story is one of those uniquely American folk tales, about a work-shy gentleman farmer who falls asleep under a tree—for 20 years. When he awakes, he finds that the world is a very different place. I read the story as a young boy, and it wasn't until recently that I

began to have some inkling of what poor Rip must have been feeling the day he finally opened his eyes and rejoined the world.

2   I'm a 22-year-old freshman at a small New England liberal-arts college. I take classes in subjects like writing and sociology. The school newspaper I write for is filled with aspiring muckrakers, and most people here followed Teddy Kennedy's re-election bid with enthusiasm. A casual outside observer might say I fit the mold of the left-wing, out-of-touch, spotted-owl-saving, liberal-loving college student. A stereotypical Generation Xer suffering from a short bout of college-induced idealism, right?

3   Not so fast. I don't and never have fit such a label. When I was 17, I enlisted for a four-year hitch in the U.S. Navy. I entered the service as a young kid—bored, complacent and cloistered. At the end of my completed time in the navy, I was a noncommissioned officer and Desert Storm veteran. My military service was a series of stark contrasts. I often worked for cruel idiots, scrubbed countless toilets and decks, and chipped away acres of paint. I also gazed at the hypnotic grin on the Mona Lisa, visited the birthplace of Mozart, stood inside the Roman Colosseum, climbed the Great Pyramid of Cheops and put my hand on the reputed tomb of Jesus Christ.

4   I'm not bragging. The day I was discharged was one of the happiest of my life. It was also my first Rip Van Winkle experience. I turned on my car radio to begin the long drive home. I realized I was listening to bands I'd never heard of. (Who the hell is Pearl Jam? Who or what is Alice in Chains?) I'd grown apart from my age group.

5   When I got home I told people about serving overseas, about how the pride we felt came of very hard work. My old friends just stared at me and said I sounded like their father. Or their grandfather. Suddenly I felt very, very old. It seemed I now possessed values that contemporaries saw as chauvinistic, archaic or hopelessly traditional. Their reaction was odd, since people in the navy considered me very liberal.

6   My first mass exposure to Generation X, which was when I hit college, accentuated my confusion. I'd never even heard the term until I got to school. I was surprised to learn that, because of my age, I was considered a member of this lazy, apathetic group of flannel-wearing misfits. At first I laughed. Then the suggestion started to bother me. I denied any complicity. Hey, I'd been away when this inane nomenclature was hatched. "No good," my fellow students said. "By virtue of your age, you're a part of it. Think about it."

7   So I did. But their claims just weren't true. The more I searched for common ground with my peers, the more I began to notice the habits that set me apart. When I'd tell friends I was in Desert Storm, I kept getting the same reaction. "Wow, what was it like? Were you scared? Wow, I could never have done that."

8   Now I'd be curious. Exactly what did that last statement mean? "Well, you know. I mean, it's not like I'd ever put on some uniform and go to war like in the movies. There's just no way."

9   That response disturbed me. When Desert Storm was going on, everyone I knew expressed total support and sympathy for the American servicepersons risking their safety to free Kuwait. Just a few years later, the idea of serving in such a way seems unthinkable to my generation. I don't believe it's because of an abundance of conscientious objectors among them. A true conscientious objector has strong, carefully thought out

convictions and acts out of sense of moral compulsion. I think those who told me they wouldn't go were just plain lazy.

10   The average age of an American combat soldier in the Korean War was 20, and in the Vietnam War, it was 19. I know there was a draft in effect, but besides the relative few who went to Canada, these young American proved that they were doers rather than talkers. Even the ones who went north *acted* on their beliefs. Today's youth, by contrast, seem willing to talk about their convictions, but not act on them.

11   I've seen other, more commonplace examples of my peers' laziness. Physical fitness was expected growing up in my family, and that attitude was reinforced in the navy. Now most of my friends look at me like I'm nuts when I say that I go to the gym regularly. Hell, forget the gym. To a lot of my fellow students, just walking a mile to the dining hall is unthinkable. Thank God for that shuttle bus, eh?

12   Sometimes, just getting out of bed is a problem. Most of the people in my college regard 8 a.m. classes as a fate between death and a world without Quentin Tarantino movies. I'm tempted to tell these people that 6 a.m. was considered "sleeping in" in the navy, but I doubt it would change anything.

13   Finally, there's the whole apathy thing. At first I felt certain that the idea of a generationwide sense of total indifference was crazy. It had to be an invention of the mass media. Unfortunately, the media assertions appear to be true. We as a generation have yet to produce any defining traits, except perhaps to show a defeatist belief that we will do worse than our parents.

14   Not that the situation is completely untenable. No living generation can honestly claim to have a general consensus on any one issue, whether the topic is politics, abortion or health-care reform. If my age group can agree to resolve its indifference before it's too late, then maybe we can go ahead to make a more constructive future. It's time to stop channel surfing and looking for new ways to procrastinate, and to desist from blaming problems on those in authority. Perhaps what's needed is a good swift kick in the rear. Playtime is over, and there is a big bad world out there. It's waiting to see what we've got, but it's also ours for the taking. Let's lose the remote and do it.

PRACTICE

Discussion

1. What is the writer's thesis? Where is it stated? Discuss the evidence supporting the thesis. What is the relevance of the writer's comparison with Rip Van Winkle?

2. Make a list of the characteristics of those students who supposedly make up Generation X. How do these characteristics act as a composite picture or *representative example* (see page 292)?

3. Discuss Janoff's use of specifics and dialogue to prove that he isn't like the other college students of Generation X. How effectively does he support his generalizations about Generation X?

4. How do his experiences as a soldier in Desert Storm contribute to his ethical appeal? How does his ethical appeal help to support his thesis?

5. Study the conclusion. How effective is his negative use of TV?

6. What is Janoff's purpose in his criticism of Generation X?

7. Make a list of the *pointers* (page 88) used by the writer. How do they help the reader follow the ideas in the essay?

8. How is the writer's use of language related to his role (see *Writer's Stance*, pages 22–24)? Note in particular

Finally, there's the whole apathy thing.

Who the hell is Pearl Jam?

There's just no way.

Vocabulary

cloistered	archaic	untenable
non-commissioned	apathetic	procrastinate
chauvinistic	complicity	

Writing

1. Using the list of characteristics you developed in number two above, write a representative example of the typical student of Generation X.

    Or, based on your experience, write a representative example of another group of students.

2. Using your experience, either refute Janoff's thesis or agree with him.

3. Everyone has had a "Rip Van Winkle" experience—a jolt when you find that some part of your world has suddenly become "a very different place." Write an essay illustrating your own special Van Winkle.

Jan Harold Brunvand

URBAN LEGENDS

In 1966, Jan Harold Brunvand was still wet behind his folklorist's ears, as he acknowledges in "Urban Legends." That year he began teaching folklore at the University of Utah in Salt Lake City, where he is currently professor of English. He is also editor of the Journal of American Folklore *and has written three books on the subject, so his ears have dried out but his enthusiasm for folklore clearly flourishes. A longer version of "Urban Legends," adapted from his book* Urban American Legends, *appeared in* Psychology Today *magazine in June, 1980. The illustrations that Brunvand scatters liberally throughout his essay are like salted peanuts: They whet your appetite for more.*

1 "A man in California saw an ad for an 'almost new' Porsche, in excellent condition— price, $50. He was certain the printers had made a typographical error, but even at $5,000 it would be a bargain, so he hurried to the address to look at the car. A nice-looking woman appeared at the front door. Yes, she had placed the ad. The price was indeed $50. 'The car is in the garage,' she said. 'Come and look at it.' The fellow was overwhelmed. It was a beautiful Porsche and, as the ad promised, nearly new. He asked if he could drive the car around the block. The woman said, 'of course,' and went with him. The Porsche drove like a dream. The young man peeled off $50 and handed it over, somewhat sheepishly. The woman gave him the necessary papers, and the car was his. Finally, the new owner couldn't stand it any longer. He had to know why the woman was selling the Porsche at such a ridiculously low price. Her reply was simple: with a half-smile, she said, 'My husband ran off with his secretary and left a note instructing me to sell the car and send him the money.'"

2 This story, which has been in circulation for years, turned up in a recent Ann Landers column. It was sent in by a reader who claimed to have seen it in the *Chicago Tribune.* Ann Landers accepted the story as true, and many of her readers probably did also. But when she checked with the *Chicago Tribune,* the paper could find no actual record of it.

3 The story seems believable at first, but when you stop to think about it, wouldn't a man running off with his secretary do so in his own Porsche? And if not, would he really trust his abandoned wife to sell such a car to help finance his departure?

4 Many people have heard stories of this kind and accepted them as true accounts of actual experiences. But scholars of contemporary American folklore recognize tales like "The Philanderer's Porsche" as characteristic examples of what they call "urban legends." ("Urban," as used by folklorists in this case, means "modern," and is not specifically related to cities.) Other widely known urban legends have titles such as "The Boyfriend's Death," "The Snake in the K-Mart," and "The Solid Cement Cadillac."

5 Urban legends are realistic stories that are said to have happened recently. Like old legends of lost mines, buried treasure, and ghosts, they usually have an ironic or supernatural twist. They belong to a subclass of folk narratives that (unlike fairy tales) are believed—or at least believable—and (unlike myths) are set in the recent past, involving ordinary human beings rather than extraordinary gods and demigods.

6 Unlike rumors, which are generally fragmentary or vague reports, legends have a specific narrative quality and tend to attach themselves to different local settings. Although they may explain or incorporate current rumors, legends tend to have a longer life and wider acceptance; rumors flourish and then die out rather quickly. Urban legends circulate, by word of mouth, among the "folk" of modern society, but the mass media frequently help to disseminate and validate them. While they vary in particular details from one telling to another, they preserve a central core of traditional themes. In some instances, these seemingly fresh stories are merely updatings of classic folklore

plots, while other urban legends spring directly from recent conditions and then develop their own traditional patterns in repeated retellings. For example, "The Vanishing Hitchhiker," which describes the disappearance of a rider picked up on a highway, has evolved from a 19th-century horse-and-buggy legend into modern variants incorporating freeway travel. A story called "Alligators in the Sewers," on the other hand, goes back no further than the 1930s and seems to be a New York City invention. Often, it begins with people who bring pet baby alligators back from Florida and eventually flush them down the drains.

7   What most interests the modern folklorist is *why* these stories recur. We suspect that the reasons will tell us something about the character of the society in which they circulate.

8   One genre of urban legend is the horror story, which seems to appeal particularly to American adolescents. Consider the well-known legend that folklorists have named "The Boyfriend's Death." The version below might typically be told in a darkened college dormitory room with fellow students sprawled on the furniture and floor:

9   *"This happened just a few years ago out on the road that turns off Highway 59 by the Holiday Inn. This couple was parked under a tree out on this road. Well, it got to be time for the girl to be back at the dorm, so she told her boyfriend that they should start back. But the car wouldn't start, so he told her to lock herself in the car and he would go down to the Holiday Inn and call for help. Well, he didn't come back and he didn't come back, and pretty soon she started hearing a scratching noise on the roof of the car. Scratch, scratch. . . scratch, scratch. She got scareder and scareder, but he didn't come back. Finally, when it was almost daylight, some people came along and stopped and helped her out of the car, and she looked up and there was her boyfriend hanging from the tree, and his feet were scraping against the roof of the car."*

10   Here is a story that has rapidly achieved nationwide oral circulation, in the process becoming structured in the typical manner of folk narratives. The traditional and fairly stable elements in it are the parked couple, the abandoned girl, the mysterious scratching, the daybreak rescue, and the horrible climax. The precise location, the reason for her abandonment, the nature of the rescuers, and the murder details may vary. For example, the rescuers may be the police, who are either called by the missing teens' parents or simply appear on the scene in the morning to check the car. In a 1969 variant from Maryland, the police utter this warning: "Miss, please get out of the car and walk to the police car with us, but don't look back." Of course the standard rule of folk-narrative plot development now applies: the taboo must be broken. The girl *does* always look back, à la Orpheus in the Underworld, and her hair may turn white from the shock of what she sees.

11   The style in which such oral narratives are told deserves attention, for a telling that is dramatic, fluid and possibly quite gripping in actual performance before a sympathetic audience may seem stiff, repetitious, and awkward when simply read. The setting of the legend-telling also plays a vital role, along with the storyteller's vocal and facial expression, gestures, and the audience's reactions.

12   However, even the bare texts retain some earmarks of effective oral performance. In "The Boyfriend's Death," notice the artful use of repetition (typical of folk-narrative style): "Well, he didn't come back and he didn't come back . . ." The repeated use of

"well" and the building of lengthy sentences with "and" are also hallmarks of oral style that give the narrator control over his performance and tend to squeeze out interruptions or lapses in attention among listeners. The scene that is set for the incident—lonely road, night, a tree looming over a car out of gas—and the sound effects—scratches or bumps on the car—all contribute to the style.

13   Many urban legends preserve the basic shock effect of classic ghost stories or horror tales. They play on the fears of physical assault or of contamination. Another significant group of legends depends on soap opera plots rather than on scare stories. In these tales, the characters are merely threatened with the discovery of a supposed infidelity or with having their naked bodies exposed, both of which they fear will amount to public proof of their foolishness.

14   Sometimes the situation is clearly one of dalliance, with someone getting caught in the act—or at least caught in preparing for the act. So realistic are the plots and so ordinary the characters that it seems completely possible not only that such adventures *could* have happened but also that they could in fact happen again to anyone.

15   I was taken in by one of these stories myself when I was still wet behind my folklorist's ears: I eventually christened it "The Solid Cement Cadillac." One day in the early summer of 1961, proud of my freshly earned Ph.D. in folklore, I lounged on a beach along Lake Michigan with family and friends and daydreamed about my first teaching job. A neighbor of my parents began to tell us about a funny incident that she said had happened recently to a cement-truck driver in Kalamazoo. Her story soon had my full attention:

16   *"It seems that the truck driver was delivering a load of wet mix to an address near his own neighborhood one day when he decided to detour slightly and say hello to his wife. When he came in sight of his home, he saw a shiny new Cadillac in the driveway, and so he parked the ready-mix truck and walked around the house to check things out. Voices were heard coming from the kitchen; when he peeped in through the window, there was his wife talking to a strange man. Without checking any further, and certainly without alerting the couple inside, the truck driver proceeded to lower a window of the new Cadillac, and he emptied the entire load of wet cement into it, filling the car completely. But when he got off work that evening and returned home, his tearful wife informed him that the new (now solid cement) car was for him—bought with her own hardearned savings—and that the stranger was merely the local Cadillac dealer who had just delivered the car and was arranging the papers on it with her."*

17   I made a mental note of the story, for even though it seemed to have some details that could be corroborated (police had been called, a wrecking company towed the car away, the name of the cement company had been mentioned), it surely had the ring of other urban legends I had heard and studied. For example, I wondered how one of those big, noisy, ready-mix trucks could have parked right outside a house—let alone unloaded—without attracting attention from the two people who were chatting quietly inside.

18   Later that summer, I received the first issue of the *Oregon Folklore Bulletin* and read this notice: "An interesting story is presently circulating in all parts of the United States. It is told as if it were right out of last week's newspaper, and concerns a cement-truck driver who stops by his own house for a midmorning cup of coffee while on the way to

deliver a load. But when he drives down his street he notices a flashy car parked in front of his house, and. . . "

19   The only variation is the story as reported from Oregon turned out to be that the driver "finds his wife and a strange man in a compromising situation and sees that he is a bit too late to intervene successfully." In the next two issues of the *Oregon Folklore Bulletin,* the editor reported on his findings about the cement-truck driver story. He described "a plethora of versions mailed from all over the country," and in the third issue of the *Bulletin* provided a summary of 43 versions then on file. The majority of the accounts contained supposed authenticating details about police, tow trucks, or newspaper reports, but no really solid documentation was ever offered. The make and model of the car varied, of course, but only two other significant changes were reported: a Utah version had it that the car belonged to the company boss who had come around to set up a surprise party for the driver for faithful service to the company; in Massachusetts the car was said to be one that the wife had just won in a raffle.

20   American folklorists did not pay much further attention to the story, except to record it regularly from their students and acquaintances. Like many urban legends, it tends to run in unpredictable cycles of popularity. Its continued appeal clearly derives from the belief that philandering spouses should "get what they deserve," a viewpoint tempered with the warning that a person ought to be absolutely sure of the evidence before doing something drastic. Thus, the truck driver, who looks like a decisive, aggressive, he-man hero at first, is shown up finally as an impulsive dummy who jumped to an incomplete conclusion before making his move.

21   A great mystery of folklore research is where oral traditions originate and who invents them. One might expect that, at least in modern folklore, we could come up with answers to such questions, but that is seldom, if ever, the case. Most leads pointing to possible authors or original events lying behind urban legends simply fizzle out.

22   Whatever their origins, the dissemination process is no mystery. Groups of age-mates, especially adolescents, form one important legend channel; other paths of transmission include gatherings of office workers and club members, or religious, recreational, and regional groups, like the Ozark hill folk or the Pennsylvania Dutch. Some people seem to specialize in knowing every recent rumor or tale and can enliven any coffee break, party, or trip with the latest supposed news. The telling of one episode inspires other people to share what they have read or heard, and in a short time, a lively exchange of details occurs, with new variants often created.

23   The difficulties in tracing a story can be illustrated by "The Snake at K-Mart," an urban legend involving a modern suburban discount store. A dangerous creature is discovered in an unexpected place; this time it's a poisonous snake, which supposedly strikes an unaware shopper who is looking at some imported rugs, blankets, or sweaters in the store.

24   Although there are dozens of oral versions of "The Snake at K-Mart," a news story in the *Dallas Morning News* (1970) illustrates the hopeless circular quest for origins that anyone hoping to track down such an urban legend as this is likely to undergo:

25   *"'I'd like some information,' a male caller told the* Dallas News City Desk *some weeks ago. It seems he'd heard about a woman who had gone to a local discount store*

to look at some fur coats imported from Mexico. When the woman put her hand in the coat pocket, she felt a sudden, sharp pain. A few minutes later her arm supposedly had started turning black and blue.

26 *"Well,' the man continued, 'they rushed her to the hospital. It seems that pain was a snake in the coat pocket. The woman's arm had to be amputated.'*

27 *"The reporter said he'd check the story. About that time a woman called with the same story, only she'd heard the woman had died right in Presbyterian Hospital's emergency ward. Presbyterian Hospital said it had no such case on record.*

28 *"'My brother is a doctor,' another caller explained. 'He's on the staff at Baylor Hospital, and he was present when they brought the woman in.'*

29 *"Baylor Hospital said it had no such case on record. Nor did the police or the health department. When the doctor was questioned, he said it wasn't actually he who was present but a friend. The friend explained that he had not been present either, but that he had just overheard two nurses talking about it.*

30 *"After about 10 calls from other 'interested' persons the fur coat turned into some material that had come in from India.*

31 *"One man gave the name of the insurance company that was handling the case. The insurance man said it wasn't actually his company, but his next door neighbor's cousin's company.*

32 *"Finally, a caller came up with the victim's name. The* News *called and the supposed victim answered the phone. She said she had never been in better health. Someone must have confused her with someone else, but she had heard the rumor. Only she had heard the snake was found in a basket of fruit."* (Probably only in Texas would so many people believe that fur coats may be purchased in discount stores.)

33 For a folklorist—unlike a journalist—the purpose of trying to trace an urban legend is not merely to validate or debunk a good story. For us, collecting a story's variations and tracing its dissemination and change through time and across space are only the beginning of an analysis. The larger theme in "The Snake at K-Mart" is the fear of danger or contamination of commercial products, as with "The Mouse in the Coke Bottle" or "The Rat in the Fried Chicken." This theme seems to grow out of the widespread anxiety about a multitude of health risks in our environment, many of them possibly caused by individual or corporate negligence. The legend sounds plausible and serves effectively as a warning against the dangers that may be lurking in terrific bargains, fast-food restaurants, and cheap goods from underdeveloped countries.

34 Along with the best-known urban legends, which circulate over a wide territory (including other countries) in various well-wrought versions, there are numerous other fragmentary rumors and stories going around—sometimes only within a specific folk group. Some of these are takeoffs on older traditional themes that come alive again suddenly after years of inactivity. Others may have intense local or regional life for a time, but fail to catch on with the general public, usually because they are too much the esoteric possession of a particular ethnic or occupational group.

35 It is tempting to take one or two of the most typical examples of urban legends as inclusive symbols of distinctive aspects of our recent history. "The Snake in the K-Mart," some have suggested, draws on our guilt stemming from the war in Vietnam and implies that the venomous intentions we fear Asian peoples may feel toward us take the

form of revenge via imported goods. Personally, I see the story simply as a new twist on the old theme of xenophobia.

36   Without denying that such themes may be implied, I believe that a great deal of the legends' continuing popularity might be explained much more simply. Goods *are* imported in quantity from some countries that have tropical climates: what if a snake or snake eggs got into them (as insects sometimes stow away in fruit shipments)?

37   In any age or with any subject, when a skilled oral storyteller begins to play around with such ideas and when members of the audience respond, repeat the stories, and begin to add their own flourishes, such legends will begin to be formed and to circulate. I expect to hear many more examples of the old favorite urban legends in the coming years and to hear many more new ones as well. And I expect that these stories will continue to suggest how people believe things have happened, or how they either hope—or fear—that things *could* happen.

PRACTICE

Discussion

1. How are urban legends different from other categories of folklore? What characteristics do they share with all folklore?

2. Why are folklorists interested in studying urban legends? How do they go about their work and share their findings? How is it significant that this essay appeared in *Psychology Today?*

3. What part do the media play in the urban legends? How do reporters and folklorists differ in their approaches to stories?

4. Although this essay appears in the section on illustration, Brunvand uses several strategies of development. Name three other strategies and cite the section of the essay where each is used.

5. What general categories of urban legends does Brunvand's essay explore? List the categories in order. What ordering principle can you perceive? Is the first illustration in or out of order? Would you change it? Why?

6. Brunvand speaks in several voices in this essay. Where does he sound like a college student? Like a teacher? Like a sociologist? Where does he use a traditional folk saying to give a lively introduction to a story about himself? How does he prevent all these voices from confusing the reader?

7. Which is more important, setting or characterization, in "The Philanderer's Porsche"? In "The Boyfriend's Death"? In "The Solid Cement Cadillac"? In each case, why? What stylistic device do they share?

8. Compare Brunvand's use of illustration with Janoff's. How do you account for the differences?

Vocabulary

typographical	genre	plethora
philanderer	Orpheus	debunk
demigods	dalliance	esoteric
disseminate	corroborated	xenophobia

Writing

1. Write out three or four urban legends with which you are familiar. Be a skilled storyteller. As Brunvand describes in his final paragraph, "play around with [the] ideas. . . and [your] own flourishes."

2. Identify a theme in some of the graffiti you have seen or can gather, and write an essay on the ideas or feelings that drive those particular scribblings. Illustrate liberally.

3. Examine folklore publications and identify some common interests of folklorists besides urban legends. Write an essay about the work of folklorists. Use illustrations from the publications you studied.

CHAPTER 17

Definition

▼ Definition

Any example of how you intend to use a word or phrase can be called a *definition.* If you clarify a usage which is common or customary, as in dictionary definitions, you give what is called a *reported definition.* The reported definition of *follower* is someone who believes (or follows) another's creed, doctrine, or teachings. If, on the other hand, you give the term a special usage in the context of your discussion, you have created a *stipulative definition.* Tom, the student who classified boys as *leaders, followers,* and *obstructionists* (see pages 271–274), stipulated his use of *followers* to mean *those boys attending summer camp who do what the leader expects, but who seldom act on their own initiative.*

It is often necessary to define terms beyond a one-sentence definition. Abstract terms, for example, require more attention. Sometimes you may want to deal with traditional ideas in a different way. Or you may wish to take a special view of a subject— and will then need to clarify your terms. So used, definition becomes one of the major methods of developing a subject, and can even be a full-length paper, if you find that the subject is large enough to warrant that much space. *Definition* can be both a method of developing a subject and a subject itself.

Consider this paragraph:

Mysteries are about *understanding;* thrillers are about *winning.* In a mystery you are never really sure who the villain is or what he is up to until the end of the book (and sometimes not even then if you have not read carefully). In a thriller you usually know what the villain wants and how he plans to get it. Often you know perfectly well how the story will end—Germany will lose World War II, de Gaulle will not be assassinated, New York will not be destroyed by the nuclear device in the closet in the Pan Am Building.

The tension comes from trying to figure out how the hero will avert disaster and survive. The task of the mystery-writer is to make you share a detective's curiosity, whereas the thriller-writer must make you share a hero's fear.

—Ken Follett, "A Moscow Mystery"

In this paragraph, we find many of the typical characteristics and uses of definition:

1. Definition works in a context of an event, situation, problem, etc. Ken Follett, in his book review of a mystery novel, clarifies his position on the differences between a mystery and a thriller in order to make his review more persuasive.

2. Definition clarifies an ambiguous situation by explaining the key term (or terms) your essay is based on. You ordinarily define in order to support a thesis convincingly and to get your reader to see the point you are making. In the article from which the paragraph is taken, Follett adopts the role of a book reviewer who tries to persuade his readers that this book is, indeed, a mystery novel, not a thriller, as the book's publishers have advertised it.

3. Definition explains, limits, and specifies. The rest of this section shows you how this is done.

4. Definition is a part of the writer's attempt to give a truthful account of what a thing, act, or idea is really like. Defining is another strategy for getting at the truth.

■■■ *Techniques of Defining*

Now that you know something about definition, here are five practical techniques for getting the ordinary jobs of defining done. We will keep our discussion of each quite brief. All of them could be expanded by adding more examples and details.

Definition by Classification (Logical Definition)

In defining by classification, you put the term to be defined in its *class* (of things, people, activities, or ideas). Then you explain how the term *differs* from other terms in the same class. Examples:

Term	Class	Differences
Epic [is]	narrative poetry	"of exalted style, celebrating heroic ventures, mythical or historical, in poems of considerable length."
		—*Oxford Companion to Classical Literature*
Bucket [is]	a domestic carrying utensil	deep and round, with a curved handle that fits into the hand, used for carrying fluids, especially water or milk.

Liberty [is]	a human condition, mainly political and mainly negative	that has to do with those freedoms that are neither social, nor religious, nor private; it consists simply of being let alone by the people who have the temporary powers of government.

For logical definitions to be useful, neither class nor differences should be too broadly stated. The class for epic is *narrative poetry,* not simply *poetry.* The class for bucket is *domestic carrying utensil,* not just *domestic utensil* or *carrying utensil.* The list of differences should be complete enough so that the term is clearly distinguished from other terms.

Definition by Negation

This method of definition explains what something is not. A *bucket* is not a "scoop." *Cool* is not "hot." *Liberty* does not mean "license." *Education* has little to do with "training." Negative definitions are useful because they allow you to narrow your general area of definition. You can use them at the beginning of an extended definition to cut out areas of meaning you do not want to deal with, as the student-writer does in this definition of the slang term *rhubarb:*

> Anyone who has ever attended a major league baseball game knows what a *rhubarb* is. For those of you who are not sports fans, you must understand that a rhubarb is not the plant from the buckwheat family. Neither is it the stalk of the pie plant from which your grandmother made sauce or pastries. Instead, it is a term used to describe the heated discussion that occurs between a baseball player (or the manager) and the umpire over a close call in baseball.

Definition by Illustration or Example

You can sometimes employ, implicitly or explicitly, *illustration* or *example* to aid in your definition. That is, you can define a thing by giving an example of it. What is an epic poem? *The Iliad, The Odyssey,* and *Paradise Lost* are examples. What do I mean by "a great baseball player"? I mean someone like Joe DiMaggio or Cal Ripkin, Jr. Defining by illustration or example gives you a simple but incomplete meaning; consequently, you should use this method with at least one of the others.

Definition by Synonym

There are no perfect synonyms. Every word is at least slightly different from every other word. But it is possible to define a word by using another word that is similar in meaning. Examples: A *herald* is a "forerunner." *Honor,* in various senses, may be "homage," "reverence," or "deference." *Cool* may mean "composed," "collected," "unruffled," "nonchalant," "unfriendly," or "not warm." Like defining by illustration or example, this is a specialized approach that you should ordinarily use with at least one of the other methods.

Definition by Operation

You define by operation when you state what something does or how it works: A bucket is a round, deep container, hung from a curved handle, that is used for carrying water, milk, or other materials. Liberty allows one to say or do what he pleases without injuring others. Education is an attempt to discipline the mind so that it can act intelligently on its own.

If sufficiently detailed, the operational definition is valuable because it gives you a practical check on the reality or truth behind a definition. For example, the word *traitor* has been defined as "someone who deserts his country." This is a limited operational definition. But the definition does not take into account the possibility that one's country might be, like certain dictatorships, deserving of desertion. This last idea gives us an *operational check* on the definition of *traitor* and allows us to add a clause to the definition: A traitor "is someone who deserts his country when his country both needs and deserves his allegiance." Observe that the added clause is itself operational. If someone does not accept our operational check on the definition of *traitor,* we can ask him to provide his own check, and then we can argue the matter.

■■■ *Avoiding Errors in Defining*

Many errors are caused by the writer's not limiting a definition sufficiently. Consider this definition, which is both logical and operational: "A belt is a thing that a man wears around his waist to keep his trousers up." As a class, *thing* is not limited enough, for it does not take into account what sort of "thing" a belt may be. One can hold up his pants with rope, but that fact does not make the rope a belt. On the other hand, the rest of the definition is too limited because it does not take into account that women often wear belts to hold up "trousers" and that belts have many other uses. The process of a limiting in the logical definition should be done in two steps—first limit the *class,* then limit the *differences.*

Perhaps the most common errors in defining are made by writers who do not realize that their definitions must fit reality. The final question to ask yourself is: Am I telling the truth about this word? If you define *monarchy* as a "contemporary government ruled by a king for his own selfish purposes," you are in danger of being untruthful; for this definition would fit badly, to give only one example, the English constitutional monarchy. The writer who defined *individualism* as "the need of every person to be honored by others" not only blurred the meaning of *individualism* but also stated an untruth about the nature of an important idea. If a student defines *fraternity* epigrammatically as "a snob co-op," is he really being truthful about the fraternities on his campus and about fraternity life in general? The fraternity man may answer that the definition does not fit fraternity life as he knows it, that the definition is not "true." This does not mean that the point is unarguable; it means rather that the students are going to have to agree on the reality behind their definitions before they can get anywhere with their debate.

Observe how a student used a variety of techniques of defining to help her explain the term *ad-lib:*

Introduction 1   There is nothing more frightening to the amateur in the theater— at least to me—than to forget my lines. After weeks of rehearsal, with my lines seemingly embedded forever in my subconscious, I cannot

Definition by classification

conceive of forgetting them. However, all actors occasionally forget a line. Then what they do is to think up another one, called an *ad-lib.* An ad-lib is a made-up response to a cue when the actor has forgotten the playwright's words. It is not part of the script. Ad-libbing requires

Definition by negation

instant extemporizing—or improvising. The word comes from the Latin *ad-libitum,* which means "as one pleases." An actor usually does not "please" to forget a line, but if one is clever the made-up lines will please the other members of the cast who may be waiting for their cues.

2   When I realize I have forgotten a line, my mind races frantically over the lines I *do* know. If I can't remember, I think of a replacement

Definition by operation

which fits the context of the scene. All of this activity is carried out in the space of about five seconds, although it may seem ten or twenty times longer to the actor. In the meantime, most of the audience may be totally oblivious to what is going on, especially if the actors are cool about the situation.

3   For the amateur, the situation is terrifying. I break out in a cold sweat, the silence is interminable, and the stage lights blinding. I feel dizzy. The other actors are in a panic, also. They try to concentrate on the forgotten line in the hope that they can transmit it by mental telepathy. When the actor finally ad-libs, everyone heaves a sigh of relief and the play continues smoothly until another actor drops a line.

4   The ad-lib requires a certain amount of creativity. Other actors may interject an ad-lib to cover for the one who has forgotten the

Definition by example

line. It may also be used when someone has forgotten to enter. The actor who is on stage alone may say something mundane such as, "I wonder where John is?" or "John must be late," or "Perhaps John didn't receive my invitation."

5   The ad-lib is an important part of performance. Actors must be trained to make up lines in order to fill those gaps that inevitably will occur when a group of amateurs get on stage to play someone else's speeches.

▼ Some Final Suggestions for Defining

In most instances, you will use definition in one of two ways. In the first way, you define a term at the beginning of a paper and then go on to develop your ideas by different methods. In the second, you devote much of your paper to an extended definition, part of which may actually supply your thesis. Sometimes you will need to combine these two ways.

Common to both of them are certain useful practices you should follow:

1. If a term you use is likely to cause confusion, define it when you first use it. If the term is important to your theme and its thesis, define it in the introduction. Don't make your reader guess at what you mean by a particular word or phrase.

2. Look to your dictionary for help, but don't use it as a crutch. Do not merely quote dictionary definitions because they are easy to copy into a paper. Before using them, make sure that they apply to your paper and to the situation you are discussing.

3. Understand the techniques of defining and how they work. Keep in mind, for example, that defining by negation is particularly useful for cutting out inapplicable areas of word meanings.

4. Make your definitions reasonably complete by using as many techniques of defining as are necessary. Remember that the techniques work very well in combination.

5. Run an "operational check" on your definition. Be sure that the definition fits reality—that it is *true.*

Most of your defining will be rather informal. Perhaps for many papers you will need no more than a few words in the first or second paragraph stating how you are using a particular word or phrase. For example: "By *teachers' union* I mean an organization similar to a trade union in which the workers organize to protect their economic interests."

▼ Writing and Revising a Definition Paper (An Example)

After she had been studying human behavior in her Psychology 101 course, Jenine wrote some comments about *competition* in her journal.

> *Competition* is a common form of aggression. Competitiveness usually exists between two or more people. It is the basis for all of our games and sports. All sports pit one or many persons against one or many other persons. Some sports also produce competition against oneself. Runners, bikers, and swimmers attempt to better their own scores, times, or distances. Competition may also be found in more subtle forms. For example, students strive to better their grades or, more importantly, to achieve better grades than their peers. Many students try to "stick" their teachers by getting high grades. This seems to be a healthy outlet for competitive aggression. In general, we all strive to exceed others in our social or age group in whatever way possible. Competitiveness, therefore, while not the most obvious, is the most common form of aggression, because most everything we do is an attempt to know more, have more, or do more in school, business, and sports, respectively.
>
> Therefore, aggression, in these forms, and its many others too numerous to mention here, seems to be the greatest facet of human nature. All of our modern problems, from the arms race to the starving Cambodians, have aggression at their roots. This may be debated, as indeed it will be. But this, I feel, is positively fundamental, if I know anything about human nature.

Rereading her journal, Jenine wasn't happy with what she wrote. For one thing, she didn't limit her definition well enough. It is true that she could define *competition* as "a common form of aggression," but she saw that she hadn't distinguished *competitive aggression* from other kinds of *aggression.* So she made some notes:

> *Competition is good aggression* unless it gets out of hand. I talk a lot about competition in sports, but I really don't show how the rules of sports dictate a "healthy outlet for competitive aggression." I must get some examples to prove that point.

Jenine continued an analysis of her journal entry, noting how many things she had omitted. When she was through she had two pages of ideas from which she planned and wrote a paper.

DEFINITION OF COMPETITION

1   Competition is a form of aggression, but aggression controlled and channelled—not antisocial, in other words. We think of pure aggression as being one-sided and antisocial: people band together and attack someone else, who may or may not deserve the attack. The attack itself may be one of several kinds, from the merely verbal to full-scale war.

2   Unlike pure aggression, competition adds a second (and balancing) side to the human equation, so that the forces of aggression are more or less equalized and each side has rights. These rights are formalized in "rules of play," which may be written down in books or simply agreed on when the competition starts. In vacant lots, you will hear young children shout: "That tree is second base. This bare spot will be home plate." And: "Any ball hit into the street is a double." As play begins, shouts of "NO FAIR!" tell us that the agreed-upon rules of aggressive play have been violated by someone.

3   In addition, competitions are usually made for a reason apart from mere aggression, especially for a prize. And there are many kinds of prizes. You can win the game, lead the league in batting, get the highest pass completion average in the conference, become the best chess player north of Division Street, win an encyclopedia, be first in your class and graduate *cum laude.*

4   Yet despite all this, the competitive person is still driven to a great extent by aggression. Indeed if he is not, he may not be successfully competitive. Something burns within the competitive person. Like quarterback Joe Montana, the true competitor never gives up. (Montana is a particularly good example because he is so controlled, even polite—his aggression is masked by good manners.)

5   What burns most in the competitive person is a fanatical desire to win. I knew a checkers champion who wanted to win so badly that when he lost he threw up. My father was so naturally competitive that if his neighbor was mowing his lawn at the same time Dad was mowing his, Dad would try to finish first—to win at lawn mowing. Dad quit playing softball in his late forties because he could no longer "win" in his own eyes, meaning he thought that he could not play aggressively enough to compete.

6   It is curious to watch how many competitive people "give off" aggressive signals in almost every direction. When they drive they shout at other drivers. In school, they are the ones who stop you in the hall after a quiz is returned to utter the cliché: "Whatja get?" You tell them. Then they say: "Oh, *I* did better than that!" The expensive car is still a major signal of successful aggression. It means: "I won in the competition of the business world, and this Cadillac (or Mercedes or whatever) is my prize."

7   Why do we accept competitiveness in men and women? Possibly for the very reason that its aggressiveness is controlled and channelled in fairly positive ways. Competition in business provides opportunity and jobs for workers. Competition in sports and films

provides entertainment. Only when the aggressive instinct gets out of hand, when individuals no longer agree to play by certain rules, whether written or not, do we worry about what happens when human beings have that sharp "competitive edge."

PRACTICE

Discussion

1. For class discussion, read the second draft of Jenine's paper, and answer the following questions:

   a. Jenine followed the conventions for good defining by classifying *competition* as a form of *aggression.* Next she limited her use of the term *aggression* to particular kinds. For instance in paragraph 1, she calls *competition* "controlled aggression." Identify other limits she has placed on her use of *aggression* in the context of her definition. Discuss the effectiveness of these limits.

   b. Compare the use of examples in her journal entry and in her final paper.

2. For class discussion write a brief analysis of each definition given below. What are the techniques of defining being used? Do you see any errors in defining? How would you improve and rewrite any definition that you consider weak or unrealistic? (You may wish to check your dictionary as you go along.)

   a. *Shortening* is something you put in a cake to make it better.

   b. *Marriage* is the ceremony of uniting two people in holy wedlock.

   c. A *dog* is a canine.

   d. *Integration* is uniting people for political freedom.

   e. A *thermocouple* is a temperature-sensing instrument made of two dissimilar metals.

   f. *Tree-skiing* is a dangerous and exciting winter sport. It is not cross-country, slalom, or downhill skiing, and it is not the sport of skiing between two trees! Some people call it *woods winding* or *trailing.*

   g. A book is *obscene* if it is totally without redeeming social importance and appeals entirely to the reader's prurient interest.

   h. When we come to accurate measurement, we find that the word "hard" has dozens of slightly different meanings. The most usual tests of hardness in steels is that of Brinell. A very hard steel ball of 10 millimetres diameter is pressed onto a steel plate for 30 seconds with a load of 3 tons. The hardness number decreases with the depth of the indentation.

   —J. B. S. Haldane, *A Banned Broadcast and Other Essays*

i. [What is meant by *life?* A thing *is alive* when] it does a minimum of four things: it eats "foreign" substances which differ to a greater or lesser degree from its own body tissue. Then it "digests" these substances, and assimilates them into its body, which produces some waste material that is ejected. Furthermore, it "grows": it increases in size and bulk up to a certain point, which is different for different life forms. Finally, it "propagates" : it produces, or reproduces, its own kind.

—Willy Ley, "Life on Other Planets"

j. The idea that, since democracy is defective, it ought to be abolished, is an example of the commonest error in political philosophy, which I call "utopianism." By "utopianism" I mean the idea that there is a perfect constitution, and politics could be perfect. The last of our democratic duties which I shall mention is to avoid utopianism. Politics are and always will be a creaking, groaning, lumbering, tottering wagon of wretched make-shifts and sad compromises and anxious guesses; and political maturity consists in knowing this in your bones.

—Richard Robinson, *An Atheist's Values*

Writing

1. Definition skills are especially important when you must write a discussion of something that you know well but your reader does not. For instance, if you are writing a proposal for insulating a house, you will have to define *loose-fill, foam,* and *blanket* insulation methods so that the reader will know what the choices are.

    Pick a subject you know fairly well and write a paper on it in which you define terms that the ordinary reader may not be familiar with—your subject can be anything from clarinet playing to fixing engines. Pick a stance, and convince your reader to do or believe something. At the beginning, define any terms necessary to your thesis.

2. Choose one of the following terms (or pick your own). Define the term in as many ways as possible, using the methods described on pages 311–313. Choose a subject that you have some feelings about or some experience with so that you can define by a long narrative example. Group your definitions, develop a thesis, and write an extended definition paper.

    — home
    — pond
    — anger
    — noun
    — ingratitude
    — tennis
    — yellow
    — surgeon

4. Below is J. Frank Dobie's operational definition of *bandana*. In it he answers the question: What does a cowboy use a bandana for? Study his techniques, then write a short operational definition of one of the following:

a. A woman's purse, a student's backpack, or a teacher's briefcase

b. A gardener's trowel or a backyard chef's apron

c. A football player's helmet, a catcher's mask, or a bicyclist's helmet

d. A dancer's shoes, a power weightlifter's belt, or a gymnast's mat

Many a cowboy has spread his bandana, perhaps none too clean itself, over dirty, muddy water and used it as a strainer to drink through; sometimes he used it as a cup towel, which he called a "drying rag." If the bandana was dirty, it was probably not so dirty as the other apparel of the cowboy, for when he came to a hole of water, he was wont to dismount and wash out his handkerchief, letting it dry while he rode along, holding it in his hand or spread over his hat. Often he wore it under his hat in order to help keep his head cool. At other times, in the face of a fierce gale, he used it to tie down his hat. The bandana made a good sling for a broken arm; it made a good bandage for a blood wound. Early Irish settlers on the Nueces River used to believe that a bandana handkerchief that had been worn by a drowned man would, if cast into a stream above a sunken body, float until it came over the body and then sink, thus locating it. Many a cowboy out on the lonely plains has been buried with a clean bandana spread over his face to keep the dirt, or the coarse blanket on which the dirt was poured, from touching it. The bandana has been used to hang men with. Rustlers used to "wave" strangers around with it, as a warning against nearer approach, though the hat was more commonly used for signaling. Like the Mexican sombrero or the four gallon Stetson, the bandana could not be made too large. When the cowboys of the West make their final parade on the grassy shores of Paradise, the guidon that leads them should be a bandana handkerchief. It deserves to be called the flag of the range country.

Pico Iyer

IN PRAISE OF THE HUMBLE COMMA

In July of 1990, Pico Iyer could be seen in a Time *magazine photo standing before the ruins of his Santa Barbara home and clutching the book manuscript he had saved. His house burned completely in one of the worst brush fires in California history. For Iyer even to have been at home to save his manuscript was remarkable, for he travels a good deal in his search for stories, recently finding himself in Japan, the Himalayas, and China. "I try to catch the inner stirrings of a country," he says. "Over the past year I observed the summer solstice in Iceland, attended the Wimbledon tennis matches, and went to Cuba for Carnaval." In the article you are about to read, Iyer turns Lilliputian, trying to catch the "inner stirrings" of that tiny squiggle, the comma.*

1   The gods, they say, give breath, and they take it away. But the same could be said—could it not?—of the humble comma. Add it to the present clause, and, of a sudden, the

mind is, quite literally, given pause to think; take it out if you wish or forget it and the mind is deprived of a resting place. Yet still the comma gets no respect. It seems just a slip of a thing, a pedant's tick, a blip on the edge of our consciousness, a kind of printer's smudge almost. Small, we claim, is beautiful (especially in the age of the microchip). Yet what is so often used, and so rarely recalled, as the comma—unless it be breath itself?

2   Punctuation, one is taught, has a point: to keep up law and order. Punctuation marks are the road signs placed along the highway of our communication—to control speeds, provide directions and prevent head-on collisions. A period has the unblinking finality of a red light; the comma is a flashing yellow light that asks us only to slow down; and the semicolon is a stop sign that tells us to ease gradually to a halt, before gradually starting up again. By establishing the relations between words, punctuation establishes the relations between the people using words. That may be one reason why schoolteachers exalt it and lovers defy it ("We love each other and belong to each other let's don't ever hurt each other Nicole let's don't ever hurt each other," wrote Gary Gilmore to his girlfriend). A comma, he must have known, "separates inseparables," in the clinching words of H.W. Fowler, King of English usage.

3   Punctuation, then, is a civic prop, a pillar that holds society upright. (A run-on sentence, its phrases piling up without division, is as unsightly as a sink piled high with dirty dishes.) Small wonder, then, that punctuation was one of the first properties of the Victorian age, the age of the corset, that the modernists threw off: the sexual revolution might be said to have begun when Joyce's Molly Bloom spilled out all her private thoughts in 36 pages of unbridled, almost unperioded and officially censored prose; and another rebellion was surely marked when E.E. Cummings first felt free to commit "God" to the lower case.

4   Punctuation thus becomes the signature of cultures. The hot-blooded Spaniard seems to be revealed in the passion and urgency of his doubled exclamation points and question marks (¡Caramba! ¿Quien sabe?"), while the impassive Chinese traditionally added to his so-called inscrutability by omitting directions from his ideograms. The anarchy and commotion of the '60s were given voice in the exploding exclamation marks, riotous capital letters and Day-Glo italics of Tom Wolfe's spray-paint prose; and in Communist societies, where the State is absolute, the dignity—and divinity—of capital letters is reserved for Ministries, Sub-Committees and Secretariats.

5   Yet punctuation is something more than a culture's birthmark; it scores the music in our minds, gets our thoughts moving to the rhythm of our hearts. Punctuation is the notation in the sheet music of our words, telling us when to rest, or when to raise our voices; it acknowledges that the meaning of our discourse, as of any symphonic composition, lies not in the units but in the pauses, the pacing and the phrasing. Punctuation is the way one bats one's eyes, lowers one's voice or blushes demurely. Punctuation adjusts the tone and color and volume till the feeling comes into perfect focus: not disgust exactly, but distaste; not lust, or like, but love.

6   Punctuation, in short, gives us the human voice, and all the meanings that lie between the words. "You aren't young, are you?" loses its innocence when it loses the question mark. Every child knows the menace of a dropped apostrophe (the parent's "Don't do that" shifting into the more slowly enunciated "Do not do that"), and every believer, the ignominy of having his faith reduced to "faith." Add an exclamation point

to "To be or not to be . . ." and the gloomy Dane has all the resolve he needs; add a comma, and the noble sobriety of "God save the Queen" becomes a cry of desperation bordering on double sacrilege.

7   Sometimes, of course, our markings may be simply a matter of aesthetics. Popping in a comma can be like slipping on the necklace that gives an outfit quiet elegance, or like catching the sound of running water that complements, as it completes, the silence of a Japanese landscape. When V.S. Naipaul, in his latest novel, writes, "He was a middle-aged man, with glasses," the first comma can seem a little precious. Yet it gives the description a spin, as well as a subtlety, that it otherwise lacks, and it shows that the glasses are not part of the middle-agedness, but something else.

8   Thus all these tiny scratches give us breadth and heft and depth. A world that has only periods is a world without inflections. It is a world without shade. It has a music without sharps and flats. It is a martial music. It has a jackboot rhythm. Words cannot bend and curve. A comma, by comparison, catches the gentle drift of the mind in thought, turning in on itself and back on itself, reversing, redoubling and returning along the course of its own sweet river music; while the semicolon brings clauses and thoughts together with all the silent discretion of a hostess arranging guests around her dinner table.

9   Punctuation, then, is a matter of care. Care for words, yes, but also, and more important, for what the words imply. Only a lover notices the small things: the way the afternoon light catches the nape of a neck, or how a strand of hair slips out from behind an ear, or the way a finger curls around a cup. And no one scans a letter so closely as a lover, searching for its small print, straining to hear its nuances, its gasps, its sighs and hesitations, poring over the secret messages that lie in every cadence. The difference between "Jane (whom I adore)" and "Jane, whom I adore," and the difference between them both and "Jane—whom I adore—" marks all the distance between ecstasy and heartache. "No iron can pierce the heart with such force as a period put at just the right place," in Isaac Babel's lovely words; a comma can let us hear a voice break, or a heart. Punctuation, in fact, is a labor of love. Which brings us back, in a way, to gods.

PRACTICE

Discussion

1. Iyer says that lovers "defy" punctuation (paragraph 2). Do you agree? Why might this be so?

2. The author believes that punctuation is related to propriety. (See paragraph 3.) Do you agree? Can you find examples in, say, an issue of *Time* (in which this essay appeared)?

3. Iyer's essay is about how he *feels* about a subject that most people don't feel anything about. Discuss the believability of his passion for the subject of punctuation.

4. Reread carefully the third sentence of the first paragraph. How does it exemplify Iyer's comment in the first sentence of the paragraph?

5. Explain the metaphor in paragraph 2, sentence 2. Is it appropriate?

6. Discuss the function of the first sentence in paragraph 3. Why could this sentence *not* be the first one in Iyer's paper?

7. What is the overall organization of Iyer's essay? *Hint:* Where do you first learn its main point? Why has Iyer arranged the essay in this fashion?

8. Iyer's main intention is to define. What technique(s) of defining does he use most? Why would he use these rather than others?

Vocabulary

pedant	demurely	[the] resolve
civic	ignominy	precious
proprieties	gloomy Dane	jackboot
[the] pacing		

Writing

1. Reread paragraph 2. Then write a short note to a dearly loved one. How is it punctuated? Why?

2. See Discussion question 3. Write an essay explaining your feelings on a particular mark of punctuation; for example, "The semicolon is a stuffy old gentleman always standing in my way."

3. The first sentence of paragraph 6 is a classic "lead" that controls the paragraph as a topic sentence. The material following this sentence gives supporting detail. Write a paragraph employing the same topic sentence but using different details and examples. Use your own experience with punctuation.

Barbara Lyles
WHAT TO CALL PEOPLE OF COLOR

Barbara Lyles is associate professor of human development and personality in the Howard University School of Education, where she has been teaching for more than a quarter century. She received her B.S. in zoology from Marietta College, Marietta, Ohio, in 1951 and her Ph.D. in human development from the University of Maryland in 1971. She has been named Professor of the Year at Howard on four occasions and received the Howard University Teacher-Scholar Award in 1981. In her letter to us, Dr. Lyles mentions that she is the mother of three children.

1   While some influential black leaders ponder the continuing relevance of "black" as a reference for people of color, I am led to recall the words of a wise old black man. "When I was a boy," said he, "I was poor. As the years passed I became 'destitute,' 'impoverished,' 'economically disadvantaged,' and 'psychosocially and culturally deprived.' Now I'm an old man and though what they call it has changed many times, I'm still poor."

2   Like the old gentleman, I've been through a number of semantic name changes over the last half century plus. As a kid, I was a "negro." My father often admonished us that "colored people" were never to be referred to in his house as "niggers." Daddy required that we familiarize ourselves with Carter G. Woodson, W.E.B. Du Bois, George Washington Carver, Paul Laurence Dunbar, Countee Cullen and lots of other renowned "negroes." I now realize that, having been exposed to "negroes" in history and "people of color" in antiquity, I had had a prefashionable instruction in the positive meaning of being colored.

3   Somewhere, in the '40s, I guess, the argument began that "negro" should be capitalized and the standard English translation of "negro" became "Negro." In 1947 I got called "nigger" for the first time by some poor white kids who probably saw my black-watch plaid skirt and white bucks as too good for me. But I was a "Negro" with a capital letter; I passed on. The typewriter, the books, the monogrammed leather notebook, the no name calling and no slang in Daddy's house had made their mark. There never was much money; what there was devoted to Paul Robeson's "Othello," Marian Anderson's concerts, Jackie Robinson's baseball debut, the Hayden Planetarium, Nedick's orange juice and cream-cheese-and-olive sandwiches from the Automat. The point is also to be made that Daddy was *there:* colored? negro? Negro?; a male image with undeniable positive influence.

4   All my life, standardized tests were given without recourse to the fact that being a "Negro" had probably damaged my mind. Nobody seemed to care; you passed or you failed. Period. Test moratoria were unknown. Daddy's notion was if you have it to do— Do it. No excuses. Sure, I've had my bruises, grades that would have been white A's were Negro B's or maybe even C's. Maybe I was naive but I just sort of plodded on. Maybe the fact that I didn't call attention to my difference made it difficult for anyone in authority to mount a sustained attack on my efforts.

5   One marriage, two degrees and one doctoral candidacy later found me in the rhetorical '60s. Washington was burning, the Kennedys were dead, Martin Luther King was dead and the horror of unbridled human rage and frustration was upon us. By now, a college professor, I found it necessary to stand up to a student activist who had decided that he had the authority to cancel my class in midlecture. Never given then to verbal obscenity, I found myself spouting words that he could understand. "This is my damn class and it will be over when I say so." Maybe he was so shocked at my nerve that he slinked away. Sure, black was beautiful. Whoever said it wasn't? Foot-wide Afros were there and a puzzle to me; they were so hard to groom when they were so long. Lots of people in my youth had worn their hair natural. So what.

6   And now we've come full circle. Our "popular" departed president suggested that black leaders are getting rich and keeping their organizations viable by claiming that prejudice exists. That sounds as if he thinks that discrimination is in the minds of black

leaders. From 1981 to 1989, he implied that homelessness was a matter of personal preference and that jobless workers were unemployed by their own choice; anyone could see
the homeless on the heating grates a few blocks away from the White House. Perhaps
President Bush will find the poor and admit that black economic and social progress has
begun to move backwards into the '60s.

7   There is something inherently obtuse about attempting to apply a name to 29 million
Americans. Emergent individualism and a refusal to be bound by semantic trivialization
may yet force the majority culture to perceive people of color as having the diversity
necessary to escape a label. It may also force the minority culture to assert itself to explore the American dream with an unlabeled right to access without the need for excuse
or permission.

8   "Colored," "negro," "Negro," "black," "Black," "Africanamerican," "Afro
American," "Afro Amerikan," "American." No matter what people of color call themselves or are called—achievement, education and economic growth are what count. But
people of color have had subliminal and mean-spirited training in learning self-con-
tempt. The idea of working together for the common good has generally been unsuccessful because historically we have been torn apart by the majority group's need to assure itself that we will never be able to unify ourselves for a concerted thrust against an
oppressive and repressive system.

9   Maybe the best way to lose the stigma attached to whatever one calls people of color
is not to call attention to difference by changing names. Let's change the strategy.
Forget the semantic absurdity of what to call people of color and get on with the business of achieving. If attention is drawn to what is done rather than who does it, names
won't matter. We did not ask to be Americans in the 1600s. Now that it is clear that we
will not return en masse to Africa, we may as well be called Americans.

PRACTICE

Discussion

1. What is the *context* of Lyles' definition?

2. Why doesn't Lyles use a dictionary definition of any of her synonyms for *black?*

3. Is Lyles trying to "clarify an ambiguous situation" (point 2, page 311)?

4. Which of the techniques of defining is Lyles employing in her essay?

5. "There is something inherently obtuse about attempting to apply a name to 29 million Americans" (paragraph 7). Discuss.

6. What term, exactly, is Lyles intending to define?

7. We emphasize in the text that a definition must fit reality. One reader has said that Lyles' essay "is almost entirely about reality." How does her "reality" support her ethical proof?

Vocabulary

semantic	automat	stigma
admonished	moratoria	en masse
antiquity	subliminal	

Writing

1. Write a response to Lyles, arguing that *black* or *African American* (or a different name) should be used for people of color.

2. "If attention is drawn to what is done rather than who does it, names won't matter." Write an argument based on the quotation. Agree or disagree.

3. ". . . Achievement, education, and economic growth are what count." Respond specifically to the quotation.

Kay S. Hymowitz

"AMERICAN COOL" IS KILLING LOVE

Ms. Hymowitz received her B.A. from Brandeis University, her M.A. from Tufts, and her M. Phil. in English from Columbia University. She taught freshman English at Parsons School of Design before she became a full-time freelance writer. She has published articles on education and children in the New Republic, Dissent, Newsday, *the New York* Times, *and the Washington Post. She is presently a contributing editor of the New York* City Journal, *where this article originally appeared. She is also a fellow at the Manhattan Institute, a public policy think tank with a special focus on urban issues. She is presently at work on a book about the American view of children.*

1   "I see no trace of the passions which make for deeper joy," wrote Stendhal about Americans in his 1822 essay "Love." "It is as if the sources of sensibility have dried up among these people. They are just, they are rational, and they are not happy at all." Imagine the Frenchman's horror if he could hear today's Americans speak of *l'amour* in what Mademoiselle magazine calls this "Post-Idealist, Neo-Pragmatic Era of Relationships."

2   Here is Wanda Urbanska, author of The Singular Generation, describing her peers in their 20's: "We . . . do not have affairs, we have 'sexual friendships.' We do not fall in love, we build relationships. We do not date, we 'see' each other." A student quoted in a recent article in the Vassar Quarterly adopts the same cool attitude. She doesn't care for the term boyfriend or lover; she speaks instead of "my special friend with whom I spent lots of quality physical time."

3   Even rock-and-roll, once a soulful forum for aching, lonely hearts or ecstatic lovers, is as likely to rap or croon a message of don't-need-nobody independence. "You gotta be bad," sings Des'ree in a recent top-ten hit: "You gotta be strong; you gotta be hard; you gotta be tough; you gotta be stronger'; you gotta be cool."

4   If love in America is not dead, it is ailing. It is suffering from the phenomenon historian Peter Stearns describes in his book "American Cool": American cool disdains intense emotions like grief, jealousy, and love, which leave us vulnerable, in favor of an "emotional style" of smooth detachment. The unintended consequences of this banal ideal are: emotional frustration, alienation, and a sexual scene that recalls the drearier imaginings of Nietzsche or Freud.

5   American cool goes hand-in-hand with a profoundly rationalistic vision of human relations that looks with suspicion on mystery, myth and strong feeling. Powerful cultural trends have combined to produce this general coarsening and flattening of the sensibilities.

6   Feminists mounted the first significant challenge to love's hold on the American imagination. They argued that romantic love is a myth inextricably tied up with women's inequality. Though this view got some airing as early as the mid–19th century, it took on angry, raw urgency in the early 1970s. Ti-Grace Atkinson argued: "The psychopathological condition of love is a euphoric state of fantasy in which the victim transforms her oppressor into the redeemer. . . . Love has to be destroyed." Love was a disease in need of a cure.

7   But the feminist critics failed to recognize that if romantic love serves to subjugate women, it does no less to men. In many countries where romantic love has not been institutionalized, men's philandering is winked at while respectable women are kept veiled and hidden. In its first institutional flowering in the guise of medieval courtly love, stylized passion turned the wandering, brutish young men of the day into sensitive, pining poets. It was as a way of sublimating the passions that romantic love was a civilizing force. A man in love was a man subdued.

8   Health experts, starting at the turn of the century, espoused theories that echo the feminist disdain for passion and fantasy. Inspired by advances in the understanding and treatment of venereal disease, the medical profession argued in favor of a demystification of sex. They began a process of the medicalization and rationalization of sex whose basic assumptions continue to control much current thinking on the subject. They became the first to advocate sex education in the schools. And they introduced the terms that continue to make the sex-ed debate so stubbornly hyperbolic: the scientifically minded and enlightened realists vs. the superstitious and religious flat-earthers.

9   Yet the social hygienists would surely be dismayed by some of what is done in the name of health today. For the idea of rationalized and demystified sex has been stretched to its logical limits, as sex mystery has given way to sex mechanics.

10   Today's sex educator sees his demystifying task as ensuring not only that kids have the information necessary to avoid disease and pregnancy but also that they have "healthy" attitudes toward sex. A healthy student is one who is "relaxed" and "comfortable" in the presence of the erotic and can speak of sex in the same tones and with the same lack of emotion he might bring to a discussion of carburetors. Giggling kids who appear to suffer from embarrassment or reticence, sure signs of "anti-sex" attitudes or irrational hangups, must undergo a program of desensitization. At a private school in Brooklyn, N.Y., fifth-graders were required to pronounce the words for the genitals at increasingly louder volume. Children calculating math problems in nearby classrooms were treated to the serenade.

11   Sexual liberals turn out to be advancing their own rigid moral strictures. Their Eros lays down an updated Puritan law: Pleasure and self-fulfillment, yes; passion, no. The authority has simply been transferred from the church to the clinic.

12   This medicalization of sex has deposed irrational Love and installed reasonable Health as king. Kids must have "healthy" attitudes; they must "make healthy, good decisions." But on what moral terms should a teen ground this good decision? Here the educators come up emptyhanded. Is it any wonder that kids today, stripped of all spiritualizing ideals and with nothing but dismal "health" to replace them, would shrug and ask, "What's the big deal?"

13   Love's most powerful enemy may well be America's obsession with individual autonomy. From this point of view, love might well signal childish weakness. "Clearly, romance can arrive with all its obsession whenever we're feeling incomplete," writes Gloria Steinem. "The truth is that finding ourselves brings more excitement and well-being than anything romance has to offer."

14   Finding ourselves is a complex task these days. It means not only developing interests and talents but also "exploring" what we have come to call "our sexuality." Watch "Oprah" or "Donahue," pick up any academic treatise on "gender," flip through any sex education curriculum, or read any self-help book, and the creed of healthy sexuality will stare you in the face. Leah P., married 18 years and interviewed on a National Public Radio show about sex and marriage, admits she would hesitate to have an affair but insists on her autonomy from any rules or institutions or even relationships: "My sexuality belongs to me. I can take it where I choose to. . . . It doesn't belong to my husband; it doesn't belong to my marriage."

15   But if sex is imagined as a meeting of free, autonomous, and creative selves, each engaged in an act of self-exploration, we are left with a problem: The lover—or partner, the current term and one better evoking the situation—is in danger of becoming an object to be used and played with. The connection between partners can then only be imagined as contractual. Some of our best and most disenchanted bureaucratic minds have gotten to work on this, as exemplified by the Antioch College sexual harassment code: "Verbal consent should be obtained with each new level of physical or sexual conduct in any given interaction. . . . The request for consent must be specific to each act."

16   Although it ostensibly prizes freedom and pleasure, the creed of "sexuality" instead produces this sort of leaden, bureaucratic vision of sex. Here, unlike the lover willing to risk opening his heart in hopes of joyful union, the partner becomes a skilled negotiator demanding and accepting conditions for his or her personal pleasure. Hence, "sexuality" inevitably restrains the emotional, truly personal connection between lovers, stifling what Stendhal called the "passions which make for deeper joy."

17   Kids raised in a world without a romantic myth to humanize the sexual demons growling and scratching below the surface of civility are not a happy sight. For girls, the result is not just the widely reported epidemic of sexually transmitted diseases and unplanned pregnancies. Also evident to many working with these young women is a sense of vacant joylessness. Fifteen-year-olds with 10 or more "partners" do not merely fail to find love—they also fail at the pursuit of pleasure, for they are almost never orgasmic. They promise to become a new generation of embittered women, resentful of men, cynical about love, and ripe for single motherhood.

18   How could they be otherwise, given the boys they have to contend with? Without any humanizing myth to help quiet the demons, boys have begun to play out the truth of Freud's observation that lust and aggression are deeply intertwined. Reports of young studs "playing rape" in a Yonkers schoolyard during recess, of nine-year-old sexual harassers and fifth-grade rapists and sodomists, have become too common to pass off as anomalous.

19   In the past, love has had the virtue not only of satisfying our longing for profound connection but of lifting us out of mundane life into enchantment. While it may not have straightened the crooked timber of humanity, it respected and nourished its tortuous imagination. Today more than ever, the sources of that nourishment seem to have dried up.

PRACTICE

"American Cool" is a classic example of a modern opinion piece that depends on definitions to make its point. The title itself suggests that the author will define *American Cool.* Furthermore, to convince her readers, the author introduces a string of defined terms that she expects her readers to accept as she develops her point.

Now, as her readers, you are to judge whether she is successful in her definitions, the basic question being: "Do they fit reality?" As you read the essay, for each term she introduces, ask yourself if you agree with the definition. Why or why not?

The terms:

American cool
romantic love (two different definitions)
demystification of sex
healthy student
sex

Discussion

1. What is the thesis of this opinion piece? Where is it stated? How necessary is the definition of *American cool* to the thesis?

2. What is the definition of *American cool,* according to a critic of the American scene, Peter Stearns? (Review page 326.) What is the defining method used? How does the writer expand the definition by discussing the consequences of *American cool* on our society? Discuss the accuracy and reality of these consequences.

3. The author defines *romantic love* as it affected women and men in the past. What method does she use? How do the effects of romantic love on men and women act as part of the definition?

4. What defining technique is used for the term *demystification of sex?* According to sex educators, what are the advantages of the demystification of sex? How do they use cause and effect to prove their successes in sex education? In what way do these effects expand the definition of the term, *demystification of sex?*

5. What has the medicalization of sex done to love? Do you agree with the author's conclusions? Why or why not?

6. How does the author define *sex?* According to Gloria Steinem, what does autonomy or "finding ourselves" have to do with romantic love?

7. Discuss Steinem's statement that "finding ourselves brings more excitement and well-being than anything romance has to offer." Is she including sex in this pronouncement? Discuss the reality of her views on romance and sex.

8. What is the effect of the demystification of sex on girls? On boys? How can these cause-effect relationships be part of the definition of the *demystification of sex?*

9. Discuss the effectiveness of this essay. Are you convinced by Hymowitz's argument?

Vocabulary

banal	Eros	sublimating
euphoric	inextricably	

Writing

1. Write a paper in which you agree or disagree with the author's conclusions about the demystification of sex.

2. Based on your experience, write your own extended definition of *American Cool.* Or write one on *Romantic Love.*

3. Write a paper, using your definitions of romantic love, that argues men and women would be happier (or not happier) if we went back to romantic love.

CHAPTER 18

Comparison and Contrast

▼ Comparison and Contrast

Comparing means "showing likenesses"; *contrasting,* "showing differences." Classification (or grouping) is an important step in comparison and contrast because, when you classify, you usually group pieces of information by the principle of similarity. However, when you compare and contrast, you identify those qualities that distinguish members of a class from each other by their individual differences. Therefore, when you make a comparison and contrast, you show *likenesses* and *differences* between two or more (but usually only two) people, ideas, actions, things, or classes—*for the purpose of making a point.* We emphasize "making a point" because you customarily employ the strategy of comparison and contrast to convince the reader of an idea you have—that A is better than B; more interesting than B; more useful than B; and so on. You may show the likenesses or the differences between two things at the paragraph level or in a longer paper.

■■■ Planning a Comparison and Contrast

For several reasons, a comparison and contrast requires particularly strong control of your point and organization. First, you usually have more material to work with—two subject areas instead of the customary one. Consequently, you should rigorously narrow your point—or thesis—for a longer comparison and contrast so that you can cover the subjects in the number of words you have allotted. Next, you have to know a good deal about both subjects. Finally, your comparison and contrast must do more than just show similarities or likenesses. This is a trap that students often fall into. They describe the two subject areas, giving plenty of detail for both but omitting the point, thus leaving the reader wondering why the paper was written in the first place.

Note how a student uses comparison and contrast for the purpose of making a decision, and thereby communicating his *point*.

OLD CAR OR NEW(ER) CAR?

Purpose of Comparison-Contrast

1   When I go back to school next semester, I will be taking a car with me. But which one—Aunt Kay's 1949 Plymouth, or Dad's 1988 Buick? Aunt Kay left the Plymouth to me when she died; Dad said I could take his Buick after he bought a new Mercury. The Buick is a top-of-the-line luxury car, with a fancy interior, air conditioning, etc. My answer may be somewhat surprising. After considering the advantages and disadvantages of each car, I am choosing the 47-year-old Plymouth over the eight-year-old Buick. Here's why.

First consideration: condition of car

2   First—although you might not think so without knowing the cars—the Plymouth is in better shape. It was Aunt Kay's favorite car. She bought it new, and it was her child. She babied it, kept it in a warm garage, and carefully replaced any part that went bad. Dad's Buick has 122,000 miles on it, heavy miles indeed, because Dad has a heavy foot. Since he also has a light wallet, he never repaired it unless it just stopped running.

Second consideration: cost of maintenance

3   Second, the old Plymouth should cost me less to maintain. Dad's last bill on the neglected Buick was over a thousand dollars. He wanted me to do some of the repairs on it, but while I'm handy, I'm not that handy. For a modern V-8, a manual just isn't enough help for an amateur. You need experience as a mechanic, fancy tools, and a diagnostic computer. The Plymouth I can work on myself; in fact this summer I replaced the clutch, which had a serious chatter. I can't get parts for the Plymouth, you say? Not true. With the help of local parts houses (like Napa) and *Hemmings Motor News*—the bible of antique car nuts—I can get anything for the Plymouth except details like plastic door-handle bezels, which I don't need. One more thing: Since the Buick is a big V-8 and the Plymouth is a small six-cylinder, I'll get better mileage with the old car.

Third consideration: fun of driving

4   My next consideration: Which is more fun to drive? The Plymouth won hands down. No, you can't drive it 80 miles an hour, but with its overdrive (Aunt Kay had the overdrive put on in 1955) it will cruise nicely at 65. The Plymouth is short, stubby, with excelllent visibility, and much easier to park than the bloated boat of a Buick. I'll miss the air conditioning of the boat, but the fresh-air vent in the hood of the Plymouth works surprisingly well.

Fourth Consideration: attention getting

5   Finally, I am picking the Plymouth because it is an attention-getter. Aunt Kay had it repainted brilliant blue a couple of years ago. You can see the car six blocks away. The chrome (there's a lot of it inside and out) is perfect, polished and shining. Drive the car down the street, and people follow you to the nearest stop sign and yell, "What is it?" And, "Where'd you get it?" And, "Do you want to sell it?" As for the Buick—no one looks even once at it.

Result: Plymouth is better choice

6   So it's the 1949 Plymouth for me. Cheaper to maintain, more fun to drive, a conversation-starter. I'm betting even the girls will notice. I'm hoping, especially the girls.

This writer has strong control of thesis and organization. He makes the contrast-comparison in order to explain his choice of transportation, and that purpose is made clear. He does not try to include irrelevant items, such as cost of licensing the cars or insuring them. He covers both cars under consideration adequately. His transitional devices (such as *first, second, my next consideration, finally, as for the Buick*) help the reader to follow the organization of the material.

▼ Organizing Comparison and Contrast

There are three basic methods of organizing *comparison and contrast.* In the "block" method, you first discuss one item thoroughly, then go on to the second, giving about equal space to each. In the second method, you list all the similarities between the two items, then all the differences. In the third "point-by-point" method, you discuss one point or feature of each item, then go on to the next, and so on. The following lists show how the three methods are organized. A and B stand for the two items being compared.

Block	**Similarities-Differences**	**Point-by-Point**
1. introduce subject	introduce subject	introduce subject
2. discuss A (transition)	discuss similarities between A and B (transition)	discuss point 1 of A and B (transition)
3. discuss B	discuss differences between A and B	discuss point 2 of A and B
4. conclude	conclude	conclude

In the three models on the following pages, you will see how the writers used these methods for organizing their writing. The second and third examples are student essays.

Block Method

Introduction 1   I think there's something wrong here, but I can't exactly put my finger on it. I recently bought quantities of two fluids.

Discussion of A 2   The first fluid was gasoline. Gasoline is derived from crude oil,
(gasoline)   which is found deep under the ground in remote sections of the earth.
1. Source   Enormous amounts of money are risked in the search for oil. Once it's found, a great deal more money is expended to extract it from the earth, to ship it to distant refineries, to refine it, to ship it via pipeline to regional distribution points, to store it, to deliver it to retail outlets and then to make it available to the retail consumer. . . .

2. Supply 3   As far as we know, the earth's supply of crude oil is limited. Once it's gone, it's gone. There may be other substances fermenting under the soil that will prove of value to future civilizations, but for the here and now our oil supplies are finite. . . .

Discussion of B 4   The other fluid was sweetened, carbonated water, infused with ar-
(soda pop)   tificial fruit flavoring. Some call it soda pop. It's made right here in

1. Source   town. As far as we know, the raw materials exist in unlimited supply. Most of it falls from the heavens at regular intervals. . . .

2. Supply   5   Almost all of it, by processes chemical and natural, will recycle back into the system. It will become sewage, will cleanse itself, will evaporate and will rain down again from the heavens at some undetermined time and place. It will come back. We can't really get rid of it. . . .

Conclusion   6   When you further consider that roughly a third of the cost of gaso-
Thesis   line is taxes, that means that soda pop costs almost three times as much per gallon as does gasoline.

—Robert Rosefsky, *Chicago Daily News*

Similarities-Differences Method

Introduction   1   What was it like for a girl to be brought up by two bachelors? When I was ten, my mother (a widow) died, and I had no one to look after me except her two brothers, Arthur and Alan. Both were in their early forties at the time. Arthur had been married once, long ago, and his wife had left him; Alan had never married and was, people said, a woman
Thesis implied   hater. Being brothers, they had several traits in common; but they were also very different. And that fact showed up in their treatment of me.

Similarities   2   For instance, neither of them wanted me to work while I was going
between A (Alan)   to high school. They were brought up to believe that a woman's place
and B (Arthur)   is in the home or, at least, in the trailer at the edge of town where we all lived. When they found out I took a job at a local drive-in, Alan
1. Attitude toward   bawled me out and made me quit, while Arthur, the more sociable of
work   the two, made a personal visit to the manager to give him hell for hiring such a young kid. Both of them could not understand why I could not get by on the $5.00 a week they gave me for spending money. And besides, they said that the job was interfering with my "schooling."

2. Attitude toward   3   School was another thing they were concerned about, and proba-
school   bly with good reason. They always wanted to see my grade reports, although they were never quite sure when they were issued. And I tried to keep them in the dark about that as much as possible. Arthur, who thought he was better educated than Alan, always wanted to help me with my homework. Just to get him off my back, I sometimes let him. About the only thing he seemed to remember from his school days were the names of the capital cities of all the states, which, of course, did not help me much. Alan was always concerned with long-term results, continually asking, "Are you going to pass this term?" "Are you going to graduate?" I think he was a little surprised when I did. But, if it had not been for their concern, I probably would not have made it past my junior year.

Difference between   4   But in other matters involving me, they had quite different atti-
A and B   tudes. Alan was very protective of me as far as boys and dating were concerned. Arthur, however, encouraged me to date because he
1. Attitude toward   wanted me to have a good time while I was young. Alan treated me
dating   like a young Farrah Fawcett who was luring every male for miles around. When male friends would stop by, he would always grill them as if they were sex maniacs, while Arthur offered them a beer and talked sports, always managing to put in a good word for his

niece. Alan was so protective that he sometimes would drive me to parties or dances, and sit outside a teen den in his pickup, waiting until I came out after the last song died away.

2. Attitude toward   5   Their concern for me also showed itself in their attitude toward
drinking   drinking. Alan did not drink much, but Arthur was an alcoholic. He not only drank, he liked other people drinking. He made me my first salty dog. He taught me that any sort of sweet stuff with bourbon was the devil's idea. Alan disapproved greatly of all this, but he was incapable of attacking his own brother, who could charm people with ease. Alan would, when I was seventeen, take a beer out of my hand if I was drinking one—only one!—with Arthur, and pour it down the sink. After Alan had gone to bed, Arthur would go to the refrigerator and get me another one. I was never more than mildly interested in alcohol, however; the sight of Arthur drunk and sick was enough to make anyone cautious.

Conclusion   6   Even though they were alike in some things and different in oth-
(with an anecdote   ers, my uncles took care of me. When I graduated from high school
that emphasizes   last year, they came to the ceremony in the pickup. Alan wore his best
their similarities   and only suit, which had been out of style twenty years ago. Arthur
and differences)   was dressed like a king, and was so drunk he had to be carried out in the middle of "Pomp and Circumstance." A strange "family," but they are all I have—and many times all I need.

Point-By-Point Method

1   Since I came to the United States from the mainland of China in 1985, I have been to church services, Bible studies, circle meetings, church organized picnics, family dinners, parties, and sales. I have learned more about the American culture and felt less lonely through these activities, thanks to all who invited me there. But at the same time I am present in these religious situations, I cannot help comparing the worship of God to that of Mao in the Cultural Revolution. Yes, that Revolution made Mao an almighty figure to us Chinese. He was worshiped before meals; in classrooms, offices, factories, train stations, the fields; and at bus stops. Now, even though this excessive Mao worship is gone, the memory of it still haunts me. When I think about whether I should become a Christian, I ask myself: "Am I going to accept another figure like Mao? Will the worship of God one day become as ridiculous as Mao worship did?"

Point 1:   2   As the one holy book at home and the church, the Bible reminds
The Bible vs.   me of the red copy of Mao's works. It was called the treasured book.
Mao's Red Book   There were four volumes of his works in all sizes, and a pocket book
(pars. 2–3)   of his quotations. Most times, one got these copies free. They were the books one brought to evening studies from 1966 to 1976. Seldom now can I think of meetings without the memory of those studies. In America, when I was at the church (in Bible studies) turning to pages in the Bible, I felt as if I were turning to pages in Mao's red book.

3   The format of some Bible studies resembles that of Mao studies. I was in grade school during the Cultural Revolution in China. I remember that for some time the school began and ended with our

reading of Mao's quotations line by line to examine what we had done on a particular day and promise what we should do the next day.

Point 2:
Self-criticism in
Bible studies and
worship of Mao
(pars. 4–6)

4   One morning, after I stood up in class and read this quotation of Mao, "Fight selfishness and repudiate revisionism," I told the class that the day before when the ice-cream cart came by, several kids and I (who were playing in the neighborhood) all wanted the red-bean icebar. But there was only one left. As I ran to the cart first, I got that bar and sucked it contentedly in front of other kids. Mao's quotation made me realize that I was being selfish. I promised to the class that next time such things happened, I would give that icebar to others. This was my simple understanding and application of Mao's quotation. I could not comprehend the latter part of the quotation, but I read it anyway.

5   The morning study of Mao's teachings usually lasted 30–50 minutes, in which time other students took turns reading a quotation of Mao and criticizing themselves just as I did. I heard then that the older kids in Chinese high schools did the same thing, except that their self-criticisms were more complicated than ours. The last period of class would repeat the format of the morning session. As each day thus repeated itself, many times I could not find any fault with myself; yet feeling I should still say something to criticize myself, I lied or exaggerated things.

6   I almost forgot this type of self-criticism until I went to Bible studies in America. At some of these studies, people would read the Bible line by line, discuss the meanings, and criticize themselves for having failed at times to do what God commands them to do. (I am not criticizing the Bible studies themselves.) At one study, for example, after we read lines 14–16 in Matthew 5 where Jesus asks his disciples to shine their light before people like a lamp on a stand, one person criticized herself for sometimes being too shy to tell non-Christians that she is a Christian and pass God's teachings to them. Immediately I thought about the exaggerated self-criticisms I had made during our Mao studies.

Point 3:
Celebrations in
Mao's China and
the Western Church
(pars. 7–8)

7   Saying grace before meals and singing songs of Jesus in the church and at Bible studies remind me of the late 1960s in China when we would sing songs in worship of Mao, read aloud his quotations, or do both before meals at camps, in the dining-halls or other public eating places. Mao was the sun, the savior, in those songs. The radio was broadcasting them all day long. The theatres were staging choirs of those songs, revolutionary operas, and dances. In fact, songs in worship of Mao or of a revolutionary nature were the only songs taught in schools. They were also the only songs taught in schools. They were also the only songs the whole nation was allowed to sing during the Cultural Revolution.

8   Last Christmas Eve, I attended the midnight service at a Baptist Church. I was impressed with the solemn decorations of the church, the special dresses of the choir, and the way they sang their songs. Yet afterwards, all this brought back to me the memory of the celebration of Mao's birthday, which is Dec. 26, a day so close to the birthday of Jesus. For some years during the Cultural Revolution,

there were special performances and gatherings in celebration of Mao's birthday in many theatres and music halls. On that particular day, there would be a long front-page editorial dedicated to Mao in the *People's Daily*. The title was always printed in big red characters.

Conclusion   9   As a child, I truly respected Mao and enjoyed participating in the songs and dances. But now that I have grown up and realized the excessiveness of Mao worship, it becomes hard for me to accept any new worship. I have discussed my feelings with some other Chinese, and they all feel the same. Perhaps it is because Mao was the first God-figure I believed in (and later on I found myself cheated) that I doubt how long the worship of God can last. Certainly, if I remain only an observer of God worship, I will not feel guilty or be laughed at when God loses His favor.

—Ming Xiao, "God and Mao"

▼ Writing and Revising a Comparison and Contrast (An Example)

Rachel, a member of the track team, has just returned from a strenuous training session in which the coach told her, "Pain is your friend." She thinks about his statement, wondering if he is really correct. She begins freewriting:

1   I would say that some kinds of physical pain are good for me. Note that I distinguish *physical* pain from other kinds. There is another kind of pain: mental. Mental pain is much worse than physical pain. It lasts longer, and instead of diminishing in a relatively short time like physical pain, it can eat at you for days, months, or perhaps an entire lifetime. If unresolved, it can build up and drive you mad.

2   Mental pain hurts. It can come from any number of situations. A friend or relative may have gone, a girlfriend or boyfriend may have broken off a relationship, you may have been under a lot of stress, or a misunderstanding may have come between friends. There is a great difference between mental and physical pain—misunderstandings can cause much mental anguish and grief, but you will never hear of a "misunderstood broken leg."

3   Coach says, "Pain is your friend." Of course, he means the physical pain caused by running. This pain while running or exercising in other ways can be your friend by telling you that you are really working. This pain should not be confused with injury, which is a definite sign that something is wrong. Injury can be caused by too much physical work, or an accident. Sometimes injury is difficult to distinguish from soreness. Soreness is another kind of pain caused by physical work. It generally occurs when you have not exercised in a while, and have just started. You may then have soreness for a few days.

4   Mental and physical pain have different effects and are caused by different things. For me, mental pain is much more unpleasant because it can linger on, while physical pain fades relatively quickly.

Later, Rachel studies her freewriting. She is now more critical of what she wrote. She sees two problems that are reflected in her freewriting:

She notes that she has a problem with her terms. She is satisfied with the term *training pain,* but she knows she can't compare that kind of pain with every kind of *mental pain.* Therefore, she reviews her experiences with runners and other athletes. She decides to limit *mental pain* to the *emotional pain* caused by losing, or from having to stay off the team as a result of injury.

As a result of thinking about her terms, she sees that she needs clearer definitions of the two kinds of pain because the terms will form the basis for her *comparison and contrast.*

After she has tied down her terms, she develops a preliminary outline in which the coverage of two kinds of pain falls naturally in a block organization (see pp. 332–333).

I. Training pain helps to condition the body.
   A. If the athlete trains carefully, the training pain will go away.
   B. Training pain is not caused by an injury.
II. Emotional pain connected with athletics affects the spirit.
   A. Emotional pain lasts longer than training pain.
   B. Emotional pain is connected with losing and with injury.

Rachel's stance:

   Role: A student member of the women's track team.

Audience: Other runners and athletes who might be interested in an analysis of pain.

   Thesis: Emotional pain is worse for an athlete than physical pain.

ATHLETES AND PAIN

1   Recently a few members of the women's track team were comparing notes on their aches and pains. I am not a masochist, but I think that the kind of pain that comes from training is good for me (and for other athletes) because it doesn't last long, and also conditions the body. But athletes sometimes suffer another kind of pain—the emotional pain that is nearly always related to losing or being taken off the team as a result of injury. Emotional pain can last longer than training pain and sometimes affects an athlete's self-esteem.

2   Our track coach often says, "Pain is your best friend." Of course he means training pain—the pain caused by intense physical conditioning. This pain is my friend because it tells me that I am really working hard and getting better at my sport. For example, the first month of training for long-distance running is the most difficult. In this period, I must establish a vigorous stride that can be maintained without pain. Before I can establish that stride, I must break through a wall of pain—a physical barrier that will finally disappear if I continue to push myself beyond it. Getting over that wall can be gratifying because I know that I am not going to experience quite as much pain in the future. In my first month of training, I was preparing for the three-hundred. As I neared the two-hundred mark, the pain became excruciating. It came from inside as though something had exploded, and my legs required all the energy and concentration I could muster.

3   However, training pain should not be confused with pain from injury. If runners are not careful to establish a schedule for running, or if they attempt long distances too soon, they will get shin splints, a bone and tendon irritation that disables runners. Any pressure on the ankles, knees, and shins will be so painful that a runner will not be able to run for weeks. Other injuries such as stress fractures, bursitis, and tendonitis will not disappear like training pain but will keep an athlete from running.

4   Emotional pain hurts too, but it is the spirit, not the body, that suffers. And emotional pain lasts longer than training pain. Emotional pain is different from training pain because the discomfort isn't transmitted through the nervous system. However, emotional pain caused by disappointment or anxiety can cause an athlete anguish and grief that will affect the spirit for weeks, months, or even years.

5   The desire to win is strong in athletes. Runners, in particular, suffer emotional pain when they lose. They usually don't have people in the stands to cheer them on, so they must depend on their own team members for emotional support. I was in a race when three of us moved neck-and-neck toward the finish tape. As I leaned for the tape. I stumbled. Lying on the track, too exhausted to get up, I learned that I had come in second, not first as I had hoped. My desire had not been enough to win. As a result of my stumble, I believed that I had let my team down because we lost the meet. My friends on the team didn't treat me differently, but I believed that I had not done my best. As a result I was disconsolate for weeks. It was only after I won the next race that my self-esteem was renewed.

6   Suffering a physical injury which keeps athletes from competing may affect the spirit. A friend of mine broke his collarbone while training for basketball. He told me that the break caused physical pain while doing the most routine tasks: dressing, lying down, or even sneezing. But the emotional pain was the most difficult to bear. The day after he suffered his injury, he watched his team practicing in a full-court scrimmage. He said that watching his friends practice the one sport he loves more than anything else made him feel left out and abandoned. Since basketball is one of the few things he looks forward to during the year, having an injury that locked him out of the team caused him more emotional pain than physical pain.

7   Athletes are bound to suffer pain, but they hope that it is training pain, not the pain from losing or the pain from staying off the team. An athlete's self-esteem is tied up with being part of a team and any fluctuation in the team as an entity or group influences an athlete's self-esteem.

PRACTICE

Discussion

Read the final version of "Athletes and Pain." Prepare the following questions for class discussion.

1. How well has Rachel supported the main points of her comparison and contrast? What recommendations would you make for improvements in her paper and support of her thesis?

2. List Rachel's transitions. How well do they help to advance her comparison and contrast? Could her use of transitions be improved?

3. You followed Rachel through the process of identifying her terms and developing a thesis. Now review her freewriting. Are there any points in her freewriting that could have been used in her second draft?

Writing

1. Pick two words or phrases that are often used in comparable ways. Write a comparison-contrast in which you show the likenesses and the differences between the meanings of the two. Suggestions:

   a. Fashion—Style

   b. Pathetic—Tragic

   b. Persuasion—Force

   d. Stink—Odor

   e. Civil disobedience—Dissent

   f. Amateur—Professional

   g. Politician—Civil servant

   h. Appetite—Hunger

   i. Pacify—Appease

   j. Practical—Practicable

   k. Exercise—Drill

   l. Movie—TV program

   m. Blocking—Tackling

   n. Housewife—Career woman

2. Choose two people you know well—friends or relatives. Make two separate lists, identifying all the qualities that are distinctive for *each* person. Analyze and group the characteristics that these two people share (or do not share). Draw a generalization about each group of characteristics. Develop a thesis or a point, and choose an organizational method. Write a comparison-contrast, trying to keep an appropriate balance between the two people so that you don't cover one more thoroughly than the other.

Alex Kozinski

TEN REASONS SKIING IS DEAD

Alex Kozinski is a judge in the U.S. Court of Appeals for the Ninth Circuit. He was born in Bucharest, Rumania in 1950, emigrating to the United States in 1962. He graduated from UCLA Law School in 1975, first in his class. He speaks four languages besides English: German, French, Rumanian, and Spanish. Even though his other publications are much more serious than his comparison and contrast of skiing and snowboarding, they often have engaging titles: What I Ate for Breakfast and Other Mysteries of Judicial Decisionmaking, Scholarship of the Absurd: Bob Bork Meets the Bald Soprano, *and* Trademarks Unplugged.

Mark my words: 25 years or so from now your grandchild will climb on your knee and ask, "Hey, Grandpa (or Grandma), I heard that when you were a kid they used to saw snowboards in half and put one piece on each foot. Why'd they do *that*?" Stumped for an answer, you'll mumble something like, "It was a plot hatched by orthopedists."

Sound ridiculous? Don't be so sure. Children, unburdened by the prejudices and vanities of their elders, are voting with their feet and deserting skiing for snowboarding in droves. My sons skied for years, but now they're out snowboarding while their skis gather dust. Curious, I decided to give snowboarding a try, and that's the last my own skis saw the slopes.

Snowboards are here to stay and, like compact disks and touch-tone phones, they'll push out the outdated technology everyone thought was irreplaceable. Here are just a few reasons why:

1. Skiing is hard; snowboarding's easy. You can spend many years and the GNP of New Guinea on lessons and still be a mediocre skier, but you can become a darn good snowboarder in no time at all. Yes, that includes klutzniks; I should know.

2. Skiing mangles knees; snowboarding doesn't. Skiing is inherently dangerous because it requires you to strap each foot to a separate object. During a fall these objects often move in different directions, putting torque on the nearest joint—usually the knee. Quick-release bindings reduce the hazard, but highly debilitating, often permanent, knee injuries continue to be a major risk of skiing. Snowboarders (or, as they prefer to be called, "riders") seldom suffer such injuries because they keep both feet firmly attached to the same object. Riders do get injured from falls and collisions, but so do skiers. You can reduce such injuries by wearing a helmet and wrist guards, a wise move no matter how you propel yourself down the mountain. But no one has yet devised foolproof protection from the debilitating joint injuries caused by skiing.

3. Skiing is work; snowboarding's fun. Just watch any good skier and you'll see his legs move as if they were disconnected from the rest of his body. This requires an immense amount of coordination and physical exertion; most skiers never get it right. Maneuvering a snowboard involves small shifts of body weight. This is not only more natural and graceful than skiing, it uses skills that can be practiced year-round in surfing, skateboarding, even bicycling.

4. Skiers hate bad terrain; snowboarders don't care. Listen to skiers after a day on the slopes and you'll hear them complain about ice, moguls, granular snow, wet snow, etc. You seldom hear such complaints from riders because snowboards are nearly as easy to use in bad conditions as in good. The only real complaint snowboarders have is about après-ski whiners.

5. Ski boots hurt; snowboard boots are comfy. Need I say more?

6. Skiers look dweeby; snowboarders look cool. Most skiers look like overstuffed neon sausages or hearty Tyrolean yodelers who just rolled off the set of "Dumb and Dumber." The only ones on the slope who look like they're having a good time are the riders.

7. Skiing is scary; snowboarding is exhilarating. Watch skiers as they approach a steep ledge. They hesitate, they survey the terrain, they pretend to be enjoying the view. What they're really doing is praying this isn't going to be the day they discover first-hand the miracle of arthroscopic surgery. Riders show no such hesitation because snowboards are designed to keep you in control no matter how steep, icy or mogully the descent. After less than a season on a snowboard, for example, I had no trouble handling any run on the back bowls at Vail.

8. Ski equipment is a pain; snowboarding gear is a breeze. To go snowboarding all you need is a snowboard, which you can sling over your shoulders as you head for the slopes. To go skiing, you have to walk from your car or condo in forward-leaning, rigid shell boots while juggling skis and poles. When you take a spill on the slope, all that equipment gets scattered about (a condition known derisively as a "yard sale"), and you then have to go chasing it, usually uphill. Your snowboard never leaves your feet, thank you.

9. Skis clutter; snowboards are neat. An adult snowboard fits within the trunk of a Ford Taurus, and has a slim profile in a ski locker. Storing and transporting skis, poles and hard boots for a family of four is a job for Bekins.

10. Skiers carry poles; snowboarders have free hands. One of the best things about snowboarding is that you don't always have your hands full. You can throw snowballs, take pictures, or just let your arms swing free. You don't carry poles in your daily life; why should you put up with them when you're having a good time?

Skiers have learned to endure a lot of risks and inconveniences, but it all seems so pointless once you've streaked down the mountain on your Burton, without fear or pain, suspended almost weightless between snow and sky. It makes you laugh out loud and wonder, why *do* all these people split snowboards in half?

Skiing is history; snowboarding rules!

PRACTICE

Reading

1. Look up the meaning of *versus.* What does *versus* imply about the relationships between skiers and snowboarders?

2. Study pages 332–336. Identify the comparison/contrast pattern Kozinski uses. Discuss its effectiveness.

3. Name the writer's *ruling principle* (see Classification, pages 268–271). Discuss the relationship between the ruling principle and the writer's use of a numbering system.

4. Is there any way that Kozinski could combine some of his points to make his comparison and contrast headings broader and more inclusive? What would be the effect of these changes?

5. The writer uses second person *you* throughout. Why doesn't Kozinski use third person—*the skier* and *the snowboarder?*

6. What is the writer's viewpoint? Just how serious is he?

7. Is the comparison/contrast evenly divided by pros and cons? Why or why not?

Vocabulary

debilitating   après-ski

torque   arthroscopic

Writing

1. If you are a skier, take each of Kozinski's ten points and add additional information so that your comparison and contrast is tilted toward skis rather than snowboards. Also, make your categories of comparison and contrast broader.

2. Write a comparison/contrast in which you compare two kinds of activities— such as acting on stage vs. acting in movies or televisions; writing for a newspaper vs. writing a short story; composing on a typewriter vs. composing on a computer.

3. Write a comparison and contrast in which you discuss two sports such as rugby (or soccer) vs. football; tennis vs. badminton; basketball vs. volleyball; handball vs. squash, or two other sports.

E. B. White
ONCE MORE TO THE LAKE

Many good prose writers wish they could write like E. B. White, and his popular revision of William Strunk's Elements of Style *(1979) has helped many student prose writers to write better. Born in 1899, educated at Cornell University, White was for many years associated with the* New Yorker *magazine. His deep caring for precision and clarity of language, along with his personal style and humor, set standards of excellence for the American essay. Children and adults alike treasure his stories for children:* Stuart Little *(1945),* Charlotte's Web *(1952), and* The Trumpet of the Swan *(1970). Publication of White's collected letters in 1976 and essays in 1977 put him again on the bestseller lists. "Once More to the Lake" was written in 1941 for White's "One Man's Meat" column in* Harper's. *As White compares past and present times in the essay, the future is also there.*

1   One summer, along about 1904, my father rented a camp on a lake in Maine and took us all there for the month of August. We all got ringworm from some kittens and had to rub Pond's Extract on our arms and legs night and morning, and my father rolled over in a canoe with all his clothes on; but outside of that the vacation was a success and from then on one none of us ever thought there was any place in the world like that lake in Maine. We returned summer after summer—always on August 1st for

one month. I have since become a salt-water man, but sometimes in summer there are days when the restlessness of the tides and the fearful cold of the sea water and the incessant wind which blows across the afternoon and into the evening make me wish for the placidity of the lake in the woods. A few weeks ago this feeling got so strong I bought myself a couple of bass hooks and a spinner and returned to the lake where we used to go, for a week's fishing and to revisit old haunts.

2   I took along my son, who had never had any fresh water up his nose and who had seen lily pads only from train windows. On the journey over to the lake I began to wonder what it would be like. I wondered how time would have marred this unique, this holy spot—the coves and streams, the hills that the sun set behind, the camps and the paths behind the camps. I was sure the tarred road would have found it out and I wondered in what other ways it would be desolated. It is strange how much you can remember about places like that once you allow your mind to return into the grooves which lead back. You remember one thing, and that suddenly reminds you of another thing. I guess I remembered clearest of all the early mornings, when the lake was cool and motionless, remembered how the bedroom smelled of the lumber it was made of and of the wet woods whose scent entered through the screen. The partitions in the camp were thin and did not extend clear to the top of the rooms, and as I was always the first up I would dress softly so as not to wake the others, and sneak out into the sweet outdoors and start out in the canoe, keeping close along the shore in the long shadows of the pines. I remembered being very careful never to rub my paddle against the gunwale for fear of disturbing the stillness of the cathedral.

3   The lake had never been what you would call a wild lake. There were cottages sprinkled around the shores, and it was in farming country although the shores of the lake were quite heavily wooded. Some of the cottages were owned by nearby farmers, and you would live at the shore and eat your meals at the farmhouse. That's what our family did. But although it wasn't wild, it was a fairly large and undisturbed lake and there were places in it which, to a child at least, seemed infinitely remote and primeval.

4   I was right about the tar: it led to within half a mile of the shore. But when I got back there, with my boy, and we settled into a camp near a farmhouse and into the kind of summertime I had known, I could tell that it was going to be pretty much the same as it had been before—I knew it, lying in bed the first morning, smelling the bedroom, and hearing the boy sneak quietly out and go off along the shore in a boat. I began to sustain the illusion that he was I, and therefore by simple transposition, that I was my father. This sensation persisted, kept cropping up all the time we were there. It was not an entirely new feeling, but in this setting it grew much stronger. I seemed to be living a dual existence. I would be in the middle of some simple act, I would be picking up a bait box or laying down a table fork, or I would be saying something, and suddenly it would be not I but my father who was saying the words or making the gesture. It gave me a creepy sensation.

5   We went fishing the first morning. I felt the same damp moss covering the worms in the bait can, and saw the dragonfly alight on the tip of my rod as it hovered a few inches from the surface of the water. It was the arrival of this fly that convinced me beyond any doubt that everything was as it always had been, that the years were a mirage and there had been no years. The small waves were the same, chucking the rowboat under the chin as we fished at anchor, and the boat was the same boat, the same color green and the ribs broken in the same places, and under the floor-boards the same fresh-water

leavings and debris—the dead helgramite, the wisps of moss, the rusty discarded fish-hook, the dried blood from yesterday's catch. We stared silently at the tips of our rods, at the dragonflies that came and went. I lowered the tip of mine into the water, tenta-tively, pensively dislodging the fly, which darted two feet away, poised, darted two feet back, and came to rest again a little farther up the rod. There had been no years between the ducking of this dragonfly and the other one—the one that was part of memory. I looked at the boy, who was silently watching his fly, and it was my hands that held his rod, my eyes watching. I felt dizzy and didn't know which rod I was at the end of.

6   We caught two bass, hauling them in briskly as though they were mackerel, pulling them over the side of the boat in a businesslike manner without any landing net, and stunning them with a blow on the back of the head. When we got back for a swim be-fore lunch, the lake was exactly where we had left it, the same number of inches from the dock, and there was only the merest suggestion of a breeze. This seemed an utterly enchanted sea, this lake you could leave to its own devices for a few hours and come back to, and find that it had not stirred, this constant and trustworthy body of water. In the shallows, the dark, watersoaked sticks and twigs, smooth and old, were undulating in clusters on the bottom against the clean ribbed sand, and the track of the mussel was plain. A school of minnows swam by, each minnow with its small individual shadow, doubling the attendance, so clear and sharp in the sunlight. Some of the other campers were in swimming, along the shore, one of them with a cake of soap, and the water felt thin and clear and unsubstantial. Over the years there had been this person with the cake of soap, this cultist, and here he was. There had been no years.

7   Up to the farmhouse to dinner through the teeming, dusty field, the road under our sneakers was only a two-track road. The middle track was missing, the one with the marks of the hooves and the splotches of dried, flaky manure. There had always been three tracks to choose from in choosing which track to walk in; now the choice was nar-rowed down to two. For a moment I missed terribly the middle alternative. But the way led past the tennis court, and something about the way it lay there in the sun reassured me; the tape had loosened along the backline, the alleys were green with plantains and other weeds, and the net (installed in June and removed in September) sagged in the dry noon, and the whole place steamed with midday heat and hunger and emptiness. There was a choice of pie for dessert, and one was blueberry and one was apple, and the wait-resses were the same country girls, there having been no passage of time, only the illu-sion of it as in a dropped curtain—the waitresses were still fifteen; their hair had been washed, that was the only difference—they had been to the movies and seen the pretty girls with the clean hair.

8   Summertime, oh summertime, pattern of life indelible, the fadeproof lake, the woods unshatterable, the pasture with the sweetfern and the juniper forever and ever, summer without end; this was the background, and the life along the shore was the design, the cottages with their innocent and tranquil design, their tiny docks with the flagpole and the American flag floating against the white clouds in the blue sky, the little paths over the roots of the trees leading from camp to camp and the paths leading back to the out-houses and the can of lime for sprinkling, and at the souvenir counters at the store the miniature birch-bark canoes and the post cards that showed things looking a little better than they looked. This was the American family at play, escaping the city heat, wonder-ing whether the newcomers in the camp at the head of the cove were "common" or

"nice," wondering whether it was true that the people who drove up for Sunday dinner at the farmhouse were turned away because there wasn't enough chicken.

9   It seemed to me, as I kept remembering all this, that those times and those summers had been infinitely precious and worth saving. There had been jollity and peace and goodness. The arriving (at the beginning of August) had been so big a business in itself, at the railway station the farm wagon drawn up, the first smell of the pine-laden air, the first glimpse of the smiling farmer, and the great importance of the trunks and your father's enormous authority in such matters, and the feel of the wagon under you for the long ten-mile haul, and at the top of the last long hill catching the first view of the lake after eleven months of not seeing this cherished body of water. The shouts and cries of the other campers when they saw you, and the trunks to be unpacked, to give up their rich burden. (Arriving was less exciting nowadays, when you sneaked up in your car and parked it under a tree near the camp and took out the bags and in five minutes it was all over, no fuss, no loud wonderful fuss about trunks.)

10   Peace and goodness and jollity. The only thing that was wrong now, really, was the sound of the place, an unfamiliar nervous sound of the outboard motors. This was the note that jarred, the one thing that would sometimes break the illusion and set the years moving. In those other summertimes all motors were inboard; and when they were at a little distance, the noise they made was a sedative, an ingredient of summer sleep. They were one-cylinder and two-cylinder engines, and some were make-and-break and some were jump-spark, but they all made a sleepy sound across the lake. The one-lungers throbbed and fluttered, and the twin-cylinder ones purred and purred, and that was a quiet sound too. But now the campers all had outboards. In the daytime, in the hot mornings, these motors made a petulant, irritable sound; at night, in the still evening when the afterglow lit the water, they whined about one's ears like mosquitoes. My boy loved our rented outboard, and his great desire was to achieve singlehanded mastery over it, and authority, and he soon learned the trick of choking it a little (but not too much), and the adjustment of the needle valve. Watching him I would remember the things you could do with the old one-cylinder engine with the heavy flywheel, how you could have it eating out of your hand if you got really close to it spiritually. Motor boats in those days didn't have clutches, and you would make a landing by shutting off the motor at the proper time and coasting in with a dead rudder. But there was a way of reversing them, if you learned the trick, by cutting the switch and putting it on again exactly on the final dying revolution of the flywheel, so that it would kick back against compression and begin reversing. Approaching a dock in a strong following breeze, it was difficult to slow up sufficiently by the ordinary coasting method, and if a boy felt he had complete mastery over his motor, he was tempted to keep it running beyond its time and then reverse it a few feet from the dock. It took a cool nerve, because if you threw the switch a twentieth of a second too soon you would catch the flywheel when it still had speed enough to go up past center, and the boat would leap ahead, charging bull-fashion at the dock.

11   We had a good week at the camp. The bass were biting well and the sun shone endlessly, day after day. We would be tired at night and lie down in the accumulated heat of the little bedrooms after the long hot day and the breeze would stir almost imperceptibly outside and the smell of the swamp drift in through the rusty screens. Sleep would come easily and in the morning the red squirrel would be on the roof, tapping out his gay routine. I kept remembering everything, lying in bed in the mornings—the small steamboat that had a long

rounded stern like the lip of a Ubangi, and how quietly she ran on the moonlight sails, when the older boys played their mandolins and the girls sang and we ate doughnuts dipped in sugar, and how sweet the music was on the water in the shining night, and what it had felt like to think about girls then. After breakfast we would go up to the store and the things were in the same place—the minnows in a bottle, the plugs and spinners disarranged and pawed over by the youngsters from the boys' camp, the fig newtons and the Beeman's gum. Outside, the road was tarred and cars stood in front of the store. Inside, all was just as it had always been, except there was more Coca-Cola and not so much Moxie and root beer and birch beer and sarsaparilla. We would walk out with a bottle of pop apiece and some-times the pop would backfire up our noses and hurt. We explored the streams, quietly, where the turtles slid off the sunny logs and dug their way into the soft bottom; and we lay on the town wharf and fed worms to the tame bass. Everywhere we went I had trouble making out which was I, the one walking at my side, the one walking in my pants.

12   One afternoon while we were there at that lake a thunderstorm came up. It was like the revival of an old melodrama that I had seen long ago with childish awe. The second-act climax of the drama of the electrical disturbance over a lake in America had not changed in any important respect. This was the big scene, still the big scene. The whole thing was so familiar, the first feeling of oppression and heat and a general air around camp of not wanting to go very far away. In midafternoon (it was all the same) a curious darkening of the sky, and a lull in everything that had made life tick; and then the way the boats sud-denly swung the other way at their moorings with the coming of a breeze out of the new quarter, and the premonitory rumble. Then the kettle drum, then the snare, then the bass drum and cymbals, then crackling light against the dark, and the gods grinning and lick-ing their chops in the hills. Afterward the calm, the rain steadily rustling in the calm lake, the return of light and hope and spirits, and the campers running out in joy and relief to go swimming in the rain, their bright cries perpetuating the deathless joke about how they were getting simply drenched, and the children screaming with delight at the new sensa-tion of bathing in the rain, and the joke about getting drenched linking the generations in a strong indestructible chain. And the comedian who waded in carrying an umbrella.

13   When the others went swimming my son said he was going in too. He pulled his drip-ping trunks from the line where they had hung all through the shower, and wrung them out. Languidly, and with no thought of going in, I watched him, his hard little body, skinny and bare, saw him wince slightly as he pulled up around his vitals the small, soggy, icy garments. As he buckled the swollen belt suddenly my groin felt the chill of death.

PRACTICE

Discussion

1. What reasons does White give for returning to the lake instead of going to the seashore? Does he fulfill his purpose? What does he discover that is most unexpected?

2. In what ways has the modern world of 1941 encroached on the backwoods area? Does White seem to be very surprised or upset by this encroachment? What aspect of change bothers him most?

3. What actions of his son remind White of himself as a boy? When does White feel like his own father? Why does he feel "the chill of death" at the end?

4. How does White prepare us for the morbid shock of the final insight?

5. What phrase does White keep repeating to stress his sense of connectedness in time? How is the use of this repetition especially effective in paragraph 12?

6. What method of comparison-contrast does White use for this essay? Would another method have been as effective? Explain.

7. How does White manage to make his memories so vivid to his readers, as well as to himself? Find examples of his appeal to each of the five senses.

8. Where does White describe an artificial process? Why does he include this section?

Vocabulary

incessant	helgramite	petulant
placidity	pensively	imperceptibly
gunwale	undulating	moorings
primeval	indelible	premonitory
mirage	tranquil	languidly
debris		

Writing

1. Write an essay comparing a place where you have lived or visited at two different points in time.

2. Write an essay comparing your perspective of an experience with that of your mother or father.

3. Describe the process you follow to make, run, or fix something and your interest in the process, and compare these with the process followed and the interest felt by an earlier generation.

Perri Klass

A WORLD WHERE TOO MANY CHILDREN DON'T GROW UP

Perri Klass earned her bachelor's degree from Radcliffe College in 1979 and her medical degree from Harvard Medical School in 1986. She completed a residency in pediatrics at The Children's Hospital in Boston. Author as well as doctor, Klass has a collection of short stories, I Am Having An Adventure, *a novel,* Recombinations, *and a collection of essays,* Other Women's Children, *to*

her credit. She has written for Discover *magazine and contributed article to the*
New York Times, Vogue, Esquire, **and** Mademoiselle. *The following account of
her experience with Indian pediatrics was written when Klass was a fourth-
year medical student at Harvard. The culture shock sent Klass sharply back to
basics. In an earlier part of the article, not included in the excerpt that follows,
Klass tells of questioning an obvious diagnosis because she mistook a ten-year-
old boy for a girl. She was unfamiliar with the Sikh custom of long coiled braids
for boys. Klass' article, which appeared in the April, 1986 issue of* Discover,
*illustrates the narrowness of the personal perspective with which we view the
world.*

1   Recently I spent some time in India, working in the pediatric department of an important New Delhi hospital. I wanted to learn about medicine outside the U.S., to work
in a pediatric clinic in the Third World, and I suppose I also wanted to test my own medical education, to find out whether my newly acquired skills are in fact transferable to
any place where there are human beings, with human bodies, subject to their range of
ills and evils.

2   But it wasn't just a question of my medical knowledge. In India, I found that my
cultural limitations often prevented me from thinking clearly about patients. Everyone
looked different, and I was unable to pick up any clues from their appearance, their
manners of speech, their clothing. This is a family of Afghan refugees. This family is
from the south of India. This child is from a very poor family. This child has a Nepalese
name. All the clues I use at home to help me evaluate patients, clues ranging from what
neighborhood they live in to what ethnic origin their names suggest, were hidden from
me in India.

3   The people don't just look different on the outside, of course. It might be more accurate to say *the population is different.* The gene pool for example: there are some genetic diseases that are much more common here than there, cystic fibrosis, say, which
you have to keep in mind when evaluating patients in Boston, but which would be a
showoffy and highly unlikely diagnosis-out-of-a-book for a medical student to suggest
in New Delhi (I know—in my innocence I suggested it).

4   And all of this, in the end, really reflects human diversity, though admittedly it's reflected in the strange warped mirror of the medical profession; it's hard to exult in the
variety of human genetic defects, or even in the variety of human culture, when you're
looking at it as a tool for examining a sick child. Still, I can accept the various implications of a world full of different people, different populations.

5   *The diseases are different.* The patient is a seven-year-old boy whose father says that
over the past week and a half he has become progressively more tired, less active, and
lately he doesn't seem to understand everything going on around him. Courteously, the
senior doctor turns to me, asks what my assessment is. He asks this in a tone that suggests that the diagnosis is obvious, and as a guest, I'm invited to pronounce it. The diagnosis, whatever it is, is certainly not obvious to me. I can think of a couple of infections
that might look like this, but no single answer. The senior doctor sees my difficulty, and
offers a maxim, one that I've heard many times back in Boston. Gently, slightly reprov-
ingly, he tells me, "Common things occur commonly. There are many possibilities, of
course, but I think it is safe to say that this is almost certainly tuberculous meningitis."

6 Tuberculous meningitis? Common things occur commonly? Somewhere in my brain (and somewhere in my lecture notes) "the complications of tuberculosis" are filed away, and, yes, I suppose it can affect the central nervous system, just as I vaguely remember that it can affect the stomach, and the skeletal system . . . To tell the truth, I've never even seen a case of straightforward tuberculosis of the lungs in a small child, let alone what I would have thought of as a rare complication.

7 And hell, it's worse than that. I've done a fair amount of pediatrics back in Boston, but there are an awful lot of things I've never seen. When I'm invited to give an opinion on a child's rash, I come up with quite a creative list of tropical diseases, because guess what? I've never seen a child with measles before. In the U.S., all children are vaccinated against measles, mumps, and rubella at the age of one year. There are occasional outbreaks of measles among college students, some of whom didn't get vaccinated 20 years ago, but the disease is now very rare in small children. ("Love this Harvard medical student. Can't recognize tuberculous meningitis. Can't recognize measles or mumps. What the hell do you think they teach them over there in pediatrics?")

8 And this, of course, is one of the main medical student reasons for going to study abroad, the chance to see diseases you wouldn't see at home. The pathology, we call it, as in "I got to see some amazing pathology while I was in India." It's embarrassing to find yourself suddenly ignorant, but it's interesting to learn all about a new range of diagnoses, symptoms, treatments, all things you might have learned from a textbook and then immediately forgotten as totally outside your own experience.

9 The difficult thing is that these differences don't in any way, however tortured, reflect the glory of human variation. They reflect instead the sad partitioning of the species, because they're almost all preventable diseases, and their prevalence is a product of poverty, of lack of vaccinations, of malnutrition and poor sanitation. And therefore, though it's all very educational for the medical student (and I'm by now more or less used to parasitizing my education off of human suffering), this isn't a difference to be accepted without outrage.

10 *The expectations are different.* The child is a seven-month-old girl with diarrhea. She has been losing weight for a couple of weeks, she won't eat or drink, she just lies there in her grandmother's arms. The grandmother explains: one of her other grandchildren has just died from very severe diarrhea, and this little girl's older brother died last year, not of diarrhea but of a chest infection . . . I look at the grandmother's face, at the faces of the baby's mother and father, who are standing on either side of the chair, where the grandmother is sitting with the baby. All these people believe in the possibility of death, the chance that the child will not live to grow up. They've all seen many children die. These parents lost a boy last year, and they know that they may lose their daughter.

11 The four have traveled for almost sixteen hours to come to this hospital, because after the son died last year, they no longer have faith in the village doctor. They're hopeful, they offer their sick baby to this famous hospital. They're prepared to stay in Delhi while she's hospitalized, the mother will sleep in the child's crib with her, the father and grandmother may well sleep on the hospital grounds. They've brought food, cooking pots, warm shawls because it's January and it gets cold at night. They're tough, and they're hopeful, but they believe in the possibility of death.

12 Back home, in Boston, I've heard bewildered, grieving parents say, essentially, "Who would have believed that in the 1980s a child could just die like that?" Even par-

ents with terminally ill children, children who spend months or years getting sicker and
sicker, sometimes have great difficulty accepting that all the art and machinery of modern medicine is completely hopeless. They expect every child to live to grow up.

13   In India, it isn't that parents are necessarily resigned, and certainly not that they love
their children less. They may not want to accept the dangers, but poor people, people
living in poor villages or in urban slums, know the possibility is there. If anything, they
may be even more terrified than American parents, just because perhaps they're picturing the death of some other loved child, imagining this living child going the way of
that dead one.

14   I don't know. This is a gap I can't cross. I can laugh at my own inability to interpret
the signals of a different culture, and I can read and ask questions and slowly begin to
learn a little about the people I'm trying to help care for. I can blush at my ignorance of
diseases uncommon in my home territory, study up in textbooks, and deplore inequalities that allow preventable diseases to ravage some unfortunate populations, while others are protected. I can try to become more discriminating in my appreciation of medical technology and its uses, understanding that the best hospital isn't the one that does
the most tests. But I can't draw my lesson from this grandmother, these parents, this
sick little girl. I can't imagine their awareness, their accommodations of what they
know. I can't understand how they live with it. I can't accept their acceptance. My medical training has taken place in a world where all children are supposed to grow up, and
the exceptions to this rule are rare horrible diseases, disastrous accidents. This is the attitude, the expectation, I demand from patients. I'm left most disturbed not by the fact
of children dying, not by the different diseases from which they die, or the differences
in the medical care they receive, but by the way their parents look at me, at my profession. Perhaps its only in this that I allow myself to take it all personally.

PRACTICE

Discussion

1. What three misdiagnoses does Klass make? Why is she mistaken in each
   case? Is she a poor medical student?

2. What insights are particularly difficult or disturbing to Klass?

3. What difference does Klass discover between the way American and Indian
   parents look on the death of their children? Does she find any similarities?

4. Into what three major sections is the essay divided? What method of
   organization is used? Why are the three parts arranged in just that order?
   How are the three sentences that conclude the three sections related?

5. How has Klass provided for transitions in her essay? Are her transitions
   clear? smooth? effective?

6. Klass takes her subject seriously, but she doesn't always take herself
   seriously. What differences of diction or construction does she employ to cut

herself down to size? In which section does she not employ these methods? Why not?

7. Study paragraph 13. Can you suggest a rearrangement of its sentences or phrases that might improve its interior logic as well as its transitions from paragraph 12 and to paragraph 14? Explain.

8. In her final paragraph (14), Klass pours out her despair and frustration at what she has experienced in India. How many of the elements of *ethical proof* (see page 5) can you find in this one paragraph?

Vocabulary

pediatric	maxim	pathology
gene pool	tuberculosis	prevalence
cystic fibrosis	meningitis	parasitizing
exult	rubella	deplore

Writing

1. Describe an experience that you have had performing a familiar activity in an unfamiliar setting.

2. Have you had the experience of visiting a foreign country with a radically different culture from your own? another section of your own country with a radically different lifestyle? Write an essay comparing and contrasting the two cultures or lifestyles. Give your essay focus and purpose.

3. Interview another person about his or her views on death, funerals, or immortality. Choose someone whose age, ethnic background, or religion is different from yours. Write an essay comparing and contrasting your views and those of the person you interview.

CHAPTER 19

Analogy

▼ Analogy

Definition: An analogy is an *extended* comparison between two "things"—ideas, actions, processes, and so on. An analogy is more than just saying A is like B. It also says (in *extending* the point) that A is like B in certain important ways and for significant reasons. Analogies are used for two major purposes: (1) to help make an argument, and (2) to help readers understand something *unknown* by reference to a *known*.

Let's look at an example of purpose (1). In the passage below, Professor Joseph Weizenbaum, Professor of Computer Science at MIT, argues that educating children in computer science is a "delusion."

1   We in the United States are in the grip of a mass delusion with respect to the education of kids with computers. The belief that it is urgent that we put computers in primary and secondary schools is based on a number of premises, of which only one is true. The true premise is that the whole world is becoming increasingly pervaded by computers. . . .

2   I would like to draw an analogy to something that is ubiquitous in our society—the electric motor. There are undoubtedly many more electric motors in the United States than there are people, and almost everybody owns a lot of electric motors without thinking about them. They are everywhere, in automobiles, food mixers, vacuum cleaners, even watches and pencil sharpeners. Yet, it doesn't require any sort of electric-motor literacy to get on with the world, or, importantly, to be able to use these gadgets.

3   Another important point about electric motors is that they're invisible. If you question someone using a vacuum cleaner, of course they know that there is an electric motor inside. But nobody says, "Well, I think I'll use an electric motor programmed to be a vacuum cleaner to vacuum the floor."

4   The computer will also become largely invisible, as it already is to a large extent in the consumer market. I believe that the more pervasive the computer becomes the more

invisible it will become. We talk about it a lot now because it is new, but as we get used to the computer, it will retreat into the background. How much hands-on computer experience will students need? The answer, of course, is not very much. The student and the practicing professional will operate special-purpose instruments that happen to have computers as components.

5   If Johnny can't read and somebody writes computer software that will improve Johnny's reading score a little bit for the present, then the easiest thing to do is to bring in the computer and sit Johnny down at it. This makes it unnecessary to ask why Johnny can't read. In other words, it makes it unnecessary to reform the school system, or for that matter the society that tolerates the breakdown of its schools.

—Joseph Weizenbaum, "Another View from MIT"

In this analogy, you observe that Weizenbaum does more than just compare the electric motor to the computer. He also extends the comparison, talking about the electric motor in vacuum cleaners and automobiles, and its invisibility in such machines. He points out that the computer will also be invisible in machinery of various kinds; indeed it is invisible already "to a large extent in the consumer market." Weizenbaum uses the analogy to *argue* that students do not need to be taught in school to use an invisible mechanical servant. And he concludes that computer study wastes time which would be better spent on other educational endeavors.

The second purpose of typical analogies is to help a reader understand an *unknown* by reference to a *known*. Here is such an analogy from a student paper:

1   A tank truck usually holds between 4,000 and 6,000 gallons of gasoline. Depending on the tanker and the oil company, there are three to six individual compartments which hold 600 to 900 gallons of gasoline apiece. The tank that contains the compartments is elliptically shaped to distribute the pressure equally and to allow a more complete flow of air when the gasoline is delivered.

2   Until recently the only way to load a tanker was to climb up on top, where the openings to the compartments are located. You can easily picture this by visualizing six pop bottles lined up in single file on a table. A man wants to fill up bottle three, so he takes the cap off. He then inserts a small hose into the neck of the bottle and turns on a faucet which is connected to the hose.

3   A gasoline tanker is loaded in a similar way, but on a much larger scale. A man climbs on top of the tanker and opens a particular compartment by removing the cap. He then takes a hose with a four-foot metal pipe extension, about three and a half inches in diameter, and inserts the pipe down into the "bottle" (the compartment hole), which measures four inches in diameter. A pump is then turned on, allowing the gasoline to flow into the compartment.

In this analogy, an engineering student explains something relatively *unknown* (loading a tanker) by using her knowledge of something *known* (filling pop bottles). If you, the reader, think that a tanker consists of one long compartment, then the engineer's analogy is valuable and useful. If, however, you knew before reading the analogy how tankers were constructed and loaded, the analogy might not be particularly informative. That means, of course, that you should base your use of analogy on the knowledge of your audience.

All of us know many things that we can use to help a reader understand an idea better. Here a geology major helps to understand how the oil seismograph works by comparing it to shouting at a cliff wall.

Introduction

1   For over twenty years, my father has worked on an oil seismograph crew. We all know about the big seismographs that detect and measure earthquakes. The oil seismograph is a small portable electronic instru-

Definition

ment that detects and measures artificial earthquakes. The purpose of the instrument is to find geological structures that may contain oil. I have worked for the past two summers on a seismograph crew. In that period of time I have learned that the oil seismograph instrument is not mysterious because it can be compared to shouting at a cliff wall.

First analogy: Echo, and relationship to distance

2   Let me begin with an occurrence that should be familiar. Imagine yourself standing near the base of a large cliff. If you shout at the cliff face, you will get an echo because the sound waves bounce back from the so-called "interface" where air meets rock. The sound waves travel at 1100 feet per second. You can find out how far you are standing from the cliff by measuring the time it takes for your shout to travel from you to the cliff and back again, and then by solving a simple formula for distance.

3   The function of the oil seismograph is to find out how far down in the earth the horizontal layers of rock are. To discover this distance, the oil seismologist digs a deep hole (usually 100–200 feet) in the surface of the ground—the purpose of the hole I will explain later. At the bottom of the hole, he explodes a heavy charge of dynamite. Ground waves travel from the explosion down to the layers of rock. At each major interface between the layers, the waves bounce back to

Echo analogy applied to seismograph

the surface. The explosion is similar to shouting at the cliff. Just as sound travels through the air at a certain speed, ground waves travel through the earth, although much faster. Ground waves bounce from rock interfaces as sound waves bounce from a cliff face. And the seismologist can determine distance just as you can determine the distance between you and the cliff.

4   Why does the seismologist dig a hole to explode the dynamite? Much of the ground surface is covered with what geologists call *weathering,* that relatively loose covering of soil, sand, clay, etc., that usually goes down to the water table. This weathering has a disastrous effect upon seismic waves in the ground; it slows them up and even disperses them. To explode a dynamite charge on top of the

Second analogy: Weathering of ground like mush

ground would be like shouting at a cliff face through a bowl of mush—no matter how loud you shouted, little of your voice would get through. So the seismologist drills through the weathering and plants the dynamite charge below it. Usually the weathering has a bad effect only on the waves at the point of explosion; the *reflected* waves will travel through the weathering to the instruments on the surface.

Differences

5   In the interests of accuracy, I should add that the analogy between air waves and seismic waves is partly literal and partly figurative. The principles are similar but the conditions are different. Air waves are relatively constant in speed because the medium varies little. Seismic waves, by contract, increase in speed with depth, and the increase is irregular and difficult to measure. Also, seismic reflections vary in

ways that no one completely understands. But the analogy is, in a basic sense, revealing and accurate enough to explain to a beginner how an oil seismograph works.

We can diagram the first basic analogy here as follows:

Shouting at cliff face	**Using a seismograph**
Point A shout ⟷	set off dynamite
Point B creates sound waves in air ⟷	creates seismic waves in earth
Point C waves travel at set rate ⟷	waves travel at various rates
Point D waves bounce back from cliff ⟷	waves bounce back from rock interface
Point E distance can be measured ⟷	distance can be measured

When you construct an analogy, make sure that the compared points *are* comparable. Cut out or explain any points that cannot be logically compared and be certain that the familiar or known side of the analogy is really familiar and known to your reader. It is useless to explain a mineral's crystal-lattice structure by reference to analytic geometry if your reader knows nothing about analytic geometry. Do not try to stretch an analogy too far. Like the fabled camel which first put his nose in the man's tent, then his head, and finally his whole body, pushing the man out of the tent, metaphor tends to creep into analogies. What starts out to be literally explanatory can become as unreal and metaphorical as a fairy tale, and no more convincing.

Sometimes you may choose to develop analogies by using figures of speech. Figurative language can help you to clarify, dramatize, or sharpen your comparison. The function of such analogies is not so much to explain one "side" of the extended comparison, but to help the reader see the whole thing in a new and fresh way. For instance, we all know what war and cancer are; they are known to us. But observe how Sydney Harris uses metaphor to argue that war is like cancer; both must be eradicated to save the species.

Introduction
The term "self-preservation" introduced

1   We say that the aim of life is self-preservation, if not for the individual, at least for the species. Granted that every organism seeks this end, does every organism know what is best for its self-preservation?

Contrast between cancer cells and normal cells

2   Consider cancer cells and noncancer cells in the human body. The normal cells are aimed at reproducing and functioning in a way that is beneficial to the body. Cancer cells, on the other hand, spread in a way that threatens and ultimately destroys the whole body. Normal cells work harmoniously, because they "know," in a sense, that their preservation depends upon the health of the body they inhabit. While they are organisms in themselves, they also act as part of a substructure, directed at the good of the whole body.

Beginning of analogy: "Cancer

3   We might say, metaphorically, that cancer cells do not know enough about self-preservation; they are, biologically, more ignorant

*cells [like warriors]
do not know about
self-preservation*

than normal cells. The aim of cancer cells is to spread throughout the body, to conquer all the normal cells—and when they reach their aim, the body is dead. And so are the cancer cells.

4   For cancer cells destroy not only all rival cells, in their ruthless biological warfare, but also destroy the large organization—the body itself—signing their own suicide warrant.

*Extension of
analogy: War and
cancer both kill*

5   The same is true of war, especially in the modern world. War is the social cancer of mankind. It is pernicious form of ignorance, for it destroys not only its "enemies," but also the whole superstructure of which it is a part—and thus eventually it defeats itself. Nations live in a state of anarchy, not in a state of law. And, like cancer cells, nations do not know that their ultimate self-interest lies in preserving the health and harmony of the whole body (that is, the community of man), for if that body is mortally wounded, then no nation can survive and flourish.

*Argument stated
in an "if . . .
then" analogy*

6   If the aim of life is self-preservation—for the species as well as for the individual—we must tame or eradicate the cancer cells of war in the social organism. And this can be done only when nations begin to recognize that what may seem to be "in the national interest" cannot be opposed to the common interest of mankind, or both the nation and mankind will die in this "conquest."

*Analogy
continued*

Conclusion

7   The life of every organism depends upon the viability of the system of which it is a member. The cancer cells cannot exist without the body to inhabit, and they must be exterminated if they cannot be reeducated to behave like normal cells. At present, their very success dooms them to failure—just as a victorious war in the atomic age would be an unqualified disaster for the dying winner.

—Sydney J. Harris, "When Winning Is Losing"

When using metaphor in an analogy, keep in mind C. S. Lewis' advice:

1. The figures [of speech] or metaphors should be well chosen by the writer.

2. The reader must be able to understand the figures.

3. Both writer and reader should understand that figurative language is being used.

▼ Writing and Revising an Analogy (An Example)

Gerry Kinder starts to write an extended analogy. He begins with a title:

Is the Greek Letter Organization Just a Country Club?

This Gerry follows with a scratch outline:

1. *Me and the Greeks*
   — they're OK

2. *Snobbery*
       and exclusiveness

3. The great life in both country club and Greek house

4. Business deals
    country club
    frat house

Gerry now begins his first draft:

1   I'm neither for nor against Greeks. My sister went through rush here two years ago and pledged Tri-Delt. She is now a happy sorority girl. I have shown some interest my first year in going Greek and have visited some of the houses and been involved in some of the entertainments. I've played football against Greeks in Touch League. I know and like many Greeks of both sexes. But something bothers me about them—even though I am not "politically" against their organization. (I am not a devout Independent either.)

2   There is too much snobbery in the Greek system. They remind me of the people I used to caddy for in the country club at home. Their major idea is to be exclusive. Exclusive. The One and Only. Their motto is: Keep others out. Otherwise, why join either the country club or a fraternity/sorority?

3   Another advantage of both is that you get to live better. In a Greek house you eat better and have a better place to sleep and have fun. Similarly a country club is the place to eat great dinners, and swim in a luxurious swimming pool. There is something very similar about the people sitting around the pool watching the golfers come in at dusk and their counterpart: the boys sitting on the front steps watching the students coming back from their late afternoon classes, the sun shining through the trees. Glamor.

4   And the deals. How many deals are completed over golf and drinks at the country club? How many friendships are cemented in the fraternity, friendships that later are used in furthering business relationships?

At the point Gerry stops. For him, this has been a "letting loose" draft, one that provides ideas and material, a rambling outline of sorts. Now he needs to think hard about the ordering of ideas and shape the whole paper more carefully. He puts down a new order of elements in the basic analogy:

1. Deals (business, etc.)

2. Live better

3. Exclusiveness: the whole point.

Now he begins on the new draft. He cuts the first paragraph entirely because it starts the paper too slowly, and he wants to see how short a paper he can write that still does the job. How vivid—yet economical—can he be? He chooses a new title and writes two new opening paragraphs that set analogous scenes. Having finished these, he simply keeps writing.

GOLDEN GHETTOES

1   They sit quietly, handsome wives beside them; drinks in their hands, the setting sun glimmering beautifully on their tanned faces. There are muted sounds of traffic from the highway a mile away and sounds of splashing from the pool a few feet away. "I parred the last one!" says a happy man walking toward the club house. He is about fifty, his fine-looking hair glowing silver in the setting sun.

2   Two-hundred miles from this scene, their sons and daughters sit quietly, tanned faces turned toward the street. A convertible pulls up in the driveway, and a young man with the arms of a sweater tied around his throat vaults gracefully over the side of the car. A girl drinks from a beer can, tilts it high, drops it carefully into a wastebasket. Another girl strides by on the sidewalk, her long legs carrying her smoothly along "I aced the geology exam!" she calls out happily. A murmur follows her down the street.

3   Here are two sides of the good life, American style. In the country club, affluent Americans play and enjoy themselves: this is what life is meant to be. In the fraternity and sorority, their sons and daughters play and enjoy themselves: practicing their skills for the life that will be theirs—some day.

4   But there is more to the uses of Greek organization and country club besides just the good life. It is well known that thousands of business deals every year are made in country clubs. On the golf course, people agree to buy this or sell that. Plans are made: "Let's talk to old Freddy about his work on the downtown mall." (As a caddy I would stand and listen; they ignored me as if I were a 19th-century slave, present but invisible.) At lunch they pull out pens and pencils and draw on napkins and add up figures. "Waiter—more napkins!" The lawyers talk to engineers, who talk to city council members, who shout across the room. "Hey, Sam, are you going to handle the Lions' Antique Show this year?"

5   In the frats, the same kind of scenes occur. The same names, the same ignoring of waiters, similar deals. But little money is involved usually, except for festive occasions. Jack Windsor chairs the Homecoming program. "Can we get THE FILTHY FIVE this year? I heard they were great at Purdue." A senior, graduating at midterm, tells his roommate: "Listen, next year call up Selkirk in my Dad's office; he may be hiring then." Meanwhile, over in a sorority, two girls plot an attack on a favored law school. "I know what you should write in your Statement on the application," says one. "They *love* to hear that you're big on sports."

6   All this is real enough, the good life and the business deals. Yet what keeps both country club and Greek organization permanently alive is more deeply psychological. It is a sense of being different by choice and warming your whole self in that choice. Members of both organizations swim happily in exclusivity. Not everybody can get in; they are the chosen few. Both organizations come with a dozen privileges that not even a Phi Beta Kappa key can get for you. The key won't allow you to ignore the slave carrying forty pounds of golf clubs; or to eat de-boned trout and drink champagne with the mayor of the city; or to date the star quarterback who (after graduation) will be worth two million dollars on June 1st. Greek house and country club: the golden ghettoes of American life.

PRACTICE

Discussion

1. Read Gerry's final draft and prepare for discussion the following questions:

   a. Diagram the analogy, following the form on page 355. Discuss the diagram in relation to the paper's organization.

    b. What is the writer's point? Is there a "known" side of the analogy?

    c. How is the organization similar to one of the *comparison and contrast* patterns?

    d. Discuss the use of dialogue in the paper.

    e. Study the discussion of the *representative example* on page 292. How has Gerry used that kind of illustrative material in his paper?

    f. How well does Gerry fulfill his goal: to write a vivid, economical paper that "does the job"?

2. Discuss each of the analogies below. Do any of them depend on figures of speech? Is the extended comparison consistently made? Do the differences between the two elements being compared weaken the analogy? Is the "known side" of he analogy familiar enough to you? How could the analogy be improved (if at all)?

    a. For a long time now, since the beginning, in fact, men and women have been sparring and dancing around with each other, each pair trying to get it together and boogie to the tune called Life. For some people, it was always a glide, filled with grace and ease. For most of us, it is a stumble and a struggle, always trying to figure out the next step, until we find a partner whose inconsistencies seem to fit with ours, and the two of us fit into some kind of rhythm. Some couples wind up struggling and pulling at cross purposes; and of course, some people never get out on the floor, just stand alone in the corners, looking hard at the dancers.

        That's the way it's always been, and probably, always will be. The only difference now is that for the past few years a group of noisy people have been standing over next to the band and yelling above it, "Hey, listen everybody! You don't have to dance to the old tune any more! You can make up your own tune! You can make up your dance steps! *The man doesn't even have to lead any more!* Forget the band! This is a whole new movement! It's called *you can make your Life whatever you want!*"

        —Jay Molishever, "Marriage"

    b. In practice, showing "respect" for machines means learning not to look on them simply as slaves. When a slave owner sees that his slaves are stronger, faster, and more efficient than himself, he is likely to fear that someday these slaves will realize their power and revolt. In the same way, so long as human beings see machines as slaves, they will continue to regard any machine that is stronger, faster, or "smarter" than themselves as a potential threat. It is only when the stereotypes are broken and an individual human being makes the effort to become thoroughly familiar with a particular machine—however complex or powerful it may be—that this fear is overcome and the machine becomes a partner rather than a slave. Just as truckers get to know their "rigs," sailors their ships, and musicians their instruments, so ordinary people in the near future may get to know their computers.

—Jennings Lane, "Computer Chess"

c. Our dependence on uncertain energy sources to power our big cars and our recreational vehicles, to heat and cool our oversized houses and ill-designed office buildings, may be as deadly in the long run as an addict's dependence on dope.

—William Raspberry

d. There is a lot at stake when a building gets sick. Architects lose their reputations. Contractors get sued. Rents plummet. And, of course, people can die. What suffers most, perhaps, is that faith we all place in anything made of concrete and steel. The fact is, the building you live in or work in, the bridge you drive across each day, is a complex system, almost alive. The Cape Hatteras Lighthouse on North Carolina's Outer Banks leans away from the sun as much as eight one hundredths of an inch, then straightens out after dark. In cool weather, the huge steel cables of the Golden Gate Bridge contract, steepening slightly the arch in the bridge's central span. Structures grow, shrink, shiver, breathe. And may not be as solid as they look. Gauging the health of huge structures can be as complex as trying to find the cause of a man's illness; more complex, in some ways, considering that when buildings get sick they don't complain, and considering, too, their sheer size. It's one thing to do a routine physical on a 150-pound man. But what do you do with a 300-million-pound bridge?

—Erik Larsen

e. It would sound ridiculous to ask, "Should robbery be studied in our schools?" Yet, if academic freedom is the sole issue rather than national survival, such a question is consistent and in order. If carpentry, why not burglary? Both are ways and means of getting a living. But carpentry is socially constructive and robbery is socially destructive. Communism is likewise socially destructive for its methods frankly include robbery, murder, arson, lying, and incitement to violence. These it defends and advocates on the basis of its working slogan that the "ends justify the means."

We protect our young people from harmful epidemic diseases of a physical nature such as smallpox, by quarantining them. We expose our young people to harmful epidemic diseases of an ideological nature, such as Communism, by a false suicidal interpretation of academic freedom. What youth does when it reaches maturity is something else again. At that time, in the interest of national security, adults should study Communism to be able to recognize it and fight it for dear life whenever and under whatever disguise it rears its hideous head.

—Ruth Alexander, "Should Communism Be Studied in Our Schools?"

PRACTICE

Writing

1. Write a paragraph or essay using one of the following theses and the analogy that it suggests; or you may use a thesis and analogy of your own choice. Specify your stance.

   a. *Thesis:* The theater department should produce some older, less contemporary plays.

   Analogy: A theater that produces only new plays is like a library that stocks only new books.

   —Martin Gottfried

   b. *Thesis:* Man should colonize space.

   Analogy: Saying that man should not colonize space because it is too dangerous is like refusing to leave a sinking ship and board a lifeboat because the open sea is too dangerous.

   c. *Thesis:* Smoking should be allowed in public buildings.

   Analogy: A person who smokes (or who breathes other people's cigarette smoke) takes in a small dose of poison each day.

   d. *Thesis:* Being able to drive a car makes a young person feel like an adult.

   Analogy: Passing one's first driving test is similar to an initiation rite.

   e. *Thesis:* Every citizen should make an effort to avoid littering the nation's roadsides, parks, and cities.

   Analogy: Destroying the nation's environment is like burning down your house.

2. The powerful and prosperous Roman empire was said to have fallen for the following reasons: (a) the rise of despotic one-man rule; (b) the lowering of the prestige of the government; (c) the devaluing of the currency and increasing taxation; (d) the creation of a welfare state; (e) the rise of military control over civil government; (f) the expansion of bureaucracy; (g) the lowering of public morality; (h) the inability of the military to repulse foreign invaders. Write a paper in which you argue by using analogy that the United States is (or is not, or partly is) going the way of ancient Rome.

3. Write a figurative analogy in which you define a term by comparing it to something else. Suggestions:

   Hysteria is like a fire.

   Human opposites are like two magnets.

Social welfare multiplies like yeast cells.

Pets are like children.

Sydney J. Harris

WHAT TRUE EDUCATION SHOULD DO

Veteran newspaperman Sydney J. Harris wrote his syndicated column "Strictly Personal" from 1941—first for the Chicago Daily News *and then for the* Chicago Sun-Times—*until his death in 1986. Although Harris was born in England in 1917, he was a thorough Chicagoan, having lived there since he was five. He attended the University of Chicago before launching a career that resulted in many honors and several books, among them* Strictly Personal *(1953), a collection of his early columns, and* The Best of Sydney J. Harris *(1975), a later counterpart. Harris wrote about American life in particular, about human nature in general. As the following selection from his "Strictly Personal" column illustrates, he knew how to draw a striking analogy to make the reader see a general point.*

1   When most people think of the word "education," they think of a pupil as a sort of animate sausage casing. Into this empty casing, the teachers are supposed to stuff "education."

2   But genuine education, as Socrates knew more than two thousand years ago, is not inserting the stuffings of information *into* a person, but rather eliciting knowledge *from* him; it is the drawing out of what is in the mind.

3   "The most important part of education," once wrote William Earnest Hocking, the distinguished Harvard philosopher, "is this instruction of a man in what he has inside of him."

4   And, as Edith Hamilton has reminded us, Socrates never said, "I know, learn from me." He said, rather, "Look into your own selves and find the spark of truth that God has put into every heart, and that only you can kindle to a flame."

5   In the dialogue called the "Meno," Socrates takes an ignorant slave boy, without a day of schooling, and proves to the amazed observers that the boy really "knows" geometry—because the principles and axioms of geometry are already in his mind, waiting to be called out.

6   So many of the discussions and controversies about the content of education are futile and inconclusive because they are concerned with what should "go into" the student rather than with what should be taken out, and how this can best be done.

7   The college student who once said to me, after a lecture, "I spend so much time studying that I don't have a chance to learn anything," was succinctly expressing his dissatisfaction with the sausage-casing view of education.

8   He was being so stuffed with miscellaneous facts, with such an indigestible mass of material, that he had no time (and was given no encouragement) to draw on his own resources, to use his own mind for analyzing and synthesizing and evaluating this material.

9   Education, to have any meaning beyond the purpose of creating well-informed dunces, must elicit from the pupil what is latent in every human being—the rules of reason, the inner knowledge of what is proper for men to be and do, the ability to sift evidence and come to conclusions that can generally be assented to by all open minds and warm hearts.

10   Pupils are more like oysters than sausages. The job of teaching is not to stuff them and then seal them up, but to help them open and reveal the riches within. There are pearls is each of us, if only we knew how to cultivate them with ardor and persistence.

PRACTICE

Discussion

1. What are the responsibilities of a teacher, according to Harris? What are the responsibilities of a student? How do current discussions of education fail to address these responsibilities?

2. Who are Hocking, Hamilton, and Socrates? What does their presence in Harris' essay tell you about his value system? His ethical proof?

3. Is Harris' view of education a bit too simple? What limitations do you perceive in his approach? Can you expand the pearl analogy to illustrate a broader view?

4. Are Harris' analogies figurative or literal? If you said figurative, suggest a literal analogy for education. If you said literal, suggest a figurative one. How might you take either of these analogies too far?

5. Is Harris still using the sausage-casing analogy in paragraph 8? Explain.

6. List every repetition of the term *put into* or a variation of the phrase that you can find in the essay. Do the same with *draw out*. Why is the variation important? How can repetition be effective? Has Harris overdone the two?

7. What is the composition of the audience at which this essay is most probably aimed? To what part of that audience are the references in paragraphs 3 and 4 like to appeal? To what part of the audience is the reference in paragraph 7 likely to appeal?

8. What figurative analogy is Socrates quoted as drawing? What literal analogy does he make? Why is analogy a strategy particularly well suited to Harris' thesis?

Vocabulary

animate	futile	latent
casing	succinctly	assented
[Socratic] dialogue	synthesizing	cultivate
axioms	elicit	ardor

Writing

1. Use a fresh analogy to explain your sense of what your education was like in elementary or secondary school compared to what it is like in college.

2. Describe a former teacher who treated you like an oyster or a sausage casing. Explain how you reacted.

3. Define the proper role and responsibilities of a student. Try to use analogy to make your definition clear.

Ann H. Zwinger

BECOMING MOM TO AN INFANT WORD PROCESSOR

Nature writer Ann H. Zwinger was born in Muncie, Indiana, in 1925. She earned a B.A. degree from Wellesley College in 1946 and an M.A. from Indiana University in 1950. Mother of three daughters as well as infant word processor, she currently lives in Colorado Springs. Her books include Land Above the Trees: A Guide to the American Alpine Tundra *(1970), which was nominated for the National Book Award;* Run, River, Run: A Naturalist's Journey Down One of the Great Rivers of the West *(1975);* A Conscious Stillness: Two Naturalists on Thoreau's River *(1982); and* A Desert Country Near the Sea *(1983). The latter two created the need for a computer. The essay that follows, which appeared in the February, 1982 issue of* Smithsonian *magazine, was, presumably, written on a word processor.*

1   A decade ago I graduated to an electric typewriter which, since I type my own manuscripts, was a godsend. Within the last year, however, I found myself with two books to finish almost simultaneously, and when my agent sent me an article about the growing number of writers using word processors, working with one seemed the answer to endless hours of arduous typing when you've just run out of available hours.

2   But becoming the mother of a work processor is not simple. It is like adopting a child. First there were preliminary interviews which, I suspect, may have indicated my fitness for leasehood, such as: Will this person be able to "think computer"? Will she take the time to train it in the way it ought to go?

3   After the order was placed (I refrained from saying I didn't care if it were a boy or girl), my workroom was checked to see if I had the proper environment for the new infant. My work desk had proper triple-pronged sockets, but cagily I did not let anyone see my pack rat's dream of a back room in which old and new manuscripts, shells and rocks, account book, index cards, unlabeled Diptera, *Gourmet* magazines back to 1970, and dictionaries all coexist in tottering equilibrium.

4   Finally the thing in question arrived. No young mother ever as proudly removed her first child from the hospital as I did the word processor from its packing, plugging numbered plugs into numbered sockets. When I turned it on the CRT (for cathode ray tube) hummed gently, a *most* satisfactory child.

5   But not the printer. The printer balked and I had to call the pedia—sorry, repairman—who spent almost a whole afternoon adjusting, tickling its rollers, and offering lollipops, until it, too, sprang into proper configuration with a triumphant whirl.

6   Then began the training period. Mine, not its. Immediately the inevitable occurred: a whole sentence simply kept spacing to the right, running down into the next line. And it

simply would not come back. I chased it by cursor and by scatological comment. Neither worked. Finally I "thought computer." I won, but not without some scars on my ego.

7   I soon discovered that I simply needed to apply a little parental guidance and all would work well. When I requested "MOVE" it queried MOVE WHAT? and then "WHERE TO?" And when I chucked it under the cursor it made typing an uninterrupted flowing delight; it moved paragraphs, created intriguing juxtapositions, and even enhanced the opportunity for creative play. And, *mirabile dictu,* it even corrected my spelling!

8   The printer got clean ribbons when necessary and was fed paper when hungry. We developed a working relationship of considerable satisfaction to all of us. Or so *I* thought.

9   Then came growing pains. The CRT spit out petulantly, "Printer error, printer error!" And the other machine grated "Ratchety ratchety BLAT!" The CRT flashed accusingly: "Printer reprinting. Check output." So, I checked.

10   After that, the inevitable: adolescence. Having been through it with assorted children, I should have been prepared. But somehow one never is. The CRT took three chapters and ran. Absconded. Three hard-worked chapters. Gone into the ether.

11   And the printer. When I stood beside it, it behaved. But let me step out of the room and, like a greedy teenager, it stuffed paper onto its roller as fast as it could. And jammed.

12   Well, what can you do but forgive, forget—and (sigh) retype? Hope your patience and forbearance will be rewarded? And at last I do believe I see signs of real maturity in the CRT. Giving a little. Seeing things my way once in a while. Not losing things so much. Growing up.

13   And just lately I've been able to fix a sandwich in relative serenity while the printer bleeps and burrs out Chapter 5. The CRT is even getting not to mind a little mayonnaise on its keys, and on arduous days, is not averse to a chocolate bar alongside.

14   I wonder: has anyone written a diet program for a matronly WP?

PRACTICE

Discussion

1. To what specific steps in a child's development does Zwinger liken her learning to use her word processor? Where does she begin a step in the analogy, pretend to hesitate, and then roll into the analogy full-tilt? Why does she pretend to hesitate?

2. How much previous experience does the author have with machines? How much experience does she have with children? How do her two types of experiences help her with her word processor?

3. What does Zwinger mean by the term "think computer?" What scars do you think she acquired on her ego in the process of learning to "think computer"?

4. How does Zwinger order the steps of her analogy? What advantages might she gain by using a different organization of points? What might she lose?

5. What is amusing about the use of dialogue in the essay? You have been advised by the authors of this text to "avoid unnecessary repetition of the

speakers' names or unnecessary descriptions of the way they speak." Should Zwinger get a "D" for dialogue? Explain.

6. In general, the longer sentences in the essay deal with what kind of content? With what content do the shorter sentences and fragments generally deal? Point out a good example of each.

7. Run a "transition check" on Zwinger's essay, i.e., list all the first words of every paragraph after the first. What interesting patterns do you perceive in the list? Are Zwinger transitions smooth? clear?

8. In the last two paragraphs, Zwinger switches from figurative to literal analogy. Explain what happens there. Is Zwinger in trouble by mixing the two types of analogy?

Vocabulary

godsend	configuration	*mirabile dictu*
arduous	cursor	absconded
Diptera	scatological	ether
cathode ray tube	chucked	

Writing

1. Pull a reversal on Zwinger's article and write an essay on "Becoming a Child to a Parental Computer."

2. Write an essay showing how using a computer is like playing a sport of your choice.

3. Write an essay about a human activity that has, in your opinion, become overly regimented and mindlessly mechanized (registering for courses, perhaps, or seeing a doctor). Use an analogy to a machine, a factory, or a mechanized process to make your point.

A. M. Rosenthal

LEGALIZING ADDICTIVE DRUGS LIKE BRINGING BACK SLAVERY

A. M. Rosenthal is best known as a New York Times *reporter and editor. As a reporter he filed stories from the United Nations, Warsaw, Geneva, and Tokyo. He won the Pulitzer Prize for international reporting in 1960. Rosenthal rose through the ranks of various editorships at the* Times, *until he was made executive editor in 1977. He is now a highly respected syndicated columnist for the newspaper. His wide experience in the world does not let him take certain subjects lightly, nor does he tend to care for "on the other hand, I see my opponent's point" arguments. Those who would legalize drugs, he believes, are simply wrong.*

1   Across the country, a scattered but influential collection of intellectuals is intensely engaged in making the case for slavery. With considerable passion, these Americans are repeatedly expounding the benefits of not only tolerating slavery but legalizing it.

2   Legalization, they say, would make life less dangerous for the free. It would save a great deal of money. And since the economies could be used to improve the lot of the slaves, in the end they would be better off. The new anti-abolitionists, like their predecessors in the 19th century, concede that those now in bondage do not themselves see the benefits of legalizing their status. But in time they will, we are assured, because the beautiful part of legalization is that slavery would be designed so as to keep slaves pacified with the very thing that enslaves them!

3   The form of slavery under discussion is drug addiction. It does not have every characteristic of more traditional forms of bondage. But they have enough in common to make the comparison morally valid—and the campaign for drug legalization morally disgusting.

4   Like the plantation slavery that was a foundation of American society for so long, drug addiction largely involves specifiable groups of people. Most of the enchained are children and adolescents of all colors and black and Hispanic adults. Like plantation slavery, drug addiction is passed on from generation to generation. And this may be the most important similarity: like plantation slavery, addiction will destroy among its victims the social resources most valuable to free people for their own betterment—family units, family traditions, family values.

5   Anti-abolitionists argue that legalization would make drugs so cheap and available that the profit for crime would be removed. Well-supplied addicts would be peaceful addicts. We would not waste billions for jails. We could spend some of the savings helping the addicted become drug-free. That would happen at the very time that new millions of Americans were being enticed into addiction by legalization.

6   Are we really foolish enough to believe that tens of thousands of drug gang members would meekly steal away, foiled by the marvels of the free market? Not likely. The pushers would cut prices, making more money than ever from the ever-growing mass market. They would immediately increase the potency and variety beyond anything available at any government-approved narcotics counters. Crime would increase. Crack produces paranoid violence. More permissiveness equals more use equals more violence. And what will legalization do to the brains of Americans drawn into drug slavery by easy availability?

7   Earlier this year, an expert drug pediatrician told me that after only a few months babies born with crack addiction seemed to recover. Now we learn that stultifying behavioral effects last at least through early childhood. Will they last forever? How long will crack affect neurological patterns in the brains of adult crack users? Dr. Gabriel Nahas of Columbia University argues in his new book, *Cocaine: The Great White Plague,* that the damage may be irreversible. Would it not be an act of simple intelligence to drop the legalization campaign until we find out?

8   Then why do a number of writers and academicians, left to right, support it? I have discussed this with anti-drug leaders like Jesse Jackson, Dr. Mitchell Rosenthal of Phoenix House and William Bennett, who search for answers themselves.

9   Perhaps the answer is that the legalizers are not dealing with reality in America. I think the reason has to do with class. Crack is beginning to move into the white middle and upper classes. That is a tragedy for those addicted. However, it has not yet destroyed the communities around which their lives revolve, not taken over every street and doorway. It has not passed generation to generation among them, killing

the continuity of family. But in ghetto communities poverty and drugs come together in a catalytic reaction that is reducing them to social rubble.

10   The anti-abolitionists, virtually all white and well-to-do, do not see or do not care. Either way, they show symptoms of the callousness of class. That can be a particularly dangerous social disorder.

PRACTICE

Discussion

1. Check again the *diagram* of an analogy (page 355). Make a similar diagram of Rosenthal's analogy.

2. Looking at your diagram, do you find any flaw in the extended comparison (analogy)?

3. Explain the *order* of points in the analogy.

4. Which side of the analogy is *known* (see page 353)? Why does the author use *this* known side, rather than some other? Suggest two or three different knowns, of varying effectiveness, that the author might have used.

5. Is the whole essay an analogy? Explain your answer.

6. What is the job of paragraphs 5–10? How do they give you confidence in the writer's knowledge and experience (ethical proof)?

7. Why does the author wait until paragraph 3 to make his main point: "The form of slavery under discussion is drug addiction"?

8. Explain the purpose of the last two sentences of paragraph 3.

Vocabulary

abolitionists	enticed	permissiveness
bondage	foiled	paranoid
pacified	potency	

Writing

1. Write a brief paper in which you *expand* Rosenthal's analogy, using more points of comparison.

2. Write an attack on Rosenthal's argument, pointing out any weaknesses you see in the analogy.

3. Write an argument using Rosenthal's historical technique of comparison on other American social problems. *Examples:* abortion, day care, America as peacekeeper for the world, crime, punishment, sex and violence, etc.

CHAPTER 20

Argument

In argument, the writer says to readers: I want to *convince* you of something. I want you to believe in the facts of a certain proposition; or I want you to take action of a particular kind. Or I want to persuade you that another person's argument is wrong (*refutation*).

Because argument tries to convince readers to believe or to act (or not to believe or act), it follows that the major rhetorical structures of argument are those of *fact, action,* and *refutation.* These structures can be independent or mixed. Some fact arguments are pure fact; they don't suggest, explicitly, any action at all. By contrast, most arguments of action evolve out of fact arguments and will mention these facts in one way or another. Refutations may depend on both fact and action arguments, interweaving them as necessary.

▼ The Fact Structure: An argument that deals with the past or present

Here we give five theses that might be employed in the fact structure. What do they have in common?

1. Abraham Lincoln's assassin was part of a federal conspiracy originating in Lincoln's own government.

2. Shakespeare's *Romeo and Juliet* is a series of brilliant scenes interlarded with long passages of flat, ordinary blank verse.

3. Judge Richard Mulvaney had the legal training to be chosen for the United States Supreme Court.

4. According to the oral evidence of their own flight recorder, the pilots on Flight 331 were negligent in their duties.

5. The engineer's report proves that the bridge on Seventh Street was obviously in need of repair just before it collapsed on November 8.

These theses—representing arguments—are alike in that they all talk about things and ideas *in the present or the past.* They rigorously avoid mentioning the future *or any suggestion for action.* But the arguments are different in that they cover a wide range of argumentative possibilities. Number 1 belongs to the realm of interpretive history. Number 2 is a literary value judgment. Number 3 is—or appears to be—a fairly cool accounting of facts about the legal training necessary to be on the Supreme Court. Number 4 is an inference based on the oral evidence found on the plane's flight recorder. Number 5 may be the most objective of the grouping, depending as it does on a written report about the condition of the bridge.

Judging the five arguments only on their theses, we might say that each is arguable—with varying degrees of probable success, depending on the quantity and quality of the evidence. The fact that number 2 is a value judgment cannot be held against it. Many arguments involve value judgments—book reviews, for instance, or debates about the effectiveness of a pitcher who just lost the final game in the World Series.

The most noteworthy thing about the argument of fact is that it can deal only with the present or past. It cannot argue anything about the future. It cannot argue for change or for an action to be taken (these occur in the future). Of course, after reading a fact argument, readers may decide that they would like to see a change of some kind.

What is the value of the distinction just described? To many young writers, argumentation often seems more difficult than it is. They can have trouble with the relationship between arguments that say "This is true" (*fact*) and those that say "I want this particular change made" (*action*). But after you have studied the two structures of argument separately, you will discover that arguing effectively is often quite easy. (Action *patterns* are presented in pages 374–375.)

Here are five typical theses for a fact argument. After each thesis, we give the time element for the argument involved.

1. People who call themselves "patriots" are not necessarily either good or intelligent people. (*past and present*)

2. Originally, the Ku Klux Klan was more than just a political group designed to intimidate blacks. (*past*)

3. The basic damage of pornography to human beings is that it turns the unthinkable into the thinkable. (*past and present*)

4. *Ten Bad Days* [a college play] was an amateurish production—badly written, badly directed, and badly acted. (*past*)

5. For many students, objective tests are harder to take than essay tests. (*past and present*)

Here is an example of the organization found in a typical structure of a fact argument:

INTRODUCTION
    thesis stated
    terms defined, if necessary
BODY OF ARGUMENT
    first main idea
        evidence and reasons   (Use more or fewer main
    second main idea   ideas, depending on
        evidence and reasons   your material)
    third main idea
        evidence and reasons
CONCLUSION

▼ Two Sample Papers Written Using the Fact Structure

1   I went to see *Ten Bad Days* for two reasons. First, as an ordinary theatre-goer, I go to plays just as other people do. Second, as a theatre major in one of the dozen biggest theatre departments in the country I feel I have a responsibility to see an all-student production—written, directed, and staged by students only. I made a serious mistake. Watching paint dry couldn't be as boring as *Ten Bad Days.* From start to finish, the play was badly done—in a word, amateurish.

2   The writing was dreadful. Granted that the writer, Karl Ladke, set himself an awesome problem trying to capture the character of Ellen Aurthur, one of the most contradictory women who ever lived. She was, for instance, both a romantic defender of the poor and a self-satisfied member of the wealthy class. But Ladke could not make Ellen Aurthur believable, nor could he create a believable theme (about her) for the play. As the student director, Paul Mindt, said in an interview, "Ladke had a very hard time trying to deal with the inconsistencies in Aurthur's life—we couldn't get a narrative handle on the character and the inconsistencies in her life." Neither writer nor director could solve that problem. The script of the play never finds a center or a conflict that you can believe in. It is a basic sign of an amateurish script when the leading character wanders around on stage looking for relevant events to happen to her.

3   The direction is equally bad. Many scenes have no emphasis, no real beginning or end. Ellen Aurthur is supposedly the center of the action, but actually the director (Mindt) usually shows her as being acted upon. Worst of all, when faced with dramatic problems as a director, Mindt chooses to drop into fatuous sentimentality. For example, more than once Aurthur and her lover get into an old car—mocked up on stage—and moon about their inability to join their lives together. Mindt actually uses romantic background music from the 1930s in each of these scenes. The whole thing is so maudlin it is embarrassing.

4   Finally, the acting is no better than highschoolish. In other productions, Leila Williams has been accused of acting with her hair. In this one, she acts with her hair, her elbows, and out of the corner of her eyes. She hides behind an accent that sounds half-Oklahoma, half-New Jersey. She totally misses the quality of Ellen Aurthur, who in her complexity had a side as hard as diamonds. As her lover, Ken Ihnen is bad in a way that

is hard to describe. In scene after scene, he seems to think he is a stage prop, standing around like a drawing in an old back-and-white cartoon.

5   The script of *Ten Bad Days* won a national student playwright award last year, which I guess was the reason the play was produced here. But on the third night of the local run, the theatre was practically empty. Word of mouth gets around fast. A dead turkey like *Ten Bad Days* smells just awful after only two bad nights.

—Bill Morse

For a refutation to this argument, see pages 377–378.

PRACTICE

Discussion

1. Which paragraphs form the introduction and conclusion? How well do these paragraphs work? Where is the *thesis* stated? Why is this placement of the thesis valuable to the *reader*? To the *writer*?

2. Check the organization of a typical *fact structure* (page 371). Does Morse follow this pattern closely? How many *main ideas* does Morse have in his argument? (Can you *prove* that your answer to the last question is true? Be specific.)

3. List the pieces of *evidence* that Morse uses under each *main idea*. Are you convinced by this evidence?

4. Rate Morse's argument as a whole. Is it *Very good, Good, Fair, Poor,* or *Failing*? Defend your answer.

5. If you rated Morse's argument as *Fair, Poor,* or *Failing,* write a letter to him explaining in detail how his argument could be improved.

Note: You will read two papers (following, and page 375) by Pearl Ralphson on the problem of smoking in the Palmer Insurance offices. Both papers are directed to Jerrold Palmer, one of the co-owners of Palmer Insurance, a local independent firm with an office suite in a mall about a mile from the community college where Pearl Ralphson goes to school.

You will see Ralphson designing both of her arguments to appeal to Jerrold Palmer. She also designs them to take into account the law in her state on the use of tobacco in a workplace. Anyone who has a bad physical response to tobacco smoke can be considered legally a "handicapped person." The state Human Rights Act protects handicapped individuals from discrimination and requires employers to make reasonable efforts to accommodate them. Jerrold Palmer, of course, knows about the Human Rights Act.

CLEAN AIR IN THE OFFICE

1   I am writing about the recent decision by the owners of Palmer Insurance not to ban cigarette smoking in our suite of offices. Would you please reconsider that decision in light of certain problems I face as I work for Palmer Insurance?

2   Seven people work in the Palmer suite—the two owners, the secretary for the owners, two junior secretaries, the company bookkeeper, and one part-time student helper—me. I work twenty hours a week. Of the seven people, four smoke. The secretary is a chain-smoker.

3   Cigarette smoke permeates the entire suite. Because I need the work time (and the money), I come in before anyone else, at seven in the morning. (I greatly appreciate Palmer letting me do this; it has been a big help.) When I open the door, the smell of stale smoke hits me in the face. Last year, I used to open all the windows and try to air out the suite. This winter, Jack Palmer told me—"reluctantly," he said—that the heating system couldn't catch up properly after an hour of cold wind in the suite. Without this airing-out process, the office smells terrible *all* the time.

4   This cigarette smoke is hurting me. My throat is sore night and day. My nose is stuffed up, and my sinuses hurt. I feel so bad sometimes that my study habits are being affected. I am having serious trouble sleeping, because when I lie down I can't breathe. Last week I went to the college infirmary, and the doctor said that I appear to have a definite allergy to tobacco, and that the allergy would only get worse if I continued to breathe smoke in the office where I work.

5   But I can't very well find a new job at this point in the term. This is a very good job, as a matter of fact. I make up my own schedule, come and go as I please, and am thoroughly trusted by all the people I work for. But I can't do Palmer Insurance work in my dorm room, a non-smoking room, by the way. I am stuck. No other job—if I can get one—will pay me as well for a schedule I have designed myself. I need the money to stay in college, but I can't continue working in the Palmer suite.

6   In your opinion, what should I do?

—Pearl Ralphson

PRACTICE

1. Is Ralphson's Paper a *fact* argument, as we describe it on pages 369–371? Why or why not?

2. Ralphson's argument is somewhat different from Morse's (pages 371–372). List any points of difference you find. Using material from both arguments, explain why Ralphson chose to make her argument different from Morse's. *Is she right in doing this?* Explain.

3. What are the *main ideas* in her argument? Are they clearly stated? Are they "reasonable"?

4. List the examples of *evidence and reasons* that support her *main ideas*. Do you find weaknesses in any of these?

5. Are *you* convinced by her argument? If you were *Jerrold Palmer,* would you be convinced?

▼ The Action Structure: An argument that deals with the future

The action argument has two major characteristics. First, it calls for a change. The whole point of the writer is: "I want something done!" The second major characteristic is that the action must take place in the *future.*

In structure, the action argument looks like this:

INTRODUCTION
    State the *problem*
    Define *terms* (if necessary)   *Use the most logical order*
    State your *thesis* (the change
       that you want made)
    Explain why the change is
       needed (a *fact* argument)
       [see the following note below]
BODY OF ARGUMENT
    First main idea concerning change
       detail: evidence and reasons   *(Use more or fewer main*
    Second main idea concerning change   *ideas, depending on*
       detail: evidence and reasons   *your material)*
    Third main idea concerning change
       detail: evidence and reasons
CONCLUSION

Note: You have to use your own judgment about explaining the need for action in your introduction. If you think that the need is obvious, you will have little or nothing to say about it. If you have already argued the need in a fact argument, there should be little reason to develop it again. Finally, you should be aware that some theses require two arguments-in-one—a need (fact) paper combined with a proposed change (action) paper. By their nature, such papers tend to be pretty long. In order to keep their assignments down to a reasonable length, most students prefer to write either fact or action arguments.

    Check with your instructor on what he or she prefers.

■■■ *Example Of An Action Structure*

This argument is a continuation of the problem in Pearl Ralphson's student paper on page 373. As before, the argument is directed to Jerrold Palmer, co-owner of Palmer Insurance Co. For necessary background, read the *Note* on page 372.

1   Thank you very much for talking to me on Tuesday about the smoking problem in the office suite. I much appreciate your taking the time to look into the issues I raised. As I understand the situation, you will consider a suggestion on my part to solve the problem, at least so far as I am concerned. So I'll suggest a specific solution, based on the facts as I see them at this time.

2   I believe we should work towards getting a completely smoke-free office. By *smoke-free office*, I mean one that is completely free of tobacco smoke 24 hours a day. Of the four people who smoke, three—as you told me on Tuesday—are willing to give up smoking in the office. But the secretary [name omitted] has pointed out that she smokes two packs between 8:00 and 5:00, and cannot leave the office to smoke and still do her work.

3   I much appreciate that three of the four smokers have agreed to smoke elsewhere. There are ashtrays on the wall in the mall hallway just outside the office. People can also smoke in the restrooms down the hall. The women's restroom is just across from the Palmer suite, and very easy to reach.

4   With your permission, I will come in next Sunday and air out the suite by opening all the windows for a few hours. I will stay the whole time so that there will be no possibility of burglars coming in through an open window. I will also spray the place with Fresh Clean.

5   The one remaining problem is with the secretary, who has said that she cannot smoke outside the suite and still do her work. I have talked directly to her about this problem. We have not become enemies over the situation, but we have not been able to reach an agreement either. She points out that she has been smoking heavily for 35 years, and to ask her to stop now might mean that she would have to leave her job. Although the law is on my side in this case, I am reluctant to push for a legal resolution, and hope that the problem can be resolved in some other way.

6   Please remember, I am not asking for these changes in the Palmer office because I have anything against smokers or the smoking habit. I am not a fanatic who wants everybody else to have no fun—to be grim and miserable. I have an illness: tobacco smoke makes me sick. My work and my future are, to some extent, at stake. No one would force me to drink alcohol on the job and become useless to your company. Why force me to inhale tobacco smoke?

—Pearl Ralphson

PRACTICE

1. Are Ralphson's attitude and tone different in this argument from those in her fact argument (page 373)? If you find differences, do you approve of them?

2. Where is her *thesis* that asks for change? Do you approve of this placement?

3. One reader of this argument has called Ralphson's definition in paragraph 2 "hamhanded and unnecessary"? Do you agree? Why or why not?

4. Do you have any trouble identifying the *details* of her proposed changes? What are they exactly, and where are they placed in the argument? Are they in the right place?

5. Are Ralphson's proposed changes reasonable and reasonably described?

6. Why isn't she more forceful about the secretary's smoking? In this situation, would you be more forceful?

7. What has Ralphson done in this argument to make *herself* look good?

8. Do you accept the analogy at the end of paragraph 6?

▼ The Refutation Structure

A refutation is an argument expressly designed to rebut—to "knock down"—an argument someone else has previously made. (We will call this someone else your opponent.) Refutations can be of several kinds, all of which are classified here into two broad types—(a) those that refute by *showing that your opponent's argument is flawed,* and (b) those that refute by *creating a different* (or somewhat different) *argument on the same topic.*

The classic instances of these types will be immediately familiar to you if you think of the courtroom dramas so popular on TV in recent years:

a. *Refutation by showing that your opponent's argument is flawed*

The defense attorney speaks, addressing a witness on the stand:

"Now, Captain Jones, you say that the gun used in the murder was a .45, but the bullet taken from the body of Joe Smith was from a .38. And you claimed earlier that the deceased had been dead five hours when the body was discovered. But our expert witness said that the condition of the body as described by the coroner places the time of death several hours earlier. And you claim that a motive for the murder was financial because the victim was robbed. Yet we have learned from witnesses that the woman—Mrs. X—accused of this murder had in effect taken a vow of poverty some years ago; her average personal income over the past five years was only $1,000 a year. Can you logically expect us to believe that such a woman would kill another human being for money?"

b. *Refutation by creating a different* (or somewhat different) *argument on the same topic*

The same defense attorney speaks:

"Ladies and Gentlemen of the Jury—I do not know what happened in the murder of Joe Smith. But I think I know what did *not* happen. No evidence places the accused, Mrs. X, at the scene of the crime. At the time Smith died, she was washing dishes in full view of an administrator at the orphanage. Furthermore, she had no motive to kill Smith, no access to the weapon (which has never been found), and no criminal record. To say that Mrs. X committed this crime is beyond all common sense. She did not do it, and she must be set free!"

You can refute your opponent by combining these two types in whatever way you see fit. A refutation is a form of legitimate attack using rhetorical weapons. It is usually most successful if you study your opponent's argument from every possible angle. Study that argument, and ask yourself:

- Is the *evidence* solid? Any weak points anywhere?
- Are the *authorities* used (or quoted) believable?
- Are the *issues* properly identified? Is it possible that your opponent has based the argument on a minor or irrelevant issue?
- Is the *thesis* clear, reasonable, unified, debatable?
- Are there any *irrelevancies* in the argument?
- Are there any *fallacies*? (See pages 380–389 for a discussion of fallacies.)
- Is there anything about your opponent's *tone* or *attitude* that is objectionable?
- Is your opponent *prejudiced*?

Warning: Don't bring up either of the last two points unless you can show— using evidence—that prejudice or poor tone exists in the written argument.

If, after studying your opponent's argument, you believe that it deserves refutation, write the refutation as objectively as you can. Throughout, be gracious to your opponent and to his or her ideas. Snideness and bad temper will seldom help you—and may hurt.

No standard outline of *refutation* arguments is satisfactory, because too much depends on the argument you are attacking and the total situation. The following example of a refutation should be helpful.

■■■ *An Example of Refutation Structure*

This refutation is written in response to Bill Morse's argument, pages 371–372.

1   Bill Morse is a very bright critic. Bill Morse is entertaining. Bill Morse is sharp-eyed, demanding, and relentless. In addition, he is not really fair to *Ten Bad Days* or to the people who did the play.

2   Of course Bill is right about some things. The script does not give a full portrait of the remarkable Ellen Aurthur. The theme of the play "wobbles," and at times you are not sure what the point is. The acting is uneven. But it is curious that Bill makes no mention of the wonderful performance of Jeri Haven, who did not get a bad notice from anybody for her acting of Miss Baillie. It was a great part and greatly played.

3   This production of the play in general was more competently handled than Bill will admit. The writer was not a complete amateur; Karl Ladke has won two awards for writing, including the one Bill mentioned. Moreover, Ladke worked very hard on the *Bad Days* script; and—with the help of the director, Paul Mindt—did six or seven drafts. The two of them wrote and rewrote the script all last semester, right up until the last day of rehearsal. The problem was, of course, that to this day no one really knows very much about the "secret" life of Ellen Aurthur. Above all, she was an actress making up her own life as she went along. Her unpublished diaries seem to be partly fiction, representing her life as she wished she was living it. Ladke's script had to be an imaginative guess from beginning to end.

4   Ladke and Mindt decided to make *Ten Bad Days* into a romance centering on the theme (according to Mindt) of how a romantic personality deals with social conventions. Bill

ignores this fact, centering his attack on the romance only. But the two main characters, as played by Leila Williams and Ken Ihnen, *were* acting out a romance—one that each character saw differently. Who was "free" (and when), and who was "hobbled by conventions"? When Bill says (negatively) that Aurthur/Williams kept "looking for relevant events to happen to her," he was partly right. Only Bill did not understand the meaning of his own observation. Williams was merely playing the part as written, based on the theme of how much freedom of action could balance against how much convention in a love affair.

5   Yes, the theatre was nearly empty the third night of *Ten Bad Days.* But we won the biggest football game of the season late that afternoon. The streets were full of celebrating students until 2:00 the next morning. The romance of football and an invitation to a bowl game won out over a romantic student production based on the diaries of an almost unknown woman from the dust bowl of Oklahoma in the 1930s. Is anybody surprised at that?

—Maureen Durdan

PRACTICE

Discussion

1. On pages 376–377 we explain the general and particular strategies of designing a refutation. Referring specifically to these strategies, explain in detail how Durdan designed her refutation to Morse's paper (pages 371–372). Do you agree with her choices? What, if anything, would you have done differently?

2. What word in Durdan's first paragraph "controls" the entire argument? What would you say to Durdan's comment that "this word is the most important word in my refutation"?

3. Explain the rhetorical "switch" in paragraph 1. Why did Durdan create the switch?

4. Paragraph 2 employs what has been called "a very common technique in refutation arguments." Employing your own words, describe this technique—and defend or attack it.

5. What point do the *details* in Durdan's refutation support? Do all of them support this point?

6. Do you approve of her conclusion? Is the reference to the football game necessary to her refutation?

7. As a whole, is Durdan's refutation successful?

PRACTICE

Discussion

Discussion the following argument as a refutation. Using details from his argument, explain how Lawrence Wade, a black newspaper columnist (syndicated), designed the refutation. How convincing is it?

Writing

If you wish to refute Wade himself, ask your instructor about writing a refutation for your class.

AFFIRMATIVE ACTION JUST RENEWS RACISM

1   Affirmative action to get blacks into sports management would insult the name of Jackie Robinson. When Robinson came to bat in 1947, it didn't mean some white guy lost his turn. None of the early black ballplayers was hired for color. Sure, color was an issue. But the real issue was, why weren't black players who were as good as whites (and often better) allowed to play? Robinson proved that he belonged. In just two years, he was named the National League's most valuable player. And for his career achievement, he joined his colleagues in the Baseball Hall of Fame.

2   Once given a chance, blacks achieved in basketball and football. Now, stars are developing even in "white" games like golf and tennis. And it hasn't taken affirmative action to get blacks into these major sports. So why assume that quotas—or quotas in disguise, called "goals and timetables"—are needed to get blacks into sports management?

3   I suspect it's because some well-meaning people believe, when it comes to the "thinking" jobs, that blacks can't compete. That's racism at its worst, and it's not supported by what's happening in football. After years of complaints about the lack of black quarterbacks, suddenly they're appearing in the professional ranks.

4   Are these affirmative-action quarterbacks? No. They're the result of market forces working on campus. In recent years, coaches have been willing to give black quarterbacks a chance. These coaches do it not because it's "the right thing to do." They do it because they like winning. Other coaches have followed suit, even if they're personally prejudiced. No one likes coaches who don't win. The same economic forces will work in the major leagues. Let a few blacks succeed in management, and more will be hired.

5   It's also important to realize that management hasn't been as attractive to black athletes as the higher-paying and personally rewarding physical jobs. How many ex-managers sell beer or rental cars on TV? Why would any truly successful player opt for the front office? And if any guy other than Merlin Olsen tried to sell flowers, he'd be called a pansy—and worse. Black athletes haven't sought management for economic reasons. But as their numbers grow, we'll see more managers. Every black ballplayer can't be a superstar. Most white managers weren't stars themselves.

6   Is there racism in baseball? Of course. But no more than in football, basketball, or a major corporation. What's needed aren't many black managers who will fail and make bigots happy. What's needed are a few Jackie Robinsons who will succeed.

—Lawrence Wade

Writing

Write a short refutation to either of the arguments presented below.

1   "What are your moral justifications for hunting?"

2   The man who asked me this is my neighbor, a well-educated and thoughtful newcomer to our little valley in northeast Vermont. He and his partner have just built a small house across the way. We want to be friends; there are going to be difficulties.

3   My first reaction is to trot out all the standard, unconvincing arguments about game management, about hunting as a last vestige of our primitive selves. It's easy, after so many years of assault, to feel defensive about this subject. Instead, I have a Socratic inspiration.

4   What are your justifications for *not* hunting?" I ask.

5   So I get to listen to *his* standard, unconvincing arguments: the sacredness of life; the obligation not to interfere with its mechanisms; the storm of death; the suffering; the continuing evolution of man.

6   The hypocrisy of all this is staggering.

7   The only opponents of hunting I'll listen to for long are vegetarians. I won't listen for a minute to meat eaters who pay the butcher and supermarket to kill, package, and distribute their meals. But even the most sophistic arguments of the vegetarians inevitably irritate me. It's funny, they all think I'm kidding when I ask if plants feel pain. Plants can fill their lives with peace, and their stomachs with nourishment; plant life fashions dazzling displays of color and shape and even responds to classical music. But when the gardener approaches with pruning shears, suddenly plants are numb and indifferent.

8   I am not a theologian who can argue complicated precepts of morality. I am, I hope, a reasonably intelligent and sensitive man who tries to think clearly about what he does. And what I do is hunt, and sometimes kill.

—John C. Dunlap

Public humiliation is a surprisingly effective and low-cost way of deterring criminals and expressing the moral order of a community. It is used by a few judges, but much too sparingly. Some jurisdictions publish the names of "Johns" who are caught frequenting prostitutes. Lincoln County in Oregon will plea-bargain with a criminal only if he first puts an advertisement in a local newspaper, apologizing for his crime. This is limited, in practice, to nonviolent criminals, including some burglars and thieves. The ad includes the criminal's picture and is paid for by him. Judges in Sarasota, Fla. and in Midwest City, Okla., have required people caught driving while under the influence to display an easy-to-see sticker on their cars: "Convicted of Drunken Driving."

—Amitai Etzioni

▼ Deception in Argument—How to Avoid Fallacies

A *fallacy* is a flaw in an argument. The word itself comes from a Latin expression meaning "to deceive." The argumentative flaws called *fallacies* are basically deceptions created by the writer, often unintentionally. A few fallacies, like the *ad hominem,* on page 381, seem to be the result of malice. Finally, some of them occur from simple carelessness on the writer's part.

Students occasionally have trouble with the study of fallacies. No wonder—the "signs" of fallacy are often ambiguous or misleading. For instance, if five students try to identify *the* fallacy in a passage, they may identify three or four different ones and finish by arguing amongst themselves to little purpose. Also, they may reject an argument completely because they find one fallacy in it. Of course, some fallacies are so bad that they will ruin an entire argument.

It may help to consider fallacies as metaphorically analogous to "flaws" in the human body—diseases, for instance, along with other ailments. Suppose you have a mild depression, a badly pulled muscle in one leg, and a deep cavity in a tooth—three "flaws" in one body, and all different. These are inconvenient enough that (with the help of a psychologist, physician, and dentist) you will try to do something about them. But you wouldn't believe that your bodily flaws are so serious you should write your will and make an appointment with the undertaker. Moreover, you can guess that one of your bodily flaws is related to the other two—you're depressed because your pulled leg muscle keeps you in bed and the cavity in your tooth hurts.

When you look for fallacies in an argument you write, (1) don't be surprised to find two or three related fallacies tangled up together, rather like the ailments in a human body. And (2) don't assume that a fallacy always wrecks an argument completely. If you can omit or rewrite the fallacious sentence or paragraph, your argument may become healthy again. On the other hand, if the fallacy-flaw is bad enough—if it permeates your thesis or the body of your argument—you may have to give the paper a decent burial and start over.

▼ Fallacies Listed and Defined

■■■ *Ad Hominem*

The Latin expression *ad hominem* means "to the man." The fallacy is that of attacking the person who makes the argument while (usually) ignoring the argument itself. An *ad hominem* fallacy is a form of rhetorical brick-throwing; the attacker is trying to hurt his opponent rather than deal with the issues or evidence in the case. Examples:

1. "I think we should all remember that Senator J— R——, who is hypocritically defending his civil rights record in the Senate, hired no minorities in his Tennessee plant until he was forced to hire them because of rights legislation in the 1970s."

   Comment: If the argument is about the senator's civil rights record in the Senate, one should argue about that record rather than attacking the Senator personally as a hypocrite. (It may be that a second, related argument can be made regarding his Tennessee plants.)

2. "What can Ms. Smythe possibly say of value about dorm life and its 'immorality'? She is just a high school graduate and has never been to college, much less lived in a dormitory."

   Comment: Cut the personal attack on Ms. Smythe and deal with her argument on the "immorality" of dorm life.

■■■ *Begging The Question*

You "beg the question" if you *assume*—even in part—that what you are arguing is true *before you have proved it.* The key problem in most examples of question begging is that of *unproved assumption,* one which may be stated or implied.

Some question-begging consists of single words that make an assumption:

1. "Such *dishonest* methods of choosing federal judges must be stopped."

   Comment: Unless you have proved that the methods are dishonest, omit the word.

2. "The principal's comments on the student riot in the high school were patently *racist.*"

   Comment: Unless you have proved that the comments were racially motivated, drop the epithet.

   Another kind of question-begging is more complex:

3. "People like us must get college degrees because we need to maintain our standard of living."

   Comment: Essentially, this argues in a circle of assumption: *People like us need college degrees to become people like us.*

4. "In these days, we must defend religion because it is necessary to have a faith that supports us."

   Comment: The words after *because* assume the necessity of a faith—without arguing it.

   The fallacy of *begging the question* sometimes uses a grammatical *question:*

5. "When are Asians going to realize that they can't hog more than their fair share of spaces in the freshman class of our major university?"

   Comment: Hog and *more than their fair share* are both question-begging. Note that the statement is also *ad hominem.*

■■■ *Either-Or Fallacy*

This fallacy is sometimes called the *black or white* fallacy. You commit it if you fail to consider the possibility of *positions* or *alternatives* between opposites. Examples:

1. "Clearly there is going to be either a big boom or a big bust in the stock market."

   Comment: Are there not possibilities that the market will take positions nearer the middle ground?

2. "If you are not against abortion, you must be pro-choice."

   Comment: This is not necessarily true. One can favor abortion in some cases, be against it in others, or be uninterested in the debate.

Note: There are also either-or-or fallacies in which a writer "locks in" three or more positions or choices: "One of three things is bound to happen—America will have a major war, we will destroy ourselves economically, or we will find ourselves completely alone and friendless in the world."

■■■ *Equivocation*

Equivocation refers to an unwarranted change in one's use of an important term. Unless you explicitly warn your reader, don't change the meaning of such a term in your argument. Examples of *equivocation:*

1. "The hardships suffered by the unemployed in the last recession meant that government intervention was required. But who addressed the hardships of teachers who worked throughout the recession without any loss of time on the job?"

   Comment: Hardships in the first sentence is not the same as *hardships* in the second. (As one steelworker put it, "The hardship of standing in souplines when you have no money is not the same thing as the hardship of standing in line at the grocery store when you *do* have some money.")

2. "Disadvantaged minorities usually get special treatment at the university. As someone with an IQ of 160 and a composite ACT of 30, I'm a minority too, and I deserve special treatment."

   Comment: Minority in the first sentence does not refer to the same group (or kind of group) as *minority* in the second sentence.

■■■ *False Analogy*

An *analogy* is a comparison, often an extended one. We reason by comparison a good deal. Indeed, it is doubtful that we can think very much on a practical level without the help of comparisons. They may be simple ones: *I won't drive on this ice-covered road tonight because it looks just like the icy road I drove on last winter when I slid off the pavement into a tree.* Or they may be more complex. For example, many Americans dread a military involvement in Bosnia because they see an extended analogy between that (possible) involvement and our military involvement in Vietnam.

Analogies are one device in learning new things. For instance, atomic structure is often explained to children by an analogy to the planets in their orbits. And figurative analogies are sometimes used as shortcut arguments:

"Why did you leave the movie before it was over?"

"One doesn't have to eat all of an egg to know that it's spoiled."

Wilma and David Ebbitt remark that a *false analogy* results "from making comparisons that aren't relevant to the issue, from pressing an analogy beyond legitimate similarities, from treating a figurative analogy as a literal one, or from insisting that analogical resemblances constitute adequate proof."

Examples of false analogy:

1. "The world is like a gigantic clock. God wound it up, set it going, and forgot it; it has been running on its own ever since."

Comment: The figurative comparison in the analogy is being treated as if it were literal. The world, whatever it may be, is not a clock. Usually the writer should simply drop the figurative element in such an analogy and be satisfied with a literal statement: "God made our world and then left it to its own devices."

2. "My community college had only 1,200 students. It charged no fees beyond tuition; but here the university makes all 20,000 undergraduates pay huge fees, including a computer fee for services most of us don't use."

Comment: The two institutions are not similar in many respects. The nature of tax support is different, as is the use of computers on the two campuses (the university in question is one of the top computer centers in the world). To make the analogy reasonably *comparable,* one might put the student's community college alongside another community college of similar size, program, student body, and tax support.

■■■ *Faulty Causation*

Because causation is often complex (*causes* for almost any phenomenon can be difficult to determine), the fallacy of *faulty cause* is common. Examples:

1. "Poverty creates crime."

Comment: The implied causation is too simple. For instance, one can find descriptions of communities with similar levels of poverty but with very different crime rates. To avoid the fallacy, one might say: "Poverty is a significant cause of certain kinds of crime in many communities."

2. "Consider this sequence of events, one coming after another: Rock and roll, the sexual revolution, and finally the dread disease of AIDS." [The writer goes on to conclude that a causal relation exists.]

Comment: While there may be some small truths here somewhere, the causal pattern is much too simple. Social historians have suggested that rock and roll and the sexual revolution occurred more together than in sequence, and that both were probably "caused" by a number of social factors. Also, one generally accepted cause of AIDS is the sharing of needles used by drug addicts, a cause unrelated to either of the other two causes mentioned in the original quotation.

Post hoc *fallacies of causation*

The full phrase is *post hoc, ergo propter hoc*—meaning "after this, therefore because of this." The *post hoc* fallacy is the error of believing that because event Z follows event Y in time, Z is *caused* by Y. Stephen Leacock, the Canadian humorist, created a deliberately comic *post hoc* fallacy when he wrote: "When I state that my lectures were followed almost immediately by the union of South Africa, the banana riots in Trinidad, and the Turco-Italian war, I think the reader can form some opinion of their importance."

We have a *post hoc* fallacy that is alive and well in our house. It is our firm belief that the 6:30 a.m. airline flight taking off over our neighborhood on its way to Chicago causes the appearance of the morning paper. On bad days, when the 6:30 flight is cancelled, we don't seem to get our paper.

■■■ Faulty Generalization

Most *faulty generalizations* result from haste (a common name for the fallacy is *hasty* generalization). Writing hastily, we may say that *Highly placed female executives do not marry,* or that *Kids who throw curves in youth baseball games will injure their arms.* We can improve these general statements by *qualifying:*

Many highly placed female executives do not marry. [The facts indicate this.]

About 25 percent of kids who throw curves *may* injure their arms, *although the injury is seldom permanent.* [Note *three* qualifications.]

It is unwise to leave a generalization until you are reasonably sure that you have qualified it enough *to fit the facts.* Consider this generalization: *Fraternities at the University of Illinois don't have housemothers.* As of this writing, the generalization does not fit the facts; one fraternity does have a housemother. So we qualify the statement, perhaps in one of the following ways:

- The *great majority* of fraternities don't have a housemother.
- *Almost* all the fraternities. . .
- All *but one* fraternity. . .
- *With one exception,* fraternities. . .

Hint: In making generalizations, don't even suggest the idea of "allness"—unless you really mean *all!*

■■■ Faulty Sampling

A *sample* is a part that represents the whole. A piece of pie can represent the whole pie; ten students can represent the freshman class; the XRG fighter plane can represent the "fighter capability" of the U.S. Air Force. We use *sampling* for obvious reasons; it is often hard to analyze the whole thing, whatever it is. Political sampling, for instance, uses the opinions of hundreds of people to represent tens of thousands of voters. And, as you know, such samples have "error factors"—usually plus or minus three to five percent.

Faulty sampling arises when a sample is seriously unrepresentative of the whole. If our sample of ten students is only of children of millionaires, then that sample does not represent the freshman class—it is *faulty.* Here are three other faulty samples:

- Twenty males aged 21–28 as a sample of voters in a small Ohio town.
- Teachers in Poland as a sample of educational workers behind the Iron Curtain.
- Data on American V8-powered cars in crash tests as a sample of data on American car-crash tests.

■■■ *Ignoring the Question*

Here, *question* refers to the point being argued, whether it is the main point of the argument or a sub-point somewhere in the paper. There are many ways to *ignore the question;* it is a common fallacy. Examples:

The Point is About. . .	Fallacy of Ignoring the Question
1. Investing money in X Corp.	1. "Avoid get-rich-quick ideas, and invest in X Corp."
2. Smith is a capable state attorney	2. "Smith is always playing ball with her kids."
3. Whether to vote for McDavid	3. "McDavid is my kind of mayor," says famous star Studs McDougald
4. Building a new dam	4. "You're either for the dam and prosperity, or against the dam and progress."

> *Comment:* Fallacy number 1 ignores the question of whether X Corp. has a good record for investors. Fallacy number 2 ignores the question of Smith's *capability,* and instead deals with the irrelevancy of her actions as a mother (she could be a devoted, mother and an incompetent state attorney). Number 3 ignores McDavid's qualifications while making an irrelevant testimonial. Number 4 ignores the evidence for or against the dam by involving us in an *either-or* fallacy.

■■■ *Non Sequitur*

Non sequitur means "It does not follow." Usually, you stumble into the fallacy when you are involved in a sequence of statements that are supposed to be logically connected:

Statement A, followed by *Statement B,* followed by *Statement C,* etc.

If, for any reason, *C* does not *follow from* ("connect to") *B,* or *B* from *A,* you have created a *non sequitur.* Examples:

1. "As soon as Jeremy started watching TV 20 hours a week, he began to stutter."

   Comment: The second clause does not necessarily follow from the first; one would have to establish a factual relation between TV watching and stuttering.

2. "Graduates who were debaters in college are more likely to understand the nature of the technological issues that face the country."

   Comment: How does the predicate of the sentence "follow" from the subject? (Is there a necessary relationship between college debating and an understanding of technological problems?)

3. "German fascism, culminating in World War II, was culturally degenerate, and it is no wonder that Germany lost the war." Whatever German "degeneracy" may have been, it does not follow that it alone was the cause of German defeat.

Note: As these examples imply, the fallacy of *non sequitur* tends to blend with other fallacies. Number 1 is also a post hoc fallacy. Numbers 2 and 3 beg the question.

PRACTICE

Discussion

Prepare notes for the discussion of any fallacies you find in the items below. First, be sure to read the *Note,* page 383.

1. (The writer who tells this tale, Robert Fuerst, calls it "a Bob Hope inference." Why?)

   A professor was discussing the dangers of alcohol with his class and presented a demonstration as follows. He set two glasses on the desk, one filled with water, the other with gin. Into each glass he dropped an earthworm. In the water glass, the worm wriggled energetically, but in the glass of alcohol, the worm wriggled once or twice and then died.

   "What do you conclude from this demonstration?" he asked the class. A student in the back raised his hand and answered, "If you drink alcohol, you won't have worms."

2. "A dog who lived in a kennel surrounded by a high fence was urinating one day when a bone was thrown over the fence. The dog thought, 'My urinating made that bone appear.' Thereafter, whenever he wanted something to eat he lifted his leg."

   —Franz Kafka

3. Arizona is a dangerous place. More people die of respiratory diseases there than in any other state.

4. An old gentleman in a rest home used to like to sleep on the porch on hot afternoons. He had a fine big beard. A joker on the staff in the rest home dabbed some limburger cheese on his beard while he was asleep. The old man awoke, sniffed, and moved to another chair, Later, he awoke, sniffed, and moved to a chair inside; later, to his bed upstairs. When he woke for dinner, he looked around angrily and said: "Good lord, the whole house stinks!"

5. Statistics indicate that students who take driver training in high school have better safety records than drivers of the same age bracket who have not taken the course.

6. "Football causes winter."

"How do you know that?"

"It's simple. Shortly after football games start in the fall, winter begins. And the end of winter comes soon after the Super Bowl. QED."

7. This generation in college is by far the most materialistic in recent memory. The continued success of the college sorority system, full of girls with material things they don't really need, attests to the fact.

8. Researchers have "discovered that younger wives appear to be the basis for a longer lifespan in men aged 50–79. The death rate for older men married to women one to 24 years younger was 13 percent lower than average for their age group. Men with older wives seemed to have a death rate 20 percent higher than average."

—Fred Saez

9. Don't waste money on college sports! College baseball isn't any good anyway. If I want to watch good baseball, I'll go see the Detroit Tigers.

10. A married couple are having an argument about women as firefighters. Ralph speaks:

   "The goodhearted federal judge in the New York City case made one of those stupefying rulings. The city has to hire 45 women as firefighters—here we go with quotas—and the department was ordered to devise a test women could pass. Terrific. That's how we ruined our schools, by designing trick tests that anybody with a heartbeat could pass. . . .

   "From now on [Ralph continues], all the fires in this house will be on the first floor, right near the door, where even a court-appointed woman can put them out. And if I'm ever trapped under a beam or something, I'll nod knowingly if a firelady stops by and says, "Sorry, I can't lift 120 pounds. The judge said that I could save three 40-pound people instead.""

—John Leo

11. From Federal and state forms:

   a. "Mark your origin: (a) white, (b) black, (c) Asian, (d) Hispanic."

   b. "Mark your origin: (a) caucasian, (b) black, (c) Hispanic."

12. *Comment only on the last sentence.* A biochemist says in a speech to laypersons: "If brain cells were hamburgers, one human brain would be equal to about six Roman Coliseums filled with hamburgers." Member of audience: "I saw a picture of the Coliseum once and it was a total wreck."

13. "Accumulated data indicates the three most common types of behavior among American males in midlife crisis: (a) They acquire mistresses. (b) They buy fire-engine-red motorcycles. (c) They become spies for the Russians."

—Mark Russell

14. On the question of being treated by a doctor who has AIDS.

    Legal Director of the American Civil Liberties Union:

    "How would you like it if someone said: 'I don't want to be treated by that doctor because he's black?'"

    Clarence Page, black journalist:

    "But there's a difference. Blackness isn't catching."

15. On pornography: "We don't put up with pollution in our cities; why should we put up with pollution in our minds?"

16. Auto mechanic: "You don't blame surgeons for heart disease; why hold mechanics responsible for car failure?"

17. Pat: "Guns don't shoot people; people shoot people."

    Mike: "Regardless of who shoots who, it hurts."

18. Fools like him can't understand religion because religious spirituality goes beyond human understanding.

19. Often remembered is the *Literary Digest's* poll, taken by telephone, which predicted the election in 1936 of Landon over Roosevelt. Roosevelt won by a big margin. What was the fallacy in the *Digest's* thinking?

20. Juvenile fiction is horrible. I read some "books for kids" my daughter brought home from the library, and they were all dirty.

Christine Davidson

WORKING TIME AND A HALF

Christine Davidson was educated at Ripon College and Boston University and the University of Exeter, Devon, England. She taught English in Boston public schools and was an instructor in nonfiction writing at Antioch-New England and the University of New Hampshire. Now employed as a copyeditor and writer, Davidson concentrates on business, social and women's issues. She lives in New Hampshire with her husband and two children. What Davidson calls "that one little essay"—reprinted below—resulted in a full-length book, Staying Home Instead, *now in its fourth printing.*

1   There she is, the working mother of America, self-assured and jaunty with her brief-case swinging at her side. Her smile seems to say she "has it all": husband, children, stimulating job, independence, fulfillment. It doesn't show guilt, frustration, weekend headaches or exhaustion. Well, I have "had it all" since my kids were in diapers, and I have finally had it.

2   A year ago I decided that being a working wife and mother was not right for me. But I would like to suggest that the image of the working woman that advertisers and the news media portray does not jibe with reality for many American women.

3   Most of us do not dress in expensive suits; we are waitresses, office workers and teachers. Few of us are executives, and few of us carry briefcases. Even if we felt they looked right with our pink uniforms and polyester pantsuits, we couldn't afford them. We make 59 cents for every dollar a man makes.

4   Those of us who work to support or help support small children often spend more than 25 percent of our paychecks on child care. We cannot work without day care, and we cannot work happily without quality day care. A businessman who cannot work without a secretary and electricity can be given a 100 percent tax deduction for these as business expenses. Yet for years we have been given only a 20 percent tax credit on $2,000 spent per child for day care, and recent legislation raises this only slightly.

5   Another factor that is inequitable, though often unavoidable, is that in two-career families most husbands do not split housework 50–50. From everything I have read and observed, I would say it is usually 70–30 at best. In our family, my husband cooked one night a week, washed dishes the nights I cooked, made his lunch and did two loads of laundry a week. With the demanding job he had, we both knew this was all he had the energy for.

6   But after a while I began to be unhappy that I did the other ten loads of wash, vacuumed and mopped, chauffeured the kids to friends' houses and the doctor and dentist, made their lunches and snacks, ran errands, paid all our bills, kept our IRS and other business files, did the clothing and food shopping, cooked six nights a week and arranged all day care (including the rearranging when a sitter called at 8 a.m. to say she wouldn't be coming at 8:30).

7   Most of these tasks were simple, but they added up and contributed to my feeling exhausted and frustrated. My jaw would be clenched by 8:45 a.m. as I drove to work.

8   When I got to work I would shut the door to my classroom and force myself to forget everything else. And I did have an interesting job. I taught English at a local college, did free-lance writing and editing and taught a night course to adults. My work was stimulating and fun. But pay for a part-time instructor was low, and I began to take on more free-lance work than was good for me.

9   Yet we continued to think of my work away from home as "just part time," and the work at home as inconsequential. In fact, I did not work "part time,"; I had a teaching job, a damp, dilapidated house to fix up on weekends, two children to care for and usually a short story or article in progress. I worked time and a half.

10   One spring day when my husband came home with a raise, the thought struck me that maybe I didn't have to. Initially I had started working so we could stay solvent and keep up our car payments and home improvement loan. My husband's raise coincided with the last payments on these loans. I could continue working so we could live more comfortably and get household help, or I could stop and we could keep our standard of living low. I quit.

11   Since then our day-to-day living has read like a column of Heloise hints. We wash wool sweaters and air suits on the clothesline instead of taking them to the cleaners. We eat soyburgers and crock-pot soup. We can and freeze our garden vegetables and store cabbages and squash in our drafty front hallway.

12   We sometimes find these and other economies a pain in the neck. And we're broke— all the time. We cannot pay a small bill and buy our children sneakers the same week. But it's OK because I can give my kids something else now. I have stopped saying, "No, not this afternoon, I have to work" or "No, not now, I'm too tired."

13   I will never know whether my working was bad for my kids; I do know it was bad for me. I never knew when one of them would contract the flu or fall from the Jungle Gym when I had a deadline to make. Illnesses and accidents are worries for any mother, but for a working mother they can be real stomach twisters. One thing for sure, none of the swinging-working-mom articles tells you how to make it to the 9 a.m. board meeting—or more correctly, the steno pool—looking fresh and alert when your baby has been vomiting in your arms at 5 a.m.

14   I can understand how working might be good for women who feel confined at home with small children or who have grown children. Women who want to work *should*— and without a 1950s condemnation from anyone. But I think we should not move from the narrow-mindedness of the '50s to another kind of narrowness in the '80s. Mothers who choose to stay home should not feel they have to justify their decision.

PRACTICE

Discussion

1. An argument like this tends to stand or fall on the convincingness of its *facts.* List five facts you find in the essay. Do you find all five convincing?

2. Is this an argument of *fact* or *action?* How can you be sure?

3. Discuss the sentence that makes up paragraph 6. Is the sentence effective? What major technique of construction does it employ?

4. Davidson doesn't blame her husband, even though he does less work at home than she does. Why might she actually blame her husband, but as a technique of argument not mention it in her essay?

5. Consider the last sentence of paragraph 9, which echoes Davidson's title. Why doesn't she place this sentence earlier?

6. The first sentence of paragraph 13 may seem odd to some readers. Most debates on this subject emphasize the effect on *children,* but Davidson ignores the issue. Does her honesty detract from or enhance her ethical proof?

7. Sample your class. How many students agree with Davidson's thesis? with the way that she narrowed her thesis? (Did she narrow it too much? Should she have employed other issues?)

8. Explain Davidson's use of the phrase *stomach twisters* (paragraph 13).

Vocabulary

jibe	inequitable	dilapidated
quality day care	inconsequential	soyburgers

Writing

1. Write a refutation to Davidson.

2. Write a *fact* argument on this subject from a typical husband's point of view.

3. Write an *action* argument based on ideas or issues in the essay.

John Russo

"REEL" VS. REAL VIOLENCE

John Russo was the producer of Night of the Living Dead, *the movie that, as critic Dave Kehr remarked, "changed the face of American horror movies. . . ." The idea of the movie was simple: "Let's make a monster movie." It took nine months to make, on practically a non-budget (ten people put up $600 each, and a meatpacker contributed animal intestines). The flesh the ghouls ate was Silly Putty. In 1990, Russo co-produced a new version of the same movie. Russo insists that movies about the living—and the unliving—dead are essentially harmless. What do you think?*

1   One day I switched on the evening news just in time to see a Pennsylvania politician waving around a .357 magnum, warning reporters to back off so they wouldn't get hurt, then sticking the gun in his mouth and . . .

2   Mercifully, the station I was watching didn't show him pulling the trigger, but I learned later that another Pittsburgh station showed the whole suicide unedited. What I saw was enough to make me ill. My stomach was in a knot, and I couldn't get the incident out of my mind. I still can't, even though three years have gone by.

3   I have a special reason for wondering and worrying about blood and violence on TV and movie screens. I write, produce and direct horror movies. I coauthored "Night of the Living Dead," the so-called "granddaddy of the splatter flicks." And since then I've made a string of movies depicting murder and mayhem.

4   I can watch these kinds of movies when they've been made by other people, and I can even help create the bloody effects in my own movies without getting a knot in my stomach. Yet I still retain my capacity to be shocked, horrified and saddened when something like this happens in real life.

5   So there must be a difference between real violence and "reel" violence. And if I didn't feel that this is true, I'd stop making the kinds of movies that I make. What are those differences?

6   My movies are scary and unsettling, but they are also cautionary tales. They might show witches at work, doing horrible things or carrying out nefarious schemes, but in doing so they convey a warning against superstition and the dementia it can spawn. They might show people under extreme duress, set upon by human or inhuman creatures, but in doing so they teach people how duress can be handled and blind, ignorant fear can be confronted and conquered. My purpose hasn't been to glorify or encourage murder and mayhem, but to give horror fans the vicarious chills and thrills they crave.

7   The most powerful and consequently financially successful horror movies—"Night of the Living Dead," "The Texas Chainsaw Massacre," "Halloween" and "Friday The 13th"—feature a small cast in a confined situation that is made terrifying by the presence of a monster/madman/murderer. Usually the victims are young, beautiful women. Often the murders are filmed from the point of view of the murderer. For all these reasons, we filmmakers have been accused of hating women and portraying them as objects to be punished for being sexually desirable. Horror fans have been accused of identifying with the psychopathic killers portrayed in these movies and deriving vicarious enjoyment from watching the killers act out the fans' dark fantasies.

8   But there are two simple, pragmatic reasons why the victims are often filmed from the point of view of the killer. First, it's an effective technique for not revealing who the killer is, thus preserving an aura of suspense. Second, it affords dramatically explicit angles for showing the victim's terror—and the horror of what the killer is doing.

9   These films *are* horrifying because they reflect—but do not create—a frightful trend in our society. Murders, assaults and rapes are being committed with more frequency and with increasing brutality. Serial killers and mass murderers are constantly making headlines. Most of these killers are men, often sexually warped men, and they most often kill women. So we filmmakers have stuck to the facts in our portrayal of them. That's why our movies are so scary. Too many of our fellow citizens are turning into monsters, and contemporary horror movies have seized upon this fear and personified it. So now we have Jason, Michael and Freddy instead of Dracula and Frankenstein. Our old-time movie monsters used to be creatures of fantasy. But today, unfortunately, they are extensions of reality.

10   Recently, at a horror convention in Albany, I was autographing videocassettes of a show I had hosted, entitled "Witches, Vampires & Zombies," and a young man asked me if the tape showed actual human sacrifices. He was disappointed when I informed him that the ceremonies on the tape were fictional depictions. He was looking for "snuff movies"—the kind that actually show people dying.

11   Unfortunately, tapes showing real death are widely available nowadays. A video of the Pennsylvania politician blowing his brains out went on sale just a few weeks after the incident was broadcast. But I don't think that the people who are morbidly fixated on this sort of thing are the same people who are in love with the horror-movie genre.

12   I'm afraid that the young man I met in Albany has a serious personality disorder. And I don't think he's really a horror fan. He didn't buy my tape, but he would have bought it if the human sacrifices had been real. "Reel" violence didn't interest him. He didn't care about the niceties of theme, plot or character development. He just wanted to see people die.

13   I haven't seen any snuff movies for sale at the horror conventions I've attended. True horror fans aren't interested. They don't go to the movies just to see artificial blood and gore, either. The films that gratuitously deliver those kinds of effects usually are box-office flops. The hit horror films have a lot more to offer. While scaring us and entertaining us, they teach us how to deal with our deepest fears, dreads and anxieties.

14   But modern horror movies aren't to blame for these fears, dreads and anxieties. They didn't create our real-life Jasons, Michaels and Freddys any more than the gangster movies of the 1920s and 1930s created Al Capone and Dutch Schultz. If the movies reflect, with disturbing accuracy, the psychic terrain of the world we live in, then it's up to us to change that world and make it a safer place.

PRACTICE

Discussion

1. Read the brief section on *ethical proof* (pages 3–9). How does Russo use ethical proof in his argument?

2. What is the thesis of the argument? Did you find it explicitly stated?

3. What is the purpose of paragraphs 10–13? Is his argument one of *fact, action,* or *refutation*?

4. What is the *occasion* for Russo's argument? Why would he—as a producer of what he calls "splatter flicks"—feel compelled to make it?

5. Note the first sentence of paragraph 9. For discussion: *If "splatter flicks" did not help to create a "frightful trend" in our society, then where did the trend come from?*

6. In paragraph 12, sentence 1, Russo uses a jargon term, perhaps the only one in the essay: *serious personality disorder.* Why didn't he employ a less jargonized expression; for example, "The young man was a *vicious psycho*"?

7. Explain the purpose of paragraph 5.

8. How much are you convinced by Russo's argument? If you wish, take it piece by piece; for instance, do you agree with the last sentence in paragraph 6? With the first sentence in paragraph 9? With the last three sentences in paragraph 12? (Do most of the people who attend splatter movies "care about the niceties of theme, plot or character development"?)

Vocabulary

nefarious	vicarious	fixated
dementia	psychopathic	gratuitously
duress	aura	

Writing

1. Read Discussion question 8. Write a paper responding to any one of the "pieces" of Russo's argument. You may agree or disagree with him. Use evidence from your own viewing of "splatter flicks."

2. John Russo appears in his essay as a particular kind of person. Write a detailed description of this person.

3. Write an action argument on the question of "splatter flicks." You might try to answer the question: What—if anything—should be done about them (or an element of them)? You might want to use a fairly limited thesis relating to questions like the following: Should young actors refuse/agree to appear in

them? Should parents encourage/discourage their pre-teen children to see them on television?

Robert Hughes

TAKE THIS REVOLUTION . . .

Robert Hughes has been the art critic of Time *magazine since 1970. He says about his relationship with* Time, *"I think of this job as the best possible periscope through which to view modern Western art." As the following essay shows, Hughes uses his periscope to view other aspects of society besides art. His best-selling Book of the Month Club selection,* The Fatal Shore *(1986), describes in chilling detail the misery of those who were doomed to spend their lives in the Australian penal colonies from 1788 until 1868.*

Born in Australia in 1938, he claims to be a descendant of a long line of prisoners or jailers—those same people he wrote about in The Fatal Shore.

Hughes graduated in 1956 from St. Ignatius College, Sydney, after which he worked as a cartoonist. In Australia and the United States, Hughes narrated and helped develop some thirty television documentaries for BBC on the subject of art. His art books include Heaven and Hell in Western Art *(1968) and* The Shock of the New *(1980).*

1   Americans are suckers for utopian promises. They have been ever since the Puritans invented the idea of radical newness, in the 17th century. We will look back on what is now claimed for the information superhighway and wonder how we ever psyched ourselves into believing all that bulldust about social fulfillment through interface and connectivity. But by then we will have some other fantasy to chase, its approaches equally lined with entrepreneurs and flacks, who will be its main beneficiaries.

2   Let me hastily assert that I am no Luddite. Luddites wanted to smash machinery, believing that it was throwing handcraftsmen out of work. Skepticism is not Luddism. I do not want to smash my PC or anyone else's—although there have been moments when, trying to get some mulish program to run, I thought of throwing it out the window. I doubt if I could now work without my IBM clone, though I treat it strictly as a typewriter and filing system with a big memory.

3   So why am I thus wasting its potential? Why is my ancient Hayes Smartmodem 1200 switched off most of the time, when it could be patching me into the Internet? Basically because there is only so much time in the day, and there are a lot of things I would rather be doing—writing, for instance, or checking the drag mechanism on a fly reel, or conversing with wife and friends, or interfacing (that word!) with Phoebe the speckled bitch, or planting peas in early spring, or looking at pictures in a museum, or, above all, reading a book—than exchanging ephemeral gossip with faceless strangers over the electronic equivalent of the backyard fence.

4   The Internet, it seems, speaks to America's unappeasable terror of loneliness, a fear that overflows into a mistrust of one of life's most precious assets, optional solitude. Americans, it is said, already watch seven to eight hours of TV a day. Now other Americans—not all

that many at present, but their numbers are growing—spend up to 25 hours a week on the Net, goggling at another kind of screen, and call it community empowerment. To them, one is tempted to say, Get a life!

5   As the virtual social space of the various networks increases, so will the real social spaces of America decay and implode. Why keep them up? The only mildly paranoid might add that although interactivity may blossom as a democratic agora of opinion, releasing us from our dependence on Big Media, it also contains unexplored possibilities of social control. In the 18th century Jeremy Bentham proposed a form of prison in which all inmates would be totally open to inspection at all times: the panopticon. This was one of the germs of the totalitarian state: virtue through surveillance. The cable that brings information into your home can also carry information out of it. Can you be sure who is on the other end of the wire? Is there a delete key for all you put on the Net?

6   We are beset by the virtual. Virtual reality, virtual neighbors, virtual history, virtual sex and now—thanks to the facile rhetoric of social rebirth emanating from Washington—virtual virtue. Some people, particularly those who like to strike prophetic attitudes about the future, feel deprived if they are not inundated by something called "information" moving in weightless bytes at the speed of light. Mostly, what they call information is just raw data of trivial significance. Personally, I find the flow of words from books, at less than warp speed, quite difficult enough to keep up with—not that anyone can.

7   Ah, them books. One of the things infobahners like to claim is that all the rest of "culture"—including books and paintings and presumably virtual-reality tours of architecture as well—will eventually be available in cyberspace: All Human Knowledge Will Be There. With a roll and a click of the mouse, we will summon Titian's *Assumption* from the Frari in Venice onto our home screen, faithful in every respect—except that it isn't, being much smaller, with different (electronic) color, no texture, no surface and no physical reality, and in no way superior (except for the opportunity to zoom in on detail) to an ink reproduction in a book. Which is fine, especially for archivists and iconographers, but how many people will realize that the only way to know Titian is to study the actual, unedited physical works of his hands, in real space, not cyberspace?

8   Thus the printed book, as a cultural delivery system (See how easy the jargon is?), will become as obsolete in a cyberspatial society as the illuminated manuscript did after Caxton and Gutenberg. People have been saying this, in books of course, for several decades. But will it? The vast majority of books have not been converted to bits and almost certainly never will be, because they have no readership big enough to "justify" the huge task of digitalizing them all. One can well imagine digitalized versions of fundamental classics like *Antony and Cleopatra* or *Moby Dick,* or popular lit-kitsch like Maya Angelou's poetry, making it onto the small screen at some point, to satisfy mass demands from English Lit courses. But (to pick out the first three titles I see on a shelf in my home office) what about the collected poems of Christopher Smart or J.C. Beaglehole's *The Exploration of the Pacific* or Camões' *Os Lusiadas?* In sum, what about the tens of millions of titles for which there is absolutely no popular demand and which can only be consulted as print on paper? *Fuhgeddabowdit.*

9   Nothing in the persuasively foreseeable future can or will replace the printed book, and the relation of cyberspace to literature hangs on a Rube Goldberg-like joke: the idea of needing an expensive electronic machine, available only to the relatively well-off and dependent on an external power source, to perform the act of reading. Besides,

there is not now and probably never will be a computer that you can get sand in and spill coffee on without impairing it, as you can with a book, a magazine or a newspaper. And the more you make information flow dependent on costly hardware, the more you separate the info rich and the info poor, thus adding new layers to America's already vicious class inequalities. Anyone and everyone can spend 50¢ on a newspaper. It is by no means certain that the digital newspaper of the projected future, the silicon sheet you can plug into a wall jack for the day's info fix, will be widely accessible in the slums, ghettos and trailer parks of America.

10   Interactivity may add much less to the sum of human knowledge than we think. But it will deluge us with entertainment, most of which will be utter schlock. There isn't enough production talent or inventiveness in America today to fill the TV networks and cable outlets with halfway-decent programming; does anyone seriously imagine that there will be enough to fill the promised 500 channels, or the threatened 50,000, with anything but electronic drivel? All the cables will lead back to an enormous, leaking landfill of vicarious crap. Incredible sums of money will be made from this. In the not too distant future, when Bill Gates realizes he has succeeded in spending $30.8 million on the only Leonardo manuscript that doesn't have a single drawing of real aesthetic significance in it, he will be able to off-load it for $60 million onto David Geffen or Michael Ovitz. Thus civilization progresses.

11   A large beneficiary, as all in the entertainment industry know but none will admit, will be pornography. Strap on your helmet and enter the wonderworld of virtual S&M; doubtless the suits are planning such things at their conferences in Aspen already. This must be why every propagandist for the zillion-channel environment talks piously about "education." Whenever an American entrepreneur invokes education in this context, it behooves the citizen to smell a rat. Education is, or ought to be, about reality, and the dark star that lurks out there in cyberspace has less to do with reality than with the infinite replication of simulacrums, a hugely overscaled way—in Neil Postman's famous phrase—of amusing ourselves to death.

PRACTICE

Discussion

1. Why has the well-known slang phrase been omitted from the title? List all the other slang used in the essay. How does Hughes' word choice and title set the tone of the essay? Judging from Hughes' use of slang would you say that he is totally or only partly serious in his objections to the Internet?

2. Hughes is *Time* magazine's art critic and a scholar. Does his use of slang undermine his *ethical proof?* Where in the essay does he establish his knowledge? Discuss whether you consider him an objective critic of the Internet.

3. What is a Luddite? What disclaimer does Hughes make by claiming that he's not a Luddite?

4. What is Hughes' thesis? Does he support it well?

5. Review Structure of Argument, pages 369–377. Is this a fact, action, or refutation argument? On what do you base your decision?

6. Hughes makes four arguments against the Internet. List them. Which argument do you believe is the strongest? Why? Which argument is the weakest? Why?

7. Do you agree or disagree that the advantages of the Internet have been hyped and oversold?

Vocabulary

utopian	Luddite
ephemeral	simulacrums

Writing

1. Hughes opens his essay with "Americans are suckers for utopian promises." Choose one social program that proves Hughes' statement about utopian promises is correct. Then, using a fact structure, write an argument that supports his view. If you disagree, write an argument using a refutation structure.

   Possible topics: Computers in schools teach students to write better; bussing improves the education of minorities; welfare cures poverty; federal public housing provides safer housing for the poor.

2. Write an action structure argument in which you propose that the government should put limits on the use of pornography and lewd messages on the Internet.

3. Write a paper in which you agree or disagree with Clifford Stoll's position on the Internet: In his book, *Silicon Snake Oil* he says, "Life in the real world is far more interesting, far more important, far richer, than anything you'll ever find on a computer screen." If you agree, use a fact structure. If you disagree, use a refutation structure.

Linda Hasselstrom

WHY ONE PEACEFUL WOMAN CARRIES A PISTOL

Linda Hasselstrom, born in 1943, is a rancher, environmentalist, and resident of western South Dakota. She is a poet and essayist. Among her many published works are those related to her experiences as a rancher: Windbreak, A Woman Rancher on the Northern Plains, *1987;* Going over East: Reflections of a Woman Rancher, *1987; and* Roadkill, *1987. Her poetry volume,* Caught by One Wing

(1990), and her collection of essays and poetry, Land Circle: Writings Collected from the Land *(1991), reflect her interest in animal life, the environment, and her feelings about issues important to women. The essay below comes from* Land Circle.

1   I'm a peace-loving woman. I also carry a pistol. For years, I've written about my decision in an effort to help other women make intelligent choices about gun ownership, but editors rejected the articles. Between 1983 and 1986, however, when gun sales to men held steady, gun ownership among women rose fifty-three percent, to more than twelve million. We learned that any female over the age of twelve can expect to be criminally assaulted some time in her life, that women aged thirty have a fifty-fifty chance of being raped, robbed, or attacked, and that many police officials say flatly that they cannot protect citizens from crime. During the same period, the number of women considering gun ownership quadrupled to nearly two million. Manufacturers began showing lightweight weapons with small grips, and purses with built-in holsters. A new magazine is called *Guns and Women,* and more than eight thousand copies of the video *A Woman's Guide to Firearms* were sold by 1988. Experts say female gun buyers are not limited to any particular age group, profession, social class, or area of the country, and most are buying guns to protect themselves. Shooting instructors say women view guns with more caution than do men, and may make better shots.

2   I decided to buy a handgun for several reasons. During one four-year period, I drove more than a hundred thousand miles alone, giving speeches, readings, and workshops. A woman is advised, usually by men, to protect herself by avoiding bars, by approaching her car like an Indian scout, by locking doors and windows. But these precautions aren't always enough. And the logic angers me: *because* I am female, it is my responsibility to be extra careful.

3   As a responsible environmentalist, I choose to recycle, avoid chemicals on my land, minimize waste. As an informed woman alone, I choose to be as responsible for my own safety as possible: I keep my car running well, use caution in where I go and what I do. And I learned about self-protection—not an easy or quick decision. I developed a strategy of protection that includes handgun possession. The following incidents, chosen from a larger number because I think they could happen to anyone, helped make up my mind.

4   When I camped with another woman for several weeks, she didn't want to carry a pistol, and police told us Mace was illegal. We tucked spray deodorant into our sleeping bags, theorizing that any man crawling into our tent at night would be nervous anyway; anything sprayed in his face would slow him down until we could hit him with a frying pan, or escape. We never used our improvised weapon, because we were lucky enough to camp beside people who came to our aid when we needed them. I returned from that trip determined to reconsider.

5   At that time, I lived alone and taught night classes in town. Along a city street I often traveled, a woman had a flat tire, called for help on her CB, and got a rapist; he didn't fix the tire either. She was afraid to call for help again and stayed in her car until morning. Also, CBs work best along line-of-sight; I ruled them out.

6   As I drove home one night, a car followed me, lights bright. It passed on a narrow bridge, while a passenger flashed a spotlight in my face, blinding me. I braked sharply.

The car stopped, angled across the bridge, and four men jumped out. I realized the locked doors were useless if they broke my car windows. I started forward, hoping to knock their car aside so I could pass. Just then, another car appeared, and the men got back in their car, but continued to follow me, passing and repassing. I dared not go home. I passed no lighted houses. Finally, they pulled to the roadside, and I decided to use their tactic: fear. I roared past them inches away, horn blaring. It worked; they turned off the highway. But it was desperate and foolish, and I was frightened and angry. Even in my vehicle I was too vulnerable.

7   Other incidents followed. One day I saw a man in the field near my house, carrying a shotgun and heading for a pond full of ducks. I drove to meet him, and politely explained that the land was posted. He stared at me, and the muzzle of his shotgun rose. I realized that if he simply shot me and drove away, I would be a statistic. The moment passed; the man left.

8   One night, I returned home from class to find deep tire ruts on the lawn, a large gas tank empty, garbage in the driveway. A light shone in the house; I couldn't remember leaving it on. I was too embarrassed to wake the neighbors. An hour of cautious exploration convinced me the house was safe, but once inside, with the doors locked, I was still afraid. I put a .22 rifle by my bed, but I kept thinking of how naked I felt, prowling around my own house in the dark.

9   It was time to consider self-defense. I took a kung fu class and learned to define the distance to maintain between myself and a stranger. Once someone enters that space without permission, kung fu teaches appropriate evasive or protective action. I learned to move confidently, scanning for possible attack. I learned how to assess danger, and techniques for avoiding it without combat.

10   I also learned that one must practice several hours every day to be good at kung fu. By that time I had married George; when I practiced with him, I learned how *close* you must be to your attacker to use martial arts, and decided a 120-pound woman dare not let a six-foot, 220-pound attacker get that close unless she is very, very good at self-defense. Some women who are well trained in martial arts have been raped and beaten anyway.

11   Reluctantly I decided to carry a pistol. George helped me practice with his .357 and .22. I disliked the .357's recoil, though I later became comfortable with it. I bought a .22 at a pawn shop. A standard .22 bullet, fired at close range, can kill, but news reports tell of attackers advancing with five such bullets in them. I bought magnum shells, with more power, and practiced until I could hit someone close enough to endanger me. Then I bought a license making it legal for me to carry the gun concealed.

12   George taught me that the most important preparation was mental: convincing myself I could shoot someone. Few of us really wish to hurt or kill another human being. But there is no point in having a gun—in fact, gun possession might increase your danger—unless you know you can use it against another human being. A good training course includes mental preparation, as well as training in safety. As I drive or walk, I often rehearse the conditions which would cause me to shoot. Men grow up handling firearms, and learn controlled violence in contact sports, but women grow up learning to be subservient and vulnerable. To make ourselves comfortable with the idea that we are capable of protecting ourselves requires effort. But it need not turn us into macho, gun-fighting broads. We must simply learn to do as men do from an early age: believe

in, and rely on, *ourselves* for protection. The pistol only adds an extra edge, an attention-getter; it is a weapon of last resort.

13   Because shooting at another person means shooting to kill. It's impossible even for seasoned police officers to be sure of only wounding an assailant. If I shot an attacking man, I would aim at the largest target, the chest. This is not an easy choice, but for me it would be better than rape.

14   In my car, my pistol is within instant reach. When I enter a deserted rest stop at night, it's in my purse, my hand on the grip. When I walk from a dark parking lot into a motel, it's in my hand, under a coat. When I walk my dog in the deserted lots around most motels, the pistol is in a shoulder holster, and I am always aware of my surroundings. In my motel room, it lies on the bedside table. At home, it's on the headboard.

15   Just carrying a pistol is not protection. Avoidance is still the best approach to trouble; watch for danger signs, and practice avoiding them. Develop your instinct for danger.

16   One day while driving to the highway mailbox, I saw a vehicle parked about halfway to the house. Several men were standing in the ditch, relieving themselves. I have no objection to emergency urination; we always need moisture. But they'd also dumped several dozen beer cans, which blow into pastures and can slash a cow's legs or stomach.

17   As I slowly drove closer, the men zipped their trousers ostentatiously while walking toward me. Four men gathered around my small foreign car, making remarks they wouldn't make to their mothers, and one of them demanded what the hell I wanted.

18   "This is private land; I'd like you to pick up the beer cans."

19   "What beer cans?" said the belligerent one, putting both hands on the car door, and leaning in my window. His face was inches from mine, the beer fumes were strong, and he looked angry. The others laughed. One tried the passenger door, locked; another put his foot on the hood and rocked the car. They circled, lightly thumping the roof, discussing my good fortune in meeting them, and the benefits they were likely to bestow upon me. I felt small and trapped; they knew it.

20   "The ones you just threw out," I said politely.

21   "I don't see no beer cans. Why don't you get out here and show them to me, honey?" said the belligerent one, reaching for the handle inside my door.

22   "Right over there," I said, still being polite, "there and over there." I pointed with the pistol, which had been under my thigh. Within one minute the cans and the men were back in the car, and headed down the road.

23   I believe this small incident illustrates several principles. The men were trespassing and knew it; their judgment may have been impaired by alcohol. Their response to the polite request of a woman alone was to use their size and numbers to inspire fear. The pistol was a response in the same language. Politeness didn't work; I couldn't intimidate them. Out of the car, I'd have been more vulnerable. The pistol just changed the balance of power.

24   My husband, George, asked one question when I told him. "What would you have done if he'd grabbed for the pistol?"

25   "I had the car in reverse; I'd have hit the accelerator, and backed up; if he'd kept coming, I'd have fired straight at him." He nodded.

26   In fact, the sight of the pistol made the man straighten up; he cracked his head on the door frame. He and the two in front of the car stepped backward, catching the attention of the fourth, who joined them. They were all in front of me then, and as the car was still running and in reverse gear, my options had multiplied. If they'd advanced again, I'd

have backed away, turning to keep the open window toward them. Given time, I'd have put the first shot into the ground in front of them, the second into the belligerent leader. It might have been better to wait until they were gone, pick up the beer cans, and avoid confrontation, but I believed it was reasonable and my right to make a polite request to strangers littering my property. Showing the pistol worked on another occasion when I was driving in a desolate part of Wyoming. A man played cat-and-mouse with me for thirty miles, ultimately trying to run my car off the road. When his car was only two inches from mine, I pointed my pistol at him, and he disappeared.

27   I believe that a handgun is like a car; both are tools for specific purposes; both can be lethal if used improperly. Both require a license, training, and alertness. Both require you to be aware of what is happening before and behind you. Driving becomes almost instinctive; so does handgun use. When I've drawn my gun for protection, I simply found it in my hand. Instinct told me a situation was dangerous before my conscious mind reacted; I've felt the same while driving. Most good drivers react to emergencies by instinct.

28   Knives are another useful tool often misunderstood and misused; some people acquire knives mostly for display, either on a wall or on a belt, and such knives are often so large as to serve no useful purpose. My pocket knives are always razor sharp, because a small, sharp knife will do most jobs. Skinning blades serve for cutting meat and splitting small kindling in camp. A *sgian dubb,* a four-inch flat blade in a wooden sheath, was easily concealed inside a Scotsman's high socks, and slips into my dress or work boots as well. Some buckskinners keep what they call a "grace knife" on a thong around their necks; the name may derive from *coup de grâce,* the welcome throat-slash a wounded knight asked from his closest friend, to keep him from falling alive into the hands of his enemies. I also have a push dagger, with a blade only three inches long, attached to a handle that fits into the fist so well that the knife would be hard to lose even in hand-to-hand combat. When I first showed it, without explanation, to an older woman who would never consider carrying a knife, she took one look and said, "Why, you could push that right into someone's stomach," and demonstrated with a flourish. That's what it's for. I wear it for decoration, because it was handmade by Jerry and fits my hand perfectly, but I am intently aware of its purpose. I like my knives, not because they are weapons, but because they are well designed, and beautiful, and because each is a tool with a specific purpose.

29   Women didn't always have jobs, or drive cars or heavy equipment, though western women did many of those things almost as soon as they arrived here. Men in authority argued that their attempt to do so would unravel the fabric of society. Women, they said, would become less feminine; they hadn't the intelligence to cope with the mechanics of a car, or the judgment to cope with emergencies. Since these ideas were so wrong, perhaps it is time women brought a new dimension to the wise use of handguns as well.

30   We can and should educate ourselves in how to travel safely, take self-defense courses, reason, plead, or avoid trouble in other ways. But some men cannot be stopped by those methods; they understand only power. A man who is committing an attack already knows he's breaking laws; he has no concern for someone else's rights. A pistol is a woman's answer to his greater power. It makes her equally frightening. I have thought of revising the old Colt slogan: "God made man, but Sam Colt made them equal" to

read "God made men *and women* but Sam Colt made them equal." Recently I have seen an ad for a popular gunmaker with a similar sentiment; perhaps this is an idea whose time has come, though the pacifist inside me will be saddened if the only way women can achieve equality is by carrying a weapon.

31   As a society, we were shocked in early 1989 when a female jogger in New York's Central Park was beaten and raped savagely and left in a coma. I was even more shocked when reporters interviewed children who lived near the victim and quoted a twelve-year-old as saying, "She had nothing to guard herself; she didn't have no man with her; she didn't have no Mace." And another sixth-grader said, "It is like she committed suicide." Surely this is not a majority opinion, but I think it is not so unusual, either, even in this liberated age. Yet there is no city or county in the nation where law officers can relax because all the criminals are in jail. Some authorities say citizens armed with handguns stop almost as many crimes annually as armed criminals succeed in committing, and that people defending themselves kill three times more attackers and robbers than police do. I don't suggest all criminals should be killed, but some can be stopped only by death or permanent incarceration. Law enforcement officials can't prevent crimes; later punishment may be of little comfort to the victim. A society so controlled that no crime existed would probably be too confined for most of us, and is not likely to exist any time soon. Therefore, many of us should be ready and able to protect ourselves, and the intelligent use of firearms is one way.

32   We must treat a firearm's power with caution. "Power tends to corrupt, and absolute power corrupts absolutely," as a man (Lord Acton) once said. A pistol is not the only way to avoid being raped or murdered in today's world, but a firearm, intelligently wielded, can shift the balance and provide a measure of safety.

PRACTICE

Discussion

1. The writer of this selection uses a variety of strategies to develop her argument. Review this chapter and identify, with paragraph numbers, at least three different strategies used. Discuss the suitability of each strategy supporting her argument.

2. Review the title and paragraphs 1–3. Who does Hasselstrom claim to be? How eager was she to buy a gun? What is the effect of this information on her *ethical proof* (pages 3–9)?

3. Who is her primary audience? What does she claim is her purpose in writing this argument? From her evidence and her purpose, infer her *thesis*.

4. Review the material on *Structures of Argument* pages 369–380. What is the primary organization of Hasselstrom's argument—*fact* or *action*? After you have identified her primary organization, outline her argument, using appropriate categories listed under either *fact* or *action* arguments.

5. In paragraph 15, Hasselstrom says, "Avoidance is still the best approach to trouble; watch for danger signs, and practice avoiding them. Develop your instinct for danger." Give two examples where she broke her own rules. How does she justify her aggressive actions? Do you believe that she was correct in breaking her own rules in these two instances?

6. Review *ethical proof,* pages 3–9. How good is Hasselstrom's ethical proof?

Vocabulary

lethal   Sam Colt

belligerent   vulnerable

confrontation

Writing

1. Write a refutation to Hasselstrom's argument for carrying a pistol, using the suggestions on pages 376–377.

2. Write an argument, using a *fact* structure, in which you prove that other alternatives for self-defense, besides guns, are practical for women.

3. Write an argument, either *fact* or *action,* on a subject of your own choice.

Martin Luther King, Jr.

LETTER FROM BIRMINGHAM JAIL*

Martin Luther King, Jr., was a central figure in the civil rights movement of the 1960s until he was shot and killed in 1968. He was born in 1929 in Atlanta, Georgia, and educated at Morehouse College (B.A.), Crozer Theological Seminary (B.D.), and Boston University (Ph.D.). From his pulpit in Montgomery, Alabama, he preached the politics of peaceful protest and became a national spokesman for the rights of American blacks as founder of the Southern Christian Leadership Conference. In 1964 he was awarded the Nobel Peace Prize. Best known for his keynote speech "I Have a Dream," given during a 1963 protest march on Washington, D.C., King also wrote Stride Toward Freedom *(1958) and*

---

*Authors Note: This response to a published statement by eight fellow clergymen from Alabama (Bishop C. C. J. Carpenter, Bishop Joseph A. Durick, Rabbi Milton L. Grafman, Bishop Paul Hardin, Bishop Nolan B. Harmon, the Reverend George M. Murray, the Reverend Edward V. Ramage, and the Reverend Earl Stallings) was composed under somewhat constricting circumstances. Begun on the margin of the newspaper in which the statement appeared while I was in jail, the letter was continued on scraps of writing paper supplied by a friendly Negro trusty, and concluded on a pad my attorneys were eventually permitted to leave me. Although the text remains in substance unaltered, I have indulged in the author's prerogative of polishing it for publication.

Why We Can't Wait *(1964), from which "Letter from Birmingham Jail—April 16, 1963" is taken. King's consummate mastery of the great rhetorical style of Southern preaching is as apparent in this letter as it is in the film clips of his famous speeches and sermons.*

April 16, 1963

My Dear Fellow Clergymen:

1   While confined here in the Birmingham city jail, I came across your recent statement calling my present activities "unwise and untimely." Seldom do I pause to answer criticism of my work and ideas. If I sought to answer all the criticism that cross my desk, my secretaries would have little time for anything other than such correspondence in the course of the day, and I would have no time for constructive work. But since I feel that you are men of genuine good will and that your criticisms are sincerely set forth, I want to try to answer your statement in what I hope will be patient and reasonable terms.

2   I think I should indicate why I am here in Birmingham, since you have been influenced by the view which argues against "outsiders coming in." I have the honor of serving as president of the Southern Christian Leadership Conference, an organization operating in every southern state, with headquarters in Atlanta, Georgia. We have some eighty-five affiliated organizations across the South, and one of them is the Alabama Christian Movement for Human Rights. Frequently we share staff, educational and financial resources with our affiliates. Several months ago the affiliate here in Birmingham asked us to be on call to engage in a nonviolent direct-action program if such were deemed necessary. We readily consented, and when the hour came we lived up to our promise. So I, along with several members of my staff, am here because I was invited here. I am here because I have organizational ties here.

3   But more basically, I am in Birmingham because injustice is here. Just as the prophets of the eighth century B.C. left their villages and carried their "thus saith the Lord" far beyond the boundaries of their home towns, and just as the Apostle Paul left his village of Tarsus and carried the gospel of Jesus Christ to the far corners of the Greco-Roman world, so am I compelled to carry the gospel of freedom beyond my own home town. Like Paul, I must constantly respond to the Macedonian call for aid.

4   Moreover, I am cognizant of the interrelatedness of all communities and states. I cannot sit idly by in Atlanta and not be concerned about what happens in Birmingham. Injustice anywhere is a threat to justice everywhere. We are caught in an inescapable network of mutuality, tied in a single garment of destiny. Whatever affects one directly, affects all indirectly. Never again can we afford to live with the narrow, provincial "outside agitator" idea. Anyone who lives inside the United States can never be considered an outsider anywhere within its bounds.

5   You deplore the demonstrations taking place in Birmingham. But your statement, I am sorry to say, fails to express a similar concern for the conditions that brought about the demonstrations. I am sure that none of you would want to rest content with the superficial kind of social analysis that deals merely with effects and does not grapple with underlying causes. It is unfortunate that demonstrations are taking place in Birmingham, but it is even more unfortunate that the city's white power structure left the Negro community with no alternative.

6   In any nonviolent campaign there are four basic steps: collection of the facts to determine whether injustices exist; negotiation; self-purification; and direct action. We have gone through all these steps in Birmingham. There can be no gainsaying the fact that racial injustice engulfs this community. Birmingham is probably the most thoroughly segregated city in the United States. Its ugly record of brutality is widely known. Negroes have experienced grossly unjust treatment in the courts. There have been more unsolved bombings of Negro homes and churches in Birmingham than in any other city in the nation. These are the hard, brutal facts of the case. On the basis of these conditions, Negro leaders sought to negotiate with the city fathers. But the latter consistently refused to engage in good-faith negotiation.

7   Then, last September, came the opportunity to talk with leaders of Birmingham's economic community. In the course of the negotiations, certain promises were made by the merchants—for example, to remove the stores' humiliating racial signs. On the basis of these promises, the Reverend Fred Shuttlesworth and the leaders of the Alabama Christian Movement for Human Rights agreed to a moratorium on all demonstrations. As the weeks and months went by, we realized that we were the victims of a broken promise. A few signs, briefly removed, returned; the others remained.

8   As in so many past experiences, our hopes had been blasted, and the shadow of deep disappointment settled upon us. We had no alternative except to prepare for direct action, whereby we would present our very bodies as a means of laying our case before the conscience of the local and the national community. Mindful of the difficulties involved, we decided to undertake a process of self-purification. We began a series of workshops on nonviolence, and we repeatedly asked ourselves: "Are you able to accept blows without retaliating?" "Are you able to endure the ordeal of jail?" We decided to schedule our direct-action program for the Easter season, realizing that except for Christmas, this is the main shopping period of the year. Knowing that a strong economic-withdrawal program would be the byproduct of direct action, we felt that this would be the best time to bring pressure to bear on the merchants for the needed change.

9   Then it occurred to us that Birmingham's mayoral election was coming up in March, and we speedily decided to postpone action until after election day. When we discovered that the Commissioner of Public Safety, Eugene "Bull" Connor, had piled up enough votes to be in the runoff, we decided again to postpone action until the day after the runoff so that the demonstrations could not be used to cloud the issues. Like many others, we waited to see Mr. Connor defeated, and to this end we endured postponement after postponement. Having aided in this community need, we felt that our direct-action program could be delayed no longer.

10   You may well ask: "Why direct action? Why sit-ins, marches and so forth? Isn't negotiation a better path?" You are quite right in calling for negotiation. Indeed, this is the very purpose of direct action. Nonviolent direct action seeks to create such a crisis and foster such a tension that a community which has constantly refused to negotiate is forced to confront the issue. It seeks so to dramatize the issue that it can no longer be ignored. My citing the creation of tension as part of the work of the nonviolent-resister may sound rather shocking. But I must confess that I am not afraid of the word "tension." I have earnestly opposed violent tension, but there is a type of constructive, nonviolent tension which is necessary to create a tension which is necessary for growth.

Just as Socrates felt that it was necessary to create a tension in the mind so that individuals could rise from the bondage of myths and half-truths to the unfettered realm of creative analysis and objective appraisal, so must we see the need for nonviolent gadflies to create the kind of tension in society that will help men rise from the dark depths of prejudice and racism to the majestic heights of understanding and brotherhood.

11   The purpose of our direct-action program is to create a situation so crisis-packed that it will inevitably open the door to negotiation. I therefore concur with you in your call for negotiation. Too long has our beloved Southland been bogged down in a tragic effort to live in monologue rather than dialogue.

12   One of the basic points in your statement is that the action that I and my associates have taken in Birmingham is untimely. Some have asked: "Why didn't you give the new city administration time to act?" The only answer that I can give to this query is that the new Birmingham administration must be prodded about as much as the outgoing one, before it will act. We are sadly mistaken if we feel that the election of Albert Boutwell as mayor will bring the millennium to Birmingham. While Mr. Boutwell is a much more gentle person than Mr. Connor, they are both segregationists, dedicated to maintenance of the status quo. I have hope that Mr. Boutwell will be reasonable enough to see the futility of massive resistance to desegregation. But he will not see this without pressure from devotees of civil rights. My friends, I must say to you that we have not made a single gain in civil rights without determined legal and nonviolent pressure. Lamentably, it is an historical fact that privileged groups seldom give up their privileges voluntarily. Individuals may see the moral light and voluntarily give up their unjust posture; but, as Reinhold Niebuhr has reminded us, groups tend to be more immoral that individuals.

13   We know through painful experience that freedom is never voluntarily given by the oppressor; it must be demanded by the oppressed. Frankly, I have yet to engage in a direct-action campaign that was "well timed" in the view of those who have not suffered unduly from the disease of segregation. For years now I have heard the word "Wait!" It rings in the ear of every Negro with piercing familiarity. This "Wait" has almost always meant "Never." We must come to see, with one of our distinguished jurists, that "justice too long delayed is justice denied."

14   We have waited for more than 340 years for our constitutional and God-given rights. The nations of Asia and Africa are moving with jetlike speed toward gaining political independence, but we still creep at horse-and-buggy pace toward gaining a cup of coffee at a lunch counter. Perhaps it is easy for those who have never felt the stinging darts of segregation to say "Wait." But when you have seen vicious mobs lynch your mothers and fathers at will and drown your sisters and brothers at whim; when you have seen hate-filled policemen curse, kick and even kill your black brothers and sisters; when you see the vast majority of your twenty million Negro brothers smothering in an airtight cage of poverty in the midst of an affluent society; when you suddenly find your tongue twisted and your speech stammering as you seek to explain to your six-year-old daughter why she can't go to the public amusement park that has just been advertised on television, and see tears welling up in her eyes when she is told that Funtown is closed to colored children, and see ominous clouds of inferiority beginning to form in her little mental sky, and see her beginning to destroy her personality by developing an unconscious bitterness toward white people; when you

have to concoct an answer for a five-year-old son who is asking: "Daddy, why do white people treat colored people so mean?"; when you take a cross-country drive and find it necessary to sleep night after night in the uncomfortable corners of your automobile because no motel will accept you; when you are humiliated day in and day out by nagging signs reading "white" and "colored"; when your first name becomes "nigger," your middle name becomes "boy" (however old you are) and your last name becomes "John," and your wife and mother are never given the respected title "Mrs."; when you are harried by day and haunted by night by the fact that you are a Negro, living constantly at tiptoe stance, never quite knowing what to expect next, and are plagued with inner fears and outer resentments; when you are forever fighting a degenerating sense of "nobodiness"—then you will understand why we find it difficult to wait. There comes a time when the cup of endurance runs over, and men are no longer willing to be plunged into the abyss of despair. I hope, sirs, you can understand our legitimate and unavoidable impatience.

15   You express a great deal of anxiety over our willingness to break laws. This is certainly a legitimate concern. Since we so diligently urge people to obey the Supreme Court's decision of 1954 outlawing segregation in the public schools, at first glance it may seem rather paradoxical for us consciously to break laws. One may well ask: "How can you advocate breaking some laws and obeying others?" The answer lies in the fact that there are two types of laws: just and unjust. I would be the first to advocate obeying just laws. One has not only a legal but a moral responsibility to obey just laws. Conversely, one has a moral responsibility to disobey unjust laws. I would agree with St. Augustine that "an unjust law is no law at all."

16   Now, what is the difference between the two? How does one determine whether a law is just or unjust? A just law is a man-made code that squares with the moral law or the law of God. An unjust law is a code that is out of harmony with the moral law. To put it in the terms of St. Thomas Aquinas: An unjust law is a human law that is not rooted in eternal law and natural law. Any law that uplifts human personality is just. Any law that degrades human personality is unjust. All segregation statutes are unjust because segregation distorts the soul and damages the personality. It gives the segregator a false sense of superiority and the segregated a false sense of inferiority. Segregation, to use the terminology of the Jewish philosopher Martin Buber, substitutes an "I-it" relationship for an "I-thou" relationship and ends up relegating persons to the status of things. Hence segregation is not only politically, economically and sociologically unsound, it is morally wrong and sinful. Paul Tillich has said that sin is separation. Is not segregation an existential expression of man's tragic separation, his awful estrangement, his terrible sinfulness? Thus it is that I can urge men to obey the 1954 decision of the Supreme Court, for it is morally right; and I can urge them to disobey segregation ordinances, for they are morally wrong.

17   Let us consider a more concrete example of just and unjust laws. An unjust law is a code that a numerical or power majority group compels a minority group to obey but does not make binding on itself. This is *difference* made legal. By the same token, a just law is a code that a majority compels a minority to follow and that it is willing to follow itself. This is *sameness* made legal.

18   Let me give another explanation. A law is unjust if it is inflicted on a minority that, as a result of being denied the right to vote, had no part in enacting or devising the law.

Who can say that the legislature of Alabama which set up that state's segregation laws was democratically elected? Throughout Alabama all sorts of devious methods are used to prevent Negroes from becoming registered voters, and there are some counties in which, even though Negroes constitute a majority of the population, not a single Negro is registered. Can any law enacted under such circumstances be considered democratically structured?

19   Sometimes a law is just on its face and unjust in its application. For instance, I have been arrested on a charge of parading without a permit. Now, there is nothing wrong in having an ordinance which requires a permit for a parade. But such an ordinance becomes unjust when it is used to maintain segregation and to deny citizens the First-Amendment privilege of peaceful assembly and protest.

20   I hope you are able to see the distinction I am trying to point out. In no sense do I advocate evading or defying the law, as would the rabid segregationist. That would lead to anarchy. One who breaks an unjust law must do so openly, lovingly, and with a willingness to accept the penalty. I submit that an individual who breaks a law that conscience tells him is unjust, and who willingly accepts the penalty of imprisonment in order to arouse the conscience of the community over its unjustice, is in reality expressing the highest respect for law.

21   Of course, there is nothing new about this kind of civil disobedience. It was evidenced sublimely in the refusal of Shadrach, Meshach, and Abednego to obey the laws of Nebuchadnezzar, on the ground that a higher moral law was at stake. It was practiced superbly by the early Christians, who were willing to face hungry lions and the excruciating pain of chopping blocks rather that submit to certain unjust laws of the Roman Empire. To a degree, academic freedom is a reality today because Socrates practiced civil disobedience. In our own nation, the Boston Tea Party represented a massive act of civil disobedience.

22   We should never forget that everything Adolf Hitler did in Germany was "legal" and everything the Hungarian freedom fighters did in Hungary was "illegal." It was "illegal" to aid and comfort a Jew in Hitler's Germany. Even so, I am sure that, had I lived in Germany at the time, I would have aided and comforted my Jewish brothers. If today I lived in a Communist country where certain principles dear to the Christian faith are supressed, I would openly advocate disobeying that country's antireligious laws.

23   I must make two honest confessions to you, my Christian and Jewish brothers. First, I must confess that over the past few years I have been gravely disappointed with the white moderate. I have almost reached the regrettable conclusion that the Negro's great stumbling block in his stride toward freedom is not the White Citizen's Counciler or the Ku Klux Klanner, but the white moderate, who is more devoted to "order" than to justice; who prefers a negative peace which is the absence of tension to a positive peace which is the presence of justice; who constantly says: "I agree with you in the goal you seek, but I cannot agree with your methods of direct action"; who paternalistically believes he can set the time table for another man's freedom; who lives by a mythical concept of time and who constantly advises the Negro to wait for a "more convenient season." Shallow understanding from people of good will is more frustrating than absolute misunderstanding from people of ill will. Lukewarm acceptance is much more bewildering than outright rejection.

24   I had hoped that the white moderate would understand that law and order exist for the purpose of establishing justice and that when they fail in this purpose they become the dangerously structured dams that block the flow of social progress. I had hoped that the white moderate would understand that the present tension in the South is a necessary phase of the transition from an obnoxious negative peace, in which the Negro passively accepted his unjust plight, to a substantive and positive peace, in which all men will respect the dignity and worth of human personality. Actually, we who engage in nonviolent direct action are not the creators of tension. We merely bring to the surface the hidden tension that is already alive. We bring it out in the open, where it can be seen and dealt with. Like a boil that can never be cured so long as it is covered up but must be opened with all its ugliness to the natural medicines of air and light, injustice must be exposed, with all the tension its exposure creates, to the light of human conscience and the air of national opinion before it can be cured.

25   In your statement you assert that our actions, even though peaceful, must be condemned because they precipitate violence. But is this a logical assertion? Isn't this like condemning a robbed man because his possession of money precipitated the evil act of robbery? Isn't this like condemning Socrates because his unswerving commitment to truth and his philosophical inquiries precipitated the act by the misguided populace in which they made him drink hemlock? Isn't this like condemning Jesus because his unique God-consciousness and never-ceasing devotion to God's will precipitated the evil act of crucifixion? We must come to see that, as the federal courts have consistently affirmed, it is wrong to urge an individual to cease his efforts to gain his constitutional rights because the quest may precipitate violence. Society must protect the robbed and punish the robber.

26   I had also hoped that the white moderate would reject the myth concerning time in relation to the struggle for freedom. I have just received a letter from a white brother in Texas. He writes: "All Christians know that the colored people will receive equal rights eventually, but it is possible that you are in too great a religious hurry. It has taken Christianity almost two thousand years to accomplish what it has. The teachings of Christ take time to come to earth." Such an attitude stems from a tragic misconception of time, from the strangely irrational notion that there is something in the very flow of time that will inevitably cure all ills. Actually, time itself is neutral; it can be used either destructively or constructively. More and more I feel that the people of ill will have used time much more effectively than have the people of good will. We will have to repent in this generation not merely for the hateful words and actions of the bad people but for the appalling silence of the good people. Human progress never rolls in on wheels of inevitability; it comes through the tireless efforts of men willing to be co-workers with God, and without this hard work, time itself becomes an ally of the forces of social stagnation. We must use time creatively, in the knowledge that the time is always ripe to do right. Now is the time to make real the promise of democracy and transform our pending national elegy into a creative psalm of brotherhood. Now is the time to lift our national policy from the quicksand of racial injustice to the solid rock of human dignity.

27   You speak of our activity in Birmingham as extreme. At first I was rather disappointed that fellow clergymen would see my nonviolent efforts as those of an extremist. I began thinking about the fact that I stand in the middle of two opposing forces in the Negro community. One is a force of complacency, made up in part of Negroes who, as

a result of long years of oppression, are so drained of self-respect and a sense of "some-bodiness" that they have adjusted to segregation; and in part of a few middle-class Negroes who, because of a degree of academic and economic security and because in some ways they profit by segregation, have become insensitive to the problems of the masses. The other force is one of bitterness and hatred, and it comes perilously close to advocating violence. It is expressed in the various black nationalist groups that are springing up across the nation, the largest and best-known being Elijah Muhammad's Muslim movement. Nourished by the Negro's frustration over the continued existence of racial discrimination, this movement is made up of people who have lost faith in America, who have absolutely repudiated Christianity, and who have concluded that the white man is an incorrigible "devil."

28   I have tried to stand between these two forces, saying that we need emulate neither the "do-nothingism" of the complacent nor the hatred and despair of the black national-ist. For there is the more excellent way of love and nonviolent protest. I am grateful to God that, through the influence of the Negro church, the way of nonviolence became an integral part of our struggle.

29   If this philosophy had not emerged, by now many streets of the South would, I am convinced, be flowing with blood. And I am further convinced that if our white brothers dismiss as "rabble-rousers" and "outside agitators" those of us who employ nonviolent direct action, and if they refuse to support our nonviolent efforts, millions of Negroes will, out of frustration and despair, seek solace and security in black-nationalist ideolo-gies—a development that would inevitably lead to a frightening racial nightmare.

30   Oppressed people cannot remain oppressed forever. The yearning for freedom even-tually manifests itself, and that is what has happened to the American Negro. Something within has reminded him of his birthright of freedom, and something with-out has reminded him that it can be gained. Consciously or unconsciously, he has been caught up by the *Zeitgeist,* and with his black brothers of Africa and his brown and yel-low brothers of Asia, South America, and the Caribbean, the United States Negro is moving with a sense of great urgency toward the promised land of racial justice. If one recognizes this vital urge that has engulfed the Negro community, one should readily understand why public demonstrations are taking place. The Negro has many pent-up resentments and latent frustrations, and he must release them. So let him march; let him make prayer pilgrimages to the city hall; let him go on freedom rides—and try to un-derstand why he must do so. If his repressed emotions are not released in nonviolent ways, they will seek expression through violence; this is not a threat but a fact of his-tory. So I have not said to my people: "Get rid of your discontent." Rather, I have tried to say that this normal and healthy discontent can be channeled into the creative outlet of nonviolent direct action. And now this approach is being termed extremist.

31   But though I was initially disappointed at being categorized as an extremist, as I con-tinued to think about the matter I gradually gained a measure of satisfaction from the label. Was not Jesus an extremist for love: "Love your enemies, bless them that curse you, do good to them that hate you, and pray for them which despitefully use you, and perse-cute you." Was not Amos an extremist for justice: "Let justice roll down like waters and righteousness like an ever-flowing stream." Was not Paul an extremist for the Christian gospel: "I bear in my body the marks of the Lord Jesus." Was not Martin Luther an ex-tremist: "Here I stand, I cannot do otherwise, so help me God." And John Bunyan: "I will stay in jail to the end of my days before I make a butchery of my conscience." And

Abraham Lincoln: "This nation cannot survive half slave and half free." And Thomas Jefferson: "We hold these truths to be self-evident, that all men are created equal. . . ." So the question is not whether we will be extremists, but what kind of extremists we will be. Will we be extremists for hate or for love? Will we be extremists for the preservation of injustice or for the extension of justice? In that dramatic scene on Calvary's hill three men were crucified. We must never forget that all three were crucified for the same crime—the crime of extremism. Two were extremists for immorality, and thus fell below their environment. The other, Jesus Christ, was an extremist for love, truth and goodness, and thereby rose above his environment. Perhaps the South, the nation and the world are in dire need of creative extremists.

32   I had hoped that the white moderate would see this need. Perhaps I was too optimistic; perhaps I expected too much. I suppose I should have realized that few members of the oppressor race can understand the deep groans and passionate yearnings of the oppressed race, and still fewer have the vision to see that injustice must be rooted out by strong, persistent and determined action. I am thankful, however, that some of our white brothers in the South have grasped the meaning of this social revolution and committed themselves to it. They are still all too few in quantity, but they are big in quality. Some—such as Ralph McGill, Lillian Smith, Harry Golden, James McBride Dabbs, Ann Braden and Sarah Patton Boyle—have written about our struggle in eloquent and prophetic terms. Others have marched with us down nameless streets of the South. They have languished in filthy, roach-infested jails, suffering the abuse and brutality of policemen who view them as "dirty nigger-lovers." Unlike so many of their moderate brothers and sisters, they have recognized the urgency of the moment and sensed the need for powerful "action" antidotes to combat the disease of segregation.

33   Let me take note of my other major disappointment. I have been so greatly disappointed with the white church and its leadership. Of course, there are some notable exceptions. I am not unmindful of the fact that each of you has taken some significant stands on this issue. I commend you, Reverend Stallings, for your Christian stand on this past Sunday, in welcoming Negroes to your worship service on a nonsegregated basis. I commend the Catholic leaders of this state for integrating Spring Hill College several years ago.

34   But despite these notable exceptions, I must honestly reiterate that I have been disappointed with the church. I do not say this as one of those negative critics who can always find something wrong with the church. I say this as a minister of the gospel, who loves the church; who was nurtured in its bosom; who has been sustained by its spiritual blessings and who will remain true to it as long as the cord of life shall lengthen.

35   When I was suddenly catapulted into the leadership of the bus protest in Montgomery, Alabama, a few years ago, I felt we would be supported by the white church. I felt that the white ministers, priests and rabbis of the South would be among our strongest allies. Instead, some have been outright opponents, refusing to understand the freedom movement and misrepresenting its leaders; all too many others have been more cautious than courageous and have remained silent behind the anesthetizing security of stained-glass windows.

36   In spite of my shattered dreams, I came to Birmingham with the hope that the white religious leadership of this community would see the justice of our cause and, with deep moral concern, would serve as the channel through which just grievances could reach

the power structure. I had hoped that each of you would understand. But again I have been disappointed.

37 I have heard numerous southern religious leaders admonish their worshippers to comply with a desegregation decision because it is the law, but I have longed to hear white ministers declare: "Follow this decree because integration is morally right and because the Negro is your brother." In the midst of blatant injustices inflicted upon the Negro, I have watched white churchmen stand on the sideline and mouth pious irrelevancies and sanctimonious trivialities. In the midst of a mightly struggle to rid our nation of racial and economical injustice, I have heard many ministers say: "Those are social issues, with which the gospel has no real concern." And I have watched many churches commit themselves to a completely otherworldly religion which makes a strange, un-Biblical distinction between body and soul, between the sacred and the secular.

38 I have traveled the length and breadth of Alabama, Mississippi and all the southern states. On sweltering summer days and crisp autumn mornings I have looked at the South's most beautiful churches and their lofty spires pointing heavenward. I have beheld the impressive outlines of her massive religious-education buildings. Over and over I have found myself asking: "What kind of people worship here? Who is their God? Where were their voices when the lips of Governor Barnett dripped with words of interposition and nullification? Where were they when Governor Wallace gave a clarion call for defiance and hatred? Where were their voices of support when bruised and weary Negro men and women decided to rise from the dark dungeons of complacency to the bright hills of creative protest?"

39 Yes, these questions are still in my mind. In deep disappointment I have wept over the laxity of the church. But be assured that my tears have been tears of love. Yes, I love the church. How could I do otherwise? I am in the rather unique position of being the son, the grandson and the greatgrandson of preachers. Yes, I see the church as the body of Christ. But, oh! How we have blemished and scarred that body through social neglect and through fear of being nonconformists.

40 There was a time when the church was very powerful—in the time when the early Christians rejoiced at being deemed worthy to suffer for what they believed. In those days the church was not merely a thermometer that recorded the ideas and principles of popular opinion; it was a thermostat that transformed the mores of society. Whenever the early Christians entered a town, the people in power became disturbed and immediately sought to convict the Christians for being "disturbers of the peace" and "outside agitators." But the Christians pressed on, in the conviction that they were "a colony of heaven," called to obey God rather than man. Small in number, they were big in commitment. They were too God-intoxicated to be "astronomically intimidated." By their effort and example they brought an end to such ancient evils as infanticide and gladiatorial contests.

41 Things are different now. So often the contemporary church is a weak, ineffectual voice with an uncertain sound. So often it is an archdefender of the status quo. Far from being disturbed by the presence of the church, the power structure of the average community is consoled by the church's silent—and even vocal—sanction of things as they are.

42 But the judgment of God is upon the church as never before. If today's church does not recapture the sacrificial spirit of the early church, it will lose its authenticity, forfeit the loyalty of millions, and be dismissed as an irrelevant social club with no meaning

for the twentieth century. Every day I meet young people whose disappointment with the church has turned into outright disgust.

43   Perhaps I have once again been too optimistic. Is organized religion too inextricably bound to the status quo to save our nation and the world? Perhaps I must turn my faith to the inner spiritual church, the church within the church, as the true *ekklesia* and the hope of the world. But again I am thankful to God that some noble souls from the ranks of organized religion have broken loose from the paralyzing chains of conformity and joined us as active partners in the struggle for freedom. They have left their secure congregations and walked the streets of Albany, Georgia, with us. They have gone down the highways of the South on tortuous rides for freedom. Yes, they have gone to jail with us. Some have been dismissed from their churches, have lost the support of their bishops and fellow ministers. But they have acted in the faith that right defeated is stronger than evil triumphant. Their witness has been the spiritual salt that has preserved the true meaning of the gospel in these troubled times. They have carved a tunnel of hope through the dark mountain of disappointment.

44   I hope the church as a whole will meet the challenge of this decisive hour. But even if the church does not come to the aid of justice, I have no despair about the future. I have no fear about the outcome of our struggle in Birmingham, even if our motives are at present misunderstood. We will reach the goal of freedom in Birmingham and all over the nation, because the goal of America is freedom. Abused and scorned though we may be, our destiny is tied up with America's destiny. Before the pilgrims landed at Plymouth, we were here. Before the pen of Jefferson etched the majestic words of the Declaration of Independence across the pages of history, we were here. For more than two centuries our forebears labored in this country without wages; they made cotton king; they built the homes of their masters while suffering gross injustice and shameful humiliation—and yet out of a bottomless vitality they continued to thrive and develop. If the inexpressible cruelties of slavery could not stop us, the opposition we now face will surely fail. We will win our freedom because the sacred heritage of our nation and the eternal will of God are embodied in our echoing demands.

45   Before closing I feel impelled to mention one other point in your statement that has troubled me profoundly. You warmly commended the Birmingham police force for keeping "order" and "preventing violence." I doubt that you would so quickly commend the policemen if you were to observe their ugly and inhumane treatment of Negroes here in the city jail; if you were to watch them push and curse old Negro women and young Negro girls; if you were to see them slap and kick old Negro men and young boys; if you were to observe them, as they did on two occasions, refuse to give us food because we wanted to sing our grace together. I cannot join you in your praise of the Birmingham police department.

46   It is true that the police have exercised a degree of discipline in handling the demonstrators. In this sense they conducted themselves rather "nonviolently" in public. But for what purpose? To preserve the evil system of segregation. Over the past few years I have consistently preached that nonviolence demands that the means we use must be as pure as the ends we seek. I have tried to make clear that it is wrong to use immoral means to attain moral ends. But now I must affirm that it just as wrong or perhaps even more so, to use moral means to preserve immoral ends. Perhaps Mr. Connor and his policemen have been rather nonviolent in public, as was Chief Pritchett in Albany,

Georgia, but they have used the moral means of nonviolence to maintain the immoral end of racial injustice. As T. S. Eliot has said: "The last temptation is the greatest treason: To do the right deed for the wrong reason."

47   I wish you had commended the Negro sit-inners and demonstrators of Birmingham for their sublime courage, their willingness to suffer and their amazing discipline in the midst of great provocation. One day the South will recognize its real heroes. They will be the James Merediths, with the noble sense of purpose that enables them to face jeering and hostile mobs, and with the agonizing loneliness that characterizes the life of the pioneer. They will be old, oppressed, battered Negro women, symbolized in a seventy-two-year-old woman in Montgomery, Alabama, who rose up with a sense of dignity and with her people decided not to ride segregated buses, and who responded with ungrammatical profundity to one who inquired about her weariness: "My feets is tired, but my soul is at rest." They will be the young high school and college students, the young ministers of the gospel and a host of their elders, courageously and nonviolently sitting in at lunch counters and willingly going to jail for conscience' sake. One day the South will know that when these disinherited children of God sat down at lunch counters, they were in reality standing up for what is best in the American dream and for the most sacred values in our Judaeo-Christian heritage, thereby bringing our nation back to those great wells of democracy which were dug deep by the founding fathers in their formulation of the Constitution and the Declaration of Independence.

48   Never before have I written so long a letter. I'm afraid it is much too long to take your precious time. I can assure you that it would have been much shorter if I had been writing from a comfortable desk, but what else can one do when he is alone in a narrow jail cell, other than write long letters, think long thoughts and pray long prayers?

49   If I have said anything in this letter that overstates the truth and indicates an unreasonable impatience, I beg you to forgive me. If I have said anything that understates the truth and indicates my having a patience that allows me to settle for anything less than brotherhood, I beg God to forgive me.

50   I hope this letter finds you strong in the faith. I also hope that circumstances will soon make it possible for me to meet each of you, not as an integrationist or a civil-rights leader but as a fellow clergyman and a Christian brother. Let us all hope that the dark clouds of racial prejudice will soon pass away and the deep fog of misunderstanding will be lifted from our fear-drenched communities, and in some not too distant tomorrow the radiant stars of love and brotherhood will shine over our great nation with all their scintillating beauty.

> Yours for the cause of Peace and Brotherhood,
> Martin Luther King, Jr.

PRACTICE

Discussion

1. Why did King place the argument about his disappointment with the white church's leadership in his refutation of *extremism?* Does it fit here?

2. How does King turn the term "extremist" to his own advantage?

3. How does King list the names of white Southerners who have helped his cause? How effective would this list be when read by the white clergy?

4. Why does King begin his criticism of the white church's leadership with compliments? Does this enhance his ethical proof?

5. Point out the places where King tells the clergy that he is one of them. Why does he say this? How do you think this affects the readers?

6. Where does King use rhetorical questions? Why? Martin Luther King was also a master of other rhetorical techniques. Note particularly the effect of the long parallel sentence beginning, "I doubt that you would so quickly commend the policemen if you were to observe. . . ." What is the effect of King's beginning the clauses that follow the semicolon with "if"?

7. Is the tone of his letter primarily pessimistic or optimistic? Give specific evidence.

8. Besides the clergy, who is the audience for this letter? How do you know? This letter has had a profound effect on readers since its publication in 1963. Why do you think it has been printed and quoted so often?

Vocabulary

affiliated	repudiated	pious
cognizant	emulate	sanctimonious
moratorium	solace	secular
status quo	manifests	interposition
relegating	latent	mores
precipitate	languished	sanction
complacency	admonish	inextricably

Writing

1. Find a letter in your newspaper with which you disagree. Refute two or three of its points.

2. Write an argument refuting a policy position taken by an institution with which you are involved: school, church, political party, civic organization, etc.

3. Choose one of the selections in this reader and refute its main points.

PART
THREE

The Handbook

HANDBOOK

"I always choose the grammatical form unless it sounds affected," said the poet Marianne Moore. This is sensible advice for you as a writer, but first you must know what the grammatical form is. To find the correct form, or simply to polish your skills in grammar, usage, and mechanics, you should use this *Handbook*. We begin with the "small" building blocks of the language, the parts of speech. If, at any point, you need to look up unfamiliar terms, turn to the glossary beginning on page 507.

▼ A Point of View On Grammar and Usage

Much of what we say or write requires no grammatical discussion, creates no argument. Only a fraction of "normal" English statements contain mistakes or debatable usages. Such are the expressions below. They are questionable (at least, they are questioned by many people):

> Do it *like* I say.
>
> I wouldn't do that if I *was* you.
>
> The committee *are* meeting tomorrow.
>
> *To badly do* that job is a mistake.
>
> It's *me*.

Why do such problems exist at all? A major reason can be found in the imperfections of the language itself. As is generally the case with languages, English has developed inconsistently and irregularly. Many of its patterns of grammar and usage are inconsistent or irregular. One great authority, Edward Sapir, remarked that "all grammars leak." By this he meant—among other things—that the grammars we have invented to describe language are imperfect. Indeed we sometimes expect too much of our grammatical explanations, which often contain contradictions and exceptions. It should be added that not everybody can be—or should be—a grammarian. What most people need are not perfect grammatical answers, but ones that work reasonably well to questions that arise when they write: answers which won't tie their brains in knots.

▼ Premises

To answer your questions about grammar and usage, then, we oversimplify, just as other textbook authors do. And, like most other authors, we work from a set of premises that experts in English have generally agreed upon. We suggest that they be your premises also. On most questions of grammar and usage, then, you should:

1. Consider the practice of good writers.

2. Consider the opinions of authorities. See the list of authorities on the next page.

3. Consult your own wish for common sense and order in the language. "For all who speak or write," says Wilson Follett in *Modern American Usage*, "the road to effective language is thinking straight."

4. Remember that there are often several ways to solve a problem in grammar and usage, not just one.

Let's discuss the last premise for a moment. Writers often say: "I have a question in grammar [or usage]. Give me the answer." But there may be two answers, or three or four; why be satisfied with one and limit your options? We are commonly asked, for example: "What word can I use to put in the place of this 'bad' one?" The question may be poorly stated. Many sentences are like brick walls. You usually can't grasp a "bad" brick from the middle of a wall, slide it out, and stick another one in. The whole structure is too firm. Instead, to replace the brick you may have to tear down the wall, and then rebuild it in one of several ways.

▼ Alternative Solutions

When you can, consider several solutions to a linguistic problem. As an example, consider the familiar problem of agreement with *either-or* and *neither-nor*. It is not hard to remember that with singular nouns in the subject, these pairs take singular verbs. You simply memorize this fact and apply it when necessary:

Neither the car *nor* the truck *was* stolen.

But what do you use when there is one car and two trucks?

Neither the car *nor* the trucks *was (?) were (?)* stolen.

Neither *was* nor *were* sounds right, although the grammatical rule says that *were* is the proper choice—"the verb should agree with the nearer of its subjects."

It is often possible to avoid such a problem (and the possibility of error) by using one of several different constructions that will say pretty much the same thing. Here are a few:

Problem: Neither the car nor the trucks *was (?) were (?)* stolen.

Solutions: The car *was* not stolen. Neither *were* the trucks.

The trucks *were* not stolen. Nor *was* the car.

The trucks and the car *were* not stolen.

The car and the trucks *were* still there.

The car *was* not stolen, and the trucks *weren't* either.

The trucks and the car *have not been* stolen.

The thieves *left* the car and the trucks.

▼ Books To Consult

This is not a book on usage alone, so in the following pages we cannot devote much space to the many irksome questions that inevitably arise in a writer's work. But help is available. When you want more information than we have space for, consult one or more of the following:

Bernstein, Theodore, *The Careful Writer: A Modern Guide to English Usage*. New York: Atheneum, 1965.

_____, *Dos, Don'ts and Maybes of English Usage*. New York: New York Times Books, 1977.

Copperud, Roy. *American Usage and Style: The Consensus*. New York: Van Nostrand Reinhold, 1980.

Ebbitt, Wilma R., and David R. Ebbitt, *Index to English*. 8th ed. New York, NY: 1990.

Evans, Bergen, and Cornelia Evans, *A Dictionary of Contemporary American Usage*. New York: Random House, 1957.

Follett, Wilson, *Modern American Usage*. New York: Hill and Wang, 1966.

Fowler, H. W., *A Dictionary of Modern English Usage*, 2nd Rev. ed. by Ernest Gowers. Oxford University Press, 1987.

Morris, William, and Mary Morris, *Harper Dictionary of Contemporary Usage*. 2nd ed. New York: Harper & Row, 1985.

GA

Grammatical Analysis

■■■ GA 1   *Learn the Parts of Speech*

The parts of speech are classified by the jobs they perform in a sentence. Memorize this table:

nouns ⎫ *name*	(Nothing else *names*.)
pronouns ⎭	
verbs *state.*	(Nothing else *states*.)
adjectives ⎫ *modify*	(Nothing else *modifies*.)
adverbs ⎭	
prepositions ⎫ *join*	(Nothing else *joins*.)
conjunctions ⎭	

To explain how the parts of speech "perform their jobs" in a sentence, let's begin by considering some typical nouns and verbs.

Typical nouns:
The **draw** you made on the last poker hand was pure luck.
His was a great **run.**
The story started in a **place** called Shenandoah.

Typical verbs:
You will never **draw** another hand like that.
He had **run** that race before.
She could not **place** Jim, although she vaguely recognized him.

Draw, *run*, and *place* are nouns in the first group of sentences because they are *naming words*. But since they are acting as *stating words* in the second group, *draw*, *run*, and *place* are verbs there. (The verb phrases are *will draw*, *had run*, and *could place*, but we will ignore such phrases for the time being.)

In the half-mad sentence below (perhaps uttered by a crazy sea captain who had dosed himself on too much rum and grammar), what parts of speech is *forward* acting as?

      1   2   3   4   5

Forward the *forward* sail *forward* the *forward forwardly!*

1. *Forward* is a verb in the "command position," as in "*Do* a good job," or "*Pick* up my books." Military order: "*Forward*, march!"

2. *Forward* is an adjective, meaning "near the front," modifying *sail*.

3. *Forward* is a preposition, meaning "near to" and implying placement, as in "*by* the bridge," "*over* the hill," "*around* the house."

4. *Forward* is a noun, designating the front end of the ship.

5. *Forwardly* is an adverb (note the -*ly*), showing how something is done; it means "boldly and eagerly."

To explain further how the parts of speech work, let's expand the information given in the table at the beginning of this section.

1. **Nouns** are naming words. They fit in the slot in this sentence: "The _____ did it." Here are some examples:

   The *dog* did it.

   The *vandals* did it.

   The *Smiths* did it.

   The *running* did it.

   Note that even though *running* appears to be a verb, it is acting as a noun, as the subject of the sentence. Therefore we call it a noun.

   We can put two or more words together to make compound nouns: *truck driver, tenderfoot, like-mindedness, lady-in-waiting.*

2. **Pronouns** are noun substitutes. They are naming words that stand for nouns (*pro* means "for"). Examples:

   We did *that* for *you*.

   This is *what* she did for *her.*

   What is *it*?

   Are *they* coming to the party? *Some* are.

3. **Verbs** state. They can fit in the slot: "The thing(s) _____ it." (*Thing* here stands for any noun acting as a subject.) Examples:

   The thing *wanted* it.

The things *were* happy.

The thing *seems to be* a rat.

The thing *will bake* a pie.

The thing *should have been allowed to win* it.

As the last three examples indicate, words used as verbs can be combined to make verb phrases.

4. **Adjectives** modify (describe, qualify, or limit) nouns and pronouns. Examples:

A *big* house, a *bigger* house, the *biggest* house

The *sharp* stick, a *sharper* stick, the *sharpest* stick

They were *young.*

Truly *able* people are usually *happy.*

It was *better.*

Middle-aged executives make the *best* managers.

NOTE: When attached to nouns, words like *the, a, an, this, those, my, her, our,* and so on can be considered as adjectives (they describe, qualify, or limit): *the* market, *my* habit, *their* lives, *a* Pontiac, *that* diamond, *those* people, *one's* trumpet.

5. **Adverbs** modify a verb, adjective, or another adverb. They often end in *-ly.* Usually they tell *how, why, when, where,* or *how much.* Examples:

The duck quacked *loudly.*

It was a *very* old duck.

Drive *slow(ly).*

Put the chair *there.*

I'll be home *early.*

6. **Prepositions** join nouns and pronouns to other elements in a sentence. The noun or pronoun is considered the *object of the preposition.* In "before the war," *before* is the preposition, and *war* the object of the preposition; in "in regard to it," *in* and *to* are prepositions, and *regard* and *it* are their objects.

   Prepositions can also appear at the end of the sentence:

Which person did you give it *to*?

I am giving the whole thing *up.*

What did you do that *for*?

7. **Conjunctions** join. But unlike prepositions, they do not employ nouns or pronouns as objects.

   a. **Coordinating conjunctions** connect word units of equal rank:

      You *and* I

      Tired *but* happy

Cubs *or* White Sox

Help us, *or* we will fail.

I saw you, *so* I knew you were there.

b. **Subordinating conjunctions** connect subordinate clauses to main clauses (see the next section for more on clauses). Examples:

When the doorknob fell off, they were trapped in the room.

If it is raining, call a cab to get home.

The tests were postponed, *even though* all the students were ready to take them.

The angel lost its wings *because* it was careless.

PRACTICE

Identify the parts of speech of the italicized words in the following sentences.

1. *Many* colleges *suffer from* high *expenses and low* enrollments.

2. When *one* sees his life *pass before him, he is* not *necessarily ready for* death *or* the grave.

3. *The law* is *what* we *make it, in fact* as well as *action.*

4. *Running, jumping,* and *breathing* are *surely* all verbs. Is that *true?*

5. *All* women are *equal* to *men* (*say the feminists, who* are determined to shatter *many stereotypes* based *on* sex).

6. If *you believe this,* will *you* act *accordingly?*

7. It is *time* to play baseball *because spring* is *here.*

8. *Concerning your* raise *see* Mr. *Partin, the general assistant* manager.

9. "*I dreamed* I *was dreaming,* and of course I had to wake up from my *dream dream,* and that woke me out of my *dream* too."

—Dwight Bolinger, *Aspects of Language*

10. *After dreaming, but* before being *entirely awake,* he *began* to snore *fast* and *loud.*

■■■ GA 2 Learn to Identify Clauses

A **clause** is a statement created by joining a noun-subject to its own verb. Without such joining, the clause cannot exist.

1. **Main clauses** make complete statements. A main clause can be a full sentence. In the following sentences, the subjects and verbs of the main clauses are italicized:

$$\overset{S}{\text{Mrs. }} \overset{V}{Canaday \; will \; be} \text{ at home on Wednesday.}$$

Mrs. *Canaday will be* at home on Wednesday.

Two *cars came* down the block to the two-story house.

The *beer froze* on the back porch.

Asthma and *pneumonia are* related conditions.

Dogs bark.

2. **Subordinate clauses** are also created by joining noun-subjects to their own verbs. But these clauses differ in two ways from main clauses: (1) they do not make complete statements; and (2) they are usually signaled by what we call here a *subordinating sign*. Here are some examples, with the subordinating signs capitalized:

IF Mrs. *Canaday will be* at home on Wednesday. . .

. . . WHEN two *cars came* down the block.

AFTER the *beer froze* on the back porch. . .

. . . EVEN THOUGH the *beer froze* on the back porch

WHAT *man has put* asunder. . .

. . . WHO *have been* usually accurate. . .

The spaced periods indicate that subordinate clauses cannot stand alone as complete sentences.

Many words can act as subordinating signs. They give readers a signal about what lies ahead in the grammar of the sentence. Here is a partial list (units of two or three words may function as one sign):

after	since	when
although	so that	whenever
as though	that	which
because	until	while
before	what	who
no matter what	whatever	whosoever

That as a subordinating sign may be omitted from its clause, but it should always be understood:

Car-makers agree [THAT] their products use too much gasoline.

The good [THAT] a person does never lasts.

Putting subordinating signs and main clauses together, we can write sentences like these (subordinating signs are capitalized):

Subordinate	*Main*

WHATEVER they decide to do, it should be of some help.

Main	*Subordinate*

The mechanic said THAT the old engine could be fixed.

Main	*Subordinate*	*Main continued*

Our singers, WHO had been practicing in the barn, moved into the church.

Main	*Subordinate*	*Subordinate*

The senator said THAT he would sue BECAUSE he had been slandered.

Main

THAT the major is honest is obvious.

Subordinate

(The subject of the main clause is "That the major is honest.")

PRACTICE

In each of the following sentences, insert a brace (⌒) over the main and subordinate clauses. Underline any subordinating signs, and insert any that are understood.

1. Annihilation is a risk we must not take.

2. A basic principle writers should follow is brevity.

3. "It is useless to go to bed to save the light, if the result is twins."

—Chinese proverb

4. Bacon was right when he said reading makes a full man.

5. The rhetoric teacher is an academic gravedigger who always has his shovel ready.

6. How one writes reflects how one feels.

7. If you are caught between despair and misery, the only way is up.

8. "When you are nine, you know that there are things that you don't know, but you know that when you know something you know it."

—Robert Penn Warren, "Blackberry Winter"

Subordinate clauses act in three ways—as *nouns, adjectives,* or *adverbs.*

a. A **noun clause** substitutes for a noun or pronoun.

> *Noun:*   *Work* is a bore.
> *Clause:* *What we do* is a bore.

> *Pronoun:* I approve of *her.*
>   *Clause:* I approve of *how she works.*

>   *Noun:*   His parents do not understand his *politics.*
>   *Clause:* His parents do not understand *why he votes Democratic.*

b. An **adjective clause** modifies a noun or pronoun.

> A woman *who has a good job* can afford some luxuries.
> Americans *who speak Japanese* are rare.
> The table, *which had been recently painted*, got wet in the rain.
> Any drug *that can cure cancer* may have dangerous side effects.
> She *who raises children* should be respected.

c. Some **adverb clauses** modify adjectives or other adverbs. A large number of adverb clauses answer questions such as *how, when, where, how much, why,* or *to what extent.* In the years that we have been teaching grammar, however, it has become plain that these questions alone often do not help identify adverb clauses. In addition to the questions, we suggest a simple "negative formula" : An adverb clause is any clause that is *not* nounal or adjectival. In other words, the adverb clause *does not* replace or modify a noun or pronoun.

> She is sure *that she will get the job.* (Modifies an *adjective*—"sure.")
> *So that you can get home easily,* I'll lend you my car. (Tells *why.)*
> She came *as soon as she got your note. (*Tells *when.)*
> They play tennis *more than I do.* (Tells *how much.)*
> I knew you stole a cookie *because you had a guilty expression.* (Tells *why.)*

PRACTICE

Identify the italicized subordinate clauses as *noun, adjective,* or *adverb*.

1. They wondered *who he could be*.

2. The fact *that America is a great country* is beside the point.

3. Mr. Smith, *who is a medical technician*, can help us.

4. *If I were you*, I would ask him to call us.

5. She said *that more women would be having children in the next decade*.

6. *When we were in New York*, we stayed at the Biltmore.

7. I go *where I want to*.

8. He will do *what you tell him*.

9. *Whose fault it is* is a serious question.

10. Is this the book *which you had studied*?

■■■ GA 3   Learn to Identify Phrases

A **phrase** is a grammatical unit larger than a single part of speech but smaller than a clause. A phrase must have at least two words in it. Unlike a clause, a phrase does not make a statement using a combination of noun subject and its own verb. Here are five phrases that, taken together, form a complete sentence:

> The black horse   with the long mane   by the corral   will be ridden   by an expert cowboy.

Phrases are classified as follows:

1. **Noun phrases:**

Puppy love strikes *many sensible people* as *a pain* in the neck.

2. **Prepositional phrases:**

On the whole, it is not a bad pain *in the neck*.

3. **Verb phrases:**

Mr. Winchell *has been biting* into every peach in the store.

The store owner *will consider* legal action.

Have you *found* any whole peaches?

4. **Verbal phrases** (phrases made from verbs) are not main verbs or verb phrases; they cannot help to make statements in clause or sentence form.

a. **Participial phrases** act as adjectives:

The wart *growing on my finger* was not painful.

The child *hurt by shrapnel* did recover.

Relinquishing their rights, they surrendered.

Born in San Antonio, he grew up with a taste for hot weather.

b. **Infinitive phrases** use the "to _____ " form:

To act well in this life is sometimes impossible.

She wanted *to replace the astronaut.*

That work is yet *to be done.*

c. **Gerund phrases** act as nouns:

Raising roses in this heat is impossible.

They considered *rearing children,* but later thought better of it.

Here are some examples of phrases, along with the jobs they are performing:

Phrase	Name of Phrase	Job Performed (*Noun, Adjective, Adverb, Verb*)
To be a cop is dangerous.	infinitive	noun (*To be a cop* is the subject of the sentence.)
Her desire *to be a cop* is commendable.	infinitive	adjective (*To be a cop* modifies the noun *desire.*)
Their hurrying through the job was a mistake.	gerund	noun (*Their hurrying* is the subject of the sentence.)
They were people *of integrity.*	prepositional	adjective (*Of integrity* modifies the noun *people.*)
Locking the house, they ran to the car.	participial	adjective (*Locking the house* modifies *they.*)
The people *locking the house* were the owners.	participial	adjective (*Locking the house* modifies *people.*)
They protected the house by *locking it up.*	gerund	noun (*Locking it up* is the object of the preposition *by.*)
Before Sunday is soon enough.	prepositional	noun (*Before Sunday* is the subject of the sentence.)
If you must chew tobacco, do it *with style.*	prepositional	adverb (*With style* modifies the verb *do.*)
She was unhappy *to see him leave.*	infinitive	adverb (*To see him leave* modifies the adjective *unhappy.*)
The bad man is my uncle.	noun	noun
This job *is being done.*	verb	verb

PRACTICE

1. First identify the italicized phrases by name: *noun, prepositional, verb*. Then describe the job (*noun, adjective, verb*) that the phrase is performing. (The numeral following each sentence indicates the number of phrases contained in it.)

   a. The fur *of the cat was rising.* (2)

   b. *By the chair* was where we found her alternately purring and snarling. (1)

   c. You *should sit* here *by me on the bench.* (3)

   d. *Light bulbs can light our dark cellar.* (3)

   e. *The comic strip* "Doonesbury" teaches *by indirection.* (2)

   f. Megaforce [a movie] *will be forgotten with considerable ease.* (2)

2. Identify the verbal phrases (*participial, infinitive,* and *gerund*) in the following sentences. Then state the job that each phrase is performing (*noun, adjective, adverb*).

   a. *Riding a bicycle* is dangerous in this city. (1)

   b. *Even double-locked*, her bike was stolen. (1)

   c. She was eager *to get it back, calling the police* three times. (2)

   d. *By warning the residents*, they prevented more injury. (1)

   e. *Warning the residents* was a good idea. (1)

   f. *To run away, leaving the area quickly*, was their only concern. (2)

   g. Off went the residents, *leaving the area quickly.* (1)

Forms Of Grammar

■■■ G 1 Possessive with Gerunds and Inanimate Objects

G 1(a) Possessive with a Gerund

A *gerund* is a verbal noun that ends in *-ing*.

> Pitch*ing* is fun.
> Learn*ing* is hard.
> His ly*ing* is hard to take.

When the emphasis is on the activity, use the *possessive form* with the *-ing* noun.

> *Problem:*   She did not object to *me hugging* her.
> *Solution:*   She did not object to *my hugging* her.

> *Problem:*   The *officer commanding* me to pull over was a surprise.
> *Solution:*   The *officer's commanding* me to pull over was a surprise.

If the emphasis is not on the activity, you may write:

> She did not object to *me* hugging her. (But she might have objected to any other person who hugged her.)
> I prefer *John* pitching. (The emphasis is on John, rather than on his activity, pitching.)

G 1(b)   Possessive with an Inanimate Object

Inanimate means "not living." When making the possessive with an inanimate object, the problem is whether you use an apostrophe and *s* or an *of*. Do you write *my coat's collar* or *the collar of my coat*? The *floor of my living room or my living room's floor*?

With most inanimate objects, you use the *of* form:

leaves of the tree; *not* tree's leaves

maker of the furniture; *not* furniture's maker

But the rule is not completely firm, partly because our reason for using the *of* form is often based on whether the possessive with *'s* is awkward—to most writers, *furniture's maker* is just that. If the construction is familiar and reasonably smooth, you can often use either kind of possessive:

the clock's hands, *or* the hands of the clock

the index of the book, *or* the book's index

NOTE: Some very common idioms use the apostrophe with inanimate objects:

the law's delay (from Shakespeare's *Hamlet*)

her wits' end

a dollar's worth

PRACTICE

Correct the following sentences for faulty possessives; then explain your correction in a sentence or two. If you think that a sentence is correct as it stands, explain why.

1. Hal Johnson writing was the best I had ever read.

2. No one appreciates Elizabeth modeling more than I do.

3. He said that he wished you had stopped him joking about our mistakes so much.

4. The oxen in the zoo were disturbed by the lion roaring.

5. We heard them roaring.

6. Father objected to him dating Susie.

7. He insists on me chaperoning poor Susie on every date.

8. She hated him interfering with her private life.

9. Natchez is the state of Mississippi's most interesting city.

10. I don't like the city council's attitude on parking problems.

■■■ G 2 Vague or Ambiguous Pronoun Reference

G 2(a) Make Your Pronoun References Clear

Problem: The dresser had glue blocks over the screw holes so that one had to remove the screws before removing the drawer supports. *This* required me to get help from my shop instructor. (What does *this* refer to?)

Solution: Since the dresser had glue blocks over the screw holes, I asked my shop instructor to help me remove the blocks without damaging the drawer supports.

Problem: Our dog knocked two lamps on the floor and broke several glasses on the lamp table. We found *them* smashed the next morning. (Does *them* refer to lamps, to glasses, or to lamps *and* glasses?)

Solution: Our dog knocked . . . We found the glasses smashed the next morning.

Problem: In discussing the language requirements, *it* made us feel that we had the wrong idea about the usefulness of a foreign language. (What does *it* refer to?)

Solution: As we were discussing the language requirements, we began to realize that we had the wrong idea about the usefulness of a foreign language.

Problem: I won a lot of money, *which* made me very happy. (It was the occurrence, not the money, which made me happy.)

Solution: Winning a lot of money made me happy.

G 2(b) Do Not Confuse the Pronoun It with the Expletive (or "Filler") It

The expletive *it* is part of a "filler phrase" and as such is not a *pronoun* referring to something:

> *It* is raining. *Or: It's* raining.

> *It* was a good idea for you to come home today.

In both of these examples, *it* is not a pronoun but rather a part of a special linguistic formula called the *expletive*.

Problem: On the island of Saint Helena, Napoleon died of cancer. *It* was, observers noted, an irony that the great general died of a common disease instead of on the battlefield. [At first, *it* appears to refer to *cancer*.]

Solution: Napoleon died on the island of Saint Helena. Observers noted that he died in a most unmilitary fashion—of the common disease of cancer.

G 2(c)   *A Pronoun Should Refer to a Noun, Not to a Modifier*

Problem: Jane preferred historical novels because *it* [meaning *history*] was always her favorite subject in school. [*It* cannot refer to *historical* because that word is an adjective.]

Solution: Jane preferred historical novels because history was always her favorite subject in school.

G 2(d)   *Use the Pronoun* You *Appropriately*

As you have noticed, we often employ *you* in this book because we are addressing the reader. Our *stance* is that of one person talking directly to other people about a subject of some concern to us all. This stance is appropriate in many subjects:

> When pressing both CLOCK buttons, be careful to press them at the same time. If you press them unevenly, the "message" may not be sent to the VCR. [*from owner's VCR manual*]

Writers also employ *you* where an older generation might have used *one* more or less impersonally:

> When *you* consider [or: *one considers*] the early spring flowers, it is not surprising that the narcissus stands out for its beauty and fragrance.

Avoid overworking *you* or using it incongruously. The sentence below appears in a paper directed at a general audience:

> When *you* pull out *your* pipe after dinner, consider the number of people who may find both *you* and *your* smoke offensive.

Not only are *you* and *your* overworked, but since women rarely smoke pipes, these pronouns refer incongruously to only half of the potential readers.

PRACTICE

Find any *vague* or *ambiguous* pronoun references, or wrong pronoun forms, in the following sentences. Then correct each error.

1. In Tent City they now have the largest city in the state. You must agree that it is a good place to live.

2. Margaret told Helen she was the wisest girl she ever knew.

3. It said in the manual that your car never needs an oil change.

4. Carter is an airline pilot, and that is the profession his son wants to follow.

5. Over vacation, we saw two VCR movies on tape, three TV plays, and two theater movies—all this was a silly lack of exercise.

6. Don't be so angry at Tom's behavior. It's not a good idea to make it seem important.

7. He can't see well. You know this is because he did not get glasses as a child.

8. Miles held on to the cat's paw, which bit him. It was a good thing the cat had its shots.

9. Mrs. Smith gave a talk on the antique business—in particular on the method of financing it and making a proper report to the IRS. It is a complicated affair.

10. The National Cemetery is your burial place if you have served honorably in the armed forces.

■■■ G 3   *Wrong Form of Pronoun*

G 3(a)   *Use the Proper Subject and Object Forms of a Pronoun*

To correct most errors in pronoun form, isolate (or set apart) the construction. Such isolation will help you to discover whether you need the *subject* or the *object* form of the pronoun.

Subject forms fit in the slot: "_____ did it."

She did it.
They did it.
He did it.

Object forms fit in the slot: "They pushed _____."

They pushed *him.*
They pushed *her.*
They pushed *them.*

Prepositions, of course, fit in this pattern: "They did it to _____."

They did it to *him.*
They did it for *her.*
They did it with *them.*

If you isolate (or set apart) the construction, you can tell whether the pronoun should go in the *subject* or *object* slot.

Problem: Would you call Brad and *he* on the phone?
Isolation: Would you call *he*? (*He* should be *him.*)
Solution: Would you call Brad and *him* on the phone?

Problem: Phyllis and *me* will walk to the library with you.
Isolation: *Me* will walk to the library with you. (*Me* should be *I.*)

Solution: Phyllis and *I* will walk to the library with you.

Problem: The movie program was specially designed for *we* college students.

Isolation: The movie program was specially designed for *we*. (*We* should be *us*.)

Solution: The movie program was specially designed for *us* college students.

G 3(b)   Use the Proper Pronoun After Than or As in a Comparison.

The problem occurs in sentences like this:

a. Della understands Margie better than *me*; as opposed to:

b. Della understands Margie better than *I* [do].

Basically, you must decide which kind of comparison you are trying to make. The one in (a) compares two people, *Margie* and *me*; the one in (b) compares two actions (involving *understanding*).

NOTE: The construction in (b) is often shortened to:

Della understands Margie better than I.

The shortened sentence omits the last part: . . . *better than I* [*do understand*].

G 3(c)   Use the Proper Pronoun with Appositives

Appositives "rename" nouns or pronouns. The problem we are discussing occurs in constructions like these: *we* two (Jack and Jill) *vs. us* two (Jack and Jill). In both cases, *we* and *us* rename Jack and Jill.

Solve the problem by determining whether the sentence requires a *subject* or *object* form (see G 3a).

In (a) below, you want a *subject* form; in (b), an *object* form:

a. A few students (particularly, *she* and *I*) decided not to write a paper for extra credit.
    [*She* and *I* decided.]

b. The tiger named Napoleon bit three trainers—Wes, Marty, and *me*. [The tiger bit *me*.]

G 3(d)   Using Who and Whom

The editor and usage authority Theodore Bernstein remarked that *whom* is "useless and senseless; the word is in addition a complicated nuisance." It is true that hardly anybody can solve some of the murkier problems of *whom*-use. On occasion, even Shakespeare used it incorrectly. Bernstein suggested a stamp, or perhaps a bumper sticker, that would read: "I FAVOR **WHOM'S** DOOM EXCEPT AFTER A PREPOSITION." Of twenty-one authorities who (whom?) Bernstein polled, fifteen agreed with him.

Following Bernstein, we suggest using *whom* with prepositions only: *for* whom, *to* whom, *beside* whom. Use *who* with everything else. Hardly anyone will notice the difference.

But if, for any reason, you must decide whether to use *whom* in nonprepositional cases, here's a memory device that will help you.

Substitute *he* and *him* in the *clause* in question; where *him* (the word ending in *m*) would work, use who*m*. Where *he* would work, use *who*. (This test won't work with *she* and *her* because neither word ends in *m*.)

> *Problem:* John, *who/whom* they said was dead, walked in the door. [*He* was dead, or *Him* was dead? Answer: *He.* Therefore, *who* is right in the sentence.]
>
> *Solution:* John, *who* they said was dead, walked in the door.

PRACTICE

Check each sentence for errors in *pronoun form*. Correct the sentences.

1. Our son James' grandparents (Jeannette and him) preferred a Catholic education for our only boy.

2. The new laws helped our family greatly—particularly Louise and I.

3. Bob is as strong as him [Tom]. (We are comparing Bob and Tom's strength.)

4. Rene likes Tom more than her. (*Her* refers to Lisa, who likes Tom less than Rene does.)

5. He regrets that decision as much as him.

6. Tell the Dean and he about the secret contract with the CIA.

7. Mark and me—for who the award was named—were told from the beginning.

8. The tennis scholarships were supposed to have gone to we team members of last year, to who it was promised.

9. Fred understands the national debt better than me.

10. I admire Arlie more than her. (*Her* is supposed to refer to a third person, Ginger, who does not admire Arlie very much.)

■■■ G 4   *Appropriate Verb Tense*

Tense refers to how the verb expresses *time*.

> *Present tense:* She *wishes* for money.
> *Past tense:* She *wished* for money.
> *Future tense:* She *will wish* for money.

> *Present perfect:* She *has wished* for money.
> *Past perfect:* She *had wished* for money.
> *Future perfect:* She *will have wished* for money.

Most questions of tense involve thinking through the logic of the time(s) you intend to put your statements in.

Problem: Then the judge *recalled* that the prosecution *stated* its objections two weeks earlier.

Solution: Then the judge *recalled* that the prosecution *had stated* its objections two weeks earlier. (The verbs logically belong in two different "times.")

Problem: He *was* a handsome man before he *became* a vampire.

Solution: He *had been* a handsome man before he *became* a vampire.

NOTE: The present tense is customarily used in literary criticism and reviews when describing action and psychological states in the literary work. But it is not used when making statements about the author or his background.

Problem: Shakespeare *sees* Hamlet as a man who *believed* in the supernatural.

Solution: Shakespeare *saw* Hamlet as a man who *believes* in the supernatural.

Problem: In *The Catcher in the Rye*, Holden Caulfield *was* a tiresome adolescent. Perhaps the author, J. D. Salinger, *does* not *understand* his own creation.

Solution: In *The Catcher in the Rye*, Holden Caulfield *is* a tiresome adolescent. Perhaps the author, J. D. Salinger, *did* not *understand* his own creation.

PRACTICE

Where necessary, change the tense of the verbs.

1. At first, Huck Finn believes that blacks are different; later he came to recognize that all human beings will share the same faults and virtues.

2. Here she was, staring angrily at me from the stage. So I say to her: "I can't hear you from the back row!"

3. Mrs. McMinn claimed that the Imperial Valley was the hottest place in California.

4. After Mr. McMinn went to California, his wife was concerned that he could be finding the heat unbearable, so she was writing him to rent an air conditioner.

5. Charles Dickens is a great writer; his *David Copperfield* is a story that every young person will be able to enjoy.

6. Mark Twain writes *Huckleberry Finn* on the top floor of his Hartford home, which he believes to be the best place to work.

7. Sandra remembers that the TV had blown a fuse on the night when we would have been watching a rerun of *Star Trek*.

■■■ G 5   *Faulty Principal Part of the Verb*

The so-called *principal parts* of the verb form this familiar pattern:

Present Tense	**Past Tense**	**Past Participle**
ask	asked	asked
ring	rang	rung
bring	brought	brought

In its past tense and past participle, *ask* does not change much, adding only -*ed* (*ask, asked, asked*). *Ring* changes form twice, but *bring* changes only once. A verb like *ask* is called *regular*; verbs like *ring* and *bring* are said to be *irregular*. Through constant usage, most of us know most of these forms; but when we come to something like *lie* and *dive*, memory often fails. Should we write "I had *lain* there for an hour" ? (One of us can never remember and so—when pushed—says, "I had *been* there for an hour.") Is it "The child *dived* in the pool" ? Or *dove*?

The answers to such questions can be found in your standard desk dictionary under the present form of the verb (*lie* and *dive*). And there's your choice: memorize the forms, avoid the verb, or look it up.

PRACTICE

In your dictionary, look up the principal parts of these verbs:

bid (command)	hang (execute)	sink
bid (offer)	lie	sit
burst	seek	spring
dive	set	swing
forget	shrink	weave
get		

■■■ G 6   *Incomplete or Faulty Verbs*

G 6(a)   *Be Sure to Add -ed and -s to the Verb (When These Endings Are Necessary)*

In the past tense and past participle of regular verbs, use the -*ed* form:

Problem: He should not have *use* the drug except under the care of a physician.

Solution: He should not have *used* the drug except under the care of a physician.

With most present-tense verbs (expressing the third-person singular), use the -*s* form of the verb:

Problem: The Parthenon *stand* in one of Nashville's great parks.

Solution: The Parthenon *stands* in one of Nashville's great parks.

G 6(b) Always Use the Complete Verb Phrase

Problem: We can now see that Ogden Nash *been* bitter about life.

Solution: We can now see that Ogden Nash *had been* bitter about life.

G 6(c) Avoid Nonstandard Forms of the Verb Phrase

Problem: Last year Ms. Kelly *have* financed the new building.

Solution: Last year Ms. Kelly *had financed* [or simply, *financed*] the new building.

G 6(d) Use Modal Auxiliaries to Fit Your Meaning

The modal auxiliaries are *shall, will, would, should, may, might, must, can, could*. Use these modals to fit your meaning. Below are two examples of ambiguous use. For giving or requesting *permission*:

Problem: *Can* we start up the computer tomorrow morning? [*Can* implies *ability* to do something.]

Solution: *May* we start up the computer tomorrow morning?

For requiring an *action*:

Problem: You *shall* start up the computer tomorrow.

Solution: You *must* start . . .
[Note that "You *should* start" expresses a weaker requirement than "You *must* start."]

PRACTICE

Check each sentence for incomplete or faulty verbs. Correct the sentences.

1. Until last year, the U.S. Forest Service had manage more than 150 forests in this country.

2. By next fall, you will received your bachelor's degree.

3. Members of the honor society are chosed on the basis of scholarship and school spirit.

4. Can we begin to sing now? [*Asking permission*]

5. The leader of the choir shall take attendance every day.

6. Love is the family tie that bind.

7. The state governor control the national guard.

8. In October, Dinosaur Cave will been open for two years.

9. Music camp was found in 1965 [*The camp started that year.*]

10. Those who had live in America before 1600 are the forgotten people.

■■■ G 7   *Proper Use of the Subjunctive*

The subjunctive is a verb form used mainly in *contrary-to-fact* statements and after *wishes*. The verb form may be *were, be,* or the verb without the final *s*.

Contrary-to-fact statements:

I would not do that if I *were* you. (I am not you.)

If she *were* true to me she would not go out with other men. (She is not true to me.)

If this *be* patriotism, I am not a patriot. (This is not patriotism.)

After wishes:

I wish I *were* rich.

Let him *live*.

My father requested that his body *be* cremated.

I demand that Smith *be* reinstated. (A demand is a strong wish.)

PRACTICE

In the following sentences, correct the faulty forms of the subjunctive.

1. If he was to live a thousand years, he would not be able to support me adequately.

2. I wish this wasn't Tuesday.

3. I'd drop that gun if I was you.

4. If he was here, we would all leave.

5. Major Burns demands that he is given a transfer to another unit.

6. I would go to Monterey if I was given the opportunity.

■■■ G 8   *Piling Up Verbs*

The English verb system is complex and flexible, made so in part by the rich array of *auxiliaries* (or *helping verbs*): "*had been* kept," "*should have been* doing," "*will have* performed." Yet helping verbs can work against a writer if they are piled up in a sentence so that verb phrases are long and awkward:

Problem: He *would have liked to have seen* the movie.

Solution: He *wanted to see* the movie.

Problem: We *did* not *desire to have become required* as participants by the coach.

Solution: We *did* not *want* the coach to make us participate.

Problem: They *had meant to have stopped* the murder.

Solution: They *had meant to stop* the murder.

■■■ G 9   Confusion of Adjectives and Adverbs

G 9(a)   Understand the Difference Between Adjectives and Adverbs

Errors with adjectives and adverbs are sometimes created when you confuse the two. For instance, if you wanted to say that someone had body odor, it would be silly to write that he smelled *badly*, for *badly* would imply that his nose wasn't working properly. Follow these suggestions for distinguishing between adjectives and adverbs:

1. Know that adjectives modify nouns and that adverbs modify verbs, adjectives, and other adverbs. (See page 424 for more discussion of adjectives and adverbs).

2. Use your dictionary to check whether a word is an adjective or an adverb.

3. Substitute the word you are in doubt about into one of these patterns:

Subject-verb-*adjective*-object:

You injured a *well* person.

You did a *good* job.

Subject-verb-object-*adverb*:

You did the job *well*.

You did it *happily*.

Subject-is-*adjective*:

She is *good*.

She is *happy*.

The substitution should tell you whether the word is an adjective or adverb.

G 9(b)   If Your Clause Has a Linking Verb, Use an Adjective Complement to Modify the Subject

Problem: The hamburger tastes *well*.

Solution: The hamburger tastes *good*.

Problem: All the students felt *badly* when the union burned down.

Solution: All the students felt *bad* when the union burned down.

■■■ G 10   Degrees of Comparison for Adjectives and Adverbs

The degrees of comparison for adjectives and adverbs are *positive*, *comparative*, and *superlative*; for example:

Positive	Comparative	Superlative
cold	colder	coldest
big	bigger	biggest
good	better	best
much	more	most

Positive	Comparative	Superlative
easily	more easily	most easily
often	more often	most often

The shorter adjectives (and a small number of adverbs) form the degrees of comparison as *cold* does: cold, cold*er*, cold*est*. A few are irregular: *bad, worse, worst.*

Many adjectives of two syllables and all of three or more syllables form the degrees of comparison with the use of *more* and *most*: beautiful, *more* beautiful, *most* beautiful. And most adverbs are formed the same way: curiously, *more* curiously, *most* curiously.

It is often claimed that certain adjectives—such as *unique, round*, and *dead*—have only one degree and logically cannot be compared. Does *dead, deader, deadest* appear logical? When used figuratively or lightheartedly, it probably does. "That was the deadest party I ever went to" expresses the idea perfectly. But in most cases, *dead*, like *pregnant*, expresses an absolute condition—you either are or you aren't. Similarly, *unique* cannot be qualified in expressions like *more unique*—the word means "one of a kind," and you can't get "one-er" than "one." Yet you might reasonably write *almost unique*— almost "one of a kind."

■■■ G 11　Misuse of Noun as Adjective

Many nouns make poor adjectives: *liability* action, *validity* record, *believability* reasons, *plot* circumstances. The solution for most of these is to change the wording or the construction.

Problem:　I will now relate the *plot circumstances*.

Solution:　I will now relate the *circumstances of the plot*.

Problem:　His experiments have a poor *validity record*.

Solution:　His experiments *seldom work out*.

As you may have guessed, such problems are usually closely related to the use of jargon. See pages 477–478 for more discussion of "nouny" writing.

PRACTICE

Correct these sentences for: (a) confusion of adjectives with adverbs, (b) the proper use of degrees of comparison, and (c) the misuse of nouns as adjectives.

1. The Maremont Corporation Harvey, Illinois research was conducted by three chemists.

2. The research was done as careful as any technician research in the lab, and it turned out to be the more useful of all the projects started there.

3. She looked beautifully and sweet in her new Levis. But she acted recklesser than she looked.

4. I run every day for endurance reasons. It is good exercise and makes me feel good.

5. Johanna's plane was built strong enough to carry an extra load of fuel easy.

6. "Hold tight to your religion beliefs," his elderly father had said.

7. Her position qualifications are most perfect for the supervisor job.

8. My high grade was the inevitably result of having a kindly teacher.

9. His ambition is the less good thing about him.

■■■ G 12   Faulty Verb Agreement

Verbs must ordinarily agree with their subjects:

Dogs are popular pets.

A *clue was* discovered.

Each of the female bears *was* found with its cub.

These *people were* innocent.

However, when in doubt, let your meaning determine subject-verb agreement.

Problem:	A *number* of these cures *was*(*?*) *were* (*?*) rejected.
Solution (1):	A *number* of these cures *were* rejected. (Obviously, *number* designates more than one cure.)
Solution (2):	*Several* of these cures *were* rejected.
Solution (3):	A *few* of these cures *were* rejected.
Solution (4):	The doctors rejected some of the cures.

Seven typical errors in agreement follow in G 12(a) through (g).

G 12(a)   Avoid Agreement Errors with Phrasal Joiners (as well as, along with, in addition to, etc.)

Problem:	My *baby, together with three other babies* in the maternity ward, *was* (*?*) *were* (*?*) saved by the nurse.
Solution (1):	My *baby*, together with three other babies in the maternity ward, *was* saved by the nurse. (The general rule is that a singular subject, immediately followed by clumsy joiners or other interrupters, takes a singular verb.)
Solution (2):	My *baby and* three other *babies* in the maternity ward *were* saved by the nurse. (Where you can, use *and* instead of clumsy joiners.)

G 12(b)   Avoid Agreement Errors with Pronouns

Problem:	She is one of those *girls who is* (*?*) *are* (*?*) always well dressed.
Solution (1):	She is one of those *girls who are* always well dressed. (Make the verb agree with the noun [*girls*] that the pronoun [*who*] stands for.)
Solution (2):	She is the kind of *girl who is* always well dressed. (Put the whole thing in the singular.)

> *Problem:* *Everyone* who belongs to the Weekend Bikers *wants* (*?*) *want* (*?*) to attend the meet this Sunday.
>
> *Solution:* *Everyone . . . wants* to attend the meet this Sunday.
>
> *Problem:* *Nobody . . .* in the whole group of police officers involved *is* (*?*) *are* (*?*) satisfied with the new contract.
>
> *Solution (1):* *Nobody . . . is* satisfied with the new contract.
>
> *Solution (2):* *All* of the police officers *are* dissatisfied with the new contract.

G 12(c) Avoid Agreement Errors with "Subject-Is-Noun" Statements

> *Problem:* The main *issue is (?) are (?)* high prices.
>
> *Solution (1):* The main *issue is* high prices. (Make the verb agree with the subject.)
>
> *Solution (2):* The main *issue is that prices are too high.* (Change subject-*is*-noun to subject-*is*-clause.)

G 12(d) Avoid Agreement Errors with Collective Nouns

> *Problem:* The team *is (?) are (?)* happy about their victory.
>
> *Solution (1):* The *team is* happy about its victory. (Consider the *team* as one group or unit.)
>
> *Solution (2):* The *members* of the team *are* happy about their victory. (Use a plural subject.)
>
> *Problem:* A *hundred feet* of electrical wire *is (?) are (?)* too much for this room.
>
> *Solution (1):* A *hundred feet* of electrical wire *is* too much for this room. (Consider a *hundred feet* as a unit.)
>
> *Solution (2):* We don't need a hundred feet of electrical wire for this room.

G 12(e) Avoid Agreement Errors with Statements That Start with There Is or There Are

Those that begin with a non-adverb or expletive *there*:

There are TREES in my yard. (TREES is the subject.)

Those that begin with an adverb of place *there*:

There [pointing] are the TREES I want cut down. (TREES is the subject.)

In both kinds of statement, the subject is delayed. But the subject still controls the number of the verb:

There is no WAY I can accept that. (filler *there*)

There [pointing] are the ROADS you should take. (adverb *there*)

> *Problem:* *There's things* to be done today.

Solution: *There are things* to be done today.

Problem: *There is (?) are (?)* happy *cowboys* in Texas.

Solution (1):   *There are* happy *cowboys* in Texas. (Make the verb agree with the subject *cowboys*.)

Solution (2):   *Some cowboys are* happy in Texas.

G 12(f)   Avoid Agreement Errors with Either-Or and Neither-Nor

Problem: *Either* the butler *or* the maid *was (?) were (?)* the murderer.

Solution: *Either* the butler *or* the maid *was* the murderer. (In such constructions, pairs of singular subjects take singular verbs.)

Problem: *Neither* the car *nor* the trucks *was (?) were (?)* stolen.

Solution (1):   *Neither* the car *nor* the trucks *were* stolen. (The verb should agree with its nearest subject.)

Solution (2):   The car and the trucks *were* not stolen. (Revise the construction to avoid the "neither-nor" problem.)

G 12(g)   Avoid Agreement Errors with (1) Titles and (2) Words Named as Words

Hard Times is [not *are*] one of Dickens' most interesting novels.

"Fakers" was [not *were*] the word she used to describe her in-laws.

PRACTICE

Correct these sentences. If you believe that a sentence is correct as it stands, state why.

1. There's lights on in my house.

2. Was any of his rabbits killed by the weasel?

3. Neither the puppy nor the kittens were responsible for making such a mess.

4. My biggest problem is C grades on papers.

5. I have heard that an army march on their stomachs.

6. There seem to be a great deal of noise coming from the next room.

7. The stadium is one of those structures that surprises you when you first see it.

8. His use of wallpaper, as well as his painting, make the living room quite pleasant.

9. *Big Winners* are a movie I want to see.

10. My list of supplies were so long that Mr. Fenwick refused to buy them.

11. The advice of both counselors, which I heard from the next room, are that you go back to the dorm and talk to the resident advisor.

12. A word like *mottoes* are spelled with or without the *e*.

13. Their main complaint is loud stereos and people partying after midnight.

14. These are many of the kinds of reasoning that is mentioned in the Bill of Rights.

■■■ G 13 Faulty Pronoun Agreement

Here is an example of faulty pronoun agreement: "*Everyone* was told to pick up *their* books and leave." Since *everyone* is singular, the pronoun *their* does not "agree" with it.

Problem:	I told *each girl* coming to the party to bring *their* own food.
Solution (1):	I told *each girl* coming to the party to bring *her* own food.
Solution (2):	I told *all the girls* coming to the party to bring *their* own food. (Instead of forcing the pronoun to agree with the expression appearing earlier in the sentence, try starting the sentence with a plural.)

NOTE: See also the discussion of the generic pronoun, page 530. Observe the typical choices in the following agreement problem:

Problem:	If you want *an employee* to work hard for you, always give *them* plenty of praise for good work.
Solution (1):	If you want *an employee* to work hard for you, always give *him* . . .
Solution (2):	If you want *employees* to work hard for you, always give *them* . . .

Problems in pronoun agreement can often be avoided by going back to the beginning of the paragraph and deciding whether you want to be in the singular or the plural throughout your discussion. Decide early, for instance, whether you want to discuss *employees* in general, or the *employee* as an individual. Then be consistent in choosing pronouns.

PRACTICE

Correct the faulty pronoun agreement in these sentences.

1. Each person rented their own costume for the dance.

2. If someone tries to ride their bike through campus, they'll run over you every time.

3. The university is proud of their lawns and parks.

4. If anyone writes to Charlotte, have them tell her she left her skis here.

5. Each of the rules for the house can be considered practical only when they are enforced.

6. Everyone likes to have more freedom for themselves than they do for others.

7. After one retires, they like to have a hobby to keep them busy.

8. When a nursing student applies for her first job after graduation, they like to know how much money they are going to make.

■■■ *G 14 Confusing the Articles—A, An, and The (For Foreign Speakers)*

G 14(a) Definitions of Terms Used

ARTICLE

There are two "articles" in English: the word *a* or *an* (the *indefinite article*); and the word *the* (the *definite article*). Both articles signal the coming of a noun in the sentence:

a [*noun*]	=	a *textbook*
an [*noun*]	=	an *owl*
the [*noun*]	=	the *treaty* (or *treaties*)

Modifiers may appear before the noun:

an *expensive* textbook

a *hooting* owl

the *badly understood* treaties

Count Nouns vs. Mass Nouns

A *count noun* is a noun that you can count—one *tree,* two *trees,* three *trees.* A *mass noun* cannot usually be counted—*water, reluctance, wheat, sword-play, rage.* Note that some nouns are, in different contexts, either count or mass nouns:

Rage is a destructive emotion [mass noun].

These *rages* of his are becoming more destructive [count noun].

G 14(b) Distinguish between the Articles A *and* An

Use *a* before *consonant sounds*:

*a t*ree

*a l*arge room

*a d*ilemma

Use *an* before *vowel sounds*:

*an e*nigma

*an e*lliptical shape

an X in her name

G 14(c)   The Article A (An) Usually Signals a Count Noun On Its "First Mention"

NOTE: For a definition of count noun, see page 449.

There is *a* button [*first mention*] missing on your coat. I will sew *the* button [*second mention*] on for you.

I saw *a* snake [*first mention*] in your bedroom. *The* snake [*second mention*] was asleep on your pillow.

There used to be *a* large brass button [*first mention*] on your coat. [Modifiers like *large* and *brass* can appear before the noun.]

I saw *an* odd-looking snake in your bedroom. [*An* is used because of the vowel *o* in *odd-looking*.]

If you cannot count the noun (making it a *mass noun*—page 449), you will not use *a* or *an* directly in front of it. You would not say, "Give me *a* bread," but "Give me *some* (or *the*) bread." Note that you can say, "Give me *a* piece of bread" because *pieces* are countable. (*Some* is also used with plural count nouns: "I ate some *oranges* yesterday.")

G 14(d)   Uses of the Article The

The can be used with any noun, *countable* or not. (See definitions of *count* and *mass* nouns, page 449.)

G 14(d1)   USE THE WHEN BOTH THE SPEAKER AND LISTENER CAN BE THINKING ABOUT THE SAME (SPECIFIC) THING

The rain is getting tiresome.

It's freezing in here; please turn on *the* heat.

I don't know where *the* car keys are.

G 14(d2)   USE THE THE SECOND TIME YOU MENTION A NOUN

Yesterday I saw a tornado. *The* tornado [second mention] passed right over Jessie's house.

Rex bought a steak. I cooked *the* steak [second mention] and ate it.

The basement was flooded by a large amount of water. My plumber pumped *the* water [second mention] out into the street.

G 14(e) When Not to Use an Article

G 14(e1) ARTICLES ARE NOT GENERALLY USED WITH PROPER NOUNS

Proper is an ancient term meaning *belonging to oneself.* A *proper noun* is something's special name—the name of a particular person, place, thing, or idea. Proper nouns are capitalized. Examples are *Mount Olympus, Lucas* (a person), *Olney* (a city), *White Fence Farm* (a particular farm), *Romanticism* (an idea), *Fourth Street* (a place). One would not write *a* Mount Olympus, *the* Lucas, *an* Olney, and so on.

When proper nouns become *countable* (see *count nouns*, page 449), you may use *the*: "*The* Fourth Street I am speaking of is in Old Town, not in the city itself." "*The* Joneses are coming for dinner."

Exception: When a *common noun* is part of the name, you use *the*: *the* Atlantic Ocean, *the* Rocky Mountains, *the* Mississippi River. Here *ocean, mountains,* and *river* are all common nouns.

G 14(e2) THE *IS NOT ORDINARILY USED WITH PLURAL OR MASS NOUNS IN GENERALIZATIONS*

For a definition of *mass* and *count nouns*, see page 449.
The italicized nouns below will not take *the*:

> *Space* is the last frontier. *But:* Fill in the *spaces* [count noun].

> We Americans have lost *faith* in ourselves.

> I never see *cowboys* in Pittsburgh anymore.

G 14(e3) A *AND* AN *ARE NOT USED WITH PLURAL NOUNS, OR (ORDINARILY) WITH MASS NOUNS*

For a definition of *mass noun*, see page 449.
A and *an* would not be used just before the italicized nouns below:

> The editor accused the reporter of engaging in *sloganeering.*

> Barker had a way of looking at *fascism* that fascinated critics.

> In the fall term, she audited *classes* [not *a* classes].

G 14(e4) ARTICLES ARE NOT ORDINARILY USED WITH OTHER NOUN MARKERS

Noun markers, which signal a noun coming in the sentence, include articles themselves; possessive nouns and pronouns (*David's, her, its*); demonstrative pronouns (*this, that, these, those*); quantifiers (*some, many*); indefinite pronouns (*each, any*); and numbers.

One would not use an article before the italicized nouns below:

> The bank advised me to take advantage of its *services.*

> Some *sailors* should never be allowed in a boat.

> Every day, I walked that *lobster* on the end of a short leash.

PRACTICE

In each of the following sentences, fill in the spaces with the proper articles.

1. Use *a* or *an*: _____ small dog; _____ E in the sign; _____ eagle; _____ weapon.

2. Use *a, an, the,* or *some*: I wept _____ tear; _____ tear rolled down my cheek. Is there _____ big tomato for me? Slice _____ biggest one for me! And please give me _____ salad dressing too.

3. Insert the proper article (speaker and listener are thinking of the same thing): Tell me what _____ murderer is doing now! Why doesn't _____ clock strike the hour?

4. Omit an improperly used article: I am from the state of the Oklahoma. The only Oklahoma I know of is north of the Texas. Can you find the Myrtle Street on this map? There must be some Democrats in the New York. The McTavishes are Scots. Mr. McTavish drowned in the Adriatic Sea.

5. Omit an unnecessary *the*: The money is necessary for life. Hand me the money from the bank. We Americans love the debt. That's why we have affection for the federal deficit.

6. Omit unnecessary articles: I think you have been talking in the circles. Mr. Johnson had lost a control of his car. A control switch in the transmission was defective. But the police said his wife had been at the controls. He wanted a additions built on to his house.

Sentence Structure

■■■ S 1 Unnecessary Shifts

In avoiding unnecessary shifts in various sentence elements, follow the "rule of consistency," which is actually only a matter of common sense: In any rhetorical unit (particularly in the sentence), continue as you began.

1. If you began in the past tense, continue in it:

Problem: Louise *stated* that the papers were filed a year ago, while her attorney *says* they were never filed.

Solution: Louise *stated* . . . her attorney *said* . . .

2. If you started with indirect discourse, stay with it:

Problem: Mrs. McMinn said she was thirsty and would I get her some water from the cooler?

Solution: Mrs. McMinn said she was thirsty and asked me to get her some water from the cooler.

3. If you started with one form of the pronoun, stick with it.

Problem: *You* cannot understand when *one* is young that marriage is full of both pains and pleasures.

Solution: When *you* are young, *you* cannot understand . . .

Pronouns are slippery, shifty beasts:

Problem: If traveling makes *one* sick, the airline provides paper bags for *you.*

Solution: If traveling makes *one* sick, the airline provides paper bags for *him.*

This solution throws both pronouns into the third person and is, at least, grammatical. You could write "... makes *one* sick ... paper bags for *one.*" But this sounds like a British aristocrat at his most pompous. The best policy is to pick out your first pronoun (or noun) and then continue in the same person:

If traveling makes *you* sick ... bags for *you.*

If traveling makes *people* sick ... bags for *them.*

Or simply avoid the slippery beast in the second clause:

For anyone who gets sick, the airline provides a paper bag.

4. Don't make awkward shifts in the subject-verb pattern in a series of sentences. Here's an example of an awkward shift:

After considering the situation at the West End store, the students decided to support the strike there. They refused to cross the picket line, and encouraged others not to pass it. A *notice* about their action *was put* in the school paper and *was paid for* by them. Finally, they sent a delegation to the management of West End. . . .

As they shift from active to passive, the italicized subject-verb patterns break the flow of development in the paragraph and disrupt its unity. The paragraph improved:

After considering the situation at the West End store, the students decided to support the strike there. They refused to cross the picket line, and encouraged others not to pass it. The school paper published a notice about their action, a notice the students paid for. Finally, they sent a delegation to the management of West End. . . .

An awkward shift of the subject-verb pattern can be particularly noticeable if it appears inside a sentence:

Awkward: Ever since *they saw* the volcano erupt, *there has been a great fear* of Mt. St. Helens in the people who live nearby.

Improved: Ever since *they saw* the volcano erupt, the people who live near Mt. St. Helens *have been* afraid. . . .

(See page 434 for more discussion of consistent pronoun use.)

PRACTICE

Correct these sentences for consistency.

1. The airplane swooped close to the ground, and he blinked his landing lights twice.

2. As they were walking, Harley remarked that most of the elms were dying, but Sheridan explains that there is a new scientific method of saving them.

3. If the elms were all alive, and the method is easily available, we could protect thousands of them in this city alone.

4. The general ordered that the flags be lowered to half-mast on Tuesday and blow taps for the men who were lost.

5. The vice-president had to recognize Mrs. Carlin's ability, but this was not done gracefully by him.

6. A legislature does not like to tax its citizens, and they will usually try to get money some other way.

7. If you want to make a sailor happy, just give them plenty of shore leave.

8. First, mark down the suits, and then you should put "50%-Off" tags on the shirts.

9. Macbeth has trouble with his conscience, but after a time he managed to kill it completely.

10. In a small town, one is never lonely; indeed, you usually feel that you know too many people.

■■■ S 2 Omissions and Incomplete Constructions

Omissions and incomplete constructions are often accidental; the writer leaves out a word on the page that his mind easily supplies for him—but not for the reader:

> Don't leave out a word on ∧ page. *(the)*
> Many have wondered what happened ∧ Marilyn Monroe. *(to)*

Other omissions are created by what might be called a "grammatical hiccup":

> Wilma saw the bartender was watering the bourbon.

Obviously, the object of *saw* should not be *bartender* but the whole noun clause:

> Wilma saw *that the bartender was watering the bourbon.*

Another example of a hiccup:

> *Problem:* Since he's working here, he's been watering the stock.
> *Solution:* Since he's *been* working here, he's been watering the stock.

Certain idioms seem to be particularly susceptible to incompleteness:

> *Problem:* He was interested but undisturbed by her revelation.
> *Solution (1):* He was interested *in* but undisturbed by her revelation.
> *Solution (2):* He was interested in her revelation but undisturbed by it.

Problem:	You must learn obedience and respect for the coach.
Solution:	You must learn obedience *to* and respect for the coach.

PRACTICE

Supply the missing parts in these sentences. Rewrite as necessary.

1. Playing classical trumpet has and always will be a poorly paid profession.

2. Whenever I see the Statue of Liberty, I get impression power and glory.

3. They agree with Mrs. Kane's interpretation but object Mr. Kane's.

4. Winnie did a good job and earned a great deal money from the Ace Housebuilding Company.

5. The fat old dog was barking, and the puppies regarding him with wonder.

6. We promised the old dog would not bothering the neighbors any more.

7. I remember a dog had a bark like that.

8. He never has and undoubtedly never will speak confidently before an audience.

■■■ S 3   *Faulty Comparison*

Comparisons should be logical and complete. Here is a faulty comparison:

Walcott's beliefs were different from Clark.

The writer is comparing the wrong things—*beliefs* and *Clark*.

Solution (1):	Walcott's beliefs were different from Clark's.
Solution (2):	Walcott's beliefs were different from those expressed by Clark.
Problem:	We are as industrious, if not more industrious, than the East Germans. (This says that we are "as industrious . . . than the East Germans.")
Solution:	We are as industrious as the East Germans, if not more so.
Problem:	Our family's house cost more than Smith.
Solution (1):	Our family's house cost more than Smith's.
Solution (2):	Our family's house cost more than the Smiths' did.
Problem:	New York City is bigger than any city in the country. (This means that it is bigger than itself, since it is one of the cities "in the country.")
Solution (1):	New York is bigger than any *other* city in the country.

Solution (2):   New York is the biggest city in the country.

As these examples imply, faulty comparisons seem to be created when the writer does not think this through: "*What (a)* am I comparing with *what (b)*?"

PRACTICE

Correct the faulty comparisons in these sentences. Rewrite as necessary.

1. Baseball talk makes Barb every bit as angry as those people who talk endlessly of ballet and Bach.

2. My boyfriend says that his writing is easier to read than his teacher.

3. Fewer people went to the movies; more and more they bought their own TV sets instead of watching their neighbors.

4. In *Catch–22*, the plot is easier to follow than the other war novels.

5. This year's Chevrolet is smaller and more expensive.

6. The Swiss make more watches and other timepieces than England or France.

7. This fat goldfish is obviously more greedy than any fish in the tank.

8. Using contractions made Miss Wimm angrier even than when she caught anybody reading comic books in class.

■■■ S 4   *Split or "Separated" Constructions*

English grammar does its job in several ways. One of these can be described by the rule of nearness: expressions that belong together are put near each other. Here are a few instances:

1. Objects are placed near their verbs, verbs near their subjects.

   Problem: She *sent* to her senator a *letter.*
   Solution: She *sent* a *letter* to her senator.

   Problem: *He* as it turned out when we found him *was* not lost at all.
   Solution: As it turned out when we found him, *he was* not lost at all.

2. Adjective clauses are placed near the expression they modify:

   Problem: Anders lost his *knife* on the seacoast *which his mother had bought for him.*
   Solution: On the seacoast, Anders lost the *knife which his mother had bought for him.*

3. The sign of the infinitive (*to*) immediately precedes its verb:

Problem:	They wanted *to* immediately and completely *pay back* the loan.
Solution:	They wanted *to pay back* the loan immediately and completely.

NOTE: It is fashionable to say that good writers occasionally split infinitives. One excellent textbook (the first edition of which we used as freshmen back in the Middle Ages) says that "many times" infinitive splitting is "not only natural but also desirable." The authors use this example: "For her *to never complain* seems unreal." Is that better than "*never to complain*"?

It is interesting to note that for every infinitive split by an accomplished writer, there will be a hundred that won't be split. The rule of nearness is not made of granite, but it is not made of Jell-O either. If you glance over the problems in S 5, S 6, and S 7 on the following pages, you will discover that violating the rule can lead to some pretty comical sentences.

PRACTICE

In the following sentences, repair the split or "separation."

1. Mrs. McMinn told Mike when he went to the grocery store on the corner of First and Main to pick up some eggs.

2. Mike promised to quickly and faithfully carry out her request.

3. We may, if there is no objection, see a double-header this afternoon.

4. The second baseman, dismayed by the spikes of the two-hundred-pound runner bearing grimly down upon him, threw wildly to first.

5. We agreed as soon as the game was over and the noise of the crowd had abated that she would speak to me again.

6. The argument that beer makes one tipsy loses at a raucous major-league ball game all possible force.

7. When you watch people drink and sweat in 115-degree heat, it is impossible to even partly believe that any alcohol reaches the brain.

■■■ S 5 *Misplaced Modifiers*

A *modifier* is a sentence element that describes, qualifies, or limits an expression. If a modifier is incorrectly placed, the resulting construction may seem illogical. Examples:

Problem:	I departed for Europe on a freighter 3,000 miles away.
Solution (1):	I departed on a freighter for Europe—3,000 miles away.
Solution (2):	I got on a freighter bound for Europe, which was 3,000 miles away.

Problem: He nearly tried to make all of his teachers happy.

Solution: He tried to make nearly all of his teachers happy.

Problem: We discovered the old well in the north corner of Marston's backyard, which was full of green, brackish water. (The yard was full of water?)

Solution: The old well that we discovered in the north corner of Marston's backyard was full of green, brackish water.

PRACTICE

Correct the misplaced modifiers in these sentences. Because some of these errors cannot be satisfactorily corrected by moving the modifier to another position, you may have to rewrite some of the sentences.

1. Her stomach felt better after drinking the orange juice.

2. The fraternities voted for the Homecoming Queen as a body.

3. Men and women walked down the aisle to receive diplomas—not youngsters.

4. The final thrill came in eating the fish he caught with fried potatoes, sliced tomatoes, and a can of beer.

5. Look carefully at that old man with a beard about a block behind.

6. The Ratched Motel is fixing an early breakfast for campers who are leaving the area at 5:00 a.m. (Assume that the campers are leaving at 7:30.)

7. I'll investigate the crime when you finish with the body for possible clues.

■■■ S 6   Squinting Modifiers

The "*squinting*" *modifier* ambiguously points in two directions at once. Example:

Running away *occasionally* makes Sam feel better.

The reader wonders whether the writer means occasionally *running away* or occasionally *makes Sam feel better.* Such problems can be solved by tying the modifier firmly to what it modifies:

Occasionally, Sam runs away, after which he feels better.

PRACTICE

Correct these squinting constructions by rewriting the sentences.

1. The umpire claimed during the game that Detroit's manager spat in his direction.

2. The manager told us before we sportswriters left to apologize to him.

3. The lawyer who represents himself in most instances is his own "foolish client."

4. They promised after the end of the term to change her grade.

5. He wrote a treatise on mountaineering in the Gobi Desert.

■■■ S 7 *Dangling Modifiers*

The typical *dangling modifier* is an introductory expression that is not "tied" logically to the main clause that follows:

Problem: Having eaten his lunch, the steamboat departed.

The "dangler" implies an action in the opening modifier, but supplies the wrong *actor* for it in the main clause. Such errors are easily corrected by creating a logical tie between both parts of the sentence. This correction can usually be made by changing the opening modifier or the main clause that follows. Sometimes it may be best to rewrite the sentence without the opener.

Solution (1):	After lunch, the steamboat departed.
Solution (2):	Having eaten his lunch, he boarded the departing steamboat.
Problem:	Coming too fast to the stop sign, the brake was applied quickly. (The *brake* was coming too fast?)
Solution (1):	Coming too fast to the stop sign, he applied the brake quickly.
Solution (2):	He applied the brake quickly when he realized he was coming too fast to the stop sign.

Some danglers have no action stated (as such) in the opener, which is an elliptical expression:

Problem:	Upon graduation, my family gave me a hundred dollars and a ticket to Hollywood. (The *family* graduated?)
Solution (1):	When I graduated, my family gave me a hundred dollars and a ticket to Hollywood.
Solution (2):	Upon graduation, I got a hundred dollars and a ticket to Hollywood from my family.

PRACTICE

Correct the dangling modifiers in these sentences:

1. Getting up from the typewriter when the water cooler exploded, my news story was completely forgotten.

2. Astonished at the intrusion, her hands fluttered wildly.

3. Inflated to an enormous size, I rode the rubber raft around the pool.

4. By stopping smoking, there was a belief that he could cure his asthma.

5. After snuggling warm on the couch all night, the dawn finally came.

6. Concentrating my orderly mind, the paper was written quickly.

7. After working all summer on the road gang, the tan that Melvin got was the envy of his friends.

8. When only a second grader, my mother was told that I was obviously nearsighted.

■■■ S 8   *Faulty Parallelism*

Parallel elements in a sentence should be (a) roughly equal in importance, and (b) written in the same grammatical form. Examples:

Roger and *Tom* were terrible at ballroom dancing.

Ballroom dancing and *square dancing* are not activities for sissies.

Some small nations preferred to *watch, listen,* and *wait.*

Faulty parallelism fails to put parallel *ideas* in parallel *form:*

Problem:	She *believes* in him, as well as *having* faith in him.
Solution:	She *believes* in him and *has* faith in him.

Problem:	That movie had too much *sex, violence,* and the *language was bad.*
Solution:	That movie had too much *sex, violence,* and *profanity.*

Use *correlative conjunctions* properly. These conjunctions are:

either . . . or

neither . . . nor

not only . . . but also

both . . . and

Put correlative conjunctions just before the parallel expressions (and make sure the expressions are really parallel):

The riddle of the Sphinx is not only *unknown* but also *unknowable.*

Not this: To earn money for college they worked *both* for the state highway program in the summer *and* janitoring part-time at night.

But this: To earn money for college they worked for *both* the state highway program in the summer *and* the local janitor service.

Not this: The movie critic *not only* dislikes the violence *but also* the obvious acting.

But this: The movie critic dislikes *not only* the violence *but also* the obvious acting.

PRACTICE

Correct the faulty parallelism in the following sentences.

1. Her mother could always depend on Trish for going to class and to be making good grades.

2. When he owned that car, he never put in oil, checked the tires, and even the windshield was never washed.

3. In the race, a Porsche came in first, a Ferrari came in second, in addition to a Lotus having come in third.

4. I neither have the money nor the time to go to the game tonight.

5. Politicians are ruining this country, as well as its being destroyed by lenient judges.

6. Making the Dean's list and his captaincy of the football team made Strawbridge very popular.

7. The new seats in Howes Stadium are wide, comfortable, and of well-built quality.

8. Not only when they live on campus but also off, they prefer a private room.

9. Ask your roommate whether she wants to go to the party besides going to the picnic.

■■■ *S 9   Proper Subordination*

Subordination allows you to shift the emphasis from one part of a sentence to another, thus making your prose smoother and more logical. An important reason for subordinating one clause to another is to show a logical relationship: "*Because we got cold, wet, and hungry,* we left the stadium at half-time." The following subordinate elements are in italics:

> Callie Marshall was unable to reach Denver, *even though she rode all night through the snow.*
>
> John Frye, *who was one of the most energetic small men we had ever known,* climbed Slew Mountain by himself.
>
> *Although he was small,* John Frye energetically climbed Slew Mountain by himself.

Note that a subordinate element can be put at the beginning, middle, or end of a sentence.

Use subordination to improve choppy or unemphatic sentences:

Problem: His name was Bellmon. He was Canadian. He was married in his sophomore year. He had two jobs that year.

Solution: Bellmon, *the Canadian married student,* had two jobs his sophomore year.

Problem: They were hungry, but there was a drought, and they lost their farms, so they decided to go to California.

Solution: They lost their farms *after the drought came. Later, driven by hunger,* they decided to go to California.

(Also see pages 94–97.)

PRACTICE

Use subordination to improve these sentences.

1. He is poor, and he has an old Chevy pickup, but it uses too much oil, and it will eventually have to be sold.

2. The members of the first team could not understand the coach. The misunderstanding became an issue with the Athletic Council.

3. Friendship is of first importance. It helps to create harmony in human relationships.

4. He earned a great deal of money in business. He never worked hard. He paid little attention to conventions of manners and dress.

5. She wanted to major in computer science. She did not have many courses in science or math.

6. Accidents keep occurring on this busy corner. Two extra policemen have been stationed to warn motorists of the danger.

7. The manufacturer gave us a new air conditioner. This occurred before we could complain to the state Consumer's Protection Bureau. He wanted to improve his relationship with customers.

■■■ S 10   *Faulty Subordination*

In subordinating one part of a sentence to another, the writer makes the sentence elements *unequal.* Unlike a main clause, a subordinated element can never stand alone. The relationship between the main and subordinated elements is both grammatical and logical. In these two sentences, note the subordinated elements (in italics):

The old lady, *who had just put on her nightgown,* would not answer the doorbell.

The old lady, *who would not answer the doorbell,* had just put on her nightgown.

The subordination in the second sentence seems illogical. Here are other examples of faulty subordination.

Problem: Just last week I used that pay phone, *which was bombed this morning.*

Solution: This morning, someone bombed the pay phone *that I used last week.*

Problem: Barksdale is a former FBI agent *who was made president of the university today.*

Solution: Barksdale, *a former FBI agent*, was made president of the university today.

Problem: The Houndogs have lost 20 games in a row, *believing that they have no ability.*

Solution: Because they believe they have no ability, the Houndogs keep losing—20 games in a row.

Problem: The old biplane burst into flames, *when the pilot dived out of the cockpit.*

Solution: *Just as the pilot dived out of the cockpit*, the old biplane burst into flames.

(Also see page 463.)

PRACTICE

Rewrite these examples of faulty subordination.

1. We are all hoping to move to a better neighborhood, believing that we now have enough money for a new house.

2. Although the grades for his papers stayed the same, most of the class did better on their papers.

3. My father was a poor man because he believed in democracy.

4. The agreement was not signed today, the workers believing it would be.

5. Cancer is related to cigarette smoking, although millions smoke.

6. Farwell, who knows how to act, has directed many plays successfully.

7. Because he had worked very hard for it, Mike was supported by most students for the Council.

8. I got my new teeth when I took Mrs. Farquhar to the theater.

■■■ S 11 *Faulty Coordination*

Coordinate elements in a sentence should be balanced against each other so that they seem "equal" in emphasis and logic. When "unequal" elements are joined, usually by a coordinating conjunction, an illogical (or faulty) coordination is the result. To correct the problem, subordinate one of the elements at the beginning, middle, or end of the sentence.

Problem: I had a lot of work to do, *and* I had a cup of coffee.
Solution: *Even though I had a lot of work to do,* I had a cup of coffee.

Problem: Liza was an excellent worker, *and* she got the best student job the college had.
Solution: Liza, *who was an excellent worker,* got the best student job the college had.

Problem: The new shingles have been nailed on the roof, and the men have not gone on lunch break.
Solution: The men have not gone to lunch, *although they have finished nailing the shingles on the roof.*

PRACTICE

Clarify the relationship between the coordinate elements in these sentences. When you can, subordinate an element at the beginning, middle, or end of the sentence.

1. Friends say that they go to Chicago as often as they used to, and it is a fairly safe city.

2. He was a handsome man and he had a short haircut.

3. There have been many students who have seen the play, and I think it is a good one.

4. The university had a poor debate team this year, and the debaters usually used incoherent arguments.

5. Tennessee is pretty, and we will visit many parts of the state on our vacation.

6. In botany, we learned about the permeability of cell walls, and surprising chemicals can pass through such walls.

7. Susan's husband has a Ph. D., and he shared the household duties with her, not without grumbling.

■■■ S 12 *Faulty Complements*

Certain statements complete their idea with a linking verb (usually a form of *be*) and a noun element. This use of *complements* (or *completers*) supplies a logical equation:

Subject	"be" form (=)	Complement
Miss *Haversham*	*is* (=)	the *Woman* of the Year.
The *material* for the seminar	*will be* (=)	the first *topic* for the committee.

If the noun elements on either side of the sentence do not "equal" each other, you will get an illogical equation, as in these sentences:

Problem: An example of good music is the famous camp at Martindale Lake in the summer. (*example of music ≠ camp*)

Solution (1): The famous camp at Martindale Lake teaches only good music.

Solution (2): When students attend Martindale Lake Camp, they learn only good music.

Problem: The Wildlife Federation is where you get free publications on saving the environment. (*Federation ≠ where*)

Solution: At the Wildlife Federation, you can get free publications on saving the environment.

Problem: Going to the war college is when the young officer learns the newest military tactics. (*Going ≠ when*)

Solution: In the war college, the young officer learns the newest military tactics.

PRACTICE

Change the faulty *complements* in these sentences. Rewrite as necessary.

1. My mother is the reason I came back to school this fall.

2. His last experiment was an engine that would run without fuel.

3. Conservation will be an important point of debate in the election.

4. A natural bridge is when water erodes soft rock under an arch of hard rock.

5. A wife's citizenship is where she has three years' residence and makes the proper petition to the government.

6. The reason for evolution was because species lose unfavorable variations while keeping favorable ones.

7. Bird watching is where you study birds and record their habits.

8. The good soil for a vineyard is the reason Ms. Templar grew such fine grapes.

9. Successful navigation is a sextant used by a competent naval officer.

10. The final result of the conflict between Spain and England was the Spanish Armada, which was smashed by the British fleet in 1588.

■■■ S 13   *Sentence Fragments*

"The umpire called him out. Although he had already crossed the plate." The second statement is incomplete—a *sentence fragment*. Essentially, fragments are pieces of a sentence that cannot stand alone. They are not independent:

> The dead squirrel on the ground.
> Melissa having a good time.
> Waiting for us to come along.

By adding material, you can turn these sentence fragments into independent statements:

> The cat avoided the dead squirrel on the ground.
> I saw Melissa having a good time.
> There was the angry bus driver, waiting for us to come along.

Many fragments can be corrected by combining them with the previous sentence:

Problem: I refused the job. Because it was not interesting.

Solution: I refused the job because it was not interesting.

Problem: Virginia did not like the proposal. Even after her friends in the club had completely approved of it.

Solution: Virginia did not like the proposal, even after her friends in the club had completely approved of it.

Problem: James Earl Ray escaped from prison. A prison that was supposed to be escape-proof.

Solution: James Earl Ray escaped from a prison that was supposed to be escape-proof.

Problem:	The administration believes that it must carry the matter through. Having come this far.
Solution:	Having come this far, the administration believes that it must carry the matter through.
Problem:	That group of citizens has finally given Congress an ultimatum. To limit the sale of handguns.
Solution:	That group of citizens has finally given Congress an ultimatum—to limit the sale of handguns.

NOTE: In professional writing, the fragment is often used for emphasis or stylistic variation:

> "Of course, there's not much in it [the movie *Bonnie and Clyde*] about the nameless, faceless dead men. *Or the orphans and widows and the never-healing scar of a man who never knew his father.*"

> —Mike Royko

Your instructor will probably object to fragments if (1) you don't know you are using them (unconscious use is a sign that you do not know what a sentence is), or (2) you overwork them. Be sure you know his or her opinions on the matter.

PRACTICE

Revise each of the following constructions so that the sentence fragment is removed.

1. Taxes should be lowered. Because citizens pay too much to the government already.

2. Furnace tape can be used to repair cloth. And many other household items.

3. What happened to the student revolutionaries? The ones who were so evident during the sixties?

4. Some Germans practiced civil disobedience during the Nazi regime. A very small number.

5. That was the final question. Which I did not know the answer to.

6. Earlier she could remember the answer. That had been emphasized in the text.

7. I do not believe in that idea of God. An angry old man with a long beard.

■■■ S 14   *Comma Splices*

Here is a *comma splice*: "I am fond of you, he is fond of you too." The error is that of "splicing" two main clauses or sentences with a comma instead of separating them properly—usually with a period or semicolon. Another example:

A word processor is actually a "computer-typewriter," it can type the same page a thousand times without the operator's touching the keys.

Sometimes a coordinating conjunction can be inserted between the two clauses spliced by a comma. Sometimes one main clause can be subordinated to the other:

A word processor is actually a "computer-typewriter," and it can type the same. . . .

A word processor, *which is actually a "computer-typewriter,"* can type the same. . . .
(The first clause is subordinated to the second.)

Here are more examples of the comma splice:

Problem: The garden was full of beans, I ate most of them that summer.

Solution (1):   The garden was full of beans; I ate most of them that summer.

Solution (2):   The garden was full of beans, so I ate most of them that summer.

Problem: I am in no way responsible for your good fortune, you earned everything you have.

Solution (1):   I am in no way responsible for your good fortune. You earned everything you have.

Solution (2):   I am in no way responsible for your good fortune because you earned everything you have. (The second clause is subordinated to the first.)

PRACTICE

Find the comma splice in these sentences. Repunctuate (or rewrite) the sentences.

1. We went to see an unusual play last night, it was about Gertrude Stein, it had only one character, Ms. Stein herself.

2. They enjoy living in that apartment, their landlord supplies more services for them than for the other tenants.

3. I heard what the professor said, however, I did not write it down in my notes.

4. When he was editor of *Fortune,* Henry Luce said that he wanted to hire poets, at least poets knew the language, he said.

5. Luce believed that he could teach poets to write about economics, this was easier than teaching economists to write clear English.

6. The comic book has lost its appeal for many children, television has taken its place.

7. The word *prithee* is archaic, I will not use it any more.

8. First we had dust storms all over the state, then came torrential rains.

9. My horse went lame, consequently I will have to ride a stable horse in Friday's show.

10. "I've been working on a road crew for three summers now," she said, "I'm tired of that kind of work."

■■■ S 15   *Fused Sentences*

"I stopped and opened my car door the pickup behind me hit it." This construction is called a *fused sentence*. It is actually made up of two sentences joined together without any punctuation or capitalization to indicate where the first sentence ends and the second begins. The problem can be solved in several ways:

Solution (1):	I stopped and opened my car door. The pickup behind me hit it.
Solution (2):	When I stopped and opened my car door, the pickup behind me hit it.
Problem:	Try not to write fused sentences they are hard to understand.
Solution (1):	Try not to write fused sentences; they are hard to understand.
Solution (2):	Your reader will find fused sentences hard to understand.
Problem:	Where are you going when are you coming back?
Solution (1):	Where are you going? When are you coming back?
Solution (2):	Tell me where you are going and when you are coming back.

PRACTICE

In order to improve these fused sentences, repunctuate or rewrite them.

1. She discovered when she was young that she had musical talent later she was sorry she had not taken advantage of it.

2. I know that the period of the 1960s was a period of social change what kind of change was most important?

3. Librarians are now under attack for buying "dirty" books they even have to defend the circulation of certain modern classics like *The Catcher in the Rye*.

4. There was no breeze on the lake this afternoon we just sat there in the boat becalmed.

5. Scientists and creationists can sometimes agree they should not always assume that they are philosophical enemies.

6. Is the crime rate increasing perhaps we don't understand the situation perhaps we are merely getting better statistics.

7. We found Manuel building a set for the play he said he did not have time to help us with the calculus problems.

■■■ S 16   *Run-On Sentences*

The *run-on sentence* has a "stringy," unemphatic effect; it is usually created by a series of main clauses tied together with *or, and, but,* or *so*:

> Punishment is a good idea, and I believe that criminals should be punished, but they should not be put to death, for capital punishment is wrong.

Most sentences of this kind can be rewritten by using subordination and a change of emphasis:

> I believe that criminals should be punished. But since capital punishment is wrong, they should not be put to death.

Problem: Jim flew to New York, and his plane was late, so he was not able to get to the meeting on time, but his boss did not get angry with him.

Solution: When Jim flew to New York, his plane was late and he missed the meeting. His boss, however, did not get angry with him.

PRACTICE

---

1. Correct these run-on sentences.

  a. You can make beer much cheaper than you can buy it, and you need a container and a few ingredients, but you have to be sure that all materials are perfectly clean.

  b. Most readers read too slowly, and they miss the overall picture of the essay or book, so they tend to misunderstand the writer's point after they finish.

  c. I am afraid of flying, and I usually take two sleeping pills when I have to fly, but the pills don't work as well as they should, so I just stay awake and shake with fear.

  d. Jigsaw puzzles are fun to work, but they take more time than our family usually has, and the puzzles just sit there on the table half-done for days.

  e. The scientists reported that there will be a new earthquake in California, but it will be further away from San Francisco this time, and it will be lower on the Richter scale, so houses and property should not be greatly damaged.

  f. A fire department gets many strange calls, and some of them are from people who are lonely, and they just want to talk to someone, but they do not want to give their names or addresses.

2. These sentences are fused or run-on, or contain a comma splice. Identify the error, and correct the sentence. Rewrite where necessary.

   a. George Orwell wrote a famous essay called "A Hanging," and in this essay he showed how cruel people could be, but in truth Orwell had never seen a hanging, for he told a friend that he had manufactured the whole story.

   b. Reasonable debate in a college class is possible, we should encourage it.

   c. Some scientists lie others lie part of the time, a few try always to tell the truth.

   d. Suicide is available to every person not every thinking person should consider it seriously.

   e. Romance shouts defiance at tradition, and tradition answers with a sneer, but the latter usually wins, for most people in the end become traditionalists in their own culture.

   f. She walked the length of the street in front of the great Miami hotels, she saw rows of the living dead propped up in their chairs.

   g. The young wisely ignore the old they think them to be prejudiced, this is not true they are merely tired of hearing the same old questions why don't you ask some new ones?

■■■ S 17   *Weak Passive*

The *passive* construction is made with a *be* verb plus a *past participle*:

Be Verb	Past Participle
is	made
was	seen
has been	accomplished
will be	redesigned

If misused, the passive can be wordy, awkward, or unemphatic:

A picnic table *was located* by Jim.

A sonata *will be played by* the orchestra.

The banquet *was held* during which speeches *were made* and songs *were sung*.

One of the most common (and serious) misuses of the passive is the gobbledygook passive, in which the writer uses vague or polysyllabic words (and usually omits the agent). Examples of gobbledygook passive:

The experimental rationale *was explained* in the Foreword and *was* more fully *detailed* in Chapter 3.

Psychological characterization *will be considered* a major factor in the present analysis of *Huck Finn.*

Improving a Bad Passive

For a bad passive—whether it is wordy, awkward, unemphatic, or so gobbledygooky that a reader simply cannot understand it—there is one major strategy for improvement: *Turn the statement into action, with the subject placed first.*

a.   *Poor:*   A picnic table was located by Jim. (7 words)

  Improved (action):   Jim located a picnic table. (5 words)

b.   *Poor:*   The banquet was held during which speeches were made and songs were sung. (13 words)

  Improved (action):   During the banquet, we heard speeches and sang songs. (9 words)

The solution to the gobbledygook passive is *never* write a sentence like this in the first place:

> It has been decided that to maintain optimum learning conditions in the library, evening hours will be extended to 2:00 A.M.

But if a sentence like this sneaks up on you in a first draft, identify the subjects in the situation, and put the idea into one or more specific actions:

> The library has announced that its evening hours will be extended to 2:00 A.M.

> Mr. Harlan Smith, Director of the Library, has announced that . . .

> Mr. Smith announced today that starting Sunday the library will close at 2:00 A.M. Smith claimed that closing the library later will allow more students to use it.

> So that more students can use the library, it will close at 2:00 A.M. from now on.

PRACTICE

Rewrite these sentences to avoid the weak passive.

1. The meeting was organized by Jane.

2. The motion to table the question was presented by Jackson.

3. On February 1, there was an inquiry made by you about Peter Winston's final grade in English 101.

4. We students were told by the computer manual to avoid the DELETE key in special circumstances.

5. The disturbance in the classroom was created by two students wearing REVOLT! T-shirts.

6. The hiring of two new full-time teaching assistants was suggested by the student committee on teaching.

7. But part-time assistants were preferred by the head of the department.

8. When the air conditioning broke down, the students' discomfort during the final exam was ignored by the proctor.

9. An hour of preparation was saved by the use of Sarkon diamond cutters.

10. The specifications for mountain bikes will be sent by the designer as soon as possible.

Editing Sentences

Only a genius gets a sentence right the first time. Most of us write . . . rewrite . . . and then write again—trying to get the proper match between meaning and structure. Revision usually improves this match; but with revision, as with other techniques in composition, you need a plan—or a set of suggestions—in order to make it more purposeful. After writing a "bad" sentence, how do you fix it? In this chapter we will offer a number of suggestions for revision, all of them based on the following premise: As you inspect your own sentences, imagine that you are a cool, objective, and slightly negative editor who does not mind telling himself to rearrange, cut, and reword.

▼ Suggestions For Revising And Editing*

1. *Think about what you've said.*   Many bad sentences are the work of writers who have failed to think about and visualize what they have written. Leo Rosten found a sentence in the *New York Times* that shows how such a failure can result in unintentional comedy:

---

*Editors and instructors often hear this complaint from writers after they have rewritten a sentence: "But you changed my meaning!" The objection has some validity, but the response to it has more: "One cannot usually make a significant improvement in a weak sentence without changing the meaning." In fact, when writers revise or edit a sentence, they try to make *meaning* more exact at the same time that they improve *structure* and *word choice*. In the sentence, everything works (or does not work) together.

There is Mr. Burton growling and grousing and endlessly chewing the lips, ears, and neck of Elizabeth Taylor as the faithless wife of a dull ambassador with whom he is having a clandestine affair.

Rosten commented: "I am glad, in a way, that Mr. Burton was endlessly chewing the neck of Miss Taylor as the faithless wife of a dull ambassador, because it probably wouldn't be fun to chew her neck as anyone else; but who is the ambassador with whom Burton, it says here, is having a clandestine affair?" Rosten quoted another sentence from the *Times*:

Among her biggest gambles was during their tempestuous courtship.

Said Rosten: "I hate to be a spoilsport, gentlemen, but you just can't 'was' during anything."

2. *Check your stance.*   Is a weak writer's stance hurting your sentence? A student wrote about a class project:

The availability of time is an important factor in the project choice.

The stance is vague here—no writer, reader, or clear point. Clarify the stance and rewrite completely:

In choosing a problem for our project, we must remember that we have only three weeks' time.

3. *Make your subject-verb relationship as clear and specific as possible.*   A vague relationship helped make a mess of this sentence:

Parental *endeavors* (subject) in regard to education *suggest* (verb) that . . .

How can endeavors *suggest*? Specify the subject and verb; then clarify the rest of the sentence:

Parents at Elm School now *insist* that their children be taught to read.

Here is another example of vague subject and verb:

One of the most important reasons for going to graduate school *is* more training.

Edit this by changing both the stance and the subject-verb relationship:

Students who want more training *should go* to graduate school.

Or:

Do you want more training? Then [*you should*] *go* to graduate school.

4. *Read your sentences aloud.*

Pedalling hard, she reached top of the hill.

That is a sentence one of us wrote several years ago. It went through our hands and the hands of an editor before the omission was found—by a proofreader reading the sentence aloud:

Pedalling hard, she reached *the* top of the hill.

Since people read hundreds of words a minute, it is easy to miss all kinds of errors—dangling modifiers, misspellings, illogicalities, vague usage, careless punctuation, omissions. *The ear will catch what the eye will not.* Human beings spoke and heard language a million years before they wrote it, which is why the best editing often combines the talents of ear and eye and voice.

5. *Use the sentence unit rule.* Check back to page 86 for a full explanation of the rule. Also see **6** below.

6. *Make sure your sentence openers logically fit the bases that follow.*

> *Faulty:* Like many specialities in engineering, you must learn . . .
> (*dangling modifier*)
>
> *Improved:* Like many kinds of engineers, you must learn . . .

> *Faulty:* To be considered for the debate team, the voice must be trained.
>
> *Improved:* To be considered for the debate team, you must first train your voice.

7. *Avoid "nouniness" and "preposition piling."* Good sentences use no more nouns than are absolutely necessary. Abstract nouns are particularly troublesome. This sentence is "nouny":

Personality analysis is the *determination* of *function defects* and *utilization* of their *cures.*

The sentence contains seven nouns—two of them used as clumsy modifiers: "*personality* analysis" and "*function* defects." This sentence is so bad it can't be edited; who knows what is means?

In a sentence, prepositions can multiply like rabbits. Such "preposition piling" occurs with nouniness and is a sign of it:

English teachers agree that personal ownership and use *of* a good dictionary is a prime necessity *for* every student *in* obtaining the maximum results *from* the study *of* English.

Rewrite, cutting some of the nouns and altering others; for example, make *ownership* and *use* into verbs. Then the prepositions can be reduced from five to zero, the nouns from ten to three:

English teachers agree that students should own and use a good desk dictionary.

Here is a portion of a satiric essay on nouniness in modern prose:

Have you noticed the new look in the English language? Everybody's using nouns as adjectives. Or to put that in the current argot, there's a modifier noun proliferation. More exactly, since the matter is getting out of hand, a modifier noun proliferation increase. In fact, every time I open a magazine these days or listen to the radio, I am struck by the modifier noun proliferation increase phenomenon. So, I decided to write—you guessed it—a modifier noun proliferation increase phenomenon article. . . .

Abstraction is the enemy both of clear expression and easy understanding. And abstract is what these strings of nouns become. And very quickly the reader or listener doesn't know what the actual relationship is. Take "Reality Therapy," the name of a new book. Do you gather that the author uses reality as a means of therapy or that the goal of his treatment is facing reality or that he has worked out some sort of therapy which he applies to reality? Take a phrase puzzled over in *Newsweek:* "antenna television systems operation." Manufacture? broadcasting? consulting? The article said that somebody was going into that field and I still don't know where he's going. I suspect that the people who turn out these phrases might insist that they are seeking greater precision, as though each new noun pinned down the matter a bit more. Wrong. Another article like this one and we'll have a modifier noun proliferation increase phenomenon article protest campaign, but will you know what you've got?

—Bruce Price, "An Inquiry into Modifier Noun Proliferation"

8. *Cut out deadwood—words and phrases that are not doing enough work in the sentence.* The sample sentence in **7**, on using the dictionary, illustrates how to cut out deadwood. Here are more examples:

Poor: A woman who was present there saw the break-in.

Improved: A woman there saw the break-in.

Poor: We are in receipt of your memo of August 14 making reference to football tickets sold by some of the players.

Improved: We received your letter of August 14 about football tickets sold by some of the players.

Poor: In relation to his idea, it does not seem to me to be a workable one.

Improved: I doubt that his idea will work.

Poor: A second area in which Brandi should have a better knowledge involves rules of attendance.

Improved: Second, Brandi should know more about rules of attendance.

9. *Rewrite to avoid monotony or lack of emphasis.*

Poor: Many favorable comments are beginning to be made about fantasy movies by the critics. These comments are long overdue and welcome to students of film.

Improved: Recently many critics have made favorable comments about fantasy movies. To students of film, these comments are welcome—and long overdue.

Poor: I took the job happily when the head of the company offered me more money because of my long experience and also technical school training in the field.

Improved: When he found out that I had both technical training and experience, the head of the company offered me the job with a higher salary. I accepted his offer happily.

The last two improved versions work well partly because they follow the three suggestions offered by the sentence unit rule (page 86).

▼ A Final Note On Editing

Recently, a student came in to see one of us about his writing problems, particularly about his weak sentences. We talked over several of them, bringing out ideas and possibilities hidden inside (or behind) them. In effect, we were co-editors, identifying, analyzing, rethinking, and rewriting some of the troublesome constructions. You can do the same job by "talking" over your own sentences with yourself. Here are two of the student's sentences, with comments about their weaknesses:

Poor sentence: The students were accused of plagiarism, and they were told in terms of their careers in academia that they should not be too hopeful.

Comments: Stance and viewpoint are weak—*who* told the students? The two passive constructions are vague. Deadwood: *in terms of. Their careers* and *in academia* are not doing much work in the sentence either. Vague: *They should not be too hopeful.*

Edited sentence: After she accused the students of plagiarism, the Assistant Dean told them that they might be expelled.

Together, we created a clearer stance, cut out the deadwood, employed an opener, changed the vague passives to active constructions, and made the whole sentence more specific.

Poor sentence: The misuse of the environment must be improved in regard to the liquor industry.

Comments: Read the sentence aloud—we must *improve* our *misuse*? This says exactly the opposite of what the writer intended. He was probably thrown off the track by several weaknesses: the poor stance; the vagueness and deadwood *in regard to the liquor industry*; the passive *misuse . . . must be improved.*

Edited sentence: Let's pass a law in this state abolishing throwaway beer bottles.

We changed the stance. Now the writer is addressing a more specific group of readers. We cut unnecessary words, changed the bad passive to an active verb, and substituted the more specific phrase *beer bottles* for the vague phrase *liquor industry*.

PRACTICE

Edit and rewrite these sentences. Don't be afraid to change them when necessary. The point is to write a *better* sentence.

a. The assassination of Lincoln had much speculation to it.

b. The fact that the new trainees at first do not get to do much work on the actual engines should not give them a feeling of demotion.

c. It must be considered a possibility that the student nurse must be able to face physical damage, broken bones, cranial disorders, pregnancy, or even death.

d. It happened at the hour of three when there is much relaxing during the coffee break.

e. The nerve center of the oboe lies in its reed, and in its bore is its soul; the need of a good reed is the bane of the player's life.

f. Mr. Coleman announced his resignation this morning. He would have liked to have stayed a while longer.

g. "Don't expire before your license do."

—from the Illinois State License Bureau

h. He only dislikes action pictures and neither does his brother.

i. The next point to make about idiom differences is one of the most difficult problems for many foreigners.

j. It is not believed that the critics show complete rationality in their judgments when they criticize the Fall Frolic.

k. After explaining my job to me, there was a car sent by the Head Ranger to take me to the office.

l. Our family has been really having huge difficulties with hard-core resentment on the girls' part, who have been claiming that we play favorites for the one boy.

m. Thus the continual success, interest, and the test of endurance are reasons why marathon bicycle racing is an important topic.

n. Although these statistics may look suspicious, it is because there is not a more specific breakdown of them.

o. In response to the attack on my report on Adventure Playgrounds, I will prove to you, the newspapers, radio, and TV its validity.

p. Perched prettily on the branches, we watched the first robin of spring.

q. Invariably the problem of the car breaking down will sometimes arise.

r. The exploration of student differences in response to the instructor's stimulus questions cause the students to return to the textbook seeking justification for their opinions and ultimately encourage the articulation of their personal views.

s. The loss of professors' credibility represents an indispensable foundation upon which authority structures are undermined.

t. The nation's domestic ills may keep, although there is a risk in deferring them.

u. Last year the campus had a great increase in narcotics arrests, most of them on a marijuana possession charge or for smoking marijuana.

Punctuation

Punctuation marks show the "joints" or joining places in your sentences. In addition to signaling sentence structure or indicating how words phrases and sentences are put together these marks also tell the reader many small things for example that a string of words is a book title italics that something belongs to somebody apostrophe that a speech is coming comma and quotation marks

Did you have trouble reading that last sentence? No wonder—we didn't punctuate it. Now read it with the punctuation marks added (in *sixteen* places):

> In addition to "signaling" sentence structure or indicating how words, phrases, and sentences are put together, these marks also tell the reader many small things—for example, that a string of words is a book title (italics); that something belongs to somebody (apostrophe); that a speech is coming (comma and quotation marks).

▼ Spacing and Placing Punctuation Marks

Here we answer questions like:

- How many *spaces* do I put between a period and the following capital letter of the next sentence?
- Does a comma go *inside* or *outside* the quotation marks?

Note the two classes of punctuation marks involved (alphabetical order):

End Marks

! exclamation mark
. period
? question mark

Non-End Marks

' apostrophe
[ ] brackets
: colon
, comma
— dash
. . . ellipsis periods (spaced)
. . . .
- hyphen
( ) parentheses
"—" quotation marks
; semicolon

■■■ *Spacing Punctuation Marks*

1. All marks coming after a word (or after another mark) come directly after it—no space.

I was agitated.   Give him air!   Why?

Red-faced, he groped for words: "Save me; you must save me!"

Did you say, "Why?"?   Dear Joan,

2. *Parentheses* and *brackets* have no space between them and the words involved.

I was angry (but she wasn't).

The letter was recieved [*sic*].

3. On most typewriters, you make a *dash* with two hyphens placed *together.* Use *no space* before or after the dash.

The human appendix is on the right side—not the left.

4. *Hyphens* use no space on either side of the mark.

space-age technology

mid-June

ex-husband

5. *Ellipsis marks* (spaced periods) in quotations:

a. When *less* than a sentence is omitted: Use one space between three periods, and also one space between the adjacent words and the periods.

"Roger . . . did wrong."

b. When *more* than a sentence is omitted: Do the same as in (a), except use four periods and no space before the first period.

"Roger did wrong. . . . He later accepted his guilt."

6. Unless other marks must be included (see **9** below), *quotation marks* go next to the words involved.

They called him "Roger" on Tuesday.

7. Between all end marks and the capital of the next sentence, use two spaces.

I want the minimum wage. Indeed, I demand it! Demand it? Yes.

8. Put *apostrophes* next to (and just after) the words showing possession or plurality.

tiger's paw   *tigers*' paws   three *q*'s   two *7*'s

■■■ *Placing Punctuation Marks When More Than One Mark Is Involved*

9. *Quotation marks*

a. Put commas and periods *inside* quotation marks.

"I see," said the vicar, "that you have arrived."

b. Put semicolons and colons outside quotation marks.

He said it was "outrageous"; I did not agree.

These elements of the play she called "superb": direction, staging, acting.

c. Exclamation and question marks go *inside* quotation marks.

"It was an antitank mine!" the general yelled.

"Are you sure it was an antitank mine?" asked the major.

Exception (when the quoted material is only part of the sentence):

Did you hear the general call it an "antitank mine"?

10. *Parentheses* and *brackets*

When they apply *to the whole sentence*, put all end marks *inside* parentheses and brackets.

The dog was called *reh pinscher*. (The expression is German for "small deer.")

But: The dog was called *reh pinscher* ("small deer").

11. *Parentheses* and *commas*

Put the comma outside the parenthetical mark.

In the fissures (veins), the company found a good supply of minerals.

12. *Parentheses* and *colons*

Put the colon outside the parenthetical mark.

I had a reason (a good one): I simply didn't know any better.

▼ Punctuation And Sentence Units

Our research indicates that punctuation is learned most easily in the context of *writing a sentence*. In other words, you write and punctuate at the same time. Generally, it is unwise to write and then punctuate later; those little marks (particularly commas) are too much a part of the sentence and its structure. Punctuating after the fact is rather like putting up a house wall—and then hammering in the nails.

We recommend that before you read pages 485–498, you look carefully at pages 79 and 84–85. This will give you an idea of the tight relationship between the marks and how they separate and "signal" structures.

KNOW WHERE YOU ARE IN A SENTENCE. As the discussion on pages 84–85 tells you, at any specific point in the words of a sentence you will be inside either a *base unit* or a *free unit.* Example:

Before reading *Mad,* he was sure he recognized satire—now he wasn't sure.

This sentence breaks down into three units (note punctuation):

A	B	C
opener	base	closer

At point A, you are in an *opening* unit; at point B, in a *base* unit; at point C, in a *closing* unit. The *punctuation marks show where the units start and stop.*

Here are more examples; can you identify each unit?

1. He thought she was right; the others agreed.

2. I made a mistake that time. But I won't next time.

3. Family reunions (even the best organized of them) are usually a bore.

4. When we had our last reunion, I refused to go.

5. There was the dusty old book, an ancient tomb full of speeches by former governors of Idaho.

Here are the units in those sentences identified:

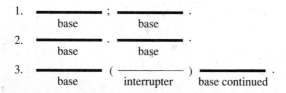

4. ──────── , ━━━━━ .
     opener   base

5. ━━━━━ , ──────── .
     base   closer

Now we will show you how to use the various punctuation marks.

▪▪▪ P 1   Use a Period When . . .

a. You end a sentence:

Thomas Jefferson was both philosopher and politician.

I don't know when I'll be back from the movies.

b. You abbreviate:

M.A. degree   etc.   10:00 p.m.   Sept.   Calif.   Mr.

▪▪▪ P 2   Use a Question Mark When . . .

You ask a question:

What did the senator do then?

What time is it?

How can I do better on the next test?

▪▪▪ P 3   Use an Exclamation Mark When . . .

You exclaim:

Fight fiercely, Harvard!

Never say die, say damn!

That's the ugliest sports coat I ever saw!

NOTE: Don't exclaim very often or very loud.

▪▪▪ P 4   Use a Comma When . . .

a. You join two main clauses with a coordinating conjunction (*and, or, but, so, for*):

The grass is bright green, *and* all the trees are beginning to bud.

The river is flooding, *but* Dad won't be there to see it.

It is extremely rainy here this season, *so* be sure to bring your raincoat.

b. You join an opening, interrupting, or closing unit to a main clause:

Since Clarice was bored in the second grade, her parents decided to let her skip a grade.

We could not shake our pursuers, *although we tried to lose them several times that day.*

That's what I want to do, *join the Army.*

Our dachshund, *who was dozing near the fire*, suddenly began to bark loudly.

You grabbed my foot, *not my hand!*

c. You use a parallel construction of three or more elements:

griffins, dragons, and *elves*

Were there *green, yellow,* or *orange* colors in the painting?

We lay on the ground, we stared at the stars, and *we thought deep thoughts.*

d. You place "equal" descriptive words before a noun:

new, nice-looking table

New and *nice-looking* describe *table,* a noun. They are "equal" because you can put *and* logically between them—"new *and* nice-looking." In the phrase "new coffee table," *new* and *coffee* are not equal: You wouldn't say "new *and* coffee table."

honest, wonderful man (honest *and* wonderful man)

hot, dark night (hot *and* dark night)

But: *last spring* semester (not last *and* spring semester)

e. You employ direct address:

John, please wash the car.

Mrs. Rosenthal, would you sit over there?

f. You supply dates and places:

Chicago, Illinois

January 15, 1990

On May 14, 1916, in Houston, Texas

He died in Nashville, Tennessee, on October 14, 1943.

g. You identify speakers in dialogue:

James said, "Where can I find my umbrella?"

"It's in the hall closet," Mom said.

"If that's the way you're faithful," said Marie angrily, "we're through!"

h. You want to prevent misreading or ambiguity:

By speaking of the dead, Lincoln in his Gettysburg Address appealed to . . .

If you write, "By speaking of the dead Lincoln . . ." your reader may be confused and have to re-read the sentence.

The deductions allowed, the taxpayer is able to . . .

("The deductions allowed the taxpayer . . . " may be confusing.)

PRACTICE

Punctuate the sentences below.

NOTE: There are more exercises on the comma on page 494.

1. I do not care for life has other attractions besides fame.

2. A mile above the mountain shook and trembled.

3. The governor of Texas said "San Antonio is the birthplace of at least one great man!"

4. "So?" said the governor of Nebraska. "Kearney is the birthplace of three great women and they are all from the same family!"

5. Ms. Crane our instructor just fainted.

6. On that hot fateful day (October 15 1943) the city of North Platte almost blew away causing many a family to flee for safety.

7. The North Platte River is the finest example of a *braiding* river in this hemisphere a geological observation I have spent 30 years trying to forget.

8. He was tiresome but honest careful but boring.

9. My roommate who has red hair is going to dye it green for St. Patrick's Day.

10. Madonna is famous talented and controversial.

11. My aunt the sister of my stepmother used to play pinochle in the afternoon a strange occupation for someone trained in the law.

12. Small children according to linguists learn to speak in a more organized more predictable way than we used to believe.

■■■ P 5   Use a Semicolon When . . .

a. You want to join two main clauses without using a coordinating conjunction:

The snows of yesterday have all gone; they have melted away.

His technique on the guitar is sloppy; he doesn't seem to care whether he hits the right notes or not.

b. You want to join two main clauses with conjunctive adverbs. (Note the comma that follows the conjunctive adverb.)

> I caught you red-handed; *therefore,* you will go to jail.
>
> Sam and Rena went to the church; *however,* they didn't get married.
>
> The company cheated on its income tax; *consequently,* the Internal Revenue Service demanded back payment of tax.

> NOTE: *A conjunctive adverb* is essentially a "sentence modifier." It says something about a sentence, and it relates the idea in the sentence to an idea expressed just before:

> Solar heating equipment is very expensive; *thus,* homeowners are still choosing more conventional methods of heating their homes.

A list of typical conjunctive adverbs:

Implies Addition	*Implies Results or Reason*	*Implies Contrast*	*Implies Similarity*
also	consequently	however	equally
besides	therefore	nevertheless	likewise
furthermore	thus	still	similarly
moreover	otherwise	yet	
	indeed		

c. You need to clarify a parallel series:

> *Unclarified:* At the meeting were Smithers the captain, Jones the first mate, and Watterson the bosun.
>
> *Clarified:* At the meeting were Smithers, the captain; Jones, the first mate; and Watterson, the bosun.
>
> *Unclarified:* My landlady tells my wife what kind of floor wax to use, the same as she uses, when to use it, the same time she does, where to set the refrigerator, the same place as hers, and, most helpful of all, when to get her husband up in the morning.
>
> *Clarified:* My landlady tells my wife what kind of floor wax to use, the same as she uses; when to use it, the same time she does; where to set the refrigerator, the same place as hers; and, most helpful of all, when to get her husband up in the morning.

d. You wish to "strengthen" a comma. Note the difference between these sentences:

> The Prime Minister was right, *but* he should have been more careful in making his appeal.

In calling for devotion to duty, the Prime Minister was right; *but* he should have been more careful in making his appeal.

Because the second sentence already has a comma in it and is more complex than the first, the writer decided to strengthen the joint between the two clauses with a semicolon. In each of the following examples, the comma ordinarily used between rather long sentence units joined by a conjunction has been strengthened to a semicolon.

These rules may seem rather harsh; *but* if you will stop to consider them carefully, you will understand that they are for the good of everybody.

Unfortunately, we don't know very much about what goes on inside the brain; *and* many surgeons, indeed some of the best ones, will refuse to operate without careful diagnosis of this condition.

Before deciding which house to buy, look very carefully at all the listings that the Multiple Service carries; *but* don't ignore other sources like newspaper ads and notices on bulletin boards.

■■■ *P 6   Use a Colon When . . .*

a. You introduce a list:

Please buy the following: butter, cheese, and bread.

It is often simpler to omit the colon and write: "Please buy butter, cheese, and bread."

b. You introduce quotations:

Toward the end of his life, Smith wrote to his son, making this plea: "Whatever you decide to do with the old property as a whole, never sell the north woods, for they meant everything to your mother."

c. You punctuate the salutation in a business letter:

Dear Dean Winkleboom:
Dear Sir:
Dear Mr. Ryan:
Dear Ms. Perez:

■■■ *P 7   Use Parentheses When . . .*

You wish to set off a word or an expression firmly from the rest of the sentence:

The man I am referring to (Jenkins) is not necessary to our plans.

There are not enough women doctors and lawyers (this is what the girl said).

When it was over the ship, the winch (which was holding up the boom) suddenly collapsed.

Parentheses *always* come in pairs. See *NOTE* in P 8 on the next page.

■■■ *P 8   Use a Dash When . . .*

You need to show a strong break in thought:

She became president only four years later—the youngest woman ever in the post.

I never want to get married—not under any circumstances.

Is there—listen to me—is there any hope for the survivors?

NOTE: Parentheses and dashes are quite helpful when you want to clarify a sentence that is loaded with too many commas. Observe how one writer, having already used commas around one interrupter, chooses to employ dashes around a second:

> Edward Cole, an engineer who owned one of the first 300 Corvettes produced in 1953, remembers that on his first long ride in the rain—from suburban Detroit 150 miles to Kalamazoo—the water rising in the cockpit compelled him to take off his shoes and roll up his pants.

—Coles Phinizy, "The Marque of Zora"

Of course, the writer could have used parentheses around either one of his interrupters. Don't rely too heavily on parentheses or dashes.

■■■ *P 9   Use an Apostrophe When . . .*

a. You use a possessive form:

the *trailer's* wheel (one trailer)

the *trailers'* wheels (more than one trailer)

Peter's arm

Persius' style

NOTE: Do not use the apostrophe with personal pronouns: "*his* car," "these are *hers*."

If you have trouble remembering whether the apostrophe goes inside or outside the *s*, simply think of this example. Take the word *dog,* add an apostrophe and the *s: dog's*. If the word already has an *s*, do the same—but drop the second *s*. And so *dogs* becomes *dog's* becomes *dogs'*. Here are a few additional examples:

"The water supply of the town" becomes "the *town*'s water supply."

"The water supply of the towns" becomes "the *towns'* water supply."

"The house belonging to Roger" becomes "*Roger's* house."

"The house belonging to the Rogers family" becomes "the *Rogers'* house."

b. You form plurals using numbers or letters:

Last semester, she got three *A's,* two *B's,* and a *C*.

There are four *3's* in the winning lottery number.

c. You form a contraction:

He'll be there.

I *can't* be at home today.

It's the thing to do.

NOTE: Do not confuse *it's* and *its* (without the apostrophe.) *Its* is a possessive pronoun like *theirs, hers, his, ours*—and does not take an apostrophe.

■■■ *P 10 Use a Hyphen When . . .*

a. You need a syllable break at the end of a line:

real-ization   *stereo-phonic*   *incor-porate*

(For more information on correct syllable breaks, see page 502.)

b. You use a prefix before a syllable starting with *e*:

pre-empt   *de-emphasize*   *re-enforce*

c. You make a compound word:

self-analysis   *cease-fire* (noun)   *mother-in-law*

d. You make a compound modifier:

a one-year clause   *a big-time* actor   *a blue-eyed* rabbit

When in doubt about the use of a hyphen, particularly for prefixes and syllable breaks, check your dictionary.

■■■ *P 11 Use Quotation Marks When . . .*

a. You quote the exact spoken or written words of someone else:

"No country on earth," shouted Senator Blanksley, "is richer than ours!"

It was John Donne who first said that "no man is an island."

b. You refer to titles of songs, paintings, and short literary works:

Faulkner wrote that short story, "A Rose for Emily."

The song is called "Stardust."

Picasso's "Guernica" is one of the most famous paintings of the twentieth century.

There is always some confusion about where quotation marks are placed in relation to other punctuation marks. The rules for such placement are actually quite simple:

1. Commas and periods that end a sentence unit always go inside the quotation marks:

He remarked, "My house is haunted."

"My house," she said, "is not haunted."

2. Colons and semicolons, when they divide the quoted material from the rest of the text, always go outside the quotation marks:

The editorial gave three reasons why Maltby would be "by far the best candidate": his experience, honesty, and fiscal conservatism.

He remarked, "My house is haunted"; he didn't say anything else.

3. Question marks and exclamation marks go inside or outside the quotation marks according to how the quoted material is being used:

Did he say, "My house is haunted"? (The question mark is placed *outside* the quotation marks because the entire sentence is the question.)

He asked, "Is my house haunted?" (The question mark goes *inside* the quotation marks because the quotation, not the entire sentence, is the question.)

Were you frightened when the ghost said "Boo!"? (The exclamation mark is part of the quotation, while the question mark indicates that the entire sentence is a question.)

NOTE: Occasionally, you may need to use a "quote within a quote." For the quote inside the quote, use single marks:

Jenny said, "I would prefer that you do not refer to me as 'that sweet little girl.' "

■■■ P 12   Use Italics (Underlining) When . . .

a. You refer to specific words or phrases:

The word *fragrance* is euphonious.

I do not understand what Marx meant by *democracy.*

b. You emphasize a word or phrase:

Do the job *right.*

I was referring to John *Adams,* not John Addison.

c. You refer to the titles of novels, stage productions, magazines, and newspapers:

Moby Dick (novel)	*Schindler's List* (movie)
Hamlet (play)	*Sports Illustrated* (magazine)
La Traviata (opera)	St. Louis *Post-Dispatch* (newspaper)

The relative length of works determines whether you use quotation marks or italics. Faulkner's short story, "A Rose for Emily," is put in quotation marks, but his novels (like *Sanctuary*) are italicized. Milton's "L'Allegro" is a short poem; his *Paradise Lost* is long—interminable.

PRACTICE

1. Punctuate the sentences below. Many of them can be punctuated in different ways—for example, students have suggested ten or so different solutions to *i.* For each sentence use the punctuation marks that seem to make it read most easily and clearly.

   a. The instructor said Read the chapter called Monopolies in Hansens book Economic Power.

   b. Burns opinion is that the word rapport is French.

   c. The boys lives are in danger so is yours.

   d. The car was new shiny and very pretty but it cost thirty thousand dollars.

   e. Lindbergh flew his airplane a high wing monoplane across the Atlantic.

   f. Before I come back you should have eaten your beans rice and honey.

   g. At the end of the semester however ones work gets easier.

   h. In the musical play Oklahoma there is a well known song called Oklahoma.

   i. At the end of Act II I stabbed him John pulled out the blood red knife and we laid his body on the floor.

   j. Its over taxed heart failing the racehorse dropped before the peoples eyes.

   k. Smith who had been there before looked around the house and moving swiftly we all searched the place.

   l. Jones father was a small time thug and politician in San Francisco in addition he was on drugs.

   m. In spite of the never ending rain however they pushed on and they finally came to the cave.

   n. Dickens wrote books for instance he wrote David Copperfield.

o. Dean Woof said his secretary the Admissions Office called and wants to know what to do with the student program requests for preregistration.

p. Steinbeck who wrote The Grapes of Wrath was a self made writer.

q. The dogs forelegs were scratched bruised and broken its eyes were perfectly all right.

r. You must return the child you must keep out of sight and you must above all not call the police.

2. In the following passage, we have numbered each space where the author originally placed a punctuation mark inside a sentence. After you have punctuated the sentences, explain or defend in a brief phrase each punctuation mark you used.

1   There are some students who can't remember how to spell a word even after they have looked it up in a dictionary. There are others who don't have much luck looking words up in a dictionary because they can't come close enough to guessing the spelling to have much chance of finding the words. Both kinds of students deserve a very limited amount of sympathy (1) especially from themselves. It is true that the English spelling system is the worst in the world (2) but it really wasn't invented out of pure malice (3) and the rules are the same for everybody. Resentment and alibis make the job of learning to spell enormously more difficult. The job does not require unusual intelligence (4) but it does require close attention and a long and patient effort. You may not think it is worth the effort (5) but on the whole the country does. Some kinds of ignorance can be concealed for years (6) but bad spelling can show up every time you write a sentence (7) and it can cost jobs and promotions as well as bad marks on English papers. Few people can afford not to learn to spell at least reasonably well.

2   If you are a really poor speller (8) the first step is to find out what method of learning a new word works best for you. Some people do best by spelling a word out loud a number of times (9) others by writing it down repeatedly (10) and still others by tracing it with a pencil after it has been correctly written. Find out whether your eyes (11) your ears (12) or your muscles help you most in this particular job. As you try each method (13) be sure you give your full attention to what you are doing. It is a pure waste of time to use any of them while you are thinking about something else. Five minutes of *real* work on spelling is worth much more than an hour of semiconscious droning or purely mechanical copying.

3   The next step is the critical one. Learn three new words a day every day for the next month (14) just everyday words that have been giving you trouble. Anybody bright enough to be in college can do this if he wants to. Most poor spellers give it up and find a new alibi before the first week is over. At first the results are slow and don't seem worth the effort (15) and if you figure that at this rate it would take you the rest of your life to learn a third of the words in your dictionary (16) the whole prospect seems pretty gloomy. But if you really work at the problem consistently and *alertly* for a month you will find that you have made real progress (17) and the ninety new words you know will be the smallest part of it. For one thing (18) you will find that you are seeing words more clearly (19) the new ones are easier to learn. For another (20) you'll have something to build on. You'll be ready to learn a good many words in groups instead of individually. This group method is so attractive that many people

want to begin with it (21) but it seldom works well until a good foundation has been laid by the simple but unpopular one at a time (22) method.

—L. M. Myers, *Guide to American English*

3. From a textbook, magazine, or other source, find a good short section of non-fiction prose. Copy two paragraphs, leaving out the punctuation, and set your copied page aside for a few hours. Then go back over it and put in your own punctuation marks. How well does your punctuation agree with that of the original? Can you defend any of your variations?

■■■ *P 13   Rhetoric of Punctuation*

So far, we have been explaining the "mechanics" of punctuation. *Mechanics* refers to those more or less firm rules that govern how you punctuate most sentences. But in addition to using punctuation marks in a mechanical way, you can use them for effect, to help create certain patterns of emotion and logic in the reader's mind. This *rhetoric* of punctuation allows you to make choices on the basis of stylistic effectiveness and interest. In order to see how rhetorical punctuation works, consider the following scene. When Mr. Smith went to his garage to finish cleaning his Mercedes, he found a terrible and bloody scene inside the trunk, which he had left open the night before. To his ten-year-old son, he said:

> The cat dragged a dead rabbit into the Mercedes trunk last night / get a
> shovel/ put the rabbit in the garbage / and clean up that mess out there.

These sentence structures, not to mention Mr. Smith's fatherly instructions, are clear as glass. But the structures can be punctuated differently, according to how you wish to create certain pauses, emphases, and effects:

> The cat dragged a dead rabbit into the Mercedes trunk last night. Get a
> shovel, put the rabbit in the garbage, and clean up that mess out there.

This is a calm father, even a dull one. He's obviously not very upset about the rabbit, for he plops down his commas and periods with bland regularity and precision. Here is another version:

> The cat dragged a dead rabbit into the Mercedes trunk last night—get a
> shovel. Put the rabbit in the garbage and clean up that mess out there!

In the first clause, this father has just seen the rabbit. He's a little sleepy, but by the time he gets out the first few words he's been pretty well awakened by the sight. It takes him a punctuational dash of time to think of the solution ("get a shovel"), after which he excitedly runs his words together in the following two main clauses and omits the comma before "and clean up."

Our third father is angry. He coldly bites off each sentence and stomps on it with a period:

> The cat dragged a dead rabbit into the Mercedes trunk last night. Get a
> shovel. Put the rabbit in the garbage. And clean up that mess out there.

The cat is going to catch it. So is the son, although he is as innocent as a lamb. The fourth father is edging on hysteria: the rabbit is bloody, and it smells:

> The *cat* dragged a *dead rabbit* into the Mercedes *trunk* last night! Get a shovel, put the rabbit in the garbage—and *clean up* that *mess* out there!

Punctuation works best when it achieves both mechanical and rhetorical effects. When you separate clauses with commas or enclose a phrase between a pair of parentheses, you do so according to precise mechanical rules of grammar and sentence structure. But when you build on these rules to help write sentences that are particularly interesting or effective, you are using a punctuational rhetoric that varies according to the situation. Consider these situations:

Simple fact; two things happen:

He looked at her, and she blushed.

Not-so-simple fact; cause-and-effect:

He looked at her; she blushed.

The same, with a little drama added:

He looked at her—she blushed.

Rapid cause-and-effect:

He looked at her, she blushed. (The comma splice may be considered acceptable here because the clauses are so brief.)

A reported afterthought:

He looked at her (and she blushed).

Deep, dark dramatic emphasis:

He looked at her and she blushed.

At this point, let's remind ourselves that like all the other forms and devices of rhetoric, punctuation can get out of hand. You can get too flashy with it. You don't want your reader to take special notice of your commas, periods, and dashes or to remark, "My, how clever this person is with the semicolon." Ideally, the main job of your punctuation marks should be to support your ideas and make easy the transmission of your thoughts to the reader. Sir Ernest Gowers, in his *Plain Words: Their ABC,* tells of a writer of a training manual for pilots who ended his comments with, "Pilots, whose minds are dull, do not usually live long." This writer's mispunctuation transmitted a thought he certainly did not intend and, as Sir Ernest commented, converted "a truism into an insult."

Good punctuation should separate with perfect clarity the parts of your sentences. In the long run of writing, such punctuation is the most effective kind there is.

PRACTICE

Here is Lincoln's Gettysburg Address—unpunctuated. If you were Lincoln, how would you punctuate it?

1   Fourscore and seven years ago our fathers brought forth on this continent a new nation conceived in liberty and dedicated to the proposition that all men are created equal.

2   Now we are engaged in a great civil war testing whether that nation or any nation so conceived and so dedicated can long endure we are met on a great battlefield of that war we have come to dedicate a portion of that field as a final resting place for those who here gave their lives that that nation might live it is altogether fitting and proper that we should do this

3   But in a larger sense we cannot dedicate we cannot consecrate we cannot hallow this ground the brave men living and dead who struggled here have consecrated it far above our poor power to add or detract the world will little note nor long remember what we say here but it can never forget what they did here it is for us the living rather to be dedicated here to the unfinished work which they who fought here have thus far so nobly advanced it is rather for us to be here dedicated to the great task remaining before us that from these honored dead we take increased devotion to that cause for which they gave the last full measure of devotion that we here highly resolve that these dead shall not have died in vain that this nation under God shall have a new birth of freedom and that government of the people by the people and for the people shall not perish from the earth

Mechanics

■■■ M 1 Abbreviations

Although abbreviations are a useful form of shorthand in some kinds of writing, you should avoid them whenever possible. Write the full form: *university,* not *univ.* or *u.*; *August,* not *Aug.*; *New York*, not *N.Y.*

There are, however, certain abbreviations that have become the standard form: *a.m.* and *p.m.* to indicate time; *e.g.* (the abbreviation of the Latin phrase for "for example"); *Dr.* for *Doctor*; and so on. (Note that *Dr.* should be used only with the person's surname or full name—*Dr. Smith* or *Dr. Jane Smith.*)

When in doubt concerning an abbreviation, first take into account its context. Considering your subject and reader, would an abbreviation be proper? Then check your dictionary for the correct form and spelling. *Ect.,* for example, is a popular mistake for *etc.* (*et cetera*—"and so forth").

■■■ M 2 Capitalization

Capital letters are used to designate the following items:

a. The first word of a sentence:

Revision is important for the writer.

Encourage them to do better.

b. Proper nouns:

Spain	Atlanta, Georgia
Mary Ann	Korean War
Chrysler Corporation	House of Representatives

c. Proper adjectives:

Shakespearean sonnet   Freudian psychology

Colombian coffee   Buddhist temple

d. Titles of articles, poems, books, magazines, stage productions, etc.:

"Ten Ways to Help Cut Inflation" (article)

"Dover Beach" (poem)

A Grammar of Modern English (book)

Good Housekeeping (magazine)

Waiting for Godot (play)

Capitalize all words in a title except, *a, an,* and *the,* and except those coordinating conjunctions and prepositions that contain fewer than five letters. If these come first or last in the title, they must be capitalized:

A Farewell to Arms

To Have and Have Not

"A Place to Return To"

e. The first word of a line in "regular" poetry:

Good friend, for Jesus' sake forbear
To dig the dust enclosed here;
Blest be the man that spares these stones,
And curst be he that moves my bones.

—William Shakespeare

■■■ M 3   *Manuscript Form*

a. Writing material:

Always use standard-size paper, 8 1/2 × 11 inches. Write on *one side* of the paper only. Use a ball-point pen with black, blue, or blue-black ink. If you type or use a word processor, choose white paper that is thick enough so that writing on a second page does not show through the first.

b. Spacing and margins:

Use double spaces between lines unless you are setting off long quotations. (For more on the format for long quotations, see pages 134–135.) When typing, allow about 1 1/2 inches of space on the left side, and about one inch on all the others. When writing in long-hand, use lined paper that has a vertical rule on the left-hand side.

c. Indentation:

Indent the first line of each paragraph about one inch in handwritten papers, five spaces in typewritten ones.

d. Titles:

Put your title on the first page of the paper, about two inches below the top. Leave about one inch between the title and the first line of the essay. Do not use quotation marks or underlining for the title. If your instructor wants you to use a title page, see the sample on page 152.

e. Numbering pages:

Whether or not you have a separate title page, number the page on which your essay begins with *1*, and the rest of the pages in sequence.

f. Appearance:

The appearance of your final draft subtly influences the reader's impression of your efforts. A sloppy paper often indicates sloppy thinking; so always be neat. When proofreading, you can line through an error or insert a small revision if you do it carefully and then check the correction. When typing, do not strike over an error unless you first erase it—neatly. If your draft contains numerous corrections, redo it.

■■■ *M 4 Numbers*

There are several general rules for the use of numbers that you should be aware of.

a. Spell out in full the following numbers:

1. Those from *one* to *ninety-nine*: *two, seventeen, twenty-three,* etc.

2. Those used as adjectives: *first, second, seventeenth, twenty-third,* etc. (not *1st, 2nd, 17th, 23rd*).

A street address, however, can be written with the endings *nd, rd, st, th*: East *75th* Street, 187 North *3rd* Street.

b. Use numerals for:

1. Numbers of more than two words:

1979   2,170 $4,560,000

2. Dates, times, addresses:

August 14, 1982	6:30 a.m.	1311 Locust Avenue
December 25, 1859	10:00 p.m. (but *ten o'clock*)	631 West 93rd Street

c. Hyphenate compound numbers:

1. From *twenty-one* to *ninety-nine:*

thirty-seven   *fifty-eight*   *seventy-two*

2. Used as adjectival fractions:

a *one-fourth* minority   a *two-thirds'* vote

d. Do not begin a sentence with a numeral:

Not: *107* people survived.

But: *One hundred and seven* people survived.

When spelling out the number at the beginning of a sentence is awkward, revise the construction:

Not: *Forty-five thousand, one hundred and eighty-six* voters are registered.

But: The total number of registered voters is *45,186*.

■■■ M 5 *Syllabication*

To keep an even margin on the right side of your paper, you will occasionally have to divide a word at the end of a line and run it over into the next. When you are in doubt about a word's syllabication, check your dictionary. Here are some general rules to keep in mind.

1. Never divide one-syllable words: *moist, hound, great, Tom, see.*

2. Divide a word with double consonants between the consonants: *wit-ty, refer-ral, com-mand.*

3. Never divide a word so that only one letter remains on a line. Try to get two—and preferably three—letters on a line:

Not: e-bullient, intrica-cy

But: ebul-lient, intri-cacy

For words that have prefixes and suffixes, divide where either joins the root: *cast-ing, pre-registration, manage-ment, dis-appear.*

Using The Dictionary

A good dictionary is important to you in many ways. But it is of special importance to you as a writer. It is a useful source for various kinds of information about words that you may need to know as you work toward improving your papers. At one time or another, you may wish to know such things as:

—the exact meaning of *ecology*
—the spelling of *capital* (*capitol*?)
—whether *overridden* should be hyphenated (*over-ridden*?)
—a synonym for *complete*
—the part of speech of *than* (is it a preposition or a conjunction?)
—when you may use *contact* as a verb
—whether you may write: "*Plus* I wanted more money for college."

Consider for a moment the last problem in the list. On pages 89–90, we discuss the employment of clear "word pointers"—such as *before, but, also, since, then*—in opening positions in your sentences. There are so many possible pointers that we could not mention them all, and you will have to depend on your dictionary for help when considering the use of certain pointers. Should you, for instance, use *plus* as you might use *and* or *also* to signal the addition of a second or third reason for doing something? The major dictionaries will indicate that in standard written English *plus* can be used as a preposition, adjective, or noun, but not as a conjunction or adverb. Grammatically speaking, dictionaries allow these usages: "X *plus* Y," "on the *plus* side," or "a definite *plus.*" But not: "*Plus* I wanted more money for college."

The following desk dictionaries have proved to be the most popular and reliable in regard to grammar, pronunciation, basic definitions, and usage. If you don't have one, you should buy one.

The American Heritage College Dictionary, 3rd ed., 1993

Funk and Wagnalls Standard Dictionary 1993

The Random House Webster's College Dictionary, 1995

Webster's New World Dictionary of the American Language, College Edition, 3rd ed., 1993

What does a typical dictionary entry tell you? Let's look at the entry for one of the most discussed words in modern English, *contact.* The source is *The American Heritage Dictionary.*

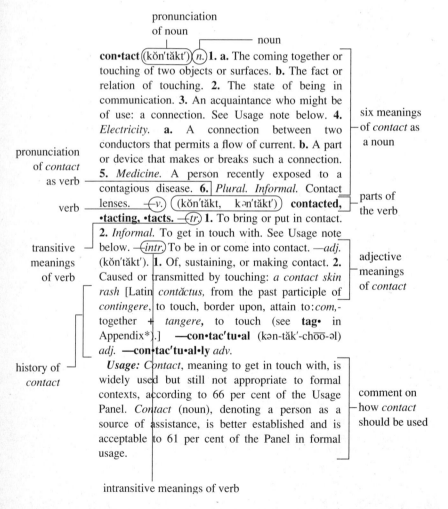

pronunciation of noun

noun

con•tact (kŏn′tăkt′) *n.* **1. a.** The coming together or touching of two objects or surfaces. **b.** The fact or relation of touching. **2.** The state of being in communication. **3.** An acquaintance who might be of use: a connection. See Usage note below. **4.** *Electricity.* **a.** A connection between two conductors that permits a flow of current. **b.** A part or device that makes or breaks such a connection. **5.** *Medicine.* A person recently exposed to a contagious disease. **6.** *Plural. Informal.* Contact lenses. —*v.* (kŏn′tăkt, kən′tăkt′) **contacted, •tacting, •tacts.** —*tr.* **1.** To bring or put in contact. **2.** *Informal.* To get in touch with. See Usage note below. —*intr.* To be in or come into contact. —*adj.* (kŏn′tăkt′). **1.** Of, sustaining, or making contact. **2.** Caused or transmitted by touching: *a contact skin rash* [Latin *contăctus,* from the past participle of *contingere,* to touch, border upon, attain to: *com,-* together + *tangere,* to touch (see **tag•** in Appendix*).] —**con•tac′tu•al** (kən-tăk′-choo-əl) *adj.* —**con•tac′tu•al•ly** *adv.*

Usage: Contact, meaning to get in touch with, is widely used but still not appropriate to formal contexts, according to 66 per cent of the Usage Panel. *Contact* (noun), denoting a person as a source of assistance, is better established and is acceptable to 61 per cent of the Panel in formal usage.

pronunciation of *contact* as verb

verb

transitive meanings of verb

history of *contact*

intransitive meanings of verb

six meanings of *contact* as a noun

parts of the verb

adjective meanings of *contact*

comment on how *contact* should be used

Here you learn that *contact* may be used as a noun, verb, or adjective. You are given different pronunciations of the word and its various meanings. You also learn the major parts of the verb form of *contact* (note the boldface **contacted, -tacting, -tacts**). The usage note at the bottom of the entry tells you that two-thirds of the *American Heritage Dictionary's* Usage Panel disapproves of the formal use of *contact* as a verb (meaning "to get in touch with"), an observation that may be helpful if you want to know whether to use that form of the word in a paper.

For most words, the standard desk dictionaries give similar information about grammar, pronunciation, and basic meanings. You'll find that dictionaries differ in regard to usage. As you've seen, the *Heritage* pretty much disapproves of *contact* in statements like "Contact your doctor before leaving work this afternoon." By contrast, the *Standard College Dictionary* remarks: "This informal usage, regarded with disfavor by some, is widely used." *Webster's New Collegiate Dictionary* and *The Random House Webster's Dictionary* give definitions of *contact* in this sense but make no comment about its proper use.

Dictionaries also supply you with synonyms for many words. Suppose you are having difficulty choosing a word for a paper. You are writing about a certain pleasant emotion you've had recently. Words come into your mind—*happiness, joy, pleasure*—but none seems quite right. Remembering that dictionaries give synonyms, you look up *pleasure* in *The Random House Webster's Dictionary* and find at the end of the entry:

> —Syn. 1. happiness, gladness, delectation. PLEASURE, ENJOYMENT, DELIGHT, JOY refer to the feeling of being pleased and happy. PLEASURE is the general term: *to take pleasure in beautiful scenery*. ENJOYMENT is a quiet sense of well-being and pleasurable satisfaction: *enjoyment at sitting in the shade on a warm day*. DELIGHT is a high degree of pleasure usually leading to active expression of it: *delight at receiving a hoped-for letter*. JOY is a feeling of delight so deep and lasting that a person radiates happiness and expresses it spontaneously: *joy at unexpected good news*. 4. luxury, voluptuousness. 7. preference, wish, inclination.

At least one of these words should work reasonably well in your sentence, and having used it you can get on with the rest of your writing.

Indeed, the dictionary is a special tool for "getting on with your writing." It not only supplies you with the kinds of knowledge that we have already mentioned, but it can also act as a small encyclopedia. Without leaving your room for the library, you can ascertain or verify many isolated facts: Who was *Pliny*? He was a Roman scholar who wrote the *Historia Naturalis*. He died in A.D. 79. What is *scrip*? It is paper money issued for temporary or emergency use. What is a *boycott*? Where did the word come from? It is an act of refusing to buy or use something; the word comes from the name of Charles Boycott, an English land agent in Ireland who was ostracized by his tenants for refusing to reduce rents. What is an *arroyo*? It is a deep, dry gulley or gulch cut out by floods or heavy rains.

As you can see, your desk dictionary is good for many things.

PRACTICE

1. Read the introductory material in your desk dictionary. Since dictionaries vary somewhat, you should know exactly what pieces of information your dictionary has and how it is organized.

2. What do *liberal* and *conservative* mean? What is their etymology or history? (*Etymology* is discussed in the introduction to your dictionary.)

Should you write, for example: "He has managed to avoid crashes for twenty-five years because he is a *liberal* [or *conservative*] pilot"?

What is the etymology of:

rape	rapture	Christian	tuxedo	noun
pencil	muscle	chivalrous	Dixie	agnostic

3. In writing essays, should you use, in their contexts, the italicized words below? In each case, give your reasons.

   a. My roommate, *yclept* Sandy, turned out to be a very friendly person.

   b. She *toted* her knapsack wherever she went, even carrying the *bloody* thing to basketball games.

   c. After *jazzing* up the engine a few times, Tinkham was satisfied with its *tune* and *killed* it.

   d. *Whither* the *paly* moon, I wondered, as I *jogged* back to the dorm in the *pitch* dark.

4. Consider this statement: "That word is not *fitting* in this context." How many synonyms can you find for *fitting* as it is used in that statement? Give synonyms for the italicized words as they are used in these contexts:

I have a *need* for a beer.

We *command* you to release your prisoners.

Why did the epidemic *happen?*

5. What is an *antonym*? After checking your dictionary, give antonyms for:

like (*verb*)	viciously	morose	light	raw
disinterested	creature	classy	sweetly	ignominious

6. Give the part of speech of the words below. If the word is a *noun,* state whether it is singular or plural; if a *verb,* give its tense.

criteria	rung (*verb*)	bade	slow	data
than	when	but	quickly	dived

7. Look up the following words to see whether they are written with a hyphen, as two words, or as one word.

drawback	drawingroom	coffeecake	Jacob'sladder
gunrunning	doublejointed	touchback	dragon'shead

8. Who or what is it?

Hapsburg	pimpernel	upbraid (*verb*)	pillory (*noun*)
Biarritz	ringworm	lug (*noun*)	Lancastrian

Glossary

This Glossary presents a list, alphabetically arranged, of troublesome words and constructions, along with certain terms that you may find useful in your writing. As we considered each problem of usage, we asked ourselves: "What would careful writers think about this? What are their choices, and how would they respond to the issue?" We have consulted many authorities (too many to list here), and confess that where they disagreed, we consulted our own experience.

Good writing is what a good writer writes. So if you find that something here contradicts your own experience and the evidence of your reading, feel free to question our advice. The rules of English usage are not carved in stone.

a, an. Use *a* before words that begin with a consonant sound: *a* pole, *a* unit (the sound is *yew*-nit), *a* history. Use *an* before words starting with a vowel sound or a silent *h*: *an* alley, *an* hour, *an* ellipse.

above, below. If you are pointing to something graphic on the page, like a chart or an illustration, *above* and *below* are useful: "The table *below* shows you how much money is spent on billiards in Marin Country." If you are referring to ideas, it is wise to use a different expression: "The facts I have just mentioned," rather than "The above facts."

absolute construction. A phrase that is linked to a sentence by logic but not by any specific grammatical "tie." It may look like a modifier but isn't one:

The play did very well, *considering the circumstances.*
My money having vanished, I decided to leave the hotel.
The last quarter of the game, *everything taken into account,* was better than we hoped.

accept, except. The verb *accept* means "to receive with approval" or "to answer in the affirmative"; the verb *except* means "to omit or exclude." The preposition *except* means, roughly, "but" or "other than": "All the women *except* Mary came from Denver."

accidentally. Commonly misspelled as *accidently.* In the correct spelling of this adverb, *-ly* is added to the adjective *accidental.*

adapt, adopt. *Adapt* means "to adjust to something." *Adopt* has several meanings; the closest to that of *adapt* is "to take or follow a course of action."

adjective. One of two basic modifiers, the other being the adverb. Adjectives modify nouns or noun elements:

small person (*Small* modifies the noun *person.*)
the woman (*The* modifies the noun *woman.*)
coach *of the year* (*Of the year* modifies the noun *coach.*)
the milk pitcher *that broke* (The adjective clause, *that broke,* modifies the noun *pitcher.*)
Flying at top speed, the squadron overtook the enemy planes. (The participial phrase, *flying at top speed,* modifies the noun *squadron.*)

administrate. See *commentate.*

adverb. One of the two basic modifiers, the other being the adjective. Adverbs modify verbs, adjectives, or other adverbs. Most adverbs end in *-ly,* but a few, like *now, very,* and *there,* do not. And not all words ending in *-ly* (the adjectives *slovenly* and *heavenly,* for example) are adverbs. Here are a few typical adverbial constructions:

They spoke *bitterly.* (*Bitterly* modifies the verb *spoke.*)
It was a *bitterly* cold night. (*Bitterly* modifies the adjective *cold.*)
They spoke *very* bitterly. (*Very* modifies the adverb *bitterly.*)
They spoke *in the heat of anger.* (The prepositional phrase is acting adverbially.)
When he beat the rug, the dust made him sneeze. (The subordinate clause is acting adverbially.)

Also see *flat adverb.*

affect, effect. As a verb, *affect* means "to bring about a change" or "to influence." As a verb, *effect* means "to do or to accomplish something." Example:

He was *affected* by her attempt to *effect* a change in policy.

As a noun, *affect* is a psychological term referring to emotion or feeling. *Effect* as a noun means "result."

agenda. A Latin word; the singular in Latin is *agendum.* In modern standard English, you can use *agenda* for the singular and *agendas* for the plural. An *agenda* is a list of things that are to be accomplished or covered at a meeting.

aggravate. For many years, *aggravate* has carried two meanings—"to make worse" and "to irritate or annoy." Both meanings are acceptable in standard English, although many good writers consider the second too *casual* in careful writing. Certainly, *irritate* or *annoy* will express the second meaning well enough.

agreement. The "matching up" of elements in gender, number, case, or person.

1. Subjects and verbs must agree:

   She is a trumpet player.
   They are the boys from Syracuse.

2. Certain adjectives (those that can change form) agree with their nouns:

   Those mice are cowards.
   This mouse is a hero.

3. A pronoun agrees with its antecedent:

   The *quarterback* broke *his* arm.
   Everyone did *his* job. (Some writers prefer *his or her job.*)
   Mrs. Tompkins had *her* way.
   Women should vote for *their* candidates.

alibi. In Latin, the word means "elsewhere." For hundreds of years, *alibi* was a technical term in law; you had an alibi for a crime if, when it was committed, you were not on the spot—but elsewhere. The meaning of the term has broadened in two ways, to mean (generally) an *excuse,* and to imply that the excuse may not be a very good one, perhaps even rather shady.

all ready, already. The first expression, used adjectivally, means "prepared": "We are *all ready* to go." *Already* is an adverb, as in "She has *already* gone ahead."

all together, altogether. Separate the implications of these words—and their spellings. *All together* means "in a group"; *altogether* means "completely, utterly, entirely."

allusion. This word is best discussed with a closely related word, *reference.* A reference is a direct remark about something: "She *referred* to his failure to pay for lunch as a sign that he was cheap." An *allusion* is indirect or oblique: "She said that he was a regular *Shylock.*" Allusions are understood only if their origin is known—in this instance, if you know that Shylock is a Shakespearean character who is tight with his money.

alot. An incorrect form for *a lot.*

alright. A nonstandard spelling; use *all right.*

alumnus, alumna. These words refer to graduates of educational institutions. The first is a male graduate, the second a female. The plural of *alumnus* is *alumni;* of *alumna, alumnae.* You will probably be better off simply using the term *graduate* in most instances.

among, between. *Between* implies two things or activities; *among* implies more than two:

He distributed the books *among* the students.
The instructor said that she would decide *between* the arguments of Joan and Carlisle.

NOTE: Between takes the object form in pronouns:

Between you and *me.*
Between *her* and *them.*

and/or. An expression that almost nobody will say a kind word for, but that some writers will use from time to time. It has an odor of legalese or of business jargon, and the careful writer tends to avoid it:

Not this: You may be fined *and /or* jailed.
But this: You may be fined or jailed, or both.

angle. When used to mean "viewpoint," "position," or "approach," the word has a faintly negative connotation, as if you were saying that the person involved is a little tricky or not quite honest. The word is also a bit too *casual* for some contexts.

anxious. (to mean *eager*). *Anxious* implies that you are worried about the future; *eager* that you expect something rather impatiently. For the sake of accuracy, it is wise to keep the two words separate.

anymore. Should be *any more:* "I don't drink coffee any more."

appositive. A noun that identifies and explains the noun it is set beside:

Mr. Smith, our *instructor,* was quite old.
Our son *John* is a rascal.
I talked to Sheila, the *director.*

apt, likely, liable. Good writers often use *apt* or *likely* when a meaning of probability is intended: "If you run in front of a car, you are *apt* (*likely*) to get hit." Used as an adjective, *apt* means "able" or "capable": "She was an *apt* student of burglary."

Liable ordinarily is restricted to matters of responsibility or legal obligation: "*liable* to imprisonment"; "*liable* for military service." Note that *liable* implies a consequence that is not usually considered pleasant.

article. *A, an,* and *the* are frequently called *articles.* In this book, however, we treat them as adjectives because they modify nouns: *a* tree, *an* omen, *the* part.

as. Properly used, *as* is a sign of subordination that implies a *time* relation: "I saw you *as* you were coming down the street." Used to indicate a causal relation, *as* is weak and ambiguous: "*As* you are going to stay in the dorm over vacation, would you keep my stereo in your room?" *Since* or *because* is better in statements that imply or show cause.

as to, in respect to. These expressions are often used as links in a sentence. "*In respect to* Smith's handling of the situation. . . . " "I can't decide *as to* the final disposition of the case." If you need a linking expression in such sentences, the word *about* is simpler and shorter. Sometimes no link is needed at all: "I can't decide the final disposition of the case."

at (as in "Where is she *at*?"). The use of *at* is nonstandard in such usages:

Tell me where they are *at.*
I know where I am *at.*
There is where it is all *at.*

author (*verb*). The careful writer does not use *author* as a verb: "Smith *authored* the new rules for the parking garage." Just say that Smith *wrote* them.

auxiliary verb. A "helping word"—like *have, had, do, might*—used with the main verb in a verb phrase. The auxiliary allows you to express tense, person, number, mood, and voice:

had written	*will be* writing	*might have been* written
do write	*was* written	*has* written

Modal auxiliaries are important because they supply you with a stock of options to express shades of meaning:

must do   *should* do   *would* do   *might* do   *could* do

Notice the difference between *had* and *must,* for example. *Had* may indicate tense (time) only, while *must* indicates not only time (the future) but also obligation.

Shall and *will* should probably be considered as "dead" modals. A clear distinction between the two no longer exists (if it ever did), and most writers appear to use them merely as signs of tense.

awful, awfully. As either intensifiers or expressions of disgust, *awful* and *awfully* are badly overworked and too *casual.* Avoid them.

backlash. A vivid and rather useful metaphorical word, *backlash* ("a violent or sudden reaction") has been worked rather hard in recent years. Try substituting *reaction,* or consider rewriting to avoid the word: "The people are growing hostile to the governor's plans for an increase in taxes."

bad, badly. With a linking verb, use *bad* (an adjective) in these situations:

It smells *bad.*
I feel *bad.*
It is *bad.*
It seems *bad.*

Use badly (an adverb) in situations where the verb is a nonlinking one:

They do it *badly.*
Standish needs the money *badly.*
She sang the aria *badly.*
I feel *badly*—my fingers don't work as they should. (Better, perhaps, would be: My fingers are numb.)

being as (to mean *because*). There are several related forms that are fairly synonymous:

Being as we were absent for the quiz . . .
I explained that *as how* we got the quiz date wrong . . .
Seeing as we received a zero that day . . .

Avoid such expressions. Ordinarily, you can substitute the word *because* for each of them.

between, among. See *among, between.*

bi-, semi-. As in *biannual, semimonthly,* etc. Authorities agree that the uses of these prefixes have become confused. *Bimonthly,* for instance, can mean "every two months," "twice a month," or "every two weeks." *Semi-* poses less of a problem—it roughly means "half" ("half-monthly" or "twice a month"). To avoid the confusion surrounding both prefixes, just say, for example, "every two months" or "twice a year."

bug. As a verb meaning "annoy" or "bother," *bug* is an effervescent little word, but too slangy for most situations.

bummer. Slang for *letdown, disappointment,* or *unpleasant occurrence.* Do not use it.

but that, but what. Both expressions seem unnecessary. Note these typical rewrites:

Not this: I do not doubt *but that* she is right.
But this: I do not doubt that she is right.

Not this: I do not know *but what* the Russians have a point in their response.
But this: I think the Russians may have a point in their response.

c., ca. Abbreviations for the Latin *circa,* these mean "about." Used with approximate dates or figures: "c. 1670."

can, may. *Can* refers to ability; *may* to permission or possibility. "I *can* do it" means "I am *able* to do it." "I *may* do it" can mean "I have *permission* to do it," or "It is *possible* that I will do it." *Can* and *may* are modal auxiliaries. See *auxiliary verb.*

cannot barely, cannot hardly, cannot help but. These are double negatives, and are considered nonstandard. Here are suggested substitutions:

Not this: I *cannot hardly* believe that.
But this: I can hardly believe that.
   Or: I cannot believe that.

Not this: I *cannot help but* wonder about the issue.
But this: I cannot help wondering about the issue.

caret. A proofreader's symbol ($_\wedge$), it is used to indicate an insertion in the written copy:

>   *that*
> I wish$_\wedge$ you were here.

case. The customary objection to the word *case* is that it is redundant in many expressions.

Not this: In some *cases,* the streets were iced over.
But this: Some streets were iced over.

Not this: Except in the *case* of Dr. Denny, the surgeons were exonerated.
But this: All the surgeons but Dr. Denny were exonerated.

Note that no satisfactory alternative has ever been found for "In case of fire, break glass."

casual, casualism. We borrow the term from Theodore M. Bernstein, who remarks in his book *The Careful Writer* that some modern acceptable writing is relaxed and familiar—in a word, *casual.* To call an expression a *casualism* is not necessarily to condemn it because there are gradations of the casual. To use Bernstein's examples, contractions such as *don't* and *can't* and colloquial terms like *face the music* and *skulduggery* may be acceptable casualisms, while *falsies* may not be. Whether a casualism is acceptable depends upon your subject and writer's stance.

censor, censure. Do not confuse these words. To *censor* means to suppress or prohibit a thing or action. To *censure* means to criticize negatively or to disapprove. Generally, ideas are censored while people are censured.

center around. Both a logical and geometrical impossibility. The *center* and the *around* of something are in different places. Write *center on,* which suggests a tight grouping; or *cluster about,* which suggests a looser grouping.

cite, site. When you *cite* (verb) people or ideas, you present them as examples, evidence, or authorities. The noun is *citation*. *Site* is a noun, referring to a place.

clause. See pages 76, 81, 425.

cliché. A *cliché* is an expression that has grown hackneyed or tired from excessive use. A surprising number of clichés are metaphorical: *slick as ice, knee high to a grasshopper.* Generally, avoid them—unless you can twist them to your advantage:

Slick as the ice in her martini-on-the-rocks.

Knee-high to a rabbit and twice as bouncy.

collective noun. A word whose form is singular but whose meaning can be singular or plural: *team, group, crowd, family, couple.* (See page 446 for advice on using singular or plural verbs with this form.)

colloquial, colloquialism. Technically *colloquial* refers merely to "the language of speech," and a *colloquialism* is an expression typical of speech. Since speech is often more informal than writing, teachers and editors have developed the habit of referring to excessively informal usages in writing as being colloquial (that is, inappropriate). This unfortunate development implies that the language of speech is necessarily inferior to the written language. In many instances, such judgment is obviously untrue: "I didn't do it" (colloquial) is obviously better than a stiffly written version like "This event was not performed by me." From Shakespeare to Hemingway and E.B. White, one finds that the colloquial is, when rightly used, lively and precise. It is objectionable only when it is inappropriate or excessively casual. See *casualism.*

comma splice. See pages 468–469.

commentate (*verb*). Not standard; use the verb *comment.* Similarly, use the verb *administer* rather than *administrate.* "I would rather *comment* on this department than *administer* it."

compare to, compare with. *Compare to* is most often used when you want to show how two things are similar (particularly in a figurative sense), as in Shakespeare's "Shall I *compare* thee *to* a summer's day?"

   Compare with is the best way to introduce a literal comparison involving both similarities and differences: "I intend to *compare* the freshman course in speech *with* the composition course in English."

comparison of adjectives and adverbs. Adjectives and adverbs change form to indicate three "degrees":

Positive	Comparative	Superlative
low	lower	lowest
good	better	best
honest	more honest	most honest
easily	more easily	most easily

complement. A grammatical term meaning "something that completes." Complements are used to complete ideas (or parts of ideas presented earlier in a sentence).

1. Direct objects as complements:
   a. You did see *her.*

      b. You did give her a *present.*

  2. Subject complements:
      a. She is *happy.*
      b. She is a happy *woman.*

  3. Object complements:
      a. They made him *king.*
      b. They appointed her *director.*
      c. I dyed the shirt *green.*

compliment, complement. As a verb, *complement* means "to complete or finish something." As a noun, it means "something that completes or rounds out another thing."

They are a perfect pair; their personalities *complement* each other.
The *complement* of 60 degrees is 30 degrees.

Compliment, as a verb, means "to say something good," usually about a person.
As a noun, it refers to the act of congratulating.

I *compliment* you on your good performance.
I gave him a *compliment.*

compound words. Words made up of two or more words that work together as a unit: *sister-in-law, crapshooter* (or *crap shooter*), *overdrive.* There are no firm rules for determining whether such words should be written separately, together, or with hyphens. When you are unsure of a particular word, check your dictionary.

comprise. Historically, *comprise* comes from an old French word that meant "comprehend" or "include." The word, in careful usage, still maintains this meaning. The whole *comprises* ("includes") its parts. You may write: "The College of Liberal Arts *comprises* four departments," not "The College of Liberal Arts *is comprised of* four departments." An alternative is to use *compose:* "Four departments *compose* (or *make up*) the College of Liberal Arts"; or "The College of Liberal Arts *is composed of* four departments."

conjugation. A listing of the forms of a verb, showing tense, person, number, voice, and mood.

Verb: To see   *Principal Parts: see, saw, seen*

ACTIVE VOICE	**PASSIVE VOICE**
	Indicative Mood

Present Tense

I, you, we, or they *see*	I *am seen,* he, she, or it *is seen*
he, she, or it *sees*	You, we, or they *are seen*

NOTE: In the rest of the table, pronouns are limited to one for each verb form.

Past Tense

I *saw*	I *was seen*
	you *were seen*

Future Tense

I *will* (or *shall*) see   I *will* (or *shall*) *be seen*

Present Perfect Tense

I *have seen*   I *have been seen*
he has *seen*   he has *been seen*

Past Perfect Tense

I *had seen*   I *had been seen*

Future Perfect Tense

I *will* (or *shall*) *have seen*   I *will* (or *shall*) *have been seen*

Subjunctive Mood

Present Tense

that I *see*   that I *be seen*

Past Tense

that I *saw*   that I *were seen*

Present Perfect Tense

that I *have seen*   that I *have been seen*

Past Perfect Tense

(Same as Indicative Mood)

Imperative Mood

Present Tense

see   *be seen*

conjunction.   The *conjunction* is a "joiner," a word that is used to connect words, phrases, clauses, or complete sentences. *Coordinating conjunctions* join words and word elements of equal grammatical rank: *and, but, or, nor, so.*

    Subordinating conjunctions act as "signs" of subordination. They typically appear just before the subject of the subordinate clause:

When you are near, . . .
Even though the spider plant needs water, . . .

    Subordinating conjunctions sometimes are formed by two words: *as if, even though,* etc. To see how the subordinating conjunction works in a sentence, see pages 424–425.

conjunctive adverb.   A rather clumsy term that grammarians have seized upon to describe what is essentially a sentence modifier:

Accordingly, Mrs. McMinn will not come to work today.
However, work on the project will continue as usual.
The mud is a foot deep across the canal; *therefore,* we will leave all the heavy equipment in the shed today. (Note the punctuation of the conjunctive adverb when it occurs between two main clauses.)

A partial list of conjunctive adverbs: *also, besides, consequently, furthermore, however, instead, likewise, moreover, still, then, therefore, thus.*

connotation, denotation. *Denotation* refers to the literal, explicit meaning of a word, *connotation* to the associations and suggestions of a word. The former madam of a bawdy house was able to employ both rhetorical devices in her book title: *A House Is Not a Home.*

consensus. A *consensus* is an agreement reached by most (but not necessarily all) of the people involved. "The consensus of the student editors was to run the editorial unchanged." *Consensus of opinion* is redundant, since the notion expressed by *of opinion* is built into the idea of *consensus.*

contact (*verb*). People have been debating the uses of this word for many years: "*Contact* Mrs. O'Leary when you get to Chicago." For those who dislike such uses, here is the typical reaction: "Really, I don't know the lady well enough to *contact* her—I will *call* her, *write* her, or *go to visit* her." Since *contact* carries the idea of touching ("the coming together or touching of two objects or surfaces," is a typical dictionary definition), the careful writer may well avoid it when touching is not meant. Many educated people consider the use of *contact* instead of *call* or *write* to be improper. (See *shibboleths of usage.*)

continual, continuous. *Continual* means that an event recurs at different times; *continuous* that the event occurs without interruption. Thus, if Jerry's bar was *continually* open from 1936 to the present, it was occasionally closed. If Jerry's stayed open *continuously,* he never closed the place.

contractions. *Contractions* (*isn't, won't, weren't,* etc.) are acceptable in standard English. They tend to be somewhat *colloquial* and *casual,* and are perhaps not suitable for very formal occasions. Yet it is impossible either to embrace or denounce contractions in any blanket fashion. Their use depends on your stance and subject—not to mention the tone and rhythm of words in the surrounding passage. It is usually true that too many contractions will make your prose seem excessively casual and familiar, and that avoiding them entirely may make you seem stuffy and Victorian. Hit a happy medium, and listen to the *sounds* of your writing.

cope. (1) *Cope* is a casualism, and you should bear that fact in mind. (2) It also requires *with*—one *copes with something.*

correlatives. These are conjunctions that are used in pairs: *either . . . or; neither . . . nor; not only . . . but also; whether . . . or not; both . . . and.*

  Generally, use the expression *whether . . . or not* only when you wish to give equal stress to both ideas: "We will vote on this issue *whether* you like it *or not.*" Otherwise, omit the *or not,* which is unnecessary here: "*Whether* Smith will be chosen is up to the committee."

could of, should of, would of. Nonstandard verb forms that incorrectly use the preposition *of* rather than the auxiliary verb *have.*

council, counsel. A *council* is a governing body. *Counsel* as a noun means "advice."

crisis. A badly overworked word. A *crisis* is a crucial point or condition, a major turning point in human affairs. A strong word for strong situations, save it for a time when the wolves are at the door. Otherwise, when you yell "Crisis!" people may merely yawn and turn away.

criterion. An overworked, voguish, and rather pedantic word. Try *standard, rule, test, judgment.* If you must use *criterion,* employ the proper form—singular: *criterion;* plural: *criteria.*

dangling modifier. See pages 458–461.

data. As used in most situations, *data* is a pompous word for *information, evidence, facts, figures,* or *statistics.* It is, in addition, one of those Latin words that usage has treated unkindly. Originally, *datum* was the singular; *data,* the plural. (Now *datum* is seldom used, except in certain technical specialties.) In modern English *data* can be both singular and plural, but usually does not sound right as either. If you must use the word, be consistent. "*This data is . . . ,*" or "*These data are.*"

decimate. An overworked expression that does not mean "to wipe out" or "to annihilate." It originally meant "to take a tenth part" of something; now it means "to kill or destroy a large part." Think twice before using the word.

deprecate, depreciate. *Depreciate* is the opposite of *appreciate,* so when you depreciate a thing you lessen it or belittle it. *Deprecate* (literally, "to pray against") means "to disapprove of or protest a thing." The distinction between the two words is narrowing, but it should still be observed.

desire (*verb*). Unless you are talking about love or passion, better use *wish, want,* or some other expression. To say "He desired a large plate of ice cream" creates a strange mental picture indeed.

dialect. "Any one of the mutually comprehensible geographic or social varieties of which a natural language consists." The definition is borrowed from the linguist Joseph Friend. A neutral term, *dialect* refers to a special grouping of linguistic features—words, forms, idioms, grammatical structures, pronunciations, etc. It is not bad to speak a dialect; everyone does.

different from, different than. *Different from* is preferred in modern English: "My belief is *different from* hers." But when the expression is followed by a clause or "condensed clause," *different than* works well enough: "Don't do this job *differently than* you used to." This is neater than "Don't do this job *differently from* the way you used to."

disinterested, uninterested. *Disinterested* means "impartial"; *uninterested* means "lacking interest." To be disinterested is to be consciously neutral about an issue; to be uninterested is to be bored or lack interest in it. *Disinterested* sounds stronger and fresher. Perhaps that is why many of us have a sneaking affection for the word, and use it when we shouldn't.

double negative. Two negatives in a sentence where only one is necessary: "She *never* had *nothing.*" Or: "They could*n't* put the sofa *nowhere.*" A common double negative is made with *hardly:* "There's *hardly nothing* in the refrigerator." All of these constructions are nonstandard. Stick to one negative:

She *never* had anything.
They could*n't* put the sofa anywhere.
There's *nothing* in the refrigerator.

double possessive. A strange construction really, because you make the possessive twice, once with an *of* and again with an *'s,* with or without the apostrophe: "a dog *of* Martha's," "a ship *of theirs,*" "a photograph *of* Ms. Smith's." Note that the double possessive can have an effect on meaning: "A photograph of Ms. *Smith's*" is different from "A photograph of Ms. *Smith.*" With pronouns, however, the double possessive is always natural: "that old gang *of mine,*" never "that old gang *of me.*"

due to. Authorities have long objected to this expression when used in this fashion: "*Due to* hard work, she succeeded." The reason usually given is that *due* is adjectival; so one should write: "Her success was *due* to hard work." If you do not find this explanation convincing, consider other options, such as, "She succeeded because she worked hard," or "Owing to hard work, she succeeded."

due to the fact that. A cumbersome and redundant expression—replace with *because.*

e.g. Abbreviation for *exempli gratia* (Latin), it means "for example." Use with a comma or colon after. If at all possible, however, use the English phrase.

　　Do not confuse *e.g.* with *i.e.,* the abbreviation of the Latin phrase meaning "that is."

elliptical construction. Such constructions have missing (but understood) parts: "We are getting tired of them, and they [*are getting tired*] of us." "[*You*] Stop doing that." "His purpose was evil and his mind [*was*] disordered." Elliptical constructions are normal in English usage.

end result. If you have a series of results, and you wish to mention the last of them, *end result* (or *final result, last result*) is not a bad choice. But in most instances, all you need is *result,* and tacking *end* to the word does not help.

enormity. Refers to something that is greatly wicked or outrageous, not to something huge or enormous in size.

enthuse. This verb is nonstandard and, therefore, not recommended. Instead of "She was enthused about going to college," write:

She was very *happy* about . . .

She was *enthusiastic* about . . .

She was *pleased* with . . .

etc. Abbreviation for *et cetera* (which implies "and other things of the same kind"). *And etc.* is redundant.

exists. Often a sign of deadwood: "a feeling like that which *exists* in the heart." This probably means: "a feeling in the heart."

expedite. Jargon. Sometimes used with modifiers, as in "to *expedite* more quickly." Since the word means "to do something faster," the modifiers are unnecessary, as are most uses of the word.

expletive. A grammarian's term for the "filler phrases" that begin sentences like these:

There is a new house going up on Bleeker Street.

It's too bad we must live in this neighborhood.

facet. Literally, a polished "cut" face on a gemstone, such as a diamond. Used figuratively, it is badly overworked for *phase* or *aspect.* Do not use unless desperate.

factor. Jargon for *cause, event, fact, idea, occurrence,* the word contributes to wordiness and vagueness: "His good looks were a great *factor* in his success."

farther, further. *Farther* usually is reserved for physical distance ("She threw the ball *farther* than anyone else"), *further* for all other uses ("That explanation couldn't be *further* from the truth").

fewer, less. Use *fewer* for items that you can count: "If you have *fewer* spoons after a friend leaves your house, he should no longer be your friend." Use *less* for degree or amount: "I have *less* money (*fewer* dollars)."

finalize. Jargon. Write *finish* or *complete.*

firstly. Write *first* (and *second, third, fourth,* etc.). *Firstly* used to be thought adverbially urbane. But *first* is a legitimate flat adverb, and the *-ly* can be awkward: *fourthly, fifthly, eleventhly, twelfthly.*

flat adverb. An adverb without the *-ly:* "Drive *slow.*" Often used in somewhat poetic contexts: "They played the song *low* and *sweet.*"

flaunt, flout. *Flaunt* means "to show off something or act ostentatiously" ("Not only was the embezzler unashamed of his crimes, he actually *flaunted* them"). *Flout* means "to show disregard or contempt for" ("If she continues to *flout* the rules, she should go elsewhere"). When using either, make sure you know the difference in meanings.

former, latter. Avoid, where possible. When you use them, you make your reader hunt back through the sentence or paragraph looking for the first thing, and then the second one; after which the reader has to find the place where you interrupted with *former* or *latter.* Using either is seldom worth the trouble.

fulsome. Can mean "offensive," "insincere," "odious," or "repulsive." It does not mean "abundant." The expression *fulsome praise,* besides being a cliché, is often misused.

fun. Never use it as an adjective: "*fun* time," "*fun* person," "*fun* course."

fused sentence. See page 470.

gender. In grammar, *gender* refers to the classifying of nouns and pronouns as masculine, feminine, or neuter.

gerund. A verbal noun that ends in *-ing:* "*Losing* worried him." "He liked *winning.*"

get. Avoid it in its slangy meanings: "I'll *get* you for that." "What do you mean? I don't *get* you." "Their way of doing things really *gets* me."

gobbledygook. Congressman Maury Maverick's term for jargon and nonsense, particularly of the bureaucratic kind. It employs expressions like *function, maximum, inoperative, in terms of, expertise,* and so on.

good, well. *Good* is ordinarily an adjective: "a *good* child," "She is *good.*" Do not use it in this fashion: "She shoveled coal *good.*" Rather, use the adverb *well:* "She shoveled it *well.*" *Good* and *well* have a complex relationship; check your dictionary if you are unsure of a particular usage.

his/her, his or her. See pages 530–531.

hopefully. Try to avoid overworking this "floating adverb" tied to the front of a sentence: "*Hopefully,* the new rule will help us do a better job." Two suggestions:

a. Tie the word to what it modifies:

She said *hopefully* that the new rule will help. . . . (This means she *said* it hopefully, that is, in a hopeful tone.)

b. Identify the person(s) being hopeful:

She hoped that the new rule . . .
They hoped that the new rule . . .
McTavish hoped that the new rule . . .

identify with. A vague cliché. Say what you mean; be specific.

Not this: She *identified with* the feminist movement.

But this: She believed that the ERA should be adopted.

if and when. Redundant. In most statements, use either *if* or *when.*

image. It can mean "a likeness," "a reflection," "a personification" ("she is the *image* of grace"), or "a mental picture." It is also a literary device. Although recently it has come to mean "reputation" or "public impression," the careful writer will avoid these vague usages:

They were worried about the company's *image.*

The child had a poor *self-image.*

impact. Use it sparingly, and only when a great force or collision is implied. To call every result or effect an *impact* is, as Theodore Bernstein remarks, to employ "a flamethrower to light a cigarette." Do not use *impact* as a verb:

They studied ways the new freeway would *impact* upon the neighborhood.

implement (*verb*). Jargon.

Not this: The library will *implement* greater use of desks in the reading room.

But this: The library will use more desks in the reading room.

imply, infer. The speaker or writer *implies* ("Wilkens *implied* that he was going to quit."); the hearer or reader *infers* ("I *inferred* from his remark that he was going to quit."). When you put forth an idea, you may also put forth *implications;* when you guess or interpret the ideas of others, you draw *inferences.*

in regard to. See *in terms of.*

in terms of. "Tripled" idioms like *in terms of, in regard to, in relation to,* etc., are usually unnecessary and wordy (they all have three parts—"tripled").

Bad: "I'll see you *in terms of* next week."
Better: "I'll see you next week."

Bad: "*In regard to* his writing, John improved."
Better: "John improved his writing."

See *as to, in respect to.*

infinitive. A verbal using this form: "*to* win," "*to* do," "*to* be," "*to* illuminate."

inside of, outside of (as compound prepositions). The *of* is redundant in these expressions: "Put it inside *of* the car." "Take it outside *of* the house."

inter-, intra-. *Inter-* (as in "*inter-* company trade") means "between units or groups." *Intra-* (as in "intra-company memos") means "within or inside of."

irony. See *sarcasm.*

irregardless. Never use; always write *regardless.*

it's, its. See page 434.

jargon. Although for some time it has meant "the special language of a group or trade," *jargon* has long implied something closer to gibberish. Its primary definition in *The American Heritage Dictionary* is "nonsensical, incoherent, or meaningless utterance." Such expressions as *conceptualize, maximization, parameters, and implementation* are examples of recent jargon.

kind of, sort of.

1. Keep the number of these pronouns straight:

    Bad: These *kind* of persons *are* a delight.

    Corrected: That *kind* of person *is* a delight.
    Those kinds of persons *are* a delight.
    Such *persons are* a delight.

2. Do not use *a* or *an* after *kind of* and *sort of:*

    Bad: That sort of *a* play won't work.
    Corrected: That sort of play won't work.

3. These usages are too *casual:*

    I'm *kind of* tired today.
    My car just *sort of* fell apart.

lend, loan. When writing about money or other material things, use the verbs *lend* in the present tense and *loaned* in the past. As a noun, *loan* is standard.

liable (to mean *likely*). Current usage suggests that *liable* should be restricted to unfortunate or unpleasant events: "The design of that airplane is so bad that it is *liable* to crash." In a legal usage, *liable* means subject to legal action: "You may well be *liable* if a neighbor's child is hurt in your swimming pool."

like, as. *Like* used as a preposition: "*Like* the Bears, the Cardinals are slowly improving." Observe that *like* takes the object form of the pronoun: "like *me*," "like *them*," "like *her.*"

When *as* is used as a conjunction, the preposition *like* should not be substituted for it:

Not this: The tree is blooming, *like* it should in the spring.
But this: The tree is blooming, *as* it should in the spring.

This sentence shows a typical distinction made between *like* and *as:*

He speaks *as* his father does, but he looks *like* his mother. (That is, he looks *like* her.)

linking verb. This type of verb ties, relates, or "links" the subject to a *complement* (a "completer") in the sentence. The test for a linking verb is to answer this question: "Can I substitute a form of *seem* for it?"

We *are* [*seem*] happy.

That *was* [*seemed*] a perfect day.

It *tasted* [*seemed*] good.

literally. *Literally* means "verbatim, word for word; prosaic." It can also mean "non-figurative." If you say, "The facts she read in the newspaper *literally* floored her," you mean that she fell down after she read them.

The word is not an intensifier and does not mean "very" or "very much." If you write "Sam's blood *literally* turned to ice water," in the next paragraph you had better mention that Sam died shortly after.

mad. Don't use for *angry, irritated,* or *annoyed. Mad* means "insane," or apparently so.

massive. Journalese for *big.* Use (only when necessary) for physical objects. Also consider using these words: *solid, bulky, heavy, huge, large.*

maximum, minimum. Both words are jargon, and ordinarily unnecessary. Instead of writing "*Maximum* effort will be put forth by the students," write "The students will work as hard as they can."

medium, media. Vogue words. Note that *media* is the plural of *medium.* Do not use these nouns as adjectives: "*media* study," "*media* analysis." It will clear the mind if you try to substitute the real things for *media: newspapers, magazines, television,* and *radio.* Given the logic of classification, you will seldom refer to all of these at once—to claim that "the media" are responsible for something or other is probably a false generalization.

misplaced modifier. See pages 458–459.

modifier. The only modifiers available in English are adjectives and adverbs. A modifier describes, qualifies, or limits another word or word group.

mood. Refers to the attitudes one has about the meaning expressed by a verb:

Indicative mood (the verb expresses *fact* or *reality*):

I *see* that you *are* here.

Imperative mood (the verb expresses a *command* or *request*):

Let me in!

Do your work immediately.

Subjunctive mood (the verb expresses a *wish* or *possibility*):

I wish that you *were* here.

If she *were* here, we would do the work.

Let the work *begin.*

Ms., ms. As a title of courtesy before a woman's name, *Ms.* has created considerable controversy. Some women dislike it intensely. One well-known American novelist, for instance, remarks that she will not accept mail addressing her as *Ms.*

Ordinarily, however, it seems safe to use *Ms.* when you don't know whether the woman addressed is single or married. We ask our own female students what they want to be called in class, and they vote about four to one in favor of *Mrs.* or *Miss.* It doesn't matter to us, of course—if it matters to the woman involved, we will accept her wishes.

Without the capital *m, ms.* is the standard abbreviation for *manuscript.*

must (*noun and adjective*).

> *Noun:* "Knowledge of mathematics is a *must* for this job."
>
> *Adjective:* "Mathematics is a *must* requirement for this job."

Both usages are fairly *casual,* and authorities disagree on whether they should be considered standard usage. Because *must* as noun and adjective is overworked, we suggest avoiding it and rewriting:

> You need to know mathematics for this job.
>
> *Or:* A knowledge of mathematics is necessary for this job.

myself (to mean *I* or *me*). Avoid this usage.

> *Not this:* Mary and *myself* agree.
>
> *But this:* Mary and *I* agree.
>
> *Not this:* Give it to Mike and *myself.*
>
> *But this:* Give it to Mike and *me.*

nice. An overworked, vague casualism. Use a more vivid and specific word.

none. Because this pronoun means "no one," it is technically singular and takes a singular verb. But usage allows the plural "none are," if the pronoun stands for more than one thing.

nonstandard English. See *standard English.*

noun. A part of speech that names something: *woman, building, sweetness, Angela, Houston, covey.*

nowhere near. Slang for *not nearly, far from.*

off of. In "He got *off of* the couch," the preposition *of* is unnecessary: "He got *off* the couch." Sometimes the construction should be changed:

> *Not this:* He fell *off of* the top of the car.

But this: He fell *from* the top of the car.

OK. *OK* (or *okay*) has been in the language for about 140 years, but it remains too slangy for all uses except the most casual.

on account of. Use *because:* "He stole the bread *because* he was hungry."

one . . . his. "*One* must do what *he* has to do" is normal and idiomatic. It is a bit stiff and old-fashioned to write "*One* must do what *one* has to do," but such constructions may be acceptable in certain contexts. For the problem of gender implied by *he,* see page 531.

only. When you can, put *only* next to the word or element that it modifies:

She likes *only* men wearing beards. (She does not like clean-shaven ones.)

Only she likes men wearing beards. (She is the sole member of the group who likes them.)

The rule is not very firm, however; and you don't have to worry much about *only* unless a reader might mistake your meaning:

She likes men wearing *only* beards. (And nothing else?)

opt. A vogue word for *choose* or *select.* Avoid it.

oral, verbal. Make a distinction between the two words. *Oral* refers only to speech; *verbal* refers to speech, writing, or both. In legal matters, a *verbal* agreement is unwritten.

out of. Retain the *of* in certain idioms meaning "away from":

She walked *out of* my life.

They stumbled *out of* the burning building.

Otherwise, avoid using *of:*

He ran *out* the door in a hurry.

overall. A vogue word for the idea expressed by *main*(ly), *general*(ly), *or usual*(ly).

Not this: Their *overall* attitude was poor.

But this: *Usually,* they had a poor attitude.

Or: Their *general* attitude was poor.

parallelism. A grammatical balancing of similar elements:

She and I are both here.

To be right and *to be righteous* are not the same thing.

Believe what we say and *watch what we do.*

See also pages 461–462.

participle. A verbal that serves as an adjective or as a part of a verb phrase; it ends usually in *-ing, -ed, -t, -en:*

Adjective	*Verb Phrase*
The *abandoned* house	They *had abandoned* it.
The *burned* (or *burnt*) toast	It *was burned* (or *burnt*).
The *running* elephant	It is *running*.
The *sunken* living room	The boat *had sunk.*

passive voice. In the passive voice the subject of the sentence receives the action:

Mrs. Blount was astonished by his appearance.

Something must be done.

The passive construction consists of a form of *be* and a past participle: *were made, will be accomplished, are riveted.* See pages 472–473 for more discussion of how the passive voice works.

pejorative. When referring to words, *pejorative* implies a negative connotation. One might write: "I do not use *communist* in a pejorative sense, but rather as a name for a philosophy of government."

person. A grammatical term that refers to the form of verb and pronoun indicating whether someone is speaking, spoken to, or spoken about:

First person:	*I see* Fritz.
Second person:	Do *you see* Fritz?
Third person:	*She sees* Fritz.

personnel. Avoid this jargon, if possible. Say *people,* or when necessary state specifically who is involved:

Not this:	Why aren't the cleaning *personnel* working on the second floor this week?
But this:	Why aren't the *janitors* working on the second floor this week?

phenomenon. Can be applied to any fact or occurrence that is observable. But in most instances, you can replace it with more exact or specific wording.

Not this:	It was a strange natural *phenomenon.*
But this:	It was the largest flood in twenty years.

And note that the plural of *phenomenon* is *phenomena.*

phrase. See pages 85–89.

predominant, predominate. *Predominant* is an adjective; *predominate* is a verb.

preposition. A part of speech that links nouns to other parts of the sentence:

He was mentioned *in* the terms *of* the will.

No one would dare go *over* the hill.

I found some old letters *among* the pages *of* the book.

Although some purists object to ending a sentence with a preposition, the construction can be idiomatic and useful:

What did you hang the picture *on*?

That is the kind of behavior I will not put *up with*.

principal, principle. A *principal* (noun) is the main thing among lesser things. A *principal* of a school runs the school; a financial *principal* that draws interest is the main sum of money involved. The adjective *principal* likewise makes a suggestion of preeminence: "The *principal* idea" refers to the main idea among lesser ones.

The noun *principle* means a rule of conduct or a general truth.

prior to. Jargon; do not use. Say *before*.

pronoun. A part of speech that "replaces" or stands for a noun (*this, she, us,* etc.).

proved, proven. Authoritative opinion is divided on the use of these words. The following advice, however, seems more or less safe: For the verb forms, use *proved:* "I have *proved* my point." For the adjective, use *proven:* "She is a *proven* candidate for the presidency."

quote (*noun*). Use the full form: *quotation.*

raise, rise (*verbs*). *Raise* means "to elevate, lift up, or increase." *Rise* means "to get up." *Raise* used to be condemned in the expression "raising children" or "raising a family," but this is considered acceptable usage now.

real (*adverb*). Should not be used as an adverb to mean "very." This is poor usage: "They did a *real* good job raising the ship from the ocean floor."

reason is because. One of the most condemned expressions in written English, yet (oddly enough) it is at certain times useful. There are two objections to it: (1) It is wordy: "The *reason* they are deserting the Army *is because* they never get leave." This can be shortened simply to "They are deserting the Army *because* they never get leave." (2) It is ungrammatical. "Because they never get leave" is technically an adverb clause, yet it is being used (in *reason . . . is because*) as a noun clause. The grammatical clause here would be: "that they never get leave."

reference. See *allusion.*

relative pronoun. A substitute for a noun that acts as a sign or signal for a subordinate clause:

I have a husband *who* never picks up a hammer.

A house *that* never needs painting would be wonderful to own.

respectfully, respectively. *Respectfully* means "acting deferentially, with respect." *Respectively* means "singly, in the order mentioned."

"I must *respectfully* tell you," she said, "that I consider your three actions yesterday *respectively* irritating, flatly unnecessary, and illegal."

résumé. A *résumé* is a short account of one's experience and qualifications. It is usually written as part of a job application. Note the accent marks. Without the accent marks, *resume* is a verb that means "to begin again."

run-on sentence. See page 471.

sarcasm, irony. *Sarcasm* is a bitter and cutting expression of contempt. If, when your roommate knocks over your study lamp, you say, "*That* was a bright thing to do," your remark is sarcasm. The meaning is clear, and your roommate is perfectly aware that you are on the attack. By contrast, *irony* is more indirect and subtle, and the reader or listener may not get its underlying meaning at the time or later. When Ambrose Bierce defined *bride* as "a woman with a fine prospect of happiness behind her," he was being ironical.

sensual, sensuous. *Sensual* refers to the gratification of the physical appetites, particularly the sexual. Typical synonyms are *carnal, voluptuous,* and *licentious. Sensuous* means "appealing to the senses." Clearly, something can be sensuous without being sensual.

sentence. A unit of expression that ordinarily presents at least one complete thought. In writing, it starts with a capital letter and ends with a period. For further discussion of the sentence, see the various entries under "Sentence Structure," pages 453–473.

shall, will. There used to be a distinction made between these two verb auxiliaries or helpers, but authorities do not accept it now. To many writers, *shall* appears more dignified (or expresses a greater degree of determination), but such opinions are more a matter of tone and style than of grammar.

shibboleths of usage. In the Bible, we learn that the Gileadites used the word *shibboleth* to distinguish the fleeing Ephraimites, who could not pronounce *sh. Shibboleth* has become a word symbolizing the idea of a password, or the "test" of a militant group or party.

Each generation has its own shibboleths of usage. For various reasons, they are used to divide writers of "good" English from writers of "bad." Some shibboleths last a long time. *Ain't* is an old one; *contact* is more recent, and *hopefully* (as in "Hopefully, it won't rain") more recent still. *Hopefully* so irritated novelist Jean Stafford that she placed this sign on the back door of her house: "The word 'hopefully' must not be misused on these premises. Violators will be humiliated."

situation. Avoid if it creates padding, as in the jargon of sports announcers: "Now we have a passing *situation.*"

slang. The mainly oral vocabulary—often employing quite popular words—found in a culture or subculture. Examples: *uptight, slap-happy, screw up, turkey* (referring to a person), *fatso, What's the diff (difference)?, smooch.* As the last two examples show, slang tends to go out of date quickly. Avoid it in your writing, except when using dialogue.

split infinitive. You "split" the infinitive by putting a word (or words) between the sign of the infinitive (*to*) and the main verb: "to *quickly* run," "to *sharply* define," "to *clearly and without ambiguity* state." The split infinitive is often awkward. Do not use the construction unless your "splitting" improves the meaning and rhythm of the sentence. See page 458.

standard English. The language that educated people generally accept as proper and suitable. Nonstandard English is often a deviation "downward" from standard—it is perhaps too casual, slangy, vulgar or otherwise inappropriate. By contrast, some nonstandard English is too formal or pedantic. See our discussion in Chapter 12.

Also see *casual, casualism; colloquial, colloquialism; dialect; jargon; shibboleths of usage; slang; vogue words.*

structure. A vogue word, often employed as a loose synonym for *organize* or *organization. The Harper Dictionary of Contemporary Usage* says: "*Structure* is very popular with people who use words like *crunch, thrust,* and *seminal.* Such people are best avoided." Perhaps the word is most usefully employed to describe physical objects like buildings.

Not this: His ideas were *unstructured.*

But this: His ideas were *disorganized.*

sure (to mean "certainly"). Example: "I'm *sure* happy you came." The word is trite and too *casual.* Rewrite:

I am very happy you came.

I am extremely happy you came.

I am overjoyed you came.

that, which, who. Much of the time these words take care of themselves, and no particular notice of them need be taken. Generally, you can rely on the old rule: *Which* refers to things, *who* to people, and *that* to people or things.

try and. Not standard; use *try to.*

Not this: Please *try and* see me tomorrow.

But this: Please *try to* see me tomorrow.

type (of). Use *type* as a noun, not as an adjective:

Not this: This *type* person is a blessing to humanity.

But this: This *type of* person is a blessing to humanity.

Not this: We need a *new-type* antenna.

But this: We need a new *type of* antenna.

unique. Means "one of a kind," and so something cannot be "more unique" or "most unique." *Unique* does not mean *unusual, remarkable,* or *excellent.*

up (*verb*). *Up* should not be used as a verb.

Not this: Please *up* my salary.

But this: Please *increase* my salary.

Not this: My final grade was *upped.*

But this: My final grade was *raised* to a B.

utilize, utilization. Jargon for *use.* Never use either word.

verb. A *verb* is a word which *states:*

They *returned.*

These *are* the questions.

I *will be* home when you *arrive.*

The old stump *had been decaying* for years.

Transitive verbs pass the action over from the subject to an object;

intransitive verbs do not pass any action to an object.

   Transitive: The farmer *plowed* his field.

   Intransitive: He *plowed* happily.

   As the examples imply, most verbs can be either transitive or intransitive, depending on whether the object is present in the sentence. Some verbs are by nature
transitive (*ignore*) or intransitive (*snore*). *Ignore* always takes an object—one always
ignores *something*—a person, a slight, a distraction. By contrast, one never "snores"
anything, at least not in normal idiom. See also *auxiliary verb* and *linking verb.*

verbal. (1) See *oral.* (2) A *verbal* is a word that is derived from a verb but that cannot
act as the main verb in a sentence. A verbal can take complements, objects, modifiers, and in some instances subjects. There are three kinds of verbals: *participles, infinitives,* and *gerunds.*

vogue words. These are words and phrases that seem to appear everywhere at once in
magazines, newspapers, public speeches, and on television and radio. Like new
clothing styles, they are a matter of fashion; and so they are picked up (and dropped)
by the public with alarming rapidity. Examples: *détente, structure* (verb), *crunch,
meaningful, thrust, Back to Basics*—several of these are going out of style even as
we write. *Relevant,* perhaps the most popular vogue word of a few years back, is
now less fashionable.

whether. See *correlatives.*

who, whom. Good writers don't appear to have much trouble with *whom,* partly because they don't use it a great deal, except with prepositions. Authorities appear to
be confused themselves and are certainly confusing to others. In his last book, however, Theodore Bernstein suggested "whom's doom," saying that *whom* is "useless
and senseless; the word is in addition a complicated nuisance." Bernstein asked 25
teachers, consultants on dictionaries, professional writers, and linguists if they
agreed. Fifteen did agree, six did not, and four were "in between" (*Dos, Dont's and
Maybes of English Usage,* 1977).

   Our own desire for order and common sense inclines us to agree with Bernstein.
So our rule is:

   Always use *who*—except with prepositions, as in: *by* whom, *for* whom, *with*
whom, *to* whom.

will. *shall, will.*

The Masculine Generic Pronoun (he, his, him)

The word *generic* refers to a class, group, or species. The English language is full of generics. Most of them we don't notice because they are so normal and idiomatic. As linguist Otto Jespersen pointed out, there are generic nouns, pronouns, adjectives, phrases, abstractions, judgments—even generic verbs and numbers, as in: "We *used to go* there every summer." And "The golf scores were all in the *70s*." Such things are built into the language; they are a part of its brick and mortar.

The generic *he* is standard, and you can use it if you want to. If you don't want to, or if you think your audience would not like it, here are other choices:

1. Avoid *he* by using plurals.

2. Avoid *he* by using *you.*

3. Use *he* or *she* sparingly. And don't repeat the phrase in clause after clause.

4. Write "around" the problem—for example, instead of writing *The student sees his chance,* write *The student sees a chance.*

5. Use the pattern *everybody . . . their.*

Don't use *he/she* or *s/he*. The slash mark (/) is not used in standard English to make such compounds.

But not one of the solutions above seems entirely satisfactory by itself. In many instances, we would prefer the pattern of *everybody . . . their*—although we don't have

530

the courage to use it very often. *Everybody* can be clearly plural in meaning, just as *none* can be. Indeed, the authorities agree that *none* is more often than not a plural, so why can't we accept *everybody* (or *anybody*) as a plural in some sentences? (Check with your instructor before using *everybody* as a plural.)

You can use *you* in a larger number of cases, like this one. We like *you* because it loosens up a writer's style, making it more conversational and direct.

He or she is all right if used sparingly. Many readers don't like it because it can be both redundant and awkward:

> As the interviewer, you may have a great deal of influence over the person's future in the company, or the choice of job that he or she will take. Therefore you should empathize with him or her and recognize that he or she may be nervous or afraid. It is up to you to put him or her at ease.

That sort of thing just won't do—it's too clumsy.

In this book, we authors have tried to replace *he* and *his* and have managed to remove most of them. The ones that remain seem more or less unavoidable. Incidently, we would not mind if we passed a law making *she* a generic pronoun—we need one of some kind. A generic is necessary in the passage just quoted, considering the logic of the passage and its context.

ACKNOWLEDGMENTS

Excerpt from "Ants," *Réalitiés*, September 1952. Reprinted by permission of Agence Photographique TOP.

Awake! "Why Mexican Jumping Beans Jump," *Awake!* September 1973.

Asimov, Isaac. Excerpt from "What Is Intelligence Anyway?" by Isaac Asimov. Reprinted by permission of the author.

Austin, James H., M.D. "Chance" adapted from "Of the *Four* Varieties of Chance Only One Is 'Pure Blind Luck,'" *Executive Health Reports*, vol. XIII, no. 8, May 1977. Copyright © 1977 by Executive Publications. Reprinted by permission of the author.

Baker, James T. "How Do We Find the Student in a World of Academic Gymnasts and Worker Ants?" by James T. Baker from *The Chronicle of Higher Education*, March 3, 1982, p. 64. Copyright © 1982 by James T. Baker. Reprinted by permission of the author.

Brunvand, Jan Harold. Abridged from "The Vanishing Hitchhiker," *American Urban Legends & Their Meanings* by Jan Harold Brunvand. Copyright © 1981 by Jan Harold Brunvand. Reprinted by permission of the author and W. W. Norton and Company, Inc.

Crews, Harry. Excerpt from *A Childhood* by Harry Crews. Copyright © 1978 by Harry Crews. Reprinted by permission of John Hawkins & Associates, Inc.

Daniels, George. Excerpt from *The Awful Handyman's Book* by George Daniels. Copyright © 1966 by George Daniels. Reprinted by permission of HarperCollins Publishers.

Davidson, Christine. "Working Time and a Half" by Christine Davidson from *Newsweek*, March 8, 1982, pp. 14–15. Copyright © 1982 by Christine Davidson. Reprinted by permission of the author.

Dowling, Claudia. Excerpt from "The Relative Explosion" by Claudia Dowling from *Psychology Today*, April 1983, pp. 54–59. Copyright © 1983 American Psychological Association. Reprinted with permission from Sussex Publishers, Inc.

Eighner, Lars. Excerpt from "On Dumpster Diving" by Lars Eighner from *Travels with Lisbeth*, 1993, pp. 11–112, 121–123. Copyright © 1993 by Lars Eighner, St. Martin's Press Inc., New York, NY. Reprinted by permission.

Elbow, Peter. "Freewriting Exercises" from *Writing Without Teachers* by Peter Elbow. Copyright © 1973 by Oxford University Press, Inc. Reprinted by permission.

Follett, Ken. Excerpt from "A Moscow Mystery" by Ken Follett from *Saturday Review*, April 1981. Copyright © 1981 by Saturday Review. All rights reserved. Reprinted with permission of General Media International.

Hale, Leon. Excerpt from "Southern Journal—My Father's World" by Leon Hale, *Southern Living*, February 1983, p. 47. Copyright © 1983 by Southern Living, Inc. Reprinted by permission.

Harris, Sydney J. "What True Education Should Do" from *On the Contrary* by Sydney J. Harris. Copyright © 1964 Publishers Syndicate by permission of King Features Syndicate.

Harris, Sydney J. "When Winning Is Losing" from *Strictly Personal* by Sydney J. Harris. Copyright © 1975 by Field Enterprises, Inc. Reprinted with permission of King Features Syndicate.

Hasselstrom, Linda, "Why One Peaceful Woman Carries a Pistol" by Linda Hasselstrom from *Land Circle: Writings Collected from the Land,* 1991, pp. 290–297. Copyright © 1991 by Linda M. Hasselstrom. Reprinted by permission of Fulcrum Publishing.

Hoff, Ron. "To Live Is to Rage Against the Dark" by Ron Hoff from the *Chicago Tribune, The Observer*, #1, June 3, 1986, p. 14. Copyright © 1986 by Ron Hoff. Reprinted by permission of the author.

Holt, Don. "Leaving the Family Farm" by Don Holt, pp. 1–8. Reprinted by permission of the author.

Hoye, R. Nicholas. Excerpt from *The Flood and the Community* by R. Nicholas Hoye. Copyright © 1976 by Corning Glass Works. Reprinted by permission.

Hubbell, Sue. Excerpt from "This Woman Learned to Manhandle a Chainsaw—Now Her Forest Thrives" by Sue Hubbell. Reprinted courtesy of *Sports Illustrated* from the April 22, 1985 issue. Copyright © 1985, Time, Inc. All rights reserved.

Hughes, Robert. Excerpt from "Take This Revolution . . ." by Robert Hughes from *Time*, Spring 1995, pp. 76–77. Copyright © 1995 Time Warner, Inc. Reprinted by permission.

Hunt, Nancy. Excerpt from "Back East They Need Lessons in Manners" by Nancy Hunt in the *Chicago Tribune*, October 13, 1980. Copyright © 1980 by The Chicago Tribune Company. All rights reserved. Used with permission.

Hymowitz, Kay S. Excerpt from "Where Has Our Love Gone?" by Kay S. Hymowitz from the *Wall Street Journal*, April 6, 1995, p. A14. Reprinted by permission of *City Journal*.

Iwata, Edward. Excerpt from "Barbed-Wire Memories" by Edward Iwata in the *San Francisco Chronicle*, May 9, 1982. Copyright © 1982 by the San Francisco Chronicle. Reprinted by permission.

Iyer, Pico. "In Praise of the Humble Comma" by Pico Iyer from *Time*, June 13, 1988, p. 80. Copyright © 1988 Time Warner, Inc. Reprinted by permission.

Janoff, Joshua B. "A Gen-X Rip Van Winkle" By Joshua B. Janoff from *Newsweek,* April 24, 1995. Copyright © 1995 by Newsweek, Inc. All rights reserved. Reprinted by permission.

Johnson, William Oscar. Excerpt from "Sports and Suds" by William Oscar Johnson. Reprinted courtesy of *Sports Illustrated* from the August 9, 1988 issue. Copyright © 1988, Time, Inc. All rights reserved.

King, Jr., Martin Luther. "Letter from Birmingham Jail" from *Why We Can't Wait* by Martin Luther King, Jr. Copyright © 1963, 1964 by Martin Luther King, Jr. Reprinted by permission of Joan Daves Agency.

Klass, Perri. Excerpt from "ZZZZZZZ(Wha'?) ZZZZZZZZZZZ(Huh?) ZZZZZZZZZ" by Perri Klass from *Discover*, December 1986, p. 18. Reprinted by permission of Maxine Grofsky Literary Agency.

Klass, Perri. "A World Where Too Many Children Don't Grow Up," reprinted by permission of G. P. Putnam from "India" in *A Not Entirely Benign Procedure* by Perri Klass. Copyright © 1987 by Perri Klass. Abridged.

Kozinski, Alex. "Skiers Beware Riders of the Apocalypse" by Alex Kozinski from the *Wall Street Journal*, March 15, 1995, Leisure & Arts, p. A12. Retitled "Ten Reasons Skiing Is Dead." Reprinted by permission of the author.

Lane, Jennings. Excerpt from "Computer Chess: Can the Machine Beat Man at His Own Game?" by Jennings Lane from *Futurist*, June 1978. Reprinted by permission of the Futurist, published by the World Future Society, 4916 St. Elmo Avenue, Washington, D.C. 20014.

Leo, John. "A Pox on All Our Houses" by John Leo from *U.S. News & World Report*, February 20, 1989, p. 65. Copyright © 1989 by U.S. News & World Report. Reprinted by permission.

Liptak, Adam. Excerpt from "Bad Reasons to Study Law" by Adam Liptak from *Newsweek on Campus*, November 1986, p. 70. Reprinted by permission of the author.

Lyles, Barbara. "What to Call People of Color" by Barbara Lyles from *Newsweek*, February 27, 1989, pp. 8–9. Copyright © 1989 by Barbara Lyles. Reprinted by permission of the author.

McClain, Leanita. "Hussies and Holes in Your Ears" by Leanita McClain, *Chicago Tribune*, April 29, 1983. Copyright © 1983 by The Chicago Tribune Company. All rights reserved. Reprinted with permission.

McManus, Patrick. "The Purist" from *A Fine and Pleasant Misery* by Patrick McManus, edited by Jack Samson. Copyright © 1978 by Patrick F. McManus. Reprinted by permission of Henry Holt and Company, Inc.

Molishever, Jay. Excerpt from "Changing Expectations of Marriage" from *Glamour Magazine*, October 1974. Copyright © 1974 by The Condé Nast Publications, Inc. Reprinted by permission of the author.

Morley, Robert. Excerpt from "The Play's Still the Thing" by Robert Morley, *Saturday Review*, June 11, 1977. Copyright © 1977 by Saturday Review magazine. Reprinted by permission of General Media International.

Nin, Anaïs. Reprinted from "The Labyrinthine City of Fez" in *In Favor of the Sensitive Man and Other Essays* by Anaïs Nin by permission of Harcourt Brace Jovanovich, Inc. Copyright © 1974 by Anaïs Nin.

Portnoy, Sharon. "My Fat Problem and Theirs" by Sharon Portnoy, *Ms.* magazine, March 1985. Reprinted by permission of the author.

Ray, Dixy Lee. Excerpt from "Who Speaks for Science?" by Dixy Lee Ray from *Imprimis*, August 1988, vol. 17, no. 8, p. 2. Reprinted by permission of *Imprimis*.

Roberts, Kenneth. "Roads of Remembrance" from *For Authors Only*. Copyright © 1929. New York: Doubleday and Company. Reprinted by permission.

Roberts, Steve. Excerpt from "An Encounter in the Woods" by Steve Roberts. Originally appeared in *Bicycle USA*, October 1985. Reprinted by permission of *Online Today* magazine, published by Compuserve, Inc.

Rosefsky, Robert. "Soda Pop" by Robert Rosefsky from the *Chicago Daily News*, February 17, 1985. Copyright © 1975 Field Enterprises, Inc., by permission of King Features Syndicate.

Rosenthal, A. M. "On My Mind: The Case for Slavery" by A. M. Rosenthal from the *New York Times*, September 26, 1989. Retitled "Legalizing Addictive Drugs Like Bringing Back Slavery." Copyright © 1989 by The New York Times Company. Reprinted by permission.

Russo, John. "'Reel' vs. Real Violence" by John Russo from *Newsweek*, February 19, 1990, p. 10. Copyright © 1990 by John Russo. Reprinted by permission of the author.

Sacks, Oliver. "The Man Who Mistook His Wife for a Hat" from *The Man Who Mistook His Wife for a Hat and Other Clinical Tales* by Oliver Sacks. Copyright © 1970, 1981, 1983, 1984, 1985 by Oliver Sacks. Reprinted by permission of Simon & Schuster.

Stewart, J. Clayton. "Growing Cold by Degrees" by J. Clayton Stewart. Reprinted courtesy of *Sports Illustrated* from the March 10, 1975 issue. Copyright © 1975, Time, Inc. All rights reserved.

Twain, Mark. "A Double-Barrelled Detective Story" by Mark Twain, 1902.

Treasure, Carole. "The Midnight Shift Does Murder Sleep" by Carole Treasure from the *Wall Street Journal*, February 15, 1989, p. A14. Copyright © 1989 by the Wall Street Journal. Reprinted by permission of the Wall Street Journal.

Wade, Lawrence. "Affirmative Action Just Renews Racism," by Lawrence Wade in *USA Today*, December 4, 1987. Reprinted by permission of Deborah Burstion-Donbraye.

Weizenbaum, Joseph. Excerpt from "Another View from MIT" by Joseph Weizenbaum from *Byte* magazine, June 1984, p. 225. Copyright © 1984 by McGraw-Hill Publishing. Reprinted by permission.

Welsch, Roger. "Shelters on the Plains" by Roger Welsch from the *National History Magazine*, vol. LXXXVI, no. 5, May 1977, pp. 48–53. Copyright © 1977 by the American Museum of Natural History. Reprinted by permission.

White, E. B. "Once More to the Lake" from *Essays of E. B. White*. Copyright © 1941 by E. B. White. Reprinted by permission of HarperCollins Publishers.

Whitebook, Budd. "Confessions of an Ex-Smoker" by Budd Whitebook, from *Harper's*, February 1976. Copyright © 1976 by Harper's Magazine. All rights reserved. Reprinted from the February 1976 issue by special permission.

Whiting, Charles S. *Creative Thinking*. Copyright © 1958 New York: Reinhold Publishing Corporation, pp. 71–72. Reprinted by permission.

Wik, Reynald M. *Henry Ford and Grass-Roots America*. Ann Arbor: The University of Michigan, 1972, pp. 32–33.

Wright, Richard. Excerpt from "The Ethics of Living Jim Crow" from *Uncle Tom's Children* by Richard Wright. Copyright © 1936 by Richard Wright. Copyright renewed © 1965 by Ellen Wright. Reprinted by permission of HarperCollins Publishers.

Zwinger, Ann H. "Becoming Mom to an Infant Word Processor" by Ann H. Zwinger, *Smithsonian*, February 1982. Copyright © 1982 by Ann H. Zwinger. Reprinted by permission of Frances Collin, Literary Agent.

Index

Key to the Handbook